CHAUCER STUDIES

ISSN 0261–9822

Previously published volumes in this series
are listed at the back of this book

Chaucer and Clothing

Clerical and Academic Costume in the General Prologue to *The Canterbury Tales*

LAURA F. HODGES

D. S. BREWER

First published 2005
D. S. Brewer, Cambridge

ISBN 1 84384 033 2

ISSN 0261–9822

D. S. Brewer is an imprint of Boydell & Brewer Ltd
PO Box 9, Woodbridge, Suffolk IP12 3DF, UK
and of Boydell & Brewer Inc.
668 Mt Hope Avenue, Rochester, NY 14620, USA
website: www.boydellandbrewer.com

A catalogue record for this book is available
from the British Library

Library of Congress Cataloging-in-Publication Data
Hodges, Laura F. (Laura Fulkerson), 1934–
    Chaucer and clothing clerical and academic costume in the general prologue
to the Canterbury tales / Laura F. Hodges.
    p. cm. – (Chaucer studies, ISSN 0261–9822 ; 34)
    Includes bibliographical references (p.) and index.
    ISBN 1–84384–033–2 (hardback : alk. paper)
    1. Chaucer, Geoffrey, d. 1400. Canterbury tales. Prologue. 2. Chaucer, Geoffrey,
d. 1400–Knowledge–Clothing and dress. 3. Clothing and dress–England–History–
Medieval, 500–1500. 4. Prologues and epilogues–History and criticism.
5. Christian pilgrims and pilgrimages in literature. 6. Clothing and dress in
literature. 7. Teachers in literature. 8. Clergy in literature. I. Title. II. Series.
PR1868.P9H627 2005
821'.1–dc22   2004010365

This publication is printed on acid-free paper

Printed in Great Britain by
Cromwell Press, Trowbridge, Wiltshire

Contents

List of Illustrations   vii

Acknowledgments   ix

Abbreviations   xiii

1.   Introduction: Clothing and Religious Rules, Society's   1
     Expectations, and Satire

2.   The Prioress, 'digne of reverence': Her Headdress and Her Habit   29

3.   Sign of Faith: The Prioress's Rosary   82

4.   A Reconsideration of the Monk's Costume   112

5.   Chaucer's Friar: 'typet' and 'semycope'   133

6.   The Clerk's 'ful thredbare . . . overeste courtepy'   160

7.   The Doctour of Phisik: Apparel for the 'parfit practisour'   199

8.   Truth and Untruth in Advertising: The Pardoner's 'cappe' with   226
     'vernycle' and the Summoner's 'gerland' and 'bokeler'

9.   The Parson Has No Clothes   258

10. Conclusion   266

Works Cited   273

Index   299

What shul these clothes thus manyfold,
   Lo this hote somers day?
After grete hete cometh cold;
   No man caste his pilche away.
      (Geoffrey Chaucer, *Proverbe of Chaucer*)

For all the companions who taught me
to lay up knowledge
against a future need

Illustrations

Color plates

Placed between pages 146 and 147

I.   St Gertrude, Benedictine nun and visionary, from *Horae beatae Virginis cum calendario, orationibus ad sanctos & aliis*, British Library.

II.   Catherine of Cleves' coral rosary, from *Horae C. de Cleves*, The Pierpont Morgan Library.

III.   The Monk, from *The Canterbury Tales*, Cambridge University Library.

IV.   A Friar, from the *Taymouth Hours*, British Library.

V.   Clerks, from *Omne bonum*, British Library.

VI.   St Cosmas or St Damian, depicted in Church of St Kenelm, Minster Lovell, Oxon.

VII.   The Pardoner, from *The Canterbury Tales*, Cambridge University Library.

VIII.   A possible case of leprosy, from *Omne bonum*, British Library.

Plates

1.   Sketch of Christ's seamless gown, after an illustration of a 'Poem on the Passion of Christ', Bodleian Library.   2

2.   Drawings of Nuns' headdresses: (a) *Liber Animarum capituli monasterii Sancti Quirini Nussiensis*, British Library; (b) Book of Hours, British Library; (c) *Omne bonum*, British Library; (d) *Sforza Book of Hours*, British Library; (e) *Le Roman de la rose*, British Library.   50

3.   The four Cardinal Virtues, from *Somme Le Roi*, British Library.   60

4.   Sketch of veil and wimple worn by Discipline, sculpture in the Museum of London, formerly on the façade of the medieval London Guildhall.   62

5.   St James in Gethsemene, St Michael's Kirche, Schwäbisch Hall, Swabia: (a) detail of St James wearing blue robe with tiraz bands; (b) gold sleeve bands with motto; (c) gold hem bands continuing motto.   86–87

6.   Sketch of St Hedwig of Silesia, from a parchment illustration,   92
     J. Paul Getty Museum.

7.   Sketch of Robert Waltham, Precentor, Salisbury Cathedral,   122
     wearing a fur hooded *almuce*, from *St Albans Golden Book*,
     British Library.

8.   Sketch of the knot emblem of Corpus Christi Guild of Leicester,   130
     after John Nichols' depiction in his *History and Antiquities of
     the County of Leicester*.

9.   Sketch of a senior cleric wearing the *vestis talaris* and three   162
     clerks in lay dress and bearing arms, from *Omne bonum*,
     British Library.

10. Sketch of a scholar wearing the *pileus*, detail from *Omne bonum*,   206
     British Library.

11. Sketch of a *cappa clausa*, worn by John Argentin, Provost,   207
     King's College, Cambridge, from his funerary brass depicted
     in H. W. Macklin's *The Brasses of England*.

12. A surgeon, in a short tunic, drawing blood from a patient, after   212
     an illustration in *The Luttrell Psalter*, British Library.

13. Sketch of a physician holding a jordan aloft, from *Omne bonum*,   224
     British Library.

14. Sketch of a youth wearing a floral wreath, from *Omne bonum*,   230
     British Library.

15. Detail of face of Christ with crown of thorns, sketched from a   255
     painting of St Veronica displaying a 'vernycle', in the Alte
     Pinakothek, Munich.

16. Sketch of a pilgrim badge of St Josse with pilgrim staff and   263
     rosary, from *The London Archaeologist*.

Acknowledgements

While, among lay persons, clothing conveniently served as a form of currency as well as a marker of social and economic status (sometimes deceptively inflated), garments worn by those in holy orders, or otherwise officially attached to the medieval church, were designed and functioned as symbols of spiritual and religious hierarchical values. These values overtly constitute the foundation of religious and academic dress and, covertly, of Chaucer's rhetoric as he names or describes these costumes as they conformed, or not, to religious rules.

Beyond the recognition of these values, if there is one overarching theme in this book, it is that of the infinite variety of Chaucer's costume imagery. He employs traditional motifs innovatively or unconventionally and generates or highlights nontraditional (at least among contemporary poets) garment and accessory details. However, I do not wish to belabor this point, deeming it sufficient to point out that each essay in this collection supports one or more of these points, sometimes all of them at the same time, and that each focuses more specifically on a given *General Prologue* pilgrim(s) and the content and broad context of his/her dress. And yet, try as I might, and with this the second of two volumes on the subject of Chaucer's costume rhetoric in his *General Prologue* and its literary, historical, social, economic, and spiritual context, I acknowledge here that I have not exhausted the subject. Even in the early 1980s when I began this project, it was clear that the topic might well be one that would unfold in the future as more research in all of the correlative subject fields is done, and as more literary scholars, with new insights, choose to apply that research as they delve into the resonance within each costume image. Therefore it is my hope that this book and its predecessor will serve other Chaucerians as stimuli for further research and publications that will illuminate Chaucer's costume images throughout his works. Should this happen, I shall be quite pleased, in the normal processes of scholarship, to find my work amplified, supported or refuted, and ultimately refined.

As is the usual case with scholarly projects, many generous friends and colleagues, some initially strangers, contributed to this exploration of costume contexts and descriptions in the *General Prologue*. I should like to thank, first, Gretchen Mieszkowski who introduced me to the rigors and the greater pleasures of medieval literary scholarship; Jane Chance who supported my research on Chaucer's clothing imagery from its earliest stage as a potential dissertation topic and has continued to encourage it for more than twenty years; Lorraine K. Stock who has debated the included essay topics with me for nearly that long; and Lois Roney who included my Kalamazoo papers on this topic in her sessions, thus insuring that I dealt with at least one pilgrim's costume a year, and who shared with me her knowledge of medieval scholars and universities, some of which I incorporate in my discussion of the Clerk's costume.

I should also like to acknowledge the wealth of assistance I have received from libraries and librarians, museums and curators, who contributed their information, artifacts, and expertise to this finished volume: the Fondren Library, William Marsh Rice University, Houston; the Huntington Library, San Marino, CA, and especially Mary L. Robertson, Chief Curator of Manuscripts, for responding to my post-research questions regarding the illuminations in the Ellesmere Manuscript; the University Research Library, University of California at Los Angeles, Los Angeles; the University of London Library, London, with many thanks to Janet Cowen, King's College London, for her assistance in securing library privileges in 1983–85, when I did a large portion of my research on the Prioress and the early stages of investigation on the remainder of the pilgrims; the Museum of London, London and notably John Clark, Curator (Medieval), Early London History and Collections, for correspondence concerning the statue known as 'Discipline', formerly at the Guildhall in London; the British Library, London, and J. Conway, Superintendent, Reference Division; the Bodleian Library, Oxford, with gratitude to the late Maureen Pemberton whose help with manuscript illuminations was invaluable; the Neuman Library, University of Houston at Clear Lake, Houston, especially the Reference Librarians including Pat Pate and Interlibrary Loan staff members; and the Freeman Memorial Library, Houston, and Interlibrary Loan librarians Jennifer Stidham, Susan Davila, and Marilyn Hopman.

In addition, I should also like to express my gratitude to Rice University for a travel and research grant, which allowed me to build a knowledgeable foundation in costume as depicted in medieval manuscript illuminations in the British Library and at the Bodleian Library, and on funerary monuments, sculptures, and wall paintings at sites throughout England.

Among the friends and colleagues who made important and generous contributions to this book are Juris Lidaka who knows how to find the most obscure sources and has the gift of demystifing strange details; Priscilla Throop who translated the Gautier de Coinci lines in Chapter 2; Richard H. Osberg who brought to my attention several articles on the Prioress; Julia Bolton Holloway who contributed valuable information concerning pilgrim hats; Thomas Hatton who sent me reading suggestions concerning the Clerk; JoAnn McNamara who shared her background knowledge of nuns' veiling; Marilyn Oliva who contributed information regarding a fifteenth-century sermon on the symbolic nature of nuns' habits; Grace Hodges Tice who mailed Xerox copies of articles on medieval medicine and the Doctour of

Phisik to me when I lived in Moscow, USSR, and had difficulty accessing Chaucer materials; B. S. Lee who helped with the final details of manuscript correction; Ken Thompson who assisted me with page proofs; Henri de Feraudy who contributed the photograph of the Oxford Doctor of Phisik (Color Plate VI); Mrs Klaus Jankofsky who kindly consented to the reproduction of pictures taken by the late Professor Klaus Jankofsky (Plate 5a–c); and Daniel Scott Henderson who made the line drawing of the surgeon bleeding his patient (Plate 12).

I am most grateful also to the late Robert Frank, Mary Hamel, and Jeanne Krochalis, whose encouragement through the years has sustained my work on Chaucer's costume rhetoric, and also to Penn State University Press for allowing me to reprint in this book two articles (Chapters 4 and 5, now expanded) that were first published in *Chaucer Review.* In addition, I gratefully acknowledge the contributions derived from listmembers on Chaucernet, medfem-l, medtextl, and medart-l who have, over the years, answered questions and participated in discussions that were both enlightening and informative. Further, I offer many thanks to all those at Boydell & Brewer Ltd whose interest, efforts, and expertise have made the publication of this book and its predecessor possible.

In conclusion, although I claim responsibility for any errors remaining in this work, I wish to express my appreciation for the most valuable resource of all – those who have critiqued, at various stages of development, some or all of the chapters in this book. My gratitude goes to Gretchen Mieszkowski for her insightful comments and questions through the years, to Lorraine Stock for access to her personal library and her knowledge of iconography, and to Lois Roney whose reading of the penultimate manuscript made a vast contribution to the final version. I also wish to thank my husband Charles Richard Hodges who has lived with the research demands of Chaucer's pilgrims as long as I have and who has been most patient throughout the journey.

Abbreviations

AN&Q	*American Notes and Queries*
Archaeol J	*Archaeological Journal*
BIHM	*Bulletin of the Institute of the History of Medicine*
BL	British Library
C&C	Laura F. Hodges, *Chaucer and Costume: The Secular Pilgrims in the General Prologue*. Chaucer Studies XXVI. Cambridge, 2000
C&L	*Christianity and Literature*
ChauN	*Chaucer Newsletter*
ChauR	*Chaucer Review*
ChauY	*Chaucer Yearbook*
CUL	Cambridge University Library
E&S	*Essays and Studies*
Econ Hist Rev	*Economic History Review*
EETS	Early English Text Society
EHR	*English Historical Review*
ELH	*English Literary History*
ELN	*English Language Notes*
ES	*English Studies*
Expl	*Explicator*
HLQ	*Huntington Library Quarterly*
JBAA	*Journal of the British Archeological Association*
JEGP	*Journal of English and Germanic Philology*
L&T	*Literature & Theology: An Interdisciplinary Journal of Theory and Criticism*
MÆ	*Medium Ævum*
MED	The Middle English Dictionary
Mediaevalia	*Mediaevalia: A Journal of Mediaeval Studies*
MLN	*Modern Language Notes*
MLQ	*Modern Language Quarterly: A Journal of Literary History*
MLS	*Modern Language Studies*
MP	*Modern Philology: A Journal Devoted to Research in Medieval and Modern Literature*
MS	*Mediaeval Studies*
N&Q	*Notes & Queries*
Neophil	*Neophilologus*
NLH	*New Literary History*

OED   The Oxford English Dictionary
PF   *The Parliament of Fowls*
PL   *Patralogia Latina*
PLL   *Papers on Language and Literature*
PMLA   *Publications of the Modern Language Association*
PP.B   *Piers Plowman: The B Version*
PQ   *Philological Quarterly*
Rom.   *The Romaunt of the rose*
RR   *Romanic Review*
SAC   *Studies in the Age of Chaucer*
SIcon   *Studies in Iconography*
SN   *Studia Neophilologica: A Journal of Germanic and
                 Romance Languages and Literature*
SP   *Studies in Philology*
Speculum   *Speculum: A Journal of Medieval Studies*
Text Hist   *Textile History*
TPB   *Tennessee Philological Bulletin*
TSE   *Tulane Studies in English*
YLS   *The Yearbook of Langland Studies*

1

Introduction:
Clothing and Religious Rules,
Society's Expectations, and Satire

In the *ideal* state of affairs envisioned by the religious orders of the medieval church in England and described in their various religious rules, all persons in holy orders would regularly dress in proper, prescribed, and somber religious habits. Metaphorically, however, they would desire to wear Christ's seamless tunic of red, banded in gold at neck, sleeves, and all edges of the garment – the red symbolizing His blood shed for the salvation of His people in His indivisible charity, and the gold signifying aspiration to the highest good – as depicted by Giotto in his painting of the *Crucifixion*.[1] This spiritual garment, depicted in Plate 1, was revered by devout Christians; it signifies the *new* garment of charity and mercy donned after discarding the 'old man' and putting on the 'new man', Christ.[2] However, Geoffrey Chaucer does not depict an ideal world in the portraits of the pilgrims in holy orders or

---

[1] See the black and white reproduction of this painting in Anne Derbes and Mark Sandona, ' "Ave charitate plena": Variations on the Theme of Charity in the Arena Chapel', *Speculum* 76.3 (2001), fig. 8, p. 618. The tunic's placement, depicted in the hands of soldiers at Christ's left, is described on pp. 619–20. Also see Annette B. Weiner and Jane Schneider, *Cloth and Human Experience* (Washington, D.C., 1989), p. 15, regarding 'continuous weaving', which 'transmits a spiritual force'; also, below, Chapter 5, n. 72.

[2] Derbes and Sandona discuss this symbolism, pp. 619–22. Regarding Christ's seamless 'coat', John 19:23 says,

> The soldiers therefore, when they had crucified him, took his garments (and they made four parts, to every soldier a part), and also his coat. Now the coat was without seam, woven from the top throughout.

Trier Cathedral claims possession of this garment relic. From 19 April through 16 May 1996, a 'Heilig-Rock' Pilgrimage was held commemorating the eight-hundredth anniversary of the consecration, by Archbishop John I, of the altar and new Eastern chancel in which the Tunic of Christ was incorporated, according to 'The "Heilig-Rock" Pilgrimage', eds Hans Casel, Christoph Rosenzweig, Hans Georg Schneider, and Alfons Waschbüsch, The Pilgrimage News Service, Episcopat Public Relations Office, Trier (n.d.). See Franz Ronig, *Trier Cathedral*, trans. M. C. Maxwell,

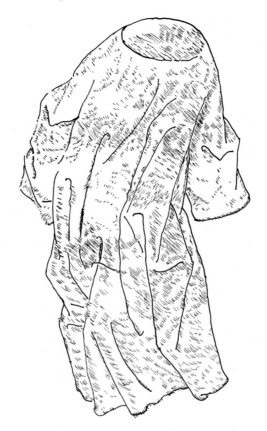

1. Sketch of Christ's seamless gown; after an illustration of a 'Poem on the Passion of Christ' in Bodleian Library MS Bodley Rolls 16.

th edn (Trier, 1986), p. 14, for a description of the Relic Chapel (the Holy Robe Chapel).

Plate 1 is a late-fifteenth-century line drawing (with some color) of the seamless tunic illustrating an English poem, 'Poem on the Passion of Christ', in MS Bodley Rolls 16, as depicted in Otto Pächt and J. J. G. Alexander, *Illuminated Manuscripts in the Bodleian Library Oxford: British, Irish, and Icelandic Schools* (Oxford, 1973), 3: pl. 105, #1126. Also, I am grateful to Alan E. Knight (e-mail to MEDTEXTL, 22 Apr. 1996) for pointing out that the Buxtehude altarpiece (c.1410), in the Kunsthalle in Hamburg, portrays Mary's four-needle knitting of the seamless gown, as illustrated in fig. 6.8, in Gail McMurry Gibson's *The Theater of Devotion: East Anglian Drama and Society in the Middle Ages* (Chicago, 1989); Gibson discusses this gown as a motif in drama, pp. 157–8. For background material and artistic representations of the seamless gown, see Ewa Kuryluk, *Veronica and her Cloth: History, Symbolism, and Structure of a 'True' Image* (Oxford, 1991), pp. 193–6, and a reproduction of the Silesian Master's *The Virgin Working on the Seamless Tunic and St Luke Painting Her* (c.1500), pl. 13.

officially affiliated with the church in his *General Prologue* to the *Canterbury Tales*. Instead, he displays pilgrims drawn from the population of the world he knew and dresses them in costume signs that illustrate a principle well known to Malory: in 'The Knight with the Two Swords', Balyn tells a damsel,

> worthynes and good tacchis [qualities, habits] and also good dedis is nat only in araymente, but manhode and worship [ys hyd] within a mannes person; and many a worshipfull knyght ys nat knowyn unto all peple. And therefore worship and hardynesse ys nat in araymente.[3]

Chaucer's costume rhetoric[4] in the *General Prologue* demonstrates clearly that what Malory says of chivalric virtues might be said for all virtues, including the virtues symbolized in garments worn by Chaucer's pilgrims affiliated with holy orders or office. Virtues are 'nat in araymente', although they may be *signified* by dress, and the same claim may be made for vices. One must look beyond the surface for essential spiritual truth. However, medieval dress codes often ignore this fact, and authors of medieval literature, among them Chaucer, often exploit it.

John Stratford, Archbishop of Canterbury, in his 1342 injunctions dealing with the issue of dress for the clergy, makes a statement that illustrates the wishful thinking behind medieval religious dress codes: 'The external costume often shows the internal character and condition of persons. . . . [T]he behaviour of clerks [in the matter of dress] ought to be an example and pattern of the laity'; then he discusses the abuse of dress codes by clerks.[5] In

---

3   Thomas Malory, 'The Knight with the Two Swords' in *Malory: Works*, 2nd edn, ed. Eugène Vinaver (Oxford, 1977), p. 39.
4   The phrase *costume rhetoric* will be used in this essay to signify the structure of '*signifying* associations' Roland Barthes posits in his 'garment system', in 'The Imagination of the Sign', in *Critical Essays*, trans. Richard Howard (Evanston, IL, 1972). These associations are made up of the individual costume signs, the basic units – the individual items of dress – that are associated within a total costume. Such basic units associated in one portrait create 'a temporary but *signifying* association, analogous to the one uniting the words of a sentence', according to Barthes, p. 206. Similarly, a structure of such 'signifying associations' makes up a rhetoric. I discuss this idea at greater length in *C&C*, pp. 1–23, esp. 4, 17–18, 23.
5   Quoted in Edward L. Cutts, *Scenes & Characters of the Middle Ages*, 7th edn (London, 1930), p. 242. Regarding the history of regulation of clerical dress, see Robert E. Rodes, Jr, *Ecclesiastical Administration in Late Medieval England: The Anglo-Saxons to the Reformation* (Notre Dame, IN, 1977), pp. 41–2. Rodes describes the Gregorian Reform, especially during the twelfth and thirteenth centuries, including the expectation that clerical dress would exemplify 'modesty and sobriety'. This dress did not differ from lay costume except for avoidance of all excess. Later, when fashions changed and long garments were shortened for laypersons, the canonists required that clerical dress retain robes down to the floor. Rodes also mentions that by 1268, among the English legatine canons of Ottobuono, there is an 'urgent' directive: that the

this statement we find a prototypical broad theory derived from a four-step process: first, a generalization about frequent occurrence – that external costume is 'often' revealing; second, an interpretation of this generalization transformed into a premise – that external costume does reveal the 'internal character and condition' of its wearer; followed by a third step, a specific application to a group, stated as a principle – that this *should* be true of clerks; and succeeded, finally, by a complaint about the abuse by clerks of this now firmly enshrined principle of dress.

Early in my medieval studies, in an analytical failure to recognize this specious rhetorical process, and in a rush to grasp at least one certainty in medieval literature, I began a study of literary costume signs in Chaucer's *General Prologue* with an important misconception. I mention this personal failure in reading costume rhetoric only because the problem is more widespread than it is particular.[6] I *misunderstood*, and took it as fact, that in medieval literature the clothing worn by a literary character literally represented his/her 'internal character and condition'. My misunderstanding was bolstered by the fact that the desirability of correct and appropriate outward representation in dress was the social principle upon which fourteenth-century civil sumptuary laws were based, and it was also the spiritual ideal expressed in numerous religious rules regarding dress requirements and restrictions for those in holy orders. In literature, medieval allegory supplied ample 'proof' of this principle, while medieval satire refuted its general application. Further, numerous articles produced by critics of medieval literature included brief comments on the costumes of the *General Prologue* pilgrims and affirmed my misapprehension that Chaucer's portraits always equated outward appearance with inner nature.[7] These critics first determined the internal character and condi-

---

'primary' effect of clerical garments should be 'to make the cleric easily distinguishable from the layman'. Failing in the effort to demonstrate sobriety and dignity through dress at all times was thought to mock God.

6   Regarding costume as a means of communication and the complexity of understanding it, see Grant McCracken, 'Clothing as Language: An Object Lesson in the Study of the Expressive Properties of Material Culture', *Material Anthropology*, eds Barrie Reynolds and Margaret A. Stott (Lanham, MD, 1987), pp. 103–28. McCracken discusses a variety of ways in which 'clothing may be seen as a concrete manifestation of "particular ideas in the mind" ', pp. 104–5, although he does not describe how images of clothing are employed and function in literature.

7   This misunderstanding remains current among many writers in the field of medieval literary costume. For example, Christopher Breward, *The Culture of Fashion* (Manchester, 1995), pp. 34–8, supports the idea that the attitude toward dress in the Middle Ages was that surface appearance (clothing) equaled the inner reality of the wearer. Clearly, we should acknowledge the common sense of S. H. Rigby, *Chaucer in Context: Society, Allegory, and Gender* (Manchester, 1996), p. 2, in considering 'what sorts of literary and non-literary conventions were at his [Chaucer's] disposal for making sense of the society around him', and specifically apply that consideration to

tion of a pilgrim and then wrote, usually briefly, that the costumes in his/her portrait supported the thesis of the pilgrim's good, bad, or indifferent nature already posited by the author. However, both historical documents and literature make it clear that all too often this principle and ideal were not maintained in practice. A reading of *Le Roman de la rose* and False Seeming's comments on his costume versus his actions forced my recognition that any automatic assumption that costume invariably represents true character was simplistic and that such simplicity had to be augmented by, at the least, one other model of costume rhetoric that recognized hypocrisy or disguise. Once my ideas of costume rhetoric were open to augmentation, other models surfaced.

Models of Costume Rhetoric[8]

False Seeming provides an example of the *False Vestments* model[9] of costume rhetoric through his monk's habit that visually proclaims him holy when in truth he is hypocrisy personified. False Seeming's commentary spells out this deliberate masquerade (lines 11011–22, 11044–58, 11076–82), culminating with the statement: 'J'aim miex devant la gent orer/ Et affubler ma renardie/ De mantiau de papelardie' ['I prefer to pray in front of people and cover my foxlike nature under a cloak of pope-holiness'] (lines 11522–4).[10] An excerpt from *Cleanness*, by the *Pearl* Poet, provides another illustration of this *False Vestments* model in which the narrator warns the reader about priests hiding personal spiritual grime under pristine holy vestments which stand for spiritual cleanness (lines 5–16, 29–38). This *False Vestments* metaphor is very important to an understanding of costume in *Cleanness*: hypocritical priests wear holy vestments as they celebrate Mass, but their souls are clothed in filth; therefore, their visible vestments are false and convey a message that is not true to those who see them.[11]

his costume rhetoric. Also see Rigby, p. x, regarding what Chaucer does not say, p. 54; and examples of a fourfold reading, p. 82.

8 Previously, in *C&C*, pp. 5–16, I have listed the models of costume rhetoric that Chaucer employs in the *General Prologue*, according to my analysis. For the convenience of the reader of this present volume, I offer a recapitulation, with altered applications pertaining to religious and academic dress.

9 Discussed, *C&C*, pp. 6–9.

10 Guillaume de Lorris and Jean de Meun, *Le Roman de la rose*, ed. Daniel Poirion (Paris, 1974); Charles Dahlberg, trans., *The Romance of the Rose* (Hanover, 1983).

11 *Cleanness*, in *Pearl, Cleanness, Patience, Sir Gawain and the Green Knight*, eds A. C. Cawley and J. J. Anderson (London, 1976), lines 5-16, 29-38. William Langland, too, makes this metaphor explicit in his many comments about friars who preach falsely while wearing holy garments, in Prologue, lines 58–65, *Piers Plowman: The B Version*,

The passage in *Cleanness*, also provides the more familiar model of costume rhetoric – costume signs which, unlike the *False Vestments* model, correctly present the wearer's spiritual state. In this case we see a *Spiritual Mirror* of a soiled soul. The concept expressed through this model eliminates the expectation that anyone might enter heaven metaphorically wearing the spiritual equivalent of torn clothes: harlot's hood; leggings torn at the knee; patched, old, and misshapen shoes; a torn tabard; as well as unwashed hands. In short, Haukyn and his uncleansed literary fellows need not apply. Thus, the *Spiritual Mirror* model of costume rhetoric may express spiritual filthiness through clothing metaphors as aptly as it expresses spiritual cleanness, for example in the shining, spotless dress of the Pearl maiden, in *Pearl*.

In costume rhetoric we find complexity where it has often been thought that only simplicity existed. Further, the recognition in these medieval works of costume-rhetoric models that work conjointly in certain respects and independently in others disproves any idea of simplicity. Beyond that, recognition of complexity increases with additional analysis and generates a longer list of models included in Chaucer's *General Prologue*, as I have previously explained. I should again stress that I do not consider this list to be exhaustive. Further, these categories overlap, and often several models are at work at one time, and on different levels, in a literary description.

For the reader's convenience, these models of costume rhetoric are repeated here with a focus on their application to religious dress:

1. *Spiritual Mirror* – a garment or accessory that symbolically represents the wearer's spiritual condition.[12] The idea behind sartorial regulations for holy habits is that the humility expressed by the garments will be a reflection of the wearer's inner spirit and that these habits will visually reflect a withdrawal from all worldly interests. The well-made cloke[13] worn by the Prioress fits the requirements of such regulations.

2. *False Vestment* – a garment or accessory having an established symbolic meaning that misrepresents a character's inner nature or estate; a spiritual or social disguise. False Seeming, Constrained Abstinence, and Pope Holiness

---

eds George Kane and E. Talbot Donaldson (University of London, 1975), hereafter referred to as *P.P.B.*

12 Secular literary examples previously mentioned include the Pearl Maiden and Haukyn. Also see Samantha Mullaney's 'Fashion and Morality in BL MS Add. 37049', *Texts and their Contexts: Papers From the Early Book Society (1997)*, eds John Scattergood and Julia Boffey (Dublin, 1997), pp. 71–86, in which she discusses fashionable dress shown in illuminations, which depict pride and worldliness versus the humble dress of Abel.

13 The page numbers for definitions of specialized costume terms may be found in the index. Those generic terms found in ordinary collegiate dictionaries will not be defined.

of *Le Roman de la rose*, illustrate this model, but it is also applicable to lay-persons dressing above their social station.

3. *Omitted Clothing*[14] – the author describes no clothing, leaving the reader to assume customary clothing; or the author omits an expected item of clothing. The omission of costume is a literary signal that the character is metaphorically clothed in his/her actions or virtues and may be judged accordingly. The obvious Chaucerian example here is the Parson for whom no garments are provided,[15] but there are other omissions of costume signs that are interesting, for example the one Chaucer openly displaces – the Pardoner's hood, which he carries in his male – as well as numerous garments customarily worn in particular religious habits but omitted from Chaucer's costume rhetoric.[16]

4. *Emblematic Dress* – a literary garment that functions as a sign, badge, or device of a kind, class, or group. Obviously, all of the particular garments worn as part of a religious habit belong in this model, and individual garments such as a nun's veil and a monk's cowl are sometimes emblematic of the entire habit.[17]

5. *Actual Garment or Accessory* – costume items described realistically at the literal level; readers might find such items described in historical records, mentioned in histories of costume, and/or present as dated artifacts (museum items, paintings, etc.). The costume signs best illustrating this idea are the Prioress's wimple, the Monk's supple boots, and the Pardoner's vernicle, as Chapters 2, 4, and 8 describe.[18]

---

[14] See *C&C*, p. 6, n. 15, regarding nakedness or nudity, or the wearing of animal skins.

[15] Lay examples include the Manciple, Harry Bailly, the Cook, and Chaucer-the-pilgrim narrator.

[16] Among the lay costumes discussed in *C&C*, and listed in the index, these omitted costume items include Chaucer's omission of the Sergeant's coif and the Knight's sword in their *General Prologue* portraits.

[17] Among the lay pilgrims, another Chaucerian example is the hip-mantel worn by the Wife of Bath, signaling her common origins. A group of signs present in the dress of affluent middle-class men appears in the portraits of the Franklin and the Guildsmen. These signs of girdle, suspended purse, and anelace or knife, which Chaucer presents in a cluster, indicate a place in the ranks of gentility, the relative places more precisely indicated by the quality of the materials used to make these items. See also Peter Corrigan's 'Interpreted, Circulating, Interpreting: The Three Dimensions of the Clothing Object', *The Socialness of Things: Essays on the Socio-Semiotics of Objects*, ed. Stephen Harold Riggings (Berlin, 1994), pp. 435–49, esp. his discussion of the three dimensions of the clothing object that indicate the wearer's job, social level, sex, ethnic origin, age category, and/or particular occasion for wearing, p. 435; and Weiner and Schneider, esp. pp. 1–4, regarding the emblematic display of cloth to represent age, gender, official and unofficial group, and status.

[18] The best example of documentable costume among the lay pilgrims is Chaucer's Merchant's unusually complete literary costume, which I have discussed at length (*C&C*).

6. *Social Mirror* – a garment or accessory that accurately reflects the wearer's social or economic status, or both. The religious habits of each of Chaucer's pilgrims in holy orders, to the extent that they are proper reflections of the appropriate religious rule, serve this purpose.[19]

7. *Generalized Costume* – a stereotypic literary description of costume, lacking detail. While, in the *General Prologue*, Chaucer is often enigmatic concerning the specific orders to which certain religious pilgrims belong, for example the Friar and the Pardoner, and also in the Pardoner's case, his specific rank within an order, he does not provide an example of the kind of *Generalized Costume* he utilizes in some of the *Tales*. For instance, in the *Knight's Tale*, Theseus is clad in royal robes. The reader must supply his/her own mental set of royal robes.

Religious Rules

Chaucer and his contemporary audience could take for granted that the folk of 'Holy Church'[20] would wear distinguishing religious costumes. The well-established consensus was that those in holy orders should be sartorially distinguishable from the rest of society. To this end and previous to Chaucer's time, each religious order had designed or chosen costumes deemed suitable for expressing their religious beliefs. The following discussion of these regulations draws on the Rules written for males and for females; however, because more sartorial details were provided in the ever-developing Rules for nuns, they quite naturally occupy more descriptive space in this chapter.

The Rule of St Benedict for monks was the basis of the habits for Benedictine nuns as well. This Rule includes several regulations concerning the quality and weights of fabric to be used, specifying that monastic garb should be suitable to local climate and seasonal needs. Further, these fabrics should be purchased locally, or from the cheapest available source. Special provisions were made for monks sent on a journey: they should receive from the wardrobe a pair of drawers, a cowl, and a tunic 'which are to be a little better than those they ordinarily wear', all of which were to be given back to the

---

[19] As one example among those pilgrims not in holy orders, the Wife of Bath's coverchiefs and 'gaye scarlet gytes' serve as literary illustrations of her profession and her economic status (*C&C*).

[20] The phrases 'folk of holy kirke' and 'men of holy chyrch' are used familiarly in *PPB* 15, line 385, and by John Mirus [John Mirk] in *Instructions for Parish Priests*, ed. Edward Peacock, EETS 31 (London, 1868; rev. 1902; rpt. 1996), p. 63. See also p. 15 below regarding the 'people of holy church' as mentioned in sumptuary legislation.

wardrobe upon return.[21] A monk's complete habit also included a belt, shoes, and stockings.[22]

Benedictine clothing regulations were concerned with maintaining economy, propriety, and climatic suitability in type of fabric used in habits as well as with prohibiting all unsuitable decoration. These concerns are echoed in the Rules for Benedictine nuns as well as for monks, friars, and nuns in other orders[23] and, as we shall see, reiterated in English monastery and convent visitation accounts continuing through the time of William Alnwick, Bishop of Lincoln in the mid-fifteenth century. Meanwhile, succeeding versions of religious rules provide more specific details of how religious Rules attempted to deal with these concerns.

Clothing Regulations

Listing garments and quality of materials, *The Northern Metrical Version of The Rule of St Benet* describes the habit of Benedictine nuns:

> **De indumentis**
> They sal be clede ful wele, we wate,
> Efter þer place es cald or hate.
> For in cald stedes who so er sted,
> Þam nedes forto be better cled;
> In who er in hate cuntre,
> Sich clething to þam may be.
> And al it sal be puruayd playne
> At þe ordinance of þeir souerayne.
> In comun places for alkins note
> Sufficis a kirtil & a cote;
> And mantels sal þai haue certayne,
> In winter dubil, in somer playne;
> And changing kirtils sal þai haue
> In nyghtes þer oþer forto saue.
> Schos þai sall haue, whor þai dwel,

21 *The Rule of St Benedict*, ed. and trans. D. Oswald Hunter Blair, 4th edn (Fort Augustus, 1934), Chapter 33, pp. 98–9, Chapter 55, pp. 144–9. See Barbara Harvey, *Monastic Dress in the Middle Ages: Precept and Practice* (Canterbury, 1988), p. 11, regarding latitude allowed in this rule; and, below, Chapter 4, pp. 112–32.

22 Revd Adrian Vigourel, *A Synthetical Manual of Liturgy*, trans. Revd John A. Nainfa (New York, 1907), p. 54; and *Rule of St Benedict: A Commentary by the Right Rev. Dom Paul Delatte*, trans. Justin McCann (New York, 1921), *cap.* 55.

23 See Gale R. Owen-Crocker, *Dress in Anglo-Saxon England* (Manchester, 1986), pp. 87–90; Francis A. Gasquet, *English Monastic Life*, 2nd edn rev. (London, 1904), Chapter 11, regarding descriptions and pictures of the various religious orders. Also see Michel Parisse, *Les nonnes au Moyen Âge* (Paris, 1983), pp. 154–9, regarding considerations for and variety of garments.

Swilk os þai may find for to sel.
Of þe farest þai sal not by,
But þe vilist ful bowsumly.   (LV, lines 2003–20)[24]

The habit of the nuns of the Benedictine Abbey at Elstow may serve as a
general model for that worn by medieval nuns. In addition to the headdress,
the habit consisted of a long white tunic or gown, called *cotte* in French,
covered by a black mantle or wide-sleeved surcoat, although the color of the
tunic, *scapular* (sleeveless outer garment falling from the shoulders), and
outer garment varied, according to the order and, perhaps, according to the
convent.[25]

---

[24] From BL Cott. MS Vespasian A. 25, in *Three Middle-English Versions of the Rule of St
Benet and Two Contemporary Rituals for the Ordination of Nuns*, ed. Ernst A. Kock,
EETS, OS 120 (London, 1902), p. 104. In succeeding lines, measurements for garments and clothes for travel are also mentioned. In this same collection, see *The Northern Prose Version of the Rule of St Benet* (Lansdowne MS 378), Chapter 55, p. 36, lines
18–28; and *The Caxton Abstract of the Rule of St Benet* (CUL, AB. 4. 64), Chapter 55,
p. 134, lines 25–35.

The account of the personal wardrobe assembled for her veiling in the nineteenth
year of Richard II's reign (22 June 1395–21 June 1396), for Joan Samborne, an Austin
nun of Lacock, describes individual garments to be made for her and the amount of
money to be spent on them. However, it also includes: 'Item paid to John Bartelot for
veils and linen cloth 102s', according to Revd W. G. Clark-Maxwell, 'The Outfit for
the Profession of an Austin Canoness at Lacock, Wilts. in the Year 1395, and Other
Memoranda', *Archaeol J*, 69, 2nd ser. 16 (1912), p. 118. This is his translation from the
Latin. The high cost mentioned here indicates that this item may have been for the
convent supply, not just for Joan.

Marilyn Oliva, *The Convent and the Community in Late Medieval England: Female
Monasteries in the Diocese of Norwich, 1350–1540*, Studies in the History of Medieval
Religion 12 (Woodbridge, 1998), p. 48, citing BL MS Egerton 3137, lists items a
novice was required to bring when she entered the Benedictine Blackborough Priory in
Norfolk: a variety of pieces of bedding, coats (4) (two each of black and white), an
outer garment (pilch) of skin or fur, (rochets) cloaks for outdoors (2), cowls (2), capes
(2), single (unlined) mantles (2), wimple (1), veils (at least 3), and other items.

[25] See Désirée Koslin, 'The Robe of Simplicity: Initiation, Robing, and Veiling of Nuns
in the Middle Ages', *Robes and Honor: The Medieval World of Investiture*, ed. Stewart
Gordon (New York, 2001), pp. 257, 261–2, for a description of monastic garments, and
p. 259, regarding illustrations of nuns' habits in pontificals. Janet Mayo, *A History of
Ecclesiastical Dress* (New York, 1984), pp. 34–6, describes individual monastic garments, shoes, and colors; and p. 48, lack of habits for the clergy. Harvey discusses garments for clerks, p. 8; for monks, pp. 14–15, 26; for nuns, p. 35; and for Poor Clares, p.
37. Gasquet, pp. 169–70, describes Augustinian nuns' clothing (1414–18) made from
materials spun, woven, and dyed at Grace Dieu convent in Leiscestershire, and also
shoes cobbled from skins from the convent supply; see his account of mending,
garment production, and cloth purchase, pp. 101–3.

Also, Oliva, p. 63, provides the text of a sermon taken from CUL MS Hh.1.11, citing
Veronica O'Mara, *A Study and Edition of Middle English Sermons* (Leeds Texts and
Monographs, 1987), pp. 199–203. This sermon lists and defines the symbolic value of
each garment in nuns' habits.

Also providing for plainness and suitability, the *Ancren Riwle* prescribes:

[Y]e may be well content with your clothes, be they white, be they black; only see they be plain and warm and well made – skins well tawed; and have as many as you need . . . [but not] any such thing that is not proper for you to have.[26]

This Rule includes black and white garments, different types of headresses, wimples,[27] and specifies plain, warm, and *well-made* garments [my emphasis]. The provisions for clothing evince a concern for good construction, suitability to local climate, and rely on common knowledge regarding what garments are appropriate for nuns.

The *Rule of Syon* forbids the wearing of anything that is 'ouer curyous'.[28] According to the MED, when the adjective *curyous* modifies things, it means 'carefully, skillfully, artistically, or elaborately designed or made; artistic, exquisite, fine; costly, sumptuous'. Apparently, religious apparel and accessories might be carefully or skillfully made, 'well made' as the *Ancren Riwle* specifies, but once a garment becomes artistically or elaborately designed, exquisite, costly or sumptuous, it might be described as 'over curious'. Embroidery in silk, gold, and silver would certainly fit this second category. It is a matter of degree, a point that is relevant to any judgment of the Monk's 'ful curious pyn', and to the Prioress's veil and wimple, as well as her rosary with pendant brooch.

Propriety and the avoidance of vanity, as signified by 'over-curious' garments, continue to be a concern in the *Additions to the Rules of Syon*. The *Additions* include a description of the duties of the Chambress who is in charge of the nuns' wardrobe and the acquisition of both clothes and bedding, including the following:

cowles . . . wymples, veyles, crounes, pynnes,[29] cappes . . . al suche other necessaryes after the disposicion of the abbes, whiche in nowyse schal be

---

26 *Ancren Riwle: A Treatise on the Duties of Monastic Life*, ed. and trans. James Morton (London, 1853), Pt 8, pp. 418–21. See also, Eileen Power, *Medieval English Nunneries*, Cambridge Studies in Medieval Life and Thought, ed. G. G. Coulton (London, 1922), pp. 530–1.

27 This Rule does not counsel against wearing a wimple (a garment that is portrayed as one means of staying warm), but does counsel against wimples worn *for the purpose of adornment only*. This reading contradicts *Riverside Chaucer* n. 151, p. 805, regarding *The Ancrene Riwle*, trans. M. B. Salu (London, 1955), p. 186.

28 Julia Bolton Holloway, *Saint Bride and Her Book: Birgitta of Sweden's Revelations* (Newburyport, MA, 1992), p. 11, discusses the habit of the Brigittine nuns.

29 Significant on this list of 'proper' items are the pins because items designated as gold and silver 'pins' are forbidden elsewhere; although the exact nature of the Syon pins is not specified, they are probably the necessary pins of non-precious metal, usually called tiring pins, for securing the headdress described in the Rule. Roberta Gilchrist describes an archeological excavation at Flixborough, Humbs., where the finds

ouer curyous, but playne and homly, witheoute weuynge of any straunge colours of sylke,[30] golde, or syluer,[31] hauynge al thynge of honeste and profyte, and nothyng of vanyte, after the rewle.[32]

We find in this Rule a number of separate items that are part of a nun's headdress: besides wimple and veil there are listed cowls, crowns, and caps. Items specifically forbidden are: colors of silk, gold, and silver, all used in a decorative manner, perhaps in such items as the belts or girdles mentioned in visitation records – confirming previous transgressions in sumptuous decoration. Significantly, the prohibited items are characterized as articles of dress that are 'ouer curyous'.[33] Most important, we note that these post-1415 *Additions* evince no concern for height of veil above eyebrows, although the rule provided meticulous directions for pinning a somewhat complicated headdress. The headdress consisted of a *fillet* or band that surrounded forehead and chin and fastened by means of pins at the back of the head. A black linen veil was provided to be worn over this fillet arrangement, and this veil was to be fastened by three pins placed at the forehead and at each ear. A white linen cap on which five pieces of red cloth were sewn, 'like five drops, allusive to the five wounds of our Saviour', was the final garment described as standard issue for these nuns. It was to be worn over the black linen veil.[34]

included straight pins of very good quality that she deems likely to be the tiring pins for securing nuns' veiling, in *Gender and Material Culture: The Archeology of Religious Women* (London, 1994), p. 30.

30 'Silk' might refer either to embroidery thread or to fabric for veils and wimples.
31 The gold and silver here may refer either to tiring pins made from these metals, or to metallic threads used in embroidery.
32 *Additions to the Rules of Syon*, in George James Aungier, *History and Antiquities of Syon Monastery, the Parish of Isleworth, and the Chapelry of Hounslow* (London, 1840), Appendix, p. 392. See also, Power, *Nunneries*, pp. 132–3.
33 *Additions to the Rules of Syon*, in Aungier, Appendix, p. 392; also Power, *Nunneries*, pp. 132–3. Koslin, pp. 264–5, discusses the sin of vanity as evidenced in these same sartorial sins.
34 Vivian Kay Hudson, 'Clothing and Adornment Imagery in "The Scale of Perfection": A Reflection of Contemplation', *Studies in Spirituality* 4 (1994), pp. 117–45, esp. 123–7, 138–40, discusses nuns' consecration ceremonies and Walter Hilton's metaphorical depiction of veiling and of nuns' habits. Aungier, Introduction, p. 11, informs us that 'The ceremony of consecration and the imposition of the veil were of very early origin' and that 'wearing veils originated with the Pontiff Soter, about the middle of the second century'. In addition, pp. 314–16, he gives us a copy of the blessing and vesting ceremony in English, taken from BL Add. MS 5208. The language of this ceremony implies no particular significance to any single garment. See *Three Middle-English Versions of The Rule of St Benet*, pp. 141–50, for ceremonies of consecration. Regarding such ceremonies, Jo Ann McNamara, *Sisters in Arms* (Cambridge, MA, 1996), p. 96, mentions Genovefa and others taking the veil. See Stewart Gordon, 'A World of Investiture', *Robes and Honor*, ed. Stewart Gordon (New York, 2001), p. 10, concern-

A survey of religious rules reveals the genuine problems concerning religious garb faced by the church hierarchy in England. To summarize: one of their concerns was that religious habits should be inexpensive or humble in materials and therefore appropriate to a religious vocation; another was that the garments illustrating such humility should be suited to both climate and particular occupation. A certain amount of attention was given to the idea that the garments should be well-made but not 'over curious'. Further, the Benedictine Rule provides that qualitatively better garments than those worn daily should be issued to anyone who made a journey. That these better clothes were returned to the general wardrobe at the conclusion of the journey is in keeping with the Rule's provisions forbidding private ownership of clothing[35] and private gifts of any sort.[36] However, as we shall see, by the end of the fourteenth century, these last two provisions were often disregarded.

While early copies of religious rules prescribed clothing in general terms, later versions became increasingly more detailed, possibly in response to the lengthening list of sartorial transgressions.[37] The Brigittine *Rule of Syon* provided that two chemises of white flannel, called *stamen* in BL MS Arundel 146, should be issued to each nun (two separate changes were allowed for alternate wearing and laundry). In addition, each was given a gown and a hood of gray cloth. The hood's sleeves were not to be longer than the middle finger and would normally hang around the hand in folds except when clasped to the arm when performing manual services. A mantle of gray cloth was also issued, 'not plaited or finely made, but tight and plain, the whole being for use, not vanity; single [unlined] in summer, but in winter lined, not with delicate skins, but with those of lambs or sheep'. This provision for a fur lining accorded with the Canons of William Corboys or Corbyl, Archbishop of Canterbury, in 1127, which decreed 'no abbess or nun should use more

ing archaic peasant dress as the models for monks' and nuns' habits received as ritual garments.

Koslin, pp. 255, 257, describes the significance of veiling; pp. 256–7, 264, 266–9, the clothing for consecration ceremonies; p. 260, nuns' dress as (anti) fashion; and p. 269, metaphors for nuns' garb after consecration. See also (Bishop of Ely) John Alcock, *(Spousage of a Virgin to Christ): An Exhortacyon Made to Relygyous Systers*, The English Experience, no. 638 (Westmynstre [Wynken de Worde], n.d.; Amsterdam, 1974; Norwood, NJ, 1974), [pp. 7–8], an address made upon the sisters' consecration; Stewart Gordon, 'Robes, Kings, and Semiotic Ambiguity', p. 382, regarding papal authority and investiture ceremonies, and Gordon, 'A World of Investiture', *Robes and Honor*, pp. 5–6, 10, concerning political and monastic investitures.

35 *The Rule of St Benedict*, ed. and trans. Blair, Chapter 33, pp. 98–9; Chapter 55, pp. 144-9.
36 *The Rule of St Benedict*, Chapter 54, pp. 144–5, 204.
37 Koslin, p. 258, discusses this process.

costly apparel than such as is made of lambs' or cats' skins'.[38] In addition each sister was allowed a *pilch* [cloaks 'of skins or fur'][39] made of either lamb or cat skins, for winter wear. The Rule specified that this pilch should be fastened at the neck with a wooden clasp, and that there should be a 'palm's breadth' between the bottom of the pilch and the ground.[40] The complete habit corresponds with the inventory listed in the duties of the Chambress who was to acquire clothing for the nuns as described in the *Additions to the Rules of Syon*. Among the items she was to keep on hand were: 'rewle cotes . . . mantelles . . . pylches, mantel furres', all of which fall under the general admonition not to be 'ouer curyous, but playne and homly'.

A concession to climate, the pilches and fur-lined mantles were considered proper. Duranti, who wrote the *Divine Offices* and *Rationale* (c. 1286), describes the tunic forerunner of this garment of fur and its linen covering, the *superpellicium* (now called surplice): the linen covering represents the robe of innocence purchased for humanity by Christ; the robe of animal skins signifies man's fallen nature, since this is, according to tradition, what Adam wore after the fall.[41] These pilches would be appropriate array for a bride of Christ as described in *The Revelations of Saint Birgitta*, which includes a discussion of the three types of fabric considered for use by a spouse of Christ: linen, wool or leather, and silk. An analogy is drawn between proper types of

38 Aungier, pp. 22-3, and nn. 2 and 1 respectively. See 'The Sisters' Clothes'; 'From *The Rule of Our Saviour*', *Women's Writing in Middle English*, ed. Alexandra Barratt (New York, 1992), p. 91, regarding furs. Barrat says that St Bridget (b.1302 or 1303, d.1373) claimed that Christ dictated the Rule of St Saviour in Latin; that fourteenth-century rule was translated into Middle English in CUL MS Ff. 6. 33, fols 43–4, in the fifteenth century, probably for the nuns of Syon Monastery. Also see Elizabeth Ewing, *Fur in Dress* (London, 1981), p. 26 regarding the pilch, and pp. 41–2 for furs worn by the clergy; Mayo, p. 38, on gifts of furs to anchorites and anchoresses, including bifle (undefined), calaber (squirrel skins from Calabria), and gris (gray back of winter squirrel).
39 James Robinson Planché, *A Cyclopaedia of Costume or Dictionary of Dress* (London, 1876), 1:398; and *An Illustrated Dictionary of Historic Costume: From the First Century B.C. to C. 1760* (Mineola, NY, 2003), p. 398.
40 Aungier also states that for summer wear, ankle-high shoes and knee-high stockings were provided; for the winter, cloth-lined knee-high boots and stockings were issued. See similar provisions for monks' foot-coverings described in Harvey, p. 15; and 'The Sisters' Clothes', p. 91.
41 *Dictum est Superpellicium, eo quod antiquitus super tunicas pellicias de pellibus mortuorum animalium factas induebantur, quod adhuc in quibusdam Ecclesiis observatur, repraesentantes quod Adam post peccatum talibus vestitus est pelliciis.*
    Duranti, *Rationale*, lib. III, *cap.* I, as quoted by Daniel Rock, *Hierugia; or, The Holy Sacrifice of the Mass*, 3rd edn rev., ed. W. H. James Weale (London, 1892), 2:256–7.
    For a history of ills deriving from costume beginning with Adam, see D'Etienne de Bourbon, *Anecdotes Historiques: Legendes et Apologues* (Paris, 1877), p. 235.

behavior and these types of fabric; silk is deemed unsuitable.[42] As for monks, regulations permitted certain furs, as well as a *pelisse* – a leather tunic, sometimes lined with fur, during cold weather.[43]

The more ascetic habits of friars were essentially based on the ideal of poverty expressed in the adoption of the clothing worn by peasants.[44] Franciscan friars, following St Francis's lead, wore one rope-girded tunic, and had one coat with a hood and a second coat without a hood, depending on need. Shoes were worn according to necessity. Only 'symple' and 'vyle' fabrics could be used for their clothing, which might be patched with similar cloth.[45]

English Civil Sumptuary Laws

A consideration of fourteenth-century English sumptuary laws completes this survey of the historical background concerned with the dress of those in holy orders. These fourteenth-century laws, although apparently not enforced, provide rules for wearing apparel and ornamentation based on factors of birth and income. They indicate the attitude of Parliament toward both lay and religious dress, and, in both cases, the economic factor is the determining one. This fact contributes to our understanding of contemporary laymen's perceptions of habits worn by those in holy orders and of livery worn by employees of the church.

In the 1337 sumptuary laws, certain fabrics and furs were prohibited to everyone except the royal family, but changes were made in the 1363 laws[46] that included 'people of Holy Church':

> Clerks, which have Degree in any Church, Cathedral, Collegial, or Schools, [or Clerk] of the King, that [hath] such Estate that requireth Furr, shall do and use according to the Constitution of the same; and all other Clerks, which have ii. C. Marks of [Land] by Year, shall wear and do as Knights of

---

42 *The Revelations of Saint Birgitta*, ed. from the fifteenth-century manuscript in the Garret Collection in Princeton University Library by William Patterson Cumming, EETS, OS 178 (London, 1929), pp. 1–2, 17–20; see also Holloway, *Saint Bride*, p. 40, nn. 9, 11; pp. 46–7, n. 14, regarding cloth and humility.

43 As described in Harvey, pp. 14–15. For furs permitted, see pp. 19–20.

44 G. G. Coulton, *The Chronicler of European Chivalry* (London, 1930), p. 15; further, G. G. Coulton, *Studies in Medieval Thought* (New York, 1965), pp. 158–60.

45 See the Middle English trans. of the Rule of St Francis in BL Cott. MS Faustina D. IV, included in *Monumenta Franciscana*, ed. Richard Howlett (London, 1882; rpt., 1965), 2.67; also this book, Chapter 5, pp. 133–59, nn. 20–1 for varieties of friars' habits. For the dress of Poor Clares, see Mayo, p. 37.

46 See Frances Elizabeth Baldwin, *Sumptuary Legislation and Personal Regulation in England*, Johns Hopkins University Studies in Historical and Political Science, Series 44, no. 1 (Baltimore, 1926), pp. 30–2, citing *Statutes of the Realm* (1910; rpt. London, 1963), 1:280–1, hereafter referred to as *Statutes*.

the same Rent; and other Clerks within the same Rent, shall wear as the Esquires of C. li. of Rent.[47]

While giving a nod to the church's governing bodies of the clergy, these 1363 civil laws clearly tied their sartorial expectations to the income of each member of the clergy. Visitation records show that some persons in holy orders wore fur, on hoods and elsewhere, and apparently some furs were inappropriately worn. With an income of less than £100, both laymen and anyone in holy orders would have been limited by the 1363 law to garments of cloth not exceeding 4½ marks per whole cloth and could not display gold, silver, precious stones, or fur.[48] Anyone '*who did not possess land or rents to the value of a hundred pounds a year*' [my italics], including esquires and gentlemen (and their families) below the rank of knights, were forbidden to wear silk and furs other than lamb, coney, cat, and fox.[49] Thus, according to secular law, income per year, rather than status attained by birth alone or status in the church hierarchy, appears to have been the deciding criterion by which, according to Parliament, a person might rightfully assume apparel designated for a given level of society. And the texts of two later laws (one of which was proposed but not passed) repeat these and similar ideas.

Although Parliament repealed this 1363 law the following year, it nevertheless clarifies prevalent attitudes in Parliament toward social status, income, and clothing during Edward III's reign. A later proposal of similar laws, although rejected by Richard II,[50] indicates that such ideas were still current among members of Parliament.

Had religious rules been followed explicitly in the late fourteenth century, those in holy orders, although drawn primarily from the ranks of the nobility, wealthy merchant class, and middle class, nevertheless would have worn habits that corresponded in expense and lack of decoration to those secular rules laid down for grooms, yeomen, and handicraftsmen, the lowest levels of society mentioned in England's sumptuary law of 1363 (37 Edward III). In this law Parliament set detailed clothing standards according to occupation, even though, once more, personal income continued to be the final determinant of what an individual might lawfully wear to avoid the threat of confiscation. Grooms and those possessing material goods valued at 40s or less were restricted to clothing made of blanket cloth, the cheapest kind of cloth, and russet, also an inferior type of cloth.[51] Such cloth would conform to the

---

47   *Statutes*, 1:381, Item XIII; see also Baldwin, p. 50.
48   *Statutes*, 1:380–1, Item X; Baldwin, pp. 48–9.
49   Baldwin, p. 48, citing 2:164–5, *Stat. L.*
50   The proposed law (1378–79) provided that cloth of silk might be worn by those who can spend £40 per year. Richard II, well known for his unparalleled personal finery, rejected this petition. It was not considered in the next parliament, according to Baldwin, p. 60, citing *Rot. Parl.*, 3:66.
51   *Statutes* 1:380–1, Items VIII and XIV; Baldwin, pp. 49–50.

requirements of the Benedictine Rule previously described. Grooms, servants of lords, 'they of mysteries and artificers', their wives, and children were not to wear a garment or hose made of cloth that cost more than two marks total per garment, or any item of clothing made with gold, silver, or silk, or that was embroidered, or enamelled, 'nor nothing pertaining to the said things'. The women could not wear veils or kerchiefs exceeding 12d in price. For yeomen and handicraftsmen, the price limit per whole cloth was 40s. It was thought necessary to stipulate that this group was forbidden 'to wear precious stones, cloth of silver, silk, girdles, knives, buttons, rings, brooches, chains, etc. of gold or silver, and embroidered or silken clothing'. Their wives and children could not wear 'silken veils or kerchiefs, nor any fur nor budge [imported lambskins], except lamb [domestic], coney, cat and fox'.[52] These restrictions form a sharp contrast with what convent visitation records say that some prioresses and abbesses wore, but they are compatible with the restrictions contained in these same records against identical items of forbidden clothing. Clearly, to be properly dressed as a nun was to give up all idea of upper-class status as acquired by birth or expressed in clothing.[53]

Literary Metaphors Signalling Improper Dress: Wide and Long Habits

Repeated religious injunctions and sumptuary legislation acknowledge an ongoing social conflict over costume manifest in all levels of society. On the one hand, religious and many secular authorities alike objected to any manner of dress judged to be extravagant, and on the other, these authorities appear to have been powerless to eliminate what they condemned. This conflict finds full expression in the literature of the period, in which characters of all social classes are castigated for spending money on decoration (embroidery, jewels, dagging – jagged, self-fringed – or scalloped edges), and most especially on any 'new' styles that required expensive or excessive amounts of fabric. Both secular and religious writers deemed that certain virtues and

---

52 Baldwin, pp. 47–8, citing *Stat. L.*, 2:164–5.
53 Nuns' clothing would not even reflect that status accorded to esquires and gentlemen below the rank of knights of the income less than £100 per annum who might wear clothing made of a somewhat better quality than did those in the category of grooms. These esquires and gentlemen might wear cloth costing up to 4½ marks per whole cloth; however, their wives were forbidden trimmings and edgings on their clothing, according to *Statutes*, 1:380, Item X; and Baldwin, pp. 48–9.
     This category appears to be sartorially well above that intended by the writers of the Benedictine Rule, since the Rule specifies locally produced fabric obtained from the cheapest source, and clearly, the price limit of 2 marks for grooms, and 40s for yeomen and handicraftsmen indicates a less expensive fabric than that allowed to esquires and gentlemen.

vices were demonstrated in costume: conservative costume proclaimed the wearer's prudence and wisdom, even chastity; extravagant costume announced vanity, pride, vainglory, and *luxuria*, or lack of chastity. The poem 'Earth to Earth' encapsulates the religious attitude toward such piling up of sartorial treasures on earth:

> He that gose appone erthe gleterande as golde,
> Lyke als erthe neuer mare goo to erthe scholde,
> And ȝitt schall erthe vnto erthe ȝa rathere þan he wolde.
> Now why þat erthe luffis earthe, wondire me thynke,
> Or why þat erthe for erthe scholde oþer swete or swynke,
> For when þat erthe appone erthe es broghte with-in brynke,
> Than schalle erthe of erthe hafe a foulle stynke.[54]

This general condemnation finds an apt metaphor, indicating excessive amounts of fabric used in the making of a garment, in the phrase *large robes*. The 'large robes' metaphor and its variants encapsulate the concept of the worldly nun, priest, monk, or friar, satirized in the literature of the later Middle Ages. Further, a knowledge of how the metaphor works aids our understanding of Chaucer's costume rhetoric.

It is worth noting the irony present in the evolution of the 'large robes' metaphor. This phrase is employed by church officials and later, with a difference, by writers of satire to describe the basic garment of the religious habit. *Vestis talaris* (also sometimes referred to as *talaris tunica* and *pellicea*) is the proper terminology for the appropriate cassock or tunic, a close-fitting garment that covered the full length of the body from the neck down to the feet, which was prescribed by the church for its religious. Prior to the end of the sixth century, it was the ordinary dress of both male and female; however, it was necessary for church officials to rule for the maintenance of this garment when fashion changed for the laity in the fourteenth century and men adopted the short tunic.[55] The church hierarchy emphasized the need for clergy and nuns to wear sober, modest clothing, and specified the length of the *vestis talaris* again and again, as, for example, in the Brigittine *Rule of Syon*, which requires space equal to the width of a hand between the bottom

---

54 'Earth to Earth', in *Religious Pieces in Prose and Verse*, ed. George G. Perry, from Robert Thornton's MS (c.1440) in the Lincoln Cathedral Library, EETS, OS 26 (London, 1867), p. 95.

55 Revd Henry J. McCloud, *Clerical Dress and Insignia of the Roman Catholic Church* (Milwaukee, 1948), pp. viii, 47; Vigourel, p. 50; David Wilkins, *Concilia Magnae Britanniae et Hiberniae* (London, 1737), 1:590–1; *A Dictionary of Christian Antiquities*, ed. William Smith and Samuel Cheetham (Hartford, CT, 1880; rpt. New York, 1968), 1:582.

of the tunic and the ground. *Monumenta Franciscana* also provides the correct measurements for Franciscan friars' habits.[56]

Yet, this very insistence became a source of literary satire, as poets described nuns who maintained chaste exteriors, such as those in Nigel De Longchamps' twelfth-century *Speculum Stultorum*, but who, beneath their proper habits and behind their convent walls, were quarrelsome, vain, and sexually immoral.[57] The poetic suggestion that such nuns hid their impropriety behind their proper habits (thus turning them into *False Vestments*) was succeeded by poetic description of the convergence of actions and costume in which the nuns' immoderate behavior was reflected in the unauthorized width or length of their religious garments (becoming *Spiritual Mirrors* of their vanities). A case in point is the satirically proposed Order of Fair-Ease, described in the poem of that name, whose members would wear gowns long enough to trail on the ground. But the 'large robes' metaphor, which could mean long, or wide, or both simultaneously, came to signify all of these deviations from the rule, as did variants of the metaphor such as the more specific description 'wide copis'. Further, the metaphor was equally applied to excessive dress worn by priests, monks, nuns, and friars.

The typical worldly religious of literature, comparable to his or her worldly counterparts in historical records, wears over-curious religious garments or accessories, and costume distinguished by unauthorized, excessive fabric, and/or sumptuous lay garments and accessories. John Wyclif plainly describes such religious stereotypes:

3if þei gederen to hem self many wast and precious cloþes bi feyned beggerie and sotil ypocrisie, and partiþ not with pore nedy men þat han nakid sidis and torne sleues and here children steruen for cold . . . hou cloþe þei nakid men, whanne bi ypocrisie þei drawen from hem þis bodily almes bi whiche þes poralis schulden be cloþid and kept fro deþ. certis þei ben cursed disceyueris boþ of pore and riche, and ben irreguler bi-for god for myschefous deþ þat þes nedy men suffren.[58]

56 See *Monumenta Franciscana*, ed. J. S. Brewer (London, 1858; Germany, 1965), 1:575–6; also *Monumenta Franciscana*, ed. Howlett, 2:88.
57 Nigel De Longchamps, *Speculum Stultorum*, ed. John H. Mozley and Robert R. Raymo (Berkeley, CA, 1960), p. 84 on 'De monialibus', and p. 171 nn. for lines 2382–2400. For an English translation, see Nigel Longchamp, *A Mirror for Fools: The Book of Burnel the Ass*, trans. J. H. Mozley (Notre Dame, IN, 1963), pp. 80–1.
58 *The English Works of Wyclif Hitherto Unprinted*, ed. F. D. Matthew, EETS, OS 74 (London, 1880), p. 14. See also Iohannis Wyclif, *Operis Evangelici Liber Tertius et Quartus sive De Antichristo Liber Primus et Secundus*, English side-notes by F. D. Matthew (London, 1896), p. 15, lines 18–29, on 'how the pharisees of to-day deceive the people in dress and ceremonies', by wearing clothing that consumed more money than was in the seamless tunic of Christ.

Friars, especially, were castigated by Wyclif for their too-wide and, therefore, too costly habits, but his attitude concerning friars' habits applies
equally to the habits of the other religious. He asks, 'lord, what helpiþ
wydnesse of habitis of þise ordris?' and answers that they aid the 'fend' and
waste God's goods, '& so ilche þreed of sich cloþis that ben two wast & too
costliche beriþ with hym a wrong boþe to god & man' because the poor
should have received the benefit from the money spent on sumptuous clothes.
He then compares the wearers of such habits to 'trees turned vpsodoun, for
roote & inward of hem benshewid wiþ-oute to þe world, and falsnesse of here
entent is hid fro men bi þis turnyng'.[59]

Most frequently, as Wyclif did, writers metaphorically express the discrep-
ancy between the ideal and the worldly religious through the description of
the latter wearing a wide habit, 'large robes'. Lydgate provides an example in
The Temple of Glas of those in holy orders who:

> Yentred were into religioun,
> Or þei hade yeris of discresioun,
> That al her life cannot but complein,
> In wide copis perfeccion to feine,
> Ful couertli to curen al hir smert,
> And shew þe contrarie outward of her hert.[60]

Rutebeuf's 'La Chanson des ordres' presents another example of the 'large
robes' metaphor. He depicts Beguines who use their 'larges robes' to hide
their improper actions. In a second poem, 'Les Ordres De Paris', Rutebeuf
again employs this metaphor in describing promiscuous Beguines who wear
robes 'large et pleniere' (41) [generous and copious].[61] 'The Court of Love'
provides yet another example of women who have taken the veil and nuns'
vows:

> *Here* thought is, thei ben in confusion:
> 'Alas', thay sayn, 'we fayne perfeccion,
> In clothes wide and lake oure libertie;
> But all the synne mote on oure frendes be'.[62]   (lines 1103–6)

These nuns place the blame for the disparity between their holy habit and
unholy liberties on those close to them who forced them to become nuns

---

59 *The English Works of Wyclif*, pp. 315–16.
60 John Lydgate, *The Temple of Glas*, ed. J. Schick, EETS, ES 60 (London, 1891), p. 8.
61 Rutebeuf, 'La Chanson des ordres', *Fabliaux et Contes Des Poètes François Des XI,
    XII, XIII, XIV et XVe siècles*, ed. E. Barbazan (Paris, 1808), 2:300, edited from
    Bibliothèque Imperiale MSS 7218 and 7633; and in the same volume, 'Les Ordres De
    Paris', p. 294.
62 This is the pseudo-Chaucerian *Court of Love* in *The Poetical Works of Geoffrey
    Chaucer*, ed. R. Morris (London, 1866), 4:38–9.

against their wishes (lines 1111–12). Nevertheless, the disparity remains, expressed in 'clothes wide'.

Naturally, these larges robes, wide and/or long, are the required habit for the satirical Order of Fair-Ease, in the previously mentioned poem of the same name. The brothers and sisters of this unholy order are said to imitate the Hospitallers in their courtly luxury:

> Un point unt tret de Hospitlers,
> Qe sunt mult corteis chevalers,
> E ount robes bien avenauntz,
> Longes desqu'al pié traynantz,
> . . .
> Si deyvent en nostre Ordre aver
> Les freres e sueres, pur veyr.

> [A point they have taken from the Hospitallers, who are very courteous knights, and have very becoming robes, so long that they drag at their feet; . . . so in our Order, in truth, the brethren and sisters must have them.][63]

In addition to employing the 'large robes' metaphor, poets who portray those in holy orders with worldly tastes in clothing occasionally describe the specific materials used in unauthorized garments. In 'A Disputation between a Christian and a Jew', the two debaters come upon a scene of feasting at a nunnery (line 198) where the table boards are decked out in 'schire clothes and schene' (lines 209–10). The nuns wear 'Dyapre dere', and are escorted by 'Squiȝers in vch a syde/ In þe wones so wyde' (lines 199–202).[64] The costly fabric known as *dyapre*, often mentioned in Old French and medieval Latin works, was 'apparently of silk, woven or flowered over the surface with gold thread'.[65]

63 'The Order of Fair-Ease', *The Political Songs of England From the Reign of John to that of Edward II*, ed. and trans. Thomas Wright (London, 1839), p. 140; from BL MS Harl. 2253, fol. 121, from the reign of Edward II.
64 'A Disputation between a Christian and a Jew', *The Minor Poems of the Vernon MS*, ed. F. J. Furnivall, EETS, OS 117 (London, 1901), Part 2, p. 490.
65 The OED advises: 'See Francisque Michel, *Recherches sur les Etoffes de Soie, d'Or et d'Argent* [Paris 1852] I. 236-244', and lists early French references to *diaspre* 'que fu fais en Constantinoble' and 'dyaspre d'Antioch and [which] associate it with other fabrics of Byzantine or Levantine origin'. Chaucer mentions this diamond-shape patterned fabric in the *Knight's Tale*: 'Couered in clooth of gold dyapered weel' (I, line 1300). Apparently, *diapre* was not always white; the OED states that in Old French *diaspre* is often described as *blanc*, a designation that would be unnecessary if the fabric was customarily white, although the name of the color might be included in literary descriptions for other reasons. However, the point of describing nuns wearing diapre in 'A Disputation' is not that they are, or are not, dressed in white, but that they wear costly fabric against the provisions of their rule.

The author of 'The Land of Cokaygne' is less specific in that he does not use a fabric name such as *diapre* to pinpoint extravagance of dress, but the nuns he describes are no less luxuriously circumstanced. They reside in a nunnery 'Whar is plente grete of silk'.[66] This poem emphasizes the sin of gluttony – the adjacent abbey is built of foods (pastry walls, cake shingles, etc.); the mention of silk is but an aside, but the juxtaposition of the two recalls the message of 'Earth to Earth', quoted above, and the final outcome of hunger for the earth's pleasures. It is no wonder that such nuns wearing silk, diapered or plain, might be described as the Kildare nuns are in 'Of Men Lif that Wonith in Lond':

> Hail be ȝe nonnes of seint mari house,
> goddes bourmaidnes and his owen spouse,
> ofte mistrediþ ȝe ȝur schone, ȝur fete beþ ful tendre,
> daþeir þe sotter þat tawiþ ȝure leþir.[67]

These nuns 'mistrediþ' and their shoes are made of skins not 'weltawed'. Did the poet suggest that these nuns walk in the wrong paths and that, thus, Satan is their cobbler who crafts, but poorly, the shoes that cause their feet to be tender? Another possible meaning is that their feet are too tender to wear the shoes prescribed by their superior.[68] In either case, the implication is that these nuns cannot live up to what their order and vows require of them, an implication expressed in terms of wearing apparel. Similarly, although on a grander, more specific scale, the worldly nun of the eleventh century '*Plangit nonna fletibus*' longs to wear ermine (royal fur), in addition to wishing for a brooch, a bridal veil, a ribbon or coronet, and a necklace.[69]

---

[66] 'The Land of Cokaygne', *Early English Poems and Lives of Saints*, ed. F. J. Furnivall, Transactions of the Philological Society (Berlin, 1858), p. 160.

[67] 'Of Men Lif that Wonith in Lond', *Early English Poems and Lives of Saints*, p. 154, edited from BL MS Harl. 913, p. 7.

[68] See Graciela S. Daichman, *Wayward Nuns in Medieval Literature* (Syracuse, NY, 1986), pp. 51–2, for this interpretation.

[69] 'Plangit nonna fletibus', ed. Peter Dronke, *Medieval Latin and the Rise of the European Love Lyric* (Oxford, 1966), 2:357, lines 19–27. Jill Mann, *Chaucer and Medieval Estates Satire: The Literature of Social Classes and the General Prologue to the Canterbury Tales* (Cambridge, 1973), p. 130, quotes, translates, and comments on these lines.

> See also the literary figure of the luxurious abbess who slept among gay coverlet, soft and delicate sheets, and furs, in *An Alphabet of Tales, An English 15th Century Translation of the Alphabetum Narrationum once attributed to Etienne de Besancon*, ed. M. M. Banks, EETS, OS 126 (London, 1904), no. 15, pp. 13–14; or the luxurious prioress in purgatory, described by J. P. Krapp, in *The Legend of St Patrick's Purgatory; Its Later Literary History* (Baltimore, 1899), pp. 75–6. Of this Prioress, the fiends in hell state,
>
>> It is wel knowen . . . at she was more cosluer in puler [fur] weryng, as of girdelles of siluer and overgilt and ringes on hir fingers, and siluer bokeles and

Thus, the metaphoric difference between correctness and incorrectness in religious costume might be expressed semantically and metaphorically in a variety of costume metaphors, but, most often, in the difference between the correct *talaris tunica* and the satiric 'large robes'.[70] The important and ironic difference may be even more emphatic when *wide* is the adjective used. Wideness implies excessive cost, in the amount of fabric consumed if two or more narrow pieces had been sewn together; alternatively it suggests the use of expensive fabric, for often cloth woven in wider measure was more costly.[71] Wideness also implies the possibility of forbidden construction methods employed in making the tunic, such as pleating and tucking,[72] which are not forbidden in wimples but are expressly forbidden in tunics.

The 'large robes' metaphor of condemning sermon and religious satire is but part of a wider convention that includes the ostentatious dress of all segments of society.[73] Complaints against costume abuses were prominent, per-

     ouergilt on hir shone, esy lieng in nyghtes as it were [a quene] or an emprise in the world, not daynyng hir for to arise to goddis servis.

70 See the discussion below of the Friar's rounded cape, Chapter 5, pp. 144–58.

71 See Harvey's discussion of fabric widths used for monastic habits, pp. 17, 23–6.

72 As mentioned previously, p. 13 in the specifications of the *Rule of Syon*, requiring tight and straight mantles lacking 'plaiting'.

73 On excess in dress see *C&C*, p. 164, and nn. 11–12. See also Caesarius of Heisterbach, *The Dialogue on Miracles*, trans. H. Von E. Scott and C. C. Swinton Bland (London, 1929), I.vii, p. 327, regarding feminine extravagance. Regarding costly masculine dress and new styles, see 'On the Deposition of Richard II', in *Political Poems and Songs Relating to English History, Composed During the Period From the Accession of Edw.III to that of Ric.III*, ed. Thomas Wright (London, 1859), 1:400; 'On the Times', from Trinity College, Dublin, MS E.5, 10(c), in *Political Poems and Songs Relating to English History*, 1:270-8; *Pricke of Conscience*, attributed to Richard Rolle de Hampole, ed. Philological Society (Berlin, 1863), pp. 43–4, lines 1522–1602. Also see *Hoccleve's Works, III: The Regement of Princes*, ed. F. J. Furnivall, EETS, ES 72 (London, 1897), pp. 15–21, in which a beggar describes clothing excesses.

    The growing extravagance of costume present in the second half of the fourteenth century is a well-established phenomenon. See a summary of the protests against costume excesses in Joseph Strutt, *A Complete View of the Dress and Habits of the People of England, from the Establishment of the Saxons in Britain to the Present Time: Illustrated by Engravings Taken from the Most Authentic Remains of Antiquity* (London, 1842; London, 1970), 2:137. John Scattergood also treats this subject in 'Fashion and Morality in the Late Middle Ages', *England in the Fifteenth Century: Proceedings of the 1986 Harlaxton Symposium*, ed. Daniel Williams (Woodbridge, 1987), esp. pp. 257–61, 264–6.

    In contrast to the luxurious and costly dress of the courtiers, the poet in 'On the Deposition of Richard II', 1:402, describes the costume of the allegorical character Wisdom as follows:

        welle homelich yhelid

        in an holsume gyse,

        not overe lenge, but ordeyned

        in the olde schappe.

vasive, and, noteworthy as regards religious habits, concerned with conspicuous consumption of fabric in a single robe. The description of religious habits that were too wide or too long proclaimed dimensions deemed to be proof of prideful excess. Conversely, as discussed in Chapter 2, literature written before and after the *General Prologue* also contains descriptions of pious religious who are perfect in habit (clothing) and habits (behavior).

Historical Records

Historical records provide plenty of evidence that in the Middle Ages those in holy orders did violate the dress restrictions of their rules.[74] The Fourth Council of Constantinople, 869–70, instituted Canon 27, requiring all religious orders to wear a habit; the canon was reaffirmed in the 1215 Fourth Council of the Lateran, under Pope Innocent III.[75] Wendy Scase describes the process of repeated attempts to regulate clerical dress from the Fourth Lateran Council of 1215 through the fifteenth century, with specifications adopted in councils and later incorporated in diocesan constitutions. The necessity of repeated conciliar discussion, and of repeated specifications with additional details, provides ample evidence that the problem of clerical dress was ongoing. These dress requirements required the cleric to wear clothing distinguished from fashionable dress so as to constitute a 'visible sign of the internal difference' between laypersons and clerics. Later religious documents specify dress differences that distinguished between 'simple priests' and the '*sublimi et litterati*'.[76]

---

[74] For example, see Mayo, pp. 35, 47–8.

[75] *New Catholic Encyclopedia* (New York, 1967), 12:286–7. See also Marion Gibbs and Jane Lang, *Bishops and Reform 1215–1272, With Special Reference to the Lateran Council of 1215* (Oxford, 1934), p. 126, regarding 'fitting garments' for clerks, and the small amount of attention that was paid to this issue; but Peter Heath, *The English Parish Clergy on the Eve of the Reformation* (London, 1969), pp. 108–9, states that a great deal of attention was paid to clerical dress in general. For examples of this attention, see David Wilkins, *Concilia Magnae Britanniae et Hiberniae, Ab Anno MCCLXVIII Ad Annum MCCCXLIX* (London, 1737; rpt. Brussels, 1964), 2:703, and *Concilia Magnae Britanniae et Hiberniae, Ab Anno MCCCL Ad Annum MDXLV* (London, 1737; rpt. Brussels, 1964), 3:619–20; also *Registrum Thome Bourgchier: Cantuariensis Archiepiscopi*, ed. F. R. H. Du Boulay (Oxford, 1957), pp. xxxi, 92, 109–11.

[76] Wendy Scase, ' "Proud Gallants and Popeholy Priests": The Context and Function of a Fifteenth-Century Satirical Poem', *MÆ* 63.2 (1994), pp. 280–1, citing *Councils and Synods*, ed. F. M. Powicke and C. R. Cheney (Oxford, 1964), II.ii, 752, and referencing D. Wilkins, *Conc.*, 2:703 and William Lyndwood, *Provinciale seu constitutiones Angliae* (Oxford, 1679), p. 120; Scase also cites *Registrum Thome Bourgchier*, p. 110. Regarding friars' dress indiscretions, see Chapter 5 below, n. 69; for monks' dress abuses, see Chapter 4, pp. 115–17.

Nuns, prioresses, and abbesses also wore a variety of costumes, some specifically violating their convent rules. These violations typically consisted of wearing caps signifying their noble estate, hoods trimmed or lined with unlawful types of fur, silken garments including veils and wimples, and gold and silver tiring pins in their veils, as well as anything 'over curious', all necessarily acquired as private property. An early example of inappropriate headdress is provided in an account of a group of nuns in the early eighth century who curled their hair with curling irons and exchanged the wearing of the dark head veil for white or colored headdresses that reached the ground and on which bows of ribbon were sewn, as described and forbidden by St Aldhelm.[77] Before and after this flagrant disregard for convent rules, bishops and archbishops struggled to maintain suitability of convent dress, a struggle that continued after Chaucer's time.

The Council of Oxford, 1222, forbade nuns to wear silken wimples, silver or gold tiring-pins in their veils, and garments made from burnet or other unlawful cloth. They were instructed to make the dimensions of their habits adequate but not superfluous,[78] an instruction that would not have been necessary had not excessive practices already been acknowledged. In 1237, monks, canons, and nuns were forbidden habits of any color other than black. Nuns' wimples are not mentioned, but they were forbidden dresses and mantles with trains and pleats,[79] or any excessive length; nuns were forbidden

---

[77] Lina Eckenstein cites St Aldhelm's *De Laudibus Virginitatis*, in *Woman under Monasticism* (Cambridge, 1896), p. 115. See 'The Prose *De Virginitate*', *Aldhelm: The Prose Works*, trans. Michael Lapidge and Michael Herren (Cambridge, 1979), pp. 127–8, regarding clothes forbidden to nuns and monks, and commentary on p. 57. See Owen-Crocker, pp. 87–90, for a discussion of the church's struggle, during the Anglo-Saxon period, to regulate nuns' habits.

[78] According to D. Wilkins, *Conc.* 1:590–1:

Adhaec, quoniam sexum muliebrem, contra versutias hostis antiqui minus fortem, multiplici remedio necesse est efficacius communiri, decernimus, ut moniales, et caeterae mulieres divino cultui dedicatae, velum vel peplum fericum non habeant, nec in velo acus argenteas vel aureas audeant deportare. Nec ipse, vel monachi seu canonici regulares habeant zonas sericas, vel auri vel argenti ornatum habentes, vel burneto vel alio panno irregulari de caetero utantur. Metiantur etiam juxta dimensionem corporis vestem suam, ita quod longitudinem corporis non excedat, sed pede, sicut decet, subducto sufficiat eis indui veste talari; et sola monialis consecrata deferat annulum, et uno solo sit contenta. Si quae autem commonita se non correxerit, regulari subjaceat disciplinae.

[79] Pleating in the long garments of a robe would add unwonted fullness, making it 'wide', and might, at this date, also be a stylish detail of construction. Stella Mary Newton, *Fashion in the Age of the Black Prince: A study of the years 1340–1365* (Woodbridge, 1980; rpt. 1999), p. 10, describes masculine 'tunics gathered (*fronciées*) at the back over their [wearer's] loins (*rains*) like women's dresses', and states, p. 16, that 'frouncing' was in fashion by 1342–43, according to wardrobe accounts. Newton adds, p. 55, that in 1361–62, frouncing in tunics was again in style, along with pleats – both

silver tiring pins in their veils.[80] Clearly these admonitions were unsuccessful because William of Wykeham finds it necessary to repeat the same rules in his 1387 injunctions to Romsey and Wherwell.[81] Buttons on the lower sleeve opening of the tunic were forbidden by Pope Clement V in 1312, and Popes Gregory IX and Benedict XII ruled again on dress for monastics.[82] Archbishop Greenfield, 1314, issued a *decretum* to the nuns of the Priory of Nunkeeling forbidding them to make themselves remarkable by wearing 'anything unsuitable to religion'.[83]

Regardless that time and again silken veils had been forbidden,[84] during a visitation of the Priory of the nuns of Rothwell in Lincoln, 1442, Sister Margaret Staple, the prioress, stated that she herself wore a silken veil.[85] Disregarding any spiritual peril, some nuns satisfied their desires for fashionable garb through several means: their annual allowance of pocket money

added fullness to garments; see also her pp. 11, 62, 102, 105. In this regard, 'The Sisters' Clothes', 'From *The Rule of Our Saviour*', p. 91, directs:
> Oon mantyl they schall have also, of grey burel as the kyrtyl and couele, which mantyl shal not be fruncyd ne pynchyd togedyr fro wythoute, nor curyously made, but on party streyte and playne.

[80] According to Wilkins, *Conc.* 1:660:
> *Item monachis et canonicis regularibus, necnon et monialibus tam vestimenta quam coopertoria interdicimus colorata, nisi fuerint nigro tincta. Et cum equitant, decentibus sellis utantur, ac fraenis ac superselliis. Moniales autem vestibus caudatis et crispatis, aut proprii corporis longitudinem excedentibus, non utantur, nec pellibus delicatis aut coloratis; nec in velo acus argenteas audeant deportare.*

[81] Power, *Nunneries*, p. 586, citing New Coll. MS, fol. 86.

[82] See Harvey's discussion of these rulings, pp. 12–13, where low-cut shoes and excessive sleeve lengths were among the topics treated.

[83] *The Victoria History of the Counties of England: Yorkshire*, ed. William Page (London, 1913), 3:120. Similarly, p. 119, Archbishop Melton, in 1318, directed the Prioress and nuns of the Priory of Nunburnholme not to wear garments 'which did not accord with religion'.

[84] See Power's description, *Nunneries*, pp. 585–7, with numerous citations. Power's summary of causes and results of this struggle between nuns and bishops, *Nunneries*, p. 316, is pertinent here:
> It seems as though the craving for a certain privacy of life, a certain minimum of private property, is a deeply rooted instinct in human nature. Certainly the attempt of monasticism to expel it with a pitchfork failed. Step by step the rule was broken down, more especially by a series of modifications in the prescribed method of feeding and clothing the community.

In particular, according to Power, p. 663, the 'world never called more seductively to medieval nuns than in contemporary fashions'. See also pp. 16, 43, 73, 207, 220, 305, 518, 624.

[85] *Visitation of Religious Houses in the Diocese of Lincoln: Alnwick's Visitations (1436–49)*, ed. Alexander Hamilton Thompson, Canterbury and York Society 33 (Oxford, 1929), 3.2:319. See also p. 361, for Prioress Dame Eleanor Cobcote's statement 'that the nuns wear silken veils and robes', in the account of the 1445 visitation of the Priory of Studley, of the Order of St Benet, of Lincoln.

(*peculium*),[86] pittances and gifts of money and goods, legacies, and wages from their own labor.[87] However, legacies were the source of much improper clothing made of expensive fabrics, some of it decorated with jewels, furs, and embroidery of silk, gold, and silver, all listed in wills along with personal jewelry and household goods. In 1404, even the Bishop of Durham, Walter Skirlaw, bequeathed to his sister, the Prioress Joan of Swine, ' "Item a robe of murrey cloth of Ypres (?yp'n) [sic] containing a mantle and hood furred with budge (?purg') [sic], another hood furred with ermine" '.[88]

Also noteworthy is the record of visitation to the Priory of Nun Monkton on 30 April 1397 made by Thomas Dalby, Archdeacon of Richmond. During this visitation, the Archdeacon learned that Prioress Margaret Fayrfax, in violation of the Rule, wore various kinds of furs, even gray, as well as silk veils. This Prioress had been the beneficiary of a will (dated 7 June 1393), made by her brother John Fayrfax, Rector of Presscot. He left her an '*armilansa* [cloak] of black cloth, furred with grey',[89] which she apparently wore in the priory. During Dalby's 1397 visitation, not only were complaints made to the Archdeacon that Prioress Margaret Fayrfax wore various kinds of furs, including grey (perhaps her inheritance?), as well as silk veils, but also, 'She frequently wore a surplice (*superpellitio*) without a mantle, in quire and elsewhere, contrary to the manner of dress of nuns and the ancient custom of the priory.' Archdeacon Dalby's injunctions, issued 8 July 1397, specifically forbade such sartorial splendor:

> None were to use silk clothes, especially not silken veils nor valuable furs
> . . . nor tunics pleated (laqueatis) . . . nor any *jupis*, anglice 'gounes', after
> the fashion of secular women.[90]

These injunctions include the mention of pleated tunics, which were forbidden, but no mention of pleating in regard to headdresses.

Monks, too, strayed sartorially. The particularities of the legislation, mentioned earlier, allow us to know that monks attempted to wear tunics made of

---

[86] *The Rule of St Benedict*, pp. 144–9, 204. See also *Three Middle English Versions of the Rule of St Benet*.

[87] See Power, *Nunneries*, p. 329, for an extensive discussion of wills and bequests to nuns which include items of value other than clothing.

[88] *Testamenta Eboracensia, or Wills Registered at York Illustrative of the History, Manners, Language, Statistics, &c., of the Province of York, From the Year MCCC Downwards*, ed. James Raine (London, 1836–1902), 1:308, 317, 322, 324. See also Oliva, pp. 103–5, concerning nuns and private property, as well as money received to buy clothes, and testamentary gifts of clothing.

[89] See *The Vic. Hist. . . . Yorkshire*, 3:122–3, n. 6, for a description of John Fayrfax's will, which is recorded in *Test. Ebor.*, 1:186.

[90] *The Vic. Hist. . . . Yorkshire*, 3:122–3.
Exceeding even these clothing violations within the convent, the apostate nun illustrates the ultimate in clothing transgressions; regarding such a nun, see Oliva, p. 211.

brightly dyed fabrics with front or side openings, outer garments of colors –
especially stripes – other than the prescribed black, garments that fitted the
body closely, and, in general, clothing that proclaimed both expense and
pride. The situation was complicated, as Westminster Abbey Muniments
indicate, because the monks were allowed to use personal money to augment
the quality of the garments they wore.[91] Barbara Harvey tells of Brother
Richard Exeter (d.1396 or 1397), who owned 'a cowl of worsted as well as
two "livery [regulation serge] cowls" ', a ' "best frock" and a "livery frock" ',
and a 'tunic with a striped lining'; similarly Brother John Canterbury possessed a worsted cowl, and something called a cloak 'for London'.[92]

For all the efforts expended, by church, university, and civil officials, upon
regulating the clothing of members of religious orders, the official dress of
clerics in academia, and those persons occupationally affiliated with the
church, deviations from the norm were common enough that they became
recognizable metaphors in literature. Chaucer's costume rhetoric reveals that
he knew these metaphors for deviations in dress codes and employed them,
but with a unique flair. Further, this flair is highlighted in his descriptions of
religious costume signs because, unlike lay costume with its intentional
social designators, many garments in religious habits were fundamentally
embued with spiritual significance. In the essays to follow, this spiritual significance, easily read by Chaucer's contemporaries, will be the foundation of
any correctness or lack of it found in Chaucer's pilgrims who are the folk of
'Holy Church'.

---

[91] Power, *Nunneries*, pp. 322–3: The *peculium*, a payment derived from 'the common
funds' rather than from a nun's independent income, functioned so that it was not called
proprietas; nevertheless, it deviated from the Benedictine rule proscribing 'the individual disposal of property' and which prescribed clothing that disallowed catering to individual tastes. See Harvey, pp. 12–14, 20–2, 25, 29, regarding private funds spent by
monks on clothing. See Chapter 4, p. 121, n. 48, below, regarding monks' special
riding cloaks and cloaks 'for London'. Also see Gasquet, pp. 100–1, for a list of proper
garments for a monk's wardrobe.

[92] Harvey, pp. 13, 20–2. In the late-fourteenth-century instructions, apparently written by
a priest to his mother, *Book to a Mother: An Edition with Commentary*, ed. Adrian
James McCarthy (Salzburg, 1981), pp. 55–7, the author lists numerous items of prideful dress for both men and women, and pp. 123–4, discusses the desiring and wearing
of 'proud' clothes as a form of lechery. See G. G. Coulton, *Five Centuries of Religion*
(Cambridge, 1923–50), 3:408, regarding nuns

> who go about in curious and costly garments, so close-fitting and so pleated that
> they can scarce be distinguished from secular ladies and girls, except perhaps by
> a curious and gauze-like veil or by a scanty scapular.

Such sins were to be dealt with in confession, as prescribed in the manual of confession, composed (possibly for nuns) between 1382 and 1419, presented in Walter
Kennedy Everett, 'A Critical Edition of the Confession Section of *The Clensyng of
Mannes Soule*', Diss., University of North Carolina at Chapel Hill, 1974, p. 80 (see
below, Chapter 9, p. 265).

2

The Prioress, 'digne of reverence': Her Headdress and Her Habit

'Reading Into' the Costume of the Prioress

There is no doubt about it – a scandalous Prioress is more interesting than a proper one. Further, and to put it bluntly, modern critics have created such a scandalous Prioress by 'reading into' Chaucer's *General Prologue* portrait. As the speculative, escalating-as-rumors-do types of critical comments built upon one another and proliferated in the early twentieth century, some critics adopted a less negative position.[1] However, the negative momentum in Prioress criticism persisted. From 1980 onward, critics adopt a variety of negative attitudes toward the Prioress, with Richard Rex providing the most defamatory reading and misreading of the text and evidence. In contrast, Mary Hardy Frank anchored her assessment of Chaucer's portrait of the Prioress in the c.1387 requirements for prioresses, thereby providing a positive and an historical reading that exonerates her. Both sides of this critical debate employed the Prioress's costume as support for their theses.

While dealing primarily with what the Prioress wears and Chaucer's particular costume rhetoric, this chapter demonstrates the manner in which evidence has been ignored while negative treatments of the Prioress have proliferated. Further, it illustrates the manner in which the chief vehicle of this escalation – pejorative diction – has become increasingly indignant in tone.

---

[1] Among them Alan T. Gaylord, 'The Unconquered Tale of the Prioress' (1962); Florence H. Ridley, *The Prioress and the Critic* (1965); and Jill Mann, *Chaucer and Medieval Estates Satire* (1973), who writes of the 'conflation of courtly lady and the nun' and the Prioress's 'fondness for nice clothes', all mentioned in Malcolm Andrew's 'Explanatory Notes' in *The General Prologue. A Variorum Edition of the Works of Geoffrey Chaucer* (Norman, OK, 1993), 2:120–1.

The Prioress's Headdress

Chaucer's Prioress wears an appropriate headdress, consistent with her interest in propriety, and illustrative of her status as nun, Prioress, and lady. This thesis challenges the voluminous and traditional defamatory criticism of this pilgrim,[2] which holds that the Prioress's veil is worn too high on her forehead and that her wimple is inappropriately 'pynched'. These critics interpret both practices as evidence of the Prioress's vanity. Several factors refute this tradition: these negative judgments regarding her headdress are anachronistic as they have a factual base in mid-fifteenth-century convent visitation records, too late to pertain to this nun. In addition, earlier historical records and other sources in the medieval arts argue against the traditional negative reading of the Prioress's headdress. Further, in depicting the Prioress, Chaucer follows the medieval rhetorical tradition of delineating ideal beauty. Thus, we may compare his rhetoric concerning her veil and wimple with representations of the ideal nun in proper headdress, represented in both literature and the visual arts, as well as in descriptions in convent rules.

Madame Eglentyne's veiling favorably contrasts with depictions of inappropriate headdresses mentioned in visitation injunctions and in literature of the late fourteenth century. Clearly, as discussed in Chapter 1, the typical worldly nun or prioress owned private property and wore it, as for example did Clemence Medforde, Prioress of Ankerwyke, in 1441. Not until the 1440s do we find the first evidence that the height of a veil is a matter of propriety or impropriety. According to her nuns' complaints written more than fifty years after *The Canterbury Tales*,

> The Prioress wears . . . silken veils, and she carries her veil too high above her forehead, so that her forehead, being entirely uncovered, can be seen of all. . . . Also she wears above her veil a cap of estate furred with budge [imported lambskin].[3]

Thus the fifteenth-century Prioress, Clemence Medforde, defies her Rule

---

2   A sampling of the much shorter list of positive readers of the Prioress's costume includes, most recently, Henry Ansgar Kelly, 'A Neo-Revisionist Look at Chaucer's Nuns', *ChauR* 31 (1996), pp. 115–32, esp. pp. 126, 128; [Mary] Hardy Long Frank, 'Seeing the Prioress Whole', *ChauR* 25.3 (1991), pp. 229–37, esp. 229–30, 235; and earlier, Sr M. Madeleva, 'Chaucer's Nuns', in *Chaucer's Nuns and Other Essays* (Port Washington, NY, 1965); and Mary Hardy Long Frank, 'Chaucer's Prioress and the Blessed Virgin', *ChauR* 13 (1979), pp. 346–62.
3   *Visitation . . . Alnwick*, 24, 2.1:3–5. See also Eileen Power, *Medieval People*, 2nd edn (Boston, 1925), pp. 77–8; and this book, Chapter 1, pp. 11–12, 25–7.

concerning appropriate habit, following in the erring footsteps of a long line of worldly nuns.

However, it is the often-cited injunction of the Bishop of Lincoln William Alnwick that contains not only the omnipresent prohibition against silk veils and silver pins (probably tiring pins[4] since they are mentioned in conjunction with veiling), but also, so far as we know, the first declaration that veils should come approximately to eyebrow level:

> None of yow, the prioresse ne none of the couente, were no vayles of sylke ne no syluere pynnes . . . ne cappes of astate abowe your vayles . . . and that ye so atyre your hedes that your vayles come downe nyghe to your yene.[5]

On the subject of veils, Alnwick was indeed fighting a losing battle. Although his injunction is untimely so far as the Prioress's headdress and Chaucer's costume rhetoric are concerned, nevertheless, because it has been so often cited, it is of particular interest. In 1440, after a visit to Langley Priory, Alnwick instructed the nuns: 'That henceforth they wear not silken veils. That they keep their veils [down] to their eye-brows. That they wear not their robes so long and flowing.' The last two instructions contain matter not mentioned in the nuns' complaints as recorded in the visitation record, and thus may have derived from Alnwick's own observations. In 1442, Alnwick visited the Priory of the nuns of Catesby, and commented that 'the nuns do not wear their veils down to their [eyebrows], but do keep their foreheads bare'. However, in the 1442–43 visitation of the Priory of Harrold, Dame Alice Decun complains to Alnwick that the nuns 'all wear their veils spread up to the top of their foreheads', yet Alnwick's injunctions to these nuns contain no mention of veils.[6] One wonders if Alnwick was being worn down by the collective disobedience of the nuns and had given up the attempt to fight this losing battle of the veil. Further, two fifteenth-century rules, *The Liber Celestis of St Bridget of Sweden* and 'The Rewle of Sustries Menouresses Enclosed',[7] a Franciscan rule, support the contention that in this century more attention is focused on the details of habit, including the position of a veil.

---

4   Described, Chapter 1, n. 29.
5   *Visitations . . . Lincoln: Alnwick*, 2.1:8.
6   See *Visitations . . . Lincoln: Alnwick*, 2:47, 118, 130, 176; also *Visitations . . . Lincoln: Alnwick*, 3.2:361.
7   *The Liber Celestis of St Bridget of Sweden*, ed. Roger Ellis, EETS, OS 291 (Oxford, 1987), 1:336 (a fifteenth-century Middle English trans. of St Bridget's *Revelations*, according to Julia Bolton Holloway, *Saint Bride and Her Book: Birgitta of Sweden's Revelations* [Newburyport, MA, 1992], pp. 130–1); *A Fifteenth-Century Courtesy Book and Two Fifteenth-Century Franciscan Rules*, eds R. W. Chambers and Walter W. Seton, EETS, OS 148 (London, 1914), p. 84.

In any case, Alnwick's injunctions, approximately fifty years later than the *General Prologue*, provide the ammunition most often used by critics castigating the Prioress's headdress, as Chaucer describes it:

> Ful semyly hir wympul pynched was,
>
> . . .
>
> But sikerly she hadde a fair forheed;
> It was almost a spanne brood, I trowe;
> For, hardily, she was nat undergrowe.   (I, lines 151, 154–6)

Simply stated, the Prioress's headdress reveals the dimensions of her forehead, and her wimple is 'ful semyly[8] . . . pynched'.

Disregarding the too-late date of Alnwick's injunctions, which actually are reactions against nuns' adoption of *fifteenth*-century styles, the Prioress's detractors persist in denigrating her veiling, although Chaucer mentions no veil. In support of his own criticism against the Prioress, Kevin S. Kiernan quotes Geoffoi de Vinsauf's remark that ' "the discretion of the wise man observes what is said through what is left unsaid" ', as being a useful idea to recall when reading Chaucer.[9] Clearly, this idea has found self-interpreted acceptance, and this veil, unmentioned by Chaucer, has spawned many negative comments concerned with Madame Eglentyne's 'fair forheed'. G. G. Coulton sums up the ongoing critical attitude toward the Prioress's veil and/or forehead in a revealing personal remark: 'This nun had no business to possess any forehead at all, so far as Chaucer was concerned.'[10] No earlier critic states this idea so plainly, even indignantly, yet many critics imply such a judgment.[11] Florence Ridley provides a vintage, but handy summary, noting that Raymond Preston, Coulton, and Eileen Power think her forehead should not be visible, an opinion echoed by more recent critics, while Thomas Blake Clark and D. W. Robertson, Jr take positions on the physiognomical implications of its broadness;[12] Gordon H. Harper posits that this broadness is pro-

---

8   Regarding seemliness, see Theresa A. Halligan, *The Booke of Gostlye Grace of Mechtild of Hackeborn* (Toronto, 1979), pp. 134–5, which describes seemliness as noble (meekness), patient, and rich in virtues.

9   Kevin S. Kiernan, 'The Art of the Descending Catalogue, and a Fresh Look at Alisoun', *ChauR* 10 (1975), pp. 3, 5.

10   G. G. Coulton, *Medieval Panorama* (New York, 1944), p. 276.

11   Most recently, Richard Rex, *'The Sins of Madame Eglentyne' and other Essays on Chaucer* (Newark, NJ, 1995), 'accords with and even *extends* the disparaging school of Prioress criticism' [my emphasis], according to Douglas Wurtele in his review of Rex's book, *SAC* 19 (1997), p. 292. For corrections of Rex's research on related topics, see Henry Ansgar Kelly, 'Bishop, Prioress, and Bawd in the Stews of Southwark', *Speculum* 75.2 (2000), pp. 349–50, 357; and Kelly, 'A Neo-Revisionist Look', pp. 123–5.

12   Regarding physiognomy and astrology, see a discussion of the forehead as evidence of alignment of the Prioress with the moon and with Cancer, and their association with the virgin goddess Diana, in 'The Book of Physiognomy' in *The World of Piers*

portionate to a body that is 'nat undergrowe', while Muriel Bowden discusses the Prioress's forehead in terms of medieval styles of beauty.[13] Bowden's point is important to Eileen Power's argument as well: Power, referring to what is a fifteenth-century, not a fourteenth-century, practice,[14] stresses the importance of high foreheads to worldly ladies who went to such lengths as shaving to achieve the desired effect. Further, she posits that in an effort to be fashionable, nuns 'could not resist lifting up and spreading out their veils'.[15] To this Power appends an interesting question: 'for how otherwise did Chaucer *know* that Madame Eglentyne had such a fair forehead?'[16] Such

Plowman, eds and trans. Jeanne Krochalis and Edward Peters (Pennsylvania, 1975), p. 222; also William Spencer, 'Are Chaucer's Pilgrims Keyed to the Zodiac?', *ChauR* 4 (1970), pp. 153–4; and Christine of Pisan, *The Epistle of Othea to Hector: or the Boke of Knyghthode*, trans. Stephen Scrope, ed. George F. Warner (London, 1904), p. 37. See Andrew's Summary, pp. 158–60.

13 Citing Walter Clyde Curry and the lover in *Confessio Amantis*, according to Florence H. Ridley, *The Prioress and the Critics* (Berkeley, CA, 1965), p. 17. Ridley's notes on the Prioress in *Riverside Chaucer*, p. 803, are somewhat at odds: her comments aver both that the Prioress 'clearly violates many of the rules of her order', and that she 'lacks most of the failings traditional in satiric portraits of nuns'. See Andrew, pp. 158–60.

14 Regarding late-fifteenth-century headdresses and foreheads shown, see Mary G. Houston, *Medieval Costume in England and France: The 13th, 14th and 15th Centuries* (New York, 1996), pp. 177–8, 180, figs 308, 309, and 312, and for earlier fifteenth-century, less extreme, versions of this style, pp. 165, 168, figs 285, 293; see also Auguste Racinet, *Racinet's Full-Color Pictorial History of Western Costume* (New York, 1987), pl. 24 for ladies in the picture at left, and pl. 33 for ladies at the right in the top picture; and Arthur Gardner, 'Hair and Head-Dress, 1050–1600', *JBAA*, series 3, 13 (1950), p. 12, regarding shaved foreheads in the fifteenth century.

15 Also responding to these extreme fifteenth-century headdress styles, the *Liber Celestis* 1:336 presents orisons for nuns to recite concerned with wearing a headdress that covers the head and forehead in order to hide their beauty from all but their heavenly spouse.

16 Power, *Medieval People*, pp. 77–8. Of Madame Eglentyne's veil, Power states,

> If she had been wearing her veil properly, it [the forehead] would have been invisible, and the father of English poetry may be observed discreetly but plainly winking the other eye when he puts in that little touch.

Power includes the brooch and 'that fetis cloak of hers' in this list of supposed garment indiscretions, in her equation of Madame Eglentyne with historical prioresses who transgressed their rules. Although it contains only *one* point of connection pertinent to her critical stance against Chaucer's Prioress, Power cites nuns' complaints about their prioress (Clemence Medforde, Prioress of Ankerwyke, in 1441), written approximately fifty years after *The General Prologue*:

> The Prioress . . . wears golden rings exceeding costly, with divers precious stones and also girdles silvered and gilded over and silken veils and *she carries her veil too high above her forehead, so that her forehead, being entirely uncovered, can be seen of all*, and she wears furs of vair. Also she wears shifts of cloth of Rennes, which costs sixteen pence the ell. Also she wears kirtles laced with silk and tiring pins of silver and silver gilt and has made all the nuns wear the like. Also she wears above her veil a cap of estate, furred with budge. Item, she

judgmental statements often cite these episcopal and convent visitation records as proof that bare foreheads were forbidden to nuns, but fail to mention that the pertinent records were dated more than half a century after the *General Prologue* was written.

In addition to this erroneous conflation of fifteenth-century styles and records with Chaucer's late fourteenth-century literary description, one word poses a special problem in the canon of criticism concerned with the Prioress's headdress: *fluted*, a term that the critics employ but Chaucer does not. F. N. Robinson notes Coulton's statement that the Prioress's wimple 'should have been plain, not fluted'.[17] Coulton's comment has evoked critical judgments about the Prioress's fluted headdress, although the fluting is nonexistent. These judgments further the predominantly negative view that the Prioress dresses in accordance with courtly practice. From this perspective, the Prioress's costume is naturally perceived as the visible result of her efforts to allure and attract men,[18] and these critics who critique the Prioress within the worldly, courtly tradition rarely fail to mention some presumed impropriety of wimple or veil.[19]

> has on her neck a long silken band, in English a lace, which hangs down below her breast. [my italics]

Although her sources do not substantiate her claim that such complaints occurred in the *fourteenth century*, Janet Mayo, *A History of Ecclesiastical Dress* (New York, 1984), p. 48, also mentions Clemence Medforde as proof that the Prioress transgresses in exposing her forehead, stating that such an abuse is common 'in the fourteenth and fifteenth centuries', citing Sacheverell Sitwell, *Monks, Nuns and Monasteries* (New York, 1965), p. 40, whose suppositions regarding Joan Blaunkfront's name and Margaret (Fayrfax) Fairfax's veiling practices are unsubstantiated. Most recently Mary A. Maleski, 'The Culpability of Chaucer's Prioress', *ChauY* 5 (1998), p. 52, lists the same costume 'sins', perpetuating this bias, although, p. 47, she states that 'bias . . . has affected our collective vision of medieval nuns'.

17 F. N. Robinson, ed., *The Poetical Works of Chaucer* (Boston, 1957), p. 756, n. 151.

18 [M.] H. L. Frank, 'Seeing the Prioress Whole', p. 230, cites Chauncey Wood, 'Chaucer's Use of Signs in his Portrait of the Prioress', *Signs and Symbols in Chaucer's Poetry*, eds John P. Hermann and John J. Burke, Jr (University, AL, 1981), pp. 81–101; she refutes his idea that the Prioress is a 'nun who wants to be a fashionable lady'. Frank states that 'surely only an insidious sexism has allowed us to entertain even a mild version of that view in face of the evidence provided us for decades'.

19 For example, Hope Phyllis Weissman, 'Antifeminism and Chaucer's Characterization of Women', in *Geoffrey Chaucer: A Collection of Original Articles*, ed. George D. Economou (New York, 1975), pp. 94–6, 104, places Madame Eglentyne in the class of the 'new woman', the lady of courtly literature, whose function it is 'to allure from her pedestal and lead men to wisdom through love', and who has 'transcending virtue' that attracts men to her tower. For Weissman, this is the function of the courtly lady, the lady she designates as the wrong new woman image, which the Prioress follows.

> In this vein, also, Gerald Morgan, 'The Universality of the Portraits in the *General Prologue* to the *Canterbury Tales*', *ES* 58 (1977), p. 489, remarks on the Prioress's 'elegance of dress and . . . physical beauty' and quotes lines I, 146–54. In his judgment,
>
> > All these details ostensibly enhance her as a courtly figure, but they have been carefully chosen to focus upon the violation of her profession as a nun, for nuns

Even the critics who see Madame Eglentyne as dressed in accordance with traditional descriptions of the Blessed Virgin Mary feel the necessity of excusing what they call her 'elegance'. For example, Mary Hardy Long Frank defends the courtly characteristics of this portrait as being unparadoxically Marian since Mary was 'in every immaculate sense of the word, mistress to the Christian world'. However, even Frank cannot find an excuse for the (theorized) bare brow of critical tradition, although she surmises that the Prioress assumes the Virgin Mary would 'excuse in a devoted servant such innocent peccadilloes as a bared brow'.[20]

Here, a definition of terms is necessary to clarify the ensuing discussion of the reputedly inappropriate height of the Prioress's veil and her wimple style. For convenience, the term *headdress* designates both veiling and wimple or barbe,[21] the entire ensemble of various styles that nuns properly wore during the Middle Ages. By *veil* we shall understand the lined or unlined cloth that covered a nun's head and did, or did not, cover all or part of her forehead. In visual representations such as illuminated manuscripts (see Color Plate I) and sculpture that reveal two veils (usually a black one over a white), these will be termed *overveil* and *underveil*. When it cannot be determined whether an underveil or a wide band across the forehead is worn, the term *underveil* will be used. Finally, *wimple* will be defined as a small garment worn in such a way that the sides of the face are covered, and the neck is covered from side to side and from the chin downward.[22] Joan Evans separates veil from

---

were not allowed to keep dogs, their wimples were to be plain and not fluted and their foreheads should not have been exposed.

S. T. Knight, ' "Almoost a spanne brood" ', *Neophil* 52 (1968), p. 179, judges that the Prioress wears her veil high on her forehead 'for the sake of a totally worldly fashion'; Joel Fredell, 'Late Gothic Portraiture: The Prioress and Philippa', *ChauR* 23.3 (1989), p. 185, describes the Prioress's headdress as exhibiting High Gothic style.

20 And the keeping of 'small dogs', as mentioned by M. H. L. Frank, 'Chaucers' Prioress', pp. 346, 355; and again in her 'The Prioress and the Puys: A Study of the Cult of the Virgin and the Medieval Puys in Relation to Chaucer's Prioress and Her Tale', Diss., University of Colorado, 1970, pp. 16 and 36, n. 88, where she acknowledges that 'excuse may be unnecessary; Chaucer never actually says that the Prioress's forehead was uncovered, merely that it was fair and broad'; see also p. 3, for a description of the courtly-Marian associations of 'simple and coy'; pp. 9–10, on Mary and physical beauty; pp. 11–13, regarding courtesy, good manners, and cleanliness; and in 'Chaucer's Prioress', pp. 348, 350, 354, regarding the rose symbolism of the Prioress's name, Madame Eglentyne, her manners as being imitative of the Virgin, and her dress as customary to the Marian tradition.

21 James Robinson Planché, *An Illustrated Dictionary of Historic Costume: From the First Century B.C. to c.1760* (Mineola, NY, 2003), p. 34, defines *barbe*: 'A piece of linen, generally plaited [pleated], worn over or under the chin, according to the rank of the lady'.

22 This differs from the OED definition: '1. A garment of linen or silk formerly worn by women, so folded as to envelop the head, chin, sides of the face, and neck: now

wimple. She dates the wimple as a fashionable item of dress for all thirteenth-century women, and asserts that, after the wimple's demise as high
fashion earlier in the fourteenth century, it continued to be worn by widows
and nuns. With a hanging veil behind, it 'was regarded as the most decorous
of head-tires'.[23] The definitions stipulated above neither cover all the possibilities for nuns' headdresses, nor always correspond to the less precise
descriptions provided in convent rules and historical records; nevertheless,
they serve as convenient descriptive terms for this study.

The Prioress and Rhetorical Traditions

Chaucer does not mention the Prioress's veil, yet as we have seen, his
comment on her fair forehead has been critically interpreted as indicative of
personal knowledge of its dimensions. Critics suppose that Chaucer observed
her veil worn high above her forehead, and they find his comment suggestive.
If there is impropriety here, however, it might well rest with the pil-
grim-narrator Chaucer who notices beauty and says so: 'But sikerly she
hadde a fair forheed;/ It was almoost a spanne brood, I trowe' (lines 154–5).
We note that Chaucer does not say, 'I know', but, instead, 'I trowe', and the
range of meaning between the two phrases is considerable. Chaucer does not
know; therefore, we need not assume that this suppositional description
unequivocally suggests only the Prioress's impropriety – the wearing of high
fashion. As narrator of the *General Prologue*, Chaucer speaks twice about the
Prioress's shape – forehead and general dimensions; otherwise her habit con-
ceals all. There is no evidence that *she* is concerned with her shape. Readers
taking the advice of *De Remediis utriusque fortunae: A Dialogue Between
Reason and Adversity* will understand that in making a moral judgment,

retained in the dress of nuns'. Subsequent quotations after 1500 sometimes mention
both wimple and veil, for example c.1530 *Court of Love* 1102: 'And eke the nonnes,
with vaile and wimple plight'.
    My definition for wimple in this study is more exclusive than some appearing else-
where. The term *wimple* has also been used to describe the two white linen bands or
fillets worn by ladies in the mid-thirteenth century in northern Europe. One band was
worn under the chin and over the crown of the head, covering the ears, and the second
went across the forehead and circled the top of the head, covering the side of the first.
For example, see Stella Mary Newton and Mary M. Giza, 'Frilled Edges', *Text Hist*
14.2 (1983), pp. 141–52.
    Because *wimple* is a somewhat nebulous term, in this study we follow the author of
Court of Love and separate wimple from veil as in the definition already stipulated, p.
35. Houston, p. 226, makes the same kind of separation in terminology, in her definition of wimple: 'A veil covering neck and chin, popular for women in the thirteenth
century and afterwards survived in the dress of many of the Religious Orders'.
23 Joan Evans, *Dress in Mediaeval France* (Oxford, 1952), pp. 23–4, 36.

shape should be a non-issue. This dialogue instructs anyone who would judge to look for virtues; if they are absent, then that *is* a problem.[24]

For the negative critics, the Prioress's fair forehead indicates impropriety in veiling. However, within the context of medieval rhetorical traditions, which included nuns described as brides of Christ,[25] or as the Virgin depicted in courtly/spiritual terms,[26] or as the beloved portrayed in Song of Songs,[27] or as the representations of the Virtues (especially Prudentia) so often depicted as nuns in manuscript illuminations,[28] other interpretations of the Prioress's forehead and veiling are possible. In short, the same rhetorical phrases employed to describe a beautiful bride are shared by secular brides and nuns who are brides of Christ. Viewing the portrait of Madame Eglentyne within such courtly/spiritual rhetorical traditions[29] offers an explanation for Chaucer's comment about both the Prioress's forehead and her 'nat undergrowe' stature that goes beyond that of a pilgrim-poet's purported open admiration for physical beauty, whether imagined or seen.

Critics who favor a rhetorical approach find the ambiguity of the Prioress's portrait fascinating. Perhaps they have not focused on a general portrayal of womanly beauty, but rather on what they conceived to be Chaucer's portrayal of a particular beautiful woman. This perspective highlights her ambiguity and generates a certain amount of critical indignation. For example, according to Kiernan, in describing a nun, Chaucer employs a rhetorical convention 'which was supposed to be used to describe a beautiful woman'. Kiernan

---

24 The comments on the 'advantages of a shapely body' make it clear that it is virtue that counts – whatever the shape of the body, in *De Remediis utriusque fortunae. English & Latin: A Dialogue Between Reason and Adversity: A Late Middle English Version of Petrarch's De Remediis*, ed. F. N. M. Diekstra (Assen, 1968), p. 3, discussing the 'advantages of a shapely body', and p. 5 concerning the body 'enduet *with* so gret a clernesse'.

25 On nuns as Christ's brides, see Vivian Kay Hudson, 'Clothing and Adornment Imagery in "The Scale of Perfection": A Reflection of Contemplation', *Studies in Spirituality* 4 (1994), pp. 123–7, and esp. 136–40.

26 M. H. L. Frank, 'The Prioress and the Puys', pp. 1–5, provides numerous illustrations.

27 See Hudson, p. 138, regarding St Bernard's comments on *Song of Songs*, citing pp. 122–4, 246, of St Bernard of Clairvaux, *Saint Bernard on the Song of Songs: Sermones in Cantica Canticorum*, trans. by A Religious of C.S.M.V. (London, 1952). Also see Ann W. Astell, *The Song of Songs in the Middle Ages* (Ithaca, NY, 1990), esp. pp. 91–104, regarding Bernard's sermons.

28 Also the possibility that Chaucer associates the Prioress, a virgin, with the moon. As 'The Book of Physiognomy' says, 'The signes of luna ben hese: þe fface is pale and clere; brode ffronte . . .', p. 222. Spencer also associates the Prioress with Luna, pp. 153–4.

29 Thomas Hahn states, 'The inventory of her features and graces draws from an older tradition of rhetorical catalogues. But its arrangement and specificity go beyond the general lists of proprieties prescribed by Latin rhetoricians, and beyond the impersonal tags of medieval lyric and romance', in 'The Performance of Gender in the Prioress', *ChauY* 1 (1992), p. 115.

claims that this usage creates discomfort because it compels the reader to concentrate on the attractive physicality of the woman, at the expense of noticing the spirituality of the nun.[30] Here there appears to be a confusion concerning authorial intent implied in Kiernan's assumption that Chaucer wished to describe 'a beautiful woman'. Instead, we should note that Chaucer follows Geoffroi de Vinsauf's directions for a convention designed 'to describe womanly beauty, *Femineum plene si vis formare decorem*', 1.567.[31] Certainly, such a description would be made in physical terms, but the emphasis is on 'womanly beauty', not on 'woman'.

The convention of a nun portrayed as a beautiful bride is important to this study of the Prioress's costume and specifically relevant to the question of the propriety of the Prioress's veil and Chaucer's praise of Madame Eglentyne's fair forehead. In this rhetorical pattern of the nun as bride, spiritual beauty is described in metaphors of physical beauty of body (feet, hands, stature), face, and speech, as illustrated in Guibert of Tournai's thirteenth-century sermons, based largely on texts from the Song of Songs and the Book of Wisdom.[32] This convention, as traditionally expressed in the description of the bride of Christ in Song of Songs,[33] was also applied to ladies in courtly literature, for example to Blanche in Chaucer's *The Book of the Duchess* (lines 818–1033) where, in contrast to the few physical details he mentions in the Prioress's portrait, Chaucer lavishes more than two hundred lines on the Black Knight's description of his lady. The tradition for such descriptions existed before Chaucer's time, and the contrast between the portrait of the Prioress and that of Blanche indicates that he knew how to vary this convention to suit the occasion. The lengthy description of Blanche also includes sensual comments on social demeanor and good character, in addition to physical beauty: specifically the bodily details of incomparable white and ruddy face; golden hair; white and smooth neck; throat like an ivory tower; fair shoulders; rounded arms; long body; red fingernails; round breasts; hips of a good breadth; straight back; and all perfectly formed limbs.

During the same time period, in less fleshly detail, this tradition was also incorporated in descriptions of the Blessed Virgin Mary.[34] Gautier de

30 Kiernan, p. 9.
31 Ernest Gallo, *The 'Poetria Nova' and its Sources in Early Rhetorical Doctrine* (The Hague, 1971), pp. 44–5. See Charles Muscatine's comments on this tradition in *Chaucer and the French Tradition: A Study in Style and Meaning* (Berkeley, CA, 1957), p. 18.
32 See Guibertus, Tornacensis, *Sermones ad oes status de novo correcti & emendati* (Ab. s. Guenyard: Lugduni [1510?]); esp. 'Ad Noniales et religiosas Sermo', as it incorporates the texts of Song of Solomon 2, 4, and 6.
33 See Gallo, pp. 182–7.
34 See 'An Orison of the Five Joys', no. 26, *Religious Lyrics of the XIVth Century*, ed. Carleton Brown, 2nd edn rev. by Revd G. V. Smithers (Oxford, 1957), pp. 29–31, which includes the phrases, 'quene of heuene', 'cortas & hende', 'fayrest of alle',

Coincy's *Le sermon en vers de la chasteé as nonnains* provides another example in this tradition. Here, God is the courtly lover; the nun is his bride who must adorn her soul as the courtly lady adorns her body in sumptuous garments. These modest nuns wear linen that is 'well pleated and tied'.[35] The description of their habits and the ideals they stand for figure largely in Gautier's poem, in which he demonstrates the spirituality exhibited in giving up worldly dress for black or white habits, and also the courtliness manifested toward their true 'friend', their spouse Christ. He posits that the beauty of this proper behavior in dress and courtliness will become the vesture of their souls. Thus they will avoid the false joy of the world, and experience true joy.[36]

'gladful was i chere', and 'Ladi, flour of alle, so rose in erber red'. This lyric is found in St John's College Cambridge MS 256, pp. 269–70.

　　Also, regarding Christ and the clothing of courtly romance, see Anne Clark Bartlett, ' "Delicious Matyr": Feminine Courtesy in Middle English Devotional Literature for Women', *Essays in Medieval Studies* 9 (1992), p. 14, <http://www.luc.edu/publications/medieval>.

[35] Gautier de Coinci, *Le sermon en vers de la chasteé as nonains*, *Suomalaisen Tiedeakatemian Toimituksia: Annales Academiae Scientiarum Fennicae* (Helsinki, 1938), Sarja B. nid. 38, no. 10, pp. 145–6, lines 404–6. Also see Jill Mann, *Chaucer and Medieval Estates Satire: The Literature of Social Classes and the General Prologue to the Canterbury Tales* (Cambridge, 1973), p. 136, for a discussion of these lines.

[36] Gautier de Coinci, pp. 180–1, lines 1059–83:

> Voz indes fleurs, vous violetes,
> Qui les grans plices d'erminetes,
> Qui la soie, le vair, le gris
> Avez laissiez por les dras bis,
> Qui por les ames faire blanches
> Vestez les fros as noires manches,
> Sachiez que Diex em paradis
> De voz fera ses fleurs de lis [actually irises].
> Voz, blanches fleurs, vois de Cistiax.
> Qui afublez ces blanz mantiax.
> Qui les pliçons et les chemises
> Por blans buriax avez jus mises,
> Ja sont ou ciel apareillies
> Blanches chemises deliies
> Et les robes a or batues
> Dont vos ames seront vestues.
> Por Dieu, por Dieu, blances et noires,
> Gardez ne prisiez pas .ij. pooires
> De cest fax mont la fause joie,
> Car toz les siens guile et fanoie.
> S'en vo biauté, s'en vo jouvent
> Tenez le veu et le couvent
> Que voz avez a Dieu pramis,

This kind of literature emphasizes the ideal of spiritual cleanness[37] through the metaphors of physical beauty, courtly terminology, and clothing used to describe the nun-brides of the courtly lover – Christ.[38] The idea of such 'aristocratic fastidiousness', or cleanness of soul, is expressed also in lines taken from *The Revelations of Saint Birgitta*: The opening section of her *Revelations* begins with the summary, 'Owr lorde Ihesu Cryst tellyth seynte Birgitte why he chesyth hyr to be hys spovse, and how as a spovse she awyth to aray hyr and be redy to hym.' And His instructions are encapsulated as

> Com vrais espeuz, com vrais amis
> De paradis voz doera.
>
> [You blue flowers, you violets/ You who have left your grand robes of ermine,/ Your silk, your vair, and Siberian squirrel/ For drab brown wool/ You who, to make your souls white,/ Dress in black-sleeved cowls:/ Know that God in paradise/ Will make lilies of you./ You, white flowers, turn from your clothes chests/ You who rig yourselves in white cloaks,/ Ruffles and fine linen shirts./ Instead of flattering heaps, have moderate dress./ Already are prepared for you in heaven/ Delicate white dresses/ And robes of beaten gold,/ With which your souls will be vested./ For God, for God, whites and blacks,/ Take care not to value two pears [OF: possessions]/ Of this false world, this false joy./ Cut from yourselves duplicity and deception/ If in your beauty, if in your youth,/ You honor the vow and keep to the convent,/ Which you have promised to God,/ As a true spouse, a true lover./ He will gratify you in paradise. (Translated by Priscilla Throop)]

37 On the subject of the correlation between physical and spiritual cleanness, see *The Book of Vices and Virtues: A Fourteenth Century English Translation of the 'Somme le Roi' of Lorens D'Orléans*, ed. W. Nelson Francis, EETS, OS 217 (London, 1942), pp. 252–4, regarding the robe of virginity that should be kept from being spotted; *The Ancrene Riwle*, ed. and trans. M. B. Salu (Notre Dame, IN, 1956), p. 70, on clean lips and conversation; Sr Mary Patrick Candon, '*The Doctrine of the Hert*, Edited from the Manuscripts with Introduction and Notes', Diss., Fordham University, 1963, pp. 45–6.
Regarding table manners, see Sandra Pierson Prior, *The Fayre Formez of the Pearl Poet*, Medieval Texts and Studies 18 (East Lansing, MI, 1996), p. 77, and n. 6 concerning the 'cleanness' of Christ's table manners. Nicholas Orme includes table manners among a list of the subjects normally included in a lady's education, in 'Chaucer and Education', *ChauR* 16 (1981), p. 42. These works refute the negative reading of fastidious table manners as they reflect on the Prioress provided by Brian Abel Ragen, in 'Chaucer, Jean de Meun, and Proverbs 30:20', *N&Q* 35.3 (Sept. 1988), pp. 295–6.
See also Francis A. Gasquet, *English Monastic Life*, 2nd edn rev. (London, 1904), p. 101, regarding provisions for monk's laundry, yet another aspect of cleanness.

38 Mann states, pp. 134–7:
> Both Guibert and Gautier see the nun not just as the bride of Christ, but as his *courtly* mistress. They attempt to turn aristocratic fastidiousness into spiritual scruple, and not to discourage a girl from romantic dreams, but to attach them to a new hero.

Mann also notes Gautier's statement that 'their flesh is sweeter than violet, rose or "eglentiers" ', suggestive of the name Chaucer gave to his Prioress.

follows: 'To the spovse þer-for it longyth to be redye when hyr spowse wyll make hys weddyng, that she be semely arayde and clene.'[39]

Considering the portrait of Madame Eglentyne within the dual rhetorical tradition of courtly/spiritual literature offers an explanation for why Chaucer mentions her fair forehead, and the texts for the sermons of Guibert de Tournai provide an example.[40] This rhetorical tradition celebrates ideal beauty such as that of the Blessed Virgin Mary who is portrayed throughout the medieval period in what Coulton terms 'supersensual loveliness'.[41]

Alan of Lille's description of *Prudentia* in *Anticlaudianus* serves as another example of this rhetorical tradition:

> Her well-ordered brows, in proper balance arranged, neither too light nor beclouded with luxuriant growth, resemble twin crescents. Her radiant eyes give forth starlight, her forehead stands forth lily-like, her nose gives balsam-odour, her teeth rival ivory, her mouth, the rose. Living colour glows upon her face and no adventitious lustre makes its disgraceful contribution to the image of a beauty so great. Lilies wedded to roses have chastened the face's brightened glow and a rosy tint prevents a cloak of paleness from overshadowing its fair. . . . No space, marked off with set measurements, impedes the movement of her body or checks it with definite limits. Now going further away, she strikes the heavens with her head. . . .
>
> Her robe was woven of fine thread; it does not fake its colour and by no trick does it deceive our eyes. . . . A white garment, woven from Egyptian papyrus, clothes her. She does not impair its beauty and its beauty does her no disservice. Raiment and beauty unite in a charming marriage and each pays its own homage to the other.[42]

This description of Prudence follows the convention of using worldly terminology to describe the delight present in spiritual qualities. In comparing this

[39] *The Revelations of Saint Birgitta*, ed. William Patterson Cumming, EETS, OS 178 (London, 1929), pp. 1–2. See above, Chapter 1, pp. 14–15, regarding the types of fabric considered suitable for wearing by a spouse of Christ.

[40] See Guibertus, *Sermones*, as mentioned in n. 32 above. A lush description of a beautiful face figures in the Song of Songs 4:1–5, 7, 10–11, verses interpreted as Christ's description of his bride, the church: 'Thy lips are as a scarlet lace: and thy speech sweet. Thy cheeks [some translations say "temples"] are as a piece of a pomegranate.' And, in 5:10–16, the bride professes her faith in Christ and employs similar details of physical beauty.

All biblical quotations derive from The Holy Bible, Douay Rheims version, 1899 edn; rpt. 1971.

[41] G. G. Coulton, *Five Centuries of Religion* (Cambridge, 1923), p. 158. Note also Mace, in (l'abbé Pierre Jean) Rousselot, 'La sainte Vierge dans la poésie française du moyen âge', *Revue du clergé français* 42 (1905), pp. 474–5. Mace, a French curate of the the early fourteenth century, treated the Virgin in that manner coexistent in poems of courtly love.

[42] Alan of Lille, *Anticlaudianus, or the Good and Perfect Man*, trans. James J. Sheridan (Toronto, 1973), pp. 56–8.

portrait with that of the Prioress, dissimilarities between them are evident –
for example, the contrast between Prudence's restrained demeanor and the
Prioress's cheer of court. However, like the Prioress, Prudence is beautiful
with 'well-ordered brows'; she is not undergrown, and her costume is (*fetis*)
well-made: 'She does not impair its beauty and its beauty does her no disser-
vice.'[43]

In this medieval rhetorical tradition, we find the proper context for a consideration of the Prioress's veil. Chaucer mentions her fair forehead as part of
his portrayal of external womanly beauty and the ideal it represents. While
her actions may not live up to this ideal outward appearance, yielding a resultant irony, this disparity in no way diminishes the lovely and proper appearance. Chaucer adopts and adapts many features of the rhetorical tradition
described above, leaving little doubt that we may read the physical description of his Prioress in the light of conventional descriptions of the nun as
bride of Christ, the Blessed Virgin Mary, and personified virtues.[44] Unless

43 Chaucer's remark about the Prioress's stature being not undergrown is rhetorically
compatible. We find one example of such a portrayal, actually comprising a summary
of this tradition, in a description of the Virgin by a Franciscan, Oswald Pelbart
(c.1475), included in the *Golden Legend*. Pelbart follows Albert the Great in declaring
that the Virgin 'had a due and proper stature, neither too great nor too small, but
according to the size of a tall woman'. This, he says, corresponds to the Song of Songs
7:6–7, which says, 'How beautiful art thou, comely, my dearest, in delights! Thy
stature is like to a palm tree.'
   Although tall like the palm tree, the Virgin is neither too fat nor too thin. Her color-
ing is the noblest, made up of red and white, and he reasons that her hair and eyes must
be dark, making up a balance of fair and dark. Pelbart describes her as having perfection of body of necessity since she conceived of the Holy Ghost and gave birth to
Christ; since Christ was 'beautiful above the sons of men', according to the laws of
nature, which say that like begets like, the Virgin must be of comparable perfection.
The description continues with an in-depth explication of her dress in *Pomerium
Sermonum de B. Virgine*, pars III, art. ii, c. I, quoted by Coulton, *Five Centuries of
Religion*, pp. 158–61.
44 If the Prioress, too, is described in the conventional rhetoric of womanly beauty, then
Chaucer's choice of her name, Madame Eglentyne, is not pejorative. In fact, Joseph A.
Dane, 'The Prioress and Her *Romanzen*', *ChauR* 24.3 (1990), pp. 219–22, refutes John
Livingston Lowes and subsequent critics accepting Lowes' thesis who claim that
Eglentyne is a name derived from twelfth- and thirteenth-century romanzen, and who
treat Madame Eglentyne as a would-be romance heroine. See M. H. L. Frank's discus-
sion of the name Eglentyne as the 'douce rose' mentioned by a Dominican friar-poet
(c.1328), in MS BN Fr. 12483, fol. 2b, ed. by Arthur Langfors, *Notice du manuscrit
française 12483 de la Bibliothèque Nationale* (Paris, 1916), pp. 19–20, in her 'The
Prioress and the Puys', pp. 4–5. She describes this 'douce rose' as 'that eternally rich
symbol of love and, more particularly, of the Virgin Mary'. See also 'An Orison of the
Five Joys', pp. 29–31, for the description of the Virgin Mary as 'Ladi, flour of alle, so
rose in erber red'. Conversely, Dolores Warwick Frese, 'The Names of Women in the
CT [sic]: Chaucer's Hidden Art of Involucral Nomenclature', negatively links names
and iconography, pp. 161–2, in *A Wyf Ther Was: Essays in Honour of Paule
Mertens-Fonck*, ed. Juliette Dor (Liège, 1992).

one actively prefers to fashion a scandalous prioress from Chaucer's portrait, it is more reasonable to assume that Madame Eglentyne's veil is appropriate than to theorize that she wears a veil draped according to a secular fashion. It is more reasonable to take Chaucer at his word, 'I trowe' that the Prioress's forehead was fair, than to conclude that he *knew*, as Power claims, because he had the Prioress's bared forehead in clear view. Beyond this, as surveys of convent rules and, later, of evidence from the visual arts of the period will show, it is quite possible that the pilgrim-Chaucer could have seen enough to formulate a judgment about the size of the Prioress's forehead *without* the Prioress being guilty of wearing an indecorous headdress.

The Prioress's Headdress and Historical Evidence

A brief survey of convent rules demonstrates that the requirements of a proper headdress for a nun were of much greater variety than literary critics have recognized. Further, the Prioress's headdress as described by Chaucer meets all of the requirements of convent rules, none of which mention specific details concerning veil height above the eyebrows or wimple style. Instead, the religious rules are concerned with maintaining economy and propriety in the type of fabric used, prohibiting all unsuitable decoration, and upholding neatness. Convent visitation records echo these concerns right up to the time of Bishop William Alnwick of Lincoln in the mid-fifteenth century.

Because of the Prioress's association with the Benedictine establishment at Stratford-at-Bowe we begin with the Benedictine Rule. This Rule includes no provision that would indicate that the Prioress's veil is inappropriate. Describing general outlines for a religious habit bespeaking humble dedication to God, it specifies locally produced, inexpensive cloth for nuns' veils and wimples, with a somewhat better quality allowed when nuns traveled away from their convents.[45] This Rule would not permit the use of silk veils for fourteenth-century English nuns since that fabric would necessarily be imported. The headdress of the nuns of the Benedictine Abbey at Elstow may serve as a general model for that worn by medieval nuns. Such a headdress consisted of a white pleated barb or draped wimple, covered by a head-veil.[46]

---

45 *The Rule of St Benedict*, ed. and trans. D. Oswald Hunter Blair, 4th edn (Fort Augustus, 1934), Chapter 33, pp. 98–9, Chapter 55, pp. 144–9; *Three Middle-English Versions of The Rule of St Benet and Two Contemporary Rituals for the Ordination of Nuns*, ed. Ernst A. Kock, EETS, OS 120 (London, 1902), pp. 36, 104–5, 109, 134, 136, and ritual taking of the veil pp. 144–7. See also Chapter 1, pp. 9–12, above.

46 See Houston, p. 152. Her fig. 266, p. 153, shows a brass of Abbess Herwy [sic], c.1525 at Elstow, Bedfordshire, which duplicates the style of habit in earlier pictures; also F. W. Fairholt, *Costume in England: A History of Dress to the End of the Eighteenth Century*, 4th edn, rev. by H. A. Dillon, 2 vols (London, 1909), pp. 197–8, and fig. 160, treats Abbess of Elstow Isabel Hervey's habit.

For purposes of comparison, the *Ancren Riwle* provides a more precise prescription for humble habits than that of the Benedictine Rule. In this Rule, it is clear that headdresses vary; they might be either black and/or white and should be plain and well-made. None of these stipulations is contrary to Chaucer's description of the Prioress's headdress.[47] The *Ancren Riwle* is concerned with propriety, and emphasizes the common knowledge of suitability. This Rule also allows, 'If ye would dispense with wimples, have warm capes, and over them black veils.'[48] Also useful for comparison, a detailed description is given of the headcovering and headdress, with proper pinning, for Bridgettine nuns in the *Rule of Syon* written for the monastery founded in 1415:[49] The gray cloth and black linen, the accepted fabrics for

47 *Ancren Riwle: A Treatise on the Duties of Monastic Life*, ed. and trans. James Morton (London, 1853), Pt 8, pp. 418–21. See also Eileen Power, *Medieval English Nunneries*, Cambridge Studies in Medieval Life and Thought, ed. G. G. Coulton (London, 1922), pp. 530–1; also Désirée Koslin's remarks, in 'The Robe of Simplicity: Initiation, Robing, and Veiling of Nuns in the Middle Ages', *Robes and Honor: The Medieval World of Investiture*, ed. Stewart Gordon (New York, 2001), pp. 264–5, regarding modifications in headdress.

48 *Ancren Riwle*, ed. Morton, Pt 8, pp. 418–21. *Wimple* here may refer to the fillets usually worn under the chin and around the head by women of this period since this work is dated c.1225–35.
    The Ancrene Riwle, trans. M. B. Salu (London, 1955), pp. 185–6, warns anchoresses against wearing a wimple for *adornment purposes only* [my emphasis]. Wearing a wimple for warmth is not forbidden.
    I must disagree with Mann's statement, as well as with the other critics who have cited her reading, that 'Pleating or "ipinchunge" of the wimple is specifically disapproved of', p. 130 in *Ancrene Wisse*, ed. J. R. R. Tolkien, EETS, OS 249 (London, 1962), edited from Cambridge MS Corpus Christi College 402, fol. 53a. Mann cites the following passage: 'Her to falleð of ueil of heaued clað. of euch oðer clað. to ouegart ace munge oðer in heowunge. oðer epinchunge. gurdlesant gurdunge o dameiseles wise.' I translate this passage as: 'Here also falls [the subject] of veiling/ veil of dyed cloth [and] of other cloth/[clothing?] [worn for the purpose of] excessive adornment either in coloring or constriction of the waist/body by girdles and binding/belting of damsels [who are] spiritually insightful.' We cannot understand from this passage that pleated or pinched wimples are forbidden, since wimples are not mentioned. Further, the MED does not define *pinching*, *epinchinge* as pleated; also, the syntax of the sentence lends itself more readily to the reading given here – that it is constricting (not pleated) girdles that are forbidden.
    I have located no other thirteenth-century manuscript of the *Ancrene Riwle* that includes this statement; this indicates that perhaps the problems of colored veils and binding girdles were not widespread. However, a copy entitled *Ancren Recluse*, cited and dated '? a1425 (c1400)' by the MED, contains the statement, 'Alle þise & many mo cleþed to ouer girt, as meninge oiþer heiȝeinge, in penchinge, in girdles girdyng of damoisels wise' (100/7).

49 By Henry V, based on the modified order of St Augustine, according to George James Aungier, *History and Antiquities of Syon Monastery, the Parish of Isleworth, and the Chapelry of Hounslow* ([London], 1840), p. 21.

these headdresses, denote humility as opposed to silk, which signified vanity.[50]

In the *Rule of Syon*, no attention is given to style of the wimple or to height of fillet over eyebrows except for the manner in which it was to be neatly secured.[51] And once again we find nothing in this later Brigittine regulation to indicate, by comparison, that Chaucer's Benedictine Prioress's headdress is in any way inappropriate. In contrast to the complicated description of the Brigittine headdress, Madame Eglentyne's veil escapes mention by Chaucer. And, unmentioned, it can neither be made of improper silk, dyed or not, nor pinned with the forbidden gold or silver tiring pins – the standard transgressions in nuns' veiling in Chaucer's day. These prohibited items would be classified as 'ouer curious', and we should note that 'curious', when applied to the clothing of the religious, carries a negative connotation.[52] Most important for our purposes is the fact that these post-1415 regulations for nuns still evince no concern for height of veil above eyebrows or particular style of wimple.

In general, convent rules are concerned with providing a headdress and a habit that symbolize the Christian ideal of spiritual cleanness represented by physical cleanness, both espoused throughout their rules. That the rules take care to prohibit expensive fabrics, colors, and decorations, including gold and silver tiring pins, tells us the nature of the specific sartorial problems confronted in real convents. Both historical records and secular literature reflect the same concerns of the period.

Historical, religious, or secular records[53] of Chaucer's time, as noted in Chapter 1, pay no attention to the height of nuns' veils nor the particular style of their wimples. In short, religious records reveal concern for the larger

[50] A fifteenth-century sermon allegorizes both wimple and veil, with the wimple representing abstinence from sin in thought and deed and the veil signifying true obedience to God through forsaking willfulness, as quoted from Cambridge University Library MS Hh.1.11, fols 131r and 131v, in V[eronica] M. O'Mara, *A Study and Edition of Selected Middle English Sermons*, Leeds Texts and Monographs, New Series 13 (1994), p. 202.

[51] Regarding neat pinning of wimple and veil, see 'The Sisters' Clothes'; 'From *The Rule of Our Saviour*', in *Women's Writing in Middle English*, ed. Alexandra Barratt (New York, 1992), p. 92:

> The araymentys of the hedde shal be a wympyl wyth which the forhede and the chekes must be unbelappyd and the face on party coveryd, whos extremytees wyth a pyn must be joynyd togedyr behynde the hede in the naterel. Upon this wympyll must be put a veyle of blacke clothe, which thre pynnys must fasten togedyr that it flowe not abrode, oon aboute the frounte and tweyne aboute bothe erys.

[52] See Chapter 1, pp. 11–14, and Chapter 4, pp. 127, 130–2, for discussion of *over curious*.

[53] Clothing transgressions listed in convent visitation records are similar in nature to sartorial presumptions, which the sumptuary laws of England attempted to regulate (see Chapter 1, pp. 15–17).

issues of Christian propriety: veils and wimples should be neatly and securely fastened with tiring-pins that are neither gold nor silver; neither veils nor wimples should be made of expensive fabrics such as silk or burnet.[54] The objective in regulating headdresses in this particular manner, and habits as a whole, was that nuns would practice the virtues of humility and prudence, as opposed to pride and vanity, which are exhibited in excessive attention to worldly things. Similarly, the literature of the Middle Ages pays little attention to nuns' headdresses other than to treat them as part of a symbolic habit, or as symbolic of the entire habit.

The Prioress's Headdress and Literary Descriptions of Nuns

The medieval poem 'Why I Can't Be a Nun' presents the idea that the nun's robe and headdress symbolize virtues that were the spiritual goals of monastic life.[55] Further, this habit stands as a sign of a nun's spiritual vows, and her subsequent spiritual state should be consistent with the holiness of her habit:

> Yowre barbe, your wympple and your vayle,
> Yowre mantelle and yowre devowte clothyng,
> Maketh men wyth-owten fayle
> To wene ȝe be holy in levyng.
> And so hyt ys an holy thyng
> To bene in habyte reguler;
> Than, as by owtewarde array in semyng,
> Beth so wyth-in, my ladyes dere.[56]   (lines 350–7)

Although, in general, medieval literature pays little specific attention to nuns' headdresses,[57] Gautier, mentioned earlier, describes modest nuns who wear linen that is 'well pleated and tied':

54 Burnet was 'a wool-dyed cloth of superior quality, orig. of dark brown colour', according to the OED.
55 John Alcock's *(Spousage of a Virgin to Christ): An Exhortacyon Made to Relygyous Systers*, The English Experience no. 638 (Westmynstre, [Wynken de Worde], n.d.; Amsterdam, 1974; Norwood, NJ, 1974), [p. 8], cites St Agnes who
    shewed that her spouse Cryste Jesu had indued her Wᵗ a garment all sett with precyous stones/that is to say/with charyte/fayth hope/humylyte/obedyens/abstynence/& prayer/& Inbroudred all thyse fayr vertues in the blake garmente of her body and soule here knytte togyder.
56 'Why I Can't Be a Nun', *Early English Poems and Lives of Saints*, ed. F. J. Furnivall (Berlin, 1858), p. 147, edited from BL MS Bibl. Cott., Vesp. D. IX, fol. 179.
    In Giovanni Boccaccio, *The Decameron* (1930; rpt. London, 1973), 2, 9th day, Novel 2, p. 233, this inward–outward consistency as a way of life is illustrated in the veil that was known to the nuns as 'the psalter' and worn by abbess and nuns in a fictional convent in Lombardy.
57 For example, they are mentioned in passing, in such brief references as 'tourel, voille on guymple', in 'Priere d'amour d'une nonnain a un jeune adolescent', *Recueil de*

Very modest, white and clean are they, and more than violets do they shrink from dirt, filth and mud. Their linen is fair and white, well pleated and tied, sweet smelling and fine and delicate.[58]

Here, again, is a reference to the manner in which nuns' headdresses are properly secured, and it is a description consistent with evidence provided from the visual arts of the period, to be discussed later. Gautier's description suggests that Chaucer's line, 'Ful semyly hir wympul pynched was', is a depiction of a wimple properly gathered or folded at the ends for pinning or tying in place.

Conversely, when a nun in medieval literature fails to live up to her vows, the medieval poet frequently indicates this by reference to her inappropriate garments, a subject to be discussed later. It is rare to find detailed literary references to an improper headdress worn by a nun. In Giovanni Boccacio's *Decameron* (II, 9th day, Novel II), although the Lombardic nuns refer to their veil as 'the psalter', the actions of both a wayward nun and the abbess belie their verbal reverence when they break their vows of chastity. This broken vow is symbolized when the abbess hastily, accidentally, places on her head not her 'psalter', but the breeches of the priest who is her lover. Here the literary character's outward appearance, her breeches-headdress, is a *Spiritual Mirror* of her inwardly sinful state. The wayward nun, who has been caught in bed with her own lover, escapes punishment when she calls attention to the telltale 'coif' of her abbess, where 'the points . . . hung down on this side and that'.[59] Nevertheless, for the majority of this story, both unchaste nun and abbess wear *False Vestments* – proper habits that symbolize spiritual cleanness, a cleanness not demonstrated in their wearers' actions; consequently, these holy habits falsely reflect the nuns' spiritual condition.

In a second literary example, an improper headdress is desired and described in 'Plangit nonna fletibus', an eleventh-century song. Here a nun longs for a bridal veil, ribbon, or coronet to wear, as well as jewelry and rich

---

poesies françoises des XVe et XVIe siècles (Paris, 1858), 8:173; and 'the nonnes with vaile and wymple plight', in the pseudo-Chaucerian *Court of Love, The Poetical Works of Geoffrey Chaucer*, ed. R. Morris (London, 1866), 4:38–9.

58   Trans. Mann, *Estates Satire*, p. 136; Gautier de Coinci, *Le sermon en vers de la chasteé as nonains*, pp. 145–6, lines 404–6:

> Mout sont sobres, blanches et netes
> Et plus assez que violetes
> Defuient tai, fumier et fanc.
> Mout sont lor chainze bel et blanc
> Et bien ride et bien lie
> Soef flairant et delie.

59   Boccaccio, p. 234.

furs.[60] Clearly, she finds the wearing of a nun's headdress unsatisfactory. However, we cannot agree with Jill Mann that the Prioress 'resembles' this description of a worldly nun.[61]

A Seemly Wimple

Chaucer informs us of Madame Eglentyne's wimple: 'Ful semyly hir wympul pynched was' (line 151). According to the OED, *seemly* means 'of a pleasing or goodly appearance, fair, well-formed, handsome, "proper" '; this term was 'in early use chiefly applied to a person of high rank or lineage', an application consistent with its use in reference to a Prioress.[62] Although he tells us that his Prioress's wimple is both pleasing and proper, some critics have deemed Chaucer's assurance of seemliness to be inadequate. They have, instead, perpetuated the erroneous idea that the Prioress's wimple is 'pynched' in an unseemly manner, that is, that this wimple 'should have been plain, not fluted', as Coulton has remarked.[63]

The most pejorative term in Coulton's comment is *fluted*. This term, referring to clothing, does not appear in the MED as a Middle English word. It

---

60 'Plangit nona fletibus', ed. Peter Dronke, *Medieval Latin and the Rise of the European Love Lyric* (Oxford, 1966), 2:357, lines 19–27.

> Fibula non perfruor,
> flammeum non capio,
> strophum assumerem,
> diadema cuperem,
> > heu misella! –
> monile arriperem
> > si valerem,
> pelles et herminie
> > libet ferre

> [I have no brooch to enjoy, can wear no bridal-veil, how I'd long to put on a ribbon or coronet – woe is me! I'd get a necklace if I could, and wearing ermine furs would be lovely (trans. Mann, p. 130).]

61 See Mann's comments on lines 19–27, p. 130.

62 Power, *Nunneries*, p. 69, states:

> Socially in all cases, and politically when their houses were large and rich, . . . prioresses ranked among the great folk of the countryside. They enjoyed the same prestige as the lords of the neighbouring manors and some extra deference on account of their religion. It was natural that the Prioress of a nunnery should be 'holden digne of reverence'.

> See also Hahn, p. 114, regarding the Prioress's social status.

> Nevertheless, such rank would represent a rise in status for some prioresses, according to data compiled and presented by Marilyn Oliva, *The Convent and the Community in Late Medieval England: Female Monasteries in the Diocese of Norwich, 1350–1540*, Studies in the History of Medieval Religion 12 (Woodbridge, 1998), p. 105.

63 Coulton, quoted by Robinson, ed., p. 756, n. 151.

appears only as part of a modern definition, and then it is applied to the preparation of pastry crust, as in 'pinching or fluting', a description that modern
readers, but not medieval women, would understand. However, coverchiefs
that present-day readers would describe as fluted or frilled were indeed worn
in the late fourteenth century.[64] Such medieval headcoverings are designated
as a 'goffered' veil, or 'nebula headdress'.[65] We are fortunate to have an
example, in a 1421 manuscript illumination, of a Benedictine nun's slightly
frilled (in the current understanding of that term) wimple; the artist shows a
tiny ripple effect along the lower and side edges of this garment (see Plate
2a).[66] This minimally goffered wimple, of necessity, was draped under the
chin and secured by unseen pins or tied.

In any case, *fluted*, which does not have an entry in the MED, is not an
appropriate synonym for Chaucer's diction, 'pynched'. The verb *pinchen is* in
the MED, defined as: 'of clothing or a wimple: pleated, gathered, having
folds or tucks'. The examples given for this definition include Chaucer's
description of the Prioress, as well as the following quotation from 'How a
Louer Prayseth Hys Lady':[67] 'The forhede playn and wommanysshe To
discryue my hert slepyth for faut of englysshe. . . . No thyng pynchyd lyke a
nonnys wymple, Ne forowyd drye lyke a nabbesse gymple' (line 326). In this
example, the speaker describes the absence of wrinkles in a forehead and uses
the pinched wimple and furrowed 'gymple' as similes for a wrinkled surface.
Such a simile appeals to common contemporary knowledge of how proper
wimples look. Thus, the MED bears out Sister Madeleva's contention that the
Prioress's pinched wimple was a normal part of her habit, and not illustrative
of vanity.[68]

[64] *C&C*, pp. 168–71 and plate 13.
[65] C. Willett Cunnington and Phillis Cunnington, *Handbook of English Mediaeval Costume* (London, 1952), pp. 94–5. See, also, Newton and Giza, 'Frilled Edges', pp. 141–52.
  Examples of goffered (fluted, or frilled) headcoverings may be seen on monumental brasses at Wood Ditton Church, Cambridge; Spilsby Church, Lincolnshire; and East Harling Church, Norfolk, as well as on the early-fourteenth-century statue of St Anne (Vienna, Staatsmuseum), and worn by the donatrix in her picture of the Crucifixion page of a c.1350 Missal possibly belonging to Louis de Male. A goffered headdress may also be seen in the *De Bohun Psalter*, Bodleian Library MS Auct. D.4.4 (c.1370), in a miniature in the initial D on the left-hand side of fol. 223v. St Mary Magdalen, in a painting (1435–40) by Roger van der Weyden, in the National Gallery, London, wears a white linen headdress with all of its edges goffered; reproduced in Françoise Piponnier and Perrine Mane, *Dress in the Middle Ages*, trans. Caroline Beamish (New Haven, CT, 1997), p. 19, pl. 6.
[66] BL Add. MS 15456, fol. 2. This edging also appears on the white underveil.
[67] From MS Bodl. Fairfax 16, fol. 306a (c.1450).
[68] Madeleva, pp. 16–17.

2. Drawings of Nuns' headdresses (a) *Liber Animarum capituli monasterii Sancti Quirini Nussiensis*, BL Add. MS 15456, fol. 2; (b) Book of Hours, BL Add. MS 28784B, fol. 10; (c) *Omne bonum*, BL MS Royal 6 E VI, fol. 27; (d) *Sforza Book of Hours*, BL Add. MS 34294, p. 420; (e) *Le Roman de la rose*, BL MS Harley 4425, fol. 108.

One has only to look at the numerous manuscript illuminations of wimples[69] to see that, when the illuminator is capable of portraying folds or gathers in a wimple, he does so. These are realistic touches, for it is impossible to drape fabric around the contours of the face and across the neck without creating folds or wrinkles. Vertical pleating (in twenty-first-century parlance), or horizontal concentric tucks, would be the most orderly treatment of fabric in such a garment, and folds or wrinkles the most natural. Most often, manuscript illuminations depict wimples hanging in the loose folds produced as the wimple accommodates contour of body and movement. However, there were several other styles of wimples, all of which, in the late fourteenth century, were deemed to be not only proper, but even the epitome of prudence, as an explication of evidence from the visual arts reveals.

The Prioress's Headdress and the Medieval Visual Arts

Numerous headdresses depicted in the visual arts of the Middle Ages make clear that Chaucer's description of the Prioress's wimple is in no way pejorative. As convent rules and historical records reveal, medieval nuns wore a variety of appropriate headdresses, and this is a circumstance that medieval visual arts illustrate, portraying appropriate headdresses in a number of different styles and combinations. With this in mind, we turn to the visual arts to provide answers to two questions: at the time of Chaucer's writing of the *General Prologue*, what was a proper height for a nun's veil? and how 'plain', borrowing Coulton's term, should a proper wimple be?

A survey of medieval manuscript illuminations in serious didactic works reveals that they depict a typical nun who is ideally beautiful in facial features and figure, in accordance with the medieval aesthetic described by Geoffroi de Vinsauf.[70] These idealized nuns exhibit a great diversity in headdresses that encompasses veils worn at a variety of heights above the eyebrows – many times high enough for an observer to be able to see the size of forehead beneath. Further, they wear several styles of wimples – draped, tucked, pleated, and goffered. Thus, we may say that nuns in manuscript illumina-

---

[69] See also Cunnington and Cunnington, *Handbook*, pl. 31, p. 76.

[70] The extent to which this ideal beauty of nuns is portrayed may be seen in *Le Sacre, Couronnement Et Entree de Claude, Royne de France* (dated 1517), BL Cott. MS Titus A. XVII, fol. 33. Here four Dominican nuns in proper habits, representing the four cardinal virtues, appear in the lower register. The nuns' faces are conventionally pretty, a prettiness enhanced by the contrast provided in the depiction, in the register above the nuns/virtues, of seven women of the court, arranged three on either side of Claude de France's daughter. Although their elaborate court costumes are delightful, the artist has given these ladies less refined features; this is particularly true of the six lady attendants. The feature most pointedly different is the nose, which juts rather than flows naturally from the contours of the face of each lady of the court.

tions possess ideal beauty and their faces are framed in headdresses made and worn in a number of different styles.

There are pitfalls inherent in using visual arts as a source. For example, we shall never know what kinds of instructions were given to the illuminators of most medieval manuscripts. Also, it is commonly known that there were sometimes discrepancies between the written text and adjacent illumination. Therefore, we could not cite the Ellesmere manuscript illuminations of the Prioress and the Second Nun as definitive visual proof of what Chaucer's pilgrims looked like and wore[71] even if the date of this manuscript was 1387 instead of 1410–30. When examining manuscript illuminations that are neither caricatures nor grotesques, we may surmise that the artist drew on both artistic tradition and personal experience in his work and that both would be subject to his ability to depict what he knew and had seen. We might assume, for example, that the depiction of a halo behind the figure of a nun-saint, or the crown on the head of such a figure known to be of royal blood, stems from artistic tradition, while the arrangement and style of her headdress may derive either from artistic tradition in which a 'standard' or 'ideal' nun is portrayed or from the artist's generalized or particular experience.

A small sample of illuminations illustrates the variance in headdresses worn by Benedictine nuns. The first example derives from a French Book of Hours (BL Add. MS).[72] The Benedictine nun in black habit on fol. 7 wears a black enveloping headcover, and white underveil and wimple, but fol. 10 shows the same headdress without a wimple (Plate 2b). Elsewhere, in the *Breviarium Romanum* (BL Harl. MS),[73] fol. 73v, a Benedictine nun wears a black overveil, and a white draped wimple, but no underveil. Her forehead is completely uncovered and delicate shading in a flesh tone shows that her brow is wrinkled. In a third example, the nun pictured in the *De Bohun Psalter* (Bodleian Library MS),[74] fol. 219v, wears neither veil nor wimple; her forehead and neck are bare, although a hood attached to her black cloak covers her head. When pictured in these manuscripts, the wimple falls in draped horizontal folds, and the veils fall in perpendicular folds that indicate the softness of the fabric and general shape of the head beneath.

---

[71] However, Samantha Mullaney, 'The Language of Costume in the Ellesmere Portraits', in *Sources, Exemplars and Copy-Texts: Influence and Transmission*, a special edition of *Trivium* 31 (1999), pp. 33–67, makes such an attempt, discounting Richard K. Emmerson's thesis that there was an 'external, guiding force' (p. 34) who knew Chaucer's text and who, therefore, accounts for the similarities between text and many of the illuminations. See Mullaney's comments on the Prioress, pp. 38–40.

[72] The c.1430–50, BL Add. MS 28784B, with thirteenth-century illuminations of Benedictine nuns, which have been cut out and pasted in.

[73] Undated, BL Harl. MS 2975.

[74] English Bodleian Library MS Auct. D.4.4, c.1370.

Dress practices concerning the baring of foreheads and necks varied in the Middle Ages, and the visual arts reflect this variety. Similar to the nuns in the *Breviarium Romanum* and the *De Bohun Psalter* are the nuns in the thirteenth-century French MS Bodley 270b, fol. 12 c 2. They, too, have bare foreheads; in addition, they wear no wimples.[75] Wimples did not become fashionable secular garments until the latter half of the thirteenth century and this illumination may depict either the nuns' headdress in pre-wimple times or their resistance to a new style.[76] Other nuns with bare foreheads may be seen in an illumination of a later date, the fourteenth-century manuscript of Jacobus's *Omne bonum* (BL MS).[77] An illumination on fol. 27 depicts a Benedictine abbess (Plate 2c) who wears a white draped wimple, black veil, and no white underveil. The foreheads of this abbess and the seven nuns she instructs are completely uncovered.[78]

An additional detail noticeable in manuscript illuminations is the position of a nun's veil relative to the eyebrows. Another early fourteenth-century Psalter in Latin (BL Roy. MS), fol. 219, provides an illustration of a Benedictine abbess blessing a nun. This line drawing with grey shading shows that both wimples are draped, and the veils of both nuns are raised an estimated one to two inches above the eyebrows[79] (I translate the difference in scale from illumination size to lifesize). Veils worn this high above the eyebrows are also shown in a Psalter (Bodleian Library MS),[80] fols 25v, 85, and 136v. Significantly, in a 1454 French manuscript (Bodleian MS),[81] fol. 16, such a veil is worn by a nun representing Continence in a scene with other virtues.

Horae beatae Virginis cum calendario, orationibus ad sanctos & aliis,[82]

---

75 Also the English Bodleian Library MS Univ. Coll., Oxford 165, *Bede's Life of St Cuthbert* (first half of the twelfth century), p. 69, depicts the Abbess Aelfflæd and a nun cured by St Cuthbert's girdle. They wear no veils or wimples; the artist has given some attention to depicting their hair, which is uncovered.

76 This illumination depicts the strife of the good (represented by monks and nuns) and the bad (men shown wearing Jewish hats).

77 BL MS 6 E VI is a c.1330–50 copy, according to the BL catalogues; however, Lucy Freeman Sandler, *Omne Bonum: A Fourteenth-Century Encyclopedia of Universal Knowledge [BL MSS Royal 6 E VI–6 E VII]* (London, 1996), 1:25, dates these manuscripts between 1360 and 1375, and Michael Camille in *Gothic Art: Glorious Visions* (New York, 1996), p. 127, concurs. Jacobus is an Englishman, possibly a Cistercian.

78 See also the exposed forehead of the Lady Abbess in the line drawing based on the Luttrell Psalter (c.1300) in John Carter, *Specimens of English Ecclesiastical Costume: From the Earliest Period Down to the Sixteenth Century* (London, 1817), pl. Class IV, upper left-hand corner, and described p. 13.

79 BL Roy. MS 2 B VII. A line drawing of this illustration may be seen in Edward L. Cutts, *Scenes & Characters of the Middle Ages*, 7th edn (London, 1930), p. 57.

80 From the second half of the thirteenth century, the northern French Bodleian Library MS Douce 118.

81 Bodleian MS Laud. Misc. 570.

82 BL Harl. MS 2962, undated.

fol. 41 (Color Plate I), provides a picture of the Benedictine nun St Gertrude wearing a white draped wimple and a black overveil; a white line around the overveil may suggest a white underveil. Allowing again for the difference in scale, approximately one inch of her forehead shows between veil and eyebrows,[83] which would be enough for an observer to estimate the breadth of her forehead.[84] Finally, the picture of a Benedictine headdress including all of the usual garments, with veil reaching down to the eyebrows, appears in the early sixteenth-century *Horae Blessed Marie Virgines, Sec. Usum Sarum* (BL Kings MS).[85] In this picture of St Etheldreda as abbess, she wears a black overveil over a white underveil and a draped wimple. Clearly, there is considerable variation in the portrayal of the veiling of Benedictine nuns in manuscript illuminations. This variety is both confirmed and expanded when illuminations of nuns of other orders are included.[86]

---

[83] The Benedictine abbess St Ethelburger is also pictured with a raised veil in the c.1425–30 *Horae Beatae Virginis*, BL Harl. MS 2900, fol. 68v. Clearly, the illuminator is combining traditions here – the accuracy of portrayal of a Benedictine abbess is combined with the symbolic tradition in which saints are portrayed in crown and royal robes. She is shown with a gold halo and crown over a black veil, under which approximately two inches of forehead show. Her white wimple drapes. Sr Marguerite De Scornay is depicted similarly in a brass commemorating her election as abbess of the Abbey of Nivelles in Belgium in 1443. She wears a nun's habit including a draped wimple, and a cloak that is fur-lined.

[84] Another noteworthy detail, in light of our interest in Chaucer's Prioress, consists of the manner in which the illuminator has chosen to portray St Gertrude's overcoming of vice. Several portraits of saints in this manuscript depict them standing over various small monsters. St Gertrude's portrait shows her standing by four tiny mice, one of which is at her hemline, while another scampers up her crozier.

R. L. P. Milburn, *Saints and Their Emblems in English Churches* (Oxford, 1957), p. 113, describes Gertrude (A.D. 620–59) as the abbess of a double monastery at Nivelles, in Brabant, and invoked to ward off rats and mice. Further, he states that she is 'occasionally shown in English churches as an abbess writing in a book, or with mice on her crozier', apparently because her feast day (17 March) occurs at the time when the hibernation of field mice is over and they begin to make a nuisance of themselves again.

[85] BL Kings MS 9, fol. 64v.

[86] For example, the fifteenth-century *Horae Sanctae Crucis*, BL Add. MS 28784A, includes pasted-in thirteenth-century illuminations that show, fol. 59, a Carmelite nun whose veil is approximately two inches higher than her eyebrows. The English Bodleian Library MS Laud. Lat. 114, fol. 148, of the third quarter of the thirteenth century, contains an illumination of a nun wearing a white draped wimple, and white band of fabric across her forehead, with a lower edge one and a half to two inches above her eyebrows.

The same amount of forehead shows in the fifteenth-century illumination of St Birgitta, fol. 117 in *The heavenly revelations unto blessed Bride, princess of Nerice in the realm of Swecie*, BL Cott. MS Claud. B. I. She wears a black habit, and a white draped wimple and veil (see also fol. 34). The contours of her forehead show plainly in the draping of her veil around her lovely face.

The abbess Heloise wears a slightly raised veil in an illumination, fol. 137, in

Just as depictions of nuns' veils show differences in style, manuscript illuminations and the other visual arts reveal a variety of wimple styles. A most intriguing variation in the most common draped wimple may be seen in *Liber Animarum capituli monasterii Sancti Quirini Nussiensis* (BL Add. MS),[87] fol. 2. Here four Benedictine nuns at prayer wear black overveils, and very interesting white underveils and wimples, which have a tiny ripple around the face and bottom edges, such as the slightest goffering produces (Plate 2a).[88] Yet another style of wimple may be found in illuminations of the fifteenth century. A saintly nun in the *Sforza Book of Hours*,[89] p. 420, wears a black veil and a white wimple that is moulded tightly to her neck in tiny folds or tucks (Plate 2d).[90] The catalogue of the range of styles in wimples is completed in the Ellesmere manuscript illuminations of the Prioress and the Second Nun, and in John Lydgate's *Pilgrimage of Man*, fol. 97v miniature of five nuns at table.[91] Their wimples fall in vertical folds resembling the pleats of a Scots kilt,[92] a type of wimple we shall discuss in more detail later.

With the exception of the Ellesmere illuminations of the Prioress and the Second Nun, the sample of manuscript illuminations described above has been chosen from religious and didactic works, rather than from 'worldly' works.[93] (One other example from a secular manuscript is the headdress of

---

Poestes De Charles, Duc D'Orleans (c.1500), which includes 'Epitres de L'Abbesse Heloys du Paraclit', BL Roy. MS 16 F II. Heloise wears a white draped wimple, with black overveil, which seems to be bordered in white (the artist's attempt to show an underveil?). Her veil is raised approximately an inch over her eyebrows and the modeling of its fabric reveals forehead contours.

87 Dated 1421, BL Add. MS 15456.

88 Fabric is said to be goffered when frills or tiny pleating is achieved by the use of a hot goffering tool (OED); however, such an effect was also achieved through a special technique of weaving. According to Newton and Giza, 'Frilled Edges', p. 141, such frills or goffering were high style in the 1360s, and the nobility wore 'veils edged with a forest of frills in airy layers almost impossible to count', which may be seen in illuminations and sculpted tombs such as the effigy of Lady Berkeley in Tewkesbury Abbey. (I am indebted to Stella Newton for her illuminating conversation on this topic, as well as for an offprint of her article with the correction of date, which I have incorporated in this note.) See also Stella Mary Newton, *Fashion in the Age of the Black Prince: A Study of the Years 1340–1365* (Woodbridge, 1980; rpt. 1999), pp. 87–8, and pl. 28. See n. 65 above for pictures of goffering.

89 BL Add. MS 34294, late fifteenth century.

90 The other nuns with her wear the same headdress with molded-by-tucks wimple. The saintly nun is shown again wearing the same style of wimple (p. 510).

91 BL MS Cott. Tib. A VII (dated 1426), reproduced in Phillis Cunnington and Catherine Lucas, *Charity Costumes of Children, Scolars, Almsfolk, Pensioners* (London, 1978), p. 42.

92 Mullaney, p. 39, apparently has not noticed the vertical folds of the Ellesmere Prioress and Second Nun illuminations' wimples.

93 Regarding worldly works, a copy of *Le Roman de la rose*, BL MS Harl. 4425, c.1500,

Constrained Abstinence[94] depicted in Plate 2e.) This sample depicts the lack of standardization in nuns' headdresses. They sometimes lack underveil, sometimes overveil, sometimes wimple. Both wimples and veils drape and sometimes reveal the contours of the wearer's head.[95] I found no illustrations of a veil worn down to the eyebrows before late fifteenth- or early sixteenth-century English and French manuscripts of the British Library and Bodleian Library.[96] Commonly, nuns' veils in earlier medieval illuminations are worn at a height of one to two inches above the eyebrows – high enough for an observer to be able to judge the breadth of forehead beneath. And we note that from the thirteenth through the fifteenth century there were diverse

contains an illumination of Strayned Abstinence, fol. 108; reproduced in a line drawing in Strutt, pl. 134, fig. 2. She is dressed as a Beguine in a draped white wimple and veil covering her eyebrows, a black cloak, and carries walking staff, book and red (coral?) rosary beads. Outwardly, all is correct; inwardly, all is false – an apt costume for the beloved of Faux Semblant: a perfect holy exterior covering a false interior, which makes her habit a *False Vestment*. Similarly, Strayned Abstinence is depicted in nun's habit, with book and pilgrim staff, in Bodleian MS Douce 332, fol. 115. Apparently, in 1490, the idea of the eyebrows as marking the appropriate level for a nun's veil had taken root, making it desirable for the illuminator to present Strayned Abstinence, wearing *False Vestments*, in suitable decorous headdress. However, another French manuscript of *Le Roman de la rose* (early fifteenth century), Bodleian Library MS Douce 188, fol. 77, shows Contrainte-Abstinence wearing a black veil or hood over white forehead band, positioned approximately two inches above her eyebrows. A copy of this same work (c.1400), the French Bodleian Library MS Douce 371, depicts Hypocrisy (Papelardie) on fol. 4, wearing nun's garb including a white draped wimple and a black overveil which also completely covers her forehead down to the eyebrows.

94 BL MS Harl. 4425.

95 A brief glance at BL Harl. MS 4425 and BL Harl. MS 621, in part, provides another explanation. Here, although the foreheads are not completely uncovered, the shape and height of the foreheads are discernible because the fabric used for the veil is soft enough to adhere to the contours of the head. Such modeling of fabric also appears in a Robert Campin portrait, c.1430, and in a Roger van der Weyden portrait, possibly of his wife, of the same time, in which the veil worn by the subject is slightly transparent, but the transparent style only serves to emphasize the molding of fabric to forehead, a modeling that is apparent in earlier pictures of opaque veils.

96 This dating is not true of nuns' veils depicted in Italian paintings. In the National Gallery, London, Italian paintings frequently depict nuns with foreheads covered down to the eyebrows. Examples are: 'A Group of Poor Clares', no. 1147, by Ambiogio Lorenzetti, painted c.1331 and deriving from the Chapter House of San Francesco, Siena; 'Christ Glorified in the Court of Heaven', no. 663, by Fra Angelico, part of an altarpiece c.1430–35 for the church of San Domenico near Florence; 'The Coronation of the Virgin', no. 569, in the style of Orcagna, painted c.1370–71 for the Benedictine Church of San Pier Maggiore in Florence; 'The Virgin and Child with Saints Catherine of Alexandria and Siena', no. 298, by Ambrogio Bergognone who was active 1481–1523.
   But see Houston, p. 40, figs 50–1; they depict thirteenth-century nuns wearing veils and wimples. Approximately three inches of forehead shows in fig. 50, and one inch in fig. 51.

wimple styles. Saints and abbesses instructing nuns, as well as ordinary nuns, all wear these styles in illuminations in serious didactic and religious works. The artists were portraying either the appearance of a 'traditional' or 'ideal' nun, in which case we must assume that such headdresses were considered to be appropriate frames for this beauty, or they were portraying nuns' head-dresses as they had seen them in actuality, and presenting them as being acceptable. Further, these styles must have been acceptable until after Chaucer's time, as visitation records manifest no official objections to raised veils of any sort until the middle of the fifteenth century and voice no com-plaints about wimple styles, so long as they were neither made of silk nor dyed.

In further answer to the questions posed earlier, concerning height of veil and plainness of wimple, we can say that the typical nun of late fourteenth- and early fifteenth-century manuscript illumination wears a draped white wimple as a frame for her delicate facial features. The other wimple styles mentioned above would also be acceptable. The draped wimple, as plain as may be found in medieval visual arts, would have been aptly described by the adjective *pynched* in fourteenth-century fashion terminology. In addition, over her head, this nun wears one or two veils, which usually, but not always, cover her forehead down to one to two inches above her eyebrows. Such a collective portrait is consistent with Chaucer's description of the Prioress, and if we cannot say that he consciously emulated this manuscript tradition, neither can we claim that he violated it. Clearly, Chaucer's knowledge of the Prioress's fair forehead might well have stemmed from casual observation of a proper veil, pinned neatly in place.[97]

Depictions of personified virtues portrayed as nuns in the visual arts of the Middle Ages provide additional support for the idea that there is no implica-tion of improper veiling in Chaucer's description of the Prioress's forehead,

---

97 An additional answer to the issue of the disposition of the Prioress's veil and how Chaucer knew the width of her forehead is suggested in Ernest Gallo's argument that if the Byzantine canon was the standard adopted by medieval painters (citing Erwin Panofsky's *Meaning in the Visual Arts* as proof), then it might well be the standard that Geoffroi de Vinsauf follows and constitutes the source of his dictum that the outline of the head should be traced by Nature's compass, p. 186. It follows then that in imitating Geoffroi de Vinsauf, Chaucer, too, emulates the Byzantine standard adopted by medi-eval painters and rhetoricians. One has only to examine several reproductions of Byzantine madonnas to see how Chaucer could know how broad the Prioress's fore-head was; the shapes, height, and breadth of the madonnas' foreheads are clearly visible beneath the fabric of their veils. See esp. the Blessed Virgin Mary in the trip-tych by Ducciodi Buoninsegna, no. 566 in the National Gallery, London, and the illu-mination of the Virgin and the Angels in BL MS Cott. Nero C. IV. Reproductions of these may be seen in Otto Demus, *Byzantine Art and the West* (New York, 1970), pp. 241, 175, figs 217 and 175. In this same work, see figs 124, 153, 155, 176, 241, and pl. 1.

and they demonstrate that the injunctions prescribing that a nun's veil should be worn down to her eyebrows responded to a fashion phenomenon in the late fifteenth century.[98] Chaucer most likely saw many Virtues figures[99] among the visual arts accessible to him, for example, the program of frescoes in the Painted Chamber of Westminster Palace,[100] the program of Triumphant Virtues figures on the portal of the Chapter House of Salisbury Cathedral (c.1280),[101] and especially the series of Seated Triumphant Virtues, c.1220, 'on the floor roundels once by the shrine of St Thomas at Canterbury',[102] as well as those he could have seen at Rheims or Strasbourg on his continental travels.[103] Beyond this, he was familiar with the rhetorical tradition of por-

[98] The one statement clearly stating this rule is Alnwick's, dated 1440, as discussed earlier in this chapter, pp. 31–2. The evidence from the visual arts suggests that completely bare foreheads were acceptable for nuns late in the fourteenth century. Regarding the history of wimples, see Houston, pp. 44, 47, 85–7, and 226, figs 63, 75, 142–3.

[99] The wide variety of twelfth- and thirteenth-century nuns' headdresses worn by Virtues figures may be seen in the following: Adolf Katzenellenbogen, *Allegories of the Virtues and Vices in Medieval Art* (Toronto, 1989), pp. 13, 24, figs 25 and 26; Herrade de Landsberg's *Hortus Deliciarum*, BL MS 42497, and *Herrade de Landsberg: Hortus Deliciarum*, eds A. Straub and G. Keller (Strassburg – Paris, 1952), pl. 38; *Speculum Virginum*, Troyes, Bibliothèque Munic. MS 252 in C. R. Dodwell's *Painting in Europe 800–1200* (Harmondsworth, 1971), pl. 199.
     Also see, at Amiens Cathedral, the headdresses of the figures of Prudence and Chastity. Concerning the headdresses of the Vice figures on these portals, see Houston, pp. 46–7, 49, who also provides illustrations from 'The Health Book', BL MS Sloane 2435, and BL Add. MS 38116, fol. 8b 13; and note other Vice figures, including Violence in the sculptures at Strasbourg Cathedral. Female figures, such as Avarice at Amiens and Luxury at Chartres, are bare-headed. Secular headresses worn by Vice figures are distinctive in form and clearly contrast with the modest head covering worn by all the Virtue figures depicted in nuns' dress.

[100] Dated 1262–77, and mentioned by Katzenellenbogen, p. 20. Paul Binski, *The Painted Chamber at Westminster* (London, 1986), provides plates depicting these Virtues figures in copies by both Crocker and Stothard; for example, see his color pl. 2 and black and white pls 6–7. The Virtues are crowned, with the crown usually worn over a single veil covering most of their hair; they wear male armor. Binski, p. 42, dates these frescoes as possibly 1267.

[101] Binski, p. 42, and pl. 39. Although he is not portraying Christian virtues, Chaucer perhaps draws on this general artistic tradition in his depiction of Fame, lines 1360–1416 in *House of Fame*, and in his description of the statues of notables, lines 1419–1514, in Fame's House.

[102] Binski, p. 41, and n. 59, citing J. Y. T. Winjum, 'The Canterbury Roundels', Diss., Michigan 1974, pp. 23ff. Binski makes it clear that this example is one of many possibilities for seeing programs of Virtues figures in England.

[103] Derek Pearsall discusses Chaucer's travels to France, Spain, and Italy, as *valettus* and as diplomat in *The Life of Geoffrey Chaucer: A Critical Biography* (Oxford, 1992; rpt. 1994), pp. 40–2, 51–5, 102–9, with references to *Chaucer Life-Records*, eds Martin M. Crow and Clair C. Olson ([Austin, TX], 1966). Neither Pearsall nor the official records of Chaucer's life determine whether or not Chaucer actually visited any Euro-

traying spiritual beauty in terms of feminine beauty, a tradition that featured mention of the forehead. In following tradition, he mentions the Prioress's forehead, and indicates that it conformed to the standards of such conventional beauty.

The treatment of costume in these traditions argues against the idea that Chaucer portrays the Prioress's physical appearance as being somehow incorrect in veil or wimple. A survey of Virtues figures portrayed as nuns in medieval visual arts discloses that the wearing of a wimple signifies the modesty becoming to a nun and to the virtue of prudence. It was a modest garment in any of its various styles: draped, slightly goffered, tucked, or pleated, and was even more conservative after it was no longer fashionable in the second half of the fourteenth century. For example, in an early fourteenth-century copy of the *Somme Le Roi* in the British Library,[104] fol. 4v (Plate 3), Prudence (upper left quadrant) is the only one of the crowned and veiled Cardinal Virtues to wear a wimple. The significance of such deviation is underscored when we note that all of the Virtues in these illuminations wear fur-lined cloaks except Sobriety (lower left quadrant). This kind of costume deviation appears in a number of illuminations of Prudence[105] who is painted wearing a wimple long after it had been out of vogue, during which time it had become the hall-mark of nuns, widows, and the elderly. In short, the wearing of a wimple of any style was a sign connoting prudence, modesty, piety, and, as such, remained a part of the habits of nuns long after secular fashion gave up this garment, indeed, until the middle of the twentieth century.

The proper attributes of the virtuous nun appear commonly as personified virtues in the visual arts of the medieval period. These images, and most frequently Prudence, were typically depicted in nuns' garb, including veil and

pean city that possessed a major public display of Virtues and Vices figures. Donald R. Howard, *Chaucer and the Medieval World* (London, 1987), discusses Chaucer's time in Rheims (pp. 70–3); his likely route to Milan and Florence via Bruges, Ghent, Strasbourg, and Basel (p. 171); his return, presumably by the same route (p. 196); and later continental voyages, which included trips to France (pp. 222–30). Katzenellenbogen's list of illustrations (pp. 85–7) mentions Virtues and Vices programs, present in the above-named sites, in friezes, mosaics, frescoes, a variety of artifacts, and numerous manuscripts, as early as A.D. 500–10 and increasing in numbers beginning in the eleventh century. The Strasboug Cathedral program was especially notable; see Katzenellenbogen, fig. 19. The other most notable site was Notre Dame de Paris.

104 BL Add. MS 28162, a French copy of the 1279 *Somme Le Roi* by Friar Laurent.
105 In BN MS 9186, fol. 304, among the four Cardinal Virtues, Prudence and Fortitude wear wimples while the other two Virtues do not; in BL Cott. MS Titus A. XVII, fol. 37v, Prudence wears a wimple when other virtues do not; and Prudence in the 1454 Bodleian Library MS Laud. Misc. 570, fol. 9v, wears a veil and wimple while the six Virtues around her are uncovered.

3. The four Cardinal Virtues, from *Somme Le Roi*, BL Add. MS 28162, fol. 4v, by permission of the British Library.

wimple.[106] However, nowhere is the equation of certain virtues and the ideal of the virtuous nun, which visual artists employ as a symbol of these virtues, more clear than in the correspondence in appearance of the Ellesmere manuscript miniature of the Prioress[107] and the statue of Discipline now in the Museum of London (Plate 4). Both date from 1400–30,[108] and both miniature and statue portray a woman in a nun's habit, which includes a wimple, with folds that we might now describe as vertical pleats. Such pleats manage the fullness of fabric that was usually allowed to fall naturally into horizontal drapery. The pleated wimple or folds must necessarily be deemed acceptable for a nun of that time because this garment is part of the habit worn by the virtue Discipline (replacing Prudence), which originally stood with three other Cardinal Virtues on the façade of the London Guildhall. Clearly, Discipline would only be represented as being correct in *habit* in every sense of that term – costume and behavior.

Presumably, costumes worn by nun-Virtues figures in the visual arts would represent appropriate habits. We cannot know if a pleated wimple, acceptable on the Guildhall statue of Discipline[109] between 1425 and 1430, would have been considered appropriate on a living Prioress in 1387, although we may

106 Examples of Virtues' veil and wimple headdresses include Prudence, in Maitre du Mansel's *Fleur des histoires*, Brussels, Bibliothèque Royale, MS 9232, fol. 448v; Faith, in N. Oresme's *Ethique d'Aristote*, vol. ii, Rouen, Bibliothèque Municipale, MS 927, fol. 17v; Ecclesiastical Power, in Bodleian MS Bodl. 338, fol. 1; the previously mentioned four Cardinal Virtues in BL Cott. MS Titus A. XVII, fol. 33; Continence, in Bodleian MS Laud. Misc. 570, fol. 16 (Continence, here, is one of the subsidiary Virtues belonging to Temperance, in a scene where both of the other two subsidiary Virtues, and Temperance as well, wear secular clothing and neither wimples nor veils); Glad Poverty, in *Boccacio de Casu illustrium virorum et feminarum*, BL MS Harl. 621, fol. 71, whose costume is cited by Joseph Strutt as being illustrative of a nun's habit, *A Complete View of the Dress and Habits of the People of England, from the Establishment of the Saxons in Britain to the Present Time: Illustrated by Engravings Taken from the Most Authentic Remains of Antiquity* (London, 1970), line drawing pl. 134); Chastity, in the French manuscript of *Le Roman de la Rose*, Bodleian MS Douce 195, fol. 63v; again, Chastity in Bodleian Library MS Douce 188, fol. 26v, of *Le Roman de la rose*.

107 For a reproduction of the Ellesmere manuscript illuminations, see *The Ellesmere Miniatures of the Canterbury Pilgrims*, ed. Theo Stemmler (Mannheim, 1977); also there is a reliable folder of these illuminations in color available in The Huntington Library gift shop, San Marino, CA.

108 However, Carter says, pp. 22–3, that this Guildhall statue was erected in the fourteenth century; a line drawing of the statue appears at the lower right-hand corner of his pl. Class VI.

109 I am grateful to John Clark, Curator (Medieval), Early London History and Collections at the Museum of London, for the following references concerning this statue of Discipline: Caroline M. Barron, *The Medieval Guildhall of London* (London, 1974), Chapter 2, pp. 25–7, 48, pls 7–10; John Edward Price, *A Descriptive Account of the Guildhall of the City of London: Its History and Associations* (London, 1836), pp. 70–3, with sketches; and Caroline M. Barron, 'Anniversary Address at the Guild-

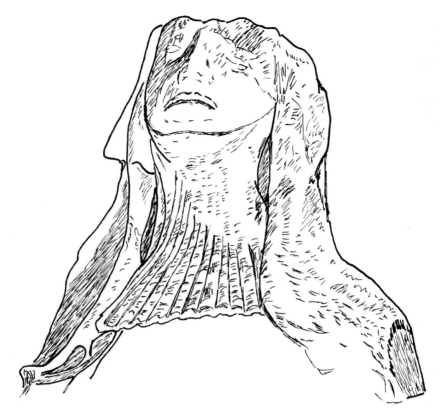

4. Sketch of the veil and wimple worn by Discipline (substituting for Prudence), full-length sculpture in the Museum of London, formerly on the facade of the medieval London Guildhall.

posit that the Ellesmere illuminator, working at approximately the same time as the Guildhall sculptor of Discipline, intended no scandal in depicting Chaucer's two nuns wearing the same wimple style with vertical folds or pleats.[110] It follows that neither the illuminator nor his sponsor found anything exceptional in Chaucer's description of Madame Eglentyne's wimple. In addition, all the evidence points to the fact that a wimple of any style, made out of suitable fabric, was considered a prudent garment. Thus Chaucer's Prioress, wearing a wimple 'pynched' 'ful semyly', would have been dressed appropriately. As for her veil, we may assume propriety there as

hall', *Transactions of the Ancient Monuments Society*, New Series 23 (1978), pp. 17–22, pls 3–5.

[110] The existence of the statue of Discipline with such a wimple refutes Mullaney's assumption, p. 39, that such a wimple was 'an irredeemably secular style'.

well, since the evidence shows that Chaucer's description of the Prioress's forehead is consonant with artistic tradition, rhetorical and visual, and finds no echo in contemporary convent costume transgressions. Such recorded veiling transgressions regarding height of veil on forehead were approximately fifty years in Chaucer's future and could not have inspired the Prioress's portrait. Instead, Chaucer tells us:

> Ful semyly hir wympul pynched was. (line 151)

The Prioress's Cloak

Chaucer provides no description of the Prioress's complete habit. Nevertheless, basing their judgments on Chaucer's depiction of the Prioress's cloak, the negative critical tradition explicated in this chapter holds that Chaucer presents Madame Eglentyne to us in 'elegant'[111] dress symbolizing her pride, vanity, and/or love of luxury. In contrast, criticism more favorably disposed toward the Prioress excuses such 'elegance' as consonant with Chaucer's portraying the Prioress as a devotee of Mary, dressed in the Marian tradition. These opposed critical stances assume that the Prioress's sartorial 'elegance' must be either condemned or excused. In contrast, this study posits that neither condemnation nor excuse is needed for Madame Eglentyne's 'elegance' because, employed as a pejorative description of her, the adjective *elegant* is anachronistic. In addition, through a comparison of Chaucer's description of the Prioress with convent rules for nuns' habits of the period, the evidence of contemporary historical records, sumptuary legislation, and other literary descriptions of nuns, we see that Chaucer implies approbation not only in the very brevity of his description of the Prioress's costume, but also in his omission of the numerous clothing abuses of nuns, so frequently included in other medieval sources.

Chaucer describes the Prioress's habit in a single clause constituting costume synechdoche:

> Ful fetys was her cloke, as I was war. (line 157)

In this line, Chaucer supplies only the image of a cloak, which covers, literally and figuratively, the remainder of her habit – smock, tunic, girdle, and scapular. According to a fifteenth-century sermon, such a cloak represents faith.[112] Although the details of Madame Eglentyne's dress cannot be known,

---

111 'Very elegant' is the first of the two glosses for *Ful fetis* provided by *Riverside Chaucer*. The second and all too often ignored gloss is 'well made'.
112 This sermon on nun's habits states,
      just as your mantle covers all other clothing and under garments, so in the same
      way will you understand all things by faith. The seams of the mantle are tokens

we might fairly assume that they are consistent with the cloak, which is 'ful fetys', a phrase that, erroneously and frequently, has been critically interpreted as pejorative.

Numerous comments concerned with the Prioress's 'ful fetys' cloak imply, or state outright, that an attractive prioress, in her person or in her clothing, should be suspect. For example, Edward Craney Jacobs equates the 'handsome cloak' with worldliness;[113] while Gerald Morgan notes the Prioress's 'elegance of dress and a [total appearance of] physical beauty', stating that the attractive details of her portrait 'have been carefully chosen to focus upon the violation of her profession as a nun'.[114] In this vein, too, Phyllis Hodgson states that 'the rich garb of the Prioress . . . would be seen as the suit of Pride' in the tradition of moral abstractions in the familiar literature of the Seven Deadly Sins.[115] Mary Hardy Long Frank, in the positive but excusatory vein, remarks on the Prioress's 'modest confusion of elegance and grace', forgiveable in light of the tradition of Mary's elaborate costumes, and says that 'more probably she reflects unabashedly the spiritual beauty of her mistress whom Chaucer himself called "Virgine, that art so noble of apparaile" '.[116] However, these three critics represent only a sample of the critical tradition illustrating the manner in which the 'ful fetys' cloak worn by the Prioress has become an 'elegant' cloak, an adjective almost invariably interpreted negatively because a modern understanding of the word, dis-

---

of Christ, your spouse's charity, how in His charity he created you, redeemed and nourishes you and endows you with the Holy Ghost for salvation.
Trans. provided by Oliva, pp. 62–3, citing CUL MS Hh.1.11. For an edition of the original text, see O'Mara, esp. pp. 199–203, also pp. 141–223.

113   Edward Craney Jacobs, 'Further Biblical Allusions for Chaucer's Prioress', *ChauR* 15 (1980), pp. 152–3.

114   Morgan, 'The Universality of the Portraits', p. 489.

115   Phyllis Hodgson, ed., *Chaucer: General Prologue, The Canterbury Tales* (London, 1969), p. 22. Hodgson reminds us that the Prioress and Idleness of *Le Roman de la rose* share many features, pp. 24–5. Her comment is certainly true of physical features, but not at all true of costume.
    Similarly, Julia Bolton Holloway, in 'The Figure of the Pilgrim in Medieval Poetry', Diss., University of California, Berkeley, 1974, p. 370, finds that the Prioress is modeled on Faux Semblant's lemman, Strayned-Abstinence, but Holloway fails to note that, whatever her actions might tell us about her spirituality, Strayned-Abstinence's Beguine habit is correct.

116   M. H. L. Frank, 'The Prioress and the Puys', p. 10. Frank also points out that it would be in character for Chaucer to write in the Marian tradition; she documents the strength of the London Puys, a literary society dedicated to the Blessed Virgin Mary that met regularly at St Mary's Guildhall in London during Chaucer's and his father's lifetime; she reminds us, as well, of Hoccleve's poetic portrait of Chaucer: 'How he thy servaunt was, mayden Marie', p. 28, quoting Thomas Hoccleve's *Governail of Princes*, ed. Wright, p. 179, stanza 713. See also Frank, pp. 133, 151.
    The Prioress is further associated with the Virgin Mary in the lengthy prayer to the Virgin at the beginning of the Prioress's *Tale*.

cussed below, turns *elegant* into a violation of the Benedictine Rule. As we shall see, subsequently, this unfavorable sense of 'elegant' and elegance has been interpreted as 'handsome', 'worldliness',[117] 'rich',[118] 'lavish', or even as 'flamboyance'.[119] In this general escalation of slanted descriptive language, a case in point is Florence H. Ridley's reference to the Prioress's love of 'ornate garb'.[120] In order to refute this negative progression, we must return to an examination of what Chaucer said and come to terms with what Eileen Power calls 'that fetis cloak'.[121]

The narrator's comment, 'Ful fetys was hir cloke, as *I was war*' (line 157) (my emphasis), colors critical apprehension of the cloak's appearance. His awareness implies an appreciation for what he sees that has, perhaps, worked against the readers' objectivity regarding what he says. He describes only the Prioress's outer garment, not a fashionable *houppeland*,[122] supertunic, or a girdle embroidered with silver or gold. He is simply aware that the cloak is 'ful fetys', that is, very 'cleverly fashioned, neat, elegant'. This MED definition of *fetis* makes 'elegant' synonymous with skill in garment making and neatness. Further, this definition is accompanied by seventeen usage examples for *fetis*, including Chaucer's description of the Prioress's cloak; sixteen of these examples are positive in connotation, and the only one that is labeled as ironic is not Chaucer's. *Elegant*, so often used as an equivalent for *fetis*, is employed as a modern definition; it does not appear as an entry in the MED, nor in dictionaries of Old French, where we find *faitis*.[123] The first OED example of *elegant* in written English is dated 1485, and at that late date it is defined as '*Tastefully* ornate in attire, *sometimes* in unfavourable sense: Dainty, foppish' [my italics]. It is this unfavorable sense of *elegant* that a number of critics have seized upon, in spite of the fact that it is a secondary definition for an early definition of a Middle English word. It is more likely that Chaucer intended 'fetys' to mean *bien fait, bien faconne, joli* [well-made, well-fashioned (and therefore) lovely], as Frédéric Godefroy defines *faitis*.

Chaucer does not say that the cloak is *curiously* fashioned, a pejorative description.[124] Nor does he say that the cloak is over-curious or excessively attractive; and he omits any mention of unauthorized fabric, decoration, or color and fur, although Madame Eglentyne might properly have worn certain

---

[117] Jacobs, pp. 152–3.
[118] Hodgson, p. 22.
[119] Regarding 'flamboyance', Charles Moorman imaginatively posits the Prioress's 'love of flamboyance', in 'The Prioress as Pearly Queen', *ChauR* 13 (1978), pp. 27, 30–2.
[120] Ridley, p. 21.
[121] Power, *Medieval People*, pp. 77–8.
[122] See Chapter 6, pp. 166–7.
[123] See Frédéric Godefroy, *Dictionnaire de L'Ancienne Langue Française et de tous ses dialectes* (Paris, 1884; rpt. New York, 1961), 3:709.
[124] As discussed earlier, in Chapter 1, and especially in regard to the Monk, Chapter 4, pp. 127, 130–2.

furs. It is most likely that Chaucer means that the Prioress wears a very neat, well-made cloak, that is a better cloak for traveling than for daily wear, which, according to the Benedictine Rule, she *should* wear.[125] This description accords with the cloak that symbolizes faith described in the sermon on nuns' habits, cited above, which describes the very seams of a nun's mantle as 'tokens of Christ'.

In addition, we may appreciate the restraint of Chaucer's description of Madame Eglentyne when we contrast his description of her cloak with other descriptions of cloaks and/or nuns' habits in the mode of either the typical historical or literary luxurious abbess or prioress. However, before contrasting the costume of this Prioress with costumes worn by nuns who broke the rules of propriety, we shall first compare it to those ideals that she emulated.

The Prioress's Habit and Historical Evidence

The *Ancren Riwle* emphasizes the idea that a religious habit should be 'well made' and uses the phrase 'skins well tawed' (processed) in what may be a metaphor to describe this phenomenon: 'only see they be plain and warm and well made – skins well tawed'.[126] The *Rule of Syon*, too, is concerned with the careful and skillful construction of nuns' garments.[127] In addition, selection of proper material, and fabric cut to the proper measure, are characteristics of a well-made habit, and these concerns are voiced in fourteenth-century Benedictine rules for nuns.[128]

Thus we see that the Prioress's 'ful fetys' cloak, so far as we know, meets all the requirements of convent rules in that it is cleverly, that is, skillfully fashioned, neat, well-made, '*bien fait, bien faconne*'. If, in meeting these requirements, the result is one that corresponds to Godefroy's third definition

---

[125] See Chapter I discussion, pp. 8–9.

[126] *Ancren Riwle*, ed. and trans. Morton, Pt 8, pp. 418–21. This Rule also comments on nuns' choices of clothing:

> Next your flesh ye shall wear no flaxen cloth, except it be of hards and of coarse canvass. Whoso will may have a stamin [a shirt made of woolen and linen, used instead of a penitentiary hair shirt. – Fosbrooke.] and whoso will may be without it. Ye shall sleep in a garment and girt. Wear no iron, nor haircloth, nor hedgehogskins; and do not beat yourselves therewith, nor with a scourge of leather thongs, nor leaded; . . .

> Let your shoes be thick and warm. In summer ye are at liberty to go and to sit barefoot, and to wear hose without vamps, and whoso liketh may lie in them. A woman may well enough wear drawers of haircloth very well tied, with the strapples reaching down to her feet, laced tightly.

[127] See Chapter 1, p. 11.

[128] *The Middle-English Versions of The Rule of St. Benet and Two Contemporary Rituals for the Ordination of Nuns*, ed. Ernst A. Kock, EETS, OS 120 (London, 1902), pp. 36, 104–5, 134.

of *faitis* as *'joli'*, attractive to the eye, the wearer of a proper religious habit can hardly be faulted for that beauty that registers in the eye of Chaucer the pilgrim-poet who says he is 'war' of it.

Had Chaucer wished to draw on contemporary examples of nuns who wore inappropriate costumes as models for an indecorous Prioress, he had a variety from which to choose. Historical records provide numerous detailed descriptions. The repetitive regulations issued by church councils depict the apparently common practice of private ownership of expensive clothing by prioresses, abbesses, and their nuns as well, and the visitation records document improper clothing practices, all of which would have provided Chaucer with ample data for satirizing a prioress through costume rhetoric. Instead, in his so brief description of the Prioress's habit epitomized only in her 'ful fetys . . . cloke', he pointedly omits all pejorative references afforded him by the long-standing struggle of church hierarchy against sartorial violations of the rules by nuns.

However carefully rules were laid down with the thought that the habit makes the nun,[129] church records suggest that it was more difficult to achieve conformity in proper religious dress – with its assumed benefits to nuns' sanctity – than the rule-makers might have originally supposed. The social and historical reality of medieval nuns' dress is revealed in church documents and wills that indicate that the bishops proposed, but the nuns disposed. As mentioned in Chapter 1, pp. 25–6, the Council of Oxford, 1222, forbade nuns to wear belts of silk, or those embroidered with silver or gold, habits made of burnet or other unlawful cloth, and habits made with superfluous fabric,[130] an instruction necessary because of evident unacceptable practices described in visitation records. In 1237, black[131] became the officially designated color of

---

[129] This idea in positive form opposes False Seeming's statement regarding monks not being made by the wearing of a monk's habit, in Guillaume de Lorris and Jean de Meun, *Le Roman de la rose*, ed. Daniel Poirion (Paris, 1974), line 11058.

[130] David Wilkins, *Concilia Magnae Britanniae et Hiberniae* (London: 1737), 1:590–1. See Chapter 1, n. 78 above, for the full Latin quotation.

[131] Cloth dyed black would have involved extra expense and, as such, violated the intent spelled out in the Benedictine Rule that the religious should wear clothing made of inexpensive cloth. Apparently, this Benedictine ruling was ignored in order to attain a more sober color for habits than that provided by the inexpensive undyed fabrics available. For numerous recipes for black dyes using a variety of dyestuffs, see the facsimile of Gioanventura Rosetti's *The Plictho: Instructions in the Art of the Dyers which Teaches the Dyeing of Woolen Cloths, Linens, Cottons, and Silk by the Great Art as Well as by the Common*, and the trans. of the 1st edn of 1548 by Sidney M. Edelstein and Hector C. Borghetty (Cambridge, MA, 1969). Kenneth G. Ponting, *A Dictionary of Dyes and Dyeing* (London, 1980), p. 18, explains why dyeing a fabric black was expensive in the medieval period. It was a problematical process made by mixing the three primary colors:

> Without doubt most blacks were dyed either by producing a very dark navy, dyed with woad and then topping with a yellow dye such as weld, or possibly a

habits for monks, canons, and nuns. Dresses with trains and pleats, or any excessive length, were forbidden to nuns, as were 'delicate or coloured furs',[132] rulings that were repeated in William of Wykeham's 1387 injunctions to Romsey and Wherwell.[133] The list of the many items of clothing forbidden to nuns is a long one: gowns with wide bottoms, sleeves turned back showing fur at the wrist, wide girdles or plaited belts that men might see, mantles and kirtles with openings in seams (decorative slashes?), large collars, barred girdles (striped or decorated with metal bands), laced shoes, red dresses, and the long supertunics of the 'secular' type, silken clothing, especially silken veils, rings other than their consecration ring, tunics that laced up or that fastened with brooches, the secular style called 'gownes' (probably *houppelandes*), and kirtles of fustian or worsted.[134]

Obviously, the worldly nuns described in historical records, who wore these garments frequently enough to have elicited these specific injunctions, were indeed followers of current fashion. Chaucer's Prioress's costume, however, is not patterned in this mode; he simply tells us that her clothing is modestly covered by her well-made cloak. In his rhetorical restraint, Chaucer implies the cloak's propriety. He mentions no wide girdle or plaited belt that men might see, no fashionable gown, no fur, no unauthorized fabrics or excessive fabric used in gown or train. However, Chaucer need not have limited himself to these transgressions of the rules. Historical records provide an even greater variety of improper details of habits he might have attributed to the Prioress.

As stated in Chapter 1, legacies were the source of much of the elaborate clothing worn by worldly nuns. Cloistered nuns frequently received clothing made of expensive fabrics and decorated with jewels, furs, and/or embroidery of silk, gold, and silver, bequeathed to them by friends and relatives, some of whom were themselves members of the church hierarchy. An example of

---

red like madder, or by dyeing a medium blue and then cross-dyeing with first
yellow (weld) and then red (madder). By this method, a good black was obtained
but the lengthy process was not good for the material.
See also Kenneth G. Ponting, *The Woolen Industry of South-West England* (Bath,
1971), p. 11.

132 D. Wilkins, *Conc.* 1:660. See Chapter 1, n. 80, for full quotation.

133 Power, *Nunneries*, p. 586, citing New Coll. MS., fol. 86. Jo Ann McNamara, *Sisters in
Arms* (Cambridge, MA, 1996), p. 364, describes costume indiscretions that illustrate
the need for such rulings:
The ladies of Saint-Cyr near Rouen . . . wore elaborate dresses and colored veils
and acted in 'farcical performances' on the feast of the Innocents and Mary
Magdalene when they danced with lay people.
(citing Eudes of Rouen, *The Register of Eudes of Rouen*, ed. and trans. Sydney M.
Brown [New York, 1964], p. 48).

134 See Power's description, *Nunneries*, pp. 585–7, with numerous citations. Also, see
Chapter 1 of this study. Regarding fabrics, see *The Cambridge History of Western
Textiles*, ed. David Jenkins (Cambridge, 2003), 1:434–5, 493–4.

such a legatee is Joan, Prioress of Swine, who benefited from the will of Anne St Quintin (1393) and received, among other things, ' "one cloak of black cloth furred with gray, . . . and ten marks of silver" '.[135] In addition, in 1404, the Bishop of Durham Walter Skirlaw, mentioned earlier in regard to his bequest of furred hoods, bequeathed furred mantles, cloaks, and robes to his sister, this same Prioress Joan of Swine: ' "Item a robe of murrey cloth of Ypres (?yp'n) containing a mantle . . . furred with budge (?purg') . . . a cloak furred with half vair, a long robe ('garnach') furred with vair" '.[136] Similarly, Margaret Fayrfax apparently wore the black *'armilansa'* furred with grey bequeathed to her by her brother, the rector of Presscot, John Fayrfax.[137]

Ladies from aristocratic backgrounds seem to have inflicted upon the bishops the largest share of fashion problems; for example Archbishop Melton, at the Priory of Hampole in 1314, found it necessary to instruct the prioress to correct her nuns for wearing fashionable clothing, the 'new-fashioned narrow-cut tunics and rochets' (loose upper garment), contrary to the rule of the order, 'whatever might be their condition or state of dignity'. These Cistercian nuns were instructed as follows:

[They should] use uncut garments of the old fashion, long time observed in the house, to the honour of religion. The archbishop also ordered that all the irregular *clamides* [mantles] of the nuns, to wit those of black colour, should be removed within half a year, and that in future they should use *clamides* of russet colour according to the old fashion of the house and institutes of the order.[138]

We may conclude, based on the list of clothing and accessory items listed above as being forbidden to nuns, that certain nuns wore some of the items they received as bequests, while other garments were refashioned into church vestments and altar cloths, and indeed some sumptuous worldly garments were bequeathed to convents for that express purpose.

Although the Benedictine Rule prohibited the possession of private prop-

135 *Testamenta Eboracensia, or Wills Registered at York Illustrative of the History, Manners, Language, Statistics, &c., of the Province of York, From the Year MCCC Downwards*, ed. James Raine (London, 1836–1902), 1:325–6, gives the Testamentum Willielmi Heghfeld De Swyn: 'Item lego eidem tria coclearia argentea, et cistam meam quae est apud Swyn, et j malesadill, et j togam longam de nigro'. Power, *Nunneries*, pp. 327–8, discusses this same bequest, citing *Test. Ebor.* 1:187–9. Further, in 1394, this same Prioress received from the will of 'Agnetis Relictae Domini Johannis De Sancto Quintino Militis' 'j quylt de serico, & j par linthiaminum de panno de reyns'. *Test. Ebor.* 1:332.
136 *Test. Ebor.* 1:308, 317, 322, 324.
137 Will dated 7 June 1393; see Chapter 1, p. 27.
138 *The Victoria History of the Counties of England: Yorkshire*, ed. William Page (London, 1913), 3:164. Here, apparently, is an attempt to eliminate the expense of dyeing garments black.

erty, in the late fourteenth century this prohibition was either no longer in force or unenforceable. The Rule provided that clothing belonged to the order and would be dispensed as required to a nun. Nevertheless, in addition to the evidence provided in the wills cited above, bequests were sometimes made with the express purpose of providing the habit for a specified nun, and not only do they indicate the extent to which nuns of the later Middle Ages possessed private property, at the same time they also specify the fabric and style of an apparently acceptable habit. For example, Elizabeth Sewardby is provided with a personal habit as well as suitable bedclothes.[139] This same will provides a list of items to be provided at a given cost of £3 13s 7½d and it lists the fabrics used.[140] However humble a toga, or cloak of russet, or a tunic of blue[141] cloth may have been, none are dyed black, the color specified for nuns' habits in *Concilia Magnae Britanniae et Hiberniae* I; they are, instead, in keeping with Archbishop Melton's 1314 instructions to the Prioress at Hampole, mentioned above. And we note that the garments listed, apparently, are to be the property of the recipient.

However, witness the account given of a wardrobe that is much more detailed and luxurious than Chaucer's description of the Prioress, assembled for Joan Samborne's veiling (22 June 1395–21 June 1396), at the Austin nunnery of Lacock. Besides the large item of 102s paid for veiling and linen cloth mentioned in Chapter 1, it includes:

> Item for a mantle 10s. Item for a furring of shankes [defined as cheap fur made from the underpart of rabbit skin according to Halliwell Philipps] for another mantle 16s. Item for white cloth for lining the first mantle 6s. 8d. Item for white cloth for a tunic 10s. Item a furring for the pilch [the

---

139   *Test. Ebor.* 3:168:
> *Expensae Factae Super et pro Elizabetha Sywardby Facta Moniali in Munkton. Et dicunt se solvisse et dedisse Priorissae Conventui de Munkton, pro quodam feodo quod dicta Priorissa et Conventus ex consuetudine clamant habere, et habere solent de qualibet moniali in ingressu suo, iij li. Et de denariis solutis pro habitu dictae Elizabethae Sywardby et pro aliis utensilibus corporis sui, una pro lecto competenti, iij li. xiij s. vij d. ob. Et in expensis factis super Priorissa et Conventus praedictis, et super. amicis dictae Elizabethae insimul commorantibus in Dominica proximo post festum Nativitatis B.M.V. anno Domini MCCCCLXX mo, iij li. xj s. iiij d.*

140   *Test. Ebor.* 3:168.
> *Et pro X paribus solularium emptis pro eadem Elizabeth, et expensis, iij s. vj d. Et pro factura unius togae cum le coler, ac pro j pari caligarum pro eadem Elizabetha, xij d. Et soluti pro ij ulnis panni ruset, emptis pro j toga facienda eidem Elizabetha, ij s. iiij d. Et pro j uln. et di. panni blodii, pro j tunica pro eadem, ij s. j d. Et pro factura dictarum togae et tunicae, et factura j paris caligarum et ij camisearum, ij s. j d.*

141   *Blodi* is defined by the MED as 'bluish, somewhat blue'. See also R. E. Latham's *Revised Medieval Word-List from British and Irish Sources* (Oxford, 1965), p. 52, for the entry *blodium*.

furlined undergarment (pellicea)] aforesaid 20s. . . . Item for another mantle of worsted bought 20s.[142]

The total cost of her habit cannot be computed because the £5 2s paid for veils and linen suggests that this purchase may have been for the entire convent rather than for Joan alone. Also, her complete habit would include shoes and/or boots, socks, and possibly some type of girdle; altogether, there are three mantles, one of worsted, a moderately priced fabric.[143] We note that Lacock was a 'royal foundation', composed of persons of good family, which customarily elevated expenses.

The earlier records of Chaucer's own century describe worldly nuns in fashionable garb,[144] and later visitation records provide additional evidence that the prohibition of private property continued to be disregarded. The previously mentioned Clemence Medforde, Prioress of Ankerwyke, in 1441, besides wearing silken veils high upon her forehead and estate caps furred with budge above these veils, owned and wore a number of other forbidden items of clothing, none of which are part of Madame Eglentyne's garb. According to the complaints,

> The Prioress wears . . . girdles silvered and gilded over . . . and she wears furs of vair. . . . Also she wears shifts of cloth of Rennes, which costs sixteen pence the ell. . . . Also she wears kirtles laced with silk and tiring pins of silver and silver gilt and has made all the nuns wear the like.[145]

Altogether, Clemence Medforde epitomizes the typical worldly nun whose fondness for things of the world manifests itself in sumptuous dress. However, she wears clothing that is no more elaborate than that of the early eighth-century nuns who wore the fine linen vests of violet under hooded scarlet tunics and sleeves striped with silk and trimmed with red fur forbidden by St Aldhelm (as well as the voluminous beribboned headdresses made

---

[142] Revd W. G. Clark-Maxwell, 'The Outfit for the Profession of an Austin Canoness at Lacock, Wilts. in the Year 1395, and Other Memoranda', *Archaeol J* 69, 2nd ser. 16 (1912), p. 118. This is his translation from the Latin and citation of H. Philipps. See Chapter 1, n. 24 regarding veiling expenses.

[143] See the discussion regarding worsted in Chapter 5, pp. 145–9 on the Friar's costume.

[144] These records include those of the Priory of Wilberfoss in 1308 whose nuns were instructed by Archbishop Greenfield's *decretum* not to 'wear red, or unsuitable clothes, nor supertunics too long, like secular women, as some had begun to do', according to *Vic. Hist. . . . Yorkshire*, 3:126. This same archbishop, in 1314, issued a *decretum* to the nuns of the Priory of Nunkeeling in which he forbade them to make themselves remarkable in their girdles or shoes, 'or anything unsuitable to religion', 3:120. And this struggle against impropriety was continued by Archbishop Melton after his 1318 visitation to the Priory of Nunburnholme. He directed the Prioress and nuns 'not to use mantles, tunics or other garments, over long or adorned in a manner which did not accord with religion', 3:119.

[145] *Visitations . . . Lincoln: Alnwick*, 2.1:3–5. See also Power, *Medieval People*, pp. 77–8.

of colored and white fabric mentioned previously).[146] Significantly, Chaucer omits all such infractions of prescribed habit in his depiction of the Prioress.

Again in the fifteenth century, Alnwick's injunction forbids other clothing excesses beyond the silken veils and silver tiring pins mentioned earlier:

> None of yow, the prioresse ne none of the couente, were . . . no gyrdles herneysed with syluere or golde . . . ne that none of yow vse no lased kyrtels, but butonede or hole be fore.[147]

We cannot ignore the possibility that it might have been common to see a nun or prioress dressed in secular, luxurious garments in the Middle Ages, although there must surely have been those who dressed according to their convent rules. The evidence presented above indicates that individual socio-economic factors, as opposed to religious rules, determined what was worn by many nuns. Some who inherited wealth in the form of garments wore their wealth contrary to the rule, but certainly not contrary to what may have been common, if not official, custom in certain convents. Yet, Chaucer presents his Prioress covered modestly by a 'ful fetys' cloak.

In addition to noting the cues about the propriety of the Prioress's cloak embodied in Chaucer's verbal restraint, we may also assess the suitability of the Prioress's cloak by another set of standards – those secular attitudes illustrated in the fourteenth-century English sumptuary legislation. A comparison of these attitudes with the historical records discussed in this chapter, coupled with the fact that this civil legislation was apparently unenforced or unenforceable, indicates that clothing restrictions were ineffective and that economic prosperity worked on all levels to subvert such rules. Considering all of these factors, and that her habit is sans fur, sans silk, sans embroidered girdle, the Prioress's costume is a model of restraint, not a model of license.

Conversely, for pious nuns, and probably the unknown majority, the religious habit was a humble one, made of humble fabric, although provisions were clearly made for protection from inclement weather and for outdoor work. Such a habit falls into that category described in secular sumptuary laws as suitable for grooms whose income was less than forty shillings a year. The length and width of nuns' habits were specifically limited – only enough fabric to reach the top of the foot and to go around the body with sufficient ease was to be used. These ideas were repeated so often that we cannot help knowing they were often abused.[148] That longer and wider fabrics (generally

---

146 As Lina Eckenstein comments, p. 115, citing St Aldhelm's *De Laudibus Virginitatis*, in *Woman under Monasticism* (Cambridge, 1896).
147 *Visitations . . . Lincoln: Alnwick*, 2.1:8.
148 See Barbara Harvey, *Monastic Dress in the Middle Ages: Precept and Practice* (Canterbury, 1988), pp. 17–21, for an account of cloth-buying and utilization practices of the Chamberlain at Westminster Abbey.

more costly) were used indicates, even if we had no records to prove it, that the transgressing nuns possessed the money or other means, such as inheritances, by which to acquire these goods. Attitudes of superiors in certain convents must have been relatively compliant, or costume violations would not be so notable in surviving records; similarly, attitudes of parliament toward income expressed in the sumptuary laws (discussed in Chapter 1, pp. 15–17) acknowledged and accepted that economic factors break down social restrictions.

However, Chaucer provides no information in his portrait of Madame Eglentyne concerning her yearly expenditures or income; he only tells us that she travels accompanied by a retinue. Following this indication of exalted status, we might expect the Prioress to dress as some of her historical counterparts did, in sumptuous clothing. Instead, Chaucer mentions no specific fabric such as double worsted, or trimming such as gray fur, to provide an index of cost. There is only his statement that the Prioress wears a 'ful fetys' cloak, a statement that must connote propriety when compared to the foregoing accounts of costume abuses in historical records.

The Prioress's Habit and Literary Descriptions of Nuns' Habits

Because so many critics have judged Madame Eglentyne to be the object of satire and have assumed the description of her costume to be part of that satire, we must analyze the Prioress's costume against the background of the 'large robes' metaphor, described in Chapter 1, pp. 17–24, often used to epitomize the costume indiscretions of the religious in medieval literature. Therefore, the questions we now address are: first, how does the Prioress's costume differ from that of other nuns and prioresses described in literature; and second, how does Chaucer's costume rhetoric differ from standard practices? In answer to both questions, we find that the Prioress's costume and Chaucer's costume rhetoric are more characteristic of the literary treatment of pious nuns, personified virtues, and the Blessed Virgin Mary than they are of satirized nuns; however, this is not to say the same for the Prioress's actions and Chaucer's description of them.[149]

Contrary to episcopal hopes, both literature and historical records make it clear that the habit did not make the nun. The medieval poem 'Why I Can't Be a Nun' states the problem succinctly:

> Yowre barbe, your wympple and your vayle,
> Yowre mantelle and yowre devowte clothyng,
> Maketh men wyth-owten fayle
> To wene ʒe be holy in levyng.

---

[149] This essay does not include an analysis of the Prioress's behavior, but does acknowledge that the critical tradition holds her culpable for a variety of reasons.

And so hyt ys an holy thyng
To bene in habyte reguler;
Than, as by owtewarde array in semyng,
Beth so wyth-in, my ladyes dere.[150]   (lines 350–7)

The author of this poem advises nuns not to frequent taverns whose doors bear the ivy garland, and not to be found drinking there, 'Ellys yowre habyte ys no trew token' (lines 358–65). The point here is that the habit is the outward sign of a nun's vows, and that her spiritual cleanness should equal this holy sign. However, implicit in 'Why I Can't Be a Nun', as it is in Chaucer's portrait of Madame Eglentyne, is the recognition that such inner–outer consistency was not always the case.[151] False Seeming in *Le Roman de la rose* argues this same point about the worldly in religious orders:

Il font un argument au monde
Ou conclusion a honteuse;
Cis a robe religieuse,
Donques est il religieus.
Cis argumens est trop fieus,
. . .
La robe, ne fait pas le moine.   (lines 11052–8)

[To the world they present an argument in which there is a shameful conclusion: this man has the robe of religion; therefore he is religious. This argument is specious . . . the habit does not make the monk.][152]

Some nuns in medieval literature – Madame Eglentyne may well be one example – present a properly dressed exterior to the world while living in a way that, to some degree, violates their vows; we shall say that such nuns, like the priests described by the *Pearl* poet in *Cleanness* (lines 5–16, 29–38),[153] are wearing *False Vestments*. Or, we may express this idea by following False Seeming's description of himself:

150 'Why I Can't Be a Nun', p. 147, edited from BL MS Bibl. Cott., Vesp. D. IX, fol. 179.
151 See also Power, *Nunneries*, p. 511, for an account of *The Nun who Loved the World*.
152 Guillaume de Lorris and Jean de Meun, *Le Roman de la rose*; Charles Dahlberg, trans., *The Romance of the Rose* by Guillaume de Lorris and Jean de Meun (Hanover, NH, 1983), p. 194.
     This idea is also expressed in an excerpt from the medieval poem 'Priere d'amour d'une nonnain a un jeune adolescent', that posits that no garment can make its wearer innocent and that clothing often creates spiritual problems, 8:173:
     It est bien vray que tourel, voille on guymple,
     Fort scapullaire ou autre habit de corps,
     Ne rend jamais homme ou femme plus simple,
     Mais rompt souvent l'union et accords
     Mectant divorce entre l'ame et le corps.
153 *Cleanness*, in *Pearl, Cleanness, Patience, Sir Gawain and the Green Knight*, eds A. C. Cawley and J. J. Anderson (London, 1976), pp. 51–2.

J'aim miex devant la gent orer
Et affubler ma renardie
De mantiau de papelardie.   (lines 11522–4)

['I prefer to pray in front of people and cover my foxlike nature
under a cloak of pope-holiness.']^[154]

Like False Seeming, wearers of false vestments cover their 'foxlike nature
under a cloak of pope-holiness'. Other nuns in medieval literature, however,
are depicted as *Spiritual Mirrors* in which their spiritual uncleanness is
reflected in their luxurious wearing apparel, and these we shall name as
worldly nuns.

The typical worldly nun of literature, as discussed in Chapter 1, wears
'large robes', or more explicitly, indulges in the luxury of excessive personal
expense in the amount of fabric and/or in the kind of fabric consumed. And,
although some works include several or more costume details, such as fancy
furs, girdles, and shoes, often medieval writers found it sufficient to mention
only one detail that represented excess or luxury in order to signify a nun
who was attached to things of the world. Perhaps they could do so because
living examples of this principle were available and furnished an array of
detail. Conversely, the typical pious nun in literature wears an appropriate
habit, demonstrating that she comprehends and values the concept expressed
in 'Earth to Earth', quoted in Chapter 1, p. 18. Such pious nuns are one part
of another tradition, that of the description of nuns as brides of Christ, and it
is worthwhile mentioning again the excerpt from Gautier de Coincy's *La
Chasteé as nonnains*, which portrays the ideal nun who wears a proper habit
for God who is her courtly lover. The nun-brides of this poem are concerned
with the enhancement of their spirituality, and the analogy made is that of the
courtly ladies preoccupied with the adornment of the body in luxurious garments, each group of ladies being concerned with their own proper sphere of
life. The nuns' spiritual 'cleanness' is symbolized in their renunciation of
secular clothing and the wearing of appropriate convent habits; their courtliness is redirected to their courtly lover and bridegroom Christ. In this
manner, their proper courtly behavior then becomes the beautiful vesture of
their souls.^[155]

In Gautier's poem, pious nuns wear clothing that signifies their piety. In
contrast, Chaucer employs pious rhetoric to depict the outer appearance of
Madame Eglentyne while at the same time describing her actions, which may
cast doubt upon the cleanness of her soul. Thus, we might say that she wears

---

154 Guillaume de Lorris and Jean de Meun, *Le Roman de la rose*; Dahlberg, trans.
155 See Gautier de Coinci's, 'La Chasteé as nonains', pp. 180–1, excerpt quoted in n. 36
     above.

False Vestments – her habits (behavior), to a degree,[156] may contradict her habit (garments), a circumstance that creates the basic opposition and fascinating tension in this portrait. Chaucer employs the same characterization technique exhibited in *Le Roman de la rose* in the descriptions of Pope- Holiness who appears, outwardly, to be a pious nun, False Seeming who hypocritically wears a 'simple robe', and Constrained Abstinence who assumes the costume of a Beguine and/or pious pilgrim, complete with psalter and rosary. In any event, when considering all costume rhetoric in the disparate literary traditions presented in this chapter, we find many more similarities between Chaucer's description of the Prioress in costume and depictions of pious nuns, the Blessed Virgin Mary, and personified virtues, than we find between Chaucer's costume rhetoric and that of typical worldly nuns in medieval literature.

Chaucer does not use the 'large robes' metaphor[157] of satire in his description of the Prioress's costume, although he is capable of doing so in subtle ways: for example, note the Friar's double worsted 'semycope', a description that indicates a short cloak made of fabric that was wider, according to law, than lesser cloths such as monks' cloth or canons' cloth. Nor does Chaucer describe the Prioress as wearing *diapre* nor any other kind of silk. She does not wear expensive fur such as the Monk's gris, or the vair and erminette that the nuns in *La Chasteé as nonnains* have also given up. She wears no shifts made of cloth of Rennes (at sixteen pence the ell), no pleated girdle, no girdle embroidered in silk, silver or gold, no kirtles laced with silk or made of fustian or worsted, no pleated gowns, no gowns of silk or with trains (and no extravagant shoes). Nor does she go about in a surplice without a mantle 'contrary to the manner of dress of nuns and the ancient custom of the priory' as the historical Prioress Margaret Fayrfax did.[158] So far as we know, in her 'ful fetys' cloak she wears acceptable fabrics, appropriate in quality, length, width, and color. We may say that the Prioress's habit is both attractive and prudent, and we affirm that these two adjectives are not mutually exclusive.

The Prioress's Habit and Medieval Illuminations

Manuscript illuminations provide ample evidence that Chaucer might have been more explicit in his description of the Prioress's habit.[159] Just as there

---

156 I leave such judgments to others.

157 If indeed the Prioress wore large robes, it would be out of the necessity for properly covering her body that was 'nat undergrowe'.

158 *Vic. Hist. . . . Yorkshire*, 3:122–3, and n. 6 for a description of her brother John Fayrfax's will, which is recorded in *Test. Ebor.* 1:186.

159 For a brief overview of nuns' habits, see the following: A headcovering may be seen in the portrait of St Clare, depicted in her *Sforza Book of Hours*, BL Add. MS 34294, pp. 418, 420, and 510. This habit style is also illustrated in *La Sainte Abbaye*, c.1300,

was great difference in styles of headdresses properly worn by medieval nuns, so was there variety in habits.[160] As previously noted, although the 1237 English Council determined that the proper color for nuns' habits was black, nevertheless, in 1314, Archbishop Melton enjoined the nuns at Hampole to return to their old habit of wearing *clamides* of russet color.[161] Elizabeth Sewardby's habit included a cloak of russet and a tunic of blue cloth;[162] and the Rule of Syon provided for gray cloth gowns, hoods, and mantles. Besides the numerous nuns in some combination of black and white garments to be found in medieval illuminations, there are quite a few variations in habits, some so distinctive that they could be identified as the habit of a particular convent. Contrasting Chaucer's simple description of Madame Eglentyne's habit with the variety of habits portrayed in the medieval visual arts provides additional support for the idea that he was portraying an ideal exterior rather than a distinctive one.

A case in point is furnished by a French manuscript, *La Sainte Abbaye*, in the British Library.[163] In this manuscript the artist has painted some nuns' habits made in the traditional style, complete with white wimple and underveil, and black overveil. However, the colors of the remainder of the nuns' garments are delicate blue, gray, orange, white, and shades of these hues, highlighted with goldleaf.[164] We find a habit of another interesting

BL Add. MS 39843; see Evans, *Dress in Mediaeval France*, pl. 74, for a reproduction.

Other illustrations of the basic habit may be seen in BL Harl. MS 4425, fol. 108, *Le Roman de la rose*, c.1490; and in BL Harl. MS 621, fol. 71, Boccaccio's 'History of Noble Men and Women'. In addition to the features described in the text, these illustrations have another merit for the purposes of this study – the nuns are dressed as religious pilgrims, as their accessories attest: the nun in BL MS Harl. 4425 carries a rosary and a book (perhaps her office?); the nun in BL MS Harl. 621 wears the pilgrim scrip or bag and a wide-brimmed hat hung by its neck cord down her back; and both carry a walking staff or bourdon. The patches on the habit of the nun in this second manuscript indicate her allegorical function as Glad Poverty. Line drawings of these nuns may be seen in Strutt, vol. 2, pl. 134, figs 2 and 4.

160 See Abbé Tiron, *Histoire et costume des ordres religieux, civils et militaires*, 2nd edn (Bruxelles, 1845), for illustrations of the variety in religious habits.

161 *Vic. Hist. . . . Yorkshire*, 3:164.

162 Power, *Nunneries*, p. 586, citing New Coll. MS, fol. 86.

163 BL Add. MS 39843, c.1300.

164 Fol. 29 reveals a nun who wears a gray-blue tunic, covered by a cloak of pale grayed orange, and a white veil and wimple. On fol. 6, the habits of pale orange alternate with those of blue-gray. There is the distinct possibility that the artist was more concerned here with aesthetic values in his variation of shades than he was in portraying the actuality of his experience. However, it is also possible that his exquisite color scheme is intended to represent habits made of humble fabric such as those provided for Elizabeth Sewardby in the will previously quoted. The date of this French manuscript (c.1300) is later than the 1237 English Council ruling that nuns should wear only black habits. It is possible either that black habits for nuns became obligatory for

color scheme in the portrait of a kneeling nun of Amesbury who is dressed in the habit of Fontevrault composed of a blue cloak over a green tunic.[165]

Another notable habit is illustrated in a British Library copy of nine books of Boccacio's *De Casu illustrium virorum et feminarum*.[166] The style of the garments on fol. 71 is that of the customary religious habit (simple outer garment, draped wimple and veil), with the exception that the habit has obvious patches on it. This costume is also arresting because the wearer carries a pilgrim wallet and walking stick, and wears a broad-brimmed pilgrim hat hanging down her back. The accompanying text reveals that this figure is Glad Poverty – hence both the patches, and the style of the clothes.[167]

Although nuns' habits did vary in color,[168] the majority of nuns appearing in medieval manuscripts appear only in some combination of black and white. The typical nun of manuscript illumination wears a tunic and cloak consistent with the prescriptions of her rule,[169] unless the artist is conflating

French nuns at a later date, or that individual ecclesiastic authorities exercised their authority in the choice of fabric and color, as did Archbishop Melton, previously described. I am most grateful to Stella Mary Newton for suggesting that the blue of these manuscript illuminations might stand for legitimate colors worn by the orders such as the gray of the Franciscan order. Her suggestion jogged my memory of the blue and russet of Elizabeth Sewardby's habit, described in Chapter 1.

165 In the c.1250 English, Salisbury, Bodleian MS All Souls College 6, fol. 6; see also fol. 4.

166 BL Harl. MS 621, fol. 71, cited by Strutt as illustrative of a medieval nun's habit; see the line drawing in his pl. 134.

167 Nothing in the text explains the artist's choice of colors – why Glad Poverty wears an orange tunic with yellow patches (unless here, again, we have a depiction of a tunic made of russet), or why the second woman in the scene, Fortune (whom the text says wears purple) wears a yellow tunic and black veil, no wimple, and a gold chain around her neck. The illuminator of this manuscript is not nearly so talented as the one who painted *La Sainte Abbaye*, and his work exhibits no sense of intricate color aesthetics; his color choices appear to be arbitrary. Still, Glad Poverty's accessories are similar to those of other nuns depicted with pilgrim accessories, especially those in illuminated copies of *Le Roman de la rose*.

168 An even greater variety in nuns' habits exists, if colors in manuscript illuminations may be believed even in part; however, demands of a particular workshop or patron sometimes dictated color choices. In any case, in an English manuscript of the second half of the thirteenth century, Bodleian Library MS Auct. D.5.9., fol. 322, a nun wears a blue cloak over a black tunic. There is some dispute about whether or not this figure is a nun; she illustrates the Canticles. Franciscan nuns wearing mauve cloaks appear on fols 25v and 85 of Bodleian Library MS Douce 118. In this same manuscript the nun on fol. 129 wears a brown cloak, while on 136v, a nun, possibly St Odile of Alsace, wears a black cloak.

169 In general, the majority of nuns identifiable in medieval illuminations are depicted in a habit that reveals few distinguishing details beyond a brief glimpse of white tunic if the black mantle is not completely closed in front, or if the wrist ends of tight tunic sleeves show below the edges of the looser sleeves of the cloak. Examples of this gen-

his depiction of the nun with that of the saint.[170] In this case, her cloak may be fur-lined or possibly trimmed with gold braid, indicating a spiritual nobility. In some cases, the saints depicted were also noblewomen, and such noble cloaks would have a dual significance. Illuminations of St Gertrude and St Ethelburger illustrate this point. St Gertrude, in BL Harley MS 2962, fol. 41 (Color Plate I), wears a white tunic under a black cloak. There are two gold lines outlining the edges of her cloak (possibly intended to depict braid). St Ethelburger, in *Horae Beatae Virginis*, also in the British Library,[171] wears a crown and royal robes, and there is a white lining to the sleeves of her black tunic. Over this tunic she wears a cloak of deep and rich blue, lined with ermine. The realistic detail of sleeve lining in this illumination may also be seen in the fifteenth-century British Library illumination of St Birgitta in *The heavenly revelations unto blessed Bride, princess of Nerice in the realm of Swecie*,[172] where she wears a black habit, with sleeves lined in a gray-blue fabric.

Chaucer, however, provides less detail about the Prioress's habit than the majority of manuscript illuminators. No ermine trim appears on her cloak such as that shown on St Ethelburger's blue cloak, and no gold braid trims its edges as is, possibly, the case for St Gertrude's black cloak, in the illuminations described above. We will never know whether Madame Eglentyne wears a russet or a white tunic because Chaucer offers no glimpse beneath her cloak, and no mention of sleeve lining, colored or otherwise, or of a fur lining for her cloak. We cannot even know for certain the color of her cloak, although we may assume that it is black, according to Benedictine custom. Given the variety of small details present in manuscript illuminations, details

---

eralization are numerous: see the illuminations of Benedictine nuns in BL Add. MS 28784B; and in BL Harl. MS 2975, fol. 73v. Also, we note the c.1490 copy of *Le Roman de la rose*, BL Harl. MS 4425, which contains an illumination of Strayned Abstinence, fol. 108; reproduced in a line drawing in Strutt, pl. 134, fig. 2: she is dressed as a nun wearing a black cloak; no tunic shows.

170 When the subject of the illumination is an abbess and/or saint, illuminations frequently show white tunics under black mantles or cloaks, as does that of a Benedictine abbess in Jacobus' *Omne bonum*, BL Roy. MS 6 E VI (1360–75), fol. 27. Similarly portrayed are the Benedictine habit of St Etheldreda as abbess in the *Horae Blessed Marie Virgines, Sec. Usum Sarum*, BL MS Kings 9 (Flanders, early sixteenth century), fol. 64v, and the habit of a saintly nun, accompanied by other nuns, in the *Sforza Book of Hours*, BL Add. MS 34294 (late fifteenth century), p. 420. The abbess Heloise, in *Poestes De Charles, Duc D'Orleans*, BL Roy. MS 16 F II (c.1500), fol. 137, which includes 'Epitres de L'Abbesse Heloys du Paraclit', is also portrayed in this manner. The color scheme is reversed in the case of Dominican nuns, such as the four representing four virtues who wear black tunics under white mantles, painted in the lower register of fol. 33, in *Le Sacre, Couronnement Et Entree de Claude, Royne de France*, BL Cott. MS Titus A. XVII (dated 1517).

171 BL Harl. MS 2900, fol. 68v.

172 BL Cott. MS Claud. B. I, fols 34, 117.

that might have been included in Chaucer's description, we find Chaucer's description sparse indeed: 'Ful fetys was hir cloke' (line 157). This partial-line treatment is comparable to his handling of her headdress, once the frequently misunderstood description of her fair forehead is properly removed from consideration: 'Ful semyly hir wympul pynched was' (line 151).

The Prioress is guilty of none of the costume abuses listed by Aldhelm, writing of monastics and ecclesiastics who illustrate 'the shameless impudence of vanity and the sleek insolence of stupidity', and who dress so 'that the bodily figure may be adorned with forbidden ornaments and charming decorations, and that the physical appearance may be glamorized'. His list of such things (for both sexes) includes, 'fine linen shirts', 'scarlet or blue tunics', 'necklines and sleeves embroidered with silk', 'shoes trimmed with red-dyed leather', curly hair, and the abandonment of 'dark-grey veils' for 'bright and coloured head-dresses, which are sewn with interlacings of ribbons and hang down as far as the ankles'.[173]

We argue neither for nor against the idea that the Prioress may be more than one virtue short of sainthood. She may not wear the virtue-jewel-bedecked robes of St Agnes, described in Johan Alcock, Bishop of Ely's *Exhortacyon*,[174] nor, conversely, the 'simple little cowl and poor mantle made of rough cloth' of St Clare, mentioned by Fra Tommaso da Celano.[175] Nevertheless, given that Chaucer states that the Prioress wished to 'ben holden digne of reverence' (line 141), and, to that end, concerns herself with proper table manners, why should we expect her to be less concerned with proper dress?

Madame Eglentyne's array is entirely proper, according to her degree as Prioress. Her 'pynched' wimple is 'ful semyly', and her cloak 'ful fetys', neat and *bien fait*, just as Chaucer stated. There is no reason to suppose that her veil was worn higher on her forehead than convent standards allowed, in a style that could have been described as unseemly. Instead, we must assume that Chaucer depicts her forehead in accordance with the traditions of both rhetoric and visual arts, the broadness of which would have been suggested to him by contemporary fashion in womanly beauty as well as by portraits of madonnas and Virtues (just as these last share her 'nat undergrowe' stature).

---

173 *Aldhelm, The Prose Works*, ed. and trans. Michael Lapidge and Michael Herren (Cambridge, 1979), pp. 127–8.
174 Alcock [p. 8].
175 Fra Tommaso da Celano, *The Life of St Clare Virgin*, trans. Catherine Bolton Magrini (Assisi, n.d.), p. 38. See the picture and description of St Clare's cape, misshapen because she cut fabric from it to patch St Francis's cowl, in Mechtild Flury-Lemberg, *Textile Conservation and Research* (Bern, 1988), pp. 314–17.

In this portrayal there is neither elegance in the modern sense of sumptuous dress, nor love of 'ornate garb'.[176] When we begin the examination of Chaucer's costume rhetoric with an analysis of the individual garment and accessory items as signs, rather than with an analysis of her character, we find no reason to suppose that Madame Eglentyne's costume is any less proper in style or form than her proper late fourteenth-century table manners.

Chaucer's costume rhetoric places the Prioress within religious, artistic, literary, and historical traditions – a juxtaposition of the ideal and the real. Equally important, an analysis of Chaucer's costume rhetoric affirms the idea that we need not see Madame Eglentyne in only one way; we may see that she visually represents virtuous religious life while falling short of perfection in her actions. Her physical description may correspond rhetorically to that ideal beauty of Prudence[177] (and to those rhetorical descriptions of other virtues as well) while her actions fall short of *prudentia*. She is both the Prioress, traveling in this world, and Madame Eglentyne, nun.

This study of Chaucer's costume rhetoric in the portrait of the Prioress illustrates the necessary part that knowledge of the culture plays in interpretation of costume descriptions in medieval literature. Further, it demonstrates the importance and pervasiveness of clothing metaphors in medieval rhetoric. From this study of her costume we may gain a kaleidoscopic view of the Prioress, seeing the external epitome of the virtuous, contemplative life, as well as the lady of courtly manners and some education, and finally the woman whose actions portray her human deficiencies. Such a view contrasts sharply with the more common understanding of Chaucer's general characterization technique, which is that outer appearance illustrates inner truth of character – a type of understanding that has, in the past, forced many critics to read into the Prioress's costume all of the imperfections they find in her actions, or else to find excuses for one or the other.

In a preliminary summary, we may now say that as the first pilgrim in holy orders to be described in the *General Prologue* in religious vocations the Prioress initiates Chaucer's explication of religious ideals and their opposite in his group of pilgrims. Further, the eclectic Chaucer employs a variety of characterization techniques, and in this process he manipulates garment metaphors to convey both blatant and subtle meaning.

---

[176] Ridley's phrase, p. 21.

[177] According to *The Book of Vices and Virtues*, p. 122, 'prudence kepeþ a man þat he ne be bi no queyntise of his enemy [the devil] bigiled'.

3

Sign of Faith: The Prioress's Rosary

Rosaries, important sacramentals in the practice of the medieval church, were produced in large numbers and in a vast variety of materials for a market that crossed all socio-economic groups. While serving as a sign of faith, their display in no way guaranteed the depth or breadth of their owner's religious devotion. Chaucer chose to include a rosary in his portrait of the Prioress, and this chapter will treat this artifact in a twofold manner: first, as a practical aid to the expression of devotion to the Virgin Mary and as a sign of such devotion; and second, as an ordinary addition to a nun's habit and to a pilgrim's garb. In the first case, the rosary is a sacramental, a religious accessory; in the second case, although it remains a sacramental, because it was so commonly carried or properly worn by nuns and pilgrims, it functions as if it were a clothing accessory, part of the religious habit or pilgrim weeds, and it makes no fashion statement. Such a religious item silently proclaims holy ideals. That its literary owner, the Prioress, may fall short of such ideals produces a kind of irony that is both visual and theoretical in impact.

The negative strain in criticism concerning the Prioress interprets her possession of a rosary with pendant brooch as automatic additional proof of her character defects. However, such a perspective is refuted by a survey of historical records of the period, which reveal no church injunctions against nuns owning rosaries made of any material, although other specific personal items, such as rings made of precious metals, are forbidden. In addition, these records indicate that medieval nuns frequently owned rosaries made from coral and other materials, some of them received as gifts from members of the clergy. A comparison of the Prioress's rosary with others in that general period reveals, also, that her rosary cannot be classified as either curious or over curious;[1] instead, it is ordinary. Also, the materials and colors of this rosary are symbolically appropriate for a prioress and for a pilgrim.[2] Similarly, objections concerning the possible impropriety of a Prioress owning a brooch of gold are dispelled when her brooch is compared to other brooches

---

1   See discussion of these terms in Chapters 1, 2, and 4, pp. 11–14, 45, 127, 130–2.
2   I do not offer a consideration here of how appropriate it is for the Prioress to be on pilgrimage, for that is an issue relevant to her actions, not her appearance.

of the time, and the ambiguity of the Latin motto on the brooch is resolved
when compared to the representation of other mottoes of the Middle Ages.
Finally, medieval illuminations of nuns bearing rosaries demonstrate that, in
describing Madame Eglentyne with rosary over her arm, as she is depicted in
the Ellesmere manuscript, Chaucer puts the finishing touch on his portrait of
a prioress, proper in appearance,[3] if less than ideal in her actions.

Chaucer devotes five lines of verse to this religious accessory and, in
doing so, attests to its significance.

> Of smal coral aboute hire arm she bar
> A peire of bedes, gauded all with grene,
> And theron heng a brooch of gold ful sheene,
> On which ther was first write a crowned A,
> And after *Amor vincit omnia*   (I, lines 158–62)

Stated simply, the Prioress's rosary, borne over her arm, is made of small
beads or bits of coral interspersed with green gauds, somewhat larger beads;
and a gold pendant, engraved with a crowned *A* and a motto, hangs from
these beads.

The critical tradition for the Prioress's rosary and pendant brooch is
chequered. The central question, as with headdress and habit, is that of propriety. Critics frequently fault the Prioress for possessing this coral rosary
and its gold brooch with motto. Such judgments stem from subjective percep-
tion of the rosary and pendant as a beautiful personal possession or even as an
item of decorative jewelry. F. N. Robinson's comment continues to be pertinent: the brooch and motto have 'often been misunderstood and the whole
spirit of the passage consequently misrepresented'. Beyond that, he acknowledges that the motto was 'applicable alike to religious and to romantic love,
and carries no implication that the Prioress was "acquainted with the gallant-
ries of her age" '.[4]

Illustrating the continuing misunderstanding to which Robinson refers,
Charles Moorman interprets the Prioress as a pretentious hen analogous to
Pertelote in the *Nun's Priest's Tale*. Further, he cites her beads and gold
brooch as evidence of her 'love of flamboyance as opposed to courtly elegance' and her liking for 'costume jewelry'.[5] In a similar vein Peter S. Taitt

---

[3]   Henry Ansgar Kelly's evaluation of the Prioress supports this idea; he advises accep-
      tance of Sr Madaleva's insights regarding the rosary and brooch, and characterizes the
      Prioress as 'a religious superior who is very attentive to religious duties and to external
      decorum', in 'A Neo-Revisionist Look at Chaucer's Nuns', *ChauR* 31 (1996), pp. 126
      and 128 respectively.

[4]   F. N. Robinson, ed., *The Poetical Works of Chaucer* (Boston, 1957), headnote, p. 755.

[5]   Charles Moorman says that such a liking is in character because Madame Eglentyne is
      a cockney, in 'The Prioress as Pearly Queen', *ChauR* 13 (1978), pp. 27, 30–2. Larry
      Sklute, 'Catalogue Form and Catalogue Style in the General Prologue of the Canter-

refers to Madame Eglentyne's rosary as a 'coral bracelet with its gold brooch'.[6] Such language on the part of a critic implies that the Prioress sins through personal vanity as medieval bracelets were generally decorative in function.[7] The gold brooch thus becomes decoration on top of decoration. Building on this interpretation, Taitt designates the 'bracelet' and motto as 'a worldly touch, a petty feminine vanity', and comments that 'its motto serves as a gentle reminder of the opposition of the ideal and real in its wearer', citing the rosary as proof that the Prioress has deviated from the path of true love of God.[8] Alan T. Gaylord agrees with Taitt's assessment that 'The Prioress has not proved she truly understands what celestial love means', and he cites the ambiguity of the rosary and the brooch's Latin motto as support for his judgment. However, Gaylord credits the Prioress with pious simplicity, in that he is certain that she would not think of *Amor* in earthly terms.[9] Although Gaylord absolves the Prioress of *intentional* ambiguity, yet the ambiguity remains because it stems from the source of the motto – Virgil's *Eclogues*, where the reference is to the love of man and woman, as John Livingston Lowes points out. Lowes also explains that in the 'strange jumble of mediaeval superstitions about Virgil' the motto began to be used to refer to

bury Tales', *SN* 52 (1980), p. 40, also mentions the Prioress's 'costume jewelry', commenting on 'the remarkably ambiguous brooch used for costume jewelry on her otherwise unexceptional habit'. Graham Landrum, 'The Convent Crowd and the Feminist Nun', *TPB* 13 (1976), p. 7, refers to the Prioress's 'gaudy jewelry', in a possible misunderstanding of her green gauds. In a restrained interpretation, Chauncey Wood, 'Chaucer's Use of Signs in His Portrait of the Prioress', *Signs and Symbols in Chaucer's Poetry*, eds John P. Hermann and John J. Burke, Jr (University, AL, 1981), p. 97, also sees the Prioress's rosary as a fashionable accessory, not as 'an outer sign of inner devotion'.

6 Peter S. Taitt, *Incubus and Ideal: Ecclesiastical Figures in Chaucer and Langland*, Salzburg Studies in English Literature, no. 44 (Salzburg, 1975), p. 61. Samantha Mullaney, 'The Language of Costume in the Ellesmere Portraits', *Sources, Exemplars and Copy-Texts: Influence and Transmission, Trivium* (special edn) 31 (1999), p. 40, also employs the term 'bracelet', stating that in the Ellesmere illumination the Prioress's 'coral beads are arranged like a bracelet', which she reads as the artist's attempt to contribute some *negative* detail in this portrait.

7 See n. 40 below concerned with their useful function; also Plate 6.

8 Taitt, pp. 61–2. Taitt's overall assessment of the Prioress, based partly on his interpretation of her costume, is clear:

The motto on her brooch seems to suggest that her pursuit of worthiness has become an end in itself, for her attention to dress and courtly manners, her sentimentalized sympathy for suffering, have pushed her aside from the path of a true love of God and her fellow men to which her calling as a nun should direct her.

9 Alan T. Gaylord, 'The Unconquered Tale of the Prioress', *Papers of the Michigan Academy of Science, Arts and Letters* 47 (1962), p. 623. Regarding ambiguity, see Francis Manley, 'Chaucer's Rosary and Donne's Bracelet: Ambiguous Coral', *MLN* 74 (1959), p. 388. John B. Friedman, 'The Prioresss' Beads "of smal coral"', *MÆ* 39 (1970), p. 301, rejects Manley's judgment because it is based on fifteenth-century data.

celestial love long before the fourteenth century, a circumstance that resulted in an 'ambiguity of convention'.[10] Significantly, this 'ambiguity of convention' may be more important to modern critics than it was to Chaucer, for it allows critics to suggest a guilt by association with source.[11]

Continuing the negative critical tradition, Edward Craney Jacobs assesses the Prioress's brooch and motto in the light of the theological tradition of several New Testament passages.[12] Jacobs finds irony in the difference between biblical injunctions regarding dress and the Prioress's garb, especially her 'elegant[13] beads, bound together by a gold brooch with such a motto, and worn band-like about her arm', when she should wear *caritatem*, which Paul defines as the ' "band of perfection" ', rather than *amorem*. Jacobs suggests that 'perhaps Chaucer found "Amor vincit omnia" so exactly right for his Prioress because it carefully subverted Paul's words [in I Corinthians 13:1–13] in a playfully ironic way'. He equates the wearing of gold, as well as her 'handsome cloak', with worldliness, but ends in equivocation, stating that St Augustine would not quarrel with such practices in dress if

---

[10] John Livingston Lowes, *Convention and Revolt in Poetry* (London, 1930), p. 44.

> Wood, p. 98, discusses both the Virgilian connotations of *amor vincit omnia* (as erotic) and the *in bono* usage as it appears in Gower's Prologue to his *Tripartite Chronicle* and in *Vox clamantis*, book 6, chapter 14, and claims that the Virgilian and erotic meaning was the prevailing one in Chaucer's day; further, that the joke is on the Prioress for not knowing that, demonstrating her 'inability to distinguish between *amor* and *caritas*, or her lack of good sense'. Further, p. 99, Wood states,

> > Insofar as the Prioress' brooch would be perceived by her to be a sign, we would probably assume (with Lowes) that she construed its legend in a good sense, and wore it as a sign of her spirituality. Of course, since it is jewelry, and prettily carved, its supposed spiritual significance is undercut. Insofar as the legend is Virgilian and carnal, the brooch is a sign without a referent, for there is nothing to indicate that the Prioress is carnal herself. She is not, after all, much like the Wife of Bath in her behavior. The brooch, then, may be a sign of the Prioress' shallow understanding of commonplace Latin tags.

> He finds that the brooch is 'womanly rather than godly' and that Chaucer's audience who knew Virgil would see it that way. But see below, p. 106, regarding William Langland's interpretation of *Amor*.

[11] Further guilt by association is attributed by Phyllis Hodgson, who reminds us that the Prioress and Idleness of *Le Roman de la rose* share many features, and that the words on her brooch are spoken by Courtesy to persuade Fair Welcome to surrender the Rose in this same work, in *Chaucer: General Prologue, The Canterbury Tales* (London, 1969), pp. 24–5.

[12] II Peter 1:1–7, I Corinthians 13:1–13, Colossians 3:12–14, I Peter 3:3–4, and I Timothy 2:9–10.

[13] See discussion of *elegant* and other slanted language such as *handsome*, *ornate*, and *flamboyance*, in Chapter 2, pp. 35, 63–7. Leger Brosnahan, 'The Pendant in the Chaucer Portraits', *ChauR* 26.4 (1992), p. 430, n. 7, mentions the 'elegance' of the Prioress's beads, but judges them to accord with her status.

5a

5. St James in Gethsemene, St Michael's Kirche, Schwäbisch Hall, Swabia, (a) detail of St James wearing blue robe with tiraz bands; (b) gold sleeve bands with motto *amor vincit omnia*; (c) gold hem bands continuing motto. Photographs by Klaus P. Jankofsky, published with the permission of Mrs Klaus P. Jankofsky.

5b

5c

they are dedicated to the love of God, and 'perhaps neither should we'.[14] Jacobs provides both the insights attainable through some careful attention to vocabulary and those inherent in theological background information. However he, too, reads the Prioress's rosary as an item of personal adornment, rather than as an aid to prayer, and this perspective colors his judgment that the Prioress wears 'elegant beads', as opposed to carrying an ordinary rosary.

The Prioress's detractors refer to her rosary and its brooch with a variety of pejorative and occasionally anachronistic language, such as 'costume jewelry', a phrase not available in fourteenth-century English, the term *costume* entering both French and English in the eighteenth century from Italian (OED). Other such judgmental terms and phrases include 'bracelet', 'gaudy jewelry', and 'elegant beads . . . worn band-like about her arm', and they imply a Prioress who tarts herself out in secular fashion. Refuting these implications, Sr Madeleva posits that *Amor vincit omnia* is a frequent and an innocent motto displayed in past and present-day convents.[15] Substantiating her claim, she mentions a ring with the same inscription found in the environs of a Benedictine convent of Chaucer's time.[16] A painting by an anonymous fifteenth-century artist from Brussels provides additional proof that a pendant brooch (such as the seven-pointed star in Color Plate II) made a serious religious statement in the Middle Ages. In 'De Lactatie van de H. Bernardus',[17] the kneeling donatrix is painted bearing a rosary to which a gold brooch is appended.

Further, the Prioress's own motto is inscribed on the borders of gold (tiraz) that edge the robes of James the apostle (Plate 5a–c) in a Gethsemene scene on the north exterior of St Michael's Church in Schwäbisch Hall, in Swabia.[18]

---

[14] Edward Craney Jacobs, 'Further Biblical Allusions for Chaucer's Prioress', *ChauR* 15 (1980), pp. 151–3.
[15] Sr M. Madeleva, 'Chaucer's Nuns', in *Chaucer's Nuns and Other Essays* (Port Washington, NY, 1965), pp. 18–19, states:
   This is one of the commonest of epigrams among religious, and I know that one could find it worked in cross stitch, or painted in all the varying forms of realistic and conventional art and framed as a motto in dozens of our convents in our very unmystical and unmedieval United States today.
   On this same topic, see Sr Mary Ernestine Whitmore, *Medieval English Domestic Life and Amusements in the Works of Chaucer* (New York, 1972), p. 184. Whitmore, p. 183, speculates that a coral rosary with green gauds may be too fine for a Prioress 'vowed to poverty', but offers no comparison shopping among medieval records for prices as proof.
[16] Madeleva, p. 19, citing *Life Records of Chaucer*, III (2nd series), p. 135.
[17] Now in the Koninglijk Museum voor Schone Kusten, in Antwerp, Belgium, catalogue no. 976.
[18] This information came from a paper entitled 'Love and Death and the Prioress's Beads', presented by Klaus P. Jankofsky at the 30th International Congress on Medieval Studies, at Western Michigan University, Kalamazoo, MI, May 1995.

Clearly, in this Gethsemane scene, the motto serves only a sacred purpose. The Prioress's brooch, as Sr Madeleva attests, was a most usual sacramental object in the medieval church. Because it is made of gold, she describes the brooch as 'a good, but not an over-elaborate, medal'.[19]

A most helpful critical approach to an understanding of the Prioress's rosary is that of John B. Friedman, who discusses it in the light of long-standing medieval medical tradition. Far from being extraordinary, the Prioress's rosary might actually 'underscore her simple piety', states Friedman. He describes the medieval belief in the apotropaic power of coral. From Friedman's survey of lapidaries, he concludes that the Prioress demonstrates knowledge of the medical properties of precious stones and that she carries coral beads as much for their apotropaic powers as for any aristocratic connotations they might have[20] (a point to which we will return later in this chapter).

The Prioress's Rosary and Historical Evidence

Convent rules, visitation records, and church council rulings provide no indication that it was inappropriate for nuns to possess rosaries.[21] Injunctions

---

[19] Madeleva, pp. 19–20. Madeleva's assurances are valuable as much for inside experience in the matter of convent attitudes toward display of religious artifacts as for her critical appraisal of the Prioress's appearance.

[20] Friedman, pp. 301–4, citing *De Naturis Rerum* (BL Roy. 12 F VI, esp. fol. 103r, Lib. XIV xv), an encyclopedia by a thirteenth-century Dominican, Thomas of Cantimpre. Of coral, Friedman states:

> It warded off phantasms from the dark side of man's mind and their concrete embodiment in the devil and demons, who continually tempt mankind to the sins of the flesh. This power belonged to coral because, in its branching state, it took the form of Christ's cross, one of the most powerful of apotropaic signs in the Middle Ages.

Also see Donald W. Lightbown, *Mediaeval European Jewellery: with a catalogue of the collection in the Victoria and Albert Museum* ([London], 1992), p. 207 and n. 13, regarding coral as a prophylactic stone, and pl. 2 of Petrus Christus's painting of St Eligius, showing coral for sale. In general, rosary beads of any material were believed to have amuletic powers 'to ward off evil', states Anne Winston-Allen, *Stories of the Rose: The Making of the Rosary in the Middle Ages* (University Park, PA, 1997), p. 116.

[21] As described earlier in Chapters 1 and 2, these documents do specifically mention, however, those items that must have been the subjects of frequent misuse: the girdles embroidered with silver, gold, and/or silk are repeatedly forbidden, as are gloves, silver and gold tiring pins, finger rings, and brooches (at the neck) worn for decoration, and anything that might be described as 'ouer curyous', such as tunics made more decorative either by pleats or by brooches (*laqueatis*).

See also 'The Sisters' Clothes', in 'From *The Rule of Our Saviour*', *Women's Writing in Middle English*, ed. Alexandra Barratt (New York, 1992), p. 91, for the specifica-

against forbidden items arose, at least in part, as a result of legacies received even by ordinary nuns.[22] From a will dated 24 August 1354, Margaret, sister of the vintner William Heyroun and a nun at Barking ('Berkyngge'), received from Isabella, widow of the London pepperer Thomas Corp, a legacy that included three gold rings, with emerald, sapphire, and diamond settings.[23] Such forbidden practices, documented in historical records, inspired literary imitations like those in *The Legend of St Patrick's Purgatory; Its Later Literary History*. Here the luxurious prioress in Purgatory wears 'ringes on hir fingers, and siluer bokeles and ouergilt on hir shone'.[24]

Again, the complaints made against Clemence Medforde, Prioress of Ankerwyke, in 1441 provide an illustration of the continuing costume indiscretions in accessories being committed by medieval nuns after Chaucer's time:

> The Prioress wears golden rings exceeding costly, with divers precious stones. . . . Also she wears . . . tiring pins of silver and silver gilt and has made all the nuns wear the like. . . . The prioress has on her neck a long silken band, in English a lace, which hangs down below her breast, and thereon a golden ring with one diamond.[25]

Clearly, the wearing of inappropriate accessories such as these were partly to blame for Alnwick's often-quoted injunction of the mid-fifteenth century:

> None of yow, the prioresse ne none of the couente, were . . . no syluere pynnes ne no gyrdles herneysed with syluere or golde, ne no mo rynges on your fyngres then oon, ye that be professed by a bysshope . . . ne that ye use

---

tions of button fastenings, esp. the 'botoun of tree' for securing a mantel at the breast, preferred to a decorative brooch.

22 See Eileen Power, *Medieval English Nunneries*, Cambridge Studies in Medieval Life and Thought, ed. G. G. Coulton (London, 1922), p. 165, for a discussion of bequests to nuns of lesser rank.

23 Besides a dozen silver spoons, a silver-plated cup with cover, and 'divers household goods', according to Reginald R. Sharpe, ed., *Calendar of Wills Proved and Enrolled in the Court of Husting, London, A.D. 1258–A.D. 1688* (London, 1889), Part I, p. 688. One example of a bequest of money to a nun is that made by Alice de Hodesdon to her daughter Margery, a nun of Haliwell, of an annual rent from a shop in All Hallows de Graschirche parish for twenty-five years or until her death; 'remainder to the Prioress & Convent of Halliwell', included in this same *Calendar*, Part I, p. 628.

24 J. P. Krapp, *The Legend of St Patrick's Purgatory; Its Later Literary History* (Baltimore, 1899); see also records in *The Victoria History of the Counties of England: Yorkshire*, ed. William Page (London, 1913), 3:122–3, 126, 181.

25 *Visitation of Religious Houses in the Diocese of Lincoln: Alnwick's Visitations (1436–49)*, ed. Alexander Hamilton Thompson, Canterbury and York Society 24 (London, 1919), 2.1:3–5. See also, Eileen Power, *Medieval People*, 2nd edn (Boston, 1925), pp. 77–8.

no lases a bowte your nekkes wythe crucyfixes or rynges hangyng by thayme.[26]

The specificity of these records leaves no doubt as to what kinds of improper accessories were common in the Middle Ages.

Alnwick excludes crucifixes worn on a neck lace; thus we may conclude that the possession and carrying of rosaries were considered appropriate since, so far as I can determine, they are not mentioned among improper items.

There is no evidence that a rosary carried by a Prioress was ever considered by anyone in the fourteenth century to be an item of personal decoration.[27] To carry a rosary over the arm, to hang it from a girdle, or to pin it with a brooch to one's clothing, as St Hedwig does in Plate 6, was ordinary usage. And the Prioress's coral and green rosary with pendant is plain indeed in comparison with Catherine of Cleves's prayer beads of large coral (Color Plate II), ending in bi-color tassles caught in gold findings beneath a multi-pearled knob, and gauded with a series of pendants – a seven-pointed gold star with coral center and pearls in each point, a gold crucifix with each arm knobbed in coral and pearls affixed in each corner of the intersection, and a small black (silk?) drawstring bag that is initialed and lined with gold (perhaps containing a relic or apotropaic stone).[28] Unlike the Prioress's

---

26 *Visitations . . . Lincoln: Alnwick*, 2.1:8.

27 This is not true of a generalized fashion scene in the late fifteenth century when 'wearing' a rosary became high fashion. Eithne Wilkins, *The Rose-Garden Game: A Tradition of Beads and Flowers, the Symbolic Background to the European Prayer-Beads* (London, 1969), pp. 48–9, discusses 'excessively grand' prayer beads, the styles of wearing them, and the status of those who did, all of which came under censure. Such ordinary rosaries as the Prioress's would not confer additional social status on a prioress whose place in society was already established. Nor would forbidding the use of coral rosaries by servants and prostitutes negate their use by a Prioress. Because the Prioress's habit is not 'gay', she wears no rings, and because we cannot *know* the extent of her devotion, we may not apply to the Prioress the fifteenth-century sermon against women with 'vain attire', who bear 'er gay bedis withe litill devocion and thereon ryngis full gay', as Richard Rex does in '*The Sins of Madame Eglentyne' and Other Essays on Chaucer* (Newark, NJ, 1995), pp. 64–5, citing Alan J. Fletcher, 'A Critical Edition of Selected Sermons from an Unpublished Fifteenth-Century *de Tempore* Sermon Cycle' (B. Litt. Thesis, Oxford University, 1978), p. 64.

28 Depicted in the Horae of Catherine de Cleves, The Pierpont Morgan Library MS 917, p. 237 (c.1440). This rosary is described on p. 347 in Lightbown. Sklute, p. 40, apparently was unaware of the custom of suspending precious objects from rosaries, as his comments, cited in n. 5 above, indicate. Lightbown, chapters 21–2, describes and pictures many pendants, some extremely elaborate; see esp. pp. 136, 138–9, pl. 19, p. 155; also of interest is p. 351 regarding relic pendants, gold beads with pendant, and coral rosary beads with pendants left to clerics in 1404; and p. 354, fourteenth-century coral prayer beads with gauds and gold pendant given to Henry VI in 1428. See also H. Clifford Smith, *Jewellery* (London, 1908; rpt. 1973), pp. 124–5.

6. Sketch of St Hedwig of Silesia, from a parchment illustration,
J. Paul Getty Museum, Los Angeles.

rosary, many rosaries were made of both precious and semi-precious stones, and because of this we may assess the Prioress's rosary of coral, green, and pendant of gold according to the descriptions of personal possessions described in sumptuary legislation in order to assess their relative merits.

That jewels served as a sign of rank[29] is evident in the sumptuary laws, laws that include members of religious orders, subject to their own religious rules. Clergy and scholars were treated as knights of the same income, and the sumptuary law of 1363 allowed knights whose income was in the range of 400 marks to £1000 to dress as they pleased with the exception of wearing ermine and 'Letuses'.[30] Apparently, jewels of all sorts were considered appropriate to this income group. Because we have no record of cases tried under these laws, they are useful only in that they reveal the attitude of the ruling classes.

Knights with incomes less than £200 per annum were not allowed to wear garments embroidered with jewels 'or anything else', and their wives could wear precious stones only in finger rings. Here and in the following group we find the groups from which some nuns ordinarily would derive. Beneath this group was that of esquires and gentlemen below the rank of knights with land or rent valued at less than £100 per annum who were forbidden to 'display harness of gold or silver, precious stones, pearls'. Socially beneath these esquires and gentlemen, yeomen and handicraftsmen were not allowed to wear 'precious stones . . . rings, brooches, chains, etc. of gold or silver'.[31] And lower still on this socio-economic scale were those described by this sumptuary law as grooms, servants of lords, and their families who were forbidden ' "for their vesture or hosing . . . anything made of gold or silver, embroidered, enamelled" '.[32]

Thus, we see that convent rules and sumptuary legislation agree that those persons who should dress humbly, whether for spiritual or secular reasons,

[29] Joan Evans, *A History of Jewellery 1100–1870* (Boston, 1970), p. 47.

[30] *The Statutes of the Realm* (London, 1910; Netherlands, 1963), 1:381, Item XII, states, 'All Knights and Ladies, which have Land or Rent over the Value of iv. C. Mark by Year, to the Sum of M.li shall wear at their Pleasure, except Ermins and Letuses'. See commentary by Frances Elizabeth Baldwin, *Sumptuary Legislation and Personal Regulation in England*, Johns Hopkins University Studies in Historical and Political Science, Series 44, no. 1 (Baltimore, 1926), p. 50.

[31] *Statutes*, Items XII, X, and IX respectively; Baldwin, pp. 48–50.

[32] Baldwin, p. 47, citing *Stat. L.*, 2:164. The later attempt to regulate clothing by legislation, made by the Parliament of 1378–79, included a petition to the king for a law that would stipulate ' "that no man or woman in the said kingdom, except knights and ladies, shall use any manner of precious stones . . . cloth of gold, or ribbon of gold . . . unless he can spend £40 a year, on pain of forfeiture or whatsoever he uses contrary to this" '. Richard II, in effect, rejected this petition, replying, ' "Le Roi s'advisera tan q a prosch' Parlement" ', and the petition was not considered in the next parliament, according to Baldwin, p. 60, citing *Rot. Parl.*, 3:66.

should not wear or display secular jewels, or gold and silver jewelry, or embroidery (and cloth made of these substances). We find a regulation forbidding display of gold and silver horse trappings; however, I have not found a rule forbidding the owning or carrying of a rosary by a prioress, whatever materials were in its composition.[33]

Chaucer lived and wrote in an age in which it was considered not only proper but commendable to create religious objects of extraordinary beauty; medieval Gothic cathedrals are monumental examples of this principle. It was not extraordinary that Madame Eglentyne should possess a lovely coral and green rosary,[34] since rosaries and paternosters were among those items most frequently bequeathed to prioresses and nuns in the Middle Ages, as numerous bequests attest. Margerie de Crioll bequeathed, in 1319, her 'pat'nost "of coral and white pearls, which the Countess of Penbrok gave me"' to Elizabeth de Pavenham, a nun of Shaftesbury;[35] and Matilda Latymer, in a will dated 1416, left coral beads to her daughter, a nun at Buckland.[36] Similarly, Sir Thomas Cumberworth (d.1451) left rosaries to the prioress of each of the following religious establishments: Coton, Irford, Legburn, and Grenefeld; he requested that each be given 'a pare bedys of corall, as far as that I haue m[a]y laste, & after yiff yam gette bedes'. Sir Thomas's will continues:

> & I will that my nese Dam Elizabet Melton hafe xl s. of the iij pound that sche ows me to by hir a pare bedes with to pray for me, & sche to giff as my [gift to] Maude & dam Johan wade & dam Elizabet Thorp to ilkon vj s. viij d. in hall the hast to by yam bedes with to pray for me opon.
>   Also, I will thar be gyfyn to the v. nones, Iohn of Cumberworth doghtyrs, & to my ij. cosyns nones in Stayn-feld [Priory] & to dam Alys Bolman &

---

33 E. Wilkins, p. 49, discusses rosaries as they relate to the user's status and describes Dominicans in 1261 who forbade lay brothers to have amber and coral beads, because these were thought to be above their status; the Augustinian Canon of Osnalbrück who castigated laypersons who wore coral rosaries around their neck in the mid-fourteenth-century; and in 1463 the Leipzig laws, again dealing with status, which forbade maid-servants either to carry or wear coral Paternosters. Lightbown, pp. 344 and 346 n. 8, dealing with these same injunctions, mentions Augustinian friars (1290) as forbidden coral and amber paternosters, but also says that by the fourteenth century gold paternosters were owned by merchants and knights as well as by princes.

34 See John Livingston Lowes, 'The Prioress's Oath', *RR* 5 (1914), pp. 373, 375, regarding St Eloy's dedication as a craftsman to making religious objects that were beautiful and, therefore, the suitability of Chaucer's choice of this saint for inclusion in the portrait of a prioress who carries a beautiful rosary.

35 *Early Lincoln Wills 1280–1547*, ed. Alfred Gibbons (Lincoln, 1888), p. 5.

36 Revd F. C. Hingeston-Randolph, *The Register of Edmund Stafford (A.D. 1395–1419)* (London, 1886), p. 416.

to Ilkon of yam a pare bedys of gete & of mony trebull of almus that schall be gyfyn to odyr nones.[37]

Among such gifts, we might also include the very generous 1498 bequests made by Lady Anne Scrope of Harling to a series of saints represented in shrines. From Lady Anne, St Thomas of Canterbury, 'our Lady of Walsyngham', 'oure Lady of Pewe', and St Edmond of Bury, each received 'x of my grete beedes of goold lassed wt sylke crymmesyn & goold, wt a grete botton of goold, and tassellyd wt the same'.[38]

From these bequests we may see that, far from being unusual for a Prioress to possess such a relatively modest rosary as Madame Eglentyne's, it was probably ordinary for her nuns to have coral rosaries as well. And it was common for pilgrims to take their rosaries along on pilgrimage. Even St Josse (by whom the Wife of Bath swore) is depicted as a pilgrim with staff and rosary in a pilgrim badge now at the Museum of London (Plate 16).[39] In fact, the medieval visual arts often depict pilgrims carrying rosaries in hand and over their arms.[40] Regarding pilgrims who wished to be fashionable, Lightbown tells us that 'small paternosters were occasionally worn attached to bracelets after these became fashionable in the late fourteenth century'.[41] Had Chaucer wished to portray the Prioress as 'stylish', he might have

[37] *Lincoln Diocese Documents, 1450–1544*, ed. Andrew Clark, EETS, OS 149 (London, 1914), p. 50. In this same section of his will, Sir Thomas leaves coral beads (or jet, if there is not enough money) to seven male heads of religious houses. Other bequests made by Sir Thomas, p. 46, include a gift of beads to the Archbishop of York, 'a pare bedys of gold meynglied with corall', and one to the Abbot of Santasse, 'a pare of bedys of xij bedys, with the gaudys gilt'.
[38] According to Diana Webb, *Pilgrims and Pilgrimage in the Medieval West* (London, 1999), pp. 146–7.
[39] My Plate 16 (p. 263) is drawn from the picture of this badge on the cover of *The London Archaeologist* 4.11 (Summer 1983). The badge was found on the Swan Lane excavations, City of London, described in an earlier issue: 4.10 (Spring 1983), p. 276.
   'A rosary of large beads, hung round the neck or arm' was a standard part of the costume of the professional pilgrim, according to Sidney Heath, *Pilgrim Life in the Middle Ages* (London, 1911), p. 121.
[40] E. Wilkins, pp. 50–1, 176–7, lists various manners of carrying a rosary: in the hand, over and between clasped hands, wrapped around the lower arm, looped around a belt, and pinned to a garment by a brooch. Another customary (although occasionally questioned) mode was that of wearing a rosary around the neck. Winston-Allen, p. 116, repeats E. Wilkin's list and specifies 'but not hanging down in back'. See also Lightbown, pp. 342–3, 352–3, regarding brooches as aids to carrying/wearing rosaries.
   Wilkins, pp. 48–9, denigrates the Prioress's brooch as 'frivolous' because it is a pendant, but fails to acknowledge that such a pendant might, and often did, also function usefully to pin a rosary to a garment, and she perhaps does not know that St Hedwig (Plate 6) is pictured with a brooch serving that purpose.
[41] Lightbown, p. 351. He describes, pp. 101, 107–9, 294–7, the popularity of bracelets in the twelfth and early thirteenth centuries, after which they ceased to be in fashion in western Europe. The fashion for bracelets was later revived.

bestowed such a bracelet upon her; instead, she carries her prayer beads in an ordinary manner – about her arm.

Nevertheless, we must consider how we might fairly evaluate the rosary carried by the Prioress. Where should it be placed on a continuum of plain to elaborate rosaries? The stock of a London jeweller, Adam Ledyard, in 1381 included 'paternoster beads of white and yellow ambers, coral, jet and silver gilt, and aves of jet and blue glass as well as cheap sets of maple-wood (mazer) and white bone for children'.[42] While an elementary rosary could be made with knotted cord,[43] a plain rosary might be made of wooden (mazer) beads, such as those on display in the Museum of London. These restrung twenty-eight beads include one large bead and two medium beads. Perhaps Chaucer holds a single strand of such beads in his portrait in BL Roy. MS 17 D VI, fol. 93v, although the color of these beads appears faintly olive green now.[44] Another portrait of Chaucer with rosary may be seen in BL Harl. MS 3866, fol. 88, where he carries a red cord holding nine beads, with his hand covering a possible tenth, of black (jet[?], a common material for less expensive rosaries). The care with which both artists portrayed Chaucer's appearance, his robe, and his characteristic penner,[45] leads inevitably to the theory that his rosary was equally and distinctively characteristic.[46]

That the Prioress carries a beautiful rosary on pilgrimage should not need defending on religious grounds, for rosaries came into more common use in the fourteenth century and, at this time, were more often made of finer materials than in the previous century.[47] They appear frequently in fourteenth-

---

[42] Evans, *History of Jewellery*, p. 50; also Lightbown, pp. 343, 349.

[43] I have seen ladies knotting such cords on the steps of the Cathedral in Barcelona. Other elementary counting devices are St Clare's pile of pebbles, mentioned by Fra Tommaso da Celano in *The Life of St Clare Virgin*, trans. Catherine Bolton Magrini (Assisi, n.d.), p. 16; and E. Wilkins, p. 33, also mentions a notched stick. Regarding knotted cord rosaries and wooden and bone beads, see Lightbown, p. 345, and fig. 195.

[44] His rosary is made up of two decades of smaller beads plus larger beads at the beginning, between decades, and at the end, all strung on red cord (silk?). The strand begins with a loop, and ends with a tassel.

[45] R. Evan Davis, 'The Pendant in the Chaucer Portraits', *ChauR* 17 (1982), pp. 193–5, suggests that what is commonly supposed to be a penner is an ampulla of St Thomas Becket's blood.

[46] The tradition of depicting Chaucer with a rosary continued into the late sixteenth century when a full-length portrait was painted of him based on the miniature in Thomas Hoccleve's c.1412 *De Regimene Principum*. This portrait, now in London's National Portrait Gallery, shows Chaucer with penner in right hand and rosary in left; his rosary is a full circle of alternating amber and black beads on a gold chain and with a pendant gold cross.

[47] Wilfrid Lescher, *The Rosary* (London, 1888), pp. 41–4. See Anne Winston, 'Tracing the Origins of the Rosary: German Vernacular Texts', *Speculum* 68.3 (1993), pp. 619–36, regarding the evolution of the rosary; and Lightbown, pp. 342–3.

century English illuminated manuscripts.[48] In addition, the Prioress's beads are not 'over curious'. We have a considerable knowledge of medieval rosaries because they are so frequently mentioned in wills, a fact that attests to their material and spiritual value. Depending on materials and workmanship, the economic value varied considerably. For example, 'two pairs of amber paternosters' worth 6s are mentioned in a London fishmonger's city house inventory of 1373;[49] a pair of beads 2s, a pair of amber beads 5s, a pair of red coral beads 6s 8d, and a pair of coral beads with an *agnus dei* 23s 4d appear in a different inventory.[50] From these accounts, we may form a somewhat limited idea of the relative value of coral beads.[51] William de Escrik, a priest, bequeaths to Alicia de Roudon 'one pair of coral beads with a gold ring appended', and the will indicates that money might be substituted, if they chose, to the amount of 6s 8d.[52] Another list of goods, belonging to Thomas Cuteler, London grocer, in 1389, includes silver paternosters valued at 3s 4d, gilt paternosters with crucifix at 4s, and amber paternosters at 20d. Here silver and gilt paternosters are worth less than the coral and amber beads listed above, although we note also that workmanship must have played some part in valuation. That it was common even for middle-class citizens to own rosaries of the types listed above is amply attested in numerous wills of the medieval period.[53]

Many descriptions of rosaries (or paternosters) owned by members of the burgess and merchant class depict prayer beads as intricate as those carried by the Prioress. Some of the more interesting descriptions include the goldsmith Robert de Walcote's 1361 bequest to John Leycestre of 'a pair of paternostres of amber with gaudes of silver and a silver fermail'; Beatrix, the

---

48 For example: BL Roy. MS 6 E VII, fols 75v, 89, 90v, 108v, 109v, and BL Add. MS 42130, fol. 53, in which there is depicted a rosary of alternating red and gold beads.

49 Edith Rickert (compiler), eds Clair C. Olson and Martin M. Crow, *Chaucer's World* (New York, 1948), pp. 59–60.

50 The inventory of articles in the house of Richard Toky, a London grocer, 1393, from London, Corporation, *Calendar of Select Pleas and Memoranda, A.D. 1381–1412*, ed. Thomas, pp. 209–13, in *Chaucer's World*, p. 64.

51 Lightbown, pp. 346–7, says that coral was prized as highly as gold and describes coral as 'costly', but does not provide evidence of the relevant or comparable monetary values of these or other prayer bead materials; therefore, we may assume that coral may have been prized for its apotropaic value. The evidence of the costs of rosaries described above indicates that coral rosaries are generally more expensive than jet or amber, less expensive than pearl and gold; coral would, therefore, fall into the middle price range of beads.

52 Canterbury, Prerogative Court, *North Country Wills, 1383–1558*, quoted in *Chaucer's World*, p. 383.

53 *Calendar of Wills . . . London*, for amber: Part I, pp. 653, 694; Part II, pp. 11, 25, 51, 214, 216, 233, 316, 599, 698; for jet: II, pp. 210, 214; for silver or silver gilt: II, pp. 25, 210, 698; with brooch, 'a *fermail*': II, pp. 214, 310. Part I covers the years 1258–1358; Part II, 1358–1688.

wife of the late vintner John de Barton's 1379 bequest to Matilda Morton of a pair of 'bedes of blak gett with gilt gaudes'; and Avice Grenyngham's 1394 bequest of a pair of paternosters with 'silver fermails hanging thereto'.[54] In 1424–25 Roger Flore bequeaths to the Maister of Manton 'my pair of bedys that I vse my self, with the x aues of siluere, and a paternoster ouer-gilt, preying him to haue mynde of me sumtime whan he seith oure lady sawter on hem'.[55] A few of the many occupations represented in these wills are those of burreller, goldsmith, draper, glazier, fishmonger, and vintner. Clearly, the mercantile class owned and bequeathed rosaries of more value than beads made of maple or other hard woods, although they may have possessed those also.

At the opposite and clearly more costly end of the rosary continuum is the late-fifteenth-century 'Langdale Rosary', in the Victoria and Albert Museum, London. Although late for our study, it nevertheless shows how elaborate rosaries became in time. The rosary is enamelled gold and consists of

> fifty oval AVE beads, six lozenge-shaped PATERNOSTER beads, and a large rounded knop. Each bead is hollow and has on its back or front a subject, either a saint or a scene from the Life of Christ, the title of which is inscribed in black-letter on the rim.[56]

From Chaucer's time, a single gold rosary bead, inscribed (Glo)ria, dated late fourteenth century, may be seen at the Museum of London, demonstrating that elaborate rosaries pre-dated the fifteenth century. Also, while Matilda Latymer, mentioned above, willed only coral beads in 1416 to her daughter, a Buckland nun, she left a more elaborate pair to Isabella Hull: 'a set of long beads of gold with large beads of coral (de longe bedys auri cum gaudeis de Corall)'.[57] In addition, Joan Evans describes fourteenth-century rosaries that serve as a contrast to the rosary carried by Chaucer's Prioress. The two belonging to Raoul de Clermont (1302) were made of jet aves with crystal paternosters, and 'Scotch pearl' aves with garnet paternosters, respectively.[58] As the century progressed, rosaries grew more varied;[59] Queen Jean

---

54 *Calendar of Wills . . . London*, 2:24–5, 209–10, and 310.

55 *The Fifty Earliest English Wills in the Court of Probate, London: A.D. 1387–1439*, ed. F. J. Furnivall, EETS, OS 78 (London, 1882), p. 58.

56 Victoria and Albert Museum catalogue no. M.30–1934. See also the rosaries of the Passion in illuminations in the fifteenth-century BL MS 15525, fols 27, 38, 49, 60, 71, 82, 93.

57 Hingeston-Randolph, p. 416.

58 'Scotch pearl' is not defined by Evans, *History of Jewellery*, p. 50.

59 The elaborate prayer beads of Yolande de Bar, Dame de Cassel (near Vermandois), were stolen in 1362. Wilkins, p. 48, describes these beads:
> a paternoster of pearls, with fifty pearls as big as peas and six large sapphires as gauds and a gold-set cameo pendant, also a gold brooch with six pearls and three balas rubies, from which the paternoster hangs.

d'Evreaux owned one, in 1372, containing a hundred pearls and ten gold 'seignaux'.[60]

A Rosary of 'smal coral' and 'grene' Gauds

Critics of the Prioress say that the Prioress's rosary – the coral, the green gauds, the gold brooch – are extraordinary,[61] but the following discussion demonstrates that the materials and style were appropriate. Because the coral of this rosary grows in a cruciform shape, it might well be illustrative of her simple piety and desire to be protected from 'phantasms from the dark side of man's mind and their concrete embodiment in the devil and demons, who continually tempt mankind to the sins of the flesh'. Thomas of Cantimpre, in *De Naturis Rerum*, says that the association of coral with the cross 'provided mediaeval men with an excellent rationale for the use of this gem in the making of rosary beads. And it was widely used by the wealthier classes, particularly for the beads of pilgrims and travelers.'[62] In discussing the Prioress's rosary, Friedman posits that she knew these properties of coral, as well as those of the emeralds (gem of chastity) and rubies (representing martyrdom), employed in her tale (VII, lines 609–10).

Beyond Friedman's evidence, early Christian lapidaries all attribute to coral both 'curative and preventative powers', and the claims for these powers increase in number in succeeding medieval lapidaries.[63] A survey of lapidar-

[60] Evans, *History of Jewellery*, p. 50. See the variety of rosaries described and pictured in Lightbown, pp. 344, 348–51. Lightbown, p. 352, mentions nuns as being forbidden luxury paternosters, but fails to say exactly what the dividing line is between acceptable and 'costly' prayer beads.

The Imperial City Museum, Rothenburg ob der Taub, Germany, includes among its collection three rosaries – a pearl rosary ending with a fillagree cross; one of jet, gauded with fillagree balls; and one of small coral, of four decades, with fillagree balls, beginning with a flat but rounded white bead with a black St Christopher figure, and ending with one coral bead and one fillagree bead in a large fillagree case that has markings of red like a clock.

[61] Rex, pp. 61–8, ignores the presence of coral rosaries in pictures of Christ and the Blessed Virgin Mary, as he utilizes secular color symbolism to support his thesis that the Prioress's 'red' rosary indicates her sinfulness, even while he admits the 'ambiguities of color symbolism'. Further, he is clearly incorrect in stating that 'no one', in a group he does not define, 'seems to have wondered why they [the gauds] were green, or why the beads were red'; see n. 71 below.

[62] Friedman, pp. 301–4, and n. 4, lists the apotropaic powers of coral; citing *De Naturis Rerum*, BL Roy. 12 F VI, fol. 103r, Lib. XIV, xv.

[63] Joan Evans, *Magical Jewels of the Middle Ages and the Renaissance, Particularly in England* (New York, 1976), pp. 29–50, 96.

Lightbown describes, p. 343, the c.1479 portrait of Walther von Rottkirchen as a pilgrim 'just returned' from Jerusalem, Sinai, and Rome, and holding in his hands his 'coral paternoster linked by two rings', reproduced in his pl. 111.

ies quickly reveals that coral, emerald, and jasper are among the most frequently mentioned stones possessing medicinal powers.[64] Such claims of medicinal value were recognized by the medieval church in, for example, the statutes of the Hotel-Dieu of Troyes (1263), which forbade any religious to carry rings or precious stones for reasons others than 'maladie'.[65] Further, Chaucer's knowledge of the healing vertues in precious stones is evident in his translation of *Le Roman de la rose*:

> Rychesse a girdel hadde upon,
> The bokel of it was of a stoon
> Of vertu greet, & mochell of might; . . .
> The mourdaunt, wrought in noble wyse,
> Was of a stoon ful precious,
> That was so fyn & vertuous,
> That hool a man it coude make
> Of palasye, & of tooth-ake.   (*Rom.*, lines 1085–98)

In addition to medicinal properties, apocalyptic gems, such as emerald and jasper, embodied spiritual significance, with emerald expressing the strength of faith in adversity, and jasper figuring the truth of faith.[66] Although not an apocalyptic gem, coral was said to embody more than one power:

> To still tempests and traverse broad rivers in safety was the privilege of one who bore either red or white coral with him. That this also staunched the flow of blood from a wound, cured madness, and gave wisdom, was said to have been experimentally proved.[67]

---

64 See 'Marbode's Lapidary', First French Version, from MS Paris, BN lat. 14470, pp. 28–69; for jaspis: p. 33; smaragdus: p. 36; coralium: p. 47, in Paul Studer and Joan Evans, *Anglo-Norman Lapidaries* (Paris, 1924). Also see the early-fifteenth-century Douce 291 (MS B), the fifteenth-century Bodleian MS Add. A106 (MS C), and the earliest English lapidary, eleventh century, BL Cott. MS Tiberias Aiii (MS A), fol. 101v, in Joan Evans and M. S. Serjeantson, *English Medieval Lapidaries*, EETS, OS 190 (Oxford, 1933), for emeraude: pp. 13, 20, 40; iaspes: p. 23; coral: p. 53.

65 'The statutes of the Hotel-Dieu of Troyes, drawn up in 1263, declared: "*Nulle (religieuse) ne doit porter anneaulx ne pierres precieuses, se ce n'est pour cause de maladie*".' See Evans, *Magical Jewels*, citing Laborde, p. 446, s. v. *Pierres*.

66 George Frederick Kunz, *The Curious Lore of Precious Stones* (Philadelphia, 1913), p. 305, citing Rabani Mauri, 'Opera Omnia', vol. v, col. 470, *Patrologia Latina*, vol. cxi, Paris, 1864. Virtuous attributions and spiritual significations abounded during the medieval period for precious and semi-precious stones: the emerald symbolized John the Evangelist, who soothed sinful, dejected souls with a divine oil, and through doctrinal grace constantly strengthened the faith of Christians; jasper symbolized St Peter, whose love for Christ was ever strong and fresh and whose fervent faith made him shepherd and leader of the Christians. See Kunz, pp. 311–12, citing *Patrologiae Graecae*, ed. Migne, vol. cvi, Paris, 1863, cols 433–8.

67 Kunz, p. 68, citing Alburtus Magnus, 'Le Grand Albert des secretz des vertus des Herbes, Pierres et Bestes'.

The traditional spiritual value of coral is further attested to by its depiction in late fifteenth- and early-sixteenth-century paintings of the Virgin and Christ-child in which Christ holds or wears a coral rosary.[68] He plays with a very long rosary in 'Virgin and Child' by Bernard van Orley (Prado Museum, Madrid); He holds a coral rosary with three pendant gold crosses in 'The Virgin and Child' by Ambrogio Berogagnone, who was active from 1481 to 1523 (National Gallery, London); He wears the rosary around His neck in 'Maria mit Kind' by Meister des Aachener Altares (Alte Penakothek, Munchen) and in 'The Virgin and Child', Flemish School (National Gallery, London); and He wears the rosary in the manner of a baldric in 'The Virgin and Child' by Gerard David (National Gallery, London). The Flemish School painting depicts a rosary that has gauds of crystal.[69] And we should note that the Blessed Virgin wears a coral rosary around her neck in what is known as 'the first rosary altarpiece'.[70]

Distributed among the Prioress's small coral bits or beads, the green gauds[71] are aids to meditation or to counting prayers, and their greenness suggests a number of possible materials from which they might be fabricated. It would be possible, although not probable, that the gauds are emeralds, signifying any number of possible virtues, among them chastity. Or the gauds might have been jasper or other material enameled in green. However, the lapidary tradition of the emerald frequently carries the phrasing that is present in the earliest English lapidary (eleventh century): 'Feortha smaragdus, se ys swith grene.'[72] Since almost identical words appear in subsequent fifteenth-century lapidaries, it is possible that the phrase 'gauds of

---

68 I wish to express my gratitude to the late Maureen Pemberton, Bodleian Library, for bringing to my attention the tradition in art of portraying Virgin and Child with coral rosary beads. Further, regarding Christ wearing a coral rosary, see Sophie McConnell (text), and Alvin Grossman (design), *Metropolitan Jewelry*, The Metropolitan Museum of Art, New York (Boston, 1991), pp. 22–3; and A. Hartshorne, 'The gold chains, the pendants, the paternosters and the zones of the Middle Ages, the Renaissance and later times', *Archaeol J* 66 (1909), p. 93.

69 See Lightbown, pp. 342–3, regarding gauds and the Joys of Mary; pp. 351–2, for fancy shapes and designs of gauds; and p. 354, for a description of gauds enameled green.

70 Dated in the second half of the fifteenth century; attributed to the Master of St Severin. See color pl. 6, opposite p. 45, in E. Wilkins. Both the Virgin and Christ handle these prayer beads.

71 Regarding gauds, see Beverly Boyd, 'Chaucer's Prioress: Her Green Gauds', *MLQ* 11 (1950), pp. 404–16. Boyd's research indicates that these gauds may not be paternosters as they would be in present-day rosaries since the prayers of the rosary did not begin to reach this form until the middle of the fifteenth century. Instead, the Prioress's gauds were likely the reminders to meditate on the five joys of the Virgin, while reciting the Aves of Our Lady's Psalter. Entire strings of beads, in the Middle Ages, were also called *Paternosters* if that was the prayer being recited repetitively. In either case, the gauds served as counters.

72 'The fourth, Emerald, is very green', in Evans and Serjeantson, p. 13.

green' would automatically signify emeralds. Alternatively, and more likely, the gauds would have been made of jasper, or even of wood painted green, or of olive wood, which might be tinted green. Eithne Wilkins posits that the Prioress's gauds are most likely green glass.[73]

As Madame Eglentyne's rosary is the final image of her portrait, one that occupies five lines of verse, and is a dominant accent to her religious habit, it is worth pursuing the green gauds one step further, although it is entirely possible that this 'grene' signifies no more than Chaucer's need for a word that rhymed with 'sheene', a term that carries connotations of spiritual spotlessness, as, for example, in the *Pearl* Poet's works. On the other hand, medieval color symbolism includes the following associations for the color green: it was the color of love; it was a color 'particularly suitable for the clothing of newly-weds'; it was the most commonly worn color of church vestments. In addition, green carried negative connotations such as inconstancy, in contrast to blue, which symbolized truth.[74] In the *Chateau d'Amour*, for example, the body of the Blessed Virgin Mary is depicted allegorically as a castle built upon a green foundation, which signifies faith:

> So is the foundement al grene
> That to the roche faste lith,
> Wel is that ther murthe isihth,
> For the greneschipe lasteth euere,
> And his heuh ne leoseth neuere.[75]

[73] E. Wilkins states that rosaries became signs of social status. While this may well be true, a prioress in the Middle Ages already possessed social status, and a coral rosary gauded with green glass was unlikely to add to, or even substantiate, that status she had. Wilkins views this rosary as a fashion accent for a 'stylish Prioress', disregarding the fact that the Prioress's garments and her manner of wearing them had not been 'in style' in the secular world for some decades at the time of the *General Prologue*'s composition. Lightbown, p. 343, also mentions glass *ave* beads.

[74] Discussing the symbolism of green are Joan Evans, *Dress in Mediaeval France* (Oxford, 1952), p. 42; Margaret Scott, *The History of Dress Series: Late Gothic Europe, 1400–1500*, ed. Aileen Ribeiro (Atlantic Highlands, NJ, 1980), p. 122; Daniel Rock, *Hierugia; or, The Holy Sacrifice of the Mass*, rev. 3rd edn, ed. W. H. James Weale (London, 1892), 2:252. See also E. G. Cuthbert F. Atchley, 'On English Liturgical Colours', *Essays on Ceremonial*, ed. Vernon Staley (London, 1904), pp. 94, 131, 143–4; and Piotr Sadowski, 'The Greeness of the Green Knight: A Study of Medieval Colour Symbolism', *Ethnologia Polona* 15–16 (1991), esp. pp. 63, 70, 72–3; Joseph Strutt, *A Complete View of the Dress and Habits of the People of England, from the Establishment of the Saxons in Britain to the Present Time: Illustrated by Engravings Taken from the Most Authentic Remains of Antiquity* (London, 1970), 2:215. For green as representing 'novelty', see Haldeen Braddy, *Geoffrey Chaucer: Literary and Historical Studies* (Port Washington, NY, 1971), p. 77; and representing 'hypocrisy' in *Summa virtutum de remediis anime*, ed. and trans. Siegfried Wenzel, The Chaucer Library (Athens, GA, 1984), p. 96.

[75] *The Middle English Translations of Robert Grosseteste's Chateau d'Amour*, ed. Kari Sajavaara (Helsinki, 1967), p. 283.

There were other associations for the color green, but none of them offers a better explanation for Chaucer's selection than these positive associations of love, bridal clothes, ecclesiastical vestments, and everlasting faith.

The Prioress's Brooch and 'Amor vincit omnia'

Despite Robinson's corrective note,[76] mentioned earlier, the Prioress's pendant brooch is often misinterpreted.[77] This gold pendant would indeed indicate 'petty feminine vanity' if it were in fact suspended from a 'bracelet',[78] as Taitt erroneously posits. And Sr Madeleva's assurance that the pendant and motto were, and are, both correct and common among the religious has not sufficed to eliminate this kind of prejudicial criticism.

Brooches with mottoes were quite ordinary in the fourteenth century. Before and after buttons became fashionable, ring brooches, with or without mottoes, were a traditional means by which tunics were fastened at the neck.[79] Clearly, many brooches are 'love gifts'; one has the message, '*IO SVI FLVR DE FIN AMVR*', or 'I am a flower of perfect love.'[80] Although, to my knowledge, it is stated only once elsewhere, an examination of artifacts and mottoes reveals a self-evident rule of thumb: secular amatory and heraldic mottoes are written in Old French,[81] and occasionally in Middle English,

---

[76] Robinson, ed., headnote, p. 755. See also John M. Steadman, 'The Prioress's Brooch and St Leonard', *ES* 44 (1963), pp. 350–3, concerning the ironic contrast between associations of the motto and the shrine of St Leonard at the Benedictine Abbey at Bromley, Middlesex.

[77] Attributed ambiguity should not be a point of debate, for people in the medieval period were well acquainted with the idea expressed in the description of the ladder of charity in *Jacob's Well*, the ladder of which 'o syde is love to god, the other syde is loue to man'. See *Jacob's Well: An Englisht Treatise on the Cleansing of Man's Conscience*, ed. A. Brandeis, EETS, OS 115 (London, 1900), p. 3.

[78] Taitt's terminology, p. 61.

[79] See the brooches worn both for non-functional reasons and as functional fastenings, by bishops and clergy, as depicted in the visual arts, in John Carter, *Specimens of English Ecclesiastical Costume: From the Earliest Period Down to the Sixteenth Century* (London, 1817), in pls of Classes II, III, and VII, on unnumbered pages.

[80] Evans describes and illustrates such brooches in *History of Jewellery*, pp. 46–7. See pp. 59–60 for amatory mottoes in Old French on heart-shaped brooches: *Sans departer, A ma vie de coer entier, A vous me lie, VOUS ESTES MA IOY MOUNDEINE, NOSTRE ET TOUT DITZ A VOSTRE PLESIR, a mon derreyne.*

Other brooches, according to Evans, p. 47, contain good wishes for the wearer, or couple an amuletic formula with an expression of love, as, for example, the brooch that reads '*AMI AMET DE LI PENCET. IHESVS NAZARENVS REX IVDAEORVM*'. For other amuletic inscriptions, see pp. 57ff.

[81] Lightbown describes, p. 100, a c.1300 brooch, fig. 79, with the motto AMOR VINCIT FORTITUDINEM (Love conquers strength), recovered in the Canterbury area. He refers to this brooch as a 'real-life predecessor' of the motto on the Prioress's brooch.

while religious mottoes are composed in Latin. An examination of the range of mottoes on posey rings[82] supports both this rule of thumb and, thus, the idea that the quite common *Amor vincit omnia* is a motto with religious intent.[83] In the British Museum, the fourteenth-century gold brooch with the motto '*AMOR VINCIT OMNIA*'[84] is the size of a United States dime and much thinner. It is less than a quarter of the size of the much heavier heart-shaped gold brooch (c. fourteenth-century) with the Old French motto '*VOUS ESTES MA IOY MOVNDEINE*' [you are my earthly joy].[85] And the smaller British Museum brooch is much less elaborate than the gold heart-shaped brooch, which is covered in ribbon patterns in enamel and engraved, 'Je suy vostre sans de partier' [I am yours for ever].[86] Other gold brooches of the thirteenth through the fifteenth centuries in the Victoria and Albert Museum,[87] London, are again both larger and more elaborate than the small gold *AMOR VINCIT OMNIA* brooch at the British Museum. However, the Victoria and Albert Museum contains one other item that sheds light on

Perhaps his acceptance of the negative literary criticism concerning the Prioress, as revealed in his scattered comments, influences his judgment of the two mottoes. This c.1300 motto surrounds a cameo depicting a faun removing a thorn from a second faun's foot – clearly a classical scene; apparently influenced by the literary association, Lightbown classifies the motto as an 'amorous device', implying worldly, not spiritual, love. He acknowledges that Latin is the language usually used for magic formulas and religious motifs, while amatory mottoes normally appear in French, but offers no other examples of clearly amorous sentiments in Latin to further his assertion that there are other exceptions. In any case, if one disregarded the negative view of the Prioress's brooch, Lightbown's fig. 79 brooch might well be interpreted as a moral warning.

Regarding a fifteenth-century inscription that includes the Old French word *amour*, Brian Spencer states, 'There can be no doubt about the amatory nature of the 15th-century pendant (or indeed of any other badge or artifact) that bears the word *amour*.' *Amour* is not a Latin word; thus Spencer's statement agrees with the rule of thumb I state in the text. He is referring to a badge in the shape of the new moon, which he says has 'talismanic intention', in *Pilgrim Souvenirs and Secular Badges*, Medieval Finds from Excavations in London 7 (London, 1998), p. 155.

82 Joan Evans, *English Posies and Posy Rings* (London, 1931).

83 See Evans, *History of Jewellery*, pp. 47, 59, 74–6, for other devotional inscriptions.

84 British Museum, Franks Bequest, 1897, M&LA AF2687. The Prioress's motto appears on several examples, which may be seen in the Museum of Shakespeare's Birthplace, the British Museum, and the Nantes Museum, according to Evans, *History of Jewellery*, p. 47, n. 1.

Oddly, Evans, pp. 46–7, includes the Prioress's brooch among her list of amatory inscriptions, although it is the only Latin motto among them. It is possible that the strength of the negative critical tradition has determined her reading of this motto.

85 Franks Bequest, 1897, M&LA AF2699. For a picture of this brooch, see Evans, *History of Jewellery*, pl. 18a.

86 MA&LA, 1967, 12–8, 8, from hoard found at Fishpool, near Mansfield, Nottinghamshire, 1966 (probably buried early in 1464).

87 See Lightbown, Chapter 16, regarding thirteenth- and fourteenth-century ring brooches at the Victoria and Albert Museum.

the Prioress's brooch; this same motto is engraved on one side of a thirteenth-century gold ring described in the catalogue as a 'projecting four-claw bezel set with a sapphire. Lion-mask shoulders. The hoop inscribed in lombardic characters: *AVE MARIA GRA* and *AMOR VINCI(T) O(M)NIA*'.[88] Here, the Prioress's motto cannot be deemed ambiguous; the link with the Blessed Virgin makes the sentiment patently religious.

A ring brooch with motto, then, may be a basic wardrobe item, having a practical function (if it is sturdy enough) as it has in Plate 6, as well as a social one (decorative and signifying status); alternatively or simultaneously, a brooch might have a mystical, or spiritual signification, as the brooch has in Color Plate II.[89] While the thin gold British Museum brooch that bears the same motto as the Prioress's brooch could never have served any practical purpose, being too small and too delicate, nevertheless, suspended from a rosary this gold medal might well have served a spiritual and prophylactic purpose. In this case, according to Evans' classification, it would not be considered *jewelry*.

Evans defines *jewelry* as belonging to 'decorative art', which consists of 'ornaments actually worn upon the person'. Certain items made of precious materials are not included among *jewelry*. Magical (or prophylactic) jewels are excluded from this category, as is 'goldwork' that is 'concerned with other things than personal ornaments'; also omitted are ecclesiastical jewels (except those of secular origin) and insignia of the Orders of Knighthood.[90] Each of these excluded items might be beautiful or costly, but their function precludes their falling into the ornamental-only category of *jewelry*.

A comparison of the inscribed pendant on Madame Eglentyne's rosary with more worldly brooches yields a broader perspective than that achieved from an examination of her brooch in isolation. Variations of the basic design for ring brooches were achieved by varying the choice of metal (gold naturally being the most expensive choice), the motto, the decoration, size and shape. Evans describes brooches that include the following shapes: an octagonal ring brooch; a silver gilt brooch of two triangles producing a star-shaped effect; a brooch with four lobes curving inward; one of eight lobes decorated with cockatrices, cabochon jewels, and projecting ribs simulating claws; and

---

88 Victoria and Albert Museum, M.181–1975, West European.
89 Donald Howard, *Writers and Pilgrims: Medieval Pilgrimage Narratives and Their Posterity* (Berkeley, CA, 1980), p. 103, states that the Prioress's brooch is 'ornamental, elegant, aristocratic, secular and religious at once as best we can divine – telling us something too complex and too objective to pin down'.
90 Evans, *History of Jewellery*, p. 40. The distinction is important because some 'jewellers' apparently also made prayer beads, for example Robert Nyke of London, described as 'jeweller and bedemaker', in Marian Campbell, 'Gold, Silver and Precious Stones', *English Medieval Industries: Craftsmen, Techniques, Products*, eds John Blair and Nigel Ramsay (London, 1991), p. 151.

brooches with projecting jewels, with clasped or praying hands, with projecting flowers of metal, and many that are elaborately jeweled. The
heart-shaped brooch was a favorite of lovers and contained obvious 'amatory'
inscriptions. One of these has a ribbon entwining the heart and, as previously
mentioned, the inscription '*VOUS ESTES MA IOY MOUNDEINE*'.[91] Clearly,
the Prioress's brooch is plain in comparison, even though it is of gold. Her
inscription is ordinary, and acceptable according to religious standards, and
its Latin is the language appropriate for religious mottoes, although its
diction attracts a secular interpretation.[92] Considering the conventions of
medieval lyric poetry, which frequently refers to the Blessed Virgin Mary in
the language of secular chivalry, we can hardly fault the Prioress for displaying a Latin motto because its diction may be read as chivalric devotion as well
as spiritual love. A language that uses one word, *Amor*, to refer to a range of
feelings – love of humankind and love of God – is at the bottom of such complaints. Her motto does not say, after all, that earthly joy conquers all.
Further, William Langland defines *Amor* clearly in Anima's discourse on
Charity: 'And whan is lele loue leely oure lord and alle oere/ Thanne is lele
loue my name, and in latyn *Amor*' (Passus 15, lines 33–4) ['and when I truly
love our Lord and all my neighbours, then my name is True Love, or in Latin,
Amor'].[93] And, later, John Lydgate affirms this definition in his 'Amor
Vincit Omnia Mentiris Quod Pecunia':

> Who seyth that Amor vincit omnia,
>   He saith ful triew, playnly to expresse,
> Nought erthely love, whiche with pecunia
>   Sette trouth aside be fraude and doublenesse;
>   But perfite love, whiche hath none interesse
> To erthly thyngges, neyther in word ne dede'
>   Suche love grounded in love and stablenesse
> Shal have of God his gwerdoun and his mede.[94]   (lines 129–36)

In addition, the rest of the brooch's engraving is not unusual, or if it is,
Chaucer does not say so. The crowned *A* may symbolize '*Amor*', of course,
but it also calls to mind the *A* of 'I am the Alpha and the Omega.' That the
love of Christ is the beginning of 'the way', 'the straight and narrow' way of
the earthly pilgrimage, is a given of Christian thought. Consider, for example,
two fourteenth-century pewter badges in the shape of a crowned *A* in the

---

91 Evans, *History of Jewellery*, pp. 58–9, pl. 18a.
92 See nn. 10–11 above for secular readings.
93 William Langland, *Piers Plowman: The B Version*, eds George Kane and E. Talbot
    Donaldson (London, 1975); trans. and notes, J. F. Goodridge, *Piers the Ploughman* by
    William Langland (New York, 1980), p. 179.
94 From BL MS Harl. 2251, leaves 46v to 48v, published in John Lydgate, *Minor Poems*,
    ed. H. N. MacCracken, EETS, OS 192 (London, 1934; rpt. 1961), p. 749, stanza 17.

Museum of London collection.[95] The museum catalogue card suggests possible attributions of 'Alban, Agnes, Amor?' [sic]. In short, no one knows for certain which pilgrim shrine the badges might represent, and the notation 'Amor?' may well represent the act of reasoning backward from the evidence provided by Chaucer. However, these pilgrim badges provide evidence that the *A* may have been a recognizable symbol for a given shrine. Thus, the Prioress's brooch may be a pilgrim badge made of a more expensive material than the more common pewter. In light of the Pardoner's 'vernycle',[96] the Yeoman's silver St Christopher medal, and the likelihood that the Wife of Bath would have worn on her large pilgrim hat badges from her numerous pilgrimages,[97] it is plausible that the Prioress should carry another such badge of religious devotion.

Nevertheless, we must still consider whether carrying a pendant of such a design indicates vanity. The Prioress's brooch, with its motto and crowned *A*, is quite plain indeed when compared to the Founder's Jewel, left by William of Wykeham to New College, Oxford, in 1404. Although brooches made in the shape of letters were fairly common in the late fourteenth century and afterward,[98] the Founder's Jewel is an elaborate example. It is a Lombardic *M*, crowned, having the Virgin and Angel of the Annunciation in a frame within the double arch of the letter. The *M* is jewelled with cabochon emeralds, rubies, and pearls. The central line of the letter is a stem of the Annunci-

---

95 Catalogue numbers 8858 and 8731. Although these brooches are kept with the pilgrim badges, there remains the possibility that they were entirely secular. I owe a debt of gratitude to John Clark of the Museum of London who kindly allowed me to see the museum's reserve collection of pilgrim badges, and to Brian Spencer of the Museum of London who made a special study of these badges and whose article 'London–St Albans Return', *The London Archaeologist* (Spring 1969), pp. 34–5, 45, answered my questions concerning the usual appearance of a St Alban's pilgrim sign.

Spencer cites crowned *M*s, standing for Maria as queen of heaven, which were quite popular in the fourteenth- and fifteenth-century badges, as well as crowned *V* badges possibly signifying the Virgin, in *Pilgrim Souvenirs and Secular Badges* (Medieval Finds . . .), pp. 155–8. See figs 166a–170; also pp. 319–21 for other letters as brooches, which Spencer classifies as secular, including one crowned *A*, which has no motto, but which Spencer associates with Chaucer's Prioress.

96 Four Vernicles are displayed on bands of colored enamel on a ring brooch in the Bargello Museum, Florence. This same brooch is inscribed *IESVS AVTEM TRANSIENS PER MED*, from Luke 4:30, a motto that was thought to protect the wearer from thieves; Evans, *History of Jewellery*, pp. 57ff., describes this and other mottoes.

97 See *C&C*, p. 177.

98 Lightbown, p. 354, discusses the vogue for letters as part of various kinds of jewelry, including those that were incorporated in prayer beads. He indicates that by 1377 such inclusion was ordinary. He classifies, p. 353, the Prioress's brooch as 'rather worldly', but offers no reason why her brooch and motto are worldly when other mottoes in Latin are not, suggesting that he merely repeats the negative literary criticism that precedes him.

ation lily, which rises from a vase made of a shaped stone. Parts of the brooch are enameled – the lilies in white, the angel's wings in green. It was donated by Wykeham as a religious jewel, and Evans comments that 'it may be that this brooch was designed as a cope clasp (morse); it is equally likely . . . that it was once a secular jewel'.[99] Other such examples described by Evans make it clear that, whatever the original secular intent of a jewel, once it was dedicated to a religious purpose, it became a religious item. Because the Prioress's brooch is suspended from a rosary, its significance may be inferred from context, and its religious intent is plain enough.

One last possibility concerning the brooch should be explored – that it served both a religious and a practical function of attaching the rosary to the Prioress's habit. A ring brooch serves this purpose for St Hedwig of Silesia (Plate 6), in a fourteenth-century German illustration of her on parchment.[100] Here, the lozenge-shaped ring brooch is pinned above the breast, and from this brooch hangs a single-strand rosary of five decades, gauded with larger beads, and ending with a tassle. Such brooches and rosaries are also found on late fourteenth-century stone effigies,[101] venues that, one would suppose, normally display only those artifacts and attitudes considered to be proper and pious.

The Prioress's brooch, as Sr Madeleva says, was a 'good, but not an over-elaborate, medal'.[102] Further, if sturdy enough, it could have served a functional purpose. Comparisons made above with other rosaries and brooches[103] of the period support this judgment.

The Rosary and Iconography in Illuminated Manuscripts

Rosaries, pictured by themselves or being handled by someone, are depicted in many medieval manuscripts of a serious didactic nature, such as Jacobus's *Omne bonum*, fol. 90v,[104] where a group of people, kneeling, pray before an altar. The Luttrell Psalter[105] also contains a miniature on fol. 53 of a pilgrim

99   Evans, *History of Jewellery*, p. 60.
100 In the J. Paul Getty Museum, Los Angeles. For reproductions, see Mary B. Deevy, *Medieval ring brooches in Ireland: A study of jewellery, dress and society*, Monograph Series no. 1 (Wicklow, 1998), opposite p. 63, pl. 34; and Michael Camille, *Gothic Art: Glorious Visions* (New York, 1996), p. 130, fig. 93.
101 Deevy, p. 56, fig. 22, and p. 58, fig. 23.
102 Madeleva, pp. 19–20.
103 For the metaphorical brooch that signified the Passion of Jesus Christ, see *Saint Bride and Her Book: Birgitta of Sweden's Revelations*, trans. Julia Bolton Holloway (Newburyport, MA, 1992), p. 66, where the Blessed Virgin Mary instructs St Birgitta to set this 'brooch' upon her breast.
104 BL MS Roy. 6 E VII, dated 1360–75. Other rosaries in this manuscript are on fols 75v, 89, 108v, 109v.
105 BL Add. MS 42130 (fourteenth century).

carrying a small child; the pilgrim carries over his wrist a rosary of thirteen to fourteen alternating red and gold beads. Further, in the Bodleian Library a Book of Hours[106] contains an illumination of a half figure of a nun, cupped in a flower and holding a rosary of red beads in her hands. Also among pictures of nuns with rosaries in serious didactic works of the late Middle Ages is that of a Benedictine nun holding a book and rosary in her hands.[107] In addition, this religious iconography of book and rosary also appears in secular contexts. Because the rosary was understood to be a pious devotional aid frequently carried by pilgrims, and because it was included in the literary description of Constrained Abstinence, it naturally served illuminators of manuscripts of *Le Roman de la rose* as a suitable additional iconographic sign for their miniatures of this personification who dresses as a nun-pilgrim. Further, the icon of a rosary was sometimes added to the figure of Papelardie, or other allegorical figures who were visually and literarily depicted as nuns, perfect in outward appearance although textually portrayed as inwardly sinful. Illuminators of these manuscripts appear to lavish pious signs on these less-than-perfect 'nuns', frequently bestowing several pious signs on one figure, such as kneeling posture, book, pilgrim staff, bare feet, and rosary. It is in this general tradition that Chaucer creates the Prioress, giving her the outward signs of spiritual cleanness in the signs of her headdress, habit, and rosary, while depicting several of her actions as falling short of the ideal she has professed in her vows and signified in her appearance.

This artistic tradition may be seen in a number of fourteenth-century manuscripts of *Le Roman de la rose*. For example, Papelardie in BL Add. MS 31840, fol. 6, kneels before an altar holding an open book in both hands. She is dressed as a nun and has a white rosary of which ten beads show. In BL MS Egerton 881, fol. 5v, this same nun figure kneels with an open book held in both hands; and she is shown in BL MS Roy. 19 B XIII, fol. 8, kneeling again at an altar with open book. This pious iconographic matrix was shared by Constrained Abstinence, leman of False Seeming, as she too appears in fourteenth- and fifteenth-century manuscripts with some or all of the outward signs of piety. In BL MS Roy. 20 A XVII, fol. 5v, Papelardie wears a black habit girdled by a knotted rope such as friars wear; Constrained Abstinence wears identical clothing, but carries a pilgrim scrip and staff, and goes barefooted. A variation of this portrayal may be seen in Bodley Library MS Douce 371 (c.1400), fol. 79v, which contains an illumination of Constrained Abstinence in nun's habit, wearing a scrip and carrying a pilgrim staff and a rosary showing twenty-five beads over her wrist and hand. An early-fifteenth-century copy of this work, Bodleian MS Douce 188, fol. 77, shows

---

106 Bodley Library MS Douce 248, in Dutch of the first half of the fifteenth century.
107 Reproduced in Elizabeth Ewing, *Women in Uniform: through the centuries* (London, 1975), in pl. 3, p. 13, from an illumination in a manuscript in the Mansell Collection.

Constrained Abstinence in nun's habit, bearing a closed red book (illustrating line 10481) and a rosary of white beads, of which fourteen beads show, which may be hanging from her wrist. In this same manuscript, fol. 23 displays Amis, in nun's clothing, instructing the Lover (representing line 3123); a rosary of ten to eleven white beads hangs from what must be her girdle. Similarly, the personification Hypocrisy is depicted in Bodleian MS Douce 195 (1487–95), fol. 4, with a rosary of red beads; and Constrained Abstinence is portrayed with pilgrim staff and a rosary of red beads on white cord, on fols 108 and 108v of BL MS Harl. 4425 (c.1490).[108]

In illuminated manuscripts, personifications such as Hypocrisy and Constrained Abstinence are efficiently depicted in nuns' habits because these habits are an outward sign denoting spiritual cleanness, a sign that these figures betray by their actions, fulfilling the nature of their allegorical names, as the text of *Le Roman de la rose* makes clear. And iconographically, a rosary functions in these illuminations as an appropriate religious accessory – further objectifying the virtues that its bearer may betray. Similarly, the good, but not 'over curious', rosary carried by the Prioress is a visual sign of devotional intent; the mere act of carrying it on pilgrimage is a prayer in action.[109] This rosary completes the discussion of iconographic signs that make up Chaucer's costume rhetoric portraying the outwardly proper Madame Eglentyne, who imitates that other most holy rose in appearance and name, if not in all actions.

We may follow the direction of Chaucer's portrait to his final point of emphasis: the rosary on the arm of the Prioress. For even though, in the worldly space of the Tabard Inn, worldly satisfactions such as 'mete' and shared cup were only an arm's reach away, yet intimations of 'celestial paradise' as represented by the rosary, and in the name Eglentyne,[110] were present, and further, they would accompany the Prioress on her Canterbury pilgrim-

---

108 This illumination is reproduced in a line drawing in Strutt, pl. 134, fig. 2.

109 E. Wilkins says, pp. 50, 176, that a rosary would be read as the mark of a Christian, a 'badge of religion', or of piety.

110 The emblem of the rose may be seen in the arcade of the north porch of Chartres Cathedral. In its depiction of the fourteen joys of body and soul in heaven, Pulchritudo is shown with the emblem of four roses. The tradition in which this emblem flourished provides the spiritual background for the Prioress' name and Chaucer's description of her beauty, dressed in nun's garb. Adolf Katzenellenbogen, *Allegories of the Virtues and Vices in Mediaeval Art: From Early Christian Times to the Thirteenth Century* (New York, 1964; Toronto, 1989), p. 69, cites the *Speculum Virginum* in his discussion of the rose. This work contains a conversation between presbyter Peregrinus and the nun Theodora, and was a widely circulated book of devotions. In it, the rose is the symbol of the 'mystical paradise', which 'flourishes in a mysterious way', and includes the cardinal and theological virtues. See also Roberta J. M. Olson, 'The Rosary and its Iconography, Part I: Background for Devotional Tondi', *Arte Cristiani* 86 (1998), esp. pp. 263–4, regarding iconography popularized in the fifteenth century.

age. As *The Book of Vices and Virtues: A Fourteenth Century English Translation of the Somme Le Roi of Lorens D'Orleans* states, citing Ambrose: 'bedes beddynges is a good scheld aȝens alle þe brennyng dartes of þe deuel'; further, 'bedes is þe remedie aȝens all temptacions of synne; renne to þe bedes þer whiles þe enemy assaileþ þe herte'.[111]

[111] *The Book of Vices and Virtues: A Fourteenth Century English Translation of the Somme Le Roi of Lorens D'Orleans*, ed. W. Nelson Francis, EETS, OS 217 (London, 1942), p. 229, citing Ambrose and Isadore. This work contains many negative references to things that are over curious and costly, including clothing.

4

A Reconsideration of the Monk's Costume[1]

Fine, expensive, fashionable, flashy, flamboyant – critics employ these adjectives to describe Chaucer's Monk's attire. Paul Beichner excuses this 'expensive' costume because such expenditure was necessary for public appearances in accordance with Daun Piers' estate as keeper of a cell and outrider,[2] while Isaac Sequeira cites it as evidence that he flouted vows of poverty and regulations of the church,[3] and Jill Mann points out details of the Monk's costume similar to those in estate satires.[4] These descriptions, predominantly condemnatory even when excuses are made for such excess,[5] polarize the issues. In contrast, this chapter will adopt a new critical stance,

---

1   An earlier, short version of this chapter was published in *ChauR* 26.2 (1991), pp. 133–46, and a shorter version was presented at the 22nd International Congress of Medieval Studies, Western Michigan University, Kalamazoo, Michigan, May 1987.

2   Paul Beichner, 'Daun Piers, Monk and Business Administrator', *Speculum* 34 (1959), pp. 611–19.

3   Isaac Sequeira, 'Clerical Satire in the Portrait of the Monk and the Prologue to *The Monk's Tale*' in *Literary Studies: Homage to Dr A. Sivaramasubramonia Aiyer*, eds K. P. K. Menon, M. Manuel and K. Ayyappa Paniker (Trivandrum, 1973), p. 40.

4   Jill Mann, *Chaucer and Medieval Estates Satire: The Literature of Social Classes and the General Prologue to the Canterbury Tales* (Cambridge, 1973), p. 23.

5   Sidney Heath characterizes the Monk as being dressed in defiance of the regulations of the church, in *Pilgrim Life in the Middle Ages* (London, 1911), pp. 143–4; Sequeira, pp. 40, 43, states that his 'flashy' costume mocks his vow of poverty; Gerald Morgan depicts the costume as 'the finest clothes that can be bought', in 'The Universality of the Portraits in the *General Prologue* to the *Canterbury Tales*', *ES* 58 (1977), p. 485; the following critics agree that the Monk's clothes are 'expensive': Peter S. Taitt, *Incubus and Ideal: Ecclesiastical Figures in Chaucer and Langland*, Salzburg Studies in English Literature 44 (Salzburg, 1975), p. 52; Edmund Reiss, 'The Symbolic Surface of the *Canterbury Tales*: The Monk's Portrait, Part I', *ChauR* 2 (1968a), p. 267; Dom David Knowles, in *The Religious Orders in England: The End of the Middle Ages* (Cambridge, 1957), 2:365; and Huling E. Ussery, in 'The Status of Chaucer's Monk: Clerical, Official, Social, and Moral', *TSE* 17 (1969), p. 29. Additionally, Mann, p. 21, finds the Monk's *grys* and boots to be illustrative of his 'weakness for fine clothing' and a sign of gluttony; while Robert B. White, Jr states that 'the elaborate bridle, the supple boots, and the gold pin are clearly more than adequate and are therefore superfluous', and that these items underscore the Monk's lack of obedience, that primary virtue, which, according to John Cassian (*PL* 49:165), monks should

different because it is neither totally censorious of the Monk's costume, nor does it excuse it. Instead, it explores the complex background against which the Monk's costume may be realistically reexamined. This background information is vital to fair judgment, for while Daun Piers is no model ascetic monk of the old school, nevertheless his costume when judged in context may be praised in comparison to many described in satires and church records and is, on the whole, acceptable when judged by varying dress regulations for religious orders of the period. A reconsideration of the Monk's costume should rest on the determination of its probable place on a continuum terminated on one end by the abandoning of monk's habit for secular clothes, the common depiction in medieval art of apostasy,[6] and on the other end by the wearing of a hair-shirt[7] under the prescribed habit of the Benedictine Rule, that outward mark of the quest for spiritual perfection. The dress of Chaucer's Monk matches neither of these extremes;[8] rather, an examination of costume details in historical context places it within the range of ordinary array worn by a late-fourteenth-century monk of his degree[9] in spite of the fact that it does not conform completely to the Benedictine Rule and subsequent sumptuary ordinances.

Certainly, Daun Piers' portrait does not reflect the monastic ideal demonstrated in the life of a contemporary of Chaucer, the premier abbot of England, Thomas de la Mare (d.1396, age 87), Abbot of St Albans, who had been 'expert' in the sports of his class as a boy, but refused, for himself and for his monks, even to watch the sports of hunting and hawking, and who wore a hair-shirt under his plain regulation habit.[10] Such an ascetic model

'put . . . even before all virtues', in 'Chaucer's Daun Piers and the Rule of St Benedict: The Failure of an Ideal', *JEGP* 70 (1971), pp. 19–20.

6   See the monk removing his habit in the Chartres Cathedral relief pictured in Charles Rufus Morey, *Mediaeval Art* (New York, 1942), pp. 203, 259, fig. 112; another example may be seen in Jacobus, *Omne bonum*, BL MS Roy. 6 E VI, fol. 115. See also Morton W. Bloomfield, *Piers Plowman as a Fourteenth-Century Apocalypse* (New Brunswick, NJ, 1962), p. 60.

7   See Morgan, p. 485; Bloomfield, pp. 100, 102, 106; Knowles, p. 46.

8   I have given due consideration to S. H. Rigby's comments on adopting a position 'somewhere in the middle' when engaged in a polarized debate, in 'The Wife of Bath, Christine de Pizan, and the Medieval Case for Women', *ChauR* 35 (2000), p. 136, citing A. Flew, *Thinking About Thinking (or, Do I Sincerely Want To Be Right?)* (Glasgow, 1975), pp. 44–6.

9   Regarding degree: see Beichner's discussion of the Monk's rank, pp. 611–19.

10 Knowles, pp. 46, 48. The funeral brass of Abbot Thomas de la Mare, engraved before 1360, shows the Abbot in eucharistic vestments. According to H. W. Macklin, *The Brasses of England* (London, 1907), p. 90, this brass is in St Albans Abbey Church. A black and white representation of this brass may be seen in *Cathedral and City: St Albans Ancient and Modern*, ed. Robert Runcie (London, 1977), p. 67, and in *The Benedictines in Britain*, British Library Series 3 (London, 1980), fig. 17.

    For renditions of monastic garments in brasses, see Herbert Druitt, *A Manual of Costume as Illustrated by Monumental Brasses* (Philadelphia, n.d.), pp. 95–7; for a line

easily available to Chaucer makes plain that the monastic ideal[11] of the Benedictine Rule was visibly alive in the late fourteenth century, at least in certain monasteries. The plain regulation habit prescribed by the Rule and worn by Abbot De la Mare consisted of tunic, cowl[12] (the thickness to be varied seasonally), belt (used for work),[13] shoes and stockings, all made of coarse, cheap material purchased in the district.[14] In addition, a scapular

drawing of a monk's habit worn over a knight's ring-mail armor (late twelfth century?), see John Carter, *Specimens of English Ecclesiastic Costume: From the Earliest Period Down to the Sixteenth Century* (London, 1817), in the Class III drawings, described p. 12; and the Beverly Minster, misericord of a cowled fox preaching to an audience of fowls.

11 According to G. G. Coulton, in *Five Centuries of Religion* (Cambridge, 1923), pp. 381–2, 476–81 (page references to this work other than in this note refer to vol. 4 in the 1950 edn), during the eleventh to the thirteenth centuries 'respect for the cloth was almost a fetish-worship', and many men who could afford to make generous gifts to a monastery arranged to take the cowl *ad succurrendum* 'in order that they might thus be found at the Last Judgment' clad in this marriage garment. Coulton cites Nicholas of Bruere who pays 10 marks to acquire 'the fraternity of the house, the daily monastic allowance of food and drink, "and, at my latter end, the habit of St Benedict" ' (pp. 90–1). Such fetishism was rejected in *The Lay Folks' Catechism* of 1357, which states that a habitual sinner cannot gain entrance simply by the wearing of a holy habit at death: 'though he had upon him in his death the clothes that Christ wore here in earth in His manhood, that by reason was never worldly cloth so holy' (EETS, OS 118 [London 1901], p. 82, line 1221, cited in Coulton, *Five Centuries*, pp. 476–7).

See also, the visual depiction of the death of Matthew Paris, made by a contemporary monk of St Albans, in which Matthew wears his woolen *staminea* and lies dying while one elbow rests on 'The Book of the Chronicles of Matthew Paris' in MS Roy. 14, Chapter VII, fol. 218v; reproduced in G. G. Coulton, *Life in the Middle Ages* (Cambridge, 1967), 1:77, and *Horda Angel Cynnan* in Joseph Strutt, *A Complete View of the Dress and Habits of the People of England, from the Establishment of the Saxons in Britain to the Present Time: Illustrated by Engravings Taken from the Most Authentic Remains of Antiquity*, 2 vols (London, 1842; 1970), pl. 35.

12 See Mechtild Flury-Lemberg, *Textile Conservation and Research* (Bern, 1988), pp. 310–13, regarding the remains of a cowl of St Anthony of Padua (d.13 June 1231), with picture #666, p. 313. Also see *The Benedictines in Britain*, p. 26, regarding the blessing of the cowl as part of a monk's investiture ceremony.

13 Revd Adrian Vigourel, *A Synthetical Manual of Liturgy* (New York, 1907), p. 54, defines the cincture:

[It] is a string of linen, silk, wool or cotton, white or of the color of the vestments, with tassels at the ends. It is used to gird up and fasten the alb [long, white, linen shirt] about the body. The one who girds himself therewith implores the grace of perfect chastity. The cincture reminds us of the cord which bound our Lord in his Passion.

See John Lydgate's *Pilgrimage of the Life of Man, From the French of Guillaume de Deguilleville, A.D. 1335*, ed. F. J. Furnivall, EETS, ES 77 (London, 1899), p. 16, lines 586ff, regarding the knotted cord used to assist friends into Jerusalem.

14 *Rule of St Benedict: A Commentary by the Right Rev. Dom Paul Delatte*, trans. Justin McCann (New York, 1921), cap. 55.

(long, usually hooded, overgarment) was included for 'working purposes'.[15] Breeches, too, were part of the monastic habit.[16] For the true monk, devotion to his habit reflected spiritual devotion and was inseparable from it, as demonstrated by Pope Benedict XII (d.1342) who wore his monk's cowl as often as papal functions allowed.[17] Characteristically, both of these exemplary fourteenth-century monks fought in the ongoing battle against *proprietas*[18] and the worldliness of numerous monks made manifest in their wearing of lay fashions.

A brief, selective history of the medieval church's fight against the wearing of worldly dress by members of religious communities provides a measure of the general deviation in costume actually practiced by the clergy, a deviation relevant to any judgment concerning Chaucer's costume rhetoric in the portrait of the Monk. As discussed in Chapter 1, pp. 24–6, the catalog of councils that attempted to deal with the issue of clergy in secular dress proves that the problem consisted of more than isolated instances. The legislative battle against such dress was officially joined during the Fourth Council of Constantinople in 869–70 when Canon 27 ordered those in religious orders to wear the habit, a canon reaffirmed by Pope Innocent III at the Fourth Council of the Lateran (1215); later, Pope Boniface VIII (1294–1303) placed the punishment of excommunication *latae sententiae* upon those in holy orders who removed their religious garb.[19] That this and succeeding laws were ineffective may easily be determined by a perusal of repetitive and additional rulings and complaints against monks who attended High Mass ' "indecently dressed – in lay garments – open in front and behind" ',[20] and against ' "certain unquiet monks from other cloisters" ' who wore the tunics usually worn by ' "irreligious nobles" ',[21] leaving little doubt that these

---

[15] According to Sr Mary Ernestine Whitmore, 'Dress and Personal Adornment', *Medieval English Domestic Life and Amusements in the Works of Chaucer* (New York, 1972), p. 163. In n. 138, Whitmore describes the scapular as 'similar to a tabard, but longer'.

[16] See Janet Mayo, *A History of Ecclesiastical Dress* (New York, 1984), p. 35, for a brief discussion of conditions for and disagreements over wearing breeches. However, Abbot Francis A. Gasquet, *English Monastic Life*, 2nd edn rev. (London, 1904), p. 101, includes both breeches and shirts among the usual garments in a monk's wardrobe.

Regarding monastic dress in general, see Mayo, pp. 33–4, 47; and Barbara Harvey, *Monastic Dress in the Middle Ages: Precept and Practice* (Canterbury, 1988), pp. 14–15.

[17] Coulton, *Life in the Middle Ages*, 2:107.

[18] Defined as owning and using private resources. See Coulton, *Five Centuries*, 4:176, regarding this important issue.

[19] *New Catholic Encyclopedia* (New York, 1967), 12:286–7.

[20] Quoted from the Chronicle of St Trond (1124–38), in Coulton, *Five Centuries*, 4:23.

[21] Coulton, *Five Centuries*, 4:21. In this vein, see the long diatribe against 'ostentatious dress [worn] by members of the church' addressed to the double monastery of Barking, listing clothes forbidden to both nuns and monks, in 'The Prose *De Virginitate*',

monks were of noble families and chose to wear their ordinary dress rather than the humble habit. The Council of Rouen (c.1238) and the Rouen synods of 1279 and 1313 decreed and reaffirmed these same objections to sartorial abuses,[22] and the chronic problem was again discussed at the Council of Constance (1415–16?) during which one participant, Peter Pulka, commented that even the clergy of the Roman Court ' "are said to . . . go about in the most indecent fashions of lay dress, with short doublets and tight hosen" '.[23]

Other fifteenth-century examples are plentiful – for instance, the account of the monk John Gedeney who sometimes left the monastery precincts publicly wearing a layman's tunic and cap, who went fowling, and who wore a white tunic when entertaining women in the monastery before and after matins. Other such examples drawn only from visitations in the Lincoln diocese include an Austin brother, Ralph Carnelle, who was accused of encouraging other brothers in the wearing of linen shirts 'next their skin' as opposed to the regulation woolen ones, as well as 'tunics fastened with laces' rather than their buttoned cassocks. And a certain prior confessed to wearing 'riding cloak and a secular hood of a black hue' at night and engaging in violence against 'divers men'; this same prior was joined in an extra-monastery outing by Brother John Overtone, 'clad in a secular gown of russet hue' worn over his surplice and 'other underclothes of his rule', on the occasion of the feast of St Bartholomew. In addition, the canons of Kirby Bellars Priory are enjoined against wearing 'on their belts or purses silver bars or orphreys', while the canons of Dorchester Abbey are forbidden to go outside the monastery wearing any clothing except 'cloaks that are closed and not open'.[24] Further, the Abbot of Peterborough Abbey (1446–47) stands accused of leaving the monastery at night with secular folk, 'having put off his regular habit, dressed in secular raiment'; this same abbot gave his mantle furred with vair to one William Parkere's wife, who was described as being 'decked out beyond her husband's estate', and with whom, among others, the

Aldhelm: The Prose Works, trans. Michael Lapidge and Michael Herren (Cambridge, 1979), pp. 127–8.

22 Coulton, *Life in the Middle Ages*, 1:79, n. 1.

23 From H. Finke, *Acta Concilii Constanciensis*, 4:460, 465, quoted in Coulton, *Five Centuries*, 4:52. Further, Whitmore, p. 164, mentions the attempts at reforming the dress of the Black Monks made by Pope Gregory IX, and again by Pope Innocent IV, which reiterated proper habits, specifying round (not pointed-toed) shoes with thong ties, and forbade colored cloaks, 'irregular' saddles and tack with decoration, gilt or silver spurs, gloves with fingers, sharp-toed boots (citing Sir William Dugdale, *Monasticon Anglicanum*, 2nd edn [1846], 2:188).

24 In *Visitations of Religious Houses in the Diocese of Lincoln: Records of Visitations Held by William Alnwick, Bishop of Lincoln A.D. 1436 to A.D. 1449*, ed. Alexander Hamilton Thompson, Canterbury & York Society 24 (Horncastle, 1919), 2.1:142–3, 81, 154–5, 168 and 76, respectively (hereafter referred to as *Visitations . . . Lincoln: Alnwick*).

Abbot is defamed.[25] Visitation records supply frequent accounts of such monks, although some complaints are less detailed.[26]

Relative to the concerns of this study, Pope Benedict XII expressly forbade, in 1337, the wearing of *grys* by all cloistered clergy, an order that was 'already ignored in Chaucer's time'.[27] And later in the fourteenth century, Abbot De la Mare continues to resist private sartorial property[28] at St Albans in a letter (probably of 1363) publishing the statutes of the provincial chapter, a letter that especially illuminates our consideration of Chaucer's Monk's costume because, with the exception of his wearing of *grys*, Daun Piers is guilty of none of the common costume abuses listed.

The Abbot's list of clothing forbidden to monks is specific in detail and revealing in length; it includes secular tunics that are split, buttoned, pleated, tight, and/or short, and surcoats, either sleeved or unsleeved. These garments were not to be worn under a monk's habit. No fur, other than black fur, was to be worn on collars and hoods. Deviations in the habits were not allowed, including garments that were too long or wide, cowls with sleeves that were wide or too long, or garments of any color besides black (green and blue[29] are specifically mentioned), as well as any non-standard cloaks or riding capes. He does not forbid boots in general, but those that are pointed[30] or too tight. In addition, belts of silk or with silver ornaments are forbidden.[31] Essentially similar lists are repeated in later injunctions over the period of the next sixty years, with the addition of a few details including red and brown as colors forbidden, a particular type of unacceptable cap, the *pilio*, as well as any

---

[25] In *Visitations of Religious Houses in the Diocese of Lincoln: Alnwick's Visitations (1436–49)*, ed. Alexander Hamilton Thompson, Canterbury & York Society 33 (Oxford, 1929), 3:286, 290–1, 293.

[26] See *Visitations . . . Lincoln: Alnwick*, 2:201, as well as *Visitations of Religious Houses in the Diocese of Lincoln: Injunctions and other Documents from the Registers of Richard Flemyng and William Gray, Bishops of Lincoln A.D. 1420–A.D. 1436*, ed. Alexander Hamilton Thompson (Horncastle, 1914), 1:71. See, also, H. S. Bennett's comments on the Bishop of Winchester's visitation of the Priory of Selborne in 1387, in 'Medieval Literature and the Modern Reader', in *Essays and Studies* 31 (1945), p. 10; and Marilyn Oliva, *The Convent and the Community in Late Medieval England: Female Monasteries in the Diocese of Norwich, 1350–1540* (Woodbridge, 1998), pp. 73, 105.

[27] As Bennett acknowledges, p. 11.

[28] On *proprietas*, see n. 18 above; also the legend of Abraham, Abbot of Prateae in Coulton, *Life in the Middle Ages*, 1:24–5.

[29] A monk wearing a dark orange tunic under a light orange cloak may be seen in MS Bodl. 247, fol. 126v (English, mid-fourteenth century).

[30] See the line drawing of pointed boots (second half of the fourteenth century) in Cecil Willett Cunnington and Phillis Cunnington, *Handbook of English Mediaeval Costume* (London, 1952), p. 84, figs e-f, hereafter referred to as *Handbook*.

[31] William Abel Pantin, ed., *Documents Illustrating the Activities of the General and Provincial Chapters of the English Black Monks 1215–1540*, 3 vols, Camden Society, 3rd Series 45, 47, 54 (1931–37), 2:66–69, hereafter referred to as *Documents*.

wearing of the cowl alone as an outer garment.[32] Another such list from an English source is that from *Concilia Magnae Britanniae* (1342), which provides additional details of forbidden costume such as ornamenting pendants, hoods with tippets of astonishing width, rings worn in public, costly girdles of marvelous magnitude, enameled and gilt purses with various images carved on them, knives worn at the sides like swords, half-boots of red, checkered green cloth, shoes with pointed toes and cut in many ways[33] (perhaps reminiscent of the rose window of St Paul's), cruppers for the saddles, and horns hanging on necks, besides cloaks made of fur.[34]

Clearly, in trying to regulate the use of fur by clergy, the church was fighting long-standing English practice. For example, according to Ellen Wedemeyer Moore, Durham Cathedral Priory, at the 1299 Boston Fair, purchased the following furs:

5	furs strandling	£1	12s 6d
8	furs squirrel	£2	4s 0d
24	furs lamb	£3	12s 0d
1	fur budge		8s 0d
5	furs miniver for hoods	£1	2s 0d
6	furs lamb for hoods		6s 0d[35]

Contrasting with the above list is the monk in John Lydgate's *Prologue to the Sege of Thebes*:

> In a Cope of blak and not of grene
> On a palfrey slender, long and lene
> With rusty brydel mad not for the sale,
> My man to forn with a voide male.[36]   (lines 73–6)

When we compare Chaucer's costume rhetoric in the Monk's portrait to the above list, and to the individual transgressions listed in visitation records, we must find that Daun Piers' costume may be relegated to the middle ground between the designation of 'worldly' and 'ascetic'. The Monk is depicted as wearing a correct Benedictine habit in both of the two illuminations now

---

32 Pantin, *Documents*, 2:111–12, 117; 3:83.

33 See line drawings of half-boots (first half of the fourteenth century), and cut-out shoes (second half of the fourteenth century) in Cunnington & Cunnington, *Handbook*, p. 59, fig. f, and p. 86, figs d–h.

34 Wilkins' 'Concilia Magnae Britanniae' (London, 1737), 2:703, quoted in J. J. Jusserand, *English Wayfaring Life in the Middle Ages: XIVth Century*, 3rd edn, trans. Lucy Toulmin Smith (London, 1923), p. 432.

35 Ellen Wedemeyer Moore, *The Fairs of Medieval England: An Introductory Study*, Studies and Texts 72 (Toronto, 1985), p. 60, Table 8 (citing J. T. Fowler, ed., *Extracts from the Account Rolls of the Abbey of Durham* [Durham, 1899], 2:484ff).

36 Whitmore, p. 164, points this out, citing Eleanor P. Hammond, *English Verse from Chaucer to Surrey* (Durham, NC, 1927), p. 121.

available to us. Significantly, the Ellesmere illumination of the Monk depicts a correct black habit, although the present smudged state of this illumination prevents our being able to determine what details might have been included. However, the illumination may never have included conspicuous details as it is common for illuminations to differ from their literary text; the miniature of the Ellesmere Knight is one case in point. The second accessible illumination of the Monk, in Cambridge University Library MS Gg.4.27, fol. 352r (Color Plate III), gives primarily a back view of a loose dark brown robe, with long loose sleeves (no fur showing), and what may be a hood hanging down his back. On his head the monk wears a broad-brimmed black hat.[37] His black footwear (with slightly pointed toes) covers his ankles, disappearing beneath the hem of his clothing.

We may place Chaucer's depiction of his costume more precisely in mid-continuum after an examination of the individual costume signs in this portrait. Chaucer tells us that the Monk wears:

> sleves purfiled at the hond
> With grys, and that the fyneste of a lond;
> And, for to festne his hood under his chyn,
> He hadde of gold ywroght a ful curious pyn;
> A love-knotte in the gretter ende ther was.
> . . .
> His bootes souple, his hors in greet estaat.   (I, lines 193–7, 203)

The Monk's wearing of *grys* has incurred a critical censure that needs reexamination in the light of the historical context and the manner in which Chaucer has limited this sartorial disobedience. While it is true that *grys* was specifically forbidden, at the same time it was worn by many members of the clergy during the reigns of Edward III and Richard II, when extremely luxurious dress, including the wearing of many fur-lined garments, was common in England as a result of success in war against the French.[38] Not only did Wyclif complain about those in religious orders wearing 'precious' and 'riche' clothes,[39] but Parliament also objected and attempted to legislate an

---

37 Samantha Mullaney, 'The Language of Costume in the Ellesmere Portraits', in special edition *Sources, Exemplars and Copy-Texts: Influence and Transmission, Trivium* 31 (1999), p. 41, interprets the Ellesmere miniaturist's provision of a hat as having 'a fashionably pronounced brim' for the Monk, but does allow that this hat was 'within acceptable limits' for monks; unfortunately, she offers no documentation for the designation of the brim as categorically fashionable.

38 Frances Elizabeth Baldwin, *Sumptuary Legislation and Personal Regulation in England*, Johns Hopkins University Studies in Historical and Political Science, Series 44, no. 1 (Baltimore, 1926), pp. 22–3, citing Society of Antiquaries of London, *Archaeologia* 20:101; Strutt, 2:251.

39 John Wyclif, *The English Works of Wyclif Hitherto Unprinted*, ed. F. D. Matthew, EETS, OS 74 (London, 1880), pp. 14, 23.

end to this *luxuria* in 1337, setting up sumptuary laws that included rules for the wearing of fur by clerks according to their incomes, clerks having an income of 200 marks or more being allowed the same fur as 'knights of the same rent'. Since knights having an income of 200 marks or less were allowed all furs except miniver and sleeves of ermine, while those having incomes of 400 marks upwards could wear all furs except ermine,[40] we must conclude that *grys* was considered suitable for knights and clerks of incomes of 400 marks and above, since it was valued at 4s a timber,[41] being less expensive than ermine, which in 1419 cost 15s to 18s a timber and, in cost, comparable to miniver at 3s 4d to 4s 6d a timber.[42] Therefore, from Parliament's point of view, *grys* was also suitable for clergy whose estate was above that of clerks. In 1363 Parliament's statute provided that 'knights and ladies with over £266. 13s. 4d. a year might wear minever and gris; less prosperous knights and clerks could wear only facings of ermine and lettice on their hoods'; however, we find that 'even women of the streets in London wore hoods lined with Baltic squirrel', and memorial brasses attest to numerous merchants who wore cloaks with fur linings, while even the poorest of the clergy might list in his will cuffs of fur, and the Bishop of Durham (d.1404) is known to have owned almost twenty furred garments.[43]

This, then, is the milieu in which Daun Piers wears his *grys*: a period in which miniver and *grys* were, indeed, the most commonly worn furs in England, as import records attest.[44] Grey fur almuces (hooded short cape) and 'quire-copes lined and edged with grey squirrel fur' were commonly worn at the Church of Blessed Peter of Irthlingborough prior to the 1442 visitation, after which their use was limited, for financial reasons, to chief festivals, while Newarke College, Leicester, maintained 'quire' habits consisting of 'a black cope, white surplice, and almuce of grys' for the canons and almuces of 'black cloth or muslin furred with black budget' for the vicars.[45] Although Lollard preachers did indeed speak out against fur-clad

---

40 Baldwin, pp. 49–50.

41 Strutt, 2:102, n. 5.

42 Elspeth M. Veale, *The English Fur Trade in the Later Middle Ages* (Oxford, 1960), p. 220; see also *The Statutes of the Realm* (London, 1910; Netherlands, 1963), 1:381, Item XII. Veale states that in 1392–93, bellies of miniver pured cost 2d per skin, while back of *gris fyn* cost 2½d, 2¼d per skin. Ordinary *grys* would cost slightly less. For other prices of fur, see James E. Thorold Rogers, *A History of Agriculture and Prices in England* (Oxford, 1892; rpt. Vaduz, 1963), 1:582–5.

43 Veale, pp. 5–6, 8–9.

44 According to Veale, pp. 69, 133–4. See also Janet Martin, *Treasure of the Land of Darkness: The Fur Trade and its Significance for Medieval Russia* (Cambridge, 1986), pp. 64–5, 68, 159, regarding England's importation of squirrel furs.

45 *Visitations . . . Lincoln: Alnwick*, 2:158. See line drawings of such fur garments in Gilbert J. French, *The Tippets of the Canons Ecclesiastical* (London, 1850), pp. 18–19, figs 31–3; also p. 16, regarding the distinction between *amice* and *almuce*, *aumess*, or *amys*.

clergy,[46] nevertheless, it is small wonder that Daun Piers, outrider, wears fur when riding out and that that fur should be, in part, *grys*. The wonder is, considering his other luxurious tastes in hunting and dining, that his sleeves are only 'purfiled' with *grys*, since purfling speaks, relatively, of economy, being the practice of using more expensive furs along the edge where they could be seen, while completing the lining with less expensive skins of the same color. For example, a gown of pured miniver purfled with ermine used 800 squirrel skins and only four or five of the more expensive ermine skins.[47] Therefore, in having purfled sleeves, Chaucer's Monk is less ostentatious than the choirs described above. Also, we note that Chaucer says only that the Monk's sleeves are purfled; there is no mention in the *General Prologue* of hood, or riding cape, or cloak such as those worn by the Black Monks at Westminster,[48] of either religious or secular style, both of which might have been purfled. The possibility exists that the purfled sleeves are part of the fur-lined sub-tunica commonly worn by the clergy,[49] which signified the skins of animals worn by Adam after the fall, over which the surplice signifying purity was worn.[50] Similarly, the purfled sleeves might belong to the hooded outer garment made of skins that many monks wore, as described by Dom Paul Delatte in his commentary on the monastic cowl.[51] Purfled sleeves, in any case, constitute a favorable contrast to Robert Waltham, precentor of Salisbury, depicted in St Albans Golden Book,[52] wearing a fur-hooded almuce with tails suspended at the lower edge (Plate 7), and those Augustinian monks shown on fifteenth-century brasses wearing not the prescribed lambskin-lined cassocks and hoods, but, instead, fur-lined cassocks and

---

46 As Gloria Cigman points out in 'Chaucer and the Goats of Creation', *L&T* 5 (1991), p. 175, citing *Lollard Sermons*, ed. Gloria Cigman, EETS, OS 294 (Oxford, 1989), 11A/211 . . . 242.

47 Veale, p. 29.

48 Harvey, pp. 14–15, mentions hoods and fur-lined hood (citing *Customary of the Benedictine Monasteries of Saint Augustine, Canterbury, and Saint Peter, Westminster*, ii, ed. E. M. Thompson [Henry Bradshaw Society, 1904], pp. 149–50). She describes, p. 22, the riding cloak belonging to an obedientiary; it was made of burnet, 'a fine cloth for which Beverly in Yorkshire was famous', and was 'probably brown, or grey, if not black', the allowed colors for a riding cloak.

49 Mary G. Houston, *Medieval Costume in England & France: The 13th, 14th and 15th Centuries* (London, 1965), p. 150; and see the discussion above, Chapter 1, pp. 14–15. Mayo, p. 35, draws attention to a satire on such fur linings by Nigel (a monk), written before 1180, entitled *Speculum Stultorum*, which is briefly described in *The Benedictines in Britain*, pp. 78–9.

50 Daniel Rock, *Hierugia; or, The Holy Sacrifice of the Mass*, rev. 3rd edn, ed. W. H. James Weale (London, 1892), 2:256–7.

51 [Delatte] *Rule of St Benedict*, pp. 348–9.

52 Dated 1380, BL MS Cott. Nero D. VII, fol. 105v, upper left corner; black and white reproduction in *The Benedictines in Britain*, p. 58, fig. 37.

7. Sketch of Robert Waltham, Precentor, Salisbury Cathedral,
wearing a fur hooded *almuce*, from *St Albans Golden Book*,
BL MS Cotton Nero D. vii, fol. 105v.

hoods of *grys* with a fringe of the tails at the hemline,[53] and to Peter
Grillinger, Salzburg canon, wearing a fur cape trimmed with squirrel tails.[54]
Further, we should note the monk Thomas Butler's funeral brass (dated 1494)
at Great Haseley, Oxon., on which he is depicted in fur cape with tails around
the edge and two long pendants at the front,[55] as well as that of John

53 John Willis Clark, ed. and trans., *The Observances in use at the Augustinian Priory of
    S. Giles and S. Andrew at Barnwell, Cambridgeshire* (Cambridge, 1897), pp. lxxv–xxx
    and fig. 3, lxxviii and sources; also cited in Ramona Bressie, ' "A Governour Wily and
    Wys" ', *MLN* 54.7 (1939), p. 487.
54 *The Bible of Peter Grillinger*, fol. 3, reproduced in Marcel Thomas, *The Golden Age*
    (New York, 1979), pl. 36.
55 Pictured in Druitt, opposite p. 87. See his description of the history (from the thirteenth
    century onward) of the fur almuce with small fur tails at lower edge, and/or long pen-
    dants.

Huntingdon (1458), in choir attire with the same kind of fur cape.[56] In the six-teenth century, funeral brasses of Robert Sutton and Geoffrey Fyche, both Deans of St Patrick's Cathedral, Dublin, depict 'amuces' of fur with pendant tails, testifying that such sartorial practice was deemed acceptable in this later century.[57]

We cannot discount the fact that the Monk wears that most commonly available, if forbidden, *grys*; the 'everybody's doing it' argument will not absolve him, of course. However, he wears only a very small amount of *grys* so far as we know, and that, possibly, on the sleeves of his monk's sub-tunic or sleeved outer garment. There is no hint here that he wears the laymen's styles mentioned above. Nor does Chaucer provide that most familiar sugges-tion of conspicuous consumption, a description of the Monk wearing a habit with sleeves or garments that are too long or too wide.[58] Given no contrary evidence, we may assume that his habit is made not of burnet or other forbid-den secular cloth, but of monk's cloth, for which width and length were speci-fied by law.[59] We may envision the Monk, as does the illuminator of the

---

56 Shown in Mayo, p. 49, fig. 18. This almuce has a fur hood. By the late fifteenth century, regulations for clergy wearing fur according to their hierarchical degree were instituted. On this subject, see Wendy Scase, 'Proud Gallants and Popeholy Priests: The Context and Function of a Fifteenth-Century Satirical Poem', *MÆ* 63.2 (1994), p. 280; Harvey, pp. 19–20; and Phillis Cunnington and Catherine Lucas, *Charity Cos-tumes of Children, Scolars, Almsfolk, Pensioners* (London, 1978), p. 84, fig. 49, showing 'Members of the College of Winchester in surplices, c. 1463. Founder, William of Wykeham, centre, wears an almuce of squirrel fur. Fellows, standing, have almuces probably lined with lambskin. One on right shows two pendant tails of fur', in a reproduction of an illustration in New College, Oxford, MS C. 288, fol. 3.

57 See also French's woodcut and description, p. 19: 'Canon in furred aumess, with a fringe of tails, from a drawing in trick [sic], engraved in the *Antiquarian Repertory*, vol. i, representing procession to the christening of Prince Arthur, son of Henry VII'.

58 As mentioned in Pantin, *Documents*, pp. 67, 117; also *English Works of Wyclif*, pp. 315–16. Such deviations are depicted in the sketches of monks wearing wide sleeves and habits of excessive length in the Monk's Sketchbook, Cambridge, Lib., Magdalen Coll. Pepys 1916, reproduced in M. R. James, *Walpole Soc Annual* 13 (Oxford, 1925); and in the illumination of John Whethamstede, Abbot of St Albans 1420–40 and 1451–65, wearing a habit that is too long, in BL MS Cott. Nero D vii.

Whitmore points out that, in *The Prologue to the Monk's Tale*, the Host asks the Monk, 'why werestow so wyd a cope?' (VII 1949). This detail, absent from the *General Prologue*, places the Monk's 'cope' within the costume tradition of large and wide garments, as I discuss in Chapter 1, pp. 17–24; alternatively this wide cope may refer to the Monk's own girth, the possible result of overeating. Whitmore, p. 161, n. 124, defines a *cope* as 'a kind of mantle of circular form sewed together in front over the neck and chest, and used as a part of the religious' full dress'. See also discussion of the Friar's 'semycope' in this book, Chapter 5, pp. 144–59; and in Mayo, pp. 53–5.

59 John James, *History of the Worsted Manufacture in England* (London, 1968), p. 74. Monks's cloths were worsted, 12 yards long at least, and 5 quarters wide, manufac-tured in dimensions suitable for habits, as were canons' cloths. Dorothy K. Burnham posits a definitive influence of cloth dimensions on the type of garments – width,

Ellesmere manuscript, wearing a standard monk's habit and add to our mental vision sleeves edged with *grys*.[60] This mental picture is a far cry from critical designations of 'flashy' or 'flamboyant', even if this bit of trim *is* the finest of its type, that is, the finest of the Baltic squirrels, not, of course, the finest of all furs.

Similarly, we need to reevaluate the Monk's supple boots. The ascetic ideal for monks of some countries, described by Dom Delatte, is practiced by going barefoot, constituting 'a sort of footgear that does not wear out, being renewed by nature'. But he lists other footgear equally acceptable elsewhere such as sandals, the *pedules* prescribed by St Benedict that are 'perhaps stockings, or socks, or light indoor footgear', *caligae* that 'are not necessarily what we call shoes, but may be military sandals bound by straps and clasping foot and ankle firmly', and the sturdier *caligae* worn for field work, such as *caligae clavatae* or nailed boots.[61] While antiquaries dispute the exact nature

length, and style – made from it; see p. 17 for religious garments in the Royal Ontario Museum publication, *Cut My Cote* (Ontario, 1973).

Harvey discusses dimensions of cloth for habits, a topic relative to length and width of garments; she also describes types of fabrics needed for different garments, including serge, worsted, Kersey, linen, frieze, wilkoc, and *stamineum* (her trans.: linsey-woolsey), pp. 17–19, 23–6.

Moore, p. 60, Table 8, lists the cloths purchased by Durham Cathedral Priory at Boston Fair, 1299: 20 ells burnet for £4 8s ½d, 5 cloths for clerics for £26 0s 1d, 4 cloths (possibly to make 3 robes) for men-at-arms for £22 7s 9d, 27 ells Lincoln says for £3 5s 6d, 4 cloths for £11 6s 9d, 11 ells cloth for tunics £1 10s 8d, 138 ells *de panno pauperum* for £5 18s 6d, 100 ells canvas for £2 1s 3d, and 2 ells muslin (*cyndon*) for 2s 8d. In 1406 at Eynsham, records kept by the chamberlain reveal that 15s per year is the usual expenditure for clothing for a monk made of 'say (or serge), burnet, silk, black cloth, linen and linsey-woolsey', according to R. H. Snape, *English Monastic Finances in the Later Middle Ages*, Cambridge Studies in Medieval Life and Thought, ed. G. G. Coulton (Cambridge, 1926), pp. 159–60, citing H. E. Salter, *Eynsham Cartulary*, ii, p. xci.

60 Mullaney, pp. 40–2, maintains that the Ellesmere illuminator consciously omits gray fur trim, as well as gold knotte brooch.

61 See ankle shoes and boot for field work (first half of the fourteenth century) in Cunnington and Cunnington, *Handbook*, p. 58, fig. a, and p. 61, figs e and f. Also see the footwear, cited by Snape, p. 160, included in the list of ' "necessaries" ' required of Ely novices when they began their novitiate; note that he defines *caligae* differently: two 'cannae', one mattress, two pairs of blankets, two pairs of straylys, three coverlets, one 'furtpane', one 'blew-bed' or say; one cowl and a frock, one black furred tunic, one black plain tunic, two white tunics, one black furred amice, one plain amice; one girdle with a pouch, and a penknife, tables, a comb, and needle and thread in 'le powch', one small girdle for nights; three 'paria staminorum' (linsey-woolsey shirts); four pairs of breeches with 'brygerdel' (an undergirding) and points, two pairs of soled hose (*caligae*), four 'paria de le sokks', two pairs of boots, one for day and one for night; one 'pilch', three 'paria flammeole' (flannel shirts?), three 'pulvinaria' or bolsters, and one white cap for nights; two towels, one dirty-clothes bag or 'pokette', one shaving-cloth; one goblet (*crater*), one '*ciphus murreus*' (probably a mazer), and a silver spoon.

of the Rule-prescribed footwear, *indumenta pedum*, the above list makes it clear that footgear was varied according to circumstances and need, just as the prescribed weight of the cowl was varied with the seasons.[62] And we know that boots were part of the prescribed habit at the New Collegiate Church of Blessed Mary at Leicester,[63] and for the Leicester monks under Abbot Clowne's jurisdiction.[64] Finally, records show that monks at Winchester wore two kinds of footcoverings: 'shoes, actually called "boots" for daytime, and slippers for nightwear', with the winter boots being lined and summer boots unlined. Such a shoe or boot, probably fourteenth-century, was found in the infirmary cloister at Winchester. Harvey describes this boot as 'designed to cover the whole of the top of the foot', having 'an opening lengthwise along the top', with leather thongs to secure the opening. The black shoe measures ten inches long and has a slightly pointed toe, but the most telling point pertinent to Chaucer's Monk is that it 'is still exceedingly oily, despite the lapse of six centuries'.[65] If after six centuries the leather was still oily, then it follows that it is also supple.[66]

An understanding that religious rules allow and cellarers provide for a variety in footwear makes some medieval satires seem to be carping. For example, Jill Mann cites a Goliardic prose satire that lists the footwear possessed by a monk: linen stockings, 'woolen shoes', leather leggings,[67] and overshoes, and states that 'The number of his footwear is not fixed, for it waxes and wanes according to the alterations of heat and cold. He has summer boots, winter boots, sandals, underlaid with three layers of felt.'[68] This list seems excessive to the satirist, but measured against the Benedictine Rule, which allowed for each abbot to dispense and collect clothing periodi-

---

62 [Delatte] *Rule of St Benedict*, pp. 346, 350–1.

63 According to visitation records of 1440 in *Visitations . . . Lincoln: Alnwick*, 2:191, n. 6.

64 According to John Nichols' quote: '*usum nigrarum botarum a nigris caligiscum nigris sotalaribus*', in *History and Antiquities of the County of Leicester* (London, 1795–1815), 1:262; see also Bressie, p. 488.

65 Harvey, p. 15. This 'boot' is pictured in her frontispiece. Also see her n. 13 regarding Winchester monks receiving money for boots. Gasquet, pp. 100–1, 112, states that usually monks were issued two pair of boots by the chamberlain of a religious house as well as one pair of 'night-boots' of thick cloth, perhaps with felt soles.

The price of footwear is listed by Rogers, 1:585. Fourteenth-century boots are priced 4s a pair in 1356 and 1358, the latter listed as ' "de aluto" ', which Rogers thinks to be a high-quality dyed leather. A third pair, described as ' "ocreæ" ', were sold for 2s 4d in 1379; two additional pairs, with spurs attached, had a combined value of 6s 8d in 1383.

66 Edmund Reiss, 'The Symbolic Surface of the *Canterbury Tales*: The Monk's Portrait, Part II', *ChauR* 3 (1968), p. 26, sees Chaucer's portrait detail of *suppleness* as part of the Monk's general unpleasantness 'oiliness, greasiness, and sweatiness', but fails to consider that monks were obliged to keep their clothing in good order.

67 See the soled hose and leather leggings/boots (first half of the fourteenth century) in Cunnington and Cunnington, *Handbook*, p. 61, fig. b, and p. 59, fig. a.

68 Translation from Latin in Mann, p. 22.

cally, depending on change of climate and activity, the satirical complaint is revealed to be mere purist preference, the statement of one who wishes monks to be holier than St Benedict.

In any case, this Goliardic complaint surely aims more at the idea of excess than at any one style of footwear, and this is a point we may apply to Daun Piers' case. Are the Monk's supple boots evidence of superfluity, as Robert B. White Jr indicates? Are they 'splendid footwear', as Jill Mann describes them? Or, are they appropriate for a monk-outrider/'business administrator', as Peter S. Taitt states in agreement with Paul Beichner?[69] The lists of forbidden wearing apparel presented earlier tell us what constitutes superfluity in footwear: pointed and too-narrow or too-tight boots, red boots, and shoes with pointed toes and cut-out designs.[70] In short, all high-style, secular footwear is forbidden, so that it is not surprising to find that the satirical *Ordre de Bel-Eyse* includes Hospitallers who wear elegant shoes.[71] But boots *per se*,[72] supple because they are either new or well cared for, are not proscribed, and therefore we may not call them superfluous, nor even 'splendid' in the sense that this means magnificent.

We may only say that boots, *caligas*, defined as leather shoes, half-boots, or soldier's boots,[73] were acceptable footgear for monks when circumstances warranted, in spite of the fact that puritanical preachers, satirists, and even certain other monks thought that boots constituted pampering. For example, William Hornyng, in 1532, complained during a visitation that another outrider, Richard Norwich, also 'cellera' to the abbot, wore boots instead of sandals when out of the monastery (*calceis et non ocreis extra monasterium*).[74]

There is no doubt that the wearing of even plain black boots contrasted with the practice of the apostles who traveled barefooted, as John V. Fleming suggests; he reads this costume sign as evidence of a monk's lack of 'sacred zeal'.[75] Such a monk wearing boots, as a satirist suggests in 'Moult a ci bele

---

69 White, p. 19; Mann, p. 23; and Taitt, p. 52. Mullaney, p. 41, calls the boots 'suitable garments for a man who would spend much of his leisure time on horseback'.
70 Pantin, *Documents*, 2:66, 68; Wilkins' 'Concilia Magnae Britanniae', quoted in Jusserand, p. 432.
71 'Ordre de Bel-Eyse' in *The Political Songs of England From the Reign of John to that of Edward II*, Old series 6, ed. and trans. Thomas Wright (London, 1839), pp. 137–48.
72 See, for example the loose buskins (first half of the fourteenth century) in Cunnington & Cunnington, *Handbook*, p. 58, fig. c.
73 Charlton T. Lewis, *Elementary Latin Dictionary* (Oxford, 1979), p. 103.
74 Ussery, p. 23, n. 85.
75 John Fleming, 'Daun Piers and Dom Pier: Waterless Fish and Unholy Hunters', *ChauR* 15.4 (1981), pp. 292–3. See also John V. Fleming, 'Gospel Asceticism: Some Chaucerian Images of Perfection', *Chaucer and Scriptural Tradition*, ed. David Lyle Jeffrey (Ottawa, 1984), p. 193, for his comments on Peter Damian's idea that 'being an "outrider" is to be dragged to "that hat which ever passes down from bad to worse" ', referring to Peter Damian's remarks in Dante's *Paradiso* 21, lines 118–20, 127–35.

compagnie', was not doing penance by enduring the cold, but neither did he deviate from the ordinary practice as a thirteenth-century poetic, non-satirical, peddler's recital makes plain: 'Si ai bottes de mostier maintes/ Netes, polies, et bien paintes' ['I have also boots for monasteries, very neat, polished and well stitched'].[76] The image of Daun Piers' boots eliminates the possibility that he could be a candidate for sainthood, but, then, we never thought he was.

Finally, in our evaluation of Chaucer's costume rhetoric in this portrait we turn to a consideration of the Monk's 'ful curious' gold pin with its 'love-knotte in the gretter ende'. Chaucer undercuts what might be considered full censure by telling us first that the pin serves a utilitarian purpose, that of fastening the hood. Brooches were, in fact, the traditional fastenings for both daily habits and for ceremonial garments; an example of the latter is the Franco-Burgundian (c.1400) Trinity Morse, worn by a bishop as a cope fastening, which depicts a colorfully enameled and sculpted grouping of the Holy Trinity in a cusped circle that measures approximately $4^3/_8$ inches across.[77] Smaller versions of such brooches worn as hood and cloak fastenings were commonplace in the late fourteenth century although they had been replaced to a large extent by the more fashionable button.[78] For example, Robert de Hereford, deacon of Sarum, wears such a pin at his neck in an illumination in BL MS Cott. Nero D VII, fol. 101. And we recall that tunics buttoned on the sleeves or on the front[79] were among those items of fashionable attire forbidden by Abbot De le Mare.[80] Thus, we find Daun Piers wearing a pin, such as those worn 'sometimes' by the Augustinians cited by Bressie.[81] Needless to say, this practice, old-fashioned as it was in the late fourteenth century, is among those deemed objectionable by satirists such as John Gower in *Mirour de l'Omme*, on the grounds that such a pin makes a show on the breast.[82] We should note, however, that Gower is concerned with

[76] 'Du Mercier' in *Satirical Songs and Poems on Costume From the 13th to the 19th Century*, ed. Frederick W. Fairholt (London, 1849), p. 11; trans. from Mann, p. 23. Regarding footwear, also see *Political Songs of England*, pp. 146, 330.

[77] In the National Gallery, London.

[78] Buttons are a device that may have originated in the form of earlier decorative rosettes, knots, or bosses, according to J. L. Nevinson, 'Buttons and Buttonholes in the Fourteenth Century', *The Journal of the Costume Society* 11 (1977), p. 38.

[79] Note the button fastenings on the cloak worn by Sir Roger, Chaplain of the chapel of the Earl of Warwick at Flamsted, pictured in St Albans Golden Book, BL MS Cott. Nero D VII, fol. 108v.

[80] Pantin, *Documents*, 2:66.

[81] Bressie, p. 487.

[82] John Gower, *Mirour de l'Omne* in *Complete Works of John Gower*, ed. G. C. Macaulay, 4 vols (Oxford, 1899–1902), 1:21020–22. See also Mann, p. 22; and J. S. P. Tatlock, 'Chaucer's Monk', *MLN* 55 (1940), p. 351, who judges the Monk's pin to be 'worldly . . . fashion'.

intent; he castigates any costume item worn by a monk *for the purpose* of making himself more attractive 'for the world', a concern that includes enameled silver jewelry worn on the hood (I.21013–24).[83] The use of a brooch as a cloak fastening clearly differs in intent from the 'broches or ouches on his hode' (line 1006), which most likely were only decorative, mentioned in the Pelican's castigation of monks' attire in *The Plowman's Tale*.[84]

The Monk's pin is all the more notable in that it is gold, the metal allowed, in the ineffective sumptuary law of 1363, only to those of knights' rank or above whose income was, or exceeded, 400 marks per annum, a ruling that was proposed again, but never passed, in 1378–79 for the same group, with spending ability specified at £40 a year.[85] Thus, in wearing a gold pin, the Monk may very well be indicating, accurately, his worldly status, for while his vows should have precluded his *owning* private property, records indicate that the practice of monks holding, inheriting, and administrating property was a common one, although this is property that belonged 'in spirit to the congregation'. This spiritual loophole reminds us forcefully that, however well they may have served God, medieval monasteries did serve the world. We should not be surprised to find this reflected in their dress, and must acknowledge that the final responsibility for what individual monks wore rested solely

83   De cest essample, dont dit ay,
          Cil moigne puet avoir esmay
          Qui pour le mond se fait jolys,
          Ne quiert la haire ainz quiert le say
          Tout le plus fin a son essay,
          Ove la fourrure vair et gris,
          Car il desdeigne le berbis;
          L'aimal d'argent n'ert pas oubliz,
          Ainz fait le moustre et pent tout gay
          Au chaperon devant le pis:
          C'est la simplesce en noz paiis
          Des moignes et de leur array.   (I, lines 21013–24)

    [From the example that I told to you, a monk can have disquiet if he beautifies himself for the world. He seeks for his use not the hair shirt, but rather the finest woolen materials, together with furs vair and gray, for he disdains sheep's fleece. Enamelled silver jewelry is not forgotten; it makes a show and hangs gaily from his hood in front of his breast. That is the simplicity of the monks and of their array in our country.]

    Mirour de l'Omme, translation by William Burton Wilson (East Lansing, 1992).
84 *The Plowman's Tale* in *Six Ecclesiastical Satires*, ed. James M. Dean (Kalamazoo, 1991), p. 90. The Pelican also complains about monks dressed in a manner 'queynte and curious' who wear mitres, rings, double worsted, and fine clothes (lines 1001–2, 1013–14).
85 Baldwin, pp. 49–50; *Statutes* 1:381, Item XII. As mentioned earlier in Chapter 1, p. 15, no records of court cases have been found; the sumptuary laws can only be seen as indicating the standards that certain members of the ruling class wished to maintain, not as standards that could be maintained.

with their abbot.[86] This is not to excuse Daun Piers from accusations of vanity, but to suggest that his costume reflects precisely that attitude of spiritual accommodation to the world revealed in his speech, and, I speculate, which possibly could have been shared, or at least tolerated, by his abbot.

This possibility gains further credence if we acknowledge the ambiguity of the love knot, which symbolizes the *summum bonum* or spiritual grace, as well as devoted worldly love. We may agree with Peter Taitt that this image 'keeps before the reader the shadow of the Ideal of service to God behind the portrait of the real Monk busy in the world of man'.[87] At the same time we acknowledge, as Ramona Bressie does, that the pin may signify the Monk's membership in a religious fraternity such as the Corpus Christi guild of Leicester (Plate 8),[88] although even this would have been deplored by Wyclif who, possibly commenting on the prescribed cincture of the religious habit, deplored 'knottis that bitokenen penaunce hongynge before fro the bodi' that 'ben signes of ypocrisie & noon other holynesse'.[89] And we know that love knots such as the Monk wears were worn for both religious and secular purposes.[90]

While we cannot ignore the possible association of Daun Piers' love knot with other amatory secular images in his portrait – for example, his 'lust' for hunting hare, the soft hunt,[91] which suggests a connection with those

---

[86] See [Delatte] *Rule of St Benedict*, pp. 246–7, 346.

[87] Taitt, p. 50; see p. 203, n. 43, for a list of love knots in secular literature.

[88] Bressie, p. 488. Nichols, 1:353–4, pl. 31, no. 14, provides a drawing of this love knot (reproduced in my Plate 8).

[89] Wyclif, *English Works*, pp. 315–16.

[90] For example, knights of the Order of 'St Esprit au Droit Désir ou du Noeud' (established at Naples by Louis of Anjou, 1352), whose motto was ' "Le Dieu Plait" ', wore a 'peculiar' embroidered knot of purple silk and gold threads, and Richard II's Queen Anne (d.1394) frequently wore an embroidered love knot badge, as may be seen on her effigy in Westminster Abbey, according to Herbert Norris, *Costume & Fashion: Senlac to Bosworth 1066–1485* (New York, 1950), 2:227, 253–4. See Ronald W. Lightbown, *Mediaeval European Jewellery: with a catalogue of the collection in the Victoria & Albert Museum* ([London]: 1992), pp. 255–6, for a discussion of the knot of Solomon worn by the Order of 'St Esprit du Droit Désir' and its significance of fraternal love that unifies all, as well as its symbolism when tied and untied. See also the iconographic uses of knots by certain families, such as the Bourchier knot on the tomb of Archbishop Thomas Bourchier at Canterbury, as mentioned by W. H. St John Hope, *Heraldry for Craftsmen and Designers* (New York, 1913), pp. 184–8; and Mayo's description, p. 51, of a black damask vestment embroidered with several designs including lovers' knots, as listed in the Benedictine nunnery at Langley in the 1485 inventory.

[91] Concerning the 'soft hunt', see D. W. Robertson, Jr, *A Preface to Chaucer* (Princeton, 1973), pp. 263–4. Dolores Warwick Frese, 'The Names of Women in the *CT* [sic]: Chaucer's Hidden Art of Involucral Nomenclature', in *A Wyf Ther Was: Essays in Honour of Paule Mertens-Fonck*, ed. Juliette Dor (Liège, 1992), pp. 161–2, symbolically links the Monk's brooch with its love knot and the Prioress's brooch, and both with the history of Abelard and Heloise.

8. Sketch of the knot emblem of Corpus Christi Guild of Leicester, after John Nichols' depiction of the engraving in *History and Antiquities of the County of Leicester*, plate 31, no. 14.

amorous monks in literature such as the one in Chaucer's *Shipman's Tale* – nevertheless, we cannot dismiss the possibility that this monk wears a gold pin with love knot in the end for both utilitarian and/or fraternal purposes. This uncertainty only serves to place the image in that middle ground discussed earlier, and to further illustrate the duality in the spiritual–secular role of monk-outrider.

One last detail of note is Chaucer's designation of the Monk's pin as 'ful curious'. Here we clearly have a derogatory comment, for elsewhere the connotations of 'curious' are mostly negative. The king's concubines in the *Pearl* Poet's *Cleanness* wear 'curious wedez' (line 1353); similarly, 'antecrist' and followers, in contrast to Christ's having no place to rest, have 'many coriouse and rich'[92] ['many' presumably refers to places to rest], according to the MED, which defines the adjective *curious*, when used to describe things, as: 'carefully, skillfully, artistically, or elaborately designed or made; artistic,

92 The MED cites *Sycl. Antichr* (2), p. cxli.

exquisite, fine; costly, sumptuous'. And while care and skill in the design or making are not objectionable, the rest of this definition explains why medieval writers found *curious* to be the proper adjective to describe the worldly possessions of concubines and antichrist. As Petrus Cantor states, 'in the superfluity and curiousness of raiment and food, the labour of nature is perverted'.[93] That Chaucer describes the Monk's pin as 'ful curious' reveals his opinion clearly.

The monk's pin, then, may be utilitarian; it may be gold in a society in which Chaucer depicts a yeoman-forester wearing a silver St Christopher medal; it may signify a religious fraternal membership, but even so, with his designation of 'ful curious' Chaucer tells us that he thinks it is too much.[94] Yet during this period such pins were frequently worn by the clergy, as witness the previously mentioned Robert Waltham (Plate 7), Precentor of Salisbury, in elbow-length fur cape (with pendant tails at the lower edge) secured at the neck by a gold pin.[95] The argument that 'many of the medieval clergy did it' does not, of course, excuse Daun Piers, but his pin, 'ful curious' though it may be, his sleeves purfled with *grys*, and his supple boots all serve to place his costume in the midst of the common clerical practice of his time. Collectively this costume is more restrained than his tastes in dining, hunting, and possibly in women, would lead us to expect.

The implications of this reconsideration of the Monk's costume are threefold. First, it acknowledges the variety of dress actually worn during the Middle Ages by those in religious orders. Secondly, it illustrates the degree to which such variety was either tolerated or embraced by many church authorities, while recognizing the humble practices of more ascetic monks. And, finally, it sheds light on Chaucer's appeal to costume associations in the minds of his fourteenth-century audience made through the complex pattern of costume rhetoric in the *General Prologue*.

[93] Trans. in Coulton, *Life in the Middle Ages* 2:25–6, from *Verbum Abbreviatum, PL* 205: 255. Petrus Cantor objects, as well, to 'bigness and curiousness and costliness' in architecture because they are excessive.

[94] Lightbown, p. 95, characterizes Chaucer's description of the Monk's pin as 'sly', and quotes the Franciscan treatise *Dives et Pauper* (written between 1405 and c.1410), that denounces men in religious orders, including monks who wear large gold or silver fastenings on their copes. But Lightbown acknowledges that 'there is evidence from wills, sources which cannot be suspected of satirical or moralising exaggeration, that many English clerics of the fourteenth and fifteenth century had jewellery'. Examples cited also include richly decorated girdles and elaborate paternosters (which Lightbown considers to be jewelry). He discusses the 'indispensable' nature of brooches, p. 136. But see Joan Evans' ideas, in *A History of Jewellery 1100–1870* (Boston, 1970), p. 40, concerning personal jewelry worn only as ornament, as distinguished from religious articles made of gems or semi-precious materials, but not termed *jewelry*, mentioned in Chapter 3, p. 105, n. 90.

[95] Golden Book of St Alban's, BL MS Cott. Nero D VII, fol. 105v (c.1380).

He does not, uniformly, give us a character type in standard illustrative clothing. This is not to say that Chaucer abandoned the literary context of estates satire in this portrait for absolute realism when he began to describe the Monk's clothing. However, Chaucer's costume rhetoric here does not bear the marks of satirical exaggeration, even though the kinds of costume signs he mentions may be found, individually and in some combinations, in satires. For example the Monk wears only a trimming of *grys* on his sleeves, not the full cloak of this fur or the secular fur-trimmed tunic described in satires. We learn that he wears boots for riding, not that he possesses an entire wardrobe of footwear (although, realistically, the storerooms of a monastery might contain such a variety of appropriate shoes for all occasions). Daun Piers wears a curious gold pin as a hood fastening, not as the ornament on his hood, a practice about which Gower complains. And Chaucer's Monk wears no non-regulation woolen fabrics such as the double worsted worn by the Friar, no russet, and no silk, fabrics often mentioned by satirists.

The fact that his sartorial deviations are lesser than those usually presented through satirical exaggeration has been obscured because the Monk does fit handily into the estates satire general mold. However, Chaucer's description, in fact, bears at least as much similarity to those in monastic visitation injunctions as it does to those in satires. Perhaps he realized that the ordinary dress of contemporary monks was ironic enough without needing exaggeration. Or, possibly, he wished to establish a hierarchy of costume deviations in which the Friar and Pardoner are guilty of the greater clothing deviations. In any case, in the portrait of the Monk, through judicious selection of costume details, Chaucer aptly portrays Daun Piers' intellectual accommodation to spiritual/worldly duties. As he serves God and man, Daun Piers wears a habit that is neither as spiritual nor as worldly as it might be.

5

Chaucer's Friar: 'typet' and 'semycope'[1]

In his *General Prologue*, Chaucer clothes Friar Huberd in a combination of garment signs surely chosen with satire in mind[2] and then amplifies this costume sentence with *systrophe*, the rhetorical technique of 'heaping up descriptions of a thing without defining it'.[3] The effect of these collective images is exceptionally strong. In this costume portrayal, Chaucer literally 'spells it out' that anyone who could be fooled by such a Friar's beguiling speech and merry manner would have to both deny the visual evidence of his dress, which flouts the fraternal ideal, and refuse to give this image the name it deserves. Rather than utilize the standard antifraternal metaphor of 'wolf in sheep's clothing', Chaucer's satire clarifies and delineates this Friar in a parade of fresh costume details, doubly damning him as a wolf in *wolf's* clothing, wearing the clearly recognizable garments of Greed that convey the signs of his vices, 'covetyse', 'doublenesse', and lechery.

Chaucer presents his description of the Friar's costume and accoutrements in two passages separated by twenty-six lines that recount his musical skill, his knowledge of taverns and their owners, his unctuous and successful prowess in begging, and his sporting on 'love-dayes'. The first costume passage describes the Friar's headgear (I, lines 233–4) while the second (lines 259–63) gives an account of his cloak. Following Chaucer's two-part division, this analysis of Chaucer's costume rhetoric, informed by examples from its historical and literary context, will deal first with the Friar's 'typet' that is

---

1 An earlier and shorter version of this chapter appeared in *ChauR* 34.3 (2000), pp. 317–43.

2 Jill Mann remarks, 'More than other satirists, Chaucer emphasizes the [Friar's] facade rather than the deceptive intent behind it', and 'we are given no firm basis for moral judgement', regarding his character and actions, in *Chaucer and Medieval Estates Satire: The Literature of Social Classes and the General Prologue to the Canterbury Tales* (Cambridge, 1973), pp. 39–40. Mann's statement may be true in general; however, in his ruthless treatment of the Friar's 'facade', specifically his costume, Chaucer more than makes up for any other comparatively gentle treatment in this portrait.

3 Definition from Richard A. Lanham, *A Handlist of Rhetorical Terms* (Berkeley, CA, 1969), p. 119.

stuffed with knives and pins, then with his bell-shaped, double worsted 'semycope', and finally with a consideration of their combination in one costume and the costume rhetoric employed by Chaucer.

In the first passage, Chaucer's multifaceted images of the Friar's tippet filled with knives and pins constitute a description that can hold its own among the most scathing antifraternal commentaries in medieval literature:

> His typet was ay farsed ful of knyves
> And pynnes, for to yeven faire wyves.   (lines 233–4)

Since the term *typet* has more than one meaning, we must first determine which of these was the most likely one behind Chaucer's choice of diction. A tippet is defined as a 'pendant streamer from the hood or from the arm' or 'a shoulder cape'.[4] If Chaucer meant 'pendant streamer', more properly called a *liripipe*, he has given the Friar a garment that, by c.1387, was not a new fashion;[5] however, such an appendage was in and out of style through the time of Henry VII.[6] Such a garment would have signified *vanitas, superbia*, and by extension *luxuria* had it been worn by a friar, for example, in 1340 when it was fashionable; even worse, by 1387 it would have suggested a comparison with fools and jesters, in whose costumes liripipes were featured.[7]

---

4   Mary G. Houston, *Medieval Costume in England & France: The 13th, 14th and 15th Centuries* (London, 1965), pp. 109, 225, and figs 197 and 198 (citing BL MS Roy. 19 D2). Muriel Bowden, *A Commentary on the General Prologue to the Canterbury Tales*, 2nd edn (New York, 1967), p. 125, citing the MED, defines a tippet as 'a long, narrow strip of cloth, either attached at one end to the hood or sleeve, or hanging loose as a scarf; it might also be a cape with hanging ends', and she speculates that the Friar's 'was probably of the first variety and must have been of two thicknesses since he employs it as an elongated pouch'. See also James Robinson Planché, *An Illustrated Dictionary of Historic Costume: From the First Century B.C. to c. 1760* (Mineola, NY, 2003), pp. 342 and 504 for definitions of *liripipe* and *tippet*; pp. 291–5 for descriptions of hoods with these appendages.

5   Herbert Norris, *Costume & Fashion: Senlac to Bosworth 1066–1485* (New York, 1950), 2:227; see rpt. *Medieval Costume and Fashion* (Mineola, NY, 1999), pp. 177, 211, 213, 227, 250, 262.

6   See also Gilbert J. French, *The Tippets of the Canons Ecclesiastical* (London, 1850), pp. 1–4, and his discussion of the length of a tippet as a sign of status. Also see F. E. Brightman's description of the hood (*caputium*) with a 'poke', as it appears on funerary brasses, quoted by Robert W. T. Günther, Preface, 'A Description of Brasses and other Funeral Monuments in the Chapel', *A Register of the Members of St. Mary Magdalen College, Oxford* n.s. 8, ed. William Dunn Macray (London, 1915), pp. v–vi.

7   Fools and jesters continued to wear these appendages. Possibly, Chaucer had this sartorial trend in mind when he bestowed a tippet upon Huberd. See Carla Casagrande and Silvana Becchio, 'Clercs et jongleurs dans la société medievale (XIIe–XIIIe siècles)', *Annales économies, sociétés, civilisations* 34.5 (1979), pp. 913–28, esp. 919–22, regarding the generally negative treatment of *jongleurs* as the image is applied to Franciscans – the image of 'jongleur de Dieu'; also Ruth Mellinkoff, *Outcasts: Signs of*

However, it is unlikely that this out-of-fashion layman's garment, completely unrelated to the fraternal habit, was the 'typet' Chaucer had in mind, even though such pendants might offer a handy storage place for the Friar's knives and pins. 'A shoulder cape', with a deep hood such as that depicted in Color Plate IV,[8] is the more likely meaning since a hood[9] is part of a friar's standard habit. The Ellesmere illumination of the Friar depicts such a deep-pointed hood, hanging halfway down his back, deep enough to transport knives and pins, but not nearly long enough to use as a scarf. In the same manuscript, the depiction of the Nun's Priest does include a tippet long enough to use as a scarf; he wears a red hat and his hood is around his neck with the tippet hanging down.

Highly significant to our analysis of Chaucer's costume rhetoric, Chaucer's employment of Huberd's tippet as a costume sign is a unique contribution to friars' costumes in the antifraternal literary tradition, c.1387. In earlier antifraternal poems, friars' habits and friars' love of fine clothing are often mentioned. The standard costume complaint against friars is that they have enlarged hems on their copes, meaning that they have used too much fabric and are therefore prideful.[10] I have found no extant poem that mentions a

Otherness in Northern European Art of the Late Middle Ages, 2 vols (Berkeley, CA, 1993), 1:231, and in vol. 2, fig. VI.56; the fool in this picture is a mocker of Christ.

8   The Taymouth Hours, BL MS Yates Thompson 13, fol. 177. See also, Kathleen Scott, Catalogue of Illustrations. *Piers Plowman: A Facsimile of Bodleian Library, Oxford, MS Douce 104*, Derek Pearsall, Introduction (Cambridge, 1992), p. xliii, regarding the chaperon with liripipe worn by the figure of Conscience in the C version of *Piers Plowman*; Francis M. Kelly and Randolph Schwabe, *A Short History of Costume and Armour Chiefly in England* (London, 1931; [New York], 1968), 1:30–1, concerning the liripipe; Dorothy R. Hartley, *Mediaeval Costume and Life* (London, 1931), pp. 89–93, for hoods and liripipes, and pl. 9 #C, for the black and white reproduction from the fourteenth-century BL MS Roy. 16 G VI, depicting a hood.

9   Concerning hoods, see W. N. Hargreaves-Mawdsley, *A History of Academical Dress in Europe until the End of the Eighteenth Century* (Oxford, 1963; rpt. Westport, CT, 1978), pp. 6–7.

10 Regarding attitudes toward religious habits that are too wide or too long illustrating pride, see Chapters 1 and 4, pp. 17–24, 123; also see John Wyclif, *The English Works of Wyclif Hitherto Unprinted*, ed. F. D. Matthew, EETS, OS 74 (London, 1880; 1896), pp. 315–16. The Pelican in *The Plowman's Tale* in *Six Ecclesiastical Satires*, ed. James M. Dean (Kalamazoo, MI, 1991), complains about religious garments that are wide because of pockets that are too wide:
    'Now ben prestes pokes so wyde
    That men must enlarge the vestement.
    The holy Gospell they done hyde,
    For they contraryen in rayment.
    Suche preestes of Lucifer ben sent:
    Lyke conquerours they ben arayde,
    The proude pendauntes at her ars ypent.
    Falsely the truthe they han betrayde'.   (lines 933–40)
See also friars in large robes discussed in *Pierce the Ploughmans Crede*, trans. and ed.

friar's hood prior to Chaucer, although, in the fifteenth century, 'The Reply of Friar Daw Topias, with Jack Upland's Rejoinder' mentions a 'grete hood' and a 'tipet':

> But if my cloth be over presciouse,
> Jakke, blame the werer;
> ffor myn ordre hath ordeyned
> al in good mesure.
> Thou axist me, Jacke, of my *grete hood.*
> What that it meneth,
> my scapelarie and my wide cope,
> and the knottide girdil.
> What meenith thi *tipet*, Jakke,
> as long as a stremer,
> that hangith longe bihinde
> and kepith thee not hoot?
> . . .
> Why is thi gowne, Jakke,
> widder than thi cote,
> and thi cloke al above
> as round as a belle.[11]   [emphasis added]

Jakke answers these questions with 'My grete coope that is so wiid,/ signifieth charite', an answer that the author of this antifraternal poem expected no one to believe.[12] Clearly, in this poem, Chaucer's original and innovative images are echoed in the 'grete hood' with its tippet and in the bell

Walter W. Skeat, EETS, OS 30 (London, 1867), lines 292–7, 340, esp. 549–53.
    For an opposing image of the large garments worn by Christ, see Sr Ritamary Bradley, 'Metaphors of Cloth and Clothing in the Showings of Julian of Norwich', *Mediaevalia* 9 (1983), pp. 272–3. As Bradley makes clear, Julian characterizes this extra size as ' "blyssefull largenesse" (51.314–17)' and symbolizes it: ' "the largnesse of his clothyng, whych was feyer flammyng about, betokenyth þat he hath becloysd in hym all hevyns and all endlesse joy and blysse" (51.155–57)'.
11 'The Reply of Friar Daw Topias, with Jack Upland's Rejoinder', *Political Poems and Songs Relating to English History, Composed During the Period From the Accession of Edw. III to that of Ric. III*, ed. Thomas Wright (London, 1859; 1861; Germany, 1965), 2:69–70. The MED dates this poem to 1402.
12 Wyclif writes of charity that 'cloþis man at domus-day wiþ bride-cloþis' necessary for any man who wishes to enter heaven and of friars who do not love these 'bride-cloþis' enough, in *The English Works*, pp. 351–2. These brideclothes are the garments of Charity. Also see William Langland, *Piers Plowman: The B Version*, eds George Kane and E. Talbot Donaldson (London, 1975), Passus 15, lines 220–1, 226, 230–1, regarding garments worn by Charity that are made of silk, homespun, sober gray, as well as grys, and with 'gilt harneis', and rags; the description includes the comment that once in St Francis's time Charity was seen wearing a friar's habit.

shape of the cloak. In addition, this conversation provides one reason why a tippet might have been considered sinful: it is superfluous, prideful because it is not used as a scarf for warmth. This suggests that a tippet with a long point to the hood, a fifteenth-century style (of the sort that might be worn wrapped about either the head or neck), is referred to in this poem.

The satire of Friar Huberd's hood benefits from the irony of Chaucer's factual depiction of a religious garment that has been converted to such usage as a peddler might give it – converted and perverted at the same time. The extent of this perversion may be seen in the contrast between Huberd's garments and the inspiration behind the original Franciscan habit.[13] St Francis conceived the plan for his order based on the idea of evangelical poverty in the biblical texts of Luke 10:1–12, as well as Matthew 10:5–15, and Mark 6:7–13.[14] According to Bonaventura's *Legenda major*, St Francis attended Mass on an apostle's feast day and heard an account of Christ's instructions for living given to the apostles:

> they were not to provide gold or silver or copper to fill their purses, . . . they were not to have a wallet for the journey or a second coat, no shoes or staff.[15] . . . There and then he [St Francis] took off his shoes and laid aside his staff. He conceived a horror of money or wealth of any kind and he wore only one tunic, changing his leather belt for a rope. The whole desire

---

13 Chaucer portrays 'the *genus Frater*', as noted by John S. P. Tatlock, 'The Date of the *Troilus* and Minor Chauceriana', *MLN* 50 (1935), p. 292. I use the story of the Franciscan habit's origin in this chapter as an example of the theology and symbolism behind fraternal habits.

14 Luke 10:1–12 presents Christ's instructions to the apostles regarding the practice of poverty as he sends them forth 'as lambs among wolves' (10:3). These instructions include the dictum, 'Carry neither purse, nor scrip, nor shoes' (10:4). Matthew 10:5–15 also provides instructions, saying, 'Do not possess gold, nor silver, nor money in your purses: Nor scrip for your journey, nor two coats, nor shoes, nor a staff' (10:9–10). Mark 6:7–13 is more lenient, stating, 'that they should take nothing for the way, but a staff only: no scrip, no bread, nor money in their purse, But . . . [they might] be shod with sandals, and that they should not put on two coats' (6:8–9). Quotations are taken from the Holy Bible, Douay Rheims Version, 1899; rpt. 1971.

15 See P. R. Szittya's comments concerning friars in the *Summoner's Tale* who carry scrip, staff, and sack, in *The Antifraternal Tradition* (Princeton, 1986), p. 243. I owe a debt of gratitude to Szittya for this book and for an additional article, cited later; his comprehensive treatment of the history of vilification of the friars known as 'the antifraternal tradition' has smoothed the way for my analysis of the costume rhetoric of the Friar's portrait. Also on the antifraternal tradition, see Nicolas Havely, 'Chaucer, Boccaccio, and the Friars', *Chaucer and the Italian Trecento*, ed. Piero Boitani (Cambridge, 1983), pp. 249–68.

For discussion of habits, violations of habits, and the rule concerning the owning of personal property, see John R. H. Moorman, *A History of the Franciscan Order* (Oxford, 1968; rpt. 1988), pp. 356–9.

of his heart was to put what he had heard into practice[16] and conform to the rule of life given to the Apostles in everything.[17]

Early Franciscan friars wore this same humble habit and practiced poverty; as a result, they 'contrasted sharply with the sometimes ostentatious worldliness of the parish clergy'.[18]

A detailed account of the Franciscan habit may be seen in *Monumenta Franciscana*:

> They whiche arre professid and haue promysed obedience shalle haue oone cote with a hode . . . and a nother withoute a hoode that wille have yt, and suche as haue nede or as ar constreynyd by necessyte may were shoone. . . . And alle the bretherne must be clothid with symple and vyle clothinge. . . . And they may pece them and amende them with pecis of sak clothe, or with other pecis,[19] with the blissyng of God.[20]

---

[16] An illustration in the margin of the *Taymouth Hours*, English c.1325, BL MS Yates Thompson 13, fol. 180v, shows St Francis in the act of constructing his own habit. Joan Evans, ed., *The Flowering of the Middle Ages* (New York, 1966), p. 31, provides a line drawing of this illustration. The pointed hood is commodious.

[17] Trans. from *St Francis of Assisi: Writings and Early Biographies*, ed. Marion Habig (Chicago, 1973), pp. 646–7, of a passage from St Bonaventura, *Opera omnia*, vol. 8 (Quaracchi, 1898), p. 510 (chapter 3, paras 1–2), as quoted in Szittya, *The Antifraternal Tradition*, pp. 43–4.

[18] Szittya, *The Antifraternal Tradition*, p. 8.

[19] St Francis's dark gray (undyed) cowl was pieced with fabric taken from St Clare's mantle, as discussed and illustrated with photographs in pp. 314–17, in Mechtild Flury-Lemberg, *Textile Conservation and Research* (Bern, 1988). Flury-Lemberg, p. 316, comments on St Francis's Rule, which allows friars 'clothing of little value' that they could 'reinforce . . . with coarse cloth'.

[20] Middle English trans. of the Rule of St Francis in BL Cott. MS Faustina D. IV, fifteenth century, included in *Monumenta Franciscana*, ed. Richard Howlett (London, 1882; rpt., 1965), 2:67; see also Sr Mary Ernestine Whitmore, *Medieval English Domestic Life and Amusements in the works of Chaucer* (New York, 1972), pp. 165–6.

The style of the Franciscan habit is shown in *Psalterium in Usum Regis Henrici VI*, BL MS Cott. Dom. A XVII, fol. 122b. Friars seated in choir stalls wear black hoods, black loose robes with loose sleeves, cord girdles with knots showing, and black sandals. Numerous manuscript illuminations contain pictures of friars. Among them are a depiction of a novice acquiring the habit in the French, late thirteenth century, BL MS Harl. 1527, fol. 33r, and four roundels illustrating the four orders of friars in the French, c.1470, MS Lat. 1176, fol. 132r, reproduced in Evans, p. 50; the picture of a Dominican friar hearing confession, fol. 74, and two Dominican friars being entertained at dinner, in the Luttrell Psalter, BL MS Add. 42130, fol. 208. Scott, pp. lix and lxviii–lxix, describes friars in the illuminations of Bodleian Library, Oxford, MS Douce 104: a Franciscan friar on fol. 46r and possibly a Carmelite friar ('false friar') on fol. 67v. Habits portrayed in illuminations illustrating the antifraternal tradition in the visual arts include Franciscan and Dominican friars with devils, illustrations in Richard FitzRalph, *De pauperie Salvatoris*, Corpus Christi College MS 180, fol. 1, reproduced in Miller, p. 254, fig. 8 (and my Color Plate IV), about which Robert P. Miller comments, 'Note the "Nicholas approach" ' (of *MT* 3276), in his edition of

'The very frock to which the Franciscans clung with an almost superstitious reverence was originally just a poor peasant's natural dress', declares G. G. Coulton.[21] While nothing in Huberd's portrait identifies him with a particular order of friars, this Middle English description of the Franciscan habit portrays the kind of simple, pious habit with hood, a hood which, according to the costume rhetoric in Chaucer's portrait, Huberd converts to the equivalent of the traveling salesman's satchel. The regulation disallowing a wallet[22] to friars obviously did not pose an obstacle to Huberd's transporting of salable items.

Precisely through this perversion of the friar's hood and in the selective naming of the goods it transports, the knives and pins, Chaucer's satire makes an innovative and telling point. Chaucer has not called the Friar a 'vaga-

---

Chaucer: Sources and Backgrounds (New York, 1977), p. 239, fig. 7.

For information on brasses of friars in habit, see H. W. Macklin, *The Brasses of England* (London, 1907), pp. 130–1, 133–5.

21 G. G. Coulton, *The Chronicler of European Chivalry* (London, 1930), p. 15. For additional comments, see G. G. Coulton's *Studies in Medieval Thought* (New York, 1965), pp. 158–60. Regarding the superstitious reverence for this 'frock', and customs allowing laypersons to wear it for burial, see Moorman, p. 355 and nn. 3–5.

Regarding regulations for proper habits, see also *Decalogus evangelice paupertatis*, ed. Michael Bihl, O.F.M., *Archivum Franciscanum Historicum* 32 (1939), pp. 330–411, esp. 333 for Ratio III.2; Edward L. Cutts, *Scenes & Characters of the Middle Ages*, 7th edn (London, 1930), p. 42 for the Franciscan habit, p. 43 for Carmelite habit, p. 44 for Austin and Crutched Friars habits. Of the Franciscan habit, he states that it includes a gray tunic with long, loose sleeves (not as loose as the Benedictines'), knotted cord for the girdle, a black hood; a friar might be barefooted or wear sandals. The color was changed from gray to dark brown in the fifteenth century. Also see Janet Mayo, *A History of Ecclesiastical Dress* (New York, 1984), pp. 33–4, regarding the cowl; pp. 37–8, concerning the habits of different preaching orders.

BL MS Harl. 1527, fol. 112b, includes a picture of the four orders of friars: Dominicans, Franciscans, Carmelites, Augustines; a line drawing of this picture is in Cutts, p. 39; see also Evans' reproduction of roundels, fol. 33r, from this same manuscript, mentioned in n. 20 above.

22 See Szittya, *The Antifraternal Tradition*, pp. 47, 49–50, for comments on carrying a bag. Chaucer does not give Huberd a purse or wallet (as he does the Pardoner); thus in the Friar's portrait he avoids the controversial issue of whether or not the Friars should carry purses and the iconographical association of Judas and purses, discussed in John V. Fleming, *An Introduction to Franciscan Literature of the Middle Ages* (Chicago, 1977), pp. 87–8. See also Fleming's comments in 'Chaucer's Ascetical Images', *C&L* 28.4 (1979), pp. 24–5, in which he cites John 12:6 on the subject of purses and notes Chaucer's knowledge of the subject expressed in the Friar's comment regarding the Summoner depicted in his tale: 'And right as Judas hadde purses smale,/ And was a theef, right swich a theef was he' (1350–1); regarding Chaucer's knowledge of the purse issue, see John V. Fleming, 'Gospel Asceticism: Some Chaucerian Images of Perfection', *Chaucer and Scriptural Tradition*, ed. David Lyle Jeffrey (Ottawa, 1984), pp. 188–9. For a discussion of the tradition of Judas' purse in the visual arts, see Mellinkoff 1:51–2, 134–5, 150–1, with corresponding color reproductions in vol. 2.

bond',[23] or a 'peddler',[24] or a 'wolf in sheep's clothing';[25] instead, he depicts Huberd, by means of the perverted hood, as a vagabond, a peddler. Peddlers are described in much the same terms as those Chaucer employs for Huberd: 'jovial', 'light-hearted', possessed of 'good humour and jollity . . . gaity',

23 John Gower, *Mirour de l'omme, Complete Works of John Gower*, ed. G. C. Macaulay (Oxford, 1899; 1968), 1:21325–84, describes friars, 'mendiantz' who go from door to door, 'Qui portera le sac derere', flattering, hearing confessions, and begging.
24 Making this charge is 'A Song Against the Friars' in Thomas Wright, ed., *Political Poems and Songs, Composed during the Period From the Accession of Edw. III. to that of Ric. III.* (London, 1859; rpt. Germany, 1965), 1:264:

> For thai have noght to lyve by,
>   thai wandren here and there,
> And dele with dyvers marcerye,
>   right as thai pedlers were.

Also, *Pierce the Ploughmans Crede* speaks of friars who have 'spicerie sprad in her purse · to parten where hem lust' (301).

See also, Szittya's comments, *The Antifraternal Tradition*, p. 227, and n. 120, for additional poetic instances of equating friars with peddlers.
25 John Gower, in *Vox clamantis, Complete Works* (1902; 1968), vol. 4, IV, 17.797–800, speaks of a friar in his habit as a wolf in sheep's clothing:

> Sic mundana tenet qui spernit in ordine mundum,
> Dum tegit hostilem vestis ouina lupum;
> Et sic ficticiis plubs incantata putabit
> Sanctos exterius, quos dolus intus habet.

Pierce the Ploughmans Crede, too, mentions 'wer-wolues' '*In vestimentis ouium*' (lines 458–9). Scott, pp. lvii–lix, discusses such images in the text and illuminations for the C version of *Piers Plowman*. See also Szittya, *The Antifraternal Tradition*, p. 54, regarding William of St Amour's use of wolves imagery; p. 176, for Wyclif's use of this image; also pp. 211–12, for Henryson's treatment that compares the wolf/friar false confessor:

> ʒour bair feit, and ʒour russet coull off gray,
> ʒour lene cheik, ʒour paill pietious face,
> Schawis to me ʒour perfite halines.   (lines 679–81)

Another animal image connected with friars is the fox. Floor tiles (nineteenth-century copies of thirteenth-century originals) in Christ Church Cathedral, Dublin, picture a fox in friar's habit, wearing a broad hat, a scrip, and carrying a 'bourdon'. These are 'begging friars', according to A. E. Stokes, *Christ Church Cathedral, Dublin*, The Irish Heritage Series, no. 12 (n.p., n.d.), pp. 2–4 (with picture). Such depictions symbolized greed, among other things. A more graphic portrayal of greed may be seen in a grotesque, possibly depicting a friar, in the right margin of the Luttrell Psalter, BL MS Add. 42130, fol. 180. The grotesque possesses the head and shoulders of a man in a tan hood, an animal body that is parti-colored with blue on the left side and white on the right. This animal has a hooked-nose animal face in place of a belly, and a fish tail protruding from its back.

Regarding the implications of the name Huberd and its associations with the *Roman de Renard* and the sin of greed, see Alain Renoir, 'Bayard and Troilus: Chaucerian Non-paradox in the Reader', *Orbis Litterarum* 36.2 (1981), p. 128; P. Burwell Rogers, 'The Names of the Canterbury Pilgrims', *Names* 16 (1968), p. 341; Charles Muscatine, 'The Name of Chaucer's Friar', *MLN* 70 (Mar. 1955), pp. 169–72.

'merry and sharp-tongued', according to J. J. Jusserand. Jusserand derives this characterization from a description in the first statute known as 'an acte for tynkers and pedlers' (5 and 6 Ed. VI) that stated:

> For as muche as it is evident that tynkers, pedlers and suche like vagrant persons are more hurtful than necessaries to the Common Wealth of this realm, . . . no person or persons commonly called pedler, tynker or petty chapman shall wander or go from one towne to another or from place to place out of the towne, parishe or village where such person shall dwell, and sell pynnes, poyntes, laces, gloves, knyves, glasses, tapes or any suche kynde of wares whatsoever, or gather connye skynnes or such like things or use or exercise the trade or occupation of a tynker . . . [unless they are licensed properly].[26]

Although this statute was enacted some time after Chaucer wrote the Friar's portrait, we note that pins and knives were still among the desirable wares[27] that itinerant peddlers hawked.

In addition, Chaucer heightens the negative effect of the peddler imagery by limiting the goods sold by Huberd, rather than naming many items of 'dyvers marcerye' such as are listed in the 'Song Against the Friars' (c.1380):

> Thai dele with purses, pynnes, and knyves,
> With gyrdles, gloves, for wenches and wyves; . . .
> Somme frers beren pelure aboute,
> For grete ladys and wenches stoute,
> To reverce with thair clothes withoute; . . .
> For somme vaire, and somme gryse,
> For somme bugee, and for somme byse,
> And also many a dyvers spyse,
> In bagges about thai bere.[28]

In having such a list of expensive merchandise, these friars have a variety of business dealings comparable to those one might expect of Chaucer's Merchant. In contrast, Chaucer depicts Friar Huberd as merely a peddler of knives and pins, which demeans him doubly. The Friar, in his perverted hood, is only a paltry peddler.

---

[26] J. J. Jusserand, *English Wayfaring Life in the Middle Ages: XIVth Century*, 3rd edn, trans. Lucy Toulmin Smith (London, 1925), pp. 234–6, citing the law enacted 5 and 6 Ed. VI, ch. 21, recorded in *Statutes*, vol. iv. part i. p. 155.

[27] Concerning the considerable persuasive powers of a gift of pins, see Mary Andere, *Old Needlework Boxes and Tools* (Plymouth, 1971), pp. 42–5. Regarding knives as 'traditional gauds', used by bawds to curry favor, see George J. Engelhardt, 'The Ecclesiastical Pilgrims of the *Canterbury Tales*: A Study in Ethology', *MS* (Toronto) 37 (1975), p. 305. See also, N. R. Havely, 'Chaucer's Friar and Merchant', *ChauR* 13 (1979), pp. 337–45, who comments on 'the mercantile language and allusions' in this portrait.

[28] 'Song Against the Friars', in *Political Poems and Songs*, 1:264–5.

This is by no means the full significance of these knives and pins, however. Of far greater import is the idea that, in this limited choice of goods, the Friar's pins and knives, which are literally instruments of penetration, Chaucer symbolizes the penetration mentioned in II Timothy 3:1–6 in the phrase '[those] who make their way into houses [*qui penetrant domos*]'. This is a point that has not previously been noted by critics. This phrase was commonly interpreted in the antifraternal tradition to characterize those friars who entered homes to corrupt wives sensually and sexually, and those who entered the ' "interior" house' of a person's conscience (through hearing confessions) without, as the secular clergy viewed the matter, the authority of proper apostolic descent, even though papal authority had been granted. In this tradition, those friars[29] constituted a sign of the approach of the end of the world.[30] These standard antifraternal ideas inform Chaucer's explanation of the Friar's knives and pins: 'for to yeven faire wyves'.

Chaucer's unique approach reflects the same ideas presented allegorically by William Langland, as P. R. Szittya comments:

> In the apocalyptic ending of *Piers Plowman*, as the forces of Antichrist muster, the door of the church is suddenly darkened by a friar with an enigmatic name: Sire *Penetrans Domos*. *Penetrans Domos* is not just a name but a text. It is a snatch from an eschatological passage in the New Testament, where St Paul warns Timothy about the dangers in the last days of the world: 'But know this, that in the last days dangerous times will come. Men will be lovers of self, covetous, haughty, proud . . . having a semblance indeed of piety, but disowning its power. Avoid these. For of such are they who make their way into houses [*qui penetrant domos*]'.
>
> (II Timothy 3:1–6)

Szittya is careful to explain that Langland's 'Sire *Penetrans Domos* is no ordinary friar', but rather he is the 'symbolic Antichrist who menaces the church at the end of Langland's poem . . . [and] a signal that the Last Days are beginning'.[31]

---

29   The antifraternal tradition included four negative biblical types with which friars were equated, although not always in specific words: the Pharisees, the pseudoapostles, the Antichrist, and 'those who violate the divine ordinance of "measure, number, and weight" of Wisdom 11.21', according to Penn R. Szittya, 'The Antifraternal Tradition in Middle English Literature', *Speculum* 52 (1977), p. 290. See also Szittya, *The Antifraternal Tradition*, pp. 34–61.

30   Szittya, *The Antifraternal Tradition*, pp. 9, 217–18, 247, 284–5. See Scott's description, pp. lxxix–lxxx, of the illumination of Sire *Penetrans Domos* in Bodleian Library MS Douce 104, fol. 111v, illustrating the C version of *PP*, Passus 22, lines 335–48; and John B. Friedman, 'The Friar Portrait in Bodleian Library MS Douce 104: Contemporary Satire', *YLS* 8 (1995), pp. 177–85, for a discussion of the jordan's significance in the illumination of fol. 111v.

31   Szittya, *The Antifraternal Tradition*, p. 3.

In contrast to Langland's work, Chaucer's portrait has no such complicated plot, but he has labeled his friar just as surely: in the perverted hood of
his religious habit, and his literal wearing/carrying of knives and pins for the
stated purpose of giving them to attractive wives, the Friar is Sire *Penetrans
Domos*, although he is called Huberd, a French name perhaps significant of
the French origin of the antifraternal tradition.[32]

Further, taken literally, the image of the Friar's tippet filled with pins and
knives equates him with a second set of negative associations attached to
peddlers, who are men of no fixed abode and therefore owe loyalty to no
fixed civil law or moral code. The disreputable lack of civil connections for
itinerants is paralleled by the lack of apostolic succession, lack of proper
place in the church hierarchy, and lack of fixed geographical locus (such as a
parish for the priest or diocese for the bishop) – all matters for which friars
are severely criticized in the large body of antifraternal literature of the late
Middle Ages, and named Sire *Penetrans Domos*.

Chaucer's subtle technique in his costume rhetoric, almost without the
reader's notice, directs attention away from the issue of type or style of
garment worn and focuses it instead on the accumulation of negative associations that might be attached to it. Regardless of the style of Huberd's tippet,
Chaucer emphasizes that what is important is the use he makes of it – to
transport gifts for wives and thus to satisfy not only his greed, but also, possibly, his lechery. This emphasis is achieved in Chaucer's *systrophe*. He amplifies the image of the tippet in the predicate adjective that describes its
function as a 'peddler's bag': 'His typet was ay farsed ful of knyves/ And
pynnes' (lines 233–4). Then, in a prepositional phrase, he makes another
amplification, providing Huberd's motivation, 'for to yeven faire wyves' (line
234). The knives and pins apparently served as door-openers, like the free
samples of modern door-to-door salesman; they serve as a key, equally a
means of penetration. To carry this idea further, Chaucer implies through
systrophe and these symbols that penetration occurs on four levels: the Friar
enters the house, he invades a Christian conscience, he gains access to his
victim's purse, and possibly he penetrates sexually.[33] Chaucer suggests that
Huberd's tactics were successful in satisfying both his greed and his lechery
when he depicts this friar as having knowledge of 'daliaunce' (line 211), as
having paid for many young women's marriages (lines 212–13), as being
beloved by 'worthy wommen of the toun' (lines 215–17), and as being able to
separate a poor widow from her last 'ferthyng' (lines 253–5), as well as

---

[32] For a discussion of the French origin of antifraternalism, see Szittya, 'The Antifraternal Tradition in Middle English Literature', pp. 293–5.

[33] A Freudian symbolic interpretation would see knives and pins as not only phallic
imagery, but also see the hood as foreskin covering instrument of penetration, penis.

mentioning his white neck (line 238), a symbol of lechery.[34] These descriptive details surround the lines concerned with the Friar's headwear. And Chaucer underscores these ideas, as well as the fourfold interpretation of the Friar's penetration, given above, in the knives/wives rhyme, just as he illustrates them in the actions of the friar in the *Summoner's Tale* who dallies with his host's wife.

Thus, Chaucer has marked the Friar with the sign of Sire *Penetrans Domos* through his tippet filled with penetrating objects. Friar Huberd is no hypocrite who covers his evil in the proper vestments of holiness (making them *False Vestments)*; instead, in his wearing of a tippet and employment of this hood for his own sinful purposes, Friar Huberd blatantly perverts his friar's habit, normally a sign of poverty and chastity. Such a tippet is a sign that only the spiritually blind could fail to see.[35]

Friar Huberd proclaims his falseness again in a clothing sign from the second passage of costume rhetoric in this portrait: his 'semycope'. In this garment choice, Chaucer diverges from standard antifraternal costume imagery at the same time that he evokes the memory of it. He employs two initial similes and three descriptive terms, one with its own simile; his *systrophe* heaps scorn upon Friar Huberd's cope:

> he was nat lyk a cloysterer
> With a thredbare cope, as is a povre scoler,
> But he was lyk a maister or a pope.
> Of double worstede was his semycope,
> That rounded as a belle out of the press.   (lines 259–63)

In Chaucer's first simile, the Friar is compared negatively to the cloisterer and scholar who do wear the dress of poverty as good friars should. The second simile compares Huberd to a master[36] or pope, but although the com-

---

34 According to Janette Richardson's note to line 238 in *Riverside Chaucer* (citing Horton, *MLN* 48, 1933, pp. 31–4).
35 I am grateful for Lorraine Stock's reminder that Chaucer explores this idea of victims who refuse to see in the *Friar's Tale* of a Summoner who is duped by the pleasant appearance of the Yeoman even though the Yeoman declares that he is the Devil. In addition, this theme is present when the Pardoner demonstrates his contempt for his victims and offers to sell his false relics to the Canterbury pilgrims, who have already been informed of their falsity.
36 See the illumination of a rotund Carmelite friar dining, in Bodleian Library, Oxford, MS Douce 104, fol. 67r, which Scott, p. lxviii, describes as illustrating *Piers Plowman C* 'a mayster, a man lyk a frere' (Passus 15, line 30) who 'was maed sitte furste' (line 39), in the place of honor at the table.
   The 'simple' priest pretending to be a 'master' and being treated accordingly was an issue taken up in the Convocation of the Province of Canterbury, 1460–61, notably in the context of clerical dress. The topic found expression in a mid-fifteenth-century satirical poem, according to Wendy Scase, 'Proud Gallants and Popeholy Priests: The Context and Function of a Fifteenth-Century Satirical Poem', *MÆ* 63.2 (1994),

parison could be true, and initially sounds favorable, the sense of it is negative. Huberd should exhibit his avowed poverty in his cope;[37] instead he
dresses in a style appropriate for someone who, Chaucer implies, has a right
to dress very well. The fact that some friars taught in universities and were
referred to as masters is treated here as if it were simply another instance of
fraternal usurpation of roles such as those of hearing confession and soliciting funds within parishes that already had pastors whose authority descended
directly from the apostles. This is a common stance regarding usurpation in
the antifraternal tradition.

Added to these negative similes are the three terms alluded to earlier:
double worstede, *semycope*, and *rounded*. None of these terms is pejorative
by definition, but when included in a description of a friar's costume, each of
them connotes censure. Taking them in order, *double worsted* is a fabric
woven in the same manner as other woolens, but woven only of threads made
from strands of long wools, carefully sorted, that have been combed (not
carded as is the case for short-haired wools) in preparation for being drafted
without a twist. Later a twist is put into these yarns. After weaving, the cloths
are not fulled as other woolens are.[38] Worsted was not a new fabric[39] in Chaucer's day; legislative action was taken by Parliament, 17 Rich. II, specifying
and confirming three traditional kinds of worsted and motley: double
worsted, half double worsted, and worsted ray.[40] It was common for those in
religious orders, and even for Lollards, to wear worsted.[41]

pp. 279–80. Scase cites *Registrum Thome Bourgchier*, ed. F. R. H. Du Boulay (Oxford,
1957), p. 92, (and provides a translation) in which the Convocation stated:
> 'simple priests and other priests over and above their grade and status openly
> wear their apparel in the manner of doctors or of other worthy men, canons of
> cathedral churches, with hoods with short streamers called "tippets" . . . and are
> not ashamed to parade in them'.

The complaint includes elements of fashionable dress as well. We should note that a
type of tippet was again fashionable at this time.

37 See S. H. Rigby's summary of Chaucer's treatment of the Friar, including his mention
of John Ashwardby's sermon, which counselled listeners not to give alms to friars
wearing 'fine copes', in *Chaucer in Context: Society, Allegory, and Gender* (Manchester, New York, 1996), pp. 13–14.

38 Kenneth G. Ponting, Introduction, *Baines's Account of the Woollen Manufacture of
England* (New York, 1970), pp. 36–8. For the process of producing worsted, see
J. Geraint Jenkins, ed., *The Wool Textile Industry in Great Britain* (London, 1972), pp.
26–7. East Norfolk is given as the primary place of production, with King's Lynn, Bury
St Edmunds and Sudbury as subsidiaries; Norwich and Great Yarmouth are specifically mentioned. The Norfolk village of Worstead is credited with giving its name to
the fabric typically produced there.

39 See John James, *History of the Worsted Manufacture in England* (London, 1968),
pp. 45–6, for the kinds of fabrics in the time of Edw. II, including *say*, a kind of
worsted; p. 81, regarding worsteds worn by all classes of people.

40 James, pp. 67–8, 75; James comments that these double worsted were 'likely the same
as stammins', p. 75.

41 Henry de Knyghton mentions Lollards wearing worsted, according to James, p. 62.

Worsted of fine quality might be woven in any of the statutorily regulated sizes,[42] although it is clear in the need for such laws that cloth sellers often enough sought to sell short measure. A statute, passed 6 Henry VI, lists worsted and dimensions.[43] John James states that *single worsted* was perhaps another name for the roll of worsted;[44] if so, then single worsted, 18 inches wide, could only have been used for religious habits if the habits had back and front seams as well as side seams, and H. L. Gray states that this fabric was likely of inferior quality and was used for export.[45]

As those in religious orders commonly wore worsted, the question remains: what is the significance of Huberd's double worsted? The issue is not whether a friar should wear single worsted as opposed to double worsted; rather it is whether he should wear double worsted instead of monks' cloth or canon cloth, that is, some form of worsted woven specifically with religious vows of poverty in mind. In general, worsted in the mid-fourteenth century

Some worsteds were specifically woven to fit the requirements of religious habits, for example 'canon cloths', and monks's cloths, p. 74; see also, monks, canons, and Lollards wearing worsted, p. 81.

See Raymond van Uytven's comment in 'Cloth in Medieval Literature of Western Europe', *Cloth and Clothing in Medieval Europe: Essays in Memory of Professor E. M. Carus-Wilson*, eds N. B. Harte and K. G. Ponting, Pasold Studies in Textile History 2 (London, 1983), p. 161, explaining the troubadour Peire Cardenal (c.1190–1271) and his antifraternal comment concerning Dominican friars' cassocks made of fine English wool, in H. Gougaud, ed., *Poémes politiques des Trobadours* (Paris, 1969), pp. 60–2.

[42] A 1428 statute, aimed at regulating size, sets the measurements of 'greatest assise' at 14 yds by 4 yds, 'mean assise' at 12 yds by 3 yds, and 'least assise' at 10 yds by 2½ yds, according to James, pp. 73–4. A 1480 inventory of Edw. IV mentions all of these sizes in red worsted: 'large' red worsted valued at 33s 4d a piece, 'middle' size red worsted at 15s 6d, and 'least' size red worsted at 10s 6d; James comments that 'from the price, considered according to the value of money in that age, these may be classed as fine worsted textures', p. 80.

[43] See n. 42. James, pp. 74–5, states that specific cloths were defined by measurements: monks' cloths, 12 yds x 5 quarters; canons's cloths, 5 yds x 7 qtrs; cloths, 6 yds x 2 yds; double worsted, 10 yds x 5 qtrs; half doubles, 6 yds x 5 qtrs; roll worsted, 30 yds x ½ yd.

See *Baines's Account*, p. 160, regarding the 'quarter' measurement. A *quarter* means 9 inches, a quarter of a yard. Thomas Baines states that it is 'the almost universal measurement for width', with normal width being 6 qtrs (54 inches), and narrow cloth width being 3 qtrs (27 inches). The standards come from the broad and narrow loom sizes. Baines, p. 157, also gives the standard measurement for cloth lengths as: Scottish – 37.2 inches; English – 45 inches; Flemish – 27 inches; and French – 54 inches.

[44] Roll-worsted 'appears to have been, under a different name, the same as the bolts of worsted', according to James, p. 75. See also James, p. 68, citing Halliwell's *Dictionary of Archaisms and Provincial Words*. H. L. Gray, 'The Production and Export of English Woolens in the Fourteenth Century', *EHR* 39 (1924), p. 18, n. 4, concurs.

[45] Gray, p. 18.

I. St Gertrude, Benedictine nun and visionary (d.1302), from *Horae beatae Virginis cum calendario, orationibus ad sanctos & aliis*, BL MS Harley 2962, fol. 41, by permission of the British Library.

II. Catherine of Cleves' large coral rosary, from *Horae C. de Cleves*, with the permission of The Pierpont Morgan Library, New York, MS M. 917, p. 237.

III. The Monk, from *The Canterbury Tales*, Cambridge University Library MS Gg.4.27, fol. 352r, by permission of the Syndics of Cambridge University Library.

IV. A Friar, from the *Taymouth Hours*, BL MS Yates Thompson 13, fol. 177, by permission of the British Library.

V. Clerks, from *Omne bonum*, BL MS Royal 6 E vii, fol. 197, by permission of the British Library.

VI. St Cosmas or St Damian depicted in the robes of an Oxford
Doctor of Phisik, in Minster Lovell: Church of St Kenelm; with
the permission of Henri De Feraudy, photographer.

Here begynnyth the Pardoner his tale

VII. The Pardoner, from *The Canterbury Tales*, Cambridge University Library MS Gg.4.27, fol. 306r, by permission of the Syndics of Cambridge University Library.

VIII. A possible case of leprosy, from *Omne bonum*, BL MS Royal 6 E vi, fol. 301, by permission of the British Library.

was counted among the 'medium-priced cloths'.[46] Lacking comparable prices for the various types of worsted, we can nevertheless illustrate the relative position of worsted in the price hierarchy of other fabrics at several different times. Records of cloth purchases, generally measured in ells,[47] made for the royal wardrobe in 1323–24, list worsted prices that may be compared to other woolens.[48]

Although records fail to supply comparable identical quantities and measurements of fabrics, it is still possible to determine that scarlets of any color and cloths dyed in grain are much more costly than worsted. In addition, in a third list prices of worsted, silk, and blanket may be compared, although unfortunately the figures for quantities purchased are often missing.[49] We note that in this list, *sindons* (a silk) are clearly more expensive than *worsted*, just as *worsted* is higher priced than *blanket* (a woolen). Again, worsted falls into the middle price range.

Textile records and such comparisons make evident that derogatory comments concerning the Friar's habit of double worsted do not take into account the facts that religious habits were commonly made of worsted, that the width of double worsted is the same as that for monks' cloth and narrower than that of canon's cloth by two quarters (18 inches), and that the length of double worsted is shorter than monks' cloth by two yards. A friar's habit (tunic and cloak) made of double worsted would actually use less fabric than was used in a standard monk's habit, and would be narrower than a canon's habit. In addition, unless some fabric was cut off the bottom, even allowing for differ-

---

46 Edward Miller, 'The Fortunes of the English Textile Industry during the Thirteenth Century', *Econ Hist Rev* 18, 2nd series (1965), p. 80. Gray, p. 18, states that a double worsted cloth, 10 yds by 1¼ yds, in 1442, was worth one half as much as broadcloth (standard measurements of 26 yds by 1½ yds). See also Ellen Wedemeyer Moore, *The Fairs of Medieval England: An Introductory Study*, Studies and Texts 72 (Toronto, 1985), p. 218; she states that certain fabrics, including worsted, 'constituted low-priced alternatives to the costly broadcloths made in the cities of England and Flanders', and that worsteds were usually sold close to where they were produced.

47 *Baines's Account*, p. 157, provides an explanation of the *ell*: a standard cloth measurement [for length]; it differs according to the country of its origin. See note 43 above.

48 From Moore, p. 44, Table 5 – Records showing cloth purchases specify unit cost, unit length, and total cost: scarlet, £6 6s 8d – £3 13s 4d, 23 ells, £13 8s; cloth dyed in grain (short), £6 ea., 23 ells, £20 10s, and (long) £5 6s 8d – £12 ea., 30 ells, £94 13s 4d. Purchases of cheaper woolens are also listed: worsted @ 2s 3d per ell, 11s 3d; serge of worsted @ 14s per piece, £2 2s.

49 From James E. Thorold Rogers, *A History of Agriculture and Prices in England*, 4 vols (Oxford, 1892; Vaduz, 1963), 2:541–2: records of fabric purchases – fabric name, quantity (if provided), cost, and date: sindon, 24/, 1365; sindon, 22/, 1367; Tantaryn (for hood), 1 yd, 3/8, 1377; sindon, 26/8, 1397; sindon, 25/, 1398; scarlet, ½ yd, @ 15/, 1379; blanket, 6 yds, @ 1/6, 1380; worsted, pro velo quadragesimali, 3 pieces, @ 5/, 1386; blanket, 8 yds, @ 1/, 1387; blanket, 26 yds, @ /6, 1392; blanket, 18¾ yds, @ /8, 1394. See also 4:570, 575, for worsted prices in the fifteenth century.

ences in height, monks' habits would be more likely to trail on the ground,[50] while the length of the double worsted, with allowance for a hood, would be approximately correct for a tunic and a cloak, with no extra fabric left over.

What, then, is the problem with Friar Huberd's double worsted? Judging from the size and price comparisons, clearly this fabric cannot be called 'opulent'[51] in the sense of rich, abundant, luxuriant. At the same time, no type of worsted would meet the criterion of 'vyle' or coarse cloth, as specified for friars' mantles.[52] We may infer from Chaucer that Huberd's garment is neither threadbare, nor, in its relatively moderate price, is it representative of the poverty friars profess. However, Chaucer goes further and implies in lines 261–2 that double worsted is a fabric suitable for a master or a pope to wear. Is this a boast about the good quality of English double worsted? or an ironic comment about the often questionable quality of exported English woolens? Although worsted was known as a 'good' and a 'sturdy' fabric, the kind of fabric worn by nearly everyone at one time or another, still it was not a 'luxury' fabric comparable to the fabric known as *scarlet*.

A more likely explanation for Chaucer's remark may be found in the politico-economic history of English worsted. A very brief sample of the history of worsted sales would indicate what Chaucer must have known: that the quality, the integrity, of worsted was questionable. For example, in 1315 merchants protested against Worsted and Aylesham cloths that failed to meet the proper standards, '20 ells being sold as 24, 25 ells as 30', and so forth, although the standard assizes of 50, 40, 30, and 24 ell lengths had been long established before that date.[53] Regardless of protests and regulations, cloth fraud continued. In 1390 a law[54] was passed that cloths had to be sold open rather than folded because western counties practiced fraud through tacking and folding, so that a cloth looked to be full measure, when it was not. However, the law was apparently insufficient to stop fraudulent practices, for in 1410 the Flemish considered inspection of all English worsted at their port of entry. Further, in general, the export of worsted decreased owing to dissatisfaction among foreign consumers.[55]

In clothing Friar Huberd in double worsted, a precise cloth term he is the first to use in antifraternal poetic satire,[56] Chaucer gave him a garment made

---

[50] Illuminations and sketches of monks in the late fourteenth century commonly show the bottom edges of monks' habits so long that they puddled in the floor around their feet. Regarding extra width or length in habits, see n. 10 above.

[51] As it is designated by Lawrence Besserman, in 'Chaucer and the Pope of Double Worsted', *ChauN* 1.1 (1979), p. 15.

[52] *Monumenta Franciscana*, 2:67.

[53] L. F. Salzman, *English Industries of the Middle Ages* (Oxford, 1923), p. 229, citing Rec. of City of Norwich, ii, 407.

[54] 13 Rich. II, in *The Statutes of the Realm*, vol. 1 (London, 1910; Netherlands, 1963).

[55] Salzman, p. 230.

[56] Boccaccio speaks of friars' stylish cloaks that are doubly thick, broad, and of luxurious

of cloth of questionable value, associated with fraudulent production and mercantile practices. In this manner, Chaucer labels the Friar as one who receives full price for short measure, and simultaneously reminds the reader that mercantile activities are not included in a friar's purview. At the same time that he strikes at mercantile deception,[57] he depicts the Friar in the garments of that deception, metaphorically as the wolf in wolf's clothing. In addition, Chaucer questions the quality of the masters and pope(s),[58] who are worthy to wear this fabric, the same church hierarchy that permits friars like Huberd to practice their chicanery. A similar insult regarding the quality of a fabric and the value of Noe as a husband, head of the family hierarchy, occurs in the Wakefield Master's *Processus Noe cum Filiis*, when Uxor exclaims to Noe, 'Bot thou were worthi be cled in Stafford blew' (line 200). In saying this, Uxor labels both husband and the cloth produced in a rival town as inferior.[59]

Not only was the reputation of double worsted questionable, but the name is also suggestive. *Double worsted* does not mean worsted double the width of other worsteds, or double value, as is often supposed; instead, the term *double worsted* simply means that its dimensions are different from *half doubles* and *single worsteds*. *Double worsted* is 10 yds long, compared to *half doubles* at 6 yds and *single worsted* at 30 yds; it is 5 qtrs[60] (45") wide, compared to *half doubles* also at 5 qtrs, and *singles* at 18". However, coupled with its checkered mercantile history discussed above, might there not be a hint regarding the Friar's character, included in Chaucer's choice of a fabric name? In its nomenclature, the term suggests the character trait of doubleness, defined by the MED as 'Duplicity, deceitfulness, treachery . . . lack of candor or sincerity; evasiveness, untrustworthiness, faithlessness'. Double worsted, then, is striking terminology in Chaucer's antifraternal satire. However, acknowledging this triple thrust – at merchants, at church hierarchy, and at friars – does not sound the depths of this costume sign;

---

fabrics. He also compares them to those of a pope, in *Decameron*, Seventh Story, Third Day, p. 388, as mentioned by Mann, p. 44. Mann also notes that *Pierce the Ploughmans Crede* has followed Chaucer's lead in clothing a fat Dominican in a cope 'Of double worstede'. However, we should note that this Dominican's cope reached 'doun to the hele' (228), unlike Huberd's short cope.

57 Note that in Langland, *P.P.B*, Passus 2, lines 232–3, friars dress Guile as a friar because he has knowledge of commerce: 'Freres wiþ fair speche fetten hym þennes;/ For knowynge of comeres coped hym as a Frere.'

58 While Chaucer was writing the *General Prologue* (c.1387), there were two elected popes at any given time (1378–1409), and between 1409 and 1417 three elected popes at a time.

59 I have discussed this insult in 'Noe's Wife: Type of Eve and Wakefield Spinner', *Equally in God's Image: Women in the Middle Ages*, eds Julia Bolton Holloway, Constance S. Wright, and Joan Bechtold (New York, 1990), p. 34 and n. 28.

60 See n. 43 above.

Chaucer's selection of this particular fabric may contain yet another implication. As discussed earlier, originally friars' habits were based on Christ's instructions to his apostles, which include Matthew 10:10, containing the admonition that they should not possess two coats. Because two full-length cloaks could be made from one piece of double worsted, a cope of such cloth suggests, although it in no way proves, the possession of two.[61] The logic of the innuendo reads as follows: given a friar who behaved like a peddler, who sold sacred services such as confession (without being in the proper line of apostolic descent) in order to serve his own greed – would such a friar feel any compunction about possessing two copes, double the specified number? And the answer is – not likely. Chaucer's portrait of the Friar follows the usual procedure of antifraternal satire: to state the worst-case scenario.

Lawrence Besserman posits yet another anticlerical thrust incorporated in Chaucer's choice of double worsted, a thrust underscored by the 'pope'/'semycope' rhyme:

> The fact that there were two popes makes lines 261–62 (ignoring the editorial full stop between them) an extension of the antipapal joke: for an instant we take *double worstede* with *pope*, and get good, comic anti-papal sense – something roughly equal to 'two Popes are worse than one'.[62]

Besserman does not elaborate; however such an interpretation draws on the idea of the Friar's doubleness, his double worsted, double the usual number of popes, in addition to the shape and length of the Friar's cope, for its bell-broadness is not matched by its length, this cope being both too wide and too short. Taking into consideration that the Pope is the descendent of that rock, Peter, on which the church was founded by Christ, the insult embedded in these two lines questions the stability of the entire hierarchical structure, metaphorically the *fabrique*,[63] of the contemporary church. From top to bottom, from Pope to mendicant friars, things are not as they should be. By extension, the entire construction or fabric of the church is wrong. Or, to be more specific *and* more interpretative, in the Pope's having given papal permission for friars to preach, hear confessions, and solicit funds, the Mantle of Church Authority, like Huberd's 'semycope', has been stretched too broadly and, as a result, has come up short.

---

61 A piece of double worsted might provide more than two 'semycopes'.
62 Besserman, 'Chaucer', p. 15. As a side note, see Lawrence Besserman, 'Girdles, Belts, and Cords: A Leitmotif in Chaucer's *General Prologue*', *PLL* 22 (1986), p. 324, where he points out that Chaucer highlights girdles in secular portraits, but pointedly omits them from the portraits of those in religious orders where they would signify the possession of 'chastity, faithfulness, truth, righteousness, and spiritual preparedness'.
63 A thirteenth-century term defined in the Larousse *dictionnaire de l'ancien français* as 'Construction religieuse'; also 'Fabrication'. The term *fabric* is used by Caxton in 1483, in the sense of edifice or structure, according to the OED.

In *semycope* – perhaps he even coins this term[64] – Chaucer makes another innovation in antifraternal costume rhetoric. This garment name is the second of the three previously mentioned terms that take on pejorative connotations. The definition of a full-size *cope* provided by the MED is straightforward: 'A cloak or mantle . . . An ecclesiastical outer garment . . . esp., the cowl or hood of a friar, monk, nun'; also the MED provides the phrase 'to get a cowl, i.e. become a friar'. Friar Huberd's cope should be a cloak with hood attached, a full-length cloak, which stands as the very sign for the eyes of the world of his being a friar.[65] The specifications of a friar's habit provide that hoods not extend below 'the shoulder boone', that habit length not be longer than needed to cover the friar wearing it full-length, that its width not exceed sixteen 'spannys' unless the warden deems there is a need for a greater width, that sleeve-length should not exceed the 'vtter joynt of the finger', and that the cope or 'mantellis' be made of 'vyle and course clothe, nat curiusly made or pynched aboute the necke, nat towching the graund by a hole spanne'.[66]

---

[64] The MED provides only one definition and one example for *semicope*: 'A short cloak. (c.1387–95) Chaucer *CT.Prol.* A.262.'

[65] 'The cope (*pluviale*) is a large cloak, to which a hood was formerly attached. It is open in front. Its original use was to protect the wearer from cold or rain in processions', according to Revd Adrian Vigourel, *A Synthetical Manual of Liturgy*, trans. Revd John A. Nainfa (New York, 1907), p. 56. Its prototype was the Roman mantle, says Daniel Rock, *Hierugia; or, The Holy Sacrifice of the Mass*, 3rd edn rev., ed. W. H. James Weale (London, 1892), 2:250–1. See also Houston: the cope as a processional vestment, p. 30, figs 25, 26; choir cope, canon's cope, Dominican cloak, pp. 38–9; and fourteenth-century *Cappa Nigra*, p. 149, fig. 41. Of fourteenth-century cloaks, Houston describes one kind that was 'open down the front and only reached to the bottom of the short tunic. It was buttoned closely from neck to hem and had a hood attached', p. 81; and cloaks from 1360 onward, p. 72. Mayo, pp. 38–9, 53–5, discusses long ceremonial copes and their origin. Line drawings of copes are provided by French, p. 18, figs 26–8, and p. 27, fig. 50.

A color plate of a processional vestment, the Syon Cope, is in Kay Staniland, *Medieval Craftsmen: Embroiderers* (Toronto, 1991), p. 21, pl. 16; see p. 18, for dimensions given for a cope: 1 3/4 yds (1/6 m.) long. Another reproduction of a cope may be seen in Margaret Rickert, *Painting in Britain: The Middle Ages*, 2nd edn (Baltimore, 1965), p. 140.

[66] The 1451 Franciscan *Statuta Generalia Edita Apud Barcinonam*, provides the following regulations for clothing:

Cum regula dicat quod fratres omnes vestimentia vilibus induantur, prout statutum bonae memoriae domini Fratris Bonaventurae contineat, statuimus et ordinamus ut vestimentorum vilitas attendatur in pretio pariter et colore. In omnibus autem, quae ad habitum fratrum spectant, ad imitationem patrum nostrorum semper in vestimentis reluceat asperitas, vilitas et paupertas. Ad majorem autem uniformitatem inter nos conservandam ordinamus, quod latitudo caputii habitus nostri non transeat a lateribus conum juncturae humerorum; et quod longitudo ipsius caputii a parte posteriori cingulum non attingat. Longitudo vero habitus talis sit, quod fratris ipsum deferentis nullo

Clearly a 'semycope' does not meet the length requirement for a proper friar's habit.[67] Additionally, a 'semycope' would fall short on the Friar's body as it falls short of propriety.[68] Precise instructions for the friars' garments of poverty were clearly not sufficient to produce properly clothed friars,[69] and in

> *modo excedat mensuram. Latitudo autem ultra sedecim palmarum mensuram non protendatur ad plus, nec minus quam xiiii. palmas habeat, nisi notabilis corpulentia alicujus in latitudine amplius requirat judicio gardiani. Longitudo vero manicarum cooperiat extremam juncturam manuum, nec ultra protendatur. Pannus vero habituum sit coloris cinerei, ut frequenter in nostris capitulis extitit declaratum. Mantellos quoque de panno vili et humili fratres habeant non rugatos circa collum vel crispos, nec usque ad terram per integram saltem palmam protensos,*

in *Monumenta Franciscana*, 2:88. *Monumenta Franciscana*, ed. J. S. Brewer (London, 1858; Germany, 1965), 1:575–6, provides the specific dimensions of the Franciscan habit as described in the Middle English trans. of the Rule in BL Cott. MS Faustina D. IV.

67 Chaucer's image is reminiscent of the reference in *P.P.B*, Passus 20, lines 218–19, to priests who wear paltocks (short garments, judging by the context):
>   Proude preestes . . .
>   In paltokes and pyked shoes, [purses and] longe knyues.

68 The idea of shortness as an indication of a lack in moral character is put to good use in *Mankind* in *The Macro Plays*, ed. Mark Eccles, EETS, ES 262 (London, 1969), as New Gyse promises Mankynde 'a fresch jakett after þe new gyse' (2.676). Later New Gyse describes this garment as 'a goode jake of fence for a mannys body' (2.719). This jacket of defense is all that remains of Mankynde's long gown after cutting off its length to provide bribes for lawyers, and the gown's shortening indicates the diminution of his reputation and piety as a result of keeping bad company. See T. W. Craik's comments on costume symbolism in *The Tudor Interlude* (Leicester, 1958), pp. 49–92, and especially pp. 83–4 for *Mankind*.

69 Richard Ruston, a friar minor, is an example of a friar who clearly did not follow the sartorial rules of his order in the number of garments he owned, although with the exception of items made of ray, a striped fabric and unsuitable for a friar, most of his garments are made of inexpensive russet. *Calendar Inquisitions Misc. 1377–88* (London, 1957), item 87, p. 63 states that on 16 Jan. 1388, his goods were evaluated and locked up at Westminster [citing Calendar of Fine Rolls, vol. X, pp. 226–7]. The list included 'a wallet worth 4d., a mantle of russet worth 4d., a cape of russet worth 12d., a "pilch" of black lambskin worth 12d., . . . a striped gown (*toga*) lined with woolen cloth worth 12d., a mantle of russet worth 20d., another mantle of russet lined with blanket worth 4d., a . . . of russet furred with white lambskin worth 4d., a tunic of blanket worth 8d., a "kertel" of "fustyan" worth 8d., . . . a ? tunic of russet worth 8d., . . . a striped tunic in poor condition worth 6d., . . . a tunic of russet worth 4d., a pair of boots (*caligarum*) of russet worth 3d., a red hood worth 1d., a shield (*parma*) worth 6d., . . . 5 "freresgerdels" worth 6d., 6 rosaries (*paria de paternosters de filo*) worth 5d., a gown partly of ray and canvas lined with woolen cloth (*pertic' raiat' et canve lin' cum panno laneo*) worth 12d., . . . a belt . . . worth 2d., a hood of russet worth 4d., . . . 3½ yards of cloth of russet worth 6s. 8d., . . . a hood of "ray" worth 2d., a cape of russet worth 8d., a tunic of russet worth 4d., a pair of boots of . . . [worth] 6d., . . . 2 "freresgerdeles" worth 4d., a belt . . . of linen cloth worth 4d., . . . an old belt worth 1d., . . . 2 belts . . . worth 2d.'; the list also included household goods.
    See also the account of Brother Hugh, an Austin friar who arrived in Dartmouth on

the late fourteenth century this issue produced a conflict that may have been known to Chaucer. John Ashwardly, a Wyclif follower and Vicar of St Mary's (University Church at Oxford) c.1380, spoke out against giving alms to any friar wearing a cope that would be classed as 'fine'. The Carmelite spokesman Richard Maidstone, John of Gaunt's confessor and well-known theologian, disputed the charges.[70] Whether or not Chaucer's inspiration derived from this debate,[71] antifraternal literature had a long history of comments on incorrect dress worn by those who used religion for their own purposes.

Semycope, Chaucer's term, summons up another possible negative association. In its opposition to a proper friar's cloak, which symbolizes a life of poverty and piety as the proper preparation for an eternal life with Christ, Huberd's 'semycope' is a phononym for seemy-coat, a coat of many seams. Indeed, this garment in its 'semy-' state is the opposite of Christ's seamless coat – his garment of perfection.[72]

Friar Huberd is not a 'whited sepulchre'; instead, he dresses in 'typet' and 'semycope' that literally and clearly convey his blackness of character. Surely

---

14 Mar. 1344, 'secretly and almost suddenly, in habit as a layman with long sword and buckler, clad in a close short coat with buttons', in G. G. Coulton, trans. and annotator, *Life in the Middle Ages* (Cambridge, 1967), 1:184.

[70] Arnold Williams, 'Two Notes on Chaucer's Friars', *MP* 54 (1956–57), pp. 117–18, suggests that this dispute may either have been known to Chaucer or that it was a commonplace known to all, and that this dispute inspired the inclusion of a cope in this portrait of a friar.

[71] Arnold Williams mentions an earlier dispute over proper clothing between 'the Spiritual Franciscans' and their 'laxer brethren' who apparently wore habits characterized by 'fullness of material', 'pleats and creases', and a 1340 document concerned with this question, in 'Chaucer and the Friars', *Speculum* 28 (1953), rpt. in *Chaucer Criticism*, eds Richard J. Schoeck and Jerome Taylor (Notre Dame, IN, 1960), 1:74–5. It may be these 'pleats and creases' that are referred to in the c.1394 poem *Pierce the Ploughmans Crede*: 'His cope þat biclypped him wel clene was it *folden*' (line 227) [my emphasis]. See also the description of the Minorite friar made by an Austin friar:
> in cotynge of his cope is more cloþ y-folden
> Þan was in Fraunces froc when he hem first made.
> And ȝet, vnder þat cope a cote haþ he furred,
> Wiþ foyns, or wiþ fitchewes oþer fyn beuer,
> And þat is cutted to þe kne & queyntly y-botend,
> Lest any spirituall man aspie þat gile. (lines 292–7)

[72] Regarding Christ's seamless gown, see John 19:23–4; and Chapter 1, p. 1, nn. 1–2, and Plate 1. According to John Harthan, *Books of Hours* (London, 1977; 1982), p. 152, pictures of pilgrim souvenirs depicting this holy tunic of Trier, Christ's seamless gown, appear three times in a roundel in the *Soane Hours*, Sir John Soane's Museum, London, MS 4, fol. 112v. See Iohannis Wyclif, *Operis evangelici liber tertius et quartus sive de antichristo liber primus et secundus*, vols 3 and 4 (London, 1896), p. 15, lines 18–29, concerning the dress of deceiving Pharisees and improperly dressed members of religious orders as being unlike Christ's seamless tunic; also John D. Sinclair's comment on the seamless garment of God in *The Divine Comedy of Dante Alighieri: III Paradiso* (New York, 1981), p. 46.

Chaucer meant his readers to understand the point – that only the spiritually blind could be taken in by a rogue whose costume advertises his roguery so flagrantly. And possibly Chaucer also satirizes the seemingly unsolvable dilemma of the church and its idea of hierarchy, as it pertained to friars. As Szittya mentions, church authority was 'a spiritually hereditary system, in which the mantle of authority could only be passed on by delegation through the properly appointed chain'.[73] In giving Friar Huberd a 'semycope', Chaucer may be stating the obvious through his costume rhetoric: Friars have the Pope's permission, but no apostolic succession; therefore, they may be seen as having only half a Mantle of Authority. In this sense, the 'semycope' is a visual joke for the mind's eye.

In addition, there may be one more 'semycope' joke in the contrast between Friar Huberd and that notable friar St Francis in their motivations for possessing only half a cloak. St Francis, wearing secular clothing, demonstrates true charity in dividing his red cloak with a beggar, as depicted in an illumination in *Psalterium et officia*.[74] It is safe to assume that Huberd had not given the lower half of his cope to a beggar. Further, no one could mistakenly view Huberd as the legitimate successor to another friar-saint: St Dominic who sold his clothes to feed the poor. In contrast, in writing 'For thogh a wydwe hadde noght a sho,/ . . . Yet wolde he have a ferthyng, er he wente' (lines 253, 255), Chaucer indicates that Huberd was far more apt to invert saintly practice and to sell (or bilk) the poor in order to buy himself more clothes.

We may agree with Mann that 'fine clothing' in antifraternal satires has been 'traditionally associated with friars';[75] however, Chaucer in his costume rhetoric has done more than take a 'documentary interest in the Friar's appearance'. In his diction, in his choice of 'semycope', Chaucer depicts a friar who does not go through the motions of looking like a proper friar;[76]

---

73 Szittya, 'The Antifraternal Tradition', p. 310.
74 Dated at the end of the fourteenth century, BL MS Harl. 2897, fol. 435. See also the miniature of St Martin of Tours dividing his cloak with a beggar in the c.1280 English *Lives of the Saints*, Fitzwilliam Museum, Cambridge, MS 370, fol. 5v, reproduced in Evans, p. 20.
75 Mann, pp. 43–4.
76 The opposite of Friar Huberd's casual treatment of his habit is the kind of religious interpretive overemphasis of the habit discussed by Wyclif. Szittya, in *The Antifraternal Tradition*, p. 159, discusses John Wyclif's position on friars and their habits as signs:

There is, charges Wyclif, too much emphasis on externals in the modern church . . . . The friars especially seem to assert that the habit, which is only a sign of religion, is religion itself [citing *De apostasia*, p. 4; cf. *Opus evangelicum*, vol. II, 4 (book 3)]. . . . They [friars] say . . . that the coloration of habits signifies aspects of the religious life: black signifies dolor about sins, white the purity of the heart, russet assiduous labor in the church militant. The Franciscans say that the knots in their rope belts signify the bodily punishment they inflict on them-

instead, he portrays Friar Huberd as a villain-friar, openly flaunting his character in a cloak made of cloth too good to suit his vows of poverty, and fashioned in an unsuitable length and width.

As if this were not enough vilification by costume rhetoric, Chaucer's term, *rounded*, implies the extra width that was a standard sartorial complaint against clergy in general; indeed, this term by itself might be construed as a costume cliché for pride, greed, and, ultimately, *luxuria*. Further, in this portrait, 'rounded' is modified by yet another of Chaucer's similes: 'as a belle out of the presse'. An understanding of the contrast between the originality of this simile expressing wideness and the tradition in antifraternal commentary and poetry dealing with excess in clothing heightens our appreciation of Chaucer's *systrophe*. Szittya explains the traditional clothing complaints:

[The] traditional charge that crystallized around verses from Matthew 23 – excesses of clothing – fused the friars' flowing habits with (a misunderstanding of) the Pharisees' phylacteries. These are mentioned in Matt. 23:5: 'Omnia vero opera sua faciunt ut videantur ab hominibus; dilatant enim phylacteria sua et magnificant fimbrias.' [All their works they do so that they might be seen by men; for they widen their phylacteries and enlarge their tassels.][77] William of St Amour had understood rightly the purpose of phylacteries and *fimbriae* in Old Testament times. But poets, lacking the helpful explanations of the *Glossa ordinaria*, made of the rare word *phylacteria* what they could. In the translation of the *Romaunt of the Rose* [including ll. 6889–922] . . . phylacteries are misunderstood as borders or hems, in the passage that renders Matt. 23:5: 'Her bordurs larger maken they,/ And make her hemmes wide alwey. (6911–12)'[78]

This kind of error in translation, Szittya posits, may have evoked Friar

selves through the poverty of the religious life [citing *Trialogus*, p. 337; *De fundatione sectarum* in *Polemical Works*, I, 27].

Szittya, p. 160, comments,

For him [Wyclif], true religion cannot be found in signs. If a physical garment in itself were a true sign of religion, an ass dressed in the habit would be a friar, and a friar taking a bath would be an apostate. Religion is rather to be found in the heart or soul, the habit of mind (habitus mentis) rather than in the corporal habit. [citing *De apostasia*, pp. 4–5; see *Opus evangelicum*, vol. II, 14 (book 3)]

Another medieval work makes the point that wearing a masculine habit does not make a friar male: *De Frere Denise* in *The French Fabliau: B.N. MS. 837*, eds and trans. Raymond Eichmann and John DuVal, Garland Library of Medieval Literature, Series A, 17 (New York, 1985), 2:246–59.

77 Trans. from Szittya, *The Antifraternal Tradition*, p. 39.

78 Szittya, *The Antifraternal Tradition*, p. 204, citing *Romaunt of the Rose*, in F. N. Robinson, ed., *The Works of Geoffrey Chaucer*, 2nd edn (Boston, 1957). Regarding the phylacteries/borders misunderstanding, see also Szittya, 'The Antifraternal Tradition', pp. 298–9. Wyclif, *Operis evangelici*, 15, lines 18–29, makes this error.

Huberd's rounded, bell-shaped cloak, and for another example,[79] he cites
Pierce the Ploughman's Crede:

> Loke nowe, leue man . beþ nouʒ þise [friars] i-lyke
> Fully to þe Farisens . in fele of þise poyntes? . . .
> And in worchipe of þe werlde . her wynnynge þei holden;
> Þei schapen her chapolories . & streccheþ hem brode,
> And launceþ heiʒe her hemmes . wiþ babelyng in stretes.
>
> (lines 546–51)

Chaucer transforms the traditional broad hems and wide borders in
antifraternal literature into an image of beauty: a short cloak 'That rounded
as a belle out of the presse'.[80] The combination of cope and bell images may
have been inspired by Dante's image of *Frate Gaudenti* wearing a leaden
cope that is gilded on the outside:

> Là giù trovammo una gente dipinta
> che giva intorno assai con lenti passi,
> piangendo e nel sembiante stanca e vinta.
> Elli avean cappe con cappucci bassi
> dinanzi a li occhi, fatte de la taglia
> che in Clugnì per li monaci fassi.
> Di fuor dorate son, sì ch'elli abbaglia;
> ma dentro tutte piombo, e gravi tanto,
> che Federigo le mettea di paglia.
> Oh in etterno faticoso manto!   (Canto 23, lines 58–67)

[There below we found a painted people who were going round
with very slow steps, weeping and in their looks tired and overcome. They wore cloaks with cowls down over their eyes, of the
cut that is made for the monks of Cluny, so gilded outside that

---

79 Szittya, *The Antifraternal Tradition*, p. 204, states, 'This traditional charge (and misunderstanding of Matt. 23:5) appears also in the Wycliffite *Tractatus de pseudo-freris*,
though here traces of Matt. 23:5 would have disappeared entirely but for the casual
mention of the Pharisees: "& þus seyen summe þat these freris habitis to whiche freris
ben þus oblishid, þat been þus large & variaunt as weren habitis of pharisees, serven þe
fend to putte in lesyngus & to destrie pore mennus goodis" ' [citing: *Tractatus*, ed.
Matthew, *English Works*, pp. 301–2, and providing the additional notes: 'For a comparison of the knots in the friars' girdles to the Pharisees' phylacteries, see Wyclif's *Opera
minora*, ed. J. Loserth (London: Wyclif Society, 1913), pp. 320–1. Boccaccio mentions
the friars' Pharisaic *fimbriae* (which he takes to be wide hems in their garments), *Il
Decameron*, ed. C. S. Singleton, I (Bari: Laterza, 1955), seventh story, third day,
p. 230, l. 12'].

80 This cloak may be the *rotundello* that was forbidden to monks, c.1363, mentioned in
Edith Rickert, comp., *Chaucer's World*, eds Clair C. Olson and Martin M. Crow (New
York, 1948), p. 339. Concerning the shape of this cloak, see also John Livingston
Lowes, 'Illustrations of Chaucer Drawn Chiefly from Deschamps', *RR* 2 (1911),
p. 118, who thinks Chaucer may have had a French style and shape in mind.

they dazzle, but within, all of lead, and so heavy that those Frederick imposed were of straw. O toilsome mantle for eternity!]

This image is further explained:

> 'Le cappe rance
> son di piombo sì grosse, che li pesi
> fan così cigolar le lor bilance.
> Frati Godenti fummo, e bolognesi'. . . .   (Canto 23, lines 100–3)

['The orange cloaks are of lead so thick that the weight thus causes their scales to creak. We were Jovial Friars, and Bolognese'. . . .][81]

In addition, in likening the Friar's cloak to a newly-made[82] bell, Chaucer evokes the image of a 'cope belle', a bell that the MED defines as 'a bell rung as a signal for choir members to put on their robes'. He furthers this choral imagery in mentioning Huberd's 'harpyng, whan that he hadde songe' (line 266). The irony is strong here, for Chaucer never mentions Friar Huberd chanting in choir; on the contrary, the foregoing portrait description leads the reader to interpret 'harpyng' in the sense of the verb 'harpen' meaning persistent repetition (MED), in terms of the begging described in lines 252–6 that follow. Consequently, the image of his eyes likened to twinkling stars on a frosty night suggests the cold glitter of greed when his 'harpyng' succeeds. In Friar Huberd's bell-cope, Chaucer reverses the readers' expectations in his picture of a lovely and gracefully rounded short cloak that in fact is the symbol of disobedience, a cloak that rounds like a bell that, visually, resonates of the old song.[83] Chaucer's costume rhetoric emphasizes the idea that

---

81 Dante Alighieri, *Inferno*, *La Commedia*, ed. Arnoldo Mondadori (1966), 2:23.50–67, 100–3; *The Divine Comedy of Dante Alighieri: Inferno*, trans. and comm. Charles S. Singleton, Bollingen Series, no. 80 (Princeton, 1970).

82 Robert Worth Frank, Jr, 'Chaucer and the London Bell-Founders', *MLN* 68 (1953), pp. 525–6, n. 4, states that, for line I, 263, ' "mould" [for making a bell] seems a better reading for "presse" than "clothes press" '.

83 Interesting, in light of the Friar's providing the funds for many young women's marriages (lines 212–13), is the association of the bell image with the 'go-between' figure in romance. In Juan Ruiz, *Libro de buen amor*, ed. Giorgio Chiarini (Milan, 1964), there are numerous suggestive bell (*canpana*) images, and both bell and clapper are among the forty-one terms (pp. 924, 926) used to refer to a talkative 'go-between'. John Dagenais, in a discussion of this issue on Medieval Texts List, 4 Aug. 1997, comments on the aptness of these bell and clapper images because they convey the idea of 'the go-between's shuttling from one party to the other, blabbing first in one direction and then in the other'. I am grateful to this discussion on medtextl in which Max Grosse, Karen Reed, Jim Marchand, and Alberto Uttranadhie also participated, and especially to Gretchen Mieszkowski whose book, concerned with the 'Go-Between' figure in medieval literature, forthcoming from Palgrave, is responsible for my initial knowledge of this image.

this is the song sung by Friar Huberd, and the song he harps. His portrait adds new meaning to the designation of friars as *joculators Dei*.[84]

In conclusion, while more than one literary critic acknowledges Friar Huberd's appealing manner and/or appearance,[85] others concentrate on his moral portrait. Peter S. Taitt notes that 'Huberd becomes, in the reader's mind, an increasingly corrupt figure',[86] while David Lyle Jeffrey comments that the Friar's deliberate greediness 'paints him in the blackest spiritual colors possible'.[87] Chaucer's costume rhetoric makes a major and unique contribution to this blackening of Huberd's character, and it does so through an innovative inversion of standard costume imagery and through the addition of new costume terms to the antifraternal literary canon.

Chaucer structures the Friar's portrait in such a way as to introduce Huberd in lines 208–32 as a friar well-liked and appreciated by all who enjoyed his company, his confessional manner, and the benefits, financial and otherwise, derived from them. Then Chaucer literally caps this false pleasantness with the tippet filled with knives and pins, the sign of Sire *Penetrans Domos*. As if the hood-turned-peddler's-bag is insufficient to mark the Friar, he then lists Huberd's actions (lines 233–58) in accordance with the directive given by False Seeming in the *Roman de la rose* who states, 'Lor fais vous estuet regarder/ Se vous vols bien d'auz garder' (lines 11789–90) ['you must look at their deeds if you really want to protect yourself from them']. And in his choice of perverted and non-standard costume for the Friar, Chaucer heeds False Seeming's warning regarding those dressed in proper religious habits, 'Ja ne les connoistrés as robes,/ Les faus traitres plains de loves' (lines 11787–8) ['You will never recognize them by their garments, these false traitors full of trickery'].[88] *Faux Semblant* may be 'a literary ancestor of the Friar'[89] in his sinfulness and in literary chronology, but *Faux Semblant* wears the garments of holiness, the better to hide his hypocrisy; this cloak of hypocrisy was also worn by *antichrist* and the *pseudoapostoli*, in the literature of antifraternal tradition. In contrast, Friar Huberd's costume owes almost nothing to this image. Chaucer follows a description of Huberd's actions with

---

84 See Coulton, *The Chronicler*, p. 17, regarding this term. See also G. G. Coulton, *Ten Medieval Studies* (Cambridge, 1930), p. 48, regarding friars being forbidden to sing.

85 For example, Williams, 'Chaucer and the Friars', p. 75; Janette Richardson, 'Friar and Summoner, The Art of Balance', *ChauR* 9 (1975), p. 227; Joseph Spencer Kennard, *The Friar in Fiction, Sincerity in Art, and Other Essays* (New York, 1923), p. 15; Gloria Cigman, 'Chaucer and the Goats of Creation', *L&T* 5 (1991), pp. 172, 176.

86 Peter S. Taitt, *Incubus and Ideal: Ecclesiastical Figures in Chaucer and Langland* (Salzburg, 1975), p. 11.

87 David Lyle Jeffrey, 'The Friar's Rent', *JEGP* 70 (1971), p. 606.

88 Guillaume de Lorris and Jean de Meun, *Le Roman de la rose*, ed. Daniel Poirion (Paris, 1974); Charles Dahlberg, trans., *The Romance of the Rose*, by Guillaume de Lorris and Jean de Meun (Hanover, NH, 1983).

89 As Janette Richardson's notes state in *Riverside Chaucer*, p. 808.

the description of the double worsted and bell-shaped 'semycope'. In effect, he provides a garment sign that should alert *anyone* to the Friar's character, even those who had overlooked the peddler's-bag tippet. Cumulatively, the Friar, his merry, sociable manner, and his actions are marked and illuminated by means of costume rhetoric and Chaucer's *systrophe*.

In dressing Friar Huberd in 'semycope' and 'typet', Chaucer bestows upon this pilgrim garments in the specified number, the 'oone cote with a hode' stipulated in the Rule of St Francis. At the same time the number of this Rule is maintained, the spirit of the Rule is violated many times in the perversion of the tippet for mercenary and lecherous purposes, and in the size, bell-shape, and quality of the too-brief cloak of double worsted. Huberd's clothing bears little resemblance to the 'symple and vyle clothinge', patched with 'pecis of sak clothe', worn by St Francis and his friars. Further, we may detect one last inverted joke in the fact that Chaucer dresses his Friar in double worsted. He never *says* that Huberd is a wolf in sheep's clothing, although in lines 210–13 he implies that Huberd indulges in 'stealing lambs', but in his inversion of the holy habit image, he costumes this outwardly charming, inwardly wolfish Friar Huberd in a woolen fabric – literally sheep's clothing.

Either 'typet' or 'semycope' in this portrait would have been sufficient to mark this friar as evil, yet Chaucer sees fit to cover – or almost cover – Huberd in two worldly garment signs of his 'covetyse', 'doublenesse', and lechery, and through vigorous *systrophy* to compound our sense of the Friar's iniquity. Through costume rhetoric Chaucer demands that we look, and see that here is a friar who *can* be easily recognized by his garments (that are *Spiritual Mirrors*); here is Friar Huberd, a wolf literally in sheep's clothing fashioned and employed as wolf's clothing.

6

The Clerk's 'ful thredbare . . . overeste courtepy'
(I, line 290)

The traditional reputation of the Clerk in the *General Prologue* as an 'ideal figure'[1] has, for a long time, influenced reader expectations of this pilgrim. Further, it is possible that familiarity with the Ellesmere miniature of the Clerk clothed in the proper clerkly[2] garments of a long robe and shoulder cape with hood, painted medium brown with a pinkish cast,[3] has worked

---

1 According to Warren S. Ginsberg's note, the Clerk is 'usually taken as an ideal figure' (*Riverside Chaucer*, p. 810). Larry Sklute states that 'there is a temptation to consider the description of the Clerk one of the ideal portraits because most people who teach and write about the General Prologue are themselves clerks', and recommends a 'dispassionate look' at the portrait, in 'Catalogue Form and Catalogue Style in the General Prologue of the *Canterbury Tales*', *SN* 52 (1980), p. 38, n. 6. S. H. Rigby describes the view of the Clerk as ideal in *Chaucer in Context: Society, Allegory, and Gender* (Manchester, 1996), p. 30. See also Malcolm Andrew, *The General Prologue. A Variorum Edition of the Works of Geoffrey Chaucer*, Explanatory Notes (Norman, OK, 1993), 2:267–70, regarding the limited amount of negative criticism in his overview of the Clerk's character, esp. remarks made by Roger Sherman Loomis, 'Was Chaucer a Laodicean?' in *Essays and Studies in Honor of Carleton Brown* (New York, 1940), pp. 140–1; J. Mitchell Morse, 'The Philosophy of the Clerk of Oxenford', *MLQ* 19 (1958), pp. 15, 20; and Jill Mann, *Chaucer and Medieval Estates Satire: The Literature of Social Classes and the 'General Prologue' to the 'Canterbury Tales'* (Cambridge, 1973), pp. 74–6, 83–5.

2 *Clerkly* is the adjective I shall use throughout this essay to designate a costume appropriate to clerks, which sets them apart from a late-fourteenth-century city population as a whole. I have borrowed *clerkly* from *The Clerk's Book of 1549*, ed. J. Wickham Legg (London, 1903). Clerkly costume indicates a clerk's status within the hierarchy of a medieval university, regardless of whether or not he is in minor orders; it is that costume that he is required to wear when attending certain university functions.

3 Muriel Bowden describes this costume as 'a violet academic gown', in *A Commentary on the General Prologue to the Canterbury Tales*, 2nd edn (New York, 1967), p. 162, in keeping with her judgment, p. 155, that the Clerk is at least in minor holy orders. In contrast, J. A. W. Bennett calls this a 'lay' costume, in *Chaucer at Oxford and at Cambridge* (Oxford, 1974), p. 13.

No conclusions may be drawn from the variety of costume colors in manuscript illuminations as this variety may be due to the vagaries of patron's choice, palette of colors available, or the necessities of artistic composition. For contemporary miniatures of

among readers to obscure what Chaucer actually says about the Clerk's costume in the *General Prologue* text: 'Ful thredbare was his overeste courtepy' (I, line 290). Accepting the Clerk's traditional repute and this widely known miniature as judgmental guide, Chaucerians generally interpret Chaucer's costume rhetoric in the Clerk's portrait as depicting the Clerk's asceticism – his eschewing of worldly goods as represented by clothing. Thus, not only is the Clerk deemed innocent of the sartorial excesses mentioned by the Parson in *The Parson's Tale* (X, lines 410–30), but, colored by this interpretation of Chaucer's costume rhetoric, he is also thought to evince no interest in clothing beyond the necessity for covering his body in public, and no concern with *fashion* at all. Such a view of this pilgrim as representing an ideal[4] finds support in the fact that the Clerk prefers books and learning over 'robes riche', as Chaucer makes clear in his depiction of the Clerk's spending preferences, desired or actual, favoring books[5] (lines 291–6). However, a careful examination of Chaucer's diction in line 290 reveals that this description of an ideal Clerk in shabby clothing also suggests several less positive characteristics in the character of the Clerk, among them *curiositas*.

clerks, see *Piers Plowman*, the C version, in Bodleian Library MS Douce 104, fol. 54r, in which a clerk wears a light tan cowl, and an academic cap of black (described p. lxiv), and fol. 63r, where a clerk, also in a black academic cap, wears a white-trimmed red cowl over a lightly tinted greyish-blue gown, topped by a hood of white (described pp. lxvii–lxviii); this clerk is *Imaginatif* in academic costume, according to Kathleen Scott, Catalogue of Illustrations, in *Piers Plowman: A Facsimile of Bodleian Library, Oxford, MS Douce 104*, Introduction by Derek Pearsall (Cambridge, 1992). A variety of colors may also be found in Jacobi's *Omne bonum*, BL MS Roy. 6 E VI, fol. 296b, where four clerks wear traveling costumes of orange, light blue, and a pinky-mauve; in fol. 300b these colors are augmented by green. Also see the 1378, *Le Songe Du Vergier*, BL MS Roy. 19 C IV, fol. 6, where the clerk is dressed in shades of red with a white fur lining; the fourteenth-century Spanish manuscript illumination, BL MS 20787, fol. 112b, of nine clerks in white robes with undertunic sleeves of light blue, dark blue, dark red, and hose of gray, black, or blue; and the end of fourteenth-century fourth volume of Froissart, BL MS Harl. 4380, fol. 10v, of a clerk wearing a brown tunic under a robe of blue with a hood lined in white.

4   One example of the interpretation of the Clerk's costume as influencing a judgment of his character as ideal is Peter Taitt's comment that 'the Clerk's moderation, his quiet demeanour, his aura of otherworldliness, are all attested to by his humble appearance and his restrained speech', in *Incubus and Ideal: Ecclesiastical Figures in Chaucer and Langland*, Salzburg Studies in English Literature 44 (Salzburg, 1975), p. 27.

5   See Sr Mary Ernestine Whitmore, *Medieval English Domestic Life and Amusements in the Works of Chaucer* (New York, 1972), p. 168, regarding the Clerk's spending. Andrew, pp. 276–7, provides a summary of the traditional debate regarding the Clerk's twenty books, considering whether or not he owns, rents, or only dreams of owning them. Twenty books is thought by all to be a large personal library. See also n. 111 below. Regarding the value of books, see Wilbur Lang Schramm, 'The Cost of Books in Chaucer's Time', *MLN* 48 (1933), pp. 139–45.

9. Sketch of a senior cleric wearing the *vestis talaris* and three clerks in lay dress and bearing arms, from *Omne bonum*, BL MS Royal 6 E VI, fol. 137.

The central issue of Chaucer's costume rhetoric in his portrait of the Clerk is the fact that the Clerk wears lay dress. This layman's dress may surprise readers whose expectations are that Chaucer would have depicted an ideal

6   This ideal includes a presumption that the Clerk is in holy orders. However, according to Hastings Rashdall, in the medieval period, 'clericality . . . did not necessarily imply even the lowest grade of minor orders'. Further, 'the adoption of the clerical tonsure and dress conferred . . . the immunities and privileges of the clerical order – exemption from the secular courts, personal inviolability and the like'. And Rashdall concludes

clerk[6] wearing a proper clerkly robe.[7] This dichotomy between expectation and the reality of the Clerk's costume finds several illustrations in illuminations of *Omne bonum*,[8] among them one rubricated 'Arma clericorum' (Plate 9). At the left of this picture a tonsured cleric wears a dark blue *vestis*

that 'it would be difficult to say what proportion of the medieval "clerks" were actually in minor orders', especially since being in orders was not mandatory for inclusion in many university activities. See his *The Universities of Europe in the Middle Ages*, rev. edn, eds F. M. Powicke and A. B. Emden (Oxford, 1936), 3:393–5, and 1:181–2, 290; also Huling E. Ussery, 'How Old is Chaucer's Clerk?', *TSE* 15 (1967), pp. 4–5, regarding Chaucer's use of the term *clerk*; and Ann Astell's definition and discussion of *clerk* in *Chaucer and the Universe of Learning* (Ithaca, NY, 1996), pp. 33, 48, 53.

7   The numerous attempts throughout the medieval period to regulate the clothing of the clergy and clerks indicate that it was an administrative task not easily achieved and that directives were quite often ignored. For clerks in minor orders, the directives urged a standard of seemliness that recognized their place within the church hierarchy. Marion Gibbs and Jane Lang, in *Bishops and Reform: 1215–1272, With Special Reference to the Lateran Council of 1215* (Oxford, 1934; rpt. 1962), p. 126, describe results of the scanty Lateran Council decrees stating that clerks should wear 'fitting garments'. Pictures of clerks' dress vary: Edward L. Cutts, *Scenes & Characters of the Middle Ages*, 7th edn (London, 1930), p. 244, describes illuminations on fol. 100v of Cott. Nero D. vii, the Golden Book of St Albans: Lawrence, a clerk in brown robe; William, a clerk in scarlet robe. Janet Mayo, *A History of Ecclesiastical Dress* (New York, 1984), pp. 47–8, makes it clear that clerics in general often violated principles of sober dress. However E. C. Clarke posits that the history of clerkly and academic costume in England, including specific garments for each stage in an academic career, begins in the thirteenth century, in 'English Academical Costume (Mediæval)', *Archaeol J* 1 (1893), pp. 73–104, 137–49, 183–209. See also Peter Heath, *The English Parish Clergy on the Eve of the Reformation* (London, 1969), pp. 108–9, for dress of the clergy and clerks.

Mary G. Houston, *Medieval Costume in England & France: The 13th, 14th and 15th Centuries* (New York, 1996), p. 153, states,

With the fifteenth century comes the first period of distinctly academic dress or habit, that is, when it can be classified with any degree of clearness. It was undoubtedly founded upon ecclesiastical and monastic dress, the schools being frequently held within the precincts of the religious houses. . . .

In medieval times the scholar was regarded as an ecclesiastic in minor orders.

Dorothy R. Hartley, *Mediaeval Costume and Life* (London, 1931), p. 13, gives directions for making a clerk's gown: 'Two lengths of cloth, each slightly gathered in the center of the neck, meet' at the shoulder. 'The high collar is a straight length of material sewn on and folded over, and forms a circle, wide enough to slip easily over the head.' See p. 15c for a black and white reproduction from the fourteenth-century BL MS Burney 275. There are slits where the sleeves should be; the arms come through those slits revealing a tight-sleeved under-tunic.

8   BL MS Roy. 6 E VI, fol. 137. This manuscript and its second volume, Roy. 6 E VII, were written and compiled by James le Palmer, and illustrated in England sometime between 1360 and 1375, according to Lucy Freeman Sandler, *Omne Bonum: A Fourteenth-Century Encyclopedia of Universal Knowledge*, 2 vols (London, 1996), 1:7–8, 13, 25; see also 1:16–34 regarding the life and identification of James le Palmer.

talaris, the usual long gown of the medieval scholar.[9] According to Stella Mary Newton's description of this illustration, he is a 'senior cleric'[10] who has 'reprimanded' the three tonsured clerks on his left who bear arms and wear 'lay dress – tight abbreviated tunics of identical cut'.[11] With his right arm bent at the elbow and his palm-up hand position, the clerk at the forefront of this threesome appears to be imparting information; in keeping with Newton's interpretation, this clerk could be offering an excuse, or explanation, or an apology for their array. The senior cleric's pose, however, with

---

[9]   The online *Catholic Encyclopedia*, vol. 4, article: 'Clerical Costume' by Herbert Thurston, provides a history of the *vestis talaris*: 'The proper dress of the medieval clergy was . . . the *vestis taleris* [sic], and over this priests and dignitaries were bidden to wear the *cappa clausa*', a ruling that was reiterated in a number of decrees passed in England, notably in 1281 and 1342. Thurston defines the *vestis talaris* as a 'tunic, reaching to the feet', and commonly referred to as 'a long gown'.

Mayo, p. 47, states that earlier in 1237 'a national council, under the Legate Otto, insisted on the *vestis talaris*, a long gown or cassock, for all clerks of the bishop's household', a provision renewed 1268 in a 'constitution' later considered to be the English rule and supported in the 1571 and 1604 canons. Bernard J. Ganter also defines and describes the *vestis talaris*, for inside and outside wear, in *Clerical Attire: A Historical Synopsis and a Commentary* (Washington, D.C., 1955), pp. 10, 19–20.

For information on the *cappa clausa*, see W. N. Hargreaves-Mawdsley's Glossary for a definition and line drawings, fig. 3a for the one-slit version, and 3b for two slits, in *A History of Academical Dress in Europe until the End of the Eighteenth Century* (Oxford, 1963; rpt. Westport, CT, 1978), pp. 190ff; Hargreaves-Mawdsley, p. 5, states that in 1222, clerks were ordered by Stephen Langton to wear the *cappa clausa* (for boots, shoes, and gloves for academics, before 1350 and later, see pp. 103–4). A 1468 *cappa clausa*, or closed cope, is depicted by Houston, fig. 271, p. 155, which represents Thomas Hylle, 1468, New College Chapel, Oxford. Houston describes this picture, p. 157: 'He wears the *round pileus* or *cap*; the *caputium*, but without the *hood*, so that it may be more correctly styled the *tippet* or *cape*, the *cappa clausa* or *closed cope* and the *sub-tunica* or *cassock*.'

However, according to Barbara Harvey, in *Monastic Dress in the Middle Ages: Precept and Practice* (Canterbury, 1988), p. 8:

until the end of the Middle Ages, the secular clergy lacked a distinctive livery or uniform, despite the attempts made from time to time by the authorities to coax them into such attire. . . . secular clerks had no single place in society but were to be found at very nearly every level of the status system: ordination did not eliminate established social differences deriving from family connections, and clerical careers themselves, being of such diverse natures, might well add others. . . . it was impossible to devise a universally recognized norm of dress.

[10]   Sandler describes this figure as 'Canonist with book' (2:53), and makes it clear that Canon Law prohibited weapon-carrying by clerks, but that officials could not prevent such disobedience.

[11]   Stella Mary Newton, illustration no. 23 (c), reproduced from *Omne bonum*, BL MS Roy. 6 E VI, fol. 137, in *Fashion in the Age of the Black Prince: A Study of the Years 1340–1365* (Woodbridge, 1980; rpt. 1999), pp. 70–1. Newton's dating of this manuscript has been corrected by Sandler (see n. 8 above).

elbows positioned in an angular fashion, book[12] clasped primly in both hands in front of his body, and his head tilted to the side, suggests that he may be a skeptical listener. Elsewhere in *Omne bonum*, under the rubric of 'Habitus (Clerical Clothing)', both acceptable and unacceptable dress are described and illustrated (see Color Plate V).[13] In 'Habitus', prideful clothing, as illustrated by the short tunics, and the carrying/bearing of arms[14] were prohibited. In this illustration, the clerics at the left wear acceptable long robes, and one wears a mantle as well, while the clerks to the right dress in the unacceptable short, close-fitting tunics and carry arms. As Newton expresses it, '[T]o dress in a fashion outside the hierarchy was . . . reprehensible', for one in any station of life.[15] However, as this chapter will discuss, historical records and the slowly evolving rules for the dress of clerks bear witness that clerks, who should have been wearing the clerical robe of scholarship[16] as their 'overeste'

---

[12] A book is the premier icon of the intellectual life. See the clerk pictured with a book on seal no. 163, in pl. 8, described as 'A clerk seated to v. [sic] holding an open book on a desk with the legend, +S'MATHEI: AL'IAI:ANGLIAI:', dated thirteenth century, in A. B. Tonnochy, *Catalogue of British Seal-dies in the British Museum* (London, 1954), p. 25.

[13] *Omne bonum*, Roy. 6 E VII, fol. 197; reproduced in Sandler, 2:206.

 According to Rashdall, 3:385–7, 'It can hardly . . . be said that in the Middle Ages there was, for the undergraduate, anything which can properly be called academical dress at all.' Italian universities wished their students to wear a black *cappa* as economical dress; universities in Paris, mindful that all students were nominally clerks, mandated both tonsure and clerical habit; in England, clerks were not supposed to wear 'indecent' or 'dissolute' dress, nor 'secular' garments such as 'trunkhose', 'puffed sleeves, pointed shoes, red or green hosen', and boots (unless these boots were hidden by long garments down to their heels). He concludes that

 no particular form of garment was prescribed by university authorities: the undergraduate's dress was in no sense an official costume. The differentia of clerical dress was apparently supposed to lie in the outer garment being of a certain length and closed in front. . . . The restriction to black is not common till even later.

[14] See Sandler, 1:106, regarding immodesty in clerical dress as pictured in *Omne bonum* and the equation of carrying swords with the practice of sexual license. See also Lynn Thorndike, *University Records and Life in the Middle Ages* (New York, 1944; rpt. 1949), pp. 78–80, regarding the prohibition of arms to clerks.

[15] Newton, p. 70.

[16] A drawing in a c.1464 manuscript at New College, Oxford, *Brevis Chronica de ortu, vita, et gestis nobilibus reverendi viri Willelmi de Wykeham*, shows a birds-eye view of the college with its members in proper habit, including three clerks. These chaplains and clerks wear surplices and 'some of them wear scarves', according to H. W. Macklin, *The Brasses of England* (London, 1907), pp. 137, 139; Macklin, pp. 135–41, describes academic costume in general, saying that the earliest example of an academical tabard in a funerary brass is 1501.

 This same drawing is reproduced, dated as 1463, and discussed by Phillis Cunnington and Catherine Lucas, *Charity Costumes of Children, Scolars, Almsfolk, Pensioners* (London, 1978), fig. 128, pp. 216–18. According to these authors, p. 217, this picture shows scholars and junior fellows who wear tabards with cape-like sleeves

garment within most areas of the university city, did at times properly dress in non-scholarly clothing in accordance with exceptions to the local rules.[17] These exceptions are pertinent as they relate to the Clerk's *courtepy*.

Clerkly sartorial rulings aside, the *courtepy* is the single garment mentioned by Chaucer in the Clerk's portrait and it is a lay garment, not part of any kind of scholarly, clerkly, or academic costume. Any present-day reader who seeks to interpret Chaucer's costume rhetoric in this image of a courtepy immediately encounters the difficulty of acquiring a precise description or definition of the Clerk's garment. The MED defines *courtepy* as a 'short woolen coat or jacket; tabard, pea jacket', and attributes its etymology to the Middle Dutch, 'corte (curte) pī-e short coat'. Among the examples of usage, the first entry is dated 1270 and the last '?c1475'. All but three of the eleven MED examples originate in legal records and wills where the descriptions indicate that a courtepy was an external garment with or without an attached hood. Two different courtepys among these eleven examples are blue in color, one being furred. In the final example, the *courtepy, cowrtby*, is synonymous with '*renale, hemitogium*'. The remaining three examples derive from medieval literature, two of which are Chaucerian – the Clerk's courtepy and Avarice's courtepy in the *Romaunt of the Rose* – while the third example is from *Piers Plowman: The B Version*.[18]

Elsewhere, *A Dictionary of English Costume: 900–1900* describes the *courtepy* as an 'upper garment akin to the Surcoat', worn by both men and women in the fourteenth and fifteenth centuries, and comments, 'Exact nature unknown'. This entry further states that the 'male garment was short and in the 15th c. may have been the same as the short Houppelande'.[19] The pursuit of a more exact definition of *courtepy* via comparisons with its synonyms produces only further reader confusion regarding length and silhouette. According to this same source, the *houppelande*[20] (deemed synonymous with the more commonly used *gown* after 1450) was worn during the end of the fourteenth and throughout the fifteenth century, and it is defined as a 'voluminous upper garment fitting the shoulders and generally falling in tubular folds. The length varied from reaching the thighs to trailing on the ground (in

and hoods that have liripipes; senior fellows who wear a pileus; and fellows (most likely masters) who wear tabards with cape-like sleeves. A 1434 scholar's gown for a boy is depicted p. 87, fig. 51; he is not designated a clerk.

17 See Ganter, pp. 12ff and p. 20, regarding the freedom to follow local custom.

18 I cite William Langland, *Piers Plowman: The B Version*, eds George Kane and E. Talbot Donaldson (University of London, 1975), hereafter referred to as *P.P.B.* The version cited by the MED is LdMisc 581, passus 6, line 191.

19 C. W. Cunnington, P. E. Cunnington, and Charles Beard, *A Dictionary of English Costume: 900–1900* (London, 1960).

20 Two line drawings are provided by Cunnington, Cunnington, and Beard. Also see the definition of *houppelande* in Susan Crane's *The Performance of Self: Ritual, Clothing and Identity During the Hundred Years War* (Philadelphia, 2002), p. 185, n. 20.

ceremonial costume).'[21] A *surcoat*, the other synonym mentioned for *courtepy*, is also designated as the more usual name for the *super tunic* in the thirteenth and fourteenth centuries; it was a ninth- through the end of the fourteenth-century garment worn by both men and women. The male version of this garment is described as a 'loose garment put on over the head and worn over the tunic or cote. The shape varied and by the fourteenth century was closer fitting. Made long if ceremonial; otherwise short to the knees'. And this entry, too, lists a variety of synonyms for the *super tunic/surcoat* including *garnashe*,[22] *garde corps*, and *tabard*. Cunnington, Cunnington, and Beard also define one last costume term, the *cote-hardie*, a unisex garment of the fourteenth to mid-fifteenth century, included in this general category of overgarments, and cite 1333 as the first reference to this garment for masculine use. Although they provide a detailed description of the *cote-hardie*, again these authors offer a disclaimer:

> Its exact nature remains obscure; the cote-hardie is thought to have been a close-fitting, knee-length overgarment with low neck; buttoned down the front to a low waist. Elbow-length sleeves with a tongue shaped extension behind. After c.1350 the cote-hardie was shortened and the elbow flap lengthened into a long narrow hanging band known as a 'tippet' or French 'coudière'. . . . A belt was always worn at hip-level.

Other costume historians provide somewhat differing descriptions. Mary G. Houston's Glossary defines *côte-hardie* only as a 'tight-fitting tunic when worn by men'.[23] Herbert Norris, too, equates a *courtepy* with a *cotehardie*. He describes a courtepy of the period of Richard II, 1377–99:

> [a] cotehardie of the latest cut – a JAQUETTE, or, as it was sometimes called, COURTEPY (German, *Curtuspije*), a very short overgarment or jacket, which was often parti-coloured or *pied*. Worn over the paltock or pourpoint, it fitted the shoulders and chest, was buttoned down the front, fastened tight round the waist, and descended only a short distance on the hips, revealing a large area of thigh.[24]

---

21 See Gervase Mathew, *The Court of Richard II* (New York, 1968), regarding both houppelande and cote-hardies, pp. 25–7, and pl. 13 of Prince Henry in a long houppelande, reproduced from the frontispiece of BL Arundel MS 38, dated before 1413, as described p. 203; Newton, Appendix I, pp. 127–8; Diana de Marly, *Fashion For Men: An Illustrated History* (New York, 1985), pp. 16–17, 21–2, regarding the houppelande and the cote or cotte hardi; also Françoise Piponnier and Perrine Mane, *Dress in the Middle Ages*, trans. Caroline Beamish (New Haven, CT, 1997), glossary regarding *haincelin* (short houppelande), and its longer version, pp. 165–6; illustration, p. 19, pl. 6.

22 Cunnington, Cunnington, and Beard provide a line drawing for a *garnache*.

23 Houston, p. 222.

24 Herbert Norris, *Medieval Costume and Fashion* (Mineola, NY, 1999), pp. 245–6, fig. 346, and pl. 13.

Norris's illustration (fig. 346) includes an innovative stand-up collar so tall that it nearly touches the earlobe. Other features are tight sleeves ending in cuffs, and the more elaborate models featured gold-thread embroidery.[25] In addition, Newton's contribution to this catalogue of descriptive definitions groups *courtpie* with *aketon* and *doublet* as like garments, in one particular case – worn when going hunting.[26]

Clearly, the variety in details of these overgarments precludes any ease, on the part of a twenty-first-century reader, in forming a clear mental image of the Clerk's 'overest'[27] garment, or outer wear. The long period from at least 1270 through '?c1475' during which *courtepy* was in use as a garment term suggests that the term itself most likely referred to an outer garment that underwent a number of stylistic changes.

The single agreed-upon characteristic of definitions specifically for *courtepy* is its shortness, for ordinary wear – although the exact dimensions are unavailable, and the length most likely varied over time. At best, the short *courtepy* lacks the social, professional, and moral authority signified by the scholarly long robe, the *vestis talaris*; and at worst a short coat implies the lack of integrity signified in Mankind's short jacket in the fifteenth-century drama of the same name.[28] The three literary examples for *courtepy* provided by the MED support this point.[29] Further, in three MED citations from literature, the *courtepy* is a garment of very poor quality.[30] In *P.P.B*, hermits hack

---

25 Norris, pp. 250–1, also describes a *courtepy/cotehardie* depicted in his fig. 352 with wide fur-edged and silk-lined sleeves, all-over embroidery, high collar with white fur edge. This is his conception of Chaucer's Squire's dress.

26 Newton, pp. 54, 27–8.

27 The MED defines *overest* as 'Upper, uppermost, highest, top; (b) outer, outermost' and cites CT Prol, A 290, including the Clerk's courtepy as an example for the (b) definition. A second example cited is CT – CY 'Ouerist sloppe' (which was not worth a mite [G 633]), from the 1500 Chaucer CT.CY. (Hrl 7333).

28 I have briefly discussed this significance in *C&C*, p. 59.

29 Nor should we forget that Chaucer chooses this short garment, 'a courtepy of green', as appropriate dress for the 'gay yeman', the self-identified 'feend', resident of 'helle', and consummate con man in *The Friar's Tale* (III, lines 1380–3, 1429–31).

30 The actual value of a courtepy would depend upon a variety of circumstances. A 1335 reference in the MED provides a price for a courtepy of 10s, probably new, quality unknown. At this price, a banneret (paid at 4s *per diem*) would serve knight's duty for 2½ days, and knights of lower rank (at 2s *per diem*) for 5 days, to pay for such a courtepy, according to 'Order for Payment of Wages for the Scottish War, 1347', *English Historical Documents*, ed. A. R. Myers (New York, 1969), 4:85–6. Further, squires (at 12d *per diem*, which is 1s) would need to serve for 10 days, and archers on horseback (at 4d) for 30 days.

    This 1335 price of a courtepy at 10s may also be compared to a 1393 inventory of previously worn items in the home of Richard Toky, London grocer: 1 cloak of *blod* lined with blanket 5s, 1 other old cloak 16d, and 1 worn-out cloak at 8d, as reported by Edith Rickert, comp., *Chaucer's World*, eds Clair C. Olson and Martin M. Crow (New

off their copes (long semi-circular outer garments) to create the workmanlike length of a courtepy:

> An heep of heremytes henten hem spades
> And kitten hir copes and courtepies hem maked
> And wente as werkmen [to wedynge] and [mowynge]
> And doluen [drit] and [dung] to [ditte out] hunger.
>
> (Passus 6, lines 187–90)

E. Talbot Donaldson translates these cut-off 'copes' as 'short coats', while J. F. Goodridge describes this garment alteration as 'a crowd of hermits, cutting their cloaks to make jerkins'.[31] The shortened length was expedient; as a result of shortening their copes, the formerly sedentary hermits would not be hindered by long clothing while engaging in the manual labor of assisting Piers to sow his field and stave off hunger.

The *Romaunt of the Rose*, Chaucer's translation of the *Roman de la rose*, provides another literary usage of a courtepy of poor quality in the portrait of Avarice (lines 209–46).

> And she was clad ful porely
> Al in an old torn courtepy,
> As she were al with doggis torn[32]   (lines 219–21)

In lines 222–3, the narrator adds that Avarice was wrapped in beggar's rags, thus characterizing all of her garments. And he provides details of her mantle, which was hanging on her clothing rod along with 'a burnet cote' 'ful old' (lines 224, 226, 230), glossed in *Riverside Chaucer* as a 'coat made of coarse brown cloth', which was lined with heavy black 'lambe-skynnes' (lines 227–9), considered to be a rude fur. Overall, her garments fit the description 'Al were it bad of woll and hewe' (line 238) telling the limits to which her clothing must deteriorate before she would replace a garment.[33]

York, 1948), pp. 62–3, citing London, Corporation, *Calendar of Select Pleas and Memoranda, A.D. 1381–1412*, ed. by Thomas, pp. 209–13.

[31] E. Talbot Donaldson, trans., *Will's Vision of Piers Plowman*. William Langland, eds Elizabeth D. Kirk and Judith H. Anderson (New York, 1990), Passus 6, line 188. J. F. Goodridge's trans. of William Langland's *Piers the Ploughman* (New York, 1959; rpt. 1980), p. 86.

[32] Chaucer's *Romaunt of the Rose*, *Riverside Chaucer*, p. 689, hereafter referred to as *Rom.*

[33] Cf. the thirteenth-century portrait by Guillaume de Lorris in *Le Roman de la rose*, ed. Daniel Poirion (Paris, 1974), pp. 48–9, lines 197–234 (portrait of Avarice); description of her clothing, lines 207–26, which mentions a 'cote', and a 'mantiau' (lines 208, 215:

> Ert elle povrement vestu:
> Cote avoit viés et derompue
> Comme s'el fust as chiens remese;
> Povre ert mout sa cote et esrese

Finally, within this trio of literary examples offered by the MED we come to Chaucer's Clerk's courtepy. His courtepy is not created by mutilation like the hermits' copes in *P.P.B*, nor does it resemble a garment rent by brawling dogs, the comparison Chaucer translates in *Rom*. Nevertheless, the Clerk's courtepy has its own distinctive characteristic, which, from a sartorial point of view, is disreputable – it is 'ful thredbare', a designation that emphasizes its age and/or near-disintegration from wear. Beyond that, this worn condition possesses its own literary implications.

In its threadbare state, the Clerk's courtepy is the opposite of what would be called foppish or dandified dress, such as is worn by Absalon, whom John Fleming names Chaucer's 'masterpiece of the type' familiarly known as 'fop' or 'dandy'. Fleming lists all the details of Absalon's foppishness – cut-out shoes (lines 3118ff); perfumes (line 3690); the 'gay' clothing he dons 'at poynt-devys' (line 3689),[34] which *Riverside Chaucer* glosses as 'dresses himself handsomely'/ 'in every detail'; and his golden curls (line 3314).[35]

> Et plene de viés paletiaus.
> Delé li pendoit uns mantiaus
> A une perchete grelete,
> Et une cote de brunete;
> Ou mantiau n'ot pas penne vere,
> Mes mout viés et de povre afere,
> D'agniaus noirs, velus et pesans.
> Bien avoit la robe vint ans,
> Mes Avarice du vestir
> Se siaut mout a tart aatir;
> Car sachies que mout li pesast
> Se cele robe point usast;
> Car s'el fust usee et mavese,
> Avarice eüst grant mesese
> De nove robe et grant disete
> Avant qu'ele eüst autre fete.

See also Charles Dahlberg's translation of Guillaume de Lorris and Jean de Meun, *The Romance of the Rose* (Hanover, NH, 1983), p. 33:

> She was . . . poorly clothed: she had an old coat, torn as if it had been among dogs, that was poor and worn out and full of old patches. Beside her, on a little thin clothespole, hung a mantle and a coat of sleazy material. The mantle had no fur linings, but very poor and shabby ones of heavy, shaggy black lamb. Her dress was at least ten years old.

34 John V. Fleming, 'Gospel Asceticism: Some Chaucerian Images of Perfection', *Chaucer and Scriptural Tradition*, ed. David Lyle Jeffrey (Ottawa, 1984), pp. 194–5. Fleming also comments upon the monastic fop, whom he names the ' "prince" of pretenders', citing Saint-Jérome, *Lettres*, ed. Jérome Labourt (Paris, 1949), 1:142 (*Epistola* xxii, 28).

35 Whitmore, p. 169, compares the Clerk to Absalon, a parish clerk in the *Miller's Tale*, as regards clothing. Absolon's clothing exhibits no poverty (*MilT*, I, lines 3314–16); he is 'appropriately clad in a kirtle', defined in Whitmore's n. 165: 'The kirtle was a kind of a tunic or surcoat. Often it was worn next the shirt and was covered by the outer cloak

Absalon, although he is a parish clerk,[36] nevertheless illustrates the principle behind the 1442 complaint about clerks at Fotheringhay College wearing 'their dress after the manner of lay-folk to the scandal of the clerkly order and the college'.[37]

The principle at issue at Fotheringhay, as it was in the previously mentioned directives and illuminations in *Omne bonum*, is that of seemliness: each preceding and succeeding directive regarding clerkly costume, through the centuries, instructed clerks to dress in a manner appropriate to their clerkly status.[38] Periodically, such vagueness is supplanted by specific

---

or cope'. Whitmore cites Joseph Strutt, *A Complete View of the Dress and Habits of the People of England, from the Establishment of the Saxons in Britain to the Present Time: Illustrated by Engravings Taken from the Most Authentic Remains of Antiquity,* Critical and explanatory notes by J. R. Planché, 2 vols (London, 1842; London, 1970), p. 349, and compares this garment to the modern cassock. Further, she describes this kirtle 'of light blue', surmounted by 'a gay surplice "as whyte as is the blosme up-on the rys" ' (quoting *MilT,* lines 3320–4). She finds Absalon's shoes 'still more striking', quoting lines 3318–19:

> With Powles window corven in his shoes,
> In hoses rede he went fetisly.

Whitmore states that these shoes 'were displayed to full advantage by the fashionable red hose worn beneath them'.

36 Whitmore notes the Parish Clerk Absolon's sociable nature, 'jolif and gay' (lines 3339, 3348). In any case, Absalon appears to fulfill many of the functions of the parish clerk in the Middle Ages: he functions as barber to 'laten blood, and clippe and shave'; as clerk-scribe to 'maken a chartre of lond or acquitaunce'; as dancer and musician and singer; as clerk carrying the 'sencer' in church services (lines 3326–33, 3340–1). Regarding parish clerks, see S. H. Rigby, *English Society in the Later Middle Ages: Class, Status and Gender* (New York, 1995), pp. 210, 213; and on the clergy order and status, pp. 206–42, esp. 206–7.

See *The Clerk's Book of 1549,* pp. xxxix–xli, regarding Absolon's clothing, including a general history of vesture for clerks, and p. xlix concerning finding a surplice for the clerk. Legg describes duties of the Parish Clerk, p. xviii, and discusses salaries, pp. lviii–lx; he states, p. xvii, that parishes customarily had such clerks, below deacon and priest in status, from St Augustine's and King Ethelbert's time. According to John Nicholls, compiler, *Illustrations of the Manners and Expences of Antient Times in England, In the Fifteenth, Sixteenth, and Seventeenth Centuries, Deduced From The Accompts of Churchwardens, and Other Authentic Documents, Collected From Various Parts of the Kingdom, with Explanatory Notes* (London, 1797; rpt. London, 1973), p. 10, extracts from Churchwardens' accounts of St Margaret's, Westminster for 1460–61 state that surplices were acquired, respectively, for the curate, costing 10s; for John More the clerk, Thomas Adams the clerk, and for the sexton, each costing 3s. Also listed, p. 37, was the purchase of 'thirteen ells of Holland more, to make surplisses for the two clarks and sextons, at 3s 4d the ell', with the total purchase price of £3 16s 8d.

37 *Visitations . . . Lincoln,* 2:111.

38 A clerk's status varied according to the stage he had reached in the educational

details, as in the case of the rules for clerks' dress that prohibited the wearing of certain clothing items at Cambridge University, King's College, rules influenced by regulations of New College, Oxford. Particularly interesting are the directives restricting fellows and scholars, except with appropriate permission, from wearing the following:

> red or green shoes secular or curved, or fancy (*modulatis*) hoods inside or outside the university, or to carry openly or secretly swords or long knives or arms for assault or defense, or belts or girdles decorated with gold or silver . . . either outside or inside the university and the city [Cambridge].[39]

Also of interest is the Ordinance on College Gowns of 1358, which is aimed at tailors. They are forbidden to make university 'gowns' (clerkly garments) that are either too brief or too scantily cut; instead, gowns were to be

> wide[40] and reaching to the ankles as they have been accustomed to wear in times past. For it is decent and consonant with reason that those to whom God had granted the privilege of mental adornment beyond the laity should also be outwardly different in dress from the laity.

The punishment for tailors who produced tight-fitting or too-short gowns was imprisonment until they corrected any such garment made 'skimpily and against the dignity of the university'.[41]

---

process. James A. Weisheipl describes this process and the stages of a clerk-scholar at Oxford University in 'Curriculum of the Faculty of Arts at Oxford in the Early Fourteenth Century', *MS* 26 (1964), pp. 143–85. See the levels of achievement listed for John Clerke by C. H. Talbot and E. A. Hammond, *The Medical Practitioners in Medieval England: A Biographical Register* (London, 1965), p. 133. Also note the stages of education and preferment achieved by John Thorp, as described by Rigby, *English Society*, p. 229, who mentions Thorp as an Oxfordian student, as clerk for the bishop of Winchester, as servant to the crown, and as archdeacon of Suffolk, among other posts held under Richard II. For the sequence of stages in holy orders and the duties of each stage, see *Pastors and the Care of Souls: in Medieval England*, eds John Shinners and William J. Dohar (Notre Dame, IN, 1998), pp. 50, 64–70.

See also Gerald Morgan, 'The Design of the *General Prologue* to the *Canterbury Tales*', *ES* 59 (1978), pp. 490–1, for a classification of the Clerk in the lowest social rank of gentils, along with the Merchant, Sergeant of Law, and Franklin.

39 Rickert, comp., pp. 129–30, citing *The Ancient Laws of the Fifteenth Century, for King's College, Cambridge, and . . . Eton College*, pp. 21, 67–8, 71, 73, 80, 83–4, 118–19, 131, 133–4.

40 *Wide* is not used here in the sense of excess fabric usage, as I discussed in Chapter 1. In this case, *wide* means not form-fitting, a style that was then fashionable.

41 Rickert, p. 133, citing Anstey, ed. *Munimenta academica*, I, 212–13.

James E. Thorold Rogers, *A History of Agriculture and Prices in England* (Oxford, 1892; rpt. Vaduz, 1963), 4:566, provides a list of fabric purchases for the personnel at King's College which indicates the hierarchy of cost and value for various academic levels. A sampling of this list shows that for the Provost (Warden), 12 yds were bought

Chaucer's costume rhetoric in the Clerk's portrait fits into neither of the two handy categories of garments previously mentioned, both illustrated in *Omne bonum* (see Color Plate V), and both also mentioned in Cambridge University records: proper clerkly-academic costume or stylish lay garb. Although the Clerk's outer garment is lay dress that may have been fashionable at one time, the threadbare condition of his courtepy effectively exonerates him from any designation of fop or dandy. Further, the worn condition of this courtepy constitutes a *Social Mirror*, sartorially placing him in the category of the 'poor scholars' familiar to readers of academic history: 'a scholar unable to support himself without assistance',[42] and described in the Friar's portrait as a 'povre scoler' who wears a 'threbare cope' instead of a 'semycope' of 'double worstede' like 'maister or pope', as the Friar himself

at 4s per yd. (48s); for each graduate fellow, 8 yds at 2s 6d per yd. (20s); for each non-graduate, 8 yds at 2s 2d per yd. (17s 4d); for each clerk (and each valet) 3½ yds at 2s (7s). Clerks and valets precede the final group of persons, the choristers and garciones, each of whom receives 2½ yds at 1s 10d.

    The Statutes of the Realm (1910; rpt. London, 1963), 1:381, item XIII, considers furs and income, and recognizes that the dress of all clerics was regulated by their church, cathedral, college, etc. However, it does say that clerks having ii. C. marks income from land per year may wear the same clothing as knights of the same income wear. Clerks having rent comparable to esquires (C. li marks) should dress as those esquires do. Beyond that, any who are legally entitled to wear wintertime fur may also wear summertime 'Linure' (lawn).

    Houston provides, p. 155, line drawings of academic dress, including esp. fig. 269, and describes, pp. 156–7, the furs depicted in a memorial brass of Richard Harward, 1493, Master of St Cross, Winchester: 'He wears the square *pileus* or *cap*, the fur *almuce* with tails and lappets, the *super-pellicum* or *surplice* and the *sub-tunica* or *cassock*. The cuffs of this latter garment show a fur lining.'

42 Bennett, p. 117, citing Rashdall's definition; see Bennett's Appendix A, pp. 117–19, regarding poor scholars. The phrases *poor scholar* and *poor clerk* appear often in university records, according to the index of Thorndike's *University Records*. Rigby, *English Society*, p. 231, estimates costs for a year of study at a university at £6–7, per annum. Also see Brian Tierney, *The Medieval Poor Law: A Sketch of Canonical Theory and Its Application in England* (Berkeley and Los Angeles, 1959), pp. 19–21, regarding the scholarly obligation to teach poor scholars who were unable to pay the usual fees; A. H. Lloyd, *The Early History of Christ's College, Cambridge* (Cambridge, 1934), Appendix A(b), p. 356, concerning the difficulty in maintaining enough teachers of grammar for King's College, Cambridge, and the request made to the king to allow poor scholars of grammar to study there without payment for housing and fees, in order to acquire grammar teachers to meet the ongoing demand; Andrew's remarks, p. 281, on the 'poor scholars'; and E. F. Jacob's essay, 'English University Clerks in the Later Middle Ages', *Essays in the Conciliar Epoch* [hereafter *Essays*], 3rd edn rev. (Manchester, 1963), pp. 207–39, esp. his definition of a poor scholar, pp. 208–9. Poor scholars were supported in earlier stages of their education also; see Nicholas Orme, *English Schools in the Middle Ages* (London, 1973), pp. 119–20, 182–6, 243–5, esp. p. 184 regarding school expenses. Ussery, 'How Old?', p. 14, states that scholars, young and old, needed and accepted donations for their upkeep; pp. 15–17, he comments on poverty as a characteristic of the 'ideal' clerk.

wears (lines 260–2). Chaucer provides two more examples of 'yonge povre scolers' in Aleyn and John, Cambridge scholars who lived in Soler Halle, in *The Reeve's Tale* (I, lines 3990, 4002, 4003, 4018), and yet a third clerk, 'hende Nicholas' (I, line 3199) of Oxford, described as 'a poure scoler', in *The Miller's Tale* (I, line 3190). However, we find that Nicholas is not quite so poor after all; he lived 'After his freendes fyndyng and his rente'; that is, his income derived both from the donations of friends and from income of his own (line 3220).[43]

Concern for poor scholars was the motivation underlying the specifications for dress laid down at the University of Toulouse. These rules were devised to protect scholars of moderate means who, rather than pay the necessary expenses of housing, food, books, and fees, tended to overspend on dress instead, a tendency that eventually caused these students to terminate their education. Consequently, in 1314, rules were duly recorded in the Statutes of the University and Faculties of Civil and Canon Law, setting limits on prices for scholars' clothing and fabric purchases, thus creating an 'approved mediocrity' for university garb. Garments of a set price were specified for scholars, bachelors, licentiates, and masters, who must wear them both inside and out of doors, throughout the city with the exception of within their own dwelling or within their dwelling's immediate surroundings for the space of twenty buildings. The garments regulated were: 'the closed overtunic, the upper tunic, excepting open overtunics, togas, hoods and tunics' worn for non-academic occasions, and 'except vests without sleeves or with sleeves which don't show and mittens, shoes and berets'. Beyond that, any garments desired might be worn while riding horseback, and garments and cloth of any cost that had been received as gifts might be worn for non-academic functions.[44] We note especially that there are no rules for what might be worn for horseback riding, and thus those scholars who were dandies might well have worn fine garments for this activity.

In the case of Chaucer's Clerk, however, such an exemption for riding, if applicable in Oxford, would only tell us that a courtepy worn while he travels by horse to Canterbury would not violate proper sartorial practice. Further, Chaucer does not say that the Clerk wears his courtepy in university congregations or disputations, thus disregarding custom as some educators and scholars did. Such violators of academic custom included University of Paris masters, whose irregular garments necessitated the institution of academic dress regulations for masters, bachelors, and scholars in 1339. These regulations proceeded from the complaint that

---

43 Nicholas Orme discusses Chaucer's several clerks, in 'Chaucer and Education', *ChauR* 16 (1981), pp. 50, 52, as 'secular clerks' in minor orders, but not yet *members* of one of the religious orders. See also Astell, p. 55.
44 Thorndike, pp. 150–4.

some masters do not shrink from attending congregations and disputations in their mantles, sleeveless tunics, or tabards, while bachelors or scholars presume to take their seats at disputations in other costume than the long-sleeved cope (*cappa*).

All of these practices were considered scandalous. The principle behind this complaint was, again, seemliness – that educators 'should be distinguished by some decency of garb' from other people.[45]

Conversely, the Clerk's wearing of a threadbare courtepy on pilgrimage, as opposed to while attending university affairs, would apparently raise few eyebrows, unless someone might have complained that 'thredbare' violates the general standard of mediocrity that was deemed seemly for clerics. In any case, clearly Whitmore sees no such violation. She compares the Clerk's costume in the *General Prologue* with that of St Richard of Chicester,

> of whom it is said that he had such love for learning 'that he cared little or nothing for food or raiment', and that he and two companions who lodged together had only one gown and their tunics between them. 'When one, therefore, went out with the gown to hear a lecture, the others sat in their room, and so they went forth alternately.'[46]

Apparently Whitmore assumed that this academic gown worn by three scholars would show its triple wear and be comparable in quality to the Clerk's courtepy; she does not qualify her judgment to account for the difference in style between an academic gown and a layman's courtepy. Thus in her comparison of the Clerk to St Richard, *thredbare* is specifically equated with great 'love for learning' and employed in support of her reading Chaucer's portrait of the Clerk as a delineation of an ideal figure.

Other favorable associations with *threadbare* include those of the virtue of humility as symbolized by Christ's clothing in Julian of Norwich's *Showings*, as explicated by Ritamary Bradley. She discusses Christ wearing 'servant's clothing', quoting Julian that He was

> 'clad symply, as a laborer whych was dysposyd to traveyle . . . hys clothyng was a whytt kyrtyll, singell, olde and all defautyd, dyed with swete of his body, streyte syttyng to hym and shorte, as it were an handfull beneth the knee, bare, semyng as it shuld sone be worne vppe, redy to be raggyd and rent' (51.165–71).

This clothing betokens who the servant is – the one man, Christ and

45 Thorndike, pp. 191–2. The correct costume for masters specified 'cope, cassock long or short, trimmed with fur'. Penalties were set for all failing to wear their proper academic costumes. Also see Rashdall, 3:389–91.
46 Whitmore, pp. 168–9, citing G. G. Coulton, *Social Life in Britain from the Conquest to the Reformation* (Cambridge, 1918), p. 61; and *Catholic Encyclopedia* 13:43.

Adam:

'. . . by the pore clothyng as a laborer stondyng nere the lyft syde is
vnderstond þe manhode of Adam with alle the myschefe and febylnesse þat
folowyth . . .' (51.226–29).

Bradley also relates Julian's extended amplification:

'the wyth kyrtyll is his fleshe; the singlehede is that ther was ryght noght
betwen/ the godhede and the manhede. The strayght nesse is povyrte, the
elde is of Adams werying. The defaultyng is the swete of Adams traveyle;
the shortness shewyth the servant laborar' (51.244–47).

According to Bradley, 'The worn condition of the clothing reflects' Christ's
willingness to wear Adam's old kyrtylle and take up the task of sacrificing
himself for humankind.[47] And Bradley continues, 'In the fourth revelation
Julian had seen the flesh of Christ as "broken on pecys as a/ cloth, and
saggynge downward, semyng as it wolde hastely haue fallen for heuynes and
for lowsenes" (17.24–26).' Bradley states that Julian unifies vision and
parable in her explication: ' "By that his kertyll was at the poynt to be ragged
is vnderstod the roddys and (the) scorgys . . . his tendyr flessch rentyng . . ."
(51.288–93).'[48] Concerning this description of Christ's garments, two points
bear emphasizing: first that the age and condition of Christ's kirtle signify
'Adams werying', or the idea of mankind's fallen nature, with the resultant
guilty assumption of clothing, and the necessity for labor; and second that
this symbolic kirtle is 'at the poynt to be ragged'. Significantly, this last
description indicates a threadbare condition – the garment has reached that
point just before holes appear and patches are needed. Although this kirtle
represents humankind's fall and need to labor, at the same time, when Christ
wears it, it represents His humility. According to D. W. Robertson and
Bernard F. Huppé, 'the humility of Christ, figured in his poverty', as signified by wearing an old garment, 'is an example to all of us' and they cite
Piers Plowman in support of their reading of this sign:

For owre ioye and owre hele   Ihesu Cryst of heuene,
In a pore mannes apparaille   pursueth vs euere,
And loketh on vs in her liknesse   and that with louely chere,

---

47 See Lynn Staley, 'The Man in Foul Clothes and a Late Fourteenth-Century Conversation About Sin', *SAC* 24 (2002), pp. 1–47, esp. the discussion of Christ's and Adam's
garments, pp. 31–4, as well as the treatment of cleanness throughout this article, which
concerns 'a late fourteenth-century English discourse about sin that uses the man in
foul clothes to explore the ecclesiastical position upon or vulnerability to the doctrine
of judgment' (p. 47).
48 Sr Ritamary Bradley, 'Metaphors of Cloth and Clothing in the Showings of Julian of
Norwich', *Mediaevalia* 9 (1983), pp. 269–82, esp. pp. 271–2, with further explication,
pp. 274–5.

> To knowen vs by owre kynde herte   and castyng of owre eyen,
> Whether we loue the lordes here   byfor owre lorde of blisse.[49]
>
> (Passus 11, lines 179–83)

Poverty and the age of a garment worn are consistent with the idea expressed in the term *threadbare*. Thus, while *threadbare*, less favorably, indicates mankind's sinful nature and fall and his subsequent status as servant and laborer, yet among the favorable interpretations of this term, it signifies a love of learning and Christian humility. The OED provides the specific denotation for this word: 'Of a garment . . . : Having the nap worn off, leaving bare the threads of the warp and woof; worn to the thread; shabby; worn out', and provides examples from Langland and Chaucer. The first of these (dated 1362), is from *PP.A*, V. 113: 'But ȝif a lous couþe lepe I con it not I-leue heo scholde wandre on þat walk hit was so þred-bare.' Chronologically, the second example (1386) is found in Chaucer's Clerk's portrait (line 290) already discussed. The MED echoes the substance of the OED definition, and provides a metaphorical usage of 'inadequate, poor; ~ of, deficient in (sth.)'. Further, the first figurative usage mentioned by both dictionaries for this term is Hoccleve's 1412 description of a person who is 'thredebare of konnynge' (*RP*, Hrl 4866) [lacks knowledge].

Threadbare literally signifies cloth or clothing in a state of deterioration only one stage removed from being ragged, while in the example above it metaphorically connotes a lack or deficiency. In portraying the Clerk's courtepy as threadbare, Chaucer's choice of diction is precise. The Clerk is not ragged, as peasants sometimes are;[50] and his courtepy is not torn by external forces such as the dogs in the simile applied to the clothing of Avarice (in *Rom.*), or by the Clerk himself as did the *PP.B.* hermits, both previously mentioned (p. 169). The Clerk's clothing was neither torn by destructive men as in the cases of the allegorical garments worn by Philosophy and Nature who are described by Boethius and Alanus de Insulis,[51] where the tears represent the viciousness and covetousness of mankind; nor torn by too

---

[49] D. W. Robertson, Jr and Bernard F. Huppé, *Piers Plowman and Scriptural Tradition* (Princeton, 1951), pp. 138, 141. See also these authors' explications of Augustine's treatment, and Scripture's allegory of poverty in *PP* Passus 11, esp. pp. 179–83, 230–4.

[50] As I have previously discussed in *C&C*, pp. 1, 15, 215–18, 220–1.

[51] Regarding these excisions, see Boethius, *The Consolation of Philosophy*, trans., introduction and notes by Richard Green (Indianapolis, IN, 1980), p. 4. Chaucer's *Boece*, *Riverside Chaucer*, p. 398, Book I, Prosa I, lines 37–41: 'Natheles handes of some men hadden korve that cloth by violence and by strengthe, and everich man of hem hadde boren awey swiche peces as he myghte geten.' Similarly, Alan of Lille, *The Plaint of Nature*, trans. and commentary by James J. Sheridan, Pontifical Institute of Mediaeval Studies (Toronto, 1980), p. 40: Nature says that the rents in her costume exist because 'vicious men have attacked Nature and torn off pieces of her garment to keep for themselves'; see also pp. 98–9 for a depiction of Nature's tunic; and Alanus de Insulis, *The Complaint of Nature*, trans. Douglas M. Moffat (New York, 1908; rpt. 1972), p. 15.

much wear, as is Enide's white linen *chainse*,[52] which represents her poverty. The Clerk's courtepy represents no particular imposed humiliation, as in the cases of the clothing of the silkworkers in *Yvaine*,[53] which highlights the deprivation of their captivity and humiliation; the old and ragged dress of the beautiful maiden in *Perceval*,[54] where the tears represent the maiden's public

---

[52] Alice Colby, *The Portrait in Twelfth Century French Literature* (Genève, 1965), p. 140, provides an explication of Enide's shabby clothes: 'Chrétien states that Enide's clothing (*robe*) consists solely of a *cheinse* and a chemise'. . . . 'the poor condition of the *cheinse* is revealed' and the syntax and rhyme stress the 'age of the garment' and also 'the connection between age and shabbiness. The exact location of the rents in the *cheinse* is thrown into relief by the anticipatory element *as costez* "at the elbows".' In addition, lines 409–10 emphasize 'the contrast between the tattered appearance of Enide's clothing and the beauty of her body'. Colby cites, pp. 138–9, the following description of Enide's clothing:

> La dame s'an est hors issue
> Et sa fille, qui fu vestu
> D'une chemise par panz lee,
> Delïee, blanche et ridee;
> Un blanc cheinse ot vestu desus,
> N'avoit robe ne mains ne plus,
> Et tant estoit li chainses viez
> Que as costez estoit perciez:
> Povre estoit la robe dehors,
> Mes desoz estoit biax li cors.   (lines 401–10)

> [The lady came out with her daughter, who was dressed in a soft white under-robe with wide skirts hanging loose in folds. Over it she wore a white linen garment, which completed her attire. And this garment was so old that it was full of holes down the sides. Poor, indeed, was her garb without, but within her body was fair. (Trans. W. W. Comfort, *Erec et Enide* by Chrétien de Troyes, *Arthurian Romances* [New York, 1975], p. 6.)]

Erec, p. 21, explaining to Guinevere why Enide comes to court dressed in such a poor fashion, characterizes her clothing as 'poor garb': 'It is poverty that has compelled her to wear this white linen garment until both sleeves are torn at the side.' John W. Baldwin defines *chainse* as 'an outer garment, usually white and of lightweight material', and mentions Enide's *chainse*, 'ragged at the elbows', in *Aristocratic Life in Medieval France: The Romances of Jean Renart and Gerbert de Montreuil, 1190–1230* (Baltimore, 2000), p. 184. See Douglas Kelly, 'The Art of Description', *The Legacy of Chrétien de Troyes*, eds Norris J. Lacy, Douglas Kelly, and Keith Busby (Amsterdam, 1987), 1:198, where Kelly attributes Enide's dress to 'the plight of nobility impoverished by war'.

[53] In *Yvain*, trans. W. W. Comfort (New York, 1975), p. 248, lines 5194–202, the young women in forced employment do gold and silk embroidery: 'But such was their poverty, that many of them wore no girdle, and looked slovenly, because so poor; and their garments were torn about their breasts and at the elbows, and their shifts were soiled about their necks.' This description of the position of these tears acknowledges that their garments had disintegrated beyond the stage of being threadbare and the threads have given way to actual tearing.

[54] *Perceval*, in *Arthurian Romances* by Chrétien de Troyes, trans. D. D. R. Owen, Everyman's Library (Rutland, VT, 1987; rpt. 1991), provides an image of ineffective

humiliation for supposed unfaithfulness; and the 'olde, roten and torne' clothes worn by Partonope,[55] which signify his self-humiliation and despair.

In another significant example of old clothing, in the *Clerk's Tale*, Griselda's prenuptial shift surely would have shown its wear, but initally, Chaucer provides no qualifying adjective such as *thredbare* nor does he mention actual tears. When Walter first sees her, her 'povere array' (IV, line 467) is a sign of her poverty and her travail. Later Walter exiles Griselda from court, and she returns home, 'in her smok, with heed and foot al bare' (line 895). The smock of her exile is noteworthy because it is a smock that Walter allows her to retain from her life as his honored wife; it is not the old smock that had been stripped from her body when she was dressed as his bride. Griselda has had to beg Walter for a boon – the retention of the smock she was wearing when he announced the end of their marriage – in order not to return naked to her father's home.[56] However, it is a small enough boon, since the phrase 'naked in her smok' is common in medieval literature, and signi-

mending. Included in a longer description, lines 3719–39, Perceval meets an unnamed lady dressed in rags: 'her breasts protruded through the rents in front [of her dress]. It was held together in places with knots and rough stitching'. Further, lines 3740ff reveal that she cannot move without incurring more tears in her clothing and showing more of her body, and lines 3831–98 indicate that the Haughty Knight of the Heath keeps her in this 'shameful' condition – wearing torn and body-revealing clothing – because he believes that she has been unfaithful to him. For another translation, see *Perceval: The Story of the Grail*, by Chrétien de Troyes, trans. Nigel Bryant (Cambridge, 1982), pp. 40–4, esp. 40–1. Jeschute's rags are again described in Wolfram von Eschenbach's *Parzival*, trans. A. T. Hatto (New York, 1980), p. 136; see also the slashed shift that Gahmuret wore over his hauberk when he died, and which his wife the queen wanted to wear to express her love and grief when she heard of his death, pp. 61–6.

55 Partonope loses himself in the woods of Ardennes in the hope that wild beasts will devour him. He is found and taken to Salence by Urake, sister of Melior, who is the lady who exiled Partonope from her company for his inconstancy. Partonope's ragged condition is described in BL Add. MS 35288, lines 10236–43, as reproduced in *The Middle-English Versions of Partonope of Blois*, ed. A. Trampe Bödtker, EETS, ES 109 (London, 1912). Here Urake speaks:

> Amonge þe wilde bestes þere I fonde
> Partonope . . .
>
> . . .
>
> Olde, roten and torne was his cloþing,
> Full bare his body, eich man myght se
> In þat ferefull place, whereof I hade pite.

56 See the account of an Italian widow who was turned out of her late husband's house without sufficient clothing to cover her honorably, pp. 224–31; the iconography of the Griselda story, pp. 228–9 and n. 58; and the discussion of customary clothing in trousseau and husband's gifts and a widow's rights regarding them in Christiane Klapisch-Zuber, *Women, Family, and Ritual in Renaissance Italy*, trans. Lydia Cochrane (Chicago, 1985), Chapter 10, 'The Griselda Complex: Dowry and Marriage Gifts in the Quattrocento', pp. 213–46.

fies humiliation – that the wearer is virtually naked and stripped of all of the social status and/or dignity that worldly goods and clothing represent.[57] In addition, as Elizabeth Salter notes in a discussion of Chaucer's *Clerk's Tale*, Griselda's father is unable to dress her in her 'olde coote' (line 913) after she has returned home following Walter's rejection of her as a wife:[58]

> But on her body myghte he it nat brynge,
> For rude was the clooth, and moore of age
> By dayes fele than at hire mariage.   (lines 915–17)

Griselda's pre-nuptial garments, called 'olde geere', are even older at this point; now they are described as 'rude and somdeel torent' (line 1012). The age and tears of these clothes signify her poverty and her loss of social and marital status.

Torn garments, a step beyond threadbare, represent some sort of degradation – moral, economic, or social – self-inflicted, inflicted on the wearer by others, or by circumstances. In other literary works, such as Chretien's *Yvain*, torn garments are the sartorial representation of the effect on the wearer of someone's death. The grief of the mourner is manifested through making rents in his/her mourning weeds, and this action is often accompanied by the tearing of hair and face.[59] The portrayal of the costume of *Tristece* in *Le Roman de la rose* is an example of the general treatment of such ritual sorrow expressed sartorially:

> Mout sembloit bien qu'el fust dolente.
> Car el n'avoir pas esté lente
> D'esgratiner toute sa chiere;
> N'el n'avoit pas sa robe chiere,
> Ains l'ot en mains leus desciree
> Cum cele qui mout fu iree.   (lines 313–18)

> [she had torn her dress in many places, until it was practically worthless, as though she had been in a violent rage.][60]

---

[57] See Laura F. Hodges, 'Sartorial Signs in *Troilus and Criseyde*', *ChauR* 35.3 (2001), p. 251, nn. 29–31, regarding the smock; and esp. E. Jane Burns, 'Ladies Don't Wear *Braies*: Underwear in the French Prose *Lancelot*', *The Lancelot-Grail Cycle*, ed. William W. Kebler (Austin, TX, 1994), p. 163. Burns states, 'the woman's *chemise* often connotes . . . seduction and nudity itself. Many women are tellingly described as being "nue en sa chemise" ("naked in her *chemise*").'
[58] See Elizabeth Salter, *Chaucer: The Knight's Tale and the Clerk's Tale*, Studies in English Literature 5, gen. ed. David Daiches (Woodbury, NY, 1962), pp. 41, 44, 47.
[59] *Yvain*, Comfort trans., pp. 195, 199.
[60] *Le Roman de la rose*, trans. Dahlberg, p. 35. Chaucer provides a translation also:
> Nor she hadde nothyng slowe be
> For to forcracchen al hir face,
> And for to rent in many place

In addition to torn garments attesting to sorrow and to ire, in one particular group of stories gathered by Laurel Broughton on a website, *Catalogue of Medieval Miracles of the Virgin*,[61] the tears in garments represent the wearers' various sins. When a wearer repents, confesses, and/or makes reparation, the clothing is restored to wholeness. Similarly, the sin of Recklessness is described in *P.P.C*: 'Recklessnesse stod forth in ragged clothes' (Passus 11, line 196), and this line is illustrated on fol. 53r of Bodleian Library MS Douce 104 by a picture of a youth wearing a tunic of orangish-red which has on all of its edges – hem and sleeves – either tatters or dagging.[62]

Further, ragged, torn, or old clothes are a sign of outcast status or otherness, according to Ruth Mellinkoff. She discusses the significance of ragged clothing in the visual arts and in medieval drama, mentioning John the Baptist portrayed in a ragged green tunic. She also points out the torn cloak worn by Synagoga, describing her tunic as 'ancient', 'plain' in hue, and her cloak as 'black and torn'.[63] Further, according to Jean MacIntyre and Garrett P. J. Epp, in stage costumes, rags portray an actor's poverty and/or remorse. They explain that stage dress for a player would accurately portray standard dress for a given social status or profession because dramatists understood the necessity for preventing any audience misunderstanding of the drama. In addition, a dramatic costume might also depict a 'moral or psychological condition'. And they provide an example of how this works: 'Fine clothes accompany the prodigal's "riotous living", which includes the sins of pride, gluttony, and lechery, while rags represent not only his poverty, but also his remorse.'[64]

In crafting his imagery depicting the Clerk's poverty, Chaucer avoids the iconography of torn cloth. He also eschews a motif that would have been familiar to his audience from everyday life and to anyone familiar with medieval art – patches. Although the Clerk may be poor, his garment is not

> Hir clothis, and for to tere hir swuire,
> As she that was fulfilled of ire.
> And al totorn lay eek hir her
> Aboute hir shuldris here and ther,
> As she that hadde it al torent
> For angre and for maltalent.   (*Rom.*, lines 322–30)

61 The website is: <http://ferment.umdl.umich.edu/cgi/b/bib/bib-idx?c= marym;cc=marym> at University of Michigan.

62 See Scott's description of this figure, p. lxiii.

63 Ruth Mellinkoff, *Outcasts: Signs of Otherness in Northern European Art of the Late Middle Ages* (Berkeley, CA, 1993), 1:7 and fig. I.3; 1: 219, citing Peter Meredith and John E. Tailby's translations in *The Staging of Religious Drama in Europe in the Later Middle Ages: Texts and Documents in English Translation* (Kalamazoo, MI, 1983).

64 Jean MacIntyre and Garrett P. J. Epp, ' "Cloathes worth all the rest": Costumes and Properties', *A New History of Early English Drama*, eds John D. Cox and David Scott Kastan (New York, 1997), p. 270.

patched in the manner of allegorical Poverty's customary depiction. For example, Lady Poverty wears a wedding gown that is both ragged and patched, in the Giotto fresco entitled *Saint Francis weds the Lady Poverty*, in the Lower Church at Assisi.[65] An additional visual example of poverty depicts Ecclesia being abandoned by the papal court that desires worldly gain and a palace in Avignon, in an illumination in a 1447 North Italian manuscript. In this illumination, the papal court is personified by a scarlet-cloaked and triple-crowned Pope Clement V, while the Roman Church is figured by a poverty-stricken Ecclesia whose white gown is also conspicuously patched.[66] And Millard Meiss informs us that two additional illustrations of Poverty, barefoot and wearing patched clothing, entitled 'Struggle between Poverty and Fortune', were produced respectively in the Cité des Dames Workshop and in the Boucicaut Workshop.[67]

Earlier examples of the motif of patches to signify poverty appear in literature. *Le Roman de la rose* details Lady Poverty's characterization by costume as follows:

> Povreté, qui un seul denier
> N'eüst pas, s'en la deüst pendre,
> Tant seü bien sa robe vendre,
> Qu'ele ere nu comme vers.
> Se le temps fust un poi diver,
> Je croi qu'el acorast de froit,
> Qu'el n'avoid qu'un viel sac estroit
> Tout plain de navés paletiaus:
> S'estoit sa robe et ses mantiaus;   (lines 441–50)

[Poverty, who wouldn't have a penny if she had to hang herself. Even if she could sell her dress, she would fare no better, for she was as naked as a worm. . . . [she might] have perished of cold, for she had only an old thin sack, full of miserable patches as her coat and her mantle.][68]

---

65 A black and white reproduction, pl. 155, p. 207, is included in Arnold Toynbee, *A Study of History*, rev. edn by Arnold Toynbee and Jane Caplan (New York, 1972), with the caption, 'Francis chose poverty as an ideal identification with Christ's rule of life'; Toynbee attributes the photo to Alinari/Mansell, p. 559.

66 Toynbee, p. 555, identifies this color pl. 33, p. 152, as a BL manuscript of 'the pseudo-Joachite prophecies on the papacy'. Toynbee, p. 153, attributes the Great Schism, including the papal residential change from Rome to Avignon, to papal 'misjudgments', which were influenced by desires for 'worldly success'.

67 See fig. 395, an illumination in the Paris, Bibl. de l'Arsenal, MS 5193, fol. 88; and fig. 396, from the New York coll. Kettaneh, both reproduced in Millard Meiss, *French Painting in the Time of Jean de Berry: The Boucicaut Master* (New York, 1968). See also fig. 486, a black and white reproduction of 'St Martin and the Begger', by Simone Martini.

68 Dahlberg, trans., p. 36.

Here Poverty's clothing is a sack that has passed that point of being merely thin (threadbare), and has given way to tears that needed to be patched; further, this one garment performs the functions ordinarily served by both a coat and a mantle. Chaucer's translation is faithful to this picture of Poverty:

> Povert al aloon,
> That not a peny hadde in wolde,
> All though she hir clothis solde,
> And though she shulde anhonged be,
> For nakid as a worm was she,
> And if the wedir stormy were,
> For cold she shulde have deyed there.
> She nadde on but a streit old sak,
> And many a clout [rag] on it ther stak:
> This was hir cote and hir mantell.   (*Rom.*, lines 451–9)

One final example of poverty exemplified by patches is provided by the relics of St Francis's cowl and St Clare's cape. Mechtild Flury-Lemberg's *Textile Conservation and Research* provides photographs of both garments that support the argument that St Francis's cowl was patched with pieces of St Clare's cape. These *Actual Garments* illustrate the Franciscan ideal that embraces poverty.[69]

In comparison with examples of patches signifying poverty and the examples of garments with emotional or demeaning rips, the Clerk's one named garment, the threadbare courtepy, signals that fine line between, on the one hand, maintaining a subsistence living with a minimum appearance of respectability and, on the other, being a victim of abject poverty or of moral or social humiliation. His threadbare courtepy, taken as a *Social Mirror*, signifies that the Clerk still has prospects, but his balance is precarious – his future studies and advancement in academia, in Theology, Law, or Medicine, might well depend upon his acquiring a benefice.[70] Further, taken as a *Spiri-*

---

[69] Mechtild Flury-Lemberg, *Textile Conservation and Research* (Bern, 1988), pp. 314–17.

[70] Regarding the processes and difficulties of acquiring patrons and benefices, see William J. Courtenay, *Schools and Scholars in Fourteenth-Century England* (Princeton, 1987), esp. pp. 119–23; see pp. 137–46 for appointments, pp. 365–8 concerning fewer jobs and rewards for theological students and more for law students in the years 1370–1400. Also, see Jacob, *Essays*, pp. 207–39, for 'English University Clerks in the Later Middle Ages', Pt 1: 'The Problem of Maintenance', and esp. Pt 2: 'Petitions for Benefices from English Universities During the Great Schism'; Pt 2 discusses the difficulties in acquiring benefices in general, getting the benefice requested, and in taking them up even if granted, esp. pp. 232–9. However, Ussery, 'How Old?', pp. 14–17, argues (with examples) that being a logician actively hampered attempts to gain a benefice in the fourteenth century and that 'it is realistically appropriate . . . that the Clerk, even as a major logician, should have neither benefice nor office'. Concern-

tual Mirror, the Clerk's threadbare courtepy suggests jeopardy on yet another plane.

Morton W. Bloomfield's discussion of the symbolism of clothing images in *Piers Plowman* as conveying very subtle meanings is equally true of Chaucer's costume rhetoric:

> Clothing is often the symbol of grace, of the new man. New or different clothes make a new and different man. Yet old clothes can be sin and corruption, the old man. . . . Like many profound symbols, clothing is an ambiguous image. . . . Clothes are man's hope and his despair. . . . Clothing as imagery, therefore, has deep moral, metaphysical, and theological implications.[71]

Despite the tradition of regarding the Clerk as one of Chaucer's 'ideal' pilgrims, we should nevertheless consider that his threadbare courtepy, weighed within that ambiguity of significations mentioned by Bloomfield, may well represent 'sin and corruption, the old man', his 'despair' rather than his 'hope'.

Elsewhere in medieval literature, and in the examples of usage included in the MED,[72] *threadbare* possesses a negative connotation. In the *Parson's Tale,* the *threadbare* condition of long gowns results from a sin of pride and its consequence – failure to practice charitable giving. The wearers trail their gowns,

> in the dong and in the mire . . . that al thilke [fabric] trailyng is verraily as in effect wasted, consumed thredbare, and roten with donge, rather than it is yeven to the povre, to greet damage of the forseyde povre folk.
> (X, line 419)

Another negative example of threadbare appears in *The Canon's Yeoman's Tale* (VIII, lines 890–1): 'thus by smellyng and threedbare array,/ If that men liste, this folk they knowe may'. In this passage the Canon's Yeoman explains the signs[73] by which people may recognize the Canon's secret alchemical

---

ing other occupational opportunities for a clerk, see Orme, *English Schools,* pp. 40–4, regarding clerks of the royal administrative offices and common clerks of towns.

71 Morton W. Bloomfield, *Piers Plowman as a Fourteenth-century Apocalypse* (New Brunswick, NJ, 1962), p. 108; see his nn. 29–30 regarding traditional sources for these ideas.

72 The MED cites from Manly-Rickert; I have altered these quotations according to the text of *Riverside Chaucer.*

73 According to the *Riverside Chaucer* explanatory note for lines 635–8, the Yeoman narrator apparently possessed experiential knowledge of alchemists. Edgar H. Duncan, 'The Literature of Alchemy and Chaucer's Canon's Yeoman's Tale: Framework, Theme, and Characters', *Speculum* 43 (1968), pp. 633–4, describes canon-alchemist William de Brumley, chaplain of Harmandsworth, and Johannes Pygas, monk in the Priory of St James, Bristol, as the only two archival examples in England of alchemists

activities – the stench of his chemical brews and the threadbare condition of his garments. An alchemist, according to the Yeoman-narrator, 'wolde hem selle and spenden on this craft./ They kan nat stynte til no thyng be laft' (lines 882–3). The threadbare condition of the Canon's clothes, then, is the direct result of his obsessive devotion to alchemy, and such compulsive behavior epitomizes the sin of *curiositas*, a word benignly defined as 'eagerness for knowledge, inquisitiveness',[74] with sin occurring when eagerness and inquisitiveness were carried to extremes.[75] Christian K. Zacher further defines this sin: '*curiositas* referred to any morally excessive and suspect interest in observing the world, seeking novel experiences, or acquiring knowledge for its own sake'. He also asserts that pilgrims were 'particularly vulnerable to that vice', and that pilgrimages and *curiositas* were 'closely identified with one another'.[76]

Although Chaucer's Canon 'clothed was in clothes blake,/ And undernethe he hadde a white surplys' (VIII, lines 557–8), garments that mark him as a Canon, any initial good impression is undercut by the flatness of his bag that allows it to be folded in half:[77] 'A male tweyfoold on his croper lay', and by

who actively practiced this science, by which we may know that this pair represents alchemists who got *caught*. John Read posits that the 'most effective' depictions of alchemists are Chaucer's and Ben Jonson's *The Alchemist*, and discusses Chaucer's Canon's clothes, as well as Hans Weiditz's c.1520 depiction of an alchemist in his lab with his garments shown as traditionally dirty, with holes and ragged edges, in his *Alchemist in Life, Literature and Art* (1947; London, n.d.), pp. 27, 30–1, 62–3, and pl. 8. However, Duncan offers a second character portrait of the alchemist, pp. 644–5; this alchemist will wear disreputable clothing in order to preserve the secrecy of his craft, to 'avoid danger and ill fame' according to Duncan, p. 646, citing the Yeoman's speech in VIII, lines 892–7.

74   Charlton T. Lewis, *An Elementary Latin Dictionary* (Oxford, 1891; 1979).
75   Thomas J. Hatton, 'Chaucer's Miller's Curious Characters', *Proceedings of the Medieval Association of the Midwest* 2 (1993), p. 83, points out St Bernard's sermon on the Canticles, giving the three improper motivations for study: 'to study merely to know "*ut sciant*", basic *curiositas*'; 'to study to be known "*ut ipse sciant*", *curiositas* compounded by *vanitas*'; and to 'study to sell their knowledge, "*ut sciantiam suam vendant*", *curiositas* stemming from avarice' (citing *In Sermones in Cantica Canticorum*, PL 183, 968, described in Christian K. Zacher, *Curiosity and Pilgrimage: The Literature of Discovery in Fourteenth-Century England* [Baltimore, 1976], p. 26). Also see Kurt Olsson, 'Grammar, Manhood, and Tears: The Curiosity of Chaucer's Monk', *MP* 76 (1978), pp. 1–17, esp. p. 3 concerning daun Piers who is guilty of 'idle curiosity, a "lust" that is exacerbated by the sloth that keeps him from "labour" and spiritual "studie" ', and p. 6, which describes knowledge, learning, and sins of the eyes.
76   Zacher, p. 4.
77   The *Riverside Chaucer* explanatory note for line 566 explains: 'male tweyfoold: A double bag; frequently taken to imply folded over and hence almost empty'.
      John Lydgate possibly had this image in mind, and also that of Chaucer's 'feend' in green of the *Friar's Tale* (III, lines 1380–3, 1429–31), when he describes a monk wearing 'a cope of blak and not of grene' (line 73), 'a wonder thred-bare hood' (line 90), and carrying a 'voide male' (line 76), in his Prologue to the *Siege of Thebes*, BL

his unseasonable 'light' summer-like garments (lines 566, 568). Further, although his attached hood and hat are clearly recognizable dress for Canons[78] (lines 571–4), he has added the homely touch of a 'clote-leef' beneath his hood, 'For swoot and for to keep his heed from heete'[79] (lines 577–8).

At second glance, this Canon[80] betrays his particular sin of *curiositas*, and his appearance inspires the Host to pose judgmental questions to the Canon's

Arundel 119, fols 1a–4a, ed. John M. Bowers, in *The Canterbury Tales: Fifteenth-Century Continuations and Additions*, TEAMS Middle English Texts Series (Kalamazoo, MI, 1992), p. 15.

78 Three types of Canons' habits existed: Black Canons (Augustinian) wore all black-habit and cloak; White Canons (Premonstratensians) wore only bleached woolen garments; male Gilbertines wore a black habit covered by a white cloak, according to Christine N. Chism, ' "I Demed Hym Som Chanoun For To Be" ', *Chaucer's Pilgrims: An Historical Guide to the Pilgrims in the Canterbury Tales*, eds Laura C. Lambdin and Robert T. Lambdin (Westport, CT, 1996), p. 342. Chism comments that, since Chaucer's Canon wore a 'white surplice and his black overcloak', it is not possible to tell which kind of Canon he might be. She speculates, pp. 342–3, that 'it is possible . . . that Chaucer gives him a piebald habit to introduce elements of all three orders – making him a kind of ur-canon, or one who plays fast and loose with his dress to show his evasion of canonical habit, or to sharpen the sense of duplicity that defines his character'.

79 An alchemist might well be accustomed to protecting himself from the heat generated by his chemical reactions coupled with the need for closed doors and windows, necessary for secrecy. The wearing of a 'clote-leaf' could be second-nature for the Canon.
  The *Clote* plant has many synonyms, including *Clot-bur*, and *burdock*. The MED defines *clote* as 'the common burdock'. *Burdock* possesses a number of traditional medicinal properties, among them leaves that 'are cooling and moderately drying and can be applied to old ulcers and sores', according to Gabriel Stoian's *An Illustrated Herbal*, http://www.magdalin.com/herbal/plants_pages/b/burdock.htm (*clote-leaf* is not mentioned). See John Gerard, *The Herball or generall historie of plantes . . .; enlarged by Thomas Johnson* (London, 1633), pp. 809–11; and *The Herbal or General History of Plants: The Complete 1633 Edition as Revised and Enlarged by Thomas Johnson* (New York, 1975), pp. 388–9 for Docke, pp. 810–11 for Clot Burre, pp. 831 for Butter-Burre, esp. p. 811 for Dioscorides' recipe for a Clot Burre seed salve to ease the pain of burnings, and p. 813 for a description of Butter-Burre's leaves 'large enough to keep a man's head from rain, and from the heat of the sun' [my regularization of spelling]. The OED defines *burdock* as 'A coarse weedy plant (*Artium Lappa*, and kindred species), common on waste ground, bearing prickly flower-heads called burs, and large leaves like those of the dock', citing Gerard's 1597 *Herbal*. Hildegard of Bingen comments on kinds of dock plants and their medicinal properties in *The Physica*, trans. Priscilla Throop (Rochester, VT, 1998), pp. 51–2, 68. I am grateful to Paul F. Schaffner and to Laurel Broughton, respectively, for the Gerard and Hildegard references. See also *The Cyrurgie of Guy de Chauliac*, ed. M. S. Ogden, EETS 265 (1971) regarding the MED citation from the ?c1425 Paris angl. 25, 119b/a: 'Laye eron a clote leef'.

80 In the explanatory note for line 557, *Riverside Chaucer*, John Reidy states, 'The Canon [is] identified as a Canon Regular of St Augustine, or Black Canon', by Marie P. Hamilton, 'The Clerical Status of Chaucer's Alchemist', *Speculum* 16 (1941): 103–8; 'he

Yeoman. He wonders why this Canon does not dress in a seemly fashion and why he

> of his worshipe rekketh so lite.
> His overslope [outer garment, cassock] nys nat worth a myte, As
> in effect, to hym, so moot I go,
> It is baudy [dirty] and totore [tattered] also.
> Why is thy lord so sluttissh [slovenly], I the preye,
> And is of power bettre clooth to beye.   (lines 632–7)

The Yeoman's response names the cause of his master's unseemly dress – the misuse of intellect:

> For whan a man hath over-greet a wit,
> Ful oft hym happeth to mysusen it.
> So dooth my lord. . . .   (lines 648–50)

Altogether, the Canon's careless dress reveals what he values most: the pursuit of alchemical knowledge in the practice of alchemy.[81] In addition, his dress echoes the sentiment expressed in Haukyn's explanation of why his heart was set on his business rather than on God: '*Vbi thesaurus tuus ibi & cor tuum*' (*P.P.B* Passus 13, line 398) ['For where thy treasure is, there is thy heart also' (Matthew 6:21)].

Clearly, in the above examples *threadbare* has derogatory connotations, and further examples of the usage of this term are equally negative. In one instance, 'The fals man walkith fro towne to towne, For the moste parte with a threadbare gowne.'[82] Another example provides an evocation of standard ugliness: 'He hath a.. berd & a flatte noose, A therde-bare gowne and a rent hoose.'[83] In fact, among the MED examples for *thredbare*, no single clearly positive example of its usage is listed.[84] In addition, in *The Testimony of William Thorpe 1407*, setting forth the exchange between Thorpe (imprisoned for Lollardy) and an Archbishop, the Archbishop judges Thorpe's threadbare clothing to be self-righteous and obvious:

---

wears a cassock, *overslope* (VIII.633), a surplice over it (558), and outermost a black cloak with hood attached (557, 571)'. But see n. 78 above.

81 Hamilton, pp. 107–8, posits that the Canon was 'an apostate from his Order, *vagabundus* in ecclesiastical Latin' and that he continued to wear his threadbare habit bears witness to the 'dire poverty to which his passion for research had driven him'. George J. Englehardt posits that the Canon's archetype is that of the 'perjurer-conjurer', in 'The Ecclesiastical Pilgrims of the *Canterbury Tales*: A Study in Ethology', *MS* 37 (1975), p. 310. See Duncan, pp. 636–7, regarding Pope John XXII's edict against alchemists as 'tricksters and *falsarii* (counterfeiters)', sinners guilty of avarice.

82 MED, citing a1500(c1477) Norton *OAlch.* (Add 10302) 324.

83 MED, ?a1525 (?a1475) *Play Sacr.* (Dub 652) 570.

84 Unless, like Whitmore and Taitt, readers interpret the Clerk's threadbare courtepy as a positive costume sign.

'Þou demest | euery preest to be proude þat wole not go arayed as þou
goist. By God, I deme hym to be more meke þat goiþ euery daie in a scarlet
gowne þan þei in þat þreedbare blew gowne!'[85]   (lines 1590–3)

Further, like the Clerk, Coueitise, in a previously mentioned example from
P.P.B, wears a threadbare coat:

> Wiþ an hood on his heed, a hat aboue,
> In a [torn] tabard of twelf wynter age;
> But if a lous couþe [lepe, I leue and I trowe],
> She sholde noȝt [wandre] on þat wel[ch]e, so was it þredbare.
>   (Passus 5, lines 194–7)

In addition to the above allegorical evocation of this sin, covetousness is
one of the numerous sins that dirty Haukyn's clothing (*P.P.B*, Passus 13, lines
271ff). His outermost garment is referred to as his 'cote of cristendom',
according to the belief of 'holy kirke'. 'Ac it was moled in many places wiþ
manye sondry plottes' (lines 273–4), and these spots represented his sins,
among which is covetousness:

> Pacience *par*ceyued of pointes [his] cote
> [Was] colomy þoruȝ coueitise and vnhynde desiryng.
> Moore to good þan to god þe gome his lou caste,
>   (Passus 13, lines 354–6)

and Haukyn proceeded, through nefarious stratagems, to acquire profits
through cheating, all the while suffering not a single pang of Conscience, and
resisting having his coat cleaned through the sacrament of Penance.

Subsequently, in Passus XIV, Haukyn explains that he has only the one
cote and has worn it night and day. Such constant wear, realistically and
morally, should make a cote threadbare, and J. F. Goodridge addresses this
idea in his translation for Passus 13, lines 354–6:

> Then Patience noticed how parts of his clothing were rotten with covetous-
> ness, and moth-eaten with unnatural greed. For he loved his goods more
> than he loved God.[86]

There is slightly more interpretation than faithfulness in Goodridge's translation, but it captures the metaphorical idea that Haukyn's sinfulness signifies
spiritual poverty, as represented in his clothing worn around the clock and,

---

85 *Two Wycliffite Texts: The Sermon of William Taylor 1406; The Testimony of William
    Thorpe 1407*, EETS, OS 301 (Oxford, 1993), pp. xiv–xxvi, 73, and note regarding the
    threadbare blue gown (line 1593), p. 126. Regarding the poor quality of Lollard dress,
    see Anne Hudson, *The Premature Reformation: Wycliffite Texts and Lollard History*
    (Oxford, 1988), pp. 144–7, esp. 146 concerning 'þat þreedbare blew gowne'.
86 Goodridge, p. 162.

so, begrimed. Haukyn's attitude perfectly illustrates Matthew 6:21, quoted above, as spoken by Haukyn to explain that his heart was focused on gaining profit and not on God.

The irony of spiritual poverty being represented in terms of earthly treasure is blatant in Langland's evocation of Haukyn. In contrast, Chaucer's portraiture is more subtle, but readers of the Clerk's portrait understand that his worldly treasure is knowledge, as demonstrated in his desire for or possession of twenty books, laid up, so to speak, at the head of his bed, and in his (usually perceived by scholarly readers as benign[87]) desire to continue learning and to teach what he has learned.

At issue here is the question of whether or not Chaucer's representation of the Clerk paints him as covetous of books and knowledge to the degree that he might be deemed guilty of *curiositas*. Is Chaucer's Clerk's threadbare courtepy the sartorial and symbolic echo of Langland's Coueitise's twelve-year-old threadbare tabard, which cannot provide cover for a louse? Is this a play on images of degree and array?

If Haukyn's begrimed 'cote of cristendom' represents his love of business affairs and profits, his avarice and coveting, then similarly, we might think of the Clerk's threadbare courtepy as signifying his incomplete education[88] as represented by his engagement with philosophy, Aristotle[89] in particular, and his desire to lay up the treasures of twenty books on that subject, which suggest his avarice[90] and *curiositas*.[91]

---

[87] For example, Engelhardt, pp. 287–8, cites Alan of Lille, *Anticlaudianus* 7.229–31, 233–44 (trans. Engelhardt), regarding 'the riches of the mind', which the Clerk accumulates via his study. Chauncey Wood argues that Chaucer makes of the Clerk an example of 'an active virtue' in exercising his learning through speaking/teaching, in 'Chaucer's Clerk and Chalcidius', *ELN* 4 (1966–67), p. 170.

[88] Concerning the insufficiency of knowing Natural Science alone, see *PPB*, Passus 12, lines 82ff, which speak of the Church knowing 'þat cristes writyng saued', and that one might acquire Christ's wisdom, 'tresor', from 'clerkes' and priests who hold the key to this treasure: 'For Clergie is kepere vnder crist of heuene'; further, knowledge of natural science is insufficient: 'his science sooþly was neuere soule ysaued/ Ne broȝt by hir bokes to blisse ne to ioye'. Also, in Passus 15, line 47–51, Will declares that, ' "by so no man were greued/ Alle þe sciences vnder somne and alle þe sotile craftes/ I wolde I knewe and kouþe kyndely in myn herte" ', and Anima responds, ' "Thanne artow imparfit . . . and oon of prides knyȝtes./ For swich a lust and likyng Lucifer fel from heuene" '. For a summary of Langland's attitude toward education, see Nicholas Orme, 'Langland and Education', *History of Education* 11 (1982), pp. 251–66.

[89] Regarding the importance of Aristotle in medieval education, see Nicholas Orme, *From Childhood to Chivalry: The Education of the English Kings and Aristocracy 1066–1550* (London, 1984), pp. 87–95.

[90] For a history of thought concerning avarice, see Richard Newhauser, *The Early History of Greed: The Sin of Avarice in Early Medieval Thought and Literature*, Cambridge Studies in Medieval Literature 41 (Cambridge, 2000).

[91] Scholars who studied pagan or secular literature often were threatened with the stigma of *curiositas*; there were as many warnings from critics like Tertullian,

At this point, it is worthwhile pausing temporarily to consider what would have been the probable educational achievements of the Clerk at the time of Chaucer's writing of his portrait. Huling Ussery reckons that the Clerk is a 'middle-aged' scholar and a professional logician.[92] In contrast, Lois Roney concludes that the Clerk is at the point of being granted his Master of Arts degree.[93] 'He is . . . most likely a bachelor,[94] giving "cursory" lectures (i.e., reading aloud and paraphrasing a required text, afternoons) and participating in the public disputations.' She posits that, considering the six to seven years devoted to studying the arts curriculum,[95] he is probably twenty-one or twenty-two years of age, having spent some time in Padua, as we learn from the *Prologue* to his *Tale* (IV, lines 27, 40).[96] After a detailed listing of the

> Ambrose, Aldhelm, and numerous medieval mystics about this as there were attempts by less puritanical spokesmen to hedge such ventures round with defensive reasons,

states Zacher, p. 30 (citing Tertullian, *Ad nationes*, *PL* 1:660; Ambrose, *De officiis ministrorum*, *PL* 16:64; Aldhelm's comments in his letter to Wiftfrid in Rudolphus Ehwald, ed., *Aldhelmi Opera* in *MGH, Auct. Ant.*, XV, 229–30).

92 Ussery, 'How Old?', pp. 1–3, n. 2, provides a summary of commentary on this issue; p. 5, he claims that the Clerk 'probably has academic status close to that of Nicholas Lynne, who lectured on theology at Oxford, and who was one of the foremost scientists of his day', and, p. 6, that being designated *philosophre* would be 'an unusual designation for a twenty-year old student'. Further, Ussery argues, pp. 7–10, 18, and n. 18, 'many fellows remained at Oxford for all, or nearly all, their adult lives', but estimates the Clerk's age at 'more than thirty and less than fifty years of age'. He expands this argument in 'Fourteenth Century English Logicians: Possible Models for Chaucer's Clerk', *TSE* 18 (1970), pp. 1–15.

93 See Weisheipl's description of this educational status, pp. 163–6.

94 See Weisheipl's description of the university Bachelor, pp. 156–63. Clarke, p. 76, states that a Bachelor 'had to wear a special dress in the lectures, which it was his duty to give, *viz.*, the *Tabard*'; also, 'he was entitled and required to wear a Hood lined with the less expensive kinds of fur'. At this time, such a hood did not designate him as a Bachelor, as it did later when it was no longer part of the costume of the Undergraduates.

95 See Orme, *From Childhood to Chivalry*, pp. 87, 156–7, regarding the seven liberal arts in medieval education.

96 Taken from a work in progress by Lois Roney, with her kind permission, working title: 'Chaucer's Clerk: Arts Education, Insoluble Tale, Expedient Ethic', p. 6. The basis for this essay is two papers, respectively presented at the Modern Language Association Conference, December 1990, and the Medieval Association of the Midwest Conference, September 1992. See Rigby, *English Society*, p. 230, concerning stages of university education; and Orme, *English Schools*, pp. 117–41, 190–3, regarding early education, esp. in the fourteenth century; and pp. 12–21 concerning educational competency among the clergy in the Middle Ages, ranging from the non-literate to the achiever of elegant style and master of Latin grammar, which affords a useful comparison to the Clerk's educational achievements. Also see Orme, 'Chaucer and Education', pp. 39, 47–54, for a summary of schools and university education as Chaucer represents it.

subject matter the Clerk would have studied during his years at Oxford,[97] Roney sums up Oxford's curriculum and the Clerk's intellectual status:

> He has just spent six or seven of his most formative years as a human being – the years from age 14 to age 21 – almost totally immersed in [a] . . . sequence of abstract, analytic readings, courses, and disputations, reasoning mostly about logic and the physical laws of the Ptolemaic universe. No educational system could have been better designed to hone the intellect and deaden the affections. Aristotelian logic, natural science, and the lecture/disputation format can develop a razor-sharp mind with a computer-like ability to analyze complicated material swiftly and accurately, make fine distinctions, and argue disputed points. But they do little to develop, and in undiluted concentration probably suppress, the student's ability to empathize with other human beings or to enrich his own spirituality.[98]

In short, Roney suggests that what she characterizes as 'the narrowly Aristotelian Oxford arts curriculum' can produce the kind of scholar who can enjoy telling a Petrarchan story (with Chaucerian changes) in which a mother's failure even to try to 'prevent or circumvent' the murders of her children may be seen as perfect obedience. Roney asks, 'Is her obedience a virtue? In Aristotelian terms, yes'. And she conjectures that, through such a portrayal of the Clerk as intellectually 'narrow', 'Chaucer may have been implying that the undergraduate arts curriculum should be broadened.'[99] Might we not metaphorically describe the deficiency of 'intellectually "narrow"' as being intellectually threadbare?

The perils of the avid pursuit of secular learning, *scientia*, as opposed to the acquisition of divine knowledge, *sapientia*, are amply explored by Zacher. In addition, he describes the accusations made by contemporaries against the avid amateur scholar, Bishop Richard de Bury, of 'covetousness (and avarice) in buying books', of 'vanity in possessing and displaying them', of taking 'excessive delight in secular literature'. De Bury's attackers also classified his scholarly activities as an 'offense against moderation', stating that de Bury's 'eagerness to delve into the contents of his treasures manifested intellectual curiosity'. Further, Zacher posits that 'professional scholars knew

---

[97] Weisheipl provides such a list, pp. 167–76.
[98] Roney, pp. 10–11.
[99] Roney, pp. 3, 17–18. Also see Mariateresa Fumagalli Beonio Brocchieri, 'The Intellectual', *Medieval Callings*, trans. Lydia G. Cochrane (Chicago, 1990), pp. 181–210, esp. p. 182 where she discusses the term *philosopher* and the 'slight suspicion of secularity it conveyed in contradistinction to someone who studied the *pagina sacra*'. Brocchieri states, p. 187, that the liberal arts were thought of as training for that study considered to be 'the highest expression of human knowledge, theology, the doctrine of the salvation of the soul'. Such liberal arts training would be preliminary – incomplete.

curiositas as an occupational hazard'.[100] Although de Bury defended his avid studies and acquisition of books with the argument that 'books are the armor of the Church's defense', and proper scholarship would only make orthodox faith stronger;[101] nevertheless, according to Zacher, in the *Philobiblon*[102] de Bury 'unconsciously represents his curiosity for books as lust of the flesh as well as of the eyes'. St Francis's and St Thomas Aquinas's views against *scientiae curiositate*, including Aquinas's discussion of curiosity as 'an offense against temperance', bolster this train of thought.[103] Finally, and specific to Chaucer's Clerk, Zacher compares de Bury to the Clerk:

> Chaucer's poor clerk . . . shared with the bishop not only a regard for Petrarch but a preference for books over other possessions:
>
> > . . . al that he myghte of his freendes hente,
> > On bookes and on lernynge he it spente,
> > And bisily gan for the soules preye[104]
> > Of hem that yaf hym wherwith to scoleye.[105]

100 Regarding scholarship and *curiositas*, see Zacher, p. 71; pp. 73–4, for a characterization of de Bury as a 'cleric [bishop], lord-chancellor, diplomat, and book-buyer' and as an early fourteenth-century humanist (in the Renaissance style), although he pre-dated this idea; p. 64, regarding John of Wales's rebuke of scholars with too much 'passion in acquiring books', with references to W. A. Pantin, 'John of Wales and Medieval Humanism', in *Medieval Studies Presented to Aubrey Gwyn, S.J.*, eds J. A. Watt et al. (Dublin, 1961), p. 301; and concerning the 'tensions between the love of learning and the desire for God', which were 'never quite resolved', citing Jean Leclercq, *The Love of Learning and the Desire for God: A Study of Monastic Culture*, trans. Catharine Misrahi (New York, 1962), pp. 22–3, and Chapter 7.
101 See Robert P. Miller, *Chaucer: Sources and Backgrounds* (New York, 1977), pp. 259–63, including an excerpt from Richard de Bury's *Philobiblon*, Chapter 6, trans. E. C. Thomas. Miller, in n. 22, posits that the Clerk behaves in the spirit of 'the first professors of evangelical poverty' who 'collecting all their force of intellect, meditating day and night on the law of the Lord' skimped on food 'to spend in buying or correcting books' (quoting from p. 261). However, Miller neglects to mention that the books these impoverished scholars were correcting were books of 'sacred scripture', to which they turned 'after some slight homage paid to secular science', while Chaucer's Clerk is engaged by and with Aristotle.
102 Regarding Chaucer's knowledge of the *Philobiblon*, see A. Wigfall Green, 'Chaucer's Clerks and the Mediaeval Scholarly Tradition as Represented by Richard de Bury's *Philobiblon*', *ELH* 18 (1951), pp. 1–6.
103 See Zacher's discussion, pp. 65–6, 69; also n. 30, p. 175, quotes Sebastian Brant's lines from *The Ship of Fools*:
> Say worthy doctours and Clerks curious:
> What moueth you of Bokes to haue such nomber.
> Syns dyuers doctrines throughe way contrarious
> Doth mannys mynde distract and sore encomber.
104 Bert Dillon interprets the Clerk's prayers for his patrons as possible evidence that the Clerk was in minor orders, 'because that would be the only way his prayers could be "effective" ', in 'A Clerk Ther Was of Oxenford Also', *Chaucer's Pilgrims: An Histor-*

Footnote 105 opposite.

Curiositas is a matter of degree, and the *General Prologue* Clerk, in his desire for or acquisition of twenty books, appears excessive. It would have been uncharacteristic of Chaucer, even if he had conceived of the comparison, to draw a clear analogy between the excess of the Clerk and that of Bishop de Bury who, in Zacher's characterization of him, constitutes 'a *curiosus* who sees book-hunting ultimately as a devout pilgrimage'.[106] However, elsewhere, in the *Parson's Tale*, the Parson does castigate *curiositas* and its excess in degree, such as the elaboration and ornamentation in dress, a manifestation of this sin that the Clerk certainly avoids. However, in the matter of intellectual activity, the Clerk seems not yet to have gotten the point of St Francis's advocation of the simplicity of the soul as being opposed to intellectual curiosity for book knowledge.[107] Consequently, in the juxtaposition of the images of too many books of philosophy and degenerating clothing, the Clerk's portrait gives new meaning to Chaucer's phrase 'degree and array': the extent of the Clerk's devotion to Aristotle, indicating *curiositas*, may be reflected in his 'cote of cristendom', symbolized by the threadbare courtepy, perhaps indicating his insufficient interest, or incomplete education, in theological studies.

Beyond this, certain words in the Clerk's portrait contribute to a matrix of diction that bolsters the impression of his being less, rather than more, of an ideal figure. His appearance is characterized by his leanness – he 'looked *holwe*' (line 289, my emphasis). Although books certainly nourish the mind in many ways, they are literally no substitute for real food, and the Clerk's 'holwe' body might well serve to illustrate the difference between mental and physical nourishment,[108] or allegorically between the nourishment provided by *scientia* or the knowledge of the world, as opposed to *sapientia*, the wisdom of God. Failure to achieve a balanced education, acquire both kinds of wisdom, would result in a kind of hollowness, which might be described as 'a lack of substance' or 'emptiness'. *Holwe* is not a term of praise, although a lean clerk could certainly be read as the favorable opposite of a corpulent cleric, such as the Monk who indulges in fat swans. In any case, coupling 'holwe' with the 'thredbare' courtepy (line 290), evokes an additional sense of things lacking – which might yield readings of the literal absence of proper substance belonging to body and fabric, or as symbolizing his intellectual

---

ical Guide to the Pilgrims in The Canterbury Tales, eds Laura C. Lambdin and Robert T. Lambdin (Westport, CT, 1996), p. 111.

[105] Zacher, p. 76, quoting Chaucer, and citing also Green, pp. 1–6, as providing additional similarities between de Bury and the Clerk.

[106] Zacher, p. 79.

[107] Concerning St Francis's comments, see Zacher's discussion, p. 79.

[108] The MED examples for *holwe* connect hollowness with physical hunger. No consideration is given to a metaphorical use of this term.

asceticism, or, metaphorically, as the deprivation (of spiritual studies) within his current status in the educational process at Oxford.[109]

Other deficiencies indicated in the diction of this portrait appear in lines 291–2, which emphasize the Clerk's lack of benefice and worldliness, and they tend to support the reading of either the Clerk's asceticism or his failure to achieve recognition. However, the following lines provide the Clerk's motivation for any deprivation of worldly comforts – it is love of books, philosophy books in particular, that drives the Clerk, and not pursuit of the wisdom of God.[110] Thus, the Clerk makes his sacrifices of 'robes riche, or fithele, or gay sautrie' (line 296) in the name of philosophical knowledge; Chaucer specifically singles out Aristotelian knowledge. His description suggests that the Clerk lusts after, rents, or might even own his own copies[111] of 'Twenty bookes, clad in blak or reed,/ Of Aristotle and his philosophie' (lines

---

[109] This could be true whether Ussery, 'How Old?', is correct that the Clerk is an aging logician, or Roney is correct that he has almost completed his undergraduate arts studies, that curriculum that was so dominated by Aristotelian thought.

[110] Dillon, p. 109, comments: 'The implication is . . . that he had persisted in his study of logic rather than moving on to the higher study of theology', an action which was 'not unusual' for the time.

[111] The possibility exists that the Clerk could have copied some or all of the twenty books mentioned by Chaucer; see Ussery, 'How Old?', pp. 6–7. On the subject of clerk-copyists, see E. F. Jacob's essay, 'The Brethren of the Common Life', *Essays*, pp. 121–6, 137, regarding clerks who were copyists while waiting to acquire a benefice; a clerk might live with the Brethren and be well-employed. In the same collection, see his 'Gerard Groote and the Beginnings of the "New Devotion" in the Low Countries', pp. 144–7, which describes Gerard buying and borrowing books to copy, esp. p. 145, regarding his institution of and participation in 'the copying tradition . . . of the brethren of the Common Life'.

The Clerk might have inherited books as did John Wetlee 'clk', who received from Robert de Austhorpe's bequest, 'totum corpus meum juris civilis', in a will dated London, xii kal. Mar. 1372, according to Alfred Gibbons, abstractor, in *Early Lincoln Wills 1280–1547* (Lincoln, 1888), pp. 26–7. Examples of large numbers of books owned by clerks include one clerk who had clearly made a success of being a school master, John Bracebrigge, 'M.A. of Oxford and master of Lincoln school'. He accumulated five grammar books, an equal number of philosophy books, ten medical books, and forty-six books on the subjects of theology, canon law, and the liturgy; post-1420, he bestowed this collection upon Syon Abbey, according to Nicholas Orme, 'Schoolmasters, 1307–1509', in *Profession, Vocation, and Culture in Later Medieval England*, ed. Cecil H. Clough (Liverpool, 1982), pp. 230–1.

Orme, 'Chaucer and Education', p. 53, comments on the Monk's ownership of one hundred tragedies (VII, lines 3161–2) and the Parson's use in his *Tale* of citations taken from Ambrose, Augustine, Isidore, the Bible, and Canon Law (X, 75, 84, 89, 97, 931), which might indicate his possession of, or access to, books. However, Orme also, in 'Education and Learning at a Medieval English Cathedral: Exeter 1380–1548', *Journal of Ecclesiastical History* 32 (1981), pp. 274–9, surveys available materials concerning book ownership among the clergy at this cathedral, finding that the adult minor clergy possessed one to three books, while the canons and dignitaries, on average, possessed five each.

293–4).[112] If purchased, twenty books would constitute a virtual fortune in books in the late fourteenth century, and we need not wonder that he had 'but litel gold in cofre' (line 298). Clearly, these books, owned or desired, represent his treasures on earth, and their abundance contrasts strongly with the accumulation of portrait images signifying deficiencies – the nearly empty coffers, the images of body and courtepy that *holwe* and *thredbare* characterize, his lack of worldliness and benefice. He spends all that his friends send on 'bookes and on lernynge' (line 300) about Aristotle. In addition, although possibly he has not yet embarked upon further studies beyond those of the liberal arts and the speculative sciences,[113] the Clerk's reading habits, whatever his age, prior to any choice among further studies of Medicine, Law, or Theology,[114] might be contrasted with William J. Courtenay's assessment of theological scholars during the second half of the fourteenth century who exhibited a marked expansion of interest in biblical studies, such endeavors being sponsored by Rome.[115]

Even Chaucer's characterization of the Clerk's speech is more consonant with that of one who studies the scientific and/or philosophical subject matter of the arts curriculum, rather than the materials of Christian theology.[116] In describing the Clerk, Chaucer emphasizes that which pertains to rhetoric and oratory, ideas that one might acquire from reading the writers featured in the arts and sciences curriculum. While a knowledge of rhetoric would be useful in teaching, Chaucer describes the Clerk's discourse as, 'Sownynge in moral vertu' (line 307), and there is no mention of piety. His speech was 'consonant with',[117] in accordance with, rather than full of moral virtue. In short – once again the cupboard seems bare of all except knowledge derived from the undergraduate program – he has the 'forme', the 'reverence', and the 'sentence' (lines 305–6), but there are no words that signify spiritual substance. That he would 'glady' learn and teach[118] is surely not so important as *what* he would learn and teach. Chaucer's audience should note that the moral virtues learned might well be Aristotelian ethics – not evil, certainly, but also not

---

112 This concentration on Aristotelian philosophy would make the Clerk eligible to be named by Brocchieri, pp. 181–210, as an intellectual, a 'lettered man', a *litterati*, a *viri scientifici*, a *speculativi*.

113 See comments by Roney, pp. 190–1 above.

114 See Rigby, *English Society*, p. 230, for the listing of higher faculties; also pp. 208–9, regarding the timing of clerks receiving the tonsure and the question of when or if they took holy orders within the stages of university education.

115 Courtenay, pp. 373–4; also pp. 41–8.

116 Mann, p. 83, mentions this.

117 *Riverside Chaucer* gloss.

118 Possibly signifying no more than what Weisheipl terms 'the twofold function of a master, *legere* and *disputare*', p. 165; for further discussion of these functions see pp. 167–85.

Christian wisdom. There is no mention in this portrait of his practicing Christian virtues for the sake of *caritas*.

Underscoring his preference for *scientia* over *sapientia*, we find in the *Prologue* to the *Clerk's Tale* that he admires Petrarch (IV, lines 27–35), whom Zacher characterizes as 'Petrarch the *curiosus*, who once admitted that "to know more was always among the first of my desires", [and who] held that man's curiosity and instability were inescapable properties of his being.' Zacher mentions Petrarch's 'lifelong vacillation between curiosity and piety', and provides examples.[119] However, there is no such vacillation in the depiction of the Clerk, neither in the *General Prologue*, nor in his *Prologue* where we learn what other pilgrims expect from him: sophist arguments and high style rhetoric with 'termes', 'colours', and 'figures' (IV, lines 5, 16–18, 26ff) And the Clerk performs as expected, giving his audience Petrarch's story of Griselda.

Zacher classes the Clerk among those Canterbury pilgrims who have appropriate motives for going on pilgrimage, as opposed to those who are guilty of *curiositas*, that is, those who 'are clearly on a holiday outing'. He has earlier mentioned the similarities between the Clerk's and Bishop de Bury's extraordinary love of books, but draws no conclusions from this connection concerning the Clerk. His only basis for exonerating the Clerk from *curiositas* appears to be his own separation of the *General Prologue* pilgrims into two groups – those who wear 'gay' clothing and those who do not.[120] Has Zacher simply accepted the 'received' 'ideal' interpretation of this pilgrim and neither questioned nor wished to question this designation? If so, no argument would be required for such an intellectual stance because this has been the traditional view.

Clearly, if Bishop Richard de Bury might be accused of 'covetousness (and avarice) in buying books', of 'vanity in possessing and displaying them', and of 'excessive delight in secular literature', all as evidence of his 'offense against moderation', *desmesure*, and if it might be said of de Bury that 'his eagerness to delve into the contents of his treasures manifested intellectual curiosity',[121] then the same might be said of Chaucer's Clerk. De Bury was only an amateur scholar, but so far as we know, at the time represented in Chaucer's portrait characterization, the Clerk is devoting his substance, not to mention his friends' contributions, to *scientia*. His threadbare, short, overest courtepy, metaphorically his 'cote of cristendom', bears witness to the incompleteness of this body of knowledge.

Medieval Christians were reminded that 'energy expended on any investigation unessential to their salvation was sinful curiosity', an idea that contin-

---

[119] Zacher, pp. 36, 38–9.
[120] Zacher, pp. 76, 87, 94–5.
[121] Arguments made by Zacher, p. 64.

ued to be emphasized well past Chaucer's time. The saving virtue for a
scholar would be *studiositas*. *Studiositas*, in Aquinas's scheme, is 'a virtue
descended from temperance', and is 'scholarly diligence tempered by spiritual vigilance'. As Aquinas noted, *studiositas* might prevent *curiositas*.[122]
Nowhere in the Clerk's portrait is there an indication that he is characterized
by spiritual vigilance. However, his scholarly career was not officially terminated at the time of Chaucer's portrait. Readers may infer that such a clerk
could or would, in time, acquire a desirable balance between intellectual and
spiritual activity,[123] and that such a balance would be reflected both in his 'cote
of cristendom', in his innermost spirit, as well as in his 'ouerest' garment.

Meanwhile, his threadbare courtepy does not sartorially signify the presence of the virtue of temperance. We have only to consider what constitutes
the golden mean in clothing as exemplified in Langland's depiction of Wit in
whom there

> Was no pruyde on his apparaille   ne pouerte noyther,
> Sadde of his semblaunt   and of soft chiere.
> I dorste meue no matere   to make hym to Iangle.
>   (*P.P.B* Passus 8, lines 116–18)

As D. W. Robertson, Jr and Bernard F. Huppé put it, 'Wit in his clothing,
appearance, and conversation shows clearly his affinity with Reason and with
its principle of measure.'[124]

In contrast, the Clerk's portrait depicts *desmesure*, as does his tale. He
writes a tale of an impoverished Griselda, wearing a worn smock, symbol of
her poverty, social position, and of her unworldliness. Once married, she is
tested for her faithfulness and obedience to her husband Walter, and he puts
her through a rags-to-riches (material, social, and familial) and back-to-rags
ordeal by means of the purported deaths of her children. Griselda, finally
having proved worthy, is rewarded by Walter with the return of her children
and a resumption of riches and marriage. The fact that her vows to her
husband constitute the treasure for which she sacrifices all else parallels the

---

122 Thomas Aquinas, *Summa Theologica*, trans. the Fathers of the English Dominican
       Province (New York, 1947–48), II.ii, q. 162, art. 4; II.ii, q. 35, art. 4; II.ii, q. 160, art.
       2; esp. II.ii, qq. 166 (on *studiositas*) and 167 (on *curiositas*), as cited by Zacher,
       pp. 28–32, including Aquinas's idea that acquisition of knowledge was sinful if the
       scholar had an excessive lust for scholarship.
123 Elton D. Higgs' more worldly and generous inference is that 'he could have gotten a
       benefice, if he had wanted it . . . he is highly respected . . . [he already] makes his con-
       tribution to society' through teaching and learning, and that his 'lean horse and the
       threadbare overcoat evoke the conventional image of a learned but dull scholar, preoc-
       cupied with books and content with an obscure and impecuniary life', in 'The Old
       Order and the "Newe World" in the General Prologue to the *Canterbury Tales*', *HLQ*
       45 (1982), p. 163.
124 Robertson and Huppé, p. 106.

idea that the Clerk's riches are his books and knowledge. When we first meet him, the Clerk may be nearing a juncture in his life, between living a life outside of holy orders or becoming a full-fledged cleric in major holy orders.[125] He might choose[126] (assuming he received adequate financial support) from among university offerings for more specialized study of Canon or Civil Law, Medicine, or Theology. At the instant of his *General Prologue* portrait, neither the narrator nor the reader know the Clerk's choices or his future. His life situation, positioned precariously between his previous education and future possibilities as determined by economic realities, finds a parallel in his courtepy, which exists in that particular suspension – its threadbare condition – between that of a garment fashioned in newly fulled fabric and its opposite, a garment that is worn, torn, and patched.

---

[125] Ussery, 'Fourteenth-Century English Logicians', p. 12, citing historical records, argues that the usual assumption that the Clerk has taken minor orders would 'not hold true for logicians. Among logicians it was usual to put off the taking of even minor orders until a benefice was assured, and some did not assume minor orders until several years after a benefice was reserved for them.' Further, 'even among those clerks who were not primarily logicians, a long period between the M.A. and the taking of orders was not unusual; though logicians seem to have been outstanding in this respect'. Most interesting to Chaucerians is Ussery's example, p. 14, of Ralph Strode, Chaucer's friend, who 'was an eminent logician, a fellow of Merton 1359–60, and an M.A. He had no benefices, and apparently never took major orders.'

[126] Astell discusses possibilities open to such a clerk, pp. 58–9.

7

The Doctour of Phisik:
Apparel for the 'parfit practisour'

In sangwyn and in pers he clad was al,
Lyned with taffata and with sendal.   (I, lines 439–40)

As numerous medieval costume complaints[1] make clear, all too often
fourteenth-century costumes proclaimed the wearer to be living beyond
both his birth status and his means, or to be dressed in a manner inconsistent
with his or her vocation. These practices violated the principle, expressed in
religious rules and in the ineffective sumptuary laws of the fourteenth
century, that clothing should be consistent with religious, social and/or economic status. Regarding the clothing of Chaucer's Doctour of Phisik, only his
probable status within the church hierarchy, as clerk or possibly as priest, or
alternatively his possible social status as a well-educated, respected member
of the upper middle class, are issues to be considered;[2] his economic status

---

[1] Regarding costume complaints, see Chapter 1, pp. 17–28, and *C&C*, pp. 58–9, nn.
11–14; pp. 163–8, esp. 165, n. 17, and 166, n. 18.

[2] Concerning the estate of a Doctor of Phisik, see the illumination depicting the hierarchy of the relative social positions of canon law (at the top), followed by the medical
profession ('fisique'), and finally civil law, in BL MS Add. 30024, fol. 1v; reproduced
in Peter Murray Jones, *Medieval Medical Miniatures* (Austin, TX, 1984), p. 57, fig. 21.
See also Huling E. Ussery's assertion that the Doctor would have been at least a clerk
or at most a priest, in *Chaucer's Physician: Medicine and Literature in Fourteenth-Century England*, TSE 19 (New Orleans, LA, 1971), pp. 29–31, 58–60, 69–72,
88, 94–114, esp. p. 115; Robert S. Gottfried, *Doctors and Medicine in Medieval
England: 1340–1530* (Princeton, 1986), pp. 57, 245–78, who classifies physicians as
'among the wealthiest bourgeoisie in England'; C. H. Talbot and E. A. Hammond, *The
Medical Practitioners In Medieval England: A Biographical Register* (London, 1965),
p. ix; Gerald Morgan, 'The Design of the *General Prologue* to the *Canterbury Tales*',
ES 59 (1978), p. 495, who ranks the Doctor with Gildsmen, Shipman, and the Wife of
Bath (highest ranked commoners) and comments on John Gower's placing physicians
among the artificers in *Mirour de Omme*. Morgan's contention opposes the traditional
view as discussed in Malcolm Andrew, ed., *The Variorum Edition of the Works of
Geoffrey Chaucer*, Vol. 2, Pt One B, Explanatory Notes, *The Canterbury Tales: The
General Prologue* (Norman, OK, 1992), p. 393, of the Doctor of Phisik as one of a

appears to be affluent, for Chaucer indicates that he acquired and retained considerable wealth tending patients during the plague.[3] Further, Chaucer's description of the specific fabrics used in the Doctor's costume substantiates this character's affinity for gold[4] and ability to accumulate wealth.[5] In addition, this physician's superior medical knowledge, attested in lines 412–14, so amply catalogued by the narrator-Chaucer in lines 429–38,[6] coupled with his

small number of well-educated physicians occupying a social position above that of craftsmen; also see p. 363 for a discussion of the Doctor as being in holy orders. Ida B. Jones, 'Popular Medical Knowledge in Fourteenth Century English Literature (Part I): Practitioners of the Healing Art', *BIHM* 5 (1937), p. 413, cites the Doctor of Phisik's expensive clothing as the basis for her conclusion that the 'physician held a high social position'.

3   Frederick F. Cartwright, *A Social History of Medicine* (New York, 1977), p. 44, describes the high death rate of medical practitioners who were in holy orders as clerks, practicing under episcopal control during the last half of the fourteenth century while the plague was raging. Regarding the plague, its effects, and its treatment, see Peter Speed, ed., *Those Who Worked: An Anthology of Medieval Sources* (New York, 1997), pp. 229–35. W. J. Bishop, 'Notes on the History of Medical Costume', *Annals of Medical History* n.s. 6.3 (May 1934), pp. 207–8, provides an interesting description and drawing of the plague costume worn by doctors as protection from infection, but not worn in England. This costume is dated 1720 by Raymond Crawfurd, *Plague and Pestilence in Literature and Art* (Oxford, 1914), pl. 28, facing p. 200; but p. 201 offers references to earlier medical dress designed to ward off infection; see also Johannes Nohl, *The Black Death*, trans. C. H. Clarke (New York, n.d.), pp. 94–5, and picture between pp. 96 and 97.

4   The Doctor prescribes gold for his patients, which medical historians agree was standard, acceptable practice for doctors in the Middle Ages. See Ida B. Jones, 'Popular Medical Knowledge in Fourteenth Century English Literature (Part II): The Theory and Practice of Medicine', *BIHM* 5 (1937), pp. 580–1; Edwin Eleazar, 'With Us Ther Was a Doctour of Phisik', *Chaucer's Pilgrims: An Historical Guide to the Pilgrims in the Canterbury Tales*, eds Laura C. Lambdin and Robert T. Lambdin (Westport, CT, 1996), p. 233, who states that John of Gaddesden 'taught that powdered gold in a solvent, or potable gold, when drunk was an effective cure for heart attacks'. As for collusion with his apothecary, George A. Renn states that this was customary and that it benefited all parties, in 'Chaucer's Doctour of Phisik', *Expl* 45.2 (1987), pp. 4–5. This cooperation is illustrated in a fifteenth-century illumination in Bologna, Biblioteca Universitaria, MS 2197, fol. 492, in the *Canon* of Avicenna (written in Hebrew), reproduced in Nancy G. Sirasi, *Medieval and Early Renaissance Medicine: An Introduction to Knowledge and Practice* (Chicago, 1990), p. 30, fig. 2.

5   In his *Romaunt of the Rose*, Chaucer amplifies the vilification of physicians and lawyers that appears in *Le Roman de la rose* by Guillaume de Lorris and Jean de Meun, ed. Daniel Poirion (Paris, 1974), lines 5091–100. Chaucer claims that they only work 'for lucre and coveitise' and 'Do right nought for charity' (lines 5738, 5744, from lines 5721–44).

6   A possible implication is that the doctor has spoken to the narrator or others in the group of his education; alternatively, we might give the narrator credit for knowing the standard authorities any doctor of medicine would have studied. Regarding medical education in the Middle Ages, see Lawrence I. Conrad, Michael Neve, Vivian Nutton,

display of wealth in his apparel indicate that the Doctor knows and practices the principles of effective public presentation.[7] Chaucer's costume rhetoric reinforces the idea that the Doctor 'was a verrey parfit practisour' of medicine through his designation of this physician's fabric and color choices, which symbolically evoke a recognition of both the physical and economic reality of medical practice as well as the eastern origin of and influence on medieval medicine.[8]

According to W. N. Hargreaves-Mawdsley, 'nearly all Masters [of Medicine; that is, doctors] were in holy orders'.[9] Historians of medicine mention a

Roy Porter, and Andrew Wear, *The Western Medical Tradition: 800 BC to AD 1800* (Cambridge, 1995), pp. 139, 153–9, 488; Cartwright, pp. 14, 47; Speed, pp. 218, 220; John A. Alford, 'Medicine in the Middle Ages; The Theory of a Profession', *The Centennial Review* 23 (1979), pp. 377–96, esp. pp. 381–6; also, E. A. Pace, 'Doctor', *The Catholic Encyclopedia*, vol. 5, online edn (1999). For the limitations of a physician's knowledge, see *The Dance of Death*, ed. Florence Warren, EETS, OS 181 (London, 1931; New York, 1971), pp. 52–5, 90–1; Aldred Scott Warthin, *The Physician of the Dance of Death* (New York, 1931), p. 20.

7 See Alford, p. 393, regarding 'The Doctrine of the Fees' and effective dress for physicians.

8 See Conrad, et al., p. 139, for the eastern influence, and the University of Salerno, pp. 140–6, and 153–9; also concerning Salerno, Cartwright, p. 14, and Speed, p. 219. In addition, William J. Courtenay, *Schools and Scholars in Fourteenth-Century England* (Princeton, 1987), p. 37, writes of medieval medicine as allied with philosophy in the Islamic and Jewish traditions. Regarding the influence on medieval medicine of translations from Arabic texts at Montpellier, see C. H. Talbot, *Medicine in Medieval England* (London, 1973), pp. 57–60.

9 W. N. Hargreaves-Mawdsley, *A History of Academical Dress in Europe until the End of the Eighteenth Century* (Oxford, 1963; rpt. Westport, CT, 1978), p. 5. Huling Ussery, 'Fourteenth Century English Logicians: Possible Models for Chaucer's Clerk', *TSE* 18 (1970), p. 12, comments on physicians taking holy orders at an earlier stage of their life than do logicians such as the Clerk. Eleazar summarizes the commentary made by the authorities on this subject, affirming this view of the Doctor being in holy orders of some sort, pp. 222–5, 227, 230. See Joseph Ziegler's comments on 'the intertwined roles of [medical] science and faith in matters of health', p. 8, in the Introduction to *Religion and Medicine in the Middle Ages*, York Studies in Medieval Theology 3, eds Peter Biller and Joseph Ziegler (York, 2001), and esp. William J. Courtenay's article 'Curers of Body and Soul: Medical Doctors as Theologians', pp. 69–75, in the same collection. Courtenay, p. 70, n. 5, cites Faye Getz, who states in 'The Faculty of Medicine before 1500', in *The History of the University of Oxford* 2, eds J. I. Catto and T. A. R. Evans (Oxford, 1992), p. 382, that of the forty scholars in medicine at Oxford in the fourteenth century, 'at least 8 studied theology', and that medicine's 'close association with arts and philosophical training allowed it to be viewed as prepatory training for "the ultimate degree, the doctorate in theology"'. In this same Biller and Ziegler collection, Michael R. McVaugh, in 'Moments of Inflation: The Careers of Arnau de Vilanova', p. 47, describes Arnau's last twenty years of life, during which he followed the dual vocations of 'academic physician' and 'lay theologian and prophet', and wrote about both. Talbot, p. 51, mentions doctors who were secular clerks (unaffil-

number of examples: English physician-scholars Adelard of Bath, Robert of Chester, and Daniel Morley were among the medical faculty at Montpellier in the twelfth century, where 'celebrated masters' busily translated Arabic medical texts into Latin.[10] Brother Matthew and Brother Warin, former students of medicine at the university at Salerno, practiced medicine at St Albans Abbey, where Warin became the Abbot. Following him in 1195 was John of Cella, called 'a Galen in medicine', who had studied medicine at the university in Paris. In John's final illness, 1214, William of Bedford, 'medical monk', cared for him; this same William eventually became Prior of Tynemouth, and after that Prior of Worcester.[11] In addition, Vivian Nutton describes physician-astronomers, all of whom must have been at least clerks, and some in higher orders, such as the c.1395 Welsh priest-physician Thomas Brown, the c.1310–72 Oxford astronomer Simon Bredon,[12] the university of Valencia-affiliated John of Bosnia (fl.1450–84) who became physician to the King of Anjou, and the 1472 Archdeacon appointee of St Andrews in Scotland, William Scheves, who incurred episcopal objections because of his background of combined astrological and medical studies at Louvain. Scheves took his complaint against these objections to Rome, was obviously successful in his argumentation, and when he returned to Scotland he was an Archbishop.[13]

Chaucer's Doctor of Phisik, having attained the degree of Master, may have been a secular clerk, or possibly even a priest, as Huling Ussery

iated with abbey or priory) and the increasing secularisation of physicians even while they were in minor orders. The history of the medieval church's involvement with and rulings on the practice of medicine by members of the clergy is described by William H. W. Fanning, in 'Medicine and Canon Law', *The Catholic Encyclopedia*, vol. 10, online edn (1999).

[10] Talbot, pp. 57ff. These physicians also practiced medicine in England and elsewhere, illustrating the mobility of trained physicians. On doctors' mobility, also see Ussery, *Chaucer's Physician*, pp. 58, 95–6; and Talbot and Hammond, pp. vii, ix, where the authors mention the large numbers of physicians and surgeons of foreign birth and education who practiced medicine in England from 1066 to the beginning of the sixteenth century.

[11] Conrad, et al., p. 148; Stanley Rubin, *Medieval English Medicine* (New York, 1974), pp. 183–4; Talbot and Hammond, pp. 130–1, 214, 372–3, 384.

[12] Simon Bredon was a doctor of medicine and theology, a mathemetician, and an astronomer, as well as a fellow of Merton College, according to Courtenay, *Schools & Scholars*, p. 37.

[13] In Conrad, et al., p. 159; Talbot and Hammond, pp. 320–2, 336, 413–14. The fact that C. David Benson felt the need to affirm that the Doctor follows the acknowledged practice of his day in his astrological prognostications attests that the historical combination of medicine and astrology continues to struggle for historical validation among modern readers; see his 'The Astrological Medicine of Chaucer's Physician and Nicholas of Lynn's *Kalendarium*', *AN&Q* 22.5–6 (1984), pp. 62–6.

posits,[14] and as such he would have been entitled to wear academical dress.[15] C. David Benson's *Riverside Chaucer* note[16] suggests that the appellation of the Doctor as also a surgeon[17] makes the Doctor entirely secular. However, this point is refuted by Ussery as he notes medieval authors of medical treatises who espouse the idea that those who practice medicine should know 'both physic and surgery', and cites Lanfrank, John de Arderne, John de Mirfeld, Henri Mondeville, and Guy de Chauliac who meet this dual requirement. This combination of phisik and surgery brought higher fees and status to a practitioner because it was rare. However, Ussery thinks that Chaucer's Doctor is not a surgeon because surgery is mentioned only once in his portrait.[18] This issue, too, may be moot, as it is possible that Chaucer never claims this dual practice for the Doctor; he says, 'In al this world ne was ther noon hym lik,/ To speke of phisik and of surgerye' (lines 412–13). This pilgrim is a Doctor of Phisik, but naturally he could *speak* of both 'phisik and surgerye', and apparently he does this very well.

Clearly, a medieval doctor might have two professional arrows in his quiver, in practice and in speaking. One such dual practitioner was the

---

14 Ussery, *Chaucer's Physician*, pp. 29–31, 95. He describes the exceptions, a small minority, to this generalization, pp. 29–30. Sirasi, *Medieval and Early Renaissance Medicine*, p. 56, states, 'the medical faculty at Oxford . . . [f]or the entire fourteenth century [includes] the names of only 40 medical masters and students . . .; all of them appear to have been beneficed clergy or members of religious orders'. Medical authors John of Gaddesden and Simon Bredon were affiliated at this time with Merton College at Oxford. Talbot and Hammond's entries throughout indicate the extent to which doctors of physic were in holy orders.

15 E. C. Clarke describes academic dress for all ranks, in 'English Academical Costume (Mediæval)', *Archaeol J* 1 (1893), pp. 73–104. There is a confusion in the attribution of this article, which was published in two parts, one of which is sometimes referred to as in *Archaeol J* 50.

16 *Riverside Chaucer*, p. 816.

17 At issue is the Fourth Lateran Council of 1215 which disallowed surgery and cauterization to all clergy. However, as Eleazar makes clear, pp. 224–5, 229–30, papal dispensations from this ruling were obtainable by secular clergy; see also Ussery, *Chaucer's Physician*, p. 31, regarding medical doctors, university teachers of medicine, medical students in holy orders, and papal dispensations for clergymen to perform such treatments as cauterization; Sirasi, *Medieval and Early Renaissance Medicine*, pp. 25–6, 178; and regarding this papal decree, exceptions, and indulgences, Fanning, 'Medicine and Canon Law', *The Catholic Encyclopedia*, vol. 10, online edn (1999). Eleazar, pp. 227, 230, mentions Montpellier as a likely place for a physician and surgeon to be educated. However, Bologna is also likely, as described by Vern L. Bullough, *The Development of Medicine as a Profession: The Contribution of the Medieval University to Modern Medicine* (Basel, 1966), pp. 62–6. See also Bullough's discussion of the separation and the integration of medical and surgical education and training, esp. pp. 59–65, 110–11, including the establishment in Paris of the College of Saints Cosmas and Damian (patron saints of surgery), as a 'corporative' organization for surgeons, pp. 83–7.

18 Ussery, *Chaucer's Physician*, pp. 59–60, 94.

Minorite friar, Brother William Appleton, who was killed by the rioters in the uprising in London in 1381; he had been physician-surgeon to John of Gaunt, as reported in *The Anonimalle Chronicle*.[19] In any case, the point of emphasis here is the probability that a physician would have been, at least, in minor orders, and, at most, a member of the beneficed clergy (regular or secular); for this reason, the Doctor of Phisik is included in this volume.[20]

A Doctor was entitled to wear academic dress,[21] and this dress, as C. H. Talbot points out, was red.[22] James Laver describes this practice as it occurs at the University of Paris:

> We know that the medical students of the University of Paris wore a black robe, and when they graduated received a red one. We also know that this 'full dress' was worn not only on state occasions, formal meetings for the granting of degrees and the like, but in ordinary life, when the doctors were attending the sick.[23]

---

[19] And as described by Speed, ed., pp. 220, 239; Talbot and Hammond, pp. 382–3; and Richard Firth Green, 'John Ball's Letters: Literary History and Historical Literature', *Chaucer's England: Literature in Historical Context*, ed. Barbara Hanawalt, Medieval Studies at Minnesota 4 (Minneapolis, MN, 1992), p. 191. On this dual practice, also see Conrad, et al., pp. 160–5.

[20] Vivian Nutton, in Conrad, et al., p. 148, states,

> In the northern European universities from 1300 onward, many medical graduates were in holy orders. . . . A religious qualification also fitted a doctor for his role as personal advisor to a wealthy patron, and helped to guarantee his honesty and fairness as a practitioner.

Further, according to Cartwright, p. 23, 'All orthodox medical practitioners were clerks but it does not follow that they were priests or monks.' A monastery might be known for its medical knowledge or a medically knowledgeable member of its community; alternatively, some monasteries hired and paid (with fees and a fur-trimmed robe) a doctor to attend inmates. These clerks who were medical practitioners 'came under episcopal jurisdiction [therefore] the bishops exercised control over orthodox practice'.

[21] The seventy-fourth canon ecclesiastical states that Doctors of Physic 'having any ecclesiastical living' have the right to wear the same dress as 'deans, masters of colleges, archdeacons, and prebendiaries, in cathedral and collegiate church, being priests or deacons', that is 'gowns with hoods or tippets of silk or sarsnet and square caps', according to Gilbert J. French, *The Tippets of the Canons Ecclesiastical* (London, 1850), p. 22, also p. 5.

[22] Talbot, p. 203. D. J. Cunningham, *The Evolution of the Graduation Ceremony* (Edinburgh, 1904), p. 18, describes the practice in Ingolstadt of those wishing to become medical doctors parading in red robes made in the style of a monastic cowl. See Sirasi, *Medieval and Early Renaissance Medicine*, fig. 8, p. 51, for a c.1400 illumination showing variations in style of long robes for doctors, from Yale Medical Library MS 18, fol. 3v.

[23] James Laver further comments on the inferior dress of surgeons who wore short clothes, reflecting their lower rank, in *Modesty in Dress* (Boston, 1967), pp. 54–5.

According to Talbot, the appropriate academical costume for a late-fourteenth-century physician included the headdress of: a round cap (*pileus rotundus*),[24] as in Plate 10, 'closed dress' (*cappa manicata*), 'shorter than the cassock with full sleeves reaching to a point behind'[25] worn for more formal wear and which was superceded by a 'voluminous dress' (*cappa clausa*), which was 'sleeveless and reaching to the feet, with one slit in the middle front for the passage of both arms, as in Plate 11, or with two side slits'[26] for normal wear. This was the 'non-liturgical garment' that Stephen Langton, Archbishop of Canterbury, at the 1222 Council of Oxford required all clerks

[24] Hargreaves-Mawdsley, p. 75, names the *pileus* 'typical clerical headgear' (citing Strickland Gibson, *Statuta Antiqua Universitatis Oxoniensis* [Oxford, 1931], p. 37). For the history of the *pileus rotundus*, see E. C. Clarke, 'College Caps and Doctors' Hats', *Archaeol J* 61 (1904), pp. 33–4. Hargreaves-Mawdsley's glossary definition, p. 194, is illustrated with a line drawing, p. 192, fig. 6. And his pl. 7, opposite p. 64, shows the black *pileus* worn by the Warden of New College, Oxford, c.1463; but also see p. 16, regarding 'a miniver *pileus*' worn at the University of Bologna, and pp. 37, 40, 52, 54, and pl. 4a. Henry J. McCloud, *Clerical Dress and Insignia of the Roman Catholic Church* (Milwaukee, 1948), p. 80, states current practice that below the rank of prelate, clerics should wear black 'skullcaps' (likely a modern term for *pileus*); Clarke, 'College Caps', p. 96, describes the advent of the skull-cap in academic costume; also see E. C. Clarke, 'English Academical Costume (Mediæval)', *Archaeol J* 50 (1893), pp. 137–49, 183–209, regarding differing types of the pileus and biretta. See also L. C. MacKinney and Harry Bober, 'A thirteenth-century medical case history in miniatures', *Speculum* 35 (1960), p. 255, for the statement that medieval illuminations provide proof that there was no standard hat for all physicians. See F. W. Fairholt, *Costume in England: A History of Dress to the End of the Eighteenth Century*, 4th edn (London, 1909), p. 203, for a description and line drawing of a physician's costume with headdress as it appears in BL Roy. MS 15 E 2. Herbert Thurston describes the early development of the biretta from a skull-cap with 'a small tuft', in 'Biretta', *The Catholic Encyclopedia*, vol. 2, online edn (1999). Cunningham, pp. 9, 11, 20, 24, 26–7, 29–31, 35, 44, 46, 50, writes of the importance of cap, pileus, and biretta in graduation ceremonies of medical doctors, from the earliest to the present times.

[25] Hargreaves-Mawdsley, definition p. 72, glossary definition p. 193; see also p. 75. Robert W. T. Günther includes F. E. Brightman's list of costume terms, including a *chimere* that fits this description as worn by Doctors of Medicine, in the preface to 'A Description of Brasses and other Funeral Monuments in the Chapel', *A Register of the Members of St Mary Magdalen College, Oxford* n.s. 8, ed. William Dunn Macray (London, 1915), p. vi. Clarke, 'English Academical Costume', pp. 103–4, describes the *cappa manicata* as a 'sleeved Cope'; and other details, p. 102.

[26] Hargreaves-Mawdsley, glossary definition, p. 190, illustrated p. 191, figs 3a and 3b; for other usage, see p. 5 regarding clerks; p. 65 concerning Doctors of Divinity. See Günther, p. vi, regarding *cappa clausa*; and Clarke, 'English Academical Costume', p. 103. This garment is illustrated in the thirteenth-century BL MS Harl. 3140, fol. 39; see reproduction in Peter Murray Jones, p. 25, fig. 6. See also Phillis Cunnington and Catherine Lucas, *Charity Costumes of Children, Scolars, Almsfolk, Pensioners* (London, 1978), p. 218, and fig. 27, p. 44, of a physician with jordan; and Herbert Thurston on proper dress of medieval clergy, in 'Clerical Costume', *The Catholic Encyclopedia*, vol. 4, online edn (1999).

10. Sketch of a scholar wearing the *pileus*, detail from *Omne bonum*, BL MS Royal 6 E vi, fol. 178.

11. Sketch of a *cappa clausa* worn by John Argentein, D.D., Provost, King's College, Cambridge, from a depiction of his funerary brass depicted in H. W. Macklin's *The Brasses of England*.

to wear. For informal apparel, doctors 'wore a sleeveless tabard[27] . . ., which later became shorter, with or without sleeves'.[28]

Chaucer's depiction of the Doctor of Physik's costume, limned only in terms of the fabrics used to construct it, neither supports nor contradicts this description of proper dress for Doctors of Medicine. Because he provides the names of both red and blue dyestuffs and of fabrics incorporated in the Doctor's garments, Chaucer's lines 439–40 inform the above-named list of garments as they are pictured in manuscript illuminations that most frequently depict doctors wearing red and blue.[29] The physician in these miniatures usually wears a 'biretta and a loose gown, with hood thrown back and tight-sleeved under-tunic. Usually the gown and biretta are red or pink, but sometimes blue.'[30] Examples of this dress appear in depictions of the physician's academic robes in the late-thirteenth- and late-fourteenth-century manuscripts, Bodleian Library MSS All Souls 71 and 72.[31] Unfortunately, we

---

[27] Hargreaves-Mawdsley, pp. 5, 75, and glossary definition, pp. 193–4, likens this tabard to a *pallium*, 'a plain, closed, sleeveless garment' worn over the basic long tunic, citing Brightman, quoted in Günther's Preface, p. vi. See Hargreaves-Mawdsley for description, p. 101; for informal wear of Doctors of Divinity in 1350, p. 65; and for Doctors of Medicine, p. 75; and Clarke, 'English Academical Costume', pp. 76, 81, 88, 92, 101–3; also see his comments on a doctor's *roba* and *habitus ordinarius*, pp. 82, 101–2. Regarding *pallium*, see E. A. Roulin, *Vestments and Vesture, A Manual of Liturgical Art*, trans. Justin McCann (Westminster, MD, 1950), p. 187, and Clarke, 'English Academical Costume', p. 137, with the tabard and *roba talaris* on pp. 139–41.

[28] Hargreaves-Mawdsley, p. 75.

[29] Colors in illuminations sometimes reflect the palate available, or the colors preferred in a given workshop, or the colors ordered by a patron. In an extensive, but not all-inclusive, survey of thirteenth- through fifteenth-century medical illuminations, I noticed that manuscripts prepared for noble patrons sometimes portrayed physicians wearing a wider range of hues, perhaps reflecting monies laid out for colors (see n. 31 below regarding: Roy. 20 C VII, fol. 78v; and Roy. 16 G VIII, fol. 32, made for Charles the Bold, Duke of Burgundy). This expansion of colors worn was true of the portrayal of peasants as well in the Luttrell Psalter, but its one medical practitioner, shown on fol. 61, is portrayed in short dress and therefore may be a surgeon rather than a physician (see n. 23 above); see Janet Backhouse, *Medieval Manuscripts in the British Library: The Luttrell Psalter* (New York, 1990), p. 45, fig. 51.

[30] Letter to author from Maureen Pemberton, Bodleian Library, 27 May 1987.

[31] An illumination in All Souls College 71, fol. 113v, shows a physician, wearing blue tunic with red cloak and biretta, giving instructions to an apothecary (frame 5 of Bodleian filmstrip 232.2); an illumination in All Souls College 72 depicts a physician in red *pileus* and cloak and white tunic, holding a flask in fol. 1 (frame 6); and a physician in red cloak and tunic with black *pileus* in fol. 67 (frame 7).
    Similarly dressed physicians appear in the 1327 BL MS Add. 47680, fol. 54v (physician in red robe, blue *pileus*), reproduced in color in Peter Murray Jones, pl. 10; in the 1345 Musée Condé, Chantilly, illuminations in Liber Notabilium Philippi VI, 'Anathomia' by Guido de Papia, reproduced in color in *Medicine: A Treasury of Art and Literature*, eds Ann G. Carmichael and Richard M. Ratzan (New York, 1991), pls 28, 29, where a physician wears a black skull-cap with red tassle with a dark red tunic

have no funerary brasses, prior to the very late sixteenth century,[32] to offer more elaborate or larger details of garment construction. In partial compensation for the lack of funerary brasses, Aldred Scott Warthin states that the figure of the Physician was a staple in dramatic representations, most likely of a religious nature, concerned with the dance of death, possibly as early as the thirteenth century. Scenes from these plays were reproduced as wall paintings in religious institutions, for example the Danse Macabre in the Cloister of the Innocents, in Paris, dated 1424, later reproduced in woodcuts by Guyot Marchant, 1485; other such scenes appear in the Block Books of Heidelberg and Munich from the early portion of the fifteenth century and later.[33] However, Chaucer's specification of both fabrics and dyes in lines 439–40 does offer more information than can be determined in small manuscript illuminations.

Chaucer's description also informs the Ellesmere illumination, which depicts a physician, designated by a jordan held aloft, who wears a red outer garment, apparently lined with dark brown (or black) fur showing at the sleeve edge. This is topped by a very dark blue hood with short shoulder cape, lined with white fur, which shows at the lower edge of the cape and on the turned-back face-edge of the hood. In addition, this doctor wears

under a lighter red fur-lined cloak that has tippets hanging from the elbows of its slightly loose sleeves. The physician in *Chroniques De Froissart*, Tom. IV. P. I, BL MS Harl. 4379, fol. 125b, wears red and blue also, and the style of his garments is fashionable rather than academic: he wears a blue robe with broad shoulders and puffed sleeves with a red chaperon (defined in Chapter 8, n. 5).

Also the late-fourteenth-century *Les Chroniques De Saint-Denis*, vol. 2, BL MS Roy. 20 C VII, fol. 78v, depicts two physicians, but their costumes vary significantly from the usual red and blue medical attire; the physician holding the urinal wears a mauve robe, green hood with white fur lining, and gray skull-cap; the second physician wears a gray robe over royal blue tunic, gray hood lined with white fur, and gray skull-cap. This illumination is reproduced in Edith Rickert's *Chaucer's World*, eds Clair C. Olson and Martin M. Crow (New York, 1948), pl. opposite p. 171.

Although the predominant colors for physicians continue to be red and blue, the trend of physicians being depicted in garments in a variety of colors also continues in fifteenth-century illuminations, for example the violet, green, blue, and red garments in the 1473 BL MS of *Les Commentaires de Julle César Traduction Jehan du Chesne*, Roy. 16 G VIII, fol. 32. Here, too, the customary fourteenth-century *pileus* is absent and a red hat shaped in the style of a fez is worn.

A variety of medical illustrations may be seen in Carl Zigrosser, *Medicine and the Artist*, 3rd enl. edn (New York, 1970).

32 'Undoubted examples' of brasses of Doctors of Medicine in academical dress are limited to three, dated 1592, 1599, and 1619, according to Hargreaves-Mawdsley, p. 76.

33 These dates are too late for Chaucer; however he could have seen earlier painted representations or versions of such religious dramas. Warthin provides a history of the development of the Danse Macabre in drama, poetry, and the visual arts; see esp. pp. 10, 12, 20, 26ff, and fig. 5, as well as numerous depictions of physicians in typical garments.

pointed-toed black shoes with a strap across the open instep,[34] where his red hose show. The illuminator's palette matches Chaucer's color description as well as being especially pertinent to Hargreaves-Mawdsley's description of the academic hoods of 'dark blue' and lined with fur worn by all Bachelors of Medicine until 1815.[35] Also of note is that the 'old Civil Law faculty colour of [navy] blue, which . . . Bachelors of Medicine wore in the fifteenth century, in common with Bachelors of Law' also became the color of choice for Masters of Surgery in the nineteenth century when they belatedly opted to have an official professional costume.[36] The fact that Hargreaves-Mawdsley designates these navy-blue hoods as 'fifteenth-century' most likely reflects the dearth of detailed records before this time, a lack which he mentions repeatedly, rather than any official adoption date. Indeed, navy-blue might have been customarily worn long before this time, and, quite possibly, authorities finally decided to make official what had been a long-standing tradition.[37] Hargreaves-Mawdsley's description of this group supports this possibility:

> The degree of Master of Surgery, formerly very rare, was until recent times considered as invariably associated with the degree of Doctor of Medicine, so that it was never mentioned on its own account, and is never considered in statutes, nor does it appear in costume plates.[38]

Also, it is possible, although not provable, that the Ellesmere illuminator's representation of the Doctor of Phisik depicts the customary wearing apparel, the academical dress, of a physician who speaks of, or practices, both 'phisik' and surgery.

In any case, Chaucer's choice of dyestuffs and fabrics appropriately represents the medical profession in the late Middle Ages. *Sanguin(e)* is defined

---

34 Hargreaves-Mawdsley, pp. 103–4, discusses boots, shoes, and gloves as prescribed in the regulations for academical dress, before 1350 and later. See also Roulin regarding *caligae* and footwear, pp. 187, 189–93.

35 After which Bachelors of Medicine officially adopted lilac silk hoods, according to Hargreaves-Mawdsley, pp. 86–7. See also L. H. Dudley Buxton and Strickland Gibson, *Oxford University Ceremonies* (Oxford, 1935), pp. 38–9, regarding blue hoods for Bachelors of Medicine. Regarding hoods worn by those with degrees of Bachelor and above, see Clarke, 'English Academical Costume', pp. 84–7, 91–2.

36 Hargreaves-Mawdsley, p. 79, n. 2.

37 Clarke, 'English Academical Costume', p. 94, states that some statutes are 'retrograde in their requirements'.

38 Hargreaves-Mawdsley, p. 79. See Speed, p. 223, concerning the status of surgeons, and the University of Bologna as being the sole university having faculty members in the field of surgery. Also see Bryon Grigsby, 'The Social Position of the Surgeon in London, 1350–1450', *Essays in Medieval Studies* 13 (1996), at <http://www.luc.edu/publications/medieval/vol13/grigsby.html>.

by the MED as a 'rich cloth[39] of blood-red color', and one example speaks of a 'bryghte sanggueyn'.[40] As already discussed, Chaucer's color choice of red and blue repeats that of medieval manuscript illuminators[41] and is symbolically apt for a physician, since blood-letting (see Plate 12) was among the common medieval procedures a doctor might order, whether or not he actually performed the procedure himself.[42] Hélène Dauby carries the symbolic connection much further in remarking that the sanguine worn by the physician evokes the idea of the blood of his patients and thus suggests the correspondence of microcosm and macrocosm. Dauby explains that, as the color red is to blood, the sanguine temperament (as determined by one of the four

---

[39] 'Cloth', in medieval England, is generally understood to be a woolen cloth; see OED def. 9, and John James, *History of the Worsted Manufacture in England* (London, 1968).

[40] This color may be the same as that *sanguigno* mentioned in the *Plictho*, pp. 26, 61, and translated in dye recipes #74, p. 116, and #145, p. 154, as 'blood'. In #74, the description, 'A tenger sanguigno debiadato', from madder and brazil, yields 'faded blood' color; but #145 provides 'blood cloth', apparently a full-strength color. See the facsimile of Gioanventura Rosetti's first edition of 1548 of *The Plictho: Instructions in the Art of the Dyers which Teaches the Dyeing of Woolen Cloths, Linens, Cottons, and Silk by the Great Art as Well as by the Common*, trans. Sidney M. Edelstein and Hector C. Borghetty (Cambridge, MA, 1969), for other recipes that produce red dyestuffs, including those described as *in grain*, *cardinal*, *crimson*, as well as various blues, such as *peacock*, *azure*, *Alexandrine* ('a navy blue'), and others, all using either indigo or woad. I was unable to locate any mention of *pers* in this work.

[41] Red is the color most frequently used for physician's clothing as depicted in medieval manuscripts. See Loren MacKinney, *Medical Illustrations in Medieval Manuscripts*, Publications of the Wellcome Historical Medical Library n.s. 5 (London, 1965), fig. 45, in which Hippocrates wears a red loose-sleeved robe with white headdress, reproduced from a north Italian ms, c.1300: Rome, Casanatense Library, MS 1382, fol. 2, at the beginning of Rolandus Parmensis, *Chirurgia*; and fig. 54, which depicts Galen in a red gown with an ermine border, which is mostly covered by a blue hooded *manicata* with white fur showing at the lower edges of the sleeves and an ermine lining around the face as well as ermine lappets at the neck, reproduced from a fifteenth-century Flanders ms, Dresden, MS Db. 92–3, fol. 320: Galen, *De flebothomia*, prologue. Surgeons wearing blue and red may be seen in figs 21 and 82a; also see figs 66, 77, 73, 81b. See color pls 1, 8, 12, of doctors dressed primarily in red in Carole Rawcliffe, *Medicine and Society in Later Medieval England* (Stroud, 1995).

[42] Eleazar, pp. 235–6, states that blood-letting (phlebotomy) was performed by a 'subculture of medical practitioners' such as 'blood-letters, leeches, barbers, and barber-surgeons'. See Talbot and Hammond's discussion of barber-surgeons, pp. vi–vii; and Claudius F. Meyer, 'A Medieval English Leechbook and its 14th Century Poem on Bloodletting', *Bulletin of the History of Medicine* 7 (1939), pp. 380–91, esp. pp. 387–91, regarding the popular medical practice of blood-letting and a poem on that subject. See also Conrad, et al., fig. 27, p. 201, for a drawing of a man with lines drawn to bubbles showing where to draw blood. This drawing is reproduced from a 1488–89 work by the Welsh poet Gutun Owain, MS Mostyn 88, p. 11, in the National Library of Wales.

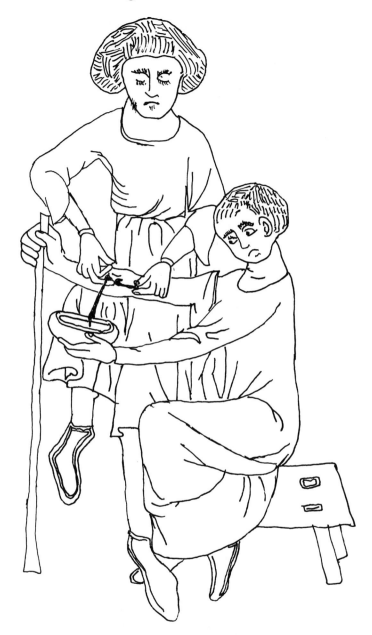

12. Line drawing of surgeon, depicted in a short tunic, drawing blood
from a patient, after the illumination in *The Luttrell Psalter*, BL Add.
MS 42130, fol. 61; drawing by Daniel Scott Henderson, included with
his permission.

humors so central to medieval practice of medicine) is to the mixture of heat and humidity, the element of air, the southern wind (presumably hot), and the god Mars.[43] In addition, medieval physicians would be concerned with the flow of blood through the body as signaled in the pulse beat, which was examined theoretically in terms of its inherent musicality, as it was thought to be allied with the Music of the Spheres and universal harmonies.[44] In general, according to Michel Pastoureau, reds of all shades, luminosity, and density were thought to have medicinal virtues.[45]

Chaucer's description of the temple of Mars in his *Knight's Tale* (I, lines 1967–2050) illustrates Mars' associaton with *sanguine* – the color red, the blood of battle and the bleeding wounds of death, and the characteristics of the sanguine humor. The Knight-narrator names this god 'Mars the rede'. His temple is described as a 'grisly place' of 'burned steel' with tumultuous winds (lines 1969, 1971, 1983, and 1985–6). The numerous images of bleeding include victims of battle, suicide, and insanity:

> with woundes al bibledde;
> Contek, with blody knyf and sharp manace.
> . . .
> His herte-blood hath bathed al his heer –
> . . .
> The careyne in the busk, with throte ycorve.
> (lines 2002–3, 2006, 2014)

Taking this association of Mars and bleeding a step further, William Spencer remarks on the astronomical implications of the planet Mars, stating that Mars ' "signifies medical practice, both surgery and other kinds of medicine" '.[46]

In addition to its mythic associations with Mars, the word *sangwyn* speaks of a dye and a cloth of quality and cost.[47] The OED provides a 1319 example

---

43 Hélène Dauby also mentions in this list the season of spring and the god Mercury, although she does not explain how they relate to the color red, in 'In Sangwyn and in pers: Les Coleurs dans le prologue général des *Canterbury Tales*', *Les couleurs au Moyen Age* (Aix-en-Provence, 1988), p. 49.

44 Nancy Sirasi explains these concepts, their origins, and subsequent histories in the study of medieval medicine, as well as their eastern advocates, in 'The Music of Pulse in the Writings of Italian Academic Physicians (Fourteenth and Fifteenth Centuries)', *Speculum* 50 (Oct. 1975), pp. 689–710.

45 See Michel Pastoureau, ' "Ceci est mon sang". Le christianisme medieval et la couleur rouge', *Le Pressoir mystique: Actes du Colloque de Recloses* (Paris, 1990), pp. 43–56.

46 William Spencer, 'Are Chaucer's Pilgrims Keyed to the Zodiac?' in *ChauR* 4.3 (1970), p. 162, citing Guido Bonatti, *De Astronomia Tractatus X* (Basileae, 1550), col. 104.

47 C.1380, sanguine cloth cost 4s 8d per yard; the same price as 'tweny medley', according to Rickert, *Chaucer's World*, pp. 343–4.
    This price may be compared with other cloths dyed red: James E. Thorold Rogers, *A*

concerned with this fabric: 'Riley *Mem. Lond.* (1858) 131 [Also two] sanguynes [(dyed) in grain, value 15 pounds].'[48] The fabric would necessarily have been of rich quality to merit the expense of this costly red dye.[49] Additional definitions in the MED include a 1397 mention of 'A coverture of sanguyn [furred with] menyver', indicating that this fabric was worthy of being furred with miniver. *Miniver* was a high-fashion and relatively expensive fur in the thirteenth and fourteenth centuries, made up of white squirrel

History of Agriculture and Prices in England (Oxford, 1892; rpt. 1963), 1:577 and 2:542, mentions a cheap red dye used to produce a cloth called 'blodium' (see below) described in records for 1388 as costing 4s 8d for 3 yds, 3s 3d for 3½ yds, 3s 10d for 5½ yds, and 3s 10d for 9 yds. Reflecting apparent variances in quality, these prices may be compared with the cost of 3s 4d for 4½ yds of green cloth. If Rogers is correct that the dye was cheap, this cannot be the same red dye used for dyeing the fabric known as 'scarlet cloth' which Rogers 1:577 quotes at 15s the yard, although the difference in price might be accounted for in the costs of the finishing required in the production of the fabric called scarlet. Regarding *scarlet cloth*, see Hodges, *C&C*, pp. 24, 51, 63–4, 85, 114, 152, 160, 173, 176, 181, 200, 227, 234; for prices, see pp. 88, 113–14, 153, 175; and see A. R. Bridbury, *Medieval English Clothmaking: An Economic Survey* (London, 1982), p. 43.

    In a discussion of cloths dyed red, the term *blodium* is confusing: 'blod', the root of *blodium*, might mean red in a document written in English, or blue in a document written in Medieval Latin. The MED provides the following: 'blod n. (1)' meaning 'blood' [and indicating the color red]; 'blod n. (2)' [comes from ML blodius] meaning '? blue color, ? blue cloth' with '(1397) *Will York* in *Sur. Soc. 4* 218: Vestimentum paled de blod & albo' and '(1432) *Will York* in *Sur. Soc. 30* 28: Unum lectum de blod', as examples. In addition, there are the following adjectives: 'blod adj. [from blod n. (1).]' meaning 'bloody, bloodstained; ? blood colored'; and 'blodi adj. [OE blodig]' meaning 'red'. Also, for *blodius* as blue, see E. G. Cuthbert F. Atchley, 'On English Liturgical Colours', *Essays on Ceremonial*, ed. Vernon Staley (London, 1904), p. 105.

    For additional examples of the red/blue confusion, see Daniel V. Thompson, *The Materials and Techniques of Medieval Painting* (New York, 1956), pp. 111ff. for discussion of red pigments; pp. 130ff. for blue; and p. 140 for a designation of *blodum* as a blue dye and a synonym for woad. Also, R. E. Latham's *Dictionary of Medieval Latin* (London, 1975), the entry for *blodius* meaning blue cloth or color, with examples including '1316 j *curtepy* de bludeo (St. Ives) *Law Merch.* I 101' and '1432 septem deifice virtutes in puella ribus effigiebus . . . solis indute jubaribus super femora [blodius] in celestina (Reventus Hen. V) MGL III 459'.

48 Compare with prices given in the chapter on the Friar's costume, p. 147, nn. 48–9, and with those given in Hodges, *C&C* regarding the prices for *scarlet*, pp. 88, 113–14, 153, 175.

49 For a discussion of *in grain*, see Hodges, *C&C*, pp. 173, n. 51, and *kermes*, p. 175, nn. 54 and 57. Two scarlet cloths are mentioned by Margaret Wade Labarge, in *A Baronial Household of the Thirteenth Century* (New York, 1965), p. 132. The scarlets, made in Lincoln, are listed in accounts for Richard of Cornwall and for the countess and her daughter respectively: 'red scarlet' and 'sanguine' scarlet, with a cost of 7s per ell (in England an ell measured 45 inches). There were several red dyestuffs in use in the Middle Ages, as Thompson makes clear, pp. 111ff. See also Stella Mary Newton, *Fashion in the Age of the Black Prince: A study of the years 1340–1365* (Woodbridge, 1980; rpt. 1999), pp. 21, 27, 31, 35, 40, 60–1, 63, 68.

bellies with only a small amount of gray left around the white.[50] It is a subtype of *vair*, which is composed of the entire skin of squirrels. However, and more pertinent to the Doctor's costume, there is a 1423 record of 'j roba domini de sangwyn', corroborating the use of this fabric for a Master's academic robe.

Chaucer's designation of *pers* as the second dyestuff or fabric worn by the Doctor matches, or possibly exceeds, sanguine in quality. The luxurious nature of *pers* is amply documented by Helen S. Houghton, who discusses the social connotations of wearing this fine fabric of deep blue color (also, according to MED def. a, 'purplish; blue-grey'),[51] that generally signified the high social rank of the wearer.[52] The c.1390 *Robert of Cisyle* (lines 234–44)

---

[50] Elspeth M. Veale, *The English Fur Trade in the Later Middle Ages* (Oxford, 1960), pp. 133–4, 228. Veale, pp. 17–18, states that 'at a time when carpenters were being paid 3*d.* a day with an allowance for food of 1½ *d.* a day, King John was paying 6*s.* to 7*s.* for linings of lambskin, 8*s.* to 10*s.* for rabbit skin, about £1 for linings of ten *tiers* of northern squirrels, £2 for a single sable skin, and £5 for a lining of ermine'. She gives 3s 4d as the price of the most expensive fur in a skinner's shop in the late fourteenth century (citing Chancery, Extents on Debts, 51, *m.* 15), while 2d–4d is the range of wages for workmen and labourers per day, and 1s 4d would be the possible cost for a gown. She reports, p. 139, that in the Great Wardrobe account (England) for 1392–93, 'minever pured' as compared to the 'gris fin' (the backs of a gray squirrel) was 2 pence per skin to 2½, 2¼. In 1407–8, this comparison was 2 pence per skin to 2½. Usually prices are computed by the timber (a timber = a bundle of 40 skins); therefore, the 1407–8 price would be 80 pence for miniver as compared with 100 pence for gris. Elsewhere, p. 221, Veale gives the 1419 cost of miniver as 3s 4d to 4s 6d per timber, while ermine was 15s to 18s; Veale discusses, pp. 4–5, the sumptuary laws that specify that miniver and *gris* might be worn by knights and ladies who possessed over £266 13s 4d, but less prosperous knights and clerks might only wear facings of ermine and lettice on their hoods, and esquires with £200 and above and merchants with £1,000 a year may wear facings of miniver on their hoods. See Gottfried, pp. 56–7, pls 15, 35, 71, regarding doctors and surgeons wearing fur.

[51] The sources of blue dyestuffs were woad, grown in many places in Europe, and indigo, imported primarily from Egypt and Syria, with the best quality originating in India. Indigo, the more expensive of the two dyes, produced the blue that the Middle Ages knew as azure; see Désirée Koslin, 'Textiles, Decorative', pp. 597–8, and Laura F. Hodges, 'Dyes and Pigments', pp. 154–6, in *Trade, Travel, and Exploration in the Middle Ages: An Encyclopedia*, eds John B. Friedman and Kristen Mossler Figg (New York, 2000).

[52] Helen S. Houghton, ' "Degree" and "Array" in Chaucer's Portrait of the Reeve: A Study of Idiom and Meaning', 2 vols, Diss., University of York, England, 1975, pp. 241–58, esp. 241, and 247. Newton discusses the problems in knowing what shade of blue is represented by *pers*, pp. 133–5. The debate as to shade of blue is set forth by Maurice Mann, 'La couleur perse en ancien française et chez Dante', *Romania* 49 (1923), pp. 186–203, and, in the same issue, by E. Hoepfner, 'Pers en ancien Française', pp. 592–7. The MED examples appear to distinguish *pers* from *ynde* and from *asure*. See Atchley for possible range of color for *pers*, p. 105; and see E. M. Carus-Wilson's comments regarding dye process and *pers* as a quality cloth, in *Medieval Merchant Venturers: Collected Studies*, 2nd edn (London, 1967), p. 216 and n. 1. Labarge cites the count-

depicts clothing made of *pers* at its best, suitable to be furred with pelts of superlative quality. In this romance, these clothes are the gift of the angel who substitutes for King Robert, meeting the messengers of Emperor Valemounde: 'Þe angel welcomede þe messagers And ȝaf hem cloþes riche of pers, Furred al wiþ ermyne.'[53] Further, Chaucer's choice of dyestuff or fabric is again appropriate for a physician who knows all of the acknowledged ancient Mediterranean and eastern authorities[54] in the field of medicine, for *pers* is associated, at least nominally, with Persia, according to the OED, which states, 'The Romanic word [for *pers*] was perh, a back-formation from *Persia*, or L *Persæ* Persians, *Persicus* Persian.'[55]

However, the name of this color or cloth of blue color may refer to Persia in another fashion: it could indicate either that the cloth was dyed in Persia, or that a certain blue cloth met the acknowledged high standards of cloths dyed in Persia. According to Malachy Postlethwayt, Persia was renowned for mastery of the dyeing process and for producing livelier colors that maintained their depth for longer periods than dyed cloths produced elsewhere. This capability was attributed to climatic conditions, and home-grown (or produced nearby), fresh dyestuffs, including lapis lazuli.[56] Thus *pers* may refer to a blue cloth originating in Persia, which exhibits the quality for which this country is famous; alternatively, it may reflect an appreciation for this quality, even when it appears in an imitation produced elsewhere. Further, *pers* might suggest a particular kind of fabric, although we cannot know which of the following this might be: the Persians were famous for their pro-

---

ess's purchase of 24½ ells of pers for servants' robes costing 42s, less than 2s per ell, and comments, 'This is so cheap that the perse must have been of particularly poor quality'. Rogers, 1:576–7, refers to a high-priced *Persetum* mentioned in records of 1284 and 1287; and see 2:536. See also Hodges, *C&C*, pp. 175, 200, 233–5, regarding *pers* as possibly both a particular color and as cloth. The MED, def. b. reads: 'one such color; cloth of such color; a kind or quality of cloth; ~bleu'.

53 *Robert of Cisyle*, in *Amis and Amiloun, Robert of Cisyle, and Sir Amadace*, ed. Edward E. Foster, TEAMS, Medieval Institute Publications (Kalamazoo, MI, 1997), pp. 96–110.

54 For a description of ancient and eastern medical authorities, see M. F. McBride, *Chaucer's Physician and Fourteenth-Century Medicine: A Compendium for Students*, University Monograph Series (Bristol, IN, 1985), pp. 44–8; for descriptions of portraits of Galen and Avicenna, see *The Story of Medicine in Art*, Exhibition, The Milwaukee Art Institute, Sept. 11–October 25, 1953 (Milwaukee, WI, 1953), p. 7.

Chaucer also mentions contemporary English authorities. In this regard, see Albert G. Nicholls, 'Medicine in Chaucer's Day', *Dalhousie Review* 12 (1932), pp. 218–30, and esp. his English candidate for a model for the Doctor's portrait, pp. 229–30; also McBride, pp. 48–9.

55 However, the OED also cites Du Cange as approving the view of Arcarisius that *perseus* was a 'deriv. of *persa*, Ital. name of marjoram, referring to the colour'.

56 Malachy Postlethwayt, *The Universal Dictionary of Trade and Commerce: Translated from the French of the Celebrated Monsieur Savary* (London, 1755), 2:444.

duction of fabrics of cotton, goats' and camels' hair, and especially silk, as well as cloths composed of a mixture of these fibers. Their silks included taffetas, tabbies, satins, and brocades, as well as gold velvets. An appealing and convenient idea is that the Doctor's *pers* actually refers to his taffeta.[57]

In any case, the Doctor of Phisik's wearing of *pers* suggests the idea of eastern *scientia*, and consequently it is culturally in keeping with many of those same authorities he is said to have mastered in his medical scholarship, as did all well-educated doctors in the Middle Ages. And clearly, if there were emblematic coats of arms for physicians, 'sangyn and pers' would be the obvious choice of symbolic colors for them.

Thus we see Chaucer's physician wearing garments made of two expensive fabrics. Further, these garments are lined with silk, a fabric known in late-fourteenth-century England as having a Mediterranean or eastern origin. Silk of all types was an import in England during this period[58] and was purchased by the ounce, costing between 10d and 1s per ounce,[59] or by the 'begen, or becket',[60] with an average price for a lining during the second half of the fourteenth century being £1 8s 1½d.[61] (We may compare this to the price a tailor charged to make a robe – 1s.) Less expensive than samite or

---

[57] Postlethwayt states, 2:444, that the Persians were renowned for their production of taffeta. Regarding taffeta in Persia, Kax Wilson states that it was produced 'in greatest quantity for costume materials', in *A History of Textiles* (Boulder, CO, 1979), p. 120. But also see Patrick Leech, 'Who Says Manchester Says Cotton: Textile Terminology in the Oxford English Dictionary (1000–1960)', *TRA linea* (1999), 2:3, 11–12, 15–16.

[58] See Labarge's account, pp. 133–5 of the thirteenth-century Italian imitation of oriental silks in Lucca and of the fourteenth-century Florentine silks, such silks being available for sale at fairs and through London and Paris merchants.

[59] Rogers 1:580; Frances Elizabeth Baldwin, *Sumptuary Legislation and Personal Regulation in England*, Johns Hopkins University Studies in Historical and Political Science, Series 44, no. 1 (Baltimore, 1926), p. 67, n. 165. See *The Statutes of the Realm* 1 (London, 1910; Netherlands, 1963), Item X, pp. 380–1, regarding the income necessary before Esquires and Gentlemen were allowed to wear silk. The *Statutes* set the standard also for Yeomen, Merchants, Citizens, and Handicraftsmen, as well as for Knights, as mentioned in Items IX, XI, and XII. Regulations for the Clergy and any 'Clerks, which have Degree in any Church, Cathedral, Collegial, or Schools' were to be commensurate with their respective 'Constitution', and they, too, were to be regulated according to individual income; however, in this source only fur is mentioned as being an issue for various ranks of the Clergy.

In *The Catholic Encyclopedia*, online edn (1999), vol. 15, Joseph Braun states, in 'Tunic', that the *tunica taleris*, a full-length tunic that reached to the feet, was made from silk in the Middle Ages. This was the ordination garment regularly provided for new sub-deacons in the fourteenth and fifteenth centuries.

[60] Rogers, 1:580, defines this as 'a measure', and states that from 2½ to 3 begens were sufficient to make a lining. Silk linings were used for summer robes, fur linings for winter.

[61] According to the calculations of Rogers, 1:580; see also 2:535, 540–2, and 4:573; and Baldwin, p. 67, n. 165.

'tartaryn', sendal[62] was a silk often used for garment linings for the robes of kings and queens, as well as for clerks' livery,[63] and 'taffata', too, was used as lining material.[64] Stella Mary Newton, writing of the 1350s, states that *cendal* 'belonged to the high categories of stuffs, in France, of which royal clothing could be made'. Sendal is also a fabric mentioned in descriptions of academical dress. E. C. Clarke states that the (1414) Ancient Statutes of Cambridge, no. 176, provide that a Bachelor may not wear a sendal lining in his tabard, hood, or other garments, and the (1342) Oxford Statute disallows sendal or *tartaran*, or other silk for anyone 'in his hood' (presumably as a

---

[62] Lisa Monnas, 'Silk Cloths Purchased for the Great Wardrobe of the Kings of England, 1325–1462', *Ancient and Medieval Textiles: Studies in Honour of Donald King*, eds Lisa Monnas and Hero Granger-Taylor, *Text Hist* 20.2 (1989), pp. 287–9, 303. Monnas cites Lucchese regulations for 1376 as listing taffeta and cendal among the cheaper silks, and tartaryn among those more expensive, a finding that is reinforced by 1392 English wardrobe accounts. The 1392–94 prices include tartaryn at 3s and 2s 1d, while taffeta is priced at 10d, 7½d, 7d, 9d and 7½d.

There is a modern confusion concerning the fibers in cendal: the MED definition for *cendal* is 'A kind of costly fabric (apparently of linen or cotton)'. Newton, p. 135, defines *cendal* as 'certainly silk'; Anna Muthesius, 'Silk in the Medieval World', in *The Cambridge History of Western Textiles*, ed. David Jenkins (Cambridge, 2003), 1:347–8, describes 'sendal' as silk.

[63] Newton, pp. 23–5, 69, 80, 132. See also Kay Staniland, 'Clothing and Textiles at the Court of Edward III 1342–1352', *Collectanea Londiniensia: Studies in London Archaeology and History Presented to Ralph Merrifield*, eds Joanna Bird, Hugh Chapman, and John Clark, London and Middlesex Archaeological Society, Special Papers 2 (London, 1978), p. 232.

[64] Taffeta is defined by William S. Beck in *The Draper's Dictionary* (London, 1882), p. 335, as

> A name once applied to plain woven silks. . . . It appears to have been first brought into this country in the 14th century, and in the eleventh year of Richard II. the Chief Justices of the King's Bench were allowed, with other rich stuffs and furs, twenty-four ells of green taffeta extra. Stubbes mentions it as among the luxuries of dress, and it was then, according to him, worn not only in gowns, but also for hoods, hats, caps, kerchiefs 'and such like'.

'Tartaryn taffata' as part of a summer robe is included in a 1379 Oxford purchase of 8½ yds of fabric priced at 5s for a robe and 'Tartaryn taffata & silk' [for a lining] amounting to 12s; and, in 1377, 16 yds of 'Green taffata' was purchased @ 10½d, with 1 yd of 'Tantaryn (for hood)' @ 3s 8d, according to records included in Rogers, 2:541. (The spelling 'Tantaryn' may be a misprint.) See also Newton, pp. 23–5, 61; Mary Ernestine Whitmore, *Medieval English Domestic Life and Amusements in the Works of Chaucer* (New York, 1972), p. 150.

Tartaryn was used in the livery for members of the Guild of Merchant Taylors, according to an entry concerning Richard II, who became an honorary member in 1385, as did his queen: 'Allowance of cloth by the Company. – First for the King 6 (yards or ells) of cloth of 8s. and 1 piece of Tartain 30s. – 3£. 18s. To the Queen 6 y^{ds} of cloth of 8s. and 1 piece of Tartain 30s. – 3£. 18s', according to C. M. Clode, comp., *Memorials of the Guild of Merchant Taylors* (London, 1875), p. 596.

lining) 'unless he be a Master or Licentiate in some Faculty or of certain birth or means'.[65]

That two different lining fabrics are mentioned signifies that Chaucer's two-line costume description refers to two different garments; the silk of lightest weight would line the garment constructed out of the lighter-weight outer fabric. There appears to be nothing unusual in a doctor wearing silk. Most likely the Act for the Reformation of Excess in Apparel of 1533 only defines long-standing custom when it allows doctors of medicine 'to use at all times "sarcenet" (silk) in the lining of their gowns, as well as satin or velvet for facings'.[66]

Knowledge of these fabric and dyestuff details tells us that the character of the Physician might be the most lavishly dressed of any of the pilgrims described in the *General Prologue*, with the possible exception of the Squire, whose embroidered gown may have been equally expensive because such labor-intensive and therefore costly embroidery was often done with silk thread and on expensive fabric. The garments of the Physician were certainly more expensive than the Friar's double worsted semicope. Sanguine, pers, taffeta, and sendal far outshine the Merchant's motley and the Man of Law's homely medley coat, even though it is worn with a barred silk girdle. And the luxurious fabrics of this Physician's costume overshadow the Monk's habit (fabric unspecified, but theoretically of monks' cloth), even with sleeves edged in gris, since implied in the purfling is an unseen lining of cheaper fur.[67] The Franklin who wears a silk purse hanging from his girdle, and the proud guildsmen dressed in livery, cannot compete in this 'best-dressed' competition because we do not know details of their robes; by the same logic, we cannot know what sartorial finery is covered by the Wife of Bath's hip mantle. And, needless to say, the Doctor's attire puts the Knight's 'bismotered' 'fustian' 'gypon' to shame.

That the Physician manifests his wealth in his costume in no way belies Chaucer's statement that the Doctor was 'but esy of dispence' (line 441) (glossed in *Riverside Chaucer* as 'moderate in [careful about] spending'), since garments were tangible property important enough to be listed individually in wills. We need not be concerned with Chaucer's sentence structure, which in the twenty-first century might suggest that the Doctor wore expensive clothing *but otherwise* spent his money carefully. In the fourteenth century, one could literally wear a fortune, *invested* in garments. Further, we need not assume that the Doctor purchased these garments, as they could have been accepted as medical fees or as gifts from wealthy patients. For example, Chaucer's contemporary John of Arderne states, 'for a case of

---

[65] Clarke, 'English Academical Costume', pp. 91–2.
[66] Hargreaves-Mawdsley, p. 75, quoting this 1533 legislation.
[67] See Chapter 4, p. 121, regarding purfling in the Monk's costume.

fistula in ano, when it is curable, the surgeon may reasonably ask of a great man 100 marks or £40 with robes and fees to the value of 100 shillings each year for the rest of his life'.[68] A second example is provided by a lifetime grant made by Isabel, daughter of Edward III, to the King's physician Master William Holme, as recorded in the Calendar of Patent Rolls, 16 November 1376, for 'an annuity of 10£ out of the manor of Cosham, Co. Wilts., with robes with fur of the suit of her clerks'.[69] In any case, the Doctor's rich costume served to advertise not only his familiarity with things eastern, but also his successful medical career, a sartorial practice that suggests that principles of dressing for success change little through the centuries.

But this costume is more than wearable wealth; it is also visual evidence that he does not wear the sober clerical robes described as suitable for doctors in, for example, such works as John Arderne's *Treatise of Fistule in Ano*, c.1376: 'Ideally, a surgeon should always be soberly dressed, not likening himself in clothing or bearing to minstrels, but rather after the, manner of a clerk [as discussed in Chapter 6]; for any discreet man clad in clerk's dress may sit at a gentleman's table.'[70] The proper dress of a scholar, physician, and professional man of the fourteenth century, according to Charles Pendrill, was a 'sober habit . . . consisting of a plain black gown reaching from the neck to the feet, buttoned closely at the throat and wrists'.[71] The dress of clerks should be 'modest and unostentatious', not 'gay and showy', nor 'embroidered with silk'. It should reflect their 'dignity', be closed at the top, and be the appropriate length; failure to meet these requirements would result in their loss of their benefice or their being prevented from gaining a desired benefice.[72] Clearly there is a disparity between the sober dress of clerks who practice medicine and Doctors, Masters of Medicine, who dress according to

---

68   John of Arderne, in *Treatise of Fistula in Ano*, ed. D'Arcy Power (EETS, OS, 1910), as reprinted in #696, 'A surgeon's code of behaviour and ethics, c. 1376', in *English Historical Documents* (New York, 1969), 4:1185. For John's biographical sketch, see Talbot and Hammond, pp. 111–12.

69   Ussery, *Chaucer's Physician*, p. 71 (citing *C.P.R. 1374–77*, p. 392); for gifts of clothing to King Richard II's physician John de Middleton, see Ussery, p. 88 (citing *Ward. Acc. Ric. II*, p. 505). For William of Holme's biographical sketch, see Talbot and Hammond, p. 403.

70   Included in *English Historical Documents*, 4:1185; also quoted in Rickert's *Chaucer's World*, p. 176; cited in Muriel Bowden, *A Reader's Guide to Geoffrey Chaucer* (New York, 1971), p. 209. See Elaine E. Whitaker, 'John of Arderne and Chaucer's Physician', *ANQ: A Quarterly Journal of Short Articles, Notes, and Reviews* 8.1 (Winter 1995), pp. 3–8. Such comments date from classical times as described by Bishop, pp. 196, 214–15; see p. 198 for his description of Roy. MS 15 E 11 miniature (mid-fifteenth century), illustrating physicians.

71   Charles Pendrill, *London Life in the 14th Century* (Port Washington, NY, 1971), p. 16.

72   According to McCloud, p. 37, speaking of clerical dress during the sixth through the fourteenth century. See also Clarke, 'English Academical Costume', pp. 80–1, describing the religious nature of the clerical habit, and the *tunica talaris*, 'a Robe reaching to

their higher rank. Otto Bettman posits that, in the Renaissance period, doctors exchanged such clerical garb for the 'rich robe of [the] Renaissance academician'.[73] However, the apparel of physicians depicted in medieval literature suggests that this exchange occurred much earlier – at least as early as the High Middle Ages.

In the place of sober clerical garb, Chaucer's Doctor wears expensive garments made of vividly dyed fabrics. However, the colors and fabrics worn by this pilgrim appear to be the standard ones for doctors of his day, as opposed to the more lavish finery worn by his literary confreres described by Petrarch, Langland, and Henryson, among others.[74] In Petrarch's opinion, physicians were objectionable in part because of 'their flaunting of costumes to which they have no right, gowns rich with purple, tricked out with various emblems, glittering rings and gilded spurs. Who would not be dazzled by such a sight?'[75] Langland's Phisik wears a 'furred ho[od]', perhaps a hood like the one pictured in the Ellesmere illumination, as previously discussed (pp. 208–10). Phisik also wears a much more luxurious 'cloke of Calabre' with 'knappes [buttons] of golde',[76] *calabre* being gray squirrel, obtained from

---

the ankles (*talaris*), decent and reputable, as suited to the clerical *status* of the wearer', and citing 1379 or 1380 ordinances.

73 Otto L. Bettman, *A Pictorial History of Medicine* (Springfield, IL, 1962), p. 95.

74 In Petrus Berchorius's negative mythographic analysis of Mercury, we have the prototypical portrait of the self-serving, eloquent physician. In William Donald Reynolds, 'The *Ovidius Moralizatus* of Petrus Berchorius: An Introduction and Translation', Diss., University of Illinois at Urbana-Champaign, 1971; Ann Arbor, MI: University Microfilms, #72–7039; see pp. 70–5; also pp. 143–5, 172–4, Berchorius states, 'Mercury was feigned to have a sleep-giving wand [the caduceus] because eloquence lulls to sleep and entraps even those who are on guard. . . . He had a cap on his head as does a merchant.' Regarding a favorable interpretation of Mercury as an honorable ecclesiastic, judge, or prelate, Berchorius again speaks of eloquence: Mercury will change gender [his nature] 'by varying his own conditions in different ways according to places, persons, and times'. However, Mercury's eloquence is also a tool of his avarice; his cap may function as concealment of his evil designs, his wingedness as evidence of 'presumption and pride', his changeability as fraudulent, and Mercury is lord of merchants, thieves, and all 'profit and growth'.

See also Jane Chance, *The Mythographic Chaucer: The Fabulation of Sexual Politics* (Minneapolis, MN, 1995), pp. 198, 219, 239, and elsewhere, for an elaboration of Mercury's character mythographically interpreted; and Bishop, p. 204.

75 Catherine Moriarty, ed., *The Voice of the Middle Ages* (New York, 1989), p. 306 (quoting and citing Petrarch's letter to Boccacio, 10 Dec. 1365, originally in Latin, pp. 305–8); see Petrarch's castigation of doctors, pp. 305–10; also Beryl Rowland's comments in 'The Physician's "Historial Thyng Notable" and the Man of Law', *ELH* 40 (1973), p. 176 and n. 35, citing Petrarch's *Invectivae contra Medicum*.

76 William Langland, *Piers Plowman, The B Text*, eds George Kane and E. Talbot Donaldson (Univ. of London, 1975), Passus 6, lines 269–70. The MED cites the c.1390 A text of *PP* (Vrn) 7.257, as well as the 1384–5 *Doc.* in *Dugdale Monasticon 8*, 1366, for 'knappes de auro' and 'de perlis'.

Calabria in Italy.[77] Also, Henryson's Doctour in phisik wears a 'hude . . . reid, heklit atour his croun', a portrait that fits Clarke's description of a headdress depicted in a miniature in a (French) manuscript of *Civitas Dei* of a Rector and a Doctor of the University of Paris, both wearing 'a soft, conical Cap without a brim, a Hood above'. And he is 'cled in scarlot goun,/ And furrit weill, as sic ane aucht to be'.[78] Because this 'scarlot' refers to the most expensive woolen fabric of the Middle Ages but specifies no color, Henryson's Doctour's well-furred gown also may be more elaborate than Chaucer's Physician's 'sangyn', a garment of blood-color but, so far as we may determine, unspecified fabric. These literary physicians are illustrated by their colleagues in the illuminations found in two late-fourteenth- century manuscripts: Chaucer's Physician finds a possible counterpart in *The Chroniques De Froissart* (Tom. IV. P. I),[79] done for Charles V of France, where the physician wears a blue robe and red chaperon. In contrast, the physicians of Petrarch, Langland, and Henryson are echoed by illuminations in *Les Chroniques De Saint-Denis* (Vol. II),[80] where the physician wears a gray skullcap, mauve robe, and green hood with white fur lining. Fifteenth-century illuminations also portray physicians in elaborate dress, including gold accessories[81] and furs.[82] Such 'luxurious clothes' are, according to Jill

---

[77] According to Veale, pp. 217–18, 224–5, this fur is Baltic squirrel classified according to its place of origin (Calabria, Italy), which arrived in England through the auspices of Hanseatic and Flemish merchants, during the time of the composition of the *General Prologue*. Her charts, p. 139, show the hierarchy of value for squirrel skins; in 1384 *lucewerk* cost £8 per one thousand skins, with *calabre* at £7^{1}/$_{8}$, *popel* at £4^{2}/$_{3}$, and *ruskyn* at £2. Regarding the wearing of squirrel, Clarke states that the Bachelor may only wear badger or lamb's wool in his hood, but that Masters and Licentiates in the Faculty or persons 'of certain birth or means' might wear miniver or 'self-coloured white or gray fur' as a lining, in 'English Academical Costume', pp. 91–2.

[78] Robert Henryson, *The Testament of Crisseid*, in Robert Kay Gordon's *The Story of Troilus* (Toronto, 1978), p. 357. See also Walter W. Skeat, ed., *Chaucerian and other Pieces*, no. 17, Supplement to *The Complete Works of Geoffrey Chaucer*, lines 250–1, 1897 edn; and 'Poem on the Evil Times of Edward II', *The Political Songs of England from the Reign of John to that of Edward II*, ed. T. Wright, EETS, OS 6, Camden Society (London, 1839), pp. 333–4.

[79] BL MS Harl. 4379, fol. 125v.

[80] BL MS Roy. 20 C VII, fol. 78v.

[81] BL MS Edgerton 2572, fol. 51, a Guild Book of Barber-Surgeons of York, shows a doctor wearing a brooch at the neck of his cloak; while decorative, this brooch also serves a utilitarian purpose. BL MS Roy. 15 E II, fol. 77b (c.1482), *Le Livre des Proprietez des Choses*, depicts an apothecary wearing a gold brooch and fur hood. In BL MS Roy. 16 G VIII, fol. 32 (1473), *Les Commentaires de Julle César*, the physician wears a gold belt.

[82] Hargreaves-Mawdsley, p. 75, notes that the Minster Lovell Church, Oxon., stained-glass window illustrating the dress of an Oxford Doctor of Medicine shows this doctor wearing robes with a miniver lining (see my Color Plate VI). Galen's robes are depicted as being 'sumptuously trimmed in ermine' in mid-fifteenth-century illuminations, according to *Medicine: A Treasury of Art and Literature*, pp. 66–7; see pl. 20.

Mann, part of the physician's 'professional "front" '.[83] In this vein, Robert M. Lumiansky assesses Chaucer's Doctor's medical education, then characterizes him as a 'fashionable medical man'.[84] But while clearly his catalogue of knowledge *is* an 'impressive show', to use Lumiansky's phrase, it is also evident that his apparel, while representing his professional standing, is somewhat more modest than other literary physicians would lead one to expect. The most obvious inferences to be drawn regarding the Doctor's sartorial practice are that Chaucer describes the Doctor's colorful silks as grand because a sumptuously dressed physician is a standard figure in estates satire,[85] and his costume illustrates the Physician's bourgeois materialism.[86] Alternatively, if we participate in Chaucer's fiction that within the parameters of vocational requirements each pilgrim 'chose' his own dress, one inference we may draw concerning this Doctor's choice is that he dresses 'in conformity with his dignity and position'.[87] And this explanation is the more likely since Chaucer's description is reinforced and illustrated by the representation of a saint, possibly St Cosmas or St Damian,[88] patron saints of physicians and surgeons,[89] wearing the regalia of an Oxford Doctor of Medicine in a stained-glass portrait (1440) in Minster Lovell Church, Oxon (color

---

83 Jill Mann, *Chaucer and Medieval Estates Satire: The Literature of Social Classes and the General Prologue to the Canterbury Tales* (Cambridge, 1973), pp. 93, 97.

84 Robert M. Lumiansky, *Of Sondry Folk: The Dramatic Principle in The Canterbury Tales* (Austin, TX, 1955), pp. 195–6.

85 George F. Jones, 'Realism and Social Satire in Heinrich Wittenwiler's Ring', Columbia Diss., University Microfilms (Ann Arbor, 1950), no. 1864, pp. 224–7, states that both doctors and druggists are literary stereotypes with a chief fault being their 'mercenary nature'. See pictures of the fox portrayed as a physician in Kenneth Varty, *Reynard the Fox: A Study of the Fox in Medieval English Art* ([Leicester?], 1967), nos. 37 and 98; ape physicians holding urinals may be seen in nos. 89, 90, 112. *The History of Reynard the Fox: Translated and Printed by William Caxton in 1481*, ed. Donald B. Sands (Cambridge, MA, 1960), pp. 3, 151–3, discusses a physician's education, his dress and wealth and classifies physicians as wily deceivers who get wealthy. John Gower depicts Fraud as an apothecary teamed up with a physician in *Mirour de l'Omme* in *Complete Works of John Gower*, ed. G. C. Macaulay (Oxford, 1899; rpt. 1968), 1:25597ff, esp. 25621–80.

   Ruth Mohl, *The Three Estates in Medieval and Renaissance Literature* (1933; rpt. New York, 1962), pp. 349–50, 356, describes the fourteenth-century reputation of physicians with a talent for making money: they are ignorant, greedy, and fraudulent.

86 See Morgan, p. 497.

87 See Nicholls, p. 219.

88 Pemberton letter to author, 19 March 1996. For a description of the portrayal of these and other medical saints, see Clarke, 'English Academical', pp. 191–4.

89 According to Gabriel Meier, 'Cosmas and Damian', *The Catholic Encyclopedia*, vol. 4, online edn (1999), they were twins and early Christian physicians, with a feast day of 27 September, commemorating their martyrdom (probably in 287). Legend has it that, unlike Chaucer's Doctor of Phisik, they refused fees for their services. This refusal would have been in keeping with a much later church ruling, 1215, which forbade clerics who practiced medicine to collect fees (although they might accept donations),

13. Sketch of a physician holding a jordan aloft, from *Omne bonum*, BL MS Royal 6 E VII, fol. 122.

Plate VI). Hargreaves-Mawdsley describes the costume: 'A Doctor of Medicine, holding the symbols of his profession, a bottle [urinal] and staff,[90] wears a crimson *cappa manicata* lined with miniver, and a black pileus.'[91] The

as described by William H. W. Fanning, 'Medicine and Canon Law', *The Catholic Encyclopedia*, vol. 10, online edn (1999).

90 See pp. 70–5, 143–5, 172–4, of Berchorius's mythographical explication regarding Mercury's chief sign – the god's wand, which has become the symbol of the medical profession – the caduceus. Mercury is described as a planet, also a god, who was portrayed as a man with winged head and heels, holding a 'staff which had the power to put men to sleep and which was wound around with snakes and a curved sword which men called hauwa'. Of his wand, this mythographer comments that it signifies that Mercury's power is directed 'through serpentine prudence', as recommended in Matthew 10:16: ' "Be wise as serpents and simple as doves".' Further, this sleep-inducing wand represents 'memory of the cross of Christ which gives sleep and sweetness to the mind' as in 'Psalm 22:4: "Your rod and your staff have comforted me".' Interpreting negatively, Berchorius reads his staff as 'deception, evil fawning, and flattery' (ability to speak persuasively).

91 Reproduced in black and white, in Hargreaves-Mawdsley, pl. 9, opposite p. 74; described p. 75.

urinal or jordan is a standard icon identifying a physician, as depicted in Plate 13. This costume is similar to that worn by the Doctor of Phisik portrayed in the Ellesmere illumination except that in the Ellesmere MS the Doctor wears a blue hood with his red robe.[92] An additional inference that may be drawn from Chaucer's portrait is that the Doctor's costume represents 'the Doctor's own estimate of himself and his abilities', as Curry suggests is true of what he assumes to be the Doctor's self-professed catalogue of knowledge.[93] Since Chaucer tells us plainly that the Doctor of Phisik kept what he earned during the plague years, such a personal opinion would be materialistically accurate. Whether or not readers are meant to think that the Doctor overstates his medical knowledge, in his costume he represents that he is a materially successful 'praktisour'.

Chaucer's Doctor dresses in a manner that accords with ordinary fourteenth-century manuscript illuminations and with the Minster Lovell stained-glass window of an Oxford Doctor of Medicine; there is nothing in Chaucer's brief costume rhetoric that disagrees with descriptions of the standard garb actually worn by medieval physicians as recorded by historians of medieval medicine and of academia. Further, his costume is less showy than some of the physicians' costumes described elsewhere in medieval literature. The Doctor of Phisik wears a costume that speaks through its fabrics and dyestuffs of the Mediterranean and the east, and thus obliquely reminds us of his knowledge of other things eastern in derivation – his medical knowledge. In color and in cost, these garments proclaim him successful; his appearance presages the modern Madison Avenue dictum that nothing succeeds like success. As the eleventh-century *Regimen Sanitatus Salernitanum*[94] proclaims,

> 'Patients always pay doctors best,
> Who make their calls in finest clothing dressed'.[95]

---

[92] Theo Stemmler, ed., *The Ellesmere Miniatures of the Canterbury Pilgrims: Poetria Mediaevalis* 2, 3rd edn (Mannheim, 1979), p. xvii, describes the Ellesmere illumination as 'a hasty routine portrait'.

[93] Walter Clyde Curry, *Chaucer and the Mediaeval Sciences*, 2nd edn (New York, 1960), p. 27, apparently deduced that this is how the narrator knows what medical authorities the Doctor has studied.

[94] A most popular medieval medical treatise, believed to derive from Salerno in the eleventh century, containing some advice that remains sound in the twenty-first century, according to Nathan Schachner, *The Medieval Universities* (New York, 1938), pp. 53–4.

[95] Quoted by Schachner, p. 55, from the French trans. by John Ordronaux of *Regimen Sanitatis Salernitanum* (Philadelphia, 1871).

8

Truth and Untruth in Advertising:
The Pardoner's 'cappe' with 'vernycle'
and the Summoner's 'gerland' and 'bokeler'

Commenting on representative dress in Elizabethan drama, G. K. Hunter writes, 'The theory of vocation came very close to making an appropriate set of clothes the precondition of a Christian identity.' Hunter's point is equally true of the Middle Ages, in which there was a strong belief in what Hunter describes as 'the underpinning religious conception of "labouring in one's vocation", which, for moralists, made the social order (discernible in clothing worn) part of the will of God'.[1] Further, nowhere was this sense of propriety and rank manifested more than in a person's headdress, its style, color, fabric, trim, and manner of wearing. This is the historical context for Chaucer's pairing of headdresses – the Pardoner's cap with vernicle and the Summoner's garland – in the *General Prologue* portraits of those traveling companions. In addition, Chaucer's costume rhetoric provides each of these pilgrims with subsidiary costume signs, the Pardoner's 'walet' and/or 'male' holding bogus relics, and the Summoner's metaphoric 'bokeleer' made of cake, signs that underscore their transgressive headgear.

Beyond this, Chaucer mentions no official ecclesiastic costume for the Pardoner, and no livery for the Summoner.[2] Manuscript illuminations provide possible clues to their dress, but we cannot know if they are accurate depictions for Chaucer's Pardoner and Summoner specifically, or for pardoners and summoners in general. In any case, it is dangerous to count on manuscript illuminations to provide accurate depictions of an individual literary and/or historical costume, even though they are, at times, both correct and

---

[1] G. K. Hunter, 'Flat-caps and Bluecoats: Visual Signals on the Elizabethan Stage', *E&S*, n.s. 33, ed. Inga-Stina Ewbank (London, 1980), p. 36.

[2] See James Keller, 'A Sumonour Was Ther With Us In That Place', *Chaucer's Pilgrims: An Historical Guide to the Pilgrims in The Canterbury Tales*, eds Laura C. Lambdin and Robert T. Lambdin (Westport, CT, 1996), pp. 307–8 regarding a summoner's duties and privileges, and p. 309 concerning his social rank. Indicative of social status, the Poll Tax of 1379 places summoners and pardoners in the lowest of four groups, according to Paul Strohm, *Social Chaucer* (Cambridge, MA, 1989), pp. 7–8.

informative if one takes into account the functional context. For instance, miniatures introduce and mark the beginning of each pilgrim's tale in the Ellesmere manuscript, and, therefore, they must iconographically identify the social position, or degree, of the individual narrators. In one such miniature, the knight at the opening of *The Knight's Tale* is not dressed to correspond with the depiction of the 'bismotered' Knight described in the *General Prologue*, but, instead, is unmistakably a nobly dressed knight. This example underscores the social status of the tale's narrator, fulfilling the function of the miniature, which need neither partly nor wholly correspond to the *General Prologue* text. Nevertheless, and with due consideration for their limitations, these illuminations serve as a contextual background for a discussion of the costume signs in Chaucer's portraits because sometimes they are all we have.

Two manuscript illuminations of a pardoner, placed at the beginning of *The Pardoner's Tale* in the Ellesmere manuscript and on fol. 306r of Cambridge University Library MS Gg.4.27 (Color Plate VII), depict him wearing red garments. In the Ellesmere miniature, a pardoner wears a three-quarter-length red coat, close-fitted with narrow sleeves. An uneven edging of white appears at the hemline, sleeve edges, and neck, suggesting the presence of a lining of white fur, possibly lamb. A broad conical-shaped pilgrim hat, most likely with the front brim turned up,[3] provides the height and a display area for a modern handkerchief-size fabric or leather vernicle. James F. Rhodes states that a vernicle is a 'standard part of the "uniform" of Pardoners', and yet he comments that the Pardoner 'does go out of his way to draw particular attention to the *vernycle* by wearing nothing else upon his head, apparently against custom, given the Narrator's notice of it'.[4] Usual or unusual, in the Ellesmere miniature, the large hat does not correspond to the 'cappe' described in the *General Prologue* portrait. Further departing from the literary text, this miniature depicts a large 'jewelled' crucifix in the Pardoner's

---

[3]   If the front brim were upturned, it would produce the tri-corn shape depicted in the Ellesmere miniature.
    See such a hat, without upturned brim, in Julia Bolton Holloway, *The Pilgrim and the Book: A Study of Dante, Langland and Chaucer* (New York, 1987), pl. Ia. Bolton states that these hats are made of black felt and were still being made for sale in Madrid in recent years (personal communication, 8 Oct. 2001). A line drawing of another broad-brimmed hat with shell badge affixed, with brim turned up in the back, is included in Cecil Willett Cunnington and Phillis Cunnington, *Handbook of English Mediaeval Costume* (London, 1952), pl. 24c. See n. 31, para 3, below regarding depiction of other such pilgrim hats.
[4]   James F. Rhodes, 'The Pardoner's *Vernycle* and his *Vera Icon*', *MLS* 13.2 (1983), p. 38, citing the *General Prologue* I, lines 680–3. Apparently, Rhodes judges what is unusual according to what he supposes to be usual as depicted by Langland's portrayal of a Palmer. He offers no source for his knowledge of the 'uniform' of a Pardoner.

hands (not in his 'male'), and a white 'walet' or 'male' suspended beneath the horse's neck on a white strap (not resting in the Pardoner's lap).

CUL MS Gg.4.27 shows the Pardoner wearing a red robe with bag sleeves, which possesses fullness through the body and is gathered to the waistline with a black belt that has either a gold boss or gold buckle. His head is covered with red drapery that suggests a shoulder cape and hood wrapped loosely in a modified fifteenth-century chaperon fashion, which, in its most fashionable form, means that the face opening and top portion of his hood were rolled up and placed on the head. For this general style, the liripipe might be either left to dangle or be wound around the head. The lower edge of the cape, now on top of the head, would produce what the Cunningtons and Beard describe as a 'cockscomb-like flopping crown'.[5] Their line drawing shows a hood with a decorative lower edge, which was up-ended and rolled. Altogether, it was an innovative, upside-down headdress for men. And it could be worn on top of another hood, or, in the case of Chaucer's Pardoner, perhaps over some kind of 'cappe'. However, in Gg.4.27, no liripipe shows, the rolled part of the hood is slight in bulk, and the remainder of the cape does not stand up upon the head, but drapes loosely about it. This depiction lacks the vernicle, crucifix, and 'walet' of the Ellesmere miniature. It is possible, but not certain, that here we have a generic fifteenth-century pardoner and his costume, whereas the Ellesmere illumination adopts and adapts some details taken from the *General Prologue* text.

These two miniatures suggest, but do not prove, that pardoners customarily wore distinctive red garments. Additional visual evidence may be offered by Douce 104, fol. 44v, in which a priest in white tunic, carrying a rose-red (outer?) garment or fabric draped across his left shoulder, passes Truth's pardon (with dangling seal) to Piers Plowman.[6] Alternatively, drawing on the

5   In the fourteenth century, *chaperon* is the 'Anglo-French term for a hood with . . . cape and dangling liripipe' [the long dangling tip of the hood]; in the fifteenth century, a *chaperon* 'derived from the hood, was a headdress consisting of a circular role of "burlet", a liripipe or tippet, sometimes left dangling, sometimes twisted round the head, and the cockscomb-like flopping crown', according to C. Willett Cunnington, Phillis Cunnington, and Charles Beard, *A Dictionary of English Costume* (London, 1960).
    See W. N. Hargreaves-Mawdsley, *A History of Academical Dress in Europe until the End of the Eighteenth Century* (Oxford, 1963; rpt. Westport, CT, 1978), p. 195, for an additional definition of *chaperon*, where *bourrelet* is described as a 'padded cap joined to the Chaperon', and p. 194, fig. 4 for a line drawing of the *chaperon*.
6   See Kathleen Scott's description of this miniature illustrating Passus 9, lines 281–93, in her Catalogue of Illustrations included in *Piers Plowman: A Facsimile of Bodleian Library, Oxford, MS Douce 104* (Cambridge, 1992). A black and white reproduction of this fifteenth-century illustration in the C-text is included in Roger Sherman Loomis, *A Mirror of Chaucer's World* (Princeton, 1965), pl. 118.

Reverend Henry J. Todd's statement that the red 'surcoat and hood' worn by the Parson in his Ellesmere miniature was the usual 'habit of a ministering priest in England, until the time of Queen Elizabeth [I]',[7] Emil Markert likens the Pardoner's dress to the Parson's, referring to both as the scarlet costume of the cleric.[8]

For the Summoner's overall dress, we have only the Ellesmere miniature to consult. The miniaturist dresses his Summoner in a somewhat dark blue paltok, with a front that either blouses outward or is gambesoned (padded). Stella Mary Newton describes the *paltok*, a garment that shows up in wardrobe accounts as a new style for court nobles in 1361 and later was issued to squires in 1363, as a male garment having laces by which hose were attached and which was likely identical to the *pourpoint*.[9] Further, this garment possesses slightly bagged sleeves and a stand-up collar where, at the neckline, a white, possibly lambskin, lining shows. The short length of the paltok would not cover the Summoner's buttocks, which may or may not be covered by his red pointed-toe hose. Attached to, or over, his girdle is a flat 'walet'-type of pouch, resembling a saddle bag, and this pouch has a design on the front flap. On his head this Summoner wears a garland made of red and white flowers of indeterminate species (possibly resembling one of those in Plate 14), but likely to be roses and reminiscent of garlands crowning the Virgin Mary in the visual arts of the period. The Summoner's right arm is extended, and he holds out a folded, sealed missive, presumably a summons.

Because there is no second miniature of the Summoner, and I have found no other pictures of summoners, there is no way to tell whether or not the basic garments worn in the Ellesmere miniature were standard dress for a summoner. And we cannot know whether the colors of red and blue were meant to represent livery colors, or were simply representative of the Ellesmere artist's palette. However, these garments constitute the ordinary secular wearing apparel for the period in which this manuscript was painted. Apparently this costume was so commonplace that the miniaturist felt

---

7   Revd Henry J. Todd, *Illustrations of the Lives and Writings of Chaucer and Gower: Collected from Authentic Documents* (London, 1810), p. 256, citing no authority for this. However, Gilbert J. French records Henry VIII's records which show him ordering fabric for travel clothes for his retinue including, 'Item xi yerds and 1 q[rter] of rede cloth for iii chaplaynes . . .', in *The Tippets of the Canons Ecclesiastical* (London, 1850), p. 12.

8   Emil Markert, *Chaucers Canterbury-Pilger und ihre Tracht* (Würzburg, 1911), pp. 85–6.

9   Stella Mary Newton, *Fashion in the Age of the Black Prince: A Study of the Years 1340–1365* (Woodbridge, 1980; rpt. 1999), p. 55; see illustrations nos. 18–20, 39–40, and entry for *Aketon*, p. 134.

   In 1357–58, Chaucer received a paltok from the Countess of Ulster. A London paltok-maker charged 4s for it, according to pp. 14 and 17, in *Chaucer Life-Records*, eds Martin M. Crow and Clair C. Olson ([Austin, TX], 1966).

14. Sketch of a youth wearing a floral wreath, from *Omne bonum*, BL MS Royal 6 E VI, fol. 236v.

obliged to provide in addition a light brown face and the distinctive attribute of folded, sealed missive or summons, in order that readers of the manuscript might know this miniature signaled the beginning of *The Somonour's Tale*. The garland as lone attribute, worn above a paler face, might have misled readers into thinking that the Summoner's painted portrait signaled a tale told by a Squire-lover. The garland itself is an unlikely headdress for either a summoner bent on his legitimate business or for any serious pilgrim, as will be discussed later in this chapter.

Accessories, especially headdresses, are frequently defining features in any consideration of costume in both the visual arts and literary texts. Chaucer's costume rhetoric in his *General Prologue* portrait makes it clear that the Pardoner's most important costume sign is the vernicle attached to his cap. In name and in fact, no more potent sign of faith existed in late medieval Christianity than the *Vera Icon*, the 'vernycle'[10] as Chaucer calls it (I, line 685).

10 Also known as the *Sudario* and *Volto Santo*, according to Herbert Thurston, *The Holy*

This holy relic, and its replicas acquired as pilgrim badges in Rome, generated a well-known and long-standing, but varied, literary tradition.[11] It is worth knowing the strength and breadth of this literary background because it informs our reading of Chaucer's rhetorical choice of icon.

According to this tradition, a cloth belonging to St Veronica,[12] which bore the imprint of Christ's face, was transported from the Holy Land to Rome by crusaders; however, accounts of this relic and its transporting differ in their details. For example, the Latin *Vindicta saluatoris*, and its rather loose Anglo-Saxon translation, tell of Volosianus who takes from Veronica the garment previously worn by Christ and given to her. Volosianus transports Christ's garment, which bore His facial image, to Rome, accompanied by Veronica who would not be parted from it:

And þæ arwurðe wyf þa Veronix ealle hyre æhta for Crystes naman forlet and wæs Volosiane æfterfyligende and samod myd hem on scyp astygende.

[And that venerable woman Veronica abandoned all her possessions in Christ's name, and followed Volosianus, and went aboard the ship with him (headed for Rome).][13]

Year of Jubilee (Westminster, MD, 1949), p. 58, and as the *Veronica*, according to Herbert L. Kessler and Johanna Zacharias, *Rome 1300: On the Path of the Pilgrim* (New Haven, CT, 2000), p. 188. Ewa Kuryluk mentions also '*acheiropoietos* (not made by hand)', *vera icon*, and *vera imago*, in *Veronica and her Cloth: History, Symbolism and Structure of a 'True' Image* (Oxford, 1991), p. 1.

11 See Kuryluk's discussion, pp. 90–142.

12 In devotional representations of St Veronica, she
    holds out the cloth which bears an image of the face of Christ, who is sometimes crowned with thorns. She may wear a turban, in allusion to her eastern origin. Veronica sometimes stands between SS Peter and Paul, the patron saints of Rome. The cloth may be carried by two angels,
    according to James Hall, *Hall's Dictionary of Subjects and Symbols in Art* (London, 1984), p. 321. See also p. 290 regarding this scene as depicted in the Stations of the Cross.
    See the (Master of Guillebert de Mets) *Saint Veronica with the Sudarium* illumination, in a c.1450–60 Flemish Book of Hours, at the J. Paul Getty Museum, MS 2, fol. 13v, in which a turbanned Veronica holds the *sudarium* in front of her. This illumination is reproduced as the cover illustration of the pamphlet publicizing the exhibit 'Illuminating the Mind's Eye: Memory and Medieval Book Arts', J. Paul Getty Museum, 1996. See also the detail of St Veronica with vernicle in *The Gospels Book of Days: According to St Matthew, St Mark, St Luke & St John* (London, 1993), pl. 16, reproduced from The Hours of Etiènne Chevalier, MS 71, fol. 19, Musée Condé, Chantilly; and St Veronica with vernicle in Roger S. Wieck, *Time Sanctified: The Book of Hours in Medieval Art and Life* (New York, 1988), described p. 105, fig. 76, reproduced from The Walters Art Gallery, MS Walters 211, fol. 82v, Cat. No. 88, from Bruges, Belgium, c.1440, by 'a painter of the Gold Scrolls group'; and pls 1, 5, and 16 of Veronica holding the vernicle, depicted by Cariani, Roger van der Weyden, and Master of Guillebert de Mets, respectively, reproduced in Kuryluk.

13 Both Latin text with modern English translation and Old English text with modern

The more usual literary representation of the vernicle, however, is more dramatic. As Christ climbed Calvary to His crucifixion, Veronica offered Him her veil or kerchief so that He could wipe His face. When He returned it to Veronica, it bore His image. Medieval pilgrims to Rome would have viewed this veil, which remains in the Vatican's possession[14] – a visual record of Christ's passion and St Veronica's compassion, representing the very essence of Christianity.

The literary potency of this Christian icon increases through the centuries as the special powers of the vernicle are celebrated and expanded in succeeding versions of the Veronica legend. As related in the late-fourteenth-century work *The Siege of Jerusalem*, once the vernicle is in the Pope's custody, twenty knights protect it and experience its powers:

> Kny3tes kepten þe cloþe . on knees fallen.
> A flauo*ur* flambeþ þer fro, . þey felleden h*it* alle,
> Was neu*er* odo*ur* ne eyr' . vpon erþe swett*er*;
> Þe kerchef clansed h*it* self . so cler' waxed,
> My3t no lede on h*it* loke . for li3t þ*at* h*it* schewed.[15]
>
> (lines 238–42)

The vernicle emits a sweet perfume; it cleans itself; and it shines with a strong light. Significantly, it cures diseases. With prayer, and with the Pope's and Veronica's assistance, the diseased Vespasian is healed by the vernicle

---

English translation are included in J. E. Cross, Denis Brearley, and Andy Orchard, trans., '*Vindicta saluatoris*: Latin text and translation; *Vindicta saluatoris*: Old English text and translation', *Two Old English Apocrypha and their Manuscript Sources*, eds J. E. Cross et al. (Cambridge, 1996) (hereafter referred to as *Two Old English Apocrypha*), pp. 248–93; see pp. 278–85, esp. ¶26. The Latin and Old English texts differ somewhat. Kessler and Zacharias also write of the transportation of the vernicle to Rome, p. 211.

14 A statue of St Veronica, by F. Mochi, exists in one of the four approximately thirty-feet-high 'niches', in the lower portion of columns reaching up to the dome of St Peter's Basilica, Rome. Above the 'niches' are chapels, constructed and designed by Bernini, where the saints' relics are preserved. The *Guide to Saint Peter's Basilica* (Rome, 1995), p. 28, provides a color photo of this statue of St Veronica stepping forward with cloth held out, as if approaching Christ. This *Guide* also recounts the tradition of the vernicle's acquisition from crusaders who brought a 'veil of Veronica' to Rome from Jerusalem. However, the chapel listed in this *Guide* is not the same one as that celebrating St Veronica in 1475, as mentioned by Thurston, pp. 152–4.
    Also see Kessler and Zacharias, p. 188; and Sidney Heath, *Pilgrim Life in the Middle Ages* (London, 1911), pp. 140–1; J. J. Jusserand, *English Wayfaring Life in the Middle Ages: XIVth Century*, trans. Lucy Toulmin Smith, 3rd edn (London, 1925), p. 365, n. 2, regarding the history of the vernicle; and Diana Webb, *Pilgrims and Pilgrimage in the Medieval West* (London, 1999), p. 66, for chronicle accounts of the 1300 jubilee regarding the *sudario*, p. 117.

15 *The Siege of Jerusalem*, eds E. Kölbing and Mabel Day, EETS, OS 188 (London, 1932), hereafter referred to as *Siege*.

(lines 243–54);[16] afterwards, this veil displays itself in the church to be seen by 'the sy*m*ple' (lines 255–6).[17]

A number of literary sources that incorporate the story of Veronica tell of miraculous cures wrought at the sight of, or contact with, the vernicle and Christ's image. These cures, coincident with conversion to Christianity, are interpreted as evidence of faith in Christ.[18] From the earliest times,[19] the Veronica stories[20] mention Veronica as a recipient of such a cure. She is identified as the woman in the Bible, Mark 5:25–9 and Luke 8:43–4, who had been afflicted with an issue of blood, which is never completely defined except that it endured for twelve years. This woman was cured through her faith, the sight of Christ, and the touching of Christ's garment.[21] The strength of her faith is the subject in the *Mors Pilati*, where, in order to keep Christ's image always before her, Veronica commissions a painting of His face, but this becomes unnecessary when Christ himself impresses His image on her veil.[22]

---

16 The Metropolitan Museum in New York possesses a Flemish tapestry (1510) illustrating Veronica curing Vespasian, according to Kuryluk, p. 121.

17 The vernicle's miraculous powers are further described in the Introduction, p. xxvii, to *Siege*: Day mentions that idols fall from their altars or pedestals 'as the Vernicle is borne through the heathen temple' (citing *Hystoria Trojana*, III, vi, 4312).

18 See Rhodes, pp. 35–6, regarding the 'inner disposition' of the person having Christ's 'presence' in his/her soul, who then is cured by the sight of Christ's face. As Stephen K. Wright puts it, 'When Veronica, Vespasian, and Tiberius accept a new allegiance to Christ, they are immediately healed', *The Vengeance of Our Lord: Medieval Dramatizations of the Destruction of Jerusalem*, Studies and Texts 89 (Toronto, 1989), p. 91.

19 Rhodes, p. 35, describes the development of the story from the fourth century forward. Thomas N. Hall, 'The *Euangelium Nichodemi* and *Vindicta saluatoris* in Anglo-Saxon England', *Two Old English Apocrypha*, pp. 66–7, states that the earliest known manuscript of *Cura sanitatis Tiberii* is eighth-century; Wright, p. 29, mentions *Vindicta Salvatoris* [sic], a Latin prose narrative dated as early as 700.

20 As recounted by Rhodes, pp. 35–6 and n. 8; Thomas N. Hall, 'The *Euangelium Nichodemi* . . . England', *Two Old English Apocrypha*, esp. pp. 44, 51, 58–9, 63–8, 71; and Wright, pp. 29–30, 54, 69, 78–80, 91, and 97.

21 Hall, 'The *Euangelium* . . . England', p. 63, and J. E. Cross, 'Saint-Omer 202 as the Manuscript Source for the Old English Texts', *Two Old English Apocrypha*, p. 103. In this same book, *Vindicta saluatoris* and the Old English text of *Vindicta saluatoris*, both with modern English translations, recount this story, p. 278 ¶22; pp. 271, 273 ¶18; p. 279 ¶22. See Rhodes, p. 35, on the development of this motif.

22 Christine Tischendorf, *Evangelica Apocrypha* (Leipzig, 1853). The cloth image of Christ later manifests miraculous healing powers of its own. See Hall, 'The *Euangelium* . . . England', p. 63.

   Another version of the legend, *St Veronica* in *The Anglo-Saxon Legends of St Andrew and St Veronica*, ed. Charles Wycliffe Goodwin (Cambridge, 1851) [hereafter referred to as *Anglo-Saxon Legends*], tells of Christ's image appearing on a garment that he had owned and then gave to Veronica. Christ's garment also figures in the Old English translation of *Vindicta saluatoris*, p. 271, 273 ¶18.

The Siege of Jerusalem provides another version of this story:

> Þrow Pilat pyned he was, . þe prouost of Rome,
> & þat worliche wife, . þat arst was ynempned,
> Haþ his visage in hir' veil, . Veronyk ʒo hatte,
> Peynted priuely & playn, . þat no poynt wanteþ;
> For loue he left hit hir' . til hir' lyues end.
> Þer is no gome [o]n þis [grounde] . þat is grym wounded,
> Meselry ne meschef, . ne man vpon erþe,
> Þat kneleþ doun to þat cloþ . on Crist leueþ,
> Bot alle hapneþ to hele . in [ane] hand whyle.   (lines 160–8)

These lines describe two points of emphasis. Besides telling of Veronica's acquisition of the vernicle to keep throughout her life, the author mentions the healing powers of this veil, available to anyone who is 'grym wounded'.

However, as Rhodes posits, the true miracle 'is that of Christ imprinting his image on the soul of the beholder',[23] and this internal image heals external ills. While Veronica's hemorrhage constitutes the initial ailment that is cured in stories about her and the *Vera Icon*, most of the healings described in literary works have to do with males who have diseases afflicting the skin and/or the face. Although in the *Cura sanitatis Tiberii* Tiberius is cured of an unnamed disease, other versions of the story tell of his 'fevers, sores, and nine kinds of leprosy', or 'leprous pustules'.[24] In another instance of facial disease, Tyrus possessed a cancer, which wreaked a destructive path from his right nostril to his eye.[25] Further, Titus suffered cancer 'which has ravaged his face',[26] variously described as 'in the lip' and 'in the nose';[27] in yet another narrative both he and his father Vespasian have facial maladies:[28]

---

23 Rhodes, p. 36.
24 As variously described by Wright, p. 29, in his discussion of a group of plays, known as 'the plays of the Vengeance of Our Lord', which were popular in the fourteenth and fifteenth centuries. In the legend of St Veronica included in *Anglo-Saxon Legends*, pp. 26–7, 46–7, Tiberius also suffers from leprosy and is cured by Veronica's relic of Christ. And see Kuryluk's discussion, pp. 201–2.
25 In both the Latin and Old English versions of *Vindicta saluatoris*, pp. 248–9 ¶1, in *Two Old English Apocrypha*.
    Also see *St Veronica, Anglo-Saxon Legends*, pp. 26–7; Tyrus's faith cures him before he sees the relic, pp. 30–1. This Anglo-Saxon legend and facing-page translation, pp. 38–9, 42–3, 46–7, make it clear that the cloth with the image is not Veronica's veil, and the image is not really that of Christ, although Veronica values it as if it were, and the pagan men who are cured think that it is. Thus, in this legend it is faith in Christ, not His image, that cures.
26 Wright, p. 29. In *St Veronica, Anglo-Saxon Legends*, pp. 32–3, Tyrus is given the baptismal name of Titus.
27 Day, Introduction, *Siege*, p. xix, in a discussion of sources for this work, including *Vindicta Salvatoris*, *Legenda Aurea*, and *De Pyloto*, pp. xix–xxiv.
28 Day discusses the tradition for this in the Introduction of *Siege*, pp. xviii, xxiv.

Tyt*us* of Rome,

. . .

He hadde a malady vn-meke . a-myd[dis] þe face:
Þe lyppe lyþ on a lu*m*pe . lynered on þe cheke;
So a canker vnclene . h*it* cloched to gedress.
Also h*is* fader' of flesche . is ferly beytide,
A biker of waspen bees . bredde on h*is* nose,
Hyued vpon h*is* hed, . he hadde he*m* of ʒouþe
And Waspasian was caled . þe waspene bees aft*er.*
Was neu*er* syknes sorer . þa*n* þ*is* sir' þoled;
For i*n* a lit*er* he lay, . laser at Rome.   (lines 25, 28–36)

In addition, Vespasian is sometimes described as being afflicted with wasps in his nose and, at other times, with leprosy and cancer.[29]

This relic with miraculous powers, the *Vera Icon*, was extensively replicated in badges made of pewter, tin, brass, and/or lead alloys, and silver, and on swatches of silk, leather, or parchment.[30] By 1350, it became the premier badge of a pilgrimage to Rome,[31] important enough to be featured in the

---

[29] In *La Destruction de Jerusalem*, and in *Legenda Aurea* and *De Pyloto*, as mentioned by Day in her discussion of the Veronica legend, in the Introduction to *Siege*, pp. xviii, xxiv.

[30] Ronald W. Lightbown describes materials used for vernicle badges and pendants in *Mediaeval European Jewellery: with a catalogue of the collection in the Victoria & Albert Museum* (London, 1992), pp. 192, 195, 229–30, 382, 510, and esp. for fig. 112, p. 211, picturing the pendant made of silver gilt and amber; also item 41, p. 505, and item 46, p. 507. Webb, p. 128, describes 'a cache of devotional objects found in the choir of the monastery of Wienhausen', which contained 'a sheet of eight woodcuts of the Veronica, not yet cut up', citing H. Appuhn, 'Der Fund kleiner Andachtsbilder des 13. bis 17. Jahrhunderts in Kloster Wienhausen', *Niederdeutsche Beiträge zir Limstgewscjocjte* 4 (1965), p. 199.

[31] Jonathan Sumption, *Pilgrimage: An Image of Medieval Religion* (Totowa, NJ, 1975), pp. 239, 242; see also pp. 222, 249. Sumption cites a 1377 account of a foreign pilgrim's entitlement to a 12,000 years indulgence for each hour spent in devotion at the altar of the vernicle. See Kessler and Zacharias, pp. 210–11, regarding 'The chapel of the Holy Face', the shrine in St Peter's, and fig. 216, reproduced from Museum nazionale del Palazzo di Venezia (Rome), depicting the Jubilee year of 1475.

About 1350, badges depicting the crossed keys, and those representing the vernicle, began to replace earlier kinds of Roman religious memorabilia. See Brian Spencer, 'Italy: SS Peter and Paul, and the Veronica, Rome', *Pilgrim Souvenirs and Secular Badges*, Medieval Finds from Excavations in London 7 (London, 1998), pp. 249–52, regarding the vernicle; pp. 21 for a vernicle painted on a square of silk as represented in a manuscript illumination; and p. 250, figs 254–254c, for depiction of metal badges, beginning with the earliest (twelfth century). The frontispiece to Brian Spencer, *Pilgrim Souvenirs and Secular Badges* [hereafter referred to as *Pilgrim Souvenirs – Salisbury*], Salisbury Museum Medieval Catalogue, Pt 2 (Salisbury, 1990), shows a detail of the picture of 'an altar-piece, dated 1487, depicting St Sebaldus as a pilgrim.

works of such authors as Dante, Petrarch, Langland, and, later, Montaigne.[32] More important, these badges, signifying the wearer's faith, were thought to possess amuletic powers. According to Nancy Armstrong,

> Amulets are objects which are believed to have special powers to protect or help the bearer. . . . [T]he Christian Church, in spite of its condemnation of primitive magical amulets . . . permitted, and eventually promoted, the wearing of medallions with a religious inscription, the carrying of reliquaries containing, perhaps, a fragment of some saint's finger-nail, the making of holy images, exactly as it adapted pagan decorations into Christian iconography.[33]

His travel souvenirs include . . . a memento of painted cloth from Rome [vernicle]. . . . Nürnberg, Germanisches Nationalmuseum, no. Gm 143.'

Joan Evans, ed., *The Flowering of the Middle Ages* (1966; 1985; New York, 1998), pp. 16–17, reproduces a portion of the 1355 fresco (Spanish Chapel, Florence) painted by Andrea da Firenze, to 'glorify the Dominican Order', in which a kneeling pilgrim, dressed in hairy tabard or sclavin, wears a gray conical hat with three pilgrim badges pinned on it in triangular positions: at the lower right is a scallop shell; at the lower left is an unidentified badge; and at the apex is a vernicle. See also the badge with keys on the pilgrim's hat in the 1559 painting *The Fight between Carnival and Lent*, by Pieter Breugel.

32 Literary allusions to the vernicle include those in Dante Alighieri (b.1265, d.1321), *Paradiso*, *The Divine Comedy*, trans. and commentary by John D. Sinclair (New York, 1981), Canto 31, line 104; and *La Vita Nuova*, trans. Barbara Reynolds (Harmondsworth, 1969; rpt. 1975), poem 40, line 1; regarding Petrarch's sonnet 14 and his description of his 1350 visit to Rome, see Thurston's comments, pp. 58–9, 138–9, 153–4; for Michel de Montaigne's 1580 account of Rome and Holy Week processions, esp. the exhibition of the vernicle on Holy Thursday evening, see Thurston, pp. 273–5.

Spencer, *Pilgrim Souvenirs – Salisbury*, pp. 43–4, states that, in earlier centuries, visitors to St Peter's at Rome usually purchased pilgrim badges which portrayed St Peter's crossed keys and tiara, triple-crowned. William Langland describes a keys of Rome badge worn by a palmer, as well as a vernicle and others, in the c.1370 *Piers Plowman: The B Version*, eds George Kane and E. Talbot Donaldson (University of London, 1975):

An hundred of Ampulles on his hat seten,
Sygnes of Synay and shelles of Galice,
And many crouch on his cloke and keyes of Rome,
And þe vernycle bifore, for men shoulde knowe
And se bi hise signes whom he souȝt hadde.   (Passus 5, lines 520–4)

However, in Bodleian Library, Oxford, MS Douce 104, fol. 33b recto, the C-text of *Piers Plowman* (Passus 7, lines 159–75), a miniature of this character illustrates the Ampulles on his hat, but no other pilgrimage signs. For a description of this miniature, see Scott, Catalogue of Illustrations, p. l.

33 Nancy Armstrong, in *Jewellery: An Historical Survey of British Styles and Jewels* (Guildford, 1973), p. 8. An example of such amuletic jewelry is the ring brooch, said to protect the wearer against thieves, in the Bargello Museum, Florence (mentioned earlier in Chapter 3), which carries the message IESVS AVTEM TRANSIENS PER MED (from Luke 4:30), in a design that includes four vernicles, as described by Joan Evans, *A History of Jewellery 1100–1870* (Boston, 1970), p. 57.

Edward I. Condren, 'The Pardoner's Bid for Existence', *Viator* 4 (1973), p. 185, dis-

The medieval visual arts and accompanying texts also attest the idea of the vernicle's powers, present even in replicas.[34] For example, the image of St Veronica with vernicle in her hands appears often in fifteenth-century Flemish Books of Hours. According to Roger S. Wieck, such illuminations were used by those who wished to gain 'generous indulgences' by gazing at this picture while repeating the prayer 'Salve sancta facies'.[35] Today, visitors to Lorenzkirche, in Nuremberg, Germany, may still see persons saying prayers in front of a c.1380 statue of St Veronica with vernicle held in front of her. Further underscoring the vernicle's importance in Christian iconography, the *Vera Icon* is included in the Arms of Christ, amid those other potent signs of His passion: rough cross, three nails, lance, crown of thorns, sponge on a reed, and triple-thonged flagella, all of which appeared on one of several shields in the fourteenth and fifteenth centuries. For example, a 1447–55 depiction of the Arms of Christ[36] includes 'an azure shield charged with the Vernicle . . . proper'.

This highly venerated holy sign worn on the 'cappe' of Chaucer's Pardoner advertises like a banner that he was 'comen fro the court of Rome' (line 671). Further, it supports the idea of his papal authority to carry pardons.[37] However, regardless of his flaunting of this true icon of Christianity, it is at best unclear whether Chaucer intended the Pardoner's authority to be deemed genuine,[38] for historical records tell of false pardoners, with forged letters of

cusses the Pardoner's use of the common belief in the power of relics in his sermons (VI, lines 352–7, 366–74). Such a belief was long-standing; Thomas N. Hall, p. 78 and n. 128, mentions the limited association of Veronica with Anglo Saxon charms, in 'The *Euangelium . . . England*', *Two Old English Apocrypha.*

34 Kuryluk, p. 115, states that 'since replicas were treated not as paintings but as new *acheiropoietoi*, churches and cloisters throughout Europe acquired their own "vernicles" and organized their own cults of the Holy Face', and pilgrimages were subsequently organized around these new copies; see also p. 214.

35 Wieck, p. 105; also Kessler and Zacharias, pp. 216–17 and fig. 224. Webb treats the subject of cures derived from pilgrim signs, pp. 125–6; and discusses indulgences in her Chapter 3, pp. 64–82, esp. p. 78 regarding a 1349 indulgence relating to the *sudarium*; also see p. 107, including a dispensation concerning the display of 'the holy Veronica'.

36 An interesting addition to these arms is Christ's Seamless Garment, used as mantling on his helm, according to Rodney Dennys, *The Heraldic Imagination* (London, 1975), p. 97; see color pl. opposite p. 80, reproduced from the Hyghalmen Roll (Coll. Arms MS 1st M.5, fols 1b, 2).

37 Concerning the Pardoner's statements (VI, lines 920, 922) that he has 'relikes and pardoun in my male,/ . . . Whiche were me yeven by the popes hond', Joseph Strutt states that the Pardoner's vernicle constitutes part of his advertisement of his wares, in *A Complete View of the Dress and Habits of the People of England, from the Establishment of the Saxons in Britain to the Present Time: Illustrated by Engravings Taken from the Most Authentic Remains of Antiquity* (1842; London, 1970), 2:168.

38 Condren states, pp. 184–5, 'so patent a fraud would not have bothered going' to Rome, and cites lines C 335–40 regarding the lengths to which the Pardoner goes, in 'demon-

authentication from the Pope. These spiritual con men preyed on the gullible by praying, preaching, and begging for alms. As the ('probably' 1377) *Register of Thomas de Brantingham, Bishop of Exeter* puts it:

> Certainly informed by public rumor and by experience of the fact, we understand that some friars of the mendicant orders and other[s] with lies assert that they have the power of hearing confessions of our subjects and absolving them of their sins, even in cases reserved to the Apostolic See and to us; and that *others, pretending to be questors* of alms and falsely fabricating and counterfeiting our seal, pretending to have letters[39] from us about indulgences which they pretend to be conceded to them, presume to set them forth in order to extort money more quickly from our subjects by such means to the deception of many souls of our subjects.[40]
>
> [my emphasis]

strating his legitimacy', which suggests to Condren that the very extent of proof supports the idea of its falseness. In addition, Condren, p. 177, notes that Chaucer's Pardoner differs from other literary pardoners as a general type in his free 'admission of fraud' and in the narrator's 'hints of sexual abnormality'.

A sampling of critical opinion about the Pardoner's sins includes: Lee Patterson, 'Chaucer's Pardoner on the Couch: Psyche and Clio in Medieval Literary Studies', *Speculum* 76.3 (2001), pp. 664–8, concerning the Pardoner's simony and sodomy; Fred Hoerner, 'Church Office, Routine, and Self-Exile in Chaucer's Pardoner', *SAC* 16 (1994), pp. 70–1, 87–8, discussing his verbal gluttony and lechery; Gloria Cigman, 'Chaucer and the Goats of Creation', *L&T* 5 (1991), p. 178, regarding the Pardoner as a 'personification of hypocrisy'; Robert E. Jungman, 'The Pardoner's Quarrel with the Host', *PQ* 55 (1976), p. 280, who discusses his *cupiditas*; J. Swart, 'Chaucer's Pardoner', *Neophil* 36 (1952), pp. 48–50, who describes his *superbia*, vanity, and hypocrisy; and Alfred L. Kellogg, 'An Augustinian Interpretation of Chaucer's Pardoner', *Speculum* 26 (1951), p. 471, who describes his *avaricia, gula,* and *luxuria*.

39 See Arnold Williams, 'Some Documents on English Pardoners, 1350–1400', *Medieval Studies in Honor of Urban Tigner Holmes, Jr.*, eds John Mahoney and John Esten Keller, University of North Carolina Studies in the Romance Languages and Literatures 56 (Chapel Hill, NC, 1965), p. 204, which includes a genuine pardoner's license, which appears in the MS Register of Richard le Scrope, Archbishop of York, in the Borthwick Institute, York, p. 221:

> On the twentieth day of the month of June in the year of Our Lord aforesaid, viz. [M] CCCC at Thorp near York the lord by his letters conceded a license to run two years from the present date to the proctors or messengers of the hospital or chapel of the most blessed Virgin Mary of Roncesvalles near Charing Cross in the city of London to publish indulgences and privileges conceded to the benefactors of the same hospital or chapel and to collect and receive alms given or to be given by any of the faithful of Christ to the said hospital or chapel throughout the archdeaconries of York, Cleveland, and Nottingham.

40 *Register of Thomas de Brantingham, Bishop of Exeter*, ed. F. C. Hingeston-Randolph (London, 1901–06), p. 380, quoted by Williams, pp. 203–4, with the caveat that perhaps this document, dated 'London 13 March 1384–5', was never issued. See also comments in *Social England: A Record of the Progress of the People*, eds H. D. Traill and J. S. Mann (New York, 1969), 2:372; J. J. Jusserand, 'Chaucer's Pardoner and the

In the *Episcopal Register of John de Grandisson, Bishop of Exeter*, such actions are referred to as 'the damnable abuses of impious questors', who bring 'scandal and infamy . . . [to] the Holy See', and who 'spiritually trick and deceive' susceptible people.[41]

The Pardoner of the *General Prologue* could be one of these thieves masquerading in Rouncivale[42] habit or livery. However, as negative a picture as this makes, it is hardly better to think of the Pardoner as authentic, bearing legitimate letters from an ecclesiastic authority, and legitimately wearing his

Pope's Pardoners', *Chaucer Society Essays*, Pt 5, Second Series 19 (London, 1884), pp. 424–36, for accounts of false pardoners portrayed in historical documents and in literature; see George F. Jones, 'Realism and Social Satire in Heinrich Wittenwiler's Ring', Diss., Columbia University, University Microfilms (Ann Arbor, MI, 1950), no. 1864, p. 239, regarding literary satires against payment for indulgences; also Patterson, p. 669 and n. 136. See John Matthews Manly, Introduction, Notes, and Glossary, *Canterbury Tales by Geoffrey Chaucer* (New York, 1928; rpt. 1947), pp. 535–6, regarding true and false pardoners; Robert N. Swanson, *Church and Society in Late Medieval England* (Oxford, 1989), pp. 243, 248–9, concerning false questors, documents, and relics, and pp. 27–88 regarding pardoners; David K. Maxfield, 'St Mary Rouncivale, Charing Cross: The Hospital of Chaucer's Pardoner', *ChauR* 28.2 (1993), pp. 149–52; Hoerner, p. 73 and n. 16, regarding the historic role of pardoners and, in some cases, the church's failure to prevent abuses of their positions.

In *The Plowman's Tale, Six Ecclesiastical Satires*, ed. James M. Dean (Kalamazoo, MI, 1991), p. 68, the Pelican speaks of false priests, summoners, and pardoners:

> 'They [false priests] taken to ferme her sompnours
>   [hire out their summoners]
> To harme the people what they may;
> To pardoners and false faytours
> Sell her seales, I dare well say;
> And all to holden great array,
> To multiply hem more metall.
> They drede full litell Domes day,
> When all such falsehode shall foul fall.'   (lines 325–32)

Also see Dante's treatment of simonists in his *Inferno* Canto 19, esp. lines 22–30, 69–72; and Langland's portrayal of false pardoners in *PP: B*, Prologue, lines 68–82, and Passus 5, lines 639–42.

41   Dated 4 March 1355 [i.e. 1356], the *Episcopal Register of John de Grandisson, Bishop of Exeter*, ed. F. C. Hingeston-Randolph (London, 1897), Pt 2, pp. 1178–9, as translated by Williams, pp. 199–202.   For the curse to be pronounced against 'Alle þat falsen þe popus selle or his letteres' and 'alle þat lettuth any man to purchase þe popus bullus or byschopp*us* letturres in defence of his rythe, and holy chyrche, & malyciously lettuth here processe', see John Mirus (Mirk), *Instructions for Parish Priests*, ed. Edward Peacock, EETS, OS 31 (London, 1868; rev. 1902; rpt. 1996), pp. 62–3.

42   Concerning Rouncivale, see Maxfield, pp. 152–5, 157–8, and esp. n. 3; Revd Richard Morris, ed., *Chaucer: The Prologue, The Knightes Tale, The Nonnes Prestes Tale, from the Canterbury Tales*, 3rd rev. edn (Oxford, 1874), p. 141, note to line 670; Revd Walter W. Skeat, ed. *The Complete Works of Geoffrey Chaucer* (Oxford, 1894), 5:55; Christine Ryan Hilary's introductory note, *Riverside Chaucer*, p. 824, and note to line 670.

ecclesiastic garb, accented by a vernicle and carrying a wallet full of
Vatican-generated pardons or indulgences, all the while carrying a 'male' full
of bogus relics.[43] Neither alternative – thief disguised as pardoner, or genuine
pardoner as thief – bodes well for the integrity of the medieval church, but the
latter possibility signals blatant betrayals of sacred trust in the Pardoner's dis-
loyalty to both his earthly lord and heavenly Lord. In any case, he is a figure
of falseness.[44]

Such a critical indictment is bolstered in that, although he provides acces-
sories, Chaucer describes no authoritative religious garments in his portrait
of the Pardoner. Because of this omission we cannot know exactly what kind
of 'noble ecclesiaste' (line 708) Chaucer intended the Pardoner to be: the
MED defines 'ecclesiastic' as 'a church official . . . a divine'; Thomas
Tyrwhitt dubs the Pardoner 'itinerant ecclesiastic'; George Lyman Kittredge,
Joseph Spencer Kennard, and Henry Barrett Hinckley think him a friar – with
Kennard specifying Franciscan, and Hinckley, Dominican;[45] Marie Padgett
Hamilton names him an Augustinian canon regular;[46] Paul E. Beichner,

---

43 On the subject of false relics, see Alan J. Fletcher, 'The Topical Hypocrisy of
Chaucer's Pardoner', *ChauR* 25 (1990), pp. 118–19; also Siegfried Wenzel, 'Chaucer's
Pardoner and His Relics', *SAC* 11 (1989), pp. 37–41, regarding false pardoners and
relics, as well as Canon Law on these issues from 1215. See also Patterson's discussion
of the Pardoner's mocking of true relics with his false ones, pp. 675–6; Jill Mann,
*Chaucer and Medieval Estates Satire: The Literature of Social Classes and the General
Prologue to the Canterbury Tales* (Cambridge, 1973), pp. 146–7, 149, regarding the
'complicity of the church authorities in the abuse of selling pardons', and, pp. 150–2,
false relics. Mann, p. 149, points out that 'In Langland, the pardoner and the priest
together cheat the "poraille" of the parish (Prol. 80–2); in Chaucer, the Pardoner
deceives both priest and people. . . . our consciousness of his victims reinforces our
sense of his nastiness.' Richard Firth Green, 'The Pardoner's Pants (and Why They
Matter)', *SAC* 15 (1993), pp. 142–5, describes the manner in which a lover's britches,
in the Friar's pants stories, become a fake relic with the complicity of all concerned,
including convent heads (with implications for the post-tale exchange following *The
Pardoner's Tale* [VI, 948–50], and for *The Tale of Beryn*).
44 The Pardoner's derivation from False Seeming in *Le Roman de la rose* is discussed by
Jane Chance, ' "Disfigured Is Thy Face": Chaucer's Pardoner and the Protean Shape-
Shifter Fals-Semblant', *PQ* 67 (1988), pp. 424–6; Condren, p. 178, disagrees that False
Seeming is the literary source for Chaucer's Pardoner, stating that they have only a
superficial resemblance to each other. Also on False Seeming as literary ancestor, see
Raymond Preston, *Chaucer* (London, 1952), p. 163.
45 Such a designation of friar would enlarge the significance of the Pardoner's hood by
making it a matter of defiance of the Franciscan or Dominican Rule when he packs the
hood in his 'male'.
46 Marie Padgett Hamilton, 'The Credentials of Chaucer's Pardoner', *JEGP* 40 (1941),
pp. 62–3, states that Augustinian canons were required to wear a hood over the
birretum (skull-cap) to symbolize they were dead to the world; but also mentions the
pileus, which she says was a part of the habit singular to canons. Hargreaves-Mawdsley
distinguishes between the *pileus* (round skull-cap, pp. 192, 195) and a *biretta* ('horned'
and rigid variety of the *pileus*, pp. 190–1).

George F. Reinecke, and others state that he is a minor ecclesiastic or in minor orders – one of which is that of clerk; however, *quaestore* is the designation most often used, with its emphasis on an administrative role in fund raising and the concomitant granting of indulgences.[47]

Thus, lacking the certainty of a particular religious order or designation of rank for the Pardoner, the evidence for a complete costume for this pilgrim of necessity, but tentatively, relies upon the visual evidence from the Ellesmere manuscript and Cambridge University Library MS Gg.4.27, as previously discussed. In any case, Chaucer speaks only of accessories, costume signs accompanying the Pardoner's vernycle – signs that represent impropriety, defiance of church authorities, and thus disorder. The Pardoner's words and actions provide the context for these accessories[48] – 'hood', 'cappe', 'walet', and 'male':

> But hood, for jolitee, wered he noon,
> For it was trussed up in his walet.
> Hym thoughte he rood al of the newe jet;
> Dischevelee, save his cappe, he rood al bare.
> . . .
> A vernycle hadde he sowed upon his cappe.

---

[47] For a summary of these positions, see Malcolm Andrew, Explanatory notes, *A Variorum Edition of the Works of Geoffrey Chaucer, Volume II: The Canterbury Tales, The General Prologue*, Pt One B (Norman, OK, and London, 1993), pp. 528–41, 547; also see Alfred L. Kellogg and Louis A. Haselmayer, 'Chaucer's Satire of the Pardoner', *PMLA* 66 (1951), pp. 251–77; rpt. in *Chaucer, Langland, Arthur: Essays in Middle English Literature* (New Brunswick, NJ, 1972), pp. 214–15, 221; Robert P. Miller, 'Chaucer's Pardoner, the Scriptural Eunuch, and the Pardoner's Tale', *Speculum* 30 (1955), p. 194; Clarence H. Miller and Roberta Bosse, 'Chaucer's Pardoner and the Mass', *ChauR* 6 (1972), p. 173, regarding whether or not the Pardoner is a priest; Joseph Spencer Kennard, *The Friar in Fiction, Sincerity in Art, and Other Essays* (New York, 1923), pp. 14–16. Regarding quaestors, see Maxfield, pp. 149–50.
The OED defines *questor* as 'An official appointed by the Pope or by a bishop to grant indulgences on the gift of alms to the Church; a pardoner' (#1); 'One who seeks or searches' (#3), with a first example dated 1887, although Shakespeare, *King Lear* III.vii.17 (dated 1605), regarding knights in hot pursuit, uses *questris*. The adjectival form, *quæstuary*, is defined as 'Connected or concerned with gain; money-making', with a first example dated 1594 and with *Questor* being 'One who seeks for gain' in a first example of 1624.

[48] John Halverson, 'Chaucer's Pardoner and the Progress of Criticism', *ChauR* 4 (1970), pp. 185–6, 188, 191–2, 196, discusses the Pardoner's character and states that his 'sordid image' is self-constructed and -projected through his own comments, except for two remarks made by the narrator-Chaucer regarding the Pardoner's belief that his headcovering was fashionable and his desire to make the parson and people 'his apes'. Halverson fails to note that, as Chaucer delineates this pilgrim, the Pardoner's choice of costume also projects the Pardoner's character.

> His walet, beforn hym in his lappe,[49]
> Bretful of pardoun comen from Rome al hoot.
>
> (lines 680–3; 685–7)

In a later line (694), Chaucer mentions the Pardoner's 'male', possibly a synonym for the previously mentioned 'walet' (line 681).[50] However, given the Pardoner's freely confessed avarice, coupled with the lines in the Summoner's portrait concerned with a 'mannes soule' being 'in his purs', and ' "Purs is the ercedekenes helle" ' (lines 656–8), even if Chaucer employs *male* as a synonym for *walet*, this synonymous repetition emphasizes the idea of multiple purses.[51] Realistically, it is hard to imagine one receptacle simultaneously holding hood, pardons, and 'relikes',[52] not to mention other pilgrimage necessities, unless this bag is quite large. Either way – one oversize bag, or two bags[53] – this porterage underscores the Pardoner's confession of

---

49 *Lappe* impinges upon this discussion of costume rhetoric only because it is the depository of the Pardoner's 'walet'. See Andrew's notes regarding the Pardoner's sexual orientation and his character in lines 675–91, in *The General Prologue . . . A Variorum Edition*, pp. 542–5, 550. See esp. pp. 543, 550, for the citations of James M. Kiehl regarding the 'sordid sexual connotations' of 'lappe' and 'walet', containing false relics, as metaphoric substitutions for the Pardoner's male sexual potency, in 'Dryden's Zimri and Chaucer's Pardoner: A Comparative Study in Verse Portraiture', *Thoth* 6 (1965), p. 6.

50 This accessory is defined, discussed, and placed within a hierarchy of types of bags, purses, and pouches in Laura F. Hodges, *Chaucer and Costume: The Secular Pilgrims in the General Prologue* [*C&C*], Chaucer Studies XXVI (Cambridge, 2000), pp. 16, 148–50; see esp. Patience's walet, pp. 149–50.

   Henry Thomas Riley, ed., Introduction, *Munimenta Gildhallae Londoniensis: Liber Albus, Liber Custumarum et Liber Horn* (London, 1859), 1:xcii, states that wallets are equated with males, bags, portmanteaus in which travellers carried their linen. They were apparently small enough to be carried beneath the traveller's arm. 'Wharfage' was not charged for them if they contained only 'necessities' defined ' "*a doos et a lyt*" "for back and bed" '. The OED compares this bag to 'a pilgrim's scrip, a knapsack, a pedlar's pack, or the like'.

51 See John V. Fleming, 'Chaucer's Ascetical Images', *C&L* 28.4 (1979), pp. 24–5, and John V. Fleming, 'Gospel Asceticism: Some Chaucerian Images of Perfection', *Chaucer and Scriptural Tradition*, ed. David Lyle Jeffrey (Ottawa, 1984), pp. 188–9, regarding the 'purse question'; and Britton J. Harwood, 'Chaucer's Pardoner: The Dialectics of Inside and Outside', *PQ* 67 (1988), pp. 409–10, on the subject of purses and bribery.

52 Also sealed indulgences, his letter from the bishop licensing his collection of alms, and/or his royal writ of protection, as discussed by Kellogg and Haselmayer, pp. 220–1.

   See *The Benedictines in Britain*, British Library Series 3 (London, 1980), pp. 58, 61, and 108, regarding a thirteenth-century pardoner's letter soliciting funds for a nunnery in exchange for indulgences.

53 Eugene Vance posits that the Pardoner has three walets or males as well as assorted 'figurative sacks', in 'Chaucer's Pardoner: Relics, Discourses, and Frames of Propriety', *NLH* 20 (1989), pp. 737–8.

greed, further marking him as a figure of Avarice.[54] If the Pardoner is con man and thief dressed in the guise of ecclesiastic garments, he blatantly signifies social and spiritual disorder;[55] if he is a legitimate emissary of the Pope or archbishop, his greed represents disorder within the church as well.

Nowhere would this disorder be more vividly expressed than in Chaucer's term 'dischevelee'. Chaucer employs this word in his description of the Pardoner as 'Dischevelee, save his cappe' (line 683), generally understood to indicate that this pilgrim wears something less than what constituted a decorous headdress. As Hamilton points out, in her argument in favor of the Pardoner's being an Augustinian Canon, 'a hood over the *birretum*' was required of Augustinians, according to the 1339 Constitutions for Austin Canons of Benedict XII.[56] And, again, Boniface IX felt it necessary to issue a December 1400 admonishment to canons in England ' "to wear . . . hoods and caps, according to the form, manner, and institutes of Augustinian canons in England" ',[57] a reproof that would have been unnecessary had canons been following the rule. Indeed, Chaucer's comments concerning the Pardoner's cap and hood would be equally irrelevant if his contemporary readers had not assumed that the Pardoner was supposed to follow some kind of holy regulations, perhaps the very ones Hamilton proposes – those of the Augustinian Canons.

A *cappe* is variously defined as 'a small head covering worn under the hood; a priest's close-fitting cap, the coif covering the tonsure; also any kind of headcovering for ecclesiastics' (MED).[58] The implication is that the Pardoner's 'cappe' saves him from being completely 'bare', but that the hood, 'trussed up in his wallet' (lines 680–1), is needed to make up a completely proper headcovering. This storage of his hood serves to emphasize the Pardoner's improper headdress at the same time this hood-hiding suggests the possibility of the proverbial 'game in my hood' trickery.[59]

---

[54] I have discussed the manner in which figures of Avarice are marked through depictions exaggerating their love of money, in *C&C*, pp. 146–7.

[55] See Lois Bragg, 'Disfigurement, Disability, and Disintegration in *Sturlunga* Saga', *alvíssmál* 4 (1994), pp. 16–17, regarding the psychology of Thorgil's negative character traits as compensatory behavior for his facial disfigurement.

[56] Hamilton, p. 62, n. 65, citing H. E. Salter, ed., *Chapters of the Augustinian Canons*, Canterbury & York Society (Woodbridge, 1922), Appendix 2, p. 247; and David Wilkins, *Concilia Magnae Britanniae et Hiberniae* (Londini, 1737), 2:629–51.

[57] Hamilton, p. 63, citing *Papal Letters pertaining to Great Britain*, 12 Boniface IX, p. 355.

[58] See the definition and description of the *pileus* in Chapter 7, n. 24.

[59] I have previously discussed *hood* as the sign of a trickster, and as Pandarus's signature costume sign, in 'Sartorial Signs in *Troilus and Criseyde*', *ChauR* 35.3 (2001), pp. 230–2. See also Sarah Stanbury Smith, ' "Game in myn hood": The Traditions of a Comic Proverb', *SIcon* 9 (1983), pp. 1–12; and the proverbial usage of *hod* in the MED. Also see the comments regarding 'sette . . . cappe' (586) in *The General Prologue . . . A Variorum Edition*, p. 485.

Although in costume rhetoric *dischevelee* is usually understood to mean 'Without a headdress, bareheaded; also, with the hair hanging loose or in disorder' (MED),[60] the circumstances surrounding Chaucer's other literary characters described as 'dischevelee' also indicate the abdication of decorum, the opposite of calmness and social or emotional order. Reinforcing this idea, in a Chaucerian scene of abandonment in *The Parliament of the Fowls*, ladies dance around a temple in the garden of love, literally letting their hair down:

> Aboute the temple daunsedyn alwey
> Women inowe, of whiche some ther weere
> Fayre of hemself, and some of hem were gay;
> In kertels, al *dishevele*, wente they there:
> That was here offyce alwey, yer by yeere.   (*PF*, lines 232–6)

Further, two instances of 'dischevelee' connoting disorder occur in *The Legend of Good Women*. Dido's hair, too, is 'dischevele' as, crying and begging, she eventually faints from her efforts to gain Aeneas's pity (lines 1314–15), her unbound hair providing mute evidence of her emotional disorder. In the legend of Lucrece, Lucrece is equally distraught, while 'al dischevele, with hire heres cleere' (line 1829), as dressed in mourning weeds, she weeps and eventually commits suicide.

Clearly, there is an affinity between lacking a proper head covering, wearing one's hair in disarray, and having one's life, circumstances, and/or emotions and intellect in disorder. The Chaucer-narrator, in a rare editorial comment, provides the motivation for the Pardoner's electing to appear with his head uncovered but for a cap – 'al dischevele'. The Pardoner violates costume decorum in his head-covering for the sake of 'jolitee' (line 680) and for being in style, for riding 'al of the newe jet' (line 682),[61] which indicates, at the very least, that he is uninterested in propriety and its contribution to social order. As Ruth Mellinkoff puts it, 'the right costume for the right person . . . was the firm rule and expectation of medieval societies', and she reaffirms Hunter's point, quoted at the beginning of this chapter, that Christian identity was predicated upon the idea of vocation and its appropriate dress.[62] Hunter's Elizabethan example illustrates a principle that is firmly rooted in the Middle Ages – Ophelia's description of Hamlet's 'unbrac'd' doublet, his 'fouled' stockings 'down-gyved to his ankle', images that accentuate the most important costume sign of 'No hat upon his head' (*Hamlet*

---

[60] The OED provides the following definition for *Dishevel*: 'Without coif or head-dress; hence with the hair unconfined and flung about in disorder. Sometimes app. in wider sense: Undressed, in dishabille'.
[61] See Halverson's comments on the Pardoner's motivation, p. 196.
[62] Ruth Mellinkoff, *Outcasts: Signs of Otherness in Northern European Art of the Late Middle Ages* (Berkeley, CA, 1993), 1:6, quoting Hunter, p. 36.

II.i.78–80). As Hunter writes, 'Ophelia's words amply define the expectation of order against which the aberrant individual makes his mark.'[63]

The Pardoner's 'cappe' and the absence of his hood clearly defy expectations of social or vocational order.[64] The various frivolous connotations of *jolitee* contribute to this impression: 'merrymaking, revelry', and 'sport' are among the less pejorative MED definitions, and Chaucer's employment of *jolitee* in *The Squire's Tale* (V, line 278) suits these definitions.[65] Examples of such joyful behavior are the opposite of serious religious activity,[66] as *The Parson's Tale* (X, line 1049) makes clear, and are associated with a variety of sins.[67] Beyond that, *jolitee* is defined as playfulness, as connected with a love affair[68] or fornication, as impudence, insolence, and presumption. To cite *jolitee* as a pardoner's motivation for appearing in public without a proper

---

63 Hunter, p. 35. He also cites King Lear's being perpetually 'unbonneted', which works to signal his abandonment of 'ritual dignity'.

64 'The Pardoner is a negative summation of the theme of disorder in the *General Prologue*. . . . almost a symbol of the Prince of Disorder himself', according to Elton D. Higgs, 'The Old Order and the "Newe World" in the *General Prologue* to the *Canterbury Tales*', *HLQ* 45 (1982), p. 169.

65 The *Riverside Chaucer* Glossary offers this example, as well as that of *The Pardoner's Tale* (VI, line 780), a tale in which we see how such *jolitee*, revelry, leads to greed and murder; *Troilus and Criseyde* (Book 1, line 559), where Pandarus complains that war has interfered with his and Troilus's pursuit of 'jolite'; and *The Parson's Tale* (X, line 1049), in which 'worldly jolitee' is said to work directly against holiness and therefore should be shunned.

66 A summary reading of all MED citations under *joie* suggests that any earthly joys are suspect, and that true *joie* is only to be found in heaven and in devotion to God. The MED provides, under *joie*, a definition 2(a) 'The perfect joy of heaven; also, one of the joys of heaven . . . ~ of god', giving an example '(c 1390) Chaucer CT. Mel. B.2700 The ioye of god, he seith, is pardurable, that is to seyn, euere lastynge'. Also, 5(a) defines *joie* as 'Praise to God, worship' from '?c 1425 Chaucer Bo. (Cmb Ii.e.21 5.pr.6.p. 179': 'To whom be goye and worshipe bi Infynyt tymes, Amen'. The final relevant spiritual definition of *joie* is 5(b): 'The glory or majesty of God', but all the examples are dated 1425 or later. In contrast to spiritual joy, definition 4(a) is 'An outward expression of pleasure or happiness; rejoicing, mirth, gaiety, music, clapping', citing an example from the celebration of not-made-in-heaven wedding in '(c.1395) Chaucer's *MerT* E.1712'.

67 The MED cites NHom. Virg. to Devil 71, 'þis kniht was ful of Jolyte, And of preyere no fors made he'; Wycl. FC Life 191, 'Song . . . stiriþ men to pride & iolite & lecherie & oþere synnys'; and the c1340 Rolle *Psalter* 2.10, 'Ta ere wickid sterynge of pride, ire, enuye, couaitis, iolifte, and other vices'.

Further, the *Riverside Chaucer* Glossary provides a definition (3) of 'attractiveness', and offers Phebus in *The Manciple's Tale* (IX, line 197) as an illustration of such usage, but this gloss does not complete a description of Phebus. He may well be physically attractive, a faithful husband, and an accomplished musician, but he is also an extremely possessive husband, capable of great ire, and a murderer.

68 The *Riverside Chaucer* Glossary includes *The Knight's Tale* (I, line 1807) in this category, equating 'jolitee' with its definition (2): 'passion, sexual desire'.

headcovering is to say that he does not take seriously the nature of his proper business: dealing with pardons and collecting alms.

As for his wishing to follow the 'newe jet', numerous medieval sermons proclaim the dangers to the soul of pursuing of changing fashion.[69] All changes in dress were decried by medieval moralists,[70] and, across the centuries of the Middle Ages, fashion complaints concerned two categories of perceived abuse – too much (conspicuous consumption), and too little (the body revealed or displayed). As Chaucer's Parson proclaims of the latter, 'desordinat scantnesse' of clothing is a sin of outward pride, which but mirrors that pride, 'withinne the herte of man' (lines 409–15). Concerning scantness, the Parson goes on to describe 'sloppes, or haynselyns' (a very

---

[69] In secular literature, see Nebugodenozar's liking for new meats and fashions in *Cleanness*, in *Pearl, Cleanness, Patience, Sir Gawain and the Green Knight*, eds A. C. Cawley and J. J. Anderson (London, 1976), line 1354; also *Mankind*, in *The Macro Plays*, ed. Mark Eccles, EETS, OS 262 (London, 1969), for the allegorical character of New Gyse who tempts Mankynde with a 'fresch jakett after þe new gyse' (line 676).

Chaucerian critics have read the Pardoner's interest in style in a variety of ways. For example, Hope Phyllis Weissman, 'The Pardoner's Vernicle, the Wife's Coverchiefs, and Saint Paul', *ChauN* 1.2 (1979), p. 10, posits an iconographic 'relationship' between the Pardoner and the Wife of Bath as a result of Chaucer's attention to styles of headcoverings. Robert P. Miller, p. 182, describes an affinity with January: 'Like January in his garden [*MerT*, lines 2025–6] the Pardoner tries to put on a gay and new exterior: with his hood folded in his walet, "Hym thoughte he rood al of the newe jet".' George J. Engelhardt, 'The Ecclesiastical Pilgrims of the *Canterbury Tales*: A Study in Ethology', *MS* 37 (1975), p. 308, remarks that the 'uncovered head, long affected by effeminate clerics, has become in the Pardoner a sign of newfangledness . . . . The avidity for the novel is a vice traditionally associated with the shameless insolence or irreverence of the *illusor*' whom he depicts as prideful, corrupt, a mocker who deludes everyone, and one who cherishes drunkenness and novelty (citing a number of biblical verses as well as Plato, *Laws* 7.797; and for a definition of *insolence*, Alan of Lille, *Summa de arte praedicatoria* 10 [PL 210.133]). An earlier reference may be found in the c.1325 'Poem on the Evil Times of Edward II', in *The Political Songs of England From the Reign of John to that of Edward II*, ed. and trans. Thomas Wright, EETS, OS 6 (London, 1839), p. 329, line 118: 'a gay wenche of the newe jet'. Regarding priests who violate chastity by wearing fashionable clothing, see John Mirus, pp. 2, 32, lines 43–4, 47–9, 1031–4; also Helmut Puff's discussion of 'Sodomite Clothes', in *The Material Culture of Sex, Procreation, and Marriage in Premodern Europe*, eds Anne L. McClanan and Karen Rosoff (New York, 2001), pp. 251–72. Mann, p. 148, states that 'reverence for the "new jet"' was generally treated with 'scorn' in texts listed in her n. 11; and Mellinkoff, 1:20–2, points out that the tormentors of Christ are artistically portrayed wearing the 'new jet' and, p. 67, that depictions of strange headgear were meant to evoke distaste for the wearer. The tradition continues beyond the Middle Ages: see Jean MacIntyre and Garrett P. J. Epp, ' "Cloathes worth all the rest": Costumes and Properties', *A New History of Early English Drama*, eds John D. Cox and David Scott Kastan (New York, 1997), pp. 276–7, regarding sixteenth- and seventeenth-century theater costuming for gallants and characters named New Guise and Newfangle.

[70] I have discussed this point in *C&C*, pp. 15, 57–60, 62, 69, 163–8, 172, 240.

short jacket or paltok such as that worn by the Summoner in the Ellesmere illumination) that 'ne covere nat the shameful membres of man, to wikked entente' (line 422).

However, the Pardoner's mere 'cappe' as head covering is another kind of scantness, perhaps less arresting than partially bared private parts or buttocks, but infinitely more subtle as costume rhetoric. The Pardoner purports to represent ecclesiastic authority, but he does so in dishabille. In contrast, correct holy habits were considered to be the visible symbol of holy vows; for Canons regular, ' "the white vestments were to remind them of the inward purity they should preserve, and the black hood that they were dead to the world and should despise it and the things that were in the world" '.[71] In any case, in his choice of incomplete headcovering, the Pardoner attracts the attention of all to his cap and to the attached vernicle, which, because of the smallness of a cap, would most likely have been a badge rather than the hand-kerchief size depicted in the Ellesmere miniature. Nevertheless, and no matter how large or small, this vernicle functions as a banner and would still look disproportionately too large on a cap. Thus he fulfills a second defini-tion of *jet* as 'a device or contrivance . . . a stratagem, trick' (MED). The Par-doner's flaunting of a replica of the *Vera Icon* is meant to attest his authenticity as a pious pilgrim from Rome, one who brings back pardons from the Pope.[72] As part of the 'stage-costume' for his public performance, the vernicle would have been an effective device.

However, at least in one instance, his vernicle is an impotent trick, and the Summoner literally provides prima facie evidence of this fact. In version after version of Veronica stories, previously mentioned, the spiritual ills of individuals manifest themselves on their faces in the form of skin diseases. For those suffering this spiritual and physical disease, the individual personal image – the ravaged face – is cured and cleared, through belief in Christ and/or at the sight of His face on the vernicle. Significantly, the Pardoner's vernicle effects no such cure[73] of the *General Prologue* pilgrim so clearly in need of it – the Summoner:

---

[71] Hamilton, p. 63, quoting G. Kettlewell, *Thomas à Kempis and the Brothers of the Common Life* (London, 1882), 1:386–7.

Hamilton's thesis that the Pardoner is an Augustinian Canon posits that he should wear such a white and black habit, a habit that does not correspond to the red robe pro-vided by the Ellesmere illuminator.

[72] As Rhodes remarks, p. 37; also see Strutt's comment in n. 37 above.

[73] Ironically, the Pardoner's curative capabilities are mentioned, jokingly, by the Host in the *Introduction to the Pardoner's Tale* (VI, lines 313–16), although he suggests that drink and a merry tale from the Pardoner will effect a cure, as Melvin Storm points out, in 'The Pardoner's Invitation: Quaestor's Bag or Becket's Shrine?' *PMLA* 97.5 (1982), p. 811.

> A Somonour was ther with us in that place,
> That hadde a fyr-reed cherubynnes face,
> For saucefleem he was, with eyen narwe.
> As hoot he was and lecherous as a sparwe,
> With scalled browes blake and piled berd.
> Of his visage children were aferd.
> Ther nas quyk-silver, lytarge, ne brymstoon,
> Boras, ceruce, ne oille of tartre noon,
> Ne oynement that wolde clense and byte,
> That hym myghte helpen of his whelkes white,
> Nor of the knobbes sittynge on his chekes.   (lines 623–33)

The description of the Summoner lists symptoms (see Color Plate VIII) that might easily have been suffered by Tiberius, Vespasian, or Titus in the Veronica stories described earlier, if all of the authors of these stories or dramas had been more detail-minded: reddened skin, pimples and pustules, swellings, swollen eyelids, loss of hair, a skin disease known as 'scall' (which is a form of leprosy known as *alopicia*),[74] or syphilis, or scabies.[75] Like Tiberius, Vespasian, and Titus, the Summoner has access to an image of Christ, although it is a replicated vernicle. In fact, his gaze would fall upon the *Vera*

---

[74] See Leviticus 13:29–30. The Douay version of the Bible describes chapter 13 as 'The law concerning leprosy in men, and in garments'. Verses 45ff concern the proper garments to wear and how to deal with the clothing of lepers.

See Terrence A. McVeigh, 'Chaucer's Portraits of the Pardoner and Summoner and Wyclif's *Tractatus De Simonia*', *Classical Folia* 29 (1975), pp. 55–6, for a description of leprosy as a metaphor for simony, which is described as spiritual sodomy. Also see 4 Kings 5:1–27, the source of the leprosy metaphor applied to the selling of God's graces, i.e., simony; Richard K. Emmerson and Ronald B. Herzman, *The Apocalyptic Imagination in Medieval Literature* (Philadelphia, 1992), for a discussion of the Pardoner's simony-sodomy, pp. 171–81, esp. 171–3; and Vance, pp. 736–43.

[75] Symptoms as listed in the *Riverside Chaucer* glosses and Explanatory Notes for these lines, and diagnoses taken from Janette Richardson's headnote and explanatory notes, *Riverside Chaucer*, pp. 822–3. For a summary of commentary on the Summoner's disease, see Andrew, Explanatory Notes, *The General Prologue . . . A Variorum Edition*, pp. 508–12, esp. regarding Walter Clyde Curry's statements characterized by Andrew as 'the classic account'; also see S. H. Rigby's summary of the physiological details in Chaucer's description of the Summoner that makes use of 'humoural physiognomy', in *Chaucer in Context: Society, Allegory, and Gender* (Manchester, 1996), pp. 8–9.

For the Latin model of *descriptio* of ugliness, depicting immorality as physical deformity or as a diseased and repulsive exterior, see Henrik Specht, 'The Beautiful, the Handsome, and the Ugly: Some Aspects of the Art of Character Portrayal in Medieval Literature', *SN* 56 (1984), pp. 135–7. For the tormentors of Christ depicted as diseased and deformed, see Mellinkoff, 1:185. Also see Cigman, p. 177, regarding the repulsive Summoner and his sins; Mann, pp. 138–44, concerning the Summoner and other literary characters whose skin problems denote sins, including lechery, harlotry in general, and simony.

Icon every time he looked at his companion, the Pardoner. However, the Summoner appears to lack a requisite ingredient for the kind of miracle-cure Tiberius, Vespasian, and Titus received. Are we to understand that no healing occurs because of the Summoner's own lack of faith? Is there no cure because, as Veronica states in the *Mors Pilati* story, 'true potency resides in the possession of the "true image" ', which exists internally, spiritually, rather than externally?[76] Is this failure further or correlative symbolic proof of the Pardoner's own lack of virility and his spiritual sterility?[77] Beyond that, might we read this failure-to-cure as evidence that the Pardoner's vernicle lacks authenticity, like the relics in his male?

> For in his male he hadde a pilwe-beer,
> Which that he seyde was Oure Lady veyl;[78]
> He seyde he hadde a gobet of the seyl
> That Seint Peter hadde, whan that he wente
> Upon the see, til Jhesu Crist hym hente.
> He hadde a croys of latoun[79] ful of stones,
> And in a glas he hadde pigges bones.   (lines 694–700)

Chaucer makes it plain that here is a pardoner, licensed or false, bearing fake relics,[80] that were unlikely – from their inherent spiritual power – to miracu-

---

76 As Rhodes points out, pp. 35–7. In *Paradiso* (Canto 31, lines 103ff) [Sinclair trans., p. 451], Dante looks at St Bernard, whose saintly, loving lifework makes *him* a *Vera Icon* of Christianity, and he thinks of pilgrims who travel great distances to gaze upon the relics of St Veronica, including the vernicle, and who question the reality of Christ's true image as depicted there. St Bernard tells Dante that there is yet greater glory that is not an image, but rather divine reality.

77 St Bernard, as mentioned in the note above, functions as a *Vera Icon*; but the Pardoner, even with his vernicle as identifying sign, is quite the opposite. In fact, especially with this holy sign worn as a misrepresentation of his own character, the Pardoner epitomizes falseness. See Rhodes's comments, p. 37, on the Pardoner's 'false imitation of Christ' and his 'outer concern with the image of Christ'; and Patterson, pp. 664–8.

78 Regarding the legendary veil of the Blessed Virgin Mary and its salvific powers, see Annemarie Weyl Carr, 'Threads of Authority: The Virgin Mary's Veil in the Middle Ages', *Robes and Honor: The Medieval World of Investiture*, ed. Stewart Gordon (New York, 2001), pp. 59–93.

79 Latoun is an alloy of brass and other metal (MED). Thus the cross is not only not gold, it is not even brass and, as an alloy, is further debased by another baser metal. We might consider here a rewriting of the familiar question, posed in the Parson's *General Prologue* portrait (line 500), as it applies to the character of the Pardoner and tarnishing: 'If gold ruste, what shal *latoun* do?'

80 Storm comments, p. 811, that Chaucer's Pardoner constitutes 'a kind of walking shrine, portable and compendious . . . peddling both ostensibly holy objects and the spiritual advantages they supposedly provide'. Yet he notes, p. 815, that lines 946–50 of *The Pardoner's Tale* and the mention of Becket's breeches of hair, usually kissed by pilgrims to Canterbury, indicate 'not only that the Pardoner's wares are debased but that they are presented as substitutes for the specific spiritual goods towards which the

lously cure their buyers' ills or to cause productive increase in worldly goods.[81] The introduction of yet another veil, that of the blessed Virgin, which is blatantly false, only emphasizes the Pardoner's improper head covering with its replica of St Veronica's veil, a vernicle that does not cure the Summoner's disease.[82]

The Pardoner's headgear is an icon of impropriety and disorder surmounted by the *Vera Icon* – the juxtaposition makes a suitable costume for a mountebank[83] who flaunts his lies and the premier emblem of Christian truth simultaneously. In addition, in carrying the image of Christ on his cap, this self-proclaimed 'ful vicious man' (VI, line 459) is superficially a Christ-bearer, oddly but erroneously reminiscent of St Christopher. At the same time, his 'male' literally holds only bogus relics, and perhaps that hood he should be wearing for decorum's sake. This ironic image further underscores the contrapuntal themes of the falseness the Pardoner lives and the truth he proclaims when he concludes his sermon with the exclamation:

> Allas! mankynde, how may it bitide
> That to thy creatour, which that the wroghte,
> And with his precious herte-blood thee boghte,
> Thou art so fals and so unkynde, allas?   (VI, lines 900–3)

If the Pardoner's headdress is inappropriate and serves as the marker for his entire demeanor and behavior, how much more so is that of the Summoner. Chaucer's description of this pilgrim portrays him as the epitomé of earthy *jolitee*:

> A gerland hadde he set upon his heed,
> As greet as it were for an ale-stake.
> A bokeleer[84] hadde he maad hym of a cake.   (lines 666–8)

---

pilgrims are journeying'. See in Morris's note for line 701, pp. 141–3, the lines from John Heywood's portrayal of a Pardoner who has a similar false set of relics.

[81] As discussed in D. W. Robertson Jr, *Preface to Chaucer: Studies in Medieval Perspectives* (Princeton, 1969; rpt. 1973), pp. 332–5.

[82] We note that in Canterbury the hospital of St Lawrence, presided over by a Prioress, housed lepers of both sexes, according to J. F. Donavan, 'IV. Leprosy in the Middle Ages', in the online *Catholic Encyclopedia*.

[83] Condren, p. 191, states that the Pardoner 'seems committed only to displaying his technical virtuosity as a performer'; he 'has sought to create a new reality out of his consummate ability to manipulate appearances', for example, 'the contradictory appearances of a professional man of God' and that of a moral reprobate. And Weissman comments, p. 10, 'The vernicle on the Pardoner's cap, in all its shame, must stand as the most substantial element of his head covering, which is otherwise conspicuous for its proudly displayed lightness.' See also Halverson, pp. 196–8, regarding the Pardoner's performance and projected image; and Hoerner, p. 70, concerning the Pardoner's 'act of self-fabrication'.

[84] A 'bokeler' is 'a small shield (round, oval, or half-moon shaped) used to ward off

Chaucer rhetorically gives the Summoner an oversize garland (lines 666–7) and provides him with a cake-buckler for his journey. These paired images achieve a bizarre correspondence with the familiar couplings of a knight wearing a helm and carrying a shield, or with a garlanded lover holding a hawk or musical instrument, or with a broad-hatted pilgrim bearing a begging bowl. However, as John V. Fleming points out, this passage describing the Summoner does not make literal sense – a garland as large as an ale-stake coupled with a cake-buckler, 'in terms of credible expectations of visual verisimilitude . . . [is] preposterous'. Fleming likens such a garland to a Christmas wreath in size, and labels the narrator's garland description as hyperbole.[85]

Clearly, the implausible buckler made of cake, flat or puffy, and of indeterminate size,[86] is metaphoric. Although such cakes were a staple of alehouses, such a buckler would have neither the solidity nor the size for martial defense; it could only fend off Hunger and/or satisfy Appetite. At the same time, the image of the ale-stake garland, composed of ivy or other greenery wound about a hoop and hung as a wreath on the end of a pole mounted on the front of taverns,[87] marks the Summoner as a consumer of that other commodity available in alehouses: alcoholic beverages. Together, these signs symbolize the excessive appetite for sensual satisfaction and greed of the Summoner, and reputed of summoners in general.[88] Fleming's comment is pertinent here:

blows' (MED). It usually has a knob or boss at the front center, which further deflects blows. I have discussed the martial and sexual connotations of the Wife of Bath's hat, 'brood as is a bokeler or a targe' (line 471), in *C&C*, pp. 177–8.

[85] John V. Fleming, 'Chaucer and the Visual Arts of His Time', *New Perspectives in Chaucer Criticism*, ed. Donald M. Ross (Norman, OK, 1981), p. 133; Fleming, pp. 133–6, discusses *General Prologue* lines 666–8.

[86] The MED describes a cake variously as a loaf or unleavened bread or griddlecake, made of oats, barley, flour, and even of medicinal ingredients (examples of recipes are fifteenth century).

[87] See MED definition 4(e). Also see Andrew's *The General Prologue . . . Variorum Edition*, p. 527, for Skeat's description of an ale-stake garland made of three hoops with ribbon decoration, as well as other critics' descriptions of green wreaths. Evans, *The Flowering of the Middle Ages*, p. 213, presents a color pl., upper right, illustrating a medieval fair in which a booth in the right-hand corner is marked with an ale-stake.

[88] Louis A. Haselmayer, 'The Apparitor and Chaucer's Summoner', *Speculum* 12 (1937), p. 55, states that 'the slight tradition of this officer [the apparitor] in literature was definite and uncompromising. The few references to or descriptions of the man were vigorously antagonistic.' On this subject see Henry Ansgar Kelly, 'Bishop, Prioress, and Bawd in the Stews of Southwark', *Speculum* 75.2 (2000), p. 376; and Thomas Hahn and Richard W. Kaeuper, 'Text and Context: Chaucer's *Friar's Tale*', *SAC* 5 (1983), pp. 67–101. Keller, pp. 306–11, sums up Chaucer's treatment of summoners and their malpractice.

Regarding summoners' alliance with greed as personified by Lady Meed, corrupt consistory court officials, and other corrupt church officials, see *PP:B*, Passus 2, lines

Purse is the archdeacon's hell,[89] and cake is no doubt the archdeacon's appetite. The Summoner who wears a pub sign on his head and carries a pastry in his hand is part of the cakes-and-ale church that Chaucer detests.

In addition, this sort of church is illustrated by the Summoner's companion, the Pardoner, 'who "wole both drinke and eten of a cake"' (VI, line 322).[90] The repetition of cakes and ale[91] images reinforces the linkage of Pardoner and Summoner and a commercialized church in which both its representatives and satisfaction of appetites are for sale.

The 'preposterous' size of the Summoner's garland would make the Summoner's headgear odd enough on its own, but Chaucer's grotesquerie does not end here. The extensive context of the term *garland* – its usual form, social and religious connotations, and literary associations – is also at issue. In the social realm, in a normal size, the garland was a simple ornament for the head worn by both men and women; garlands were 'low, not tall, and, if they had fleurons these tended to be small'. However, elaborate floral garlands were made of gold and jewels, and ornamental garlands of all sorts, natural and manufactured, were associated with courtly love, and celebra-

---

59, 169–77; Passus 3, line 134; Passus 4, line 167; and Passus 15, lines 129–32. Of *PP*, Mann, p. 140, comments that 'the sins that Langland associates with the summoner are those traditionally assigned to officials of the consistory courts; they are financially corrupt, and are particularly lenient with sexual offenders'. Muriel Bowden, *A Commentary on the General Prologue to the 'Canterbury Tales'*, 2nd edn (New York, 1967), p. 269, points out negative characteristics of summoners in the C version of *PP*: Passus 3, lines 59, 187, and Passus 4, line 171. A 'Satyre on the Consistory Courts', *The Political Songs of England: From the Reign of John to that of Edward II*, ed. and trans. Thomas Wright, Camden Society 6 (London, 1839), p. 157, presents the following fourteenth-century view:

> 3et ther sitteth somenours syexe other sevene,
> Mys motinde men alle by here evene,
>   And recheth forth heore rolle;
> Hyrd-men hem hatieth, and uch mones hyne,
> For everuch a parosshe heo polketh in pyne,
>   And clastreth with heore colle.

This same collection includes the thirteenth-century 'Song of the Corruptions of the Time', p. 32, which describes an archdeacon's administration of justice as corrupt and susceptible to bribes.

89 See Mann, pp. 141–2, for a discussion of sources for Chaucer's use of this phrase.
90 Fleming, 'Chaucer and the Visual Arts', p. 135.
91 The standard fare and behaviors in alehouses were common knowledge in the Middle Ages and later. For example, see William Shakespeare, *Twelfth Night* in *The Complete Signet Classic Shakespeare* (New York, 1972), 2.3, lines 89–92, in which Malvolio asks Sir Toby Belch, Sir Andrew, and Feste, the clown, 'Do ye make an alehouse of my lady's house, that ye squeak out your coziers' catches without any mitigation or remorse of voice?' Sir Toby's response equates their rowdiness with those products most often sold in alehouses: 'Dost thou think, because thou art virtuous,/ There shall be no more cakes and ale?' (lines 116–17).

tions such as weddings and other festive occasions.[92] In some cases, it is difficult to tell from historical records the precise difference, if any, between the terms *garland, chaplet, bandeau, coronal,* and *circlet*.[93] But one thing is clear – both the size and connotation of *garland*, in its usual usage, are entirely different from that of a wreath perched at the end of an *ale-stake*, which, together, make up the usual sign for a medieval establishment where alcoholic beverages and bread were sold.

In addition, a garland is often one of the attributes of the Virgin Mary in the visual arts, and the set of prayers devoted to her was referred to as a garland, or the rosary. This idea was visually represented in portraits of Mary wearing a garland, or framed by a garland, each floret representing an Ave.[94] Instant irony is achieved through even brief reflection upon the image of Mary crowned with a garland of roses, contrasted with that of the Summoner possibly similarly bedecked. An exemplum from *Mirk's Festial* illuminates such a contrast in depicting a Reeve whose character and circumstances surrounding his wearing a garland are the opposite of the Summoner's. This Reeve, in fear of losing his life to thieves, prays to the Virgin Mary for protection. Unseen by the Reeve, the Virgin crowns him with a garland and sets a rose that 'schon as bright as a sterre' in the garland for each Ave he prays. This shining rose garland and the Virgin are seen by the hidden master thief, who, in awe of this miracle, spares the Reeve's life and also asks for his prayers to this beautiful and powerful Lady.[95] Needless to say, Chaucer's Summoner wears no such miraculous garland. Chaucer, however, does not tell what kind of garland the Summoner wears, and the Ellesmere illuminator's choice of red and white flowers[96] of indeterminate species moves us no

---

92 Lightbown, pp. 112, 118–19. See esp. p. 380 for English custom. Apparently, pp. 377–8, garlands were worn by the bourgeoisie as well as by nobles. Lightbown's description accords with MED definitions 1 (a), and 2 (b).

93 Lightbown, pp. 68, 108, 112.

94 See Anne Winston-Allen, *Stories of the Rose: The Making of the Rosary in the Middle Ages* (University Park, PA, 1997), pp. 41, 43–5, 82, 100–2, for text and pictures representing garlands of prayers and of flowers, specifically roses. Also see Eithne Wilkins, *The Rose-Garden Game: The Symbolic Background to the European Prayer-Beads* (London, 1969), regarding the symbolic background to European prayer beads, and the metaphoric connection to garlands and gardens, esp. pp. 28–9.

95 [John Mirk], *Mirk's Festial: A Collection of Homilies by Johannes Mirkus*, ed. Theodor Erbe, EETS, ES 96 (London: 1905; rpt. 1987), pp. 16–17.

96 The illumination of the Ellesmere manuscript occurred at about the same time that *Mirk's Festial* was compiled.
   It is possible that this choice of rose garland was suggested to the illuminator by Chaucer's diction 'saucefleem', denoting a red face, which, according to the *Riverside Chaucer* note for line 625, sometimes was called *gutta rosacea*. See also Thomas Garbáty's diagnoses of the Summoner as having *Rosacea*-like *Secondary Syphiloderm* and Acne Rosacea, included in Andrew's explanatory notes for the *Variorum Edition . . . General Prologue*, p. 509; see also notes, pp. 511–12, regarding 'sawceflewm'.

closer to knowing. If, given the religious context of pilgrimage and the cultural juxtaposition of garland with aves, rosaries, rose gardens, and the Blessed Virgin Mary, we cannot help *thinking* 'roses' when reading of the Summoner's 'gerland', this notion but adds to the sense of Chaucer's rhetorical ambiguity and to untold ironic possibilities.

Frequently in literature, a garland is one iconographical detail of a lover's costume.[97] Here, too, it seems inevitable that readers think of roses, and Mann suggests that the Summoner's garland is a parody of that worn by the lover in the *Roman de la rose*. Such a lover's garland would have been highly decorative if worn by Chaucer's attractive young Squire, although it still would have been inappropriate for a pilgrimage. However, in the Ellesmere miniature of the Summoner, where the artist paints a typical floral wreath of red and white flowers perched above the Summoner's diseased countenance, this attribute only accentuates the negative. We cannot know if the Chaucer-narrator intends his audience to understand the Summoner's garland as a lover's garland, indicative of the nature of his relationship with the Pardoner. However, other associations of Chaucer's imagery indicate that it signals his willingness to take a bribe,[98] a further aspect of his greed: Chaucer's ale-stake comparison equates the garland with a wine-bribe bestowed upon the Summoner by any 'good felawe'[99] who wants to maintain or 'have his concubyn' (lines 649–50) without interference from moral authorities.[100] In wearing this garland, the Summoner has, thus, made of *himself* an ale-stake, advertising that what is within himself (morality, ethics, integrity) is for sale for earthly pleasures of various sorts.[101] By extension, the ecclesiastic estab-

---

97   Mann, p. 276, n. 1. See the wreath of roses bestowed by a lady upon Count Krafft von Toggenburg, minnesinger, in response to his song extolling her attributes, in the early-fourteenth-century Manese Codex, pal. germ. 848, in the University Library, Heidelberg; illustration reproduced in Eithne Wilkins's color pl. 14, p. 145.

98   See Mann, pp. 142–4, for a discussion of drink as the Summoner's bribe.

99   *Good felawe* is defined as a derogatory term in V. J. Scattergood, '*The Two Ways*: An Unpublished Religious Treatise by Sir John Clanvowe', *English Philological Studies* 10 (1967), pp. 49–50:

But now swiche as been synful men and wacches of þe feend been cleped of the world goode felawes/ For þei þat woln waaste þe goodis þat god hath sent hem/ in pruyde of the world/ and in lustes of here flessh and goon to þe tauerne . . . and drynken [other sins listed] . . . and been bandes for here felawes/ And lyuen al in synne and in vanitee þei been hoolde goode felawes. . . .

Regarding the phrase above, 'been bandes for here felawes', perhaps 'bandes' should have been *baudes*.

100   As Keller points out, p. 308.

101   The critical debate about the sexuality and sexual involvement of the Summoner and Pardoner is long and involved; I leave the discussion of the obvious phallic connotations of the ale-stake with garland finial metaphor to those critics who have carried this debate.

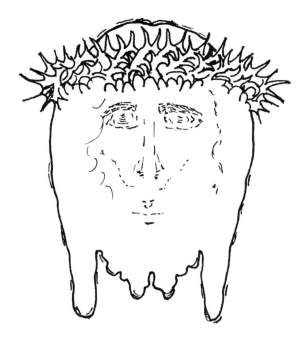

15. Detail of the face of Christ wearing a crown of thorns sketched from a painting of Saint Veronica displaying a 'vernycle', painted by the Master of Saint Veronica; now in the Alte Pinakothek, Munich.

lishment to which he is attached, the Archdeacon's Court, is likened to a tavern in which one may barter for heavenly pardon while purchasing earthly comforts.[102]

As George J. Engelhardt puts it,

The Summoner rides on the pilgrimage crowned with a garland like the reprobates crowned with roses whom the Book of Wisdom (1–2) bequeaths

[102] See the c.1300 *Lanercost Chronicle* report of an archdeacon, the master of a summoner, who fined peasants for sins of overindulgence in food, drink, and women at a local tavern. They had to pay him a 'ransom', which prevented their payment of rents to their Knight (a knight of the King of Scotland), Lord Robert of Robertstone of an Annandale mannerhouse, as recounted in G. G. Coulton, *Life in the Middle Ages* (Cambridge, 1928), 3:23–4. Also, regarding false accusations made and bribes taken by summoners, see Carter Revard, 'The Lecher, the Legal Eagle, and the Papelard Priest: Middle English Confessional Satires in MS. Harley 2253 and Elsewhere', *His Firm Estate: Essays in Honor of Franklin James Eikenberry by Former Students*, The University of Tulsa Department of English 2, ed. Donald E. Hayden (Tulsa, OK, 1967), pp. 54–71.

to the devil because they make a covenant with death and do not spare the widow nor refrain from detraction, but lie in wait for the just man and test him with contumely.[103]

Engelhardt's comment inspires one final peculiar mental image: how much more visually ironic the partnering of Pardoner and Summoner would be, as they journey side-by-side, if we but knew that the Pardoner's vernicle depicted Christ's visage surmounted with the crown of thorns (see Plate 15).[104] And we note that in *The Shewings of Julian of Norwich*[105] (VII, lines 243–4), Julian calls this wreath of thorns a 'garland', commenting that Christ's 'grete dropis of blode fel downe from under the garland like pellots semand as it had cum out of the veynis'. If we knew that the Pardoner's vernicle depicted Christ crowned with thorns, this image would then be juxtaposed and contrasted with the Summoner's 'saucefleem', 'whelkes', and 'knobbes', crowned by his 'greet' ale-stake-garland of flowers and greenery. These wreaths, the thorn-crown of Christ and the garland of an ale lover, respectively signify the sacred and the profane, spiritual passion and earthly appe-

---

103 Engelhardt, p. 307. This Bible passage may provide the impetus for the Ellesmere illuminator's choice of floral garland.

104 This line drawing was sketched from a plate in James Snyder, *Northern Renaissance Art: Painting, Sculpture, The Graphic Arts From 1350 to 1575* (New York, 1985), fig. 78. Snyder, pp. 80–1, describes this c.1400 *Saint Veronica*, by the Master of St Veronica, Staatsgemäldesammlungen, Alte Pinakothek, Munich. See also Brigitte Corley, *Painting and Patronage in Cologne 1300–1500* (Turnhout, Belgium, 2000), for both color (pl. 9) and black-and-white (p. 74, pl. 45) reproductions of this same painting; chapter 5 includes a number of pictures of Christ wearing the crown of thorns, including p. 94, pl. 61, and p. 95, pl. 62. Also, see Kuryluk, pls 24, and 32, the latter of which reproduces a c.1370 *Pietà*, Christ wearing a crown of thorns, by the Silesian Master.

   The MED classifies the crown of thorns as a garland in definition 1 (c).

   According to Spencer's *Pilgrim Souvenirs – Salisbury*, figs 116–17, other attributes of badges from Rome included Christ's crown of thorns, and a shield of arms:

   On two closely related Canterbury finds (figs 118–19), however, the *infulae* ['pendants at the back of the tiara'] are swept upwards above a face, a representation of the vernicle, which after the burial-places of St Peter and St Paul, was Rome's principal attraction to pilgrims in the late Middle Ages.

   Vernicles of Christ wearing the crown of thorns appear in a number of medieval wall paintings in Danish churches included in a website: www.danish-medieval-art.net. The website photos are dated from 1425 to as late as 1535. The c.1500 Raaby picture of only the veil with image is especially dramatic; other depictions include St Veronica.

105 Julian of Norwich, *A Book of Showings to the Anchoress Julian of Norwich*, 2 vols, eds Edmund Colledge and James Walsh, *Studies and Texts* 35 (Toronto, 1928); also <http://www.lib.rochester.edu/camelot/teams/julianfr.htm> for the TEAMS online version of *The Shewings of Julian of Norwich*.

tite. In any case, given the circumstances of Chaucer's portraits of the Pardoner and the Summoner, these costume signs indicate that even in the Middle Ages the modern dictum of 'It pays to advertise' was comprehended by hucksters.

9

The Parson Has No Clothes

In one of Chaucer's most evocative metaphors in the *Canterbury Tales*, the narrator-Parson depicts both his philosophy of dress and his attitude toward the 'two maneres of Pride', the Pride that is 'withinne the herte of man' and the Pride's outward manifestation, its sign. In this metaphoric analogy, excessive and/or fashionable clothing functions 'right as the gaye leefsel atte taverne is signe of the wyn that is in the celer' (X, line 410). Such an equation of outer sign and inner spiritual state parallels that theory of medieval dress with which Chapter 1 (pp. 1–4) begins – a simplistic and idealistic philosophy of dress in which each person should wear the clothing appropriate to his/her estate. Once he states his thesis equating Pride and excessive dress, the Parson enumerates and denounces examples of contemporary prideful fashions (lines 414–30).

Medieval satirists requite such sermons by making the dress of the clergy the frequent butt of sartorial critiques. In the *General Prologue* portrait of the Parson, on the other hand, Chaucer does not avail himself of this opportunity – he describes no clothes. Because in medieval literature detailed costume signs are the most common means of denoting Pride, for example in the Parson's own comments (X, lines 408–30), and because Chaucer provides a contextual catalogue of the Parson's devoted practice of Christianity in the Parson's care for his parishioners, his omission of any costume description in the Parson's portrait (*Omitted Clothing*) signifies the absence of this spiritual blemish. Consequently, readers simply assume that, although his portrait lacks garment signs, the Parson is nevertheless appropriately dressed for this pilgrimage. Further, we might posit that, metaphorically, the Parson is spiritually clothed in his charity, his good works, his deeds,[1] signifying that he is

---

[1] The 'povre Persoun of a Toun' is only one among several of his Canterbury Pilgrims whose traveling costumes Chaucer leaves to the reader's imagination – the narrator-Chaucer, the Second Nun, the Manciple, the Host, the Cook, and the Prioress's extra priests. The lack of costume signs leaves the reader who registers this absence to rely only on the pilgrims' actions, or, taking this absence further, to assume that these pilgrims are metaphorically clothed in their deeds, their virtues or sins.

clothed in the virtue that is the opposite of Pride – Humility, in its strongest and most favorable sense.[2]

In its least favorable sense, Humility connotes the possession or consciousness of personal defects or position; the lowly person acknowledges a lack of self-respect, his humiliation, in his non-assertive actions. Yet the possession of Humility, understood favorably, constitutes the spiritual strength manifest in the kind of service – the charitable good shepherding and the abandonment of Pride – about which SS Paul and Peter preach. St Paul speaks of serving the Lord 'with all humility' in spite of obstacles that have to be overcome (Acts 20:19), while St Peter instructs both priests and laymen to practice humility and 'watchfulness': 'Feed the flock of God which is among you, taking care of it, not by constraint, but willingly, according to God: not for filthy lucre's sake, but voluntarily'; and 'do you all insinuate humility one to another, for *God resisteth the proud, but to the humble he giveth grace*' (I Pet. 5:2–5; my emphasis). St Peter promises that the heavenly reward will be a 'crown of glory' for the earthly practice of Humility. Further, St Paul elaborates on this virtue and its companion virtues, and he does so in a clothing metaphor. He exhorts the Colossians to put off the old man and to put on the new,

> stripping yourselves of the old man with his deeds . . . And putting on the new, him who is renewed unto knowledge, according to the image of him who created him. . . . Put ye on therefore, as the elect of God, holy, and beloved, the bowels of mercy, benignity, humility, modesty, patience. . . . But above all these things have charity, which is the bond of perfection.
>
> (Col. 3:9–14)

St Peter, too, speaks of spiritual clothing when he says not to adorn oneself with clothes but with being submissive to God. He especially mentions 'having compassion one of another, being lovers of the brotherhood, merciful, modest, humble', and the necessity to do good and avoid evil, to pursue peace (I Pet. 3:3–12). Underscoring these admonishments to practice Humility and to be humble before God is Proverbs 15:33: 'The fear of the Lord *is* the lesson of wisdom: and humility goeth before glory.' In the proper fear and awe of God, then, it is wise to practice Humility, to eschew earthly display and pomp, and the person who does so will be rewarded with heavenly glory. Such beliefs portray Humility as an integral aspect of Wisdom and as a spiritual strength, a strength possessed by Chaucer's Parson as he ministers to and

---

2   See the MED definitions of *humility* as 'humble behavior or conduct', and *humble* as denoting obedience, respectfulness, submissiveness, reverence – all of which are, in the Parson's case, aspects of his priestly relationship with his God, and demonstrated in his treatment of his parishioners.

serves as a leader of his parishioners while he displays no outward sign of Pride in action or garb. He is spiritually wise.

Normally, in dealing with the other models of costume metaphors listed in Chapter 1 (pp. 5–8), I find it preferable first to explore associations with and possible implications of a literary costume before assessing how that information informs an understanding of a character in context.[3] In an example of *Omitted Clothing*, however, readers must do what many readers have traditionally done with all literary characters – decide on matters of character and afterward assume (or judge) a costume to suit. In the specific case of Chaucer's *General Prologue* Parson, the questions arise as to how we might accurately determine what he most likely would have worn on pilgrimage, as well as the limits of such a determination.

Chaucer's contemporary readers, who regularly saw traveling priests of all degree, were surely equal to the task of mentally supplying proper garments for the Parson,[4] while modern readers will possibly picture this costume in accordance with the familiar miniature of the Parson found in the Ellesmere manuscript, fol. 206v, where the illuminator portrays him in a long outer garment with tight sleeves, shoulder cape with hood, all red, and black shoes cut low enough to reveal matching red hose. His red robe is belted by a decorated black girdle at the waist. This Parson appears to wear what may be the characteristic garments of medieval parish priests.[5]

---

3   In this regard, see S. H. Rigby, in *Chaucer in Context: Society, Allegory, and Gender* (Manchester, 1996), p. 16, who poses a number of questions about how to read Chaucer, from which I single out, 'what is the relationship between individual morality and the wider social order' in terms of Chaucer's confrontation of the 'broader social, political and religious questions' of his time?

4   See Robert E. Rodes, *Ecclesiastical Administration in Medieval England* (Notre Dame, IN, 1977), pp. 41–2, regarding clerical dress. All clerics were expected to dress in accordance with their status. For a discussion of the Parson's probable status, both economic and within the church hierarchy, see Robert N. Swanson, 'Chaucer's Parson and Other Priests', *SAC* 13 (1991), pp. 41–80.

5   Regarding priestly garments in the Middle Ages, see Chapter 8, p. 229 and nn. 7–8. Richard K. Emmerson, 'Text and Image in the Ellesmere Portraits of the Tale-Tellers', *The Ellesmere Chaucer: Essays in Interpretation*, eds Martin Stevens and Daniel Woodward (San Marino, CA, 1995), p. 146, states that red is 'a traditional color for [the garments of] priests'. Samantha Mullaney, 'The Language of Costume in the Ellesmere Portraits', *Sources, Exemplars and Copy-Texts: Influence and Transmission*, special edn, *Trivium* 31 (1999), pp. 49–51, posits that the artist has dressed the Parson 'in perfect accordance with his estate and degree, neither more nor less'. She states that 'red was more commonly worn by parish priests of the period', but offers no documentation for this claim and an additional claim that the Ellesmere miniaturist has given the Parson a very large spur, which symbolizes his capability of castigating his parishioners when needed as well as his own discipline.

Finally, in the Tudor period, a measure of support emerges for the idea of red as the standard color for priests' garb: Henry VIII ordered fabric for clothes for persons accompanying him on a journey, and the records list 'Item xi yerds and 1 q^{rter} of rede

On the other hand, parish priests, when not wearing official church vestments, apparently wore lay styles.[6] Although it will not completely answer the question of what such a parson would wear on pilgrimage, an 'Inventory of the movable property of a deceased country parson, 1430' provides an accounting of the garments possessed by one parson. He owned 1 green gown (worth 8s 6d), 1 worsted doublet (1s), 2 gowns (2s each), 1 'vestment with appurtenances for the church' (20s), and 1 vest (est. 1s).[7] Miniatures of numerous clerics of all degree wearing a variety of styles and colors appear in the Golden Book of St Albans, known officially as the *Catalogus Benefactorum Monasterii S. Albani.*[8] Significantly, Chaucer's Parson himself is a benefactor – he gives of his own funds to parishoners who are needy, in contrast to certain parish priests who officially curse (excommunicate) parishioners who fail to pay their tithes:

> Ful looth were hym to cursen for his tithes,
> But rather wolde he yeven, out of doute,
> Unto his povre parisshens aboute
> Of his offryng and eek of his substaunce.   (I, lines 486–9)

Line 486 does not eliminate the possibility that the Parson might curse a parishioner if the reason for a curse was strong enough, but it does make clear that he was not eager to curse a poor parishioner who failed to tithe, even though he would be entitled to do so.[9] In addition, even under adverse conditions, and on foot, he visited his people in his far-flung parish. Given the Parson's habitual self-sacrifice in forgoing tithe collecting and in giving money to needy parishioners, he is unlikely to have worn layman's dress that was ostentatious.

Although Chaucer omits dress in the Parson's portrait, nevertheless, through his inclusion of one image, he treats the subject of the Parson's array fully. In this single sign – the walking staff taken with him as he walks the rounds in his parish and ministers to his parishioners – Chaucer provides the Parson with an accessory well-known as part of the pious pilgrim tradition;[10] further, this single sign functions as a *Spiritual Mirror* encompassing all aspects of Chaucer's description of the Parson's pastoral practices that portray

---

cloth for iii chaplaynes', according to Gilbert J. French, *The Tippets of the Canons Ecclesiastical* (London, 1850), p. 12.

6   See Chapter 1, pp. 18–21, 24, 27–8.

7   According to *English Historical Documents* (New York, 1969), 4:442.

8   BL MS Cott. Nero D VII.

9   Regarding the authority for and form of such a curse, see John Mirus (John Myrc), *Instructions for Parish Priests*, ed. Edward Peacock, EETS, OS 31 (London, 1868; rev. 1902), pp. 61–7, and for tithes esp., pp. 64–5. Mirus's *Instructions* is dated 1450.

10 See Laura F. Hodges, *Chaucer and Costume: The Secular Pilgrims in the General Prologue [C&C]*, Chaucer Studies XXVI (Cambridge, 2000), pp. 10–14, esp. n. 31.

him as a good shepherd.[11] In this context of 'signifying associations',[12] the staff functions as both costume accessory and metaphor.

Numerous walking staves appear in medieval visual arts. Some are hooked at the top, having a similarity to the crozier in Color Plate I, but with a greater likeness to the staff in Plate 16;[13] others might be topped with a knob,[14] or with a hollow ball. Sidney Heath describes walking staves with one or more hollow balls used as musical instruments.[15] Some walking staves are plain, or tapered to the bottom, which ends in a point, while others display carpentry skills and artful turnings. We cannot know what style of walking staff the Parson carries on his parish rounds, but his diatribe against ornamentation in his *Tale* (X, lines 410–30), coupled with the 'good shepherd' imagery in Chaucer's portrait of him, argues against the likelihood of the Parson's use of any style except the plainest, utilitarian shepherd's crook or knobbed staff.

Chaucer's description of the Parson's behavior as parish priest and 'good shepherd' suggests that he is clothed according to traditional Augustinian clothing metaphors in which good works clothe the soul[16] and, as we have

---

[11] I Timothy 3:1–9 lists the characteristics of those who would serve God as good shepherds of His people: free from blame, faithful, sober, prudent, well-behaved, chaste, hospitable, moderate in drinking, physically gentle, modest, uncontentious, not covetous, orderly in his home, seasoned in his calling, not prideful, of good repute, not 'double-tongued', not greedy for more; he must teach, and he must hold 'the mystery of faith in a pure conscience'. Also see the rules for priests included in *Pastors and the Care of Souls: in Medieval England*, eds John Shinners and William J. Dohar (Notre Dame, IN, 1998), pp. 8–9, 21–3, and esp. as they pertain to clothing; pp. 64–70 deals with the duties of each clerical order.

George J. Engelhardt, 'The Ecclesiastical Pilgrims of the *Canterbury Tales*: A Study in Ethology', *MS* 37 (1975), p. 314, describes 'the ethos of the perfect priest embodied in the Parson' and provides the scriptural background for this judgment. Also see Iohannes Wyclif, *Sermones*, sermon 15, ed. J. Loserth (London, 1889; New York, 1966), 3:114ff on the thirteen 'garments' necessary for the Christian *viator*, with F. D. Matthew providing the sidenotes identifying the 'garments', which are actually virtues: Bowels of mercy: esp. spiritual mercy, Kindness, Humility, Modesty, Patience, Forbearance, Forgiveness, Love, The exultant peace of God, Indwelling of the word of Christ, Teaching in all wisdom, Mutual admonition, Doing all in the name of the Lord Jesus.

[12] Roland Barthes's phrase, in 'The Imagination of the Sign', *Critical Essays*, trans. Richard Howard (Evanston, IL, 1972), p. 206.

[13] St Josse pilgrim badge (by whom the Wife of Bath swore), sketched from the cover photograph of *The London Archaeologist* 4, no. 11 (1983).

[14] As in pl. 1, p. 11 of *C&C*.

[15] Sidney Heath, *Pilgrim Life in the Middle Ages* (London, 1911), p. 121. See also H. D. Traill and J. S. Mann, eds, *Social England: A Record of the Progress of the People* (New York, 1969), 2:375; an extract from *Sarum Missal* quoted by Alan Kendall, *Medieval Pilgrims* (London, 1970), pp. 36–7; and Edward L. Cutts, *Scenes & Characters of the Middle Ages*, 7th edn (London, 1930), p. 177.

[16] As discussed in *C&C*, pp. 4–5, 9, 124. In brief, Augustine's garment metaphors make up a structure of 'associations'; see Jean Pépin, 'Saint Augustin et le symbolisme

16. Sketch of a pilgrim badge of St Josse with pilgrim staff and rosary, from the cover photograph on *The London Archaeologist* 4, no. 11 (1983).

seen, according to the clothing metaphors in the excerpts from Colossians and I Peter cited above. Further, Chaucer was likely to have known Wyclif's analogy of good works that express charity (*caritas*) that clothes the soul. In this analogy Wyclif equates *caritas* with the brideclothes that the good man wears as he approaches God:

> Þis vertu cloþis man at domus-day wiþ bride-cloþis, & þis cloþe may neuere be lost in þis world ne in þe toþure. for noman may come to heuene but he haue þis cloþinge, ne no man may haue þis clothe, but if he come to heuen.[17]

The clothing of virtue, the brideclothes – surely Chaucer's Parson has earned these spiritual garments.

While we cannot know what the Parson wears as a traveling costume en route to Canterbury, we can nevertheless be certain that he is not clothed in *False Vestments* because Chaucer emphasizes, with a statement and restatement, the Parson's spiritual authenticity: 'first he wroghte, and afterward he taughte' (line 497); and 'He taughte, but first he folwed it hymselve' (line 528). Fortunately, the Parson's teachings on the subject of humility are available: he defines *humility* or *meekness*, which he employs as a synonym for humility, as the 'remedie' against the sin of Pride, virtues that oblige a person to be always mindful of his own spiritual 'freletee'. Further, he enumerates at length the aspects of humility or meekness in such detail (X, lines 474–82) that we comprehend why the heavenly reward for being 'poor in spirit' and meek is to enter the kingdom of heaven and to possess the land, according to Matt. 5:3–4.

If Chaucer's Parson dramatizes the medieval concept that each soul is clothed according to and in its spiritual health, *clannes*,[18] or, conversely, in filthiness, depending on the soul's 'habits',[19] then we must assume that his garments are not 'bismotered', and that he does not wear a torn hat or anything concomitant with a harlot's hood, as mentioned in the opening passage of *Cleanness* by the *Pearl* Poet.[20] Chaucer's Parson bears no resemblance to those priests mentioned in the 'Ballad Against Excess in Apparel, Especially in the Clergy', described as 'poope holy prestis full of presomcion', who wear 'wyde fueryd hodes' against the instruction in their own preaching, as well as

neoplatonicien de la veture', in *Augustinus Magister, Congrès international augustinien, Paris*, Septembre 1954 (Paris, [1954–55]), pp. 293–306.

17 *The English Works of Wyclif Hitherto Unprinted*, ed. F. D. Matthew, EETS, OS 74 (London, 1880), p. 351. Brideclothes are discussed in *C&C*, p. 9.

18 See discussion of *clannes*, pp. 40, 45 74, 109–10.

19 A costume metaphor previously discussed in *C&C*, pp. 7–13, 15–17.

20 Signs of sin in *Cleanness*, in *Pearl, Cleanness, Patience, Sir Gawain and the Green Knight*, eds A. C. Cawley and J. J. Anderson (London, 1976), pp. 51–2, lines 5–16, 29–38.

short tunics, larger hats, fashionable padded doublets, and plaid gowns, practices that lessen the devotion among their congregation.[21] Nor will he need the words to make a confession for pride of dress such as these included in *The Clensyng of Mannes Soule*:

> Also for pompe and pride I haue be to curiouse in myn owne apparaile *and* in oþere mennes in vsy*n*g more ricchesse in aray of cloþing. perri pelour and oþer*e* wiseþ an my power was. or [my] degre or staat askid/ Also in makyng myn arai more semeli more schapli to oþer*e* mennes siʒt. for þis entent and such entent et *cetera*.[22]

And we may also assume that he properly and honestly wears the required pristine church vestments while he says Mass, unlike the sinful priests described by the *Pearl* Poet who hide their spiritual filth under clean holy garments (*Cleanness*, lines 5–16). In contrast, the Parson's holy vestments would convey to those attending Mass a visual message that is true. He is also the spiritual opposite of Langland's false preaching friars who dress in rich copes (*P.P.B*, Prologue, lines 58–65), and of the priest-Parson Sloth, prior to his repentance (*P.P.B*, Passus 5, lines 385–440).

In the life-pilgrimage of his daily ministry, symbolized in his walking staff, it is clear that the Parson has received and derived full benefit from a blessing that is part of a 'liturgy for departing pilgrims': such a pilgrim kneels then rises to receive from the bishop a pilgrim scrip and a walking staff. As the presentation of the staff is made, the bishop or priest says,

> In the name of our Lord Jesus Christ, . . . 'Receive . . . this staff, the support of your jou[r]ney and the labour of the path of your pilgrimage, so that you may overcome all the traps of the enemy and arrive safely at the shrine of the blessed apostle Peter and Paul [and others] which you desire to reach, and having completed the appointed course return to us joyfully. With the aid of Our Lord'.[23]

---

21 'Ballad Against Excess in Apparel, Especially in the Clergy', *Satirical Songs and Poems on Costume: From the 13th to the 19th Century*, ed. F. W. Fairholt (London, 1849), pp. 55–7.

22 Included in Walter Kennedy Everett, 'A Critical Edition of the Confession Section of *The Clensyng of Mannes Soule*', Diss., University of North Carolina at Chapel Hill, 1974, p. 80; see above, Chapter 1, n. 92, concerning this work.

23 Quoted by Diana Webb, in *Pilgrims and Pilgrimage in the Medieval West* (London, 1999), p. 47, citing the Missal of Vich, of 1038, and *Peregrinaciones*, 3, pp. 146–7.

10

Conclusion

The polysemous reading I have previously espoused[1] for Chaucer's portrayal of the lay pilgrims in the *General Prologue* may be even more helpful when employed in comprehending the portraits of those pilgrims in holy orders or otherwise in service and/or associated in a variety of ways with the medieval church. Heightened signification occurs because the church itself set a standard of morals and behavior, and authors of religious rules and institutional dress codes incorporated within their works the details of costume that they expected would be both behavioral habits and sartorial habits exemplary of this standard, or to proper variation within it, according to the various orders. Thus, in contrast with Chaucer's other pilgrims, the particular group of pilgrims treated within this volume – the folk of 'Holy Church' – were socially and spiritually bound by an additional set of costume rules. Ideally, at the highest level of social and spiritual expectation and per-formance, such pilgrims so closely affiliated with the church would have exemplified holiness, wearing holy habits and professional dress – with many garments designating a specific religious and symbolic value, their dress habits truthfully representing their life and spiritual habits.

In *Chaucer and Costume: The Secular Pilgrims in the General Prologue*, I reached four conclusions concerning Chaucer's pattern of costume rhetoric derived from a study of his depictions of lay costumes; and, although dress standards set by the church add an additional rhetorical dimension, these con-clusions hold true for the costume rhetoric in Chaucer's descriptions of pil-grims vocationally affiliated with the church. Those four conclusions are:

1. that Chaucer's costume rhetoric 'is Gothic[2] in its variety';

---

[1] Throughout [*C&C*], summarized in Chapter 10.

[2] Discussed in *C&C*, p. 21. Arnold Hauser, in *The Social History of Art* I (New York, 1952), pp. 272–3, defines *Gothic* as pertaining to art:

The basic form of Gothic art is juxtaposition. . . . it is always the principle of expansion and not of concentration, of co-ordination and not of subordination, of the open sequence and not of the closed geometric form, by which it is

2. that when he selects traditional costume motifs, he 'enhances them with enriched meaning' and he also generates new garment imagery;
3. that he is discriminating in his choice of diction;
4. that 'the scope of Chaucer's costume rhetoric is broader' than it had earlier appeared to be.

Within the grouping of the pilgrims foregrounded in this book, these previously discussed conclusions remain valid regarding religious habits, but with different applications, as pointed out in Chapter 1 and explained in succeeding chapters.

Firstly, Chaucer's verbal pictures of holy habits and professional dress for this group of pilgrims illustrate the variation in, and deviation from, the equating of inner spirituality with its outward manifestation in dress as mentioned above. The prescribed religious costumes, as may be seen in Chapter 1, are Gothic in their variety, and Chaucer does justice to this diversity in his evocation of colors, fabrics, construction details, and ornamentation.

Without specific terms being mentioned, certain colors – black, brown, gray, and white – are obviously evoked when Chaucer mentions or suggests any religious order. For example, in the case of the Benedictine Prioress, we, as did Chaucer's contemporary audience, know without being told that her mantle and overveil are black, and her underveil and wimple are white. For this austere black and white ensemble Chaucer provides vivid accents in the coral and green rosary and its gold pendant. The Monk's costume, also, is assumedly black although its color, too, is unstated. Touches of color relieve this sober darkness – the gray of the *grys* purfiling on his sleeves, and the gold shine of his 'ful curious pyn'. Chaucer is noncommital about the order to which the Friar belongs, and as a result, and by means of the Friar's verbal portrait, he summons to mind – and lambasts – all fraternal orders whether they wear brown, black, gray, or white. Similarly, the Pardoner's ecclesiastical costume, so far as Chaucer tells us, is colorless, as is his Summoner-companion's, lacking identifiable livery colors. And finally, in the case of the Parson, Chaucer's failure to give him a costume also means that he provides no color imagery; Chaucer's contemporary readers would mentally dress this good priest in accordance with customary practice, while modern readers of allegory may clothe him in his translucent saintly behavior. As for the academics, who are most likely in either major or minor holy orders, Chaucer bestows both red and blue garments upon the Doctor of Phisik, the colors most often given to physicians depicted in the visual arts and representative of their social and professional status. However, he provides no color imagery

dominated. . . . Gothic art leads the onlooker from one detail to another and causes him . . . to 'unravel' the successive parts of the work one after the other.

to relieve the threadbare condition of the Clerk's courtepy, although if one accepts the theorized German etymology (see Chapter 6, p. 167), this short garment is 'pied', thus having at least two shades or colors,[3] although they are unnamed. Clearly, Chaucer's bestowal of color imagery within this group of pilgrim portraits is discretionary. If he mentions no particular holy order or color, he may yet verbally tint friars, pardoners, and summoners with a degree of darkness commensurate with his portraits' contexts. In a reversal of this effect, the Parson's non- costume paints him in his lack of Pride and in the resultant glow of his Humility, Charity, and Wisdom.

In addition to his judicious evocation of colors for religious habits and professional or academic dress, Chaucer is particular in his naming, or omitting the names, of fabrics and their quality. He mentions no fabric for the Prioress; her cloak is 'ful fetys', and that speaks adequately for quality. The Monk wears garments whose fabrics are unnamed, leaving the reader to surmise that they are constructed from the standard monks' cloth, but his sleeves are purfiled with *grys* described as the 'fynest of a lond'. More specific, the Friar's garments are made of double worsted, a medium-priced woolen, qualitatively described, perhaps ironically, as the equivalent of fabric worn by a master or a pope, although this characterization still does not take it out of the range of middle price and quality. Meanwhile, Chaucer emphasizes the affluence of the Doctor in specifying that he dresses in '*sangwyn* and in *pers*', terms that most likely signify woolen cloth dyed in red and blue, made into garments lined with the silks called *taffeta* and *sendal* in either matching or contrasting colors. This is a costume that might constitute the 'robes riche' eschewed by the Clerk. We cannot know the fabric used in the Clerk's courtepy, but Chaucer makes clear this fabric's threadbare quality at the time of the pilgrimage; whatever its quality when newly woven, this substance has not withstood wear over time. Clearly, in Chaucer's attributions of fabrics and their qualities, both socio-economic and spiritual qualities are manifest, although, for these members of the church, the economic implications of their costumes are subservient to any moral inferences that might be drawn.

Chaucer also provides evocative garment construction and ornamentation details. With his phrase 'ful fetys' he tells us that the Prioress's cloak is both constructed in the correct style and fabric and that it is very well-made, as required for propriety. Following this, and in the order of deepening criticism, Chaucer bestows upon the Monk an outer garment with *grys* purfiling the sleeve that, while not a departure from current custom among *religieux*, nevertheless fails to display the standard of plainness advocated by the

---

3   When such a courtepy was new and fashionable, the hose customarily worn with it would have been bi- or multi-colored as well.

Benedictine Rule. Further, the exact nature of the Monk's gold 'pyn' is undetermined; we cannot *know* if it is a religious fraternal emblem, only an old-fashioned garment fastening, or a personal object illustrating his pride. In the Friar's portrait, however, Chaucer's criticism escalates in describing the Friar's double worsted 'semycope' that is too short and fashioned in a round bell-like style. Beyond that, the Friar's tippet, possibly perfect in construction, is perverted in its peddler usage. Additionally, the Pardoner fails to wear proper headcovering, constituting the flouting of ecclesiastical dress regulations; and his companion, the Summoner, who likely would have been dressed in his Archdeacon's livery, carries this flouting of proper headgear to the extreme in his wearing of an oversized garland. In garment construction, the Doctor's robes include linings of silken fabric evocative of the east, where both these fabrics and so much medieval medical knowledge originated. Chaucer does not tell us that other garments in the *General Prologue* are lined, but we might speculate that the Monk's *grys* purfiling signifies, as was customary, a fur lining of less expensive fur – perhaps lamb or coney (rabbit). As for the poor scholar, the Clerk, we know only that his courtepy is likely to be short and it is in need of replacement. All of these construction and ornamentation details speak to the question of order within the church and as represented among these members of the church – each pilgrim as verbally constructed by the poet-narrator, and ultimately fashioned by Chaucer himself. These pilgrims make up the social and spiritual fabric of Chaucer's literary church.

With regard to my second conclusion – Chaucer's costume rhetoric for the pilgrims discussed in this book necessarily had to work within and against the official dress codes of religious orders and institutions, and therefore, the traditional motifs of religious garments are present in his portraits, although he enhances these images with details and sometimes entirely reinterprets them. At the same time, he highlights details that convey his criticism of ongoing practice in the church, while he avoids the adoption of a critical tone of high dudgeon when describing religious costume. Instead, the range of his costume sketches stretches from the uncostumed Parson, in context signifying this priest's lack of interest in earthly treasures, to the Prioress, who wishes to be reverenced and who, to this end, surely wears a proper habit. Alternatively, he portrays the Monk, who dresses in accordance with more lenient practices of his time in garments illustrative of an 'outrider' for his cell, although this deviates from strict ascetic standards; then Chaucer tops this deviation with the perversion of the Friar's habit utilized as peddler's garb.

As mentioned in my third conclusion, Chaucer's diction is discriminating both in his addition and expansion of images of costume in the canon of religious dress, images later adopted by other authors. Further, he is never more rhetorically careful than when he is withholding information. Having earlier described the Prioress and Monk as Benedictines, Chaucer becomes less forthcoming in his designation of holy orders, beginning with the Friar. As interesting as the Friar's costume might be in its fabric, style, and knife- and pin-filled tippet, we cannot tell from Chaucer's description which order of friars Huberd represents. Thus Chaucer deflects his castigation of Huberd, a kind of ur-friar, among all friars. Similarly, we know nothing of the religious order, nor even what type of ecclesiastic the Pardoner might be, and his disarray illustrates his lack of specific conformity; as a result, pardoners in general are enveloped in the taint of Roncivale. The Summoner further depicts this disorder, illustrating the axiom that the wage of dissolute behaviour is disease, a concept highlighted, even celebrated, by his huge garland. The Summoner's description includes no livery with designating colors, nor any authoritative badge of the archdeaconate he represents. Thus visually, he, too, constitutes a general criticism of church laxity.

In the portrait of the Doctor of Phisik Chaucer provides color, fabric, and construction images, enough to establish that this physician is economically well-off and to place him within the satirical category of greedy physicians, but not detailed enough to place him within any particular holy order, although a profession of vows is likely, or to designate him a graduate of any particular medieval university. In a reversal of this procedure, Chaucer states that the Clerk is from Oxenford. Beyond that, the Clerk appears to be an example of the medieval 'poor scholar' or poor logician and to be of indeterminate age. His layman's courtepy – a single threadbare garment – illustrates his economic poverty, and may well, in allegorical parlance, illuminate his educational and/or spiritual poverty. As this brief list makes clear, fresh and innovative costume details appear in each of these portraits as Chaucer deploys precise diction where he chooses and leaves provocative descriptive lacunae elsewhere.

Concerning my fourth conclusion regarding the broader scope of Chaucer's costume rhetoric, these characters from the medieval church mingle with the lay pilgrims in Chaucer's *General Prologue*, and illustrate the Wycliffite complaint made by William Thorpe against pilgrimages:

> I knowe wel þat whanne dyuerse men and wymmen wolen goen þus aftir her owne willis and fyndingis out on pilgrimageyngis, þei wolen ordeyne beforehonde to haue wiþ hem boþe men and wymmen þat kunnen wel synge rowtinge songis, and also summe of þese pilgrimes wolen haue wiþ hem baggepipis so þat in eche toun þat þei comen þoru3, what wiþ noyse of her syngynge, and wiþ þe soun of her pipinge, and wiþ þe gingelynge of her Cantirbirie bellis, and wiþ þe berkynge out of dogges aftir hem, þese maken more noyse þan if þe king came þere awey wiþ his clarioneris and manye oþer mynstrals. And if þese men and wymmen ben a moneþe oute in her pilgrymage, manye of hem an half 3eere aftir schulen be greete iangelers, tale tellers and lyeris.

Archbishop Arundel disputed this complaint in his reply:

Lewid losel, þou seest not fer inowȝ in þis mateer, for þou considrist not þe grete traueil of pilgrymes, and þerfore þou blamest þat þing þat is preisable. I seie to þee þat is rizt wel don þat pilgrimes haue wiþ hem boþe syngeris and also baggepipes, þat, whanne oon of hem þat gon barfot smytiþ his too aȝens a stoon and hurtiþ him soore and makiþ him blede, it is wel done þat he or his felowe take þanne vp a songe, eiþer ellis take out of her bosum a baggepipe for to dryue awei wiþ siche myrþe þe hurt of his sore, for wiþ sich solace þe traueile and werinesse of pilgrymes is liȝtli and myrili brouȝt forþ.[4]

These passages are alive with the details, especially in aural images, of such a mingling of pilgrims, but they give no description of fabrics, colors, or garment styles. Chaucer supplies those details and, deliberately or not, forms his costume descriptions in accordance with Geoffrey de Vinsauf's procedural directions for amplification – that are themselves couched in costume metaphors:

If you choose an amplified form, proceed first of all by this step: although the meaning is one, let it not come content with one set of apparel. Let it vary its robes and assume different raiment. Let it take up again in other words what has already been said; let it reiterate in a number of clauses, a single thought. Let one and the same thing be concealed under multiple forms – be varied and yet the same.[5]

While Geoffrey de Vinsauf counsels presentation of a single idea in various guises, Thomas Malory's Balyn, advises observers to pay attention to the diverse qualities within each person:

worthynes and good tacchis [qualities, habits] and also good dedis is not only in arayments, but manhode and worship [ys hyd] within a mannes person; and many a worshipfull knyght ys nat knowyn unto all peple. And therefore worship and hardynesse ys nat in araymente.[6]

These two sets of directions offer instructions for the author seeking to achieve a single effect through amplification and for a reader who should comprehend that creative methodology and decode the author's descriptions. Just as 'worship and hardynesse [or any other virtue] ys nat in arayments', so too must a reader determine just how and what a description of costume communicates within a character portrait. The reading of Chaucer's costume

---

4 From William Thorpe's autobiography in *Two Wycliffite Texts: The Sermon of William Taylor 1406, The Testimony of William Thorpe 1407*, ed. Anne Hudson, EETS, OS 301 (Oxford, 1993), pp. 64–5.
5 'The *Poetria Nova* of Geoffrey of Vinsauf', in *Medieval Eloquence*, ed. James J. Murphy (Berkeley, CA, 1978), lines 219–25.
6 From 'The Knight with the Two Swords', by Thomas Malory, in *Malory: Works*, ed. Eugène Vinaver, 2nd edn (Oxford, 1977), p. 39.

rhetoric depicting his literary folk of the church is especially complex because nearly every garment worn signifies a prescribed holy and symbolic value within the spiritual ideation of the medieval church.[7] As a result, an author could set up a conflict between the value traditionally represented by a particular religious or professional garment and the actions of the character wearing it, as Chaucer does in his depictions of the Friar's tippet and the Pardoner's vernicle, to mention only two blatant examples. In contrast, because the literally uncostumed Parson demonstrates his love for God and mankind through his actions, we can therefore know that he is dressed and enclosed in divine love as described in garment imagery by Julian of Norwich: 'He is our clotheing, that for love wrappeth us, halsyth us and all becloseth us for tender love, that He may never leeve us.'[8]

---

7 For example, see Chapter 1, n. 25, and Chapter 2, nn. 55–6 regarding the symbolic meaning given to each garment in a nun's habit; Chapter 2, nn. 49–50 describing the significance of color and fabric choices in headdresses in the *Rule of Syon*; Chapter 2, n. 112 concerning the cloak as symbol of religious faith; Chapter 1, n. 41, and Chapter 4, p. 121, nn. 49–50 regarding the description of the pilch as signifying man's fallen nature and man's innocence purchased by Christ; Chapter 4, n. 13 concerned with the cincture representing chastity; Chapter 5, nn. 13–14 describing the ethos of the Franciscan habit as it represents evangelical poverty; and Chapter 8, p. 247, n. 71 depicting holy habits as the visible symbol of holy vows, with color selections that further this symbolism.
    Also see Chapter 2, n. 55 for the metaphoric depiction of virtue-jewel-bedecked robes of St Agnes.
8 *The Shewings of Julian of Norwich*, ed. Georgia Ronan Crampton, TEAMS Middle English Texts Series (Kalamazoo, MI, 1993), Chapter 5, p. 43.

Works Cited

Editions of Chaucer's Works

The Complete Works of Geoffrey Chaucer. Ed. Revd Walter W. Skeat. 6 vols. Oxford, 1894.
The Poetical Works of Chaucer. Ed. F. N. Robinson. Boston, 1957.
The Riverside Chaucer. 3rd edn. Ed. Larry D. Benson. Boston, 1987.

General Bibliography

Alan of Lille. *Anticlaudianus, or The Good and Perfect Man.* Trans. James J. Sheridan. Toronto, 1973.
———. *The Plaint of Nature.* Trans. and commentary, James J. Sheridan. Pontifical Institute of Mediaeval Studies. Toronto, 1980.
Alanus de Insulis. *The Complaint of Nature.* Trans. Douglas M. Moffat. New York, 1908.
Alcock, John. *(Spousage of a Virgin to Christ): An Exhortacyon Made to Relygyous Systers.* The English Experience, no. 638. Westmynstre (Wynken de Worde), n.d.; Norwood, NJ, 1974.
Aldhelm. 'The Prose *De Virginitate*'. *Aldhelm: The Prose Works.* Ed. and trans. Michael Lapidge and Michael Herren. Cambridge, 1979.
Alford, John A. 'Medicine in the Middle Ages; The Theory of a Profession'. *The Centennial Review* 23 (1979): 377–96.
Alighieri, Dante. *La Commedia, Inferno.* Vol. 2. Ed. Arnoldo Mondadori. 1966.
———. *The Divine Comedy.* Trans. and commentary, John D. Sinclair. New York, 1981.
———. *The Divine Comedy: Inferno.* Trans. and commentary, Charles S. Singleton. Bollingen Series, no. 80. Princeton, 1970.
———. *La Vita Nuova.* Trans. Barbara Reynolds. Harmondsworth, 1969; rpt. 1975.
An Alphabet of Tales, An English 15th Century Translation of the Alphabetum Narrationum once attributed to Etienne de Besancon. Ed. M. M. Banks. EETS, OS 126. London, 1904.
The Ancrene Riwle. Trans. M. B. Salu. Introduction, Dom Gerard Sitwell O.S.B. Preface, J. R. R. Tolkien. London, 1955.
The Ancrene Riwle. Ed. and trans. M. B. Salu. Notre Dame, 1956.
Ancren Riwle: A Treatise on the Rules and Duties of Monastic Life. Ed. and trans. James Morton. London, 1853.
Ancrene Wisse. Ed. J. R. R. Tolkien. EETS, OS 249. London, 1962.
Andere, Mary. *Old Needlework Boxes and Tools.* Plymouth, 1971.
Andrew, Malcolm. Explanatory notes. *A Variorum Edition of the Works of Geoffrey*

Chaucer, Volume II: The Canterbury Tales, The General Prologue. Pt One B. Norman, OK, 1993.

The Anglo-Saxon Legends of St Andrew and St Veronica. Ed. Charles Wycliffe Goodwin. Cambridge, 1851.

Armstrong, Nancy. *Jewellery: An Historical Survey of British Styles and Jewels.* Guildford, 1973.

Astell, Ann. *Chaucer and the Universe of Learning.* Ithaca, NY, 1996.

———. *The Song of Songs in the Middle Ages.* Ithaca, NY, 1990.

Atchley, E. G. Cuthbert F. 'On English Liturgical Colours'. *Essays on Ceremonial.* Ed. Vernon Staley. London, 1904, 87–176.

Aungier, George James. *History and Antiquities of Syon Monastery, the Parish of Isleworth, and the Chapelry of Hounslow.* [London], 1840.

Backhouse, Janet. *Medieval Manuscripts in the British Library: The Luttrell Psalter.* New York, 1990.

Baines's Account of the Woollen Manufacture of England. Introduction, Kenneth G. Ponting. New York, 1970.

Baldwin, Frances Elizabeth. *Sumptuary Legislation and Personal Regulation in England.* John Hopkins University Studies in Historical and Political Science Series 44, no. 1. Baltimore, 1926.

Baldwin, John W. *Aristocratic Life in Medieval France.* Baltimore, 2000.

'Ballad Against Excess in Apparel, Especially in the Clergy'. *Satirical Songs and Poems on Costume: From the 13th to the 19th Century.* Ed. F. W. Fairholt. London, 1849, 55–7.

Barron, Caroline M. 'Anniversary Address at the Guildhall'. *Transactions of the Ancient Monuments Society,* New Series 23 (1978): 17–24.

———. *The Medieval Guildhall of London.* London, 1974.

Barthes, Roland. 'The Imagination of the Sign'. *Critical Essays.* Trans. Richard Howard. Evanston, IL, 1972, 205–11.

Bartlett, Anne Clark. ' "Delicious Matyr": Feminine Courtesy in Middle English Devotional Literature for Women'. *Essays in Medieval Studies* 9 (1992): 9–18.

Beck, S. William. *The Draper's Dictionary.* London, 1882.

Beichner, Paul. 'Daun Piers, Monk and Business Administrator'. *Speculum* 34 (1959): 611–19.

The Benedictines in Britain. British Library Series 3. London, 1980.

Bennett, H. S. 'Medieval Literature and the Modern Reader'. *E&S* 31 (1945): 7–18.

Bennett, J. A. W. *Chaucer at Oxford and at Cambridge.* Oxford, 1974.

Benson, C. David. 'The Astrological Medicine of Chaucer's Physician and Nicholas of Lynn's *Kalendarium'. AN&Q* 22.5–6 (1984): 62–6.

Besserman, Lawrence. 'Chaucer and the Pope of Double Worsted'. *ChauN* 1.1 (1979): 15–16.

———. 'Girdles, Belts, and Cords: A Leitmotif in Chaucer's *General Prologue'. PLL* 22 (1986): 322–5.

Bettmann, Otto L. *A Pictorial History of Medicine.* Springfield, IL, 1962.

Binski, Paul. *The Painted Chamber at Westminster.* London, 1986.

Bishop, W. J. 'Notes on the History of Medical Costume'. *Annals of Medical History,* n.s. 6.3 (May 1934): 193–218.

Bloomfield, Morton W. *Piers Plowman as a Fourteenth-Century Apocalypse.* New Brunswick, NJ, 1962.

Boccaccio, Giovanni. *The Decameron.* Trans. J. M. Rigg. Vol. 2. 1930; London, 1973.

Boethius. *The Consolation of Philosophy.* Trans. Richard Green. The Library of Liberal Arts. Indianapolis, IN, 1980.

'The Book of Physiognomy'. *The World of Piers Plowman.* Eds and trans. Jeanne Krochalis and Edward Peters. Philadelphia, 1975, 218–28.

The Book of Vices and Virtues: a Fourteenth Century English Translation of the Somme Le Roi of Lorens D'Orleans. Ed. W. Nelson Francis. EETS, OS 217. London, 1942.

Book to a Mother: An Edition with Commentary. Ed. Adrian James McCarthy. Salzburg, 1981.

Bowden, Muriel. *A Commentary on the General Prologue to the Canterbury Tales.* 2nd edn. New York, 1967.

————. *A Reader's Guide to Geoffrey Chaucer.* New York, 1971.

Boyd, Beverly. 'Chaucer's Prioress: Her Green Gauds'. *MLQ* 11 (1950): 404–16.

Braddy, Haldeen. *Geoffrey Chaucer: Literary and Historical Studies.* Port Washington, NY, 1971.

Bradley, Sr Ritamary. 'Metaphors of Cloth and Clothing in the Showings of Julian of Norwich'. *Mediaevalia* 9 (1983): 269–82.

Bragg, Lois. 'Disfigurement, Disability, and Disintegration in *Sturlunga* Saga'. *alvissmál* 4 (1994): 15–32.

Bressie, Ramona. ' "A Governour Wily and Wys" '. *MLN* 54.7 (1939): 477–90.

Breward, Christopher. *The Culture of Fashion.* Manchester, 1995.

Bridbury, A. R. *Medieval English Clothmaking: An Economic Survey.* London, 1982.

Brocchieri, Mariateresa Fumagalli Beonio. 'The Intellectual'. *Medieval Callings.* Trans. Lydia G. Cochrane. Chicago, 1990, 181–210.

Brosnahan, Leger. 'The Pendant in the Chaucer Portraits'. *ChauR* 26.4 (1992): 424–31.

Broughton, Laurel. Catalogue of Medieval Miracles of the Virgin. <http://ferment.umdl.umich.edu/cgi/b/bib/bib-idx?c=marym;cc=marym>.

Bullough, Vern L. *The Development of Medicine as a Profession: The Contribution of the Medieval University to Modern Medicine.* Basel, 1966.

Burnham, Dorothy K. *Cut My Cote.* Ontario, 1973.

Burns, E. Jane. 'Ladies Don't Wear *Braies*: Underwear in the French Prose *Lancelot*'. *The Lancelot-Grail Cycle.* Ed. William W. Kibler. Austin, TX, 1994, 152–74.

Buxton, L. H. Dudley, and Strickland Gibson. *Oxford University Ceremonies.* Oxford, 1935.

Caesarius of Heisterbach. *The Dialogue on Miracles.* Vol. I. Trans. H. Von E. Scott and C. C. Swinton Bland. London, 1929.

Calendar Inquisitions Misc.: 1377–88. London, 1957.

Calendar of Wills Proved and Enrolled in the Court of Husting, London, A.D. 1258–A.D. 1688. Ed. Reginald R. Sharpe. 2 vols. London, 1889–90.

Cambridge History of Western Textiles. Vol. 1. Ed. David Jenkins. Cambridge, 2003.

Camille, Michael. *Gothic Art: Glorious Visions.* New York, 1996.

Campbell, Marian. 'Gold, Silver and Precious Stones'. *English Medieval Industries: Craftsmen, Techniques, Products.* Eds John Blair and Nigel Ramsay. London, 1991, 107–66.

Candon, Sr Mary Patrick. '*The Doctrine of the Hert*, Edited from the Manuscripts with Introduction and Notes'. Diss., Fordham University, 1963.

Carr, Annemarie Weyl. 'Threads of Authority: The Virgin Mary's Veil in the Middle Ages'. *Robes and Honor: The Medieval World of Investiture*. Ed. Stewart Gordon. New York, 2001, 59–93.

Carter, John. *Specimens of English Ecclesiastical Costume: From the Earliest Period Down to the Sixteenth Century*. London, 1817.

Cartwright, Frederick F. *A Social History of Medicine*. New York, 1977.

Carus-Wilson, E. M. *Medieval Merchant Adventurers: Collected Studies*. 2nd edn. London, 1967.

Casagrande, Carla, and Silvana Becchio. 'Clercs et jongleurs dans la société medievale (XIIe–XIIIe siècles)'. *Annales économies, sociétés, civilisations* 34.5 (1979): 913–28.

Cathedral and City: St Albans Ancient and Modern. Ed. Robert Runcie. London, 1977.

Catholic Encyclopedia. Online edn. Ed. Kevin Knight. 1999.

Chance, Jane. ' "Disfigured Is Thy Face": Chaucer's Pardoner and the Protean Shape-Shifter Fals-Semblant'. *PQ* 67 (1988): 423–35.

———. *The Mythographic Chaucer: The Fabulation of Sexual Politics*. Minneapolis, MN, 1995.

Chapters of the Augustinian Canons. Ed. H. E. Salter. Canterbury & York Society. [Woodbridge], 1922.

Chaucer Life-Records. Eds Martin M. Crow and Clair C. Olson. Austin, TX, 1966.

Chism, Christine N. ' "I Demed Hym Som Chanoun For To Be".' *Chaucer's Pilgrims: An Historical Guide to the Pilgrims in The Canterbury Tales*. Eds Laura C. Lambdin and Robert T. Lambdin. Westport, CT, 1996, 340–56.

Chrétien de Troyes. *Erec et Enide. Arthurian Romances*. Trans. W. W. Comfort. New York, 1975.

———. *Perceval. Arthurian Romances*. Trans. D. D. R. Owen. Everyman's Library. Rutland, VT, 1987; rpt. 1991.

———. *Perceval: The Story of the Grail*. Trans. Nigel Bryant. Cambridge, 1982.

———. *Yvain. Arthurian Romances*. Trans. W. W. Comfort. New York, 1975.

Christine of Pisan. *The Eipstle of Othea to Hector: or the Boke of Knyghthode*. Trans. Stephen Scrope. Ed. George F. Warner. London, 1904.

Cigman, Gloria. 'Chaucer and the Goats of Creation'. *L&T* 5 (1991): 162–80.

Clark, John Willis, ed. and trans. *The Observances in use at the Augustinian Priory of S. Giles and S. Andrew at Barnwell, Cambridgeshire*. Cambridge, 1897.

Clark-Maxwell, Revd W. G. 'The Outfit for the Profession of an Austin Canoness at Lacock, Wilts. in the Year 1395, and Other Memoranda'. *Archaeol J* 69, 2nd series 16 (1912): 117–24.

Clarke, E. C. 'College Caps and Doctors' Hats'. *Archaeol J* 61 (1904): 33–73.

———. 'English Academical Costume (Mediæval)'. *Archaeol J* 1 [50] (1893): 73–104, 137–49, 183–209.

Cleanness. Pearl, Cleanness, Patience, Sir Gawain and the Green Knight. Eds A. C. Cawley and J. J. Anderson. London, 1976.

The Clerk's Book of 1549. Ed. J. Wickham Legg. London, 1903.

Clode, C. M., comp. *Memorials of the Guild of Merchant Taylors*. London, 1875.

Colby, Alice. *The Portrait in Twelfth-Century French Literature*. Geneva, 1965.

Condren, Edward I. 'The Pardoner's Bid for Existence'. *Viator* 4 (1973): 177–205.

Conrad, Lawrence I., Michael Neve, Vivian Nutton, Roy Porter, and Andrew Wear. *The Western Medical Tradition: 800 BC to AD 1800*. Cambridge, 1995.

Corley, Brigitte. *Painting and Patronage in Cologne 1300–1500*. Turnhout, 2000.

Corrigan, Peter. 'Interpreted, Circulating, Interpreting: The Three Dimensions of the Clothing Object'. *The Socialness of Things: Essays on the Socio-Semiotics of Objects*. Ed. Stephen Harold Riggings. Berlin, 1994, 435–49.

Coulton, G. G. *The Chronicler of European Chivalry*. London, 1930.

——. *Five Centuries of Religion*. 4 vols. Cambridge, 1923–50.

——, trans. and annotator. *Life in the Middle Ages*. Vols 1–2. Cambridge, 1967.

——. *Medieval Panorama*. New York, 1944.

——. *Social Life in Britain from the Conquest to the Reformation*. Cambridge, 1918.

——. *Studies in Medieval Thought*. New York, 1965.

——. *Ten Medieval Studies*. Cambridge, 1930.

The Court of Love. The Poetical Works of Geoffrey Chaucer. Ed. R. Morris. London, 1866.

Courtenay, William J. 'Curers of Body and Soul: Medical Doctors as Theologians'. *Religion and Medicine in the Middle Ages*. Eds Peter Biller and Joseph Ziegler. York Studies in Medieval Theology 3. York, 2001, 69–75.

——. *Schools & Scholars in Fourteenth-Century England*. Princeton, 1987.

Craik, T. W. *The Tudor Interlude*. Leicester, 1958.

Crane, Susan. *The Performance of Self: Ritual, Clothing and Identity During the Hundred Years War*. Philadelphia, 2002.

Crawfurd, Raymond. *Plague and Pestilence in Literature and Art*. Oxford, 1914.

Cross, J. E. 'Saint-Omer 202 as the Manuscript Source for the Old English Texts'. *Two Old English Apocrypha and their Manuscript Sources*. Eds J. E. Cross et al. Cambridge, 1996, 82–104.

Cross, J. E., Denis Brearley, and Andy Orchard, trans. '*Vindicta saluatoris*: Latin text and translation; *Vindicta saluatoris*: Old English text and translation'. *Two Old English Apocrypha and their Manuscript Sources*. Eds J. E. Cross et al. Cambridge, 1996, 248–93.

Cunningham, D. J. *The Evolution of the Graduation Ceremony*. Edinborough, 1904.

Cunnington, C. Willett, and Phillis Cunnington. *Handbook of English Mediaeval Costume*. London, 1952.

Cunnington, C. W., and P. E., and Charles Beard. *A Dictionary of English Costume: 900–1900*. London, 1960.

Cunnington, Phillis, and Catherine Lucas. *Charity Costumes of Children, Scolars, Almsfolk, Pensioners*. London, 1978.

Curry, Walter Clyde. *Chaucer and the Mediaeval Sciences*. 2nd edn. New York, 1960.

Cutts, Edward L. *Scenes & Characters of the Middle Ages*. 7th edn. London, 1930.

The Cyrugie of Guy de Chauliac I. Ed. M. S. Ogden. EETS, OS 265. 1971.

Daichman, Graciela S. *Wayward Nuns in Medieval Literature*. Syracuse, NY, 1986.

The Dance of Death. Ed. Florence Warren. EETS, OS 181. London, 1931; New York, 1971.

Dane, Joseph A. 'The Prioress and Her *Romanzen*'. *ChauR* 24 (1990): 219–22.

Danish Medieval Art website. <www.danish-medieval-art.net>.

Dauby, Hélène. 'In Sangwyn and in pers: Les Coleurs dans le prologue général des *Canterbury Tales*'. *Les Couleurs au Moyen Age*. Aix-en-Provence, 1988, 47–56.

Davis, R. Evan. 'The Pendant in the Chaucer Portraits'. *ChauR* 17 (1982): 193–5.

Decalogus evangelice paupertatis. Ed. Michael Bihl. *Archivum Franciscanum Historicum* 32 (1939): 330–411.

Deevy, Mary B. *Medieval ring brooches in Ireland: A study of jewellery, dress and society*. Monograph Series no. 1. Wicklow, 1998.

Demus, Otto. *Byzantine Art and the West*. New York, 1970.

Dennys, Rodney. *The Heraldic Imagination*. London, 1975.

Derbes, Anne, and Mark Sandona. ' "Ave charitate plena": Variations on the Theme of Charity in the Arena Chapel'. *Speculum* 76 (2001): 599–637.

A Dictionary of Christian Antiquities. 2 vols. Eds William Smith and Samuel Cheetham. Hartford, CT, 1880; rpt. New York, 1968.

Dillon, Bert. ' "A Clerk Ther Was of Oxenford Also" '. *Chaucer's Pilgrims: An Historical Guide to the Pilgrims in The Canterbury Tales*. Eds Laura C. Lambdin and Robert T. Lambdin. Westport, CT, 1996, 108–15.

'A Disputation between a Christian and a Jew'. *The Minor Poems of the Vernon MS*. Pt 2. Ed. F. J. Furnivall. EETS, OS 117. London, 1901, 484–93.

Dodwell, C. R. *Painting in Europe 800–1200*. Harmondsworth, 1971.

Donaldson, E. Talbot, trans. *Will's Vision of Piers Plowman*. William Langland. Eds Elizabeth D. Kirk and Judith H. Anderson. New York, 1990.

Druitt, Herbert. *A Manual of Costume as Illustrated by Monumental Brasses*. Philadelphia, n.d.

Duncan, Edgar H. 'The Literature of Alchemy and Chaucer's Canon's Yeoman's Tale: Framework, Theme, and Characters', *Speculum* 43 (1968): 633–56.

'Earth to Earth'. *Religious Pieces in Prose and Verse*. Ed. George G. Perry. EETS, OS 26. London, 1867, 95.

Eckenstein, Lina. *Woman Under Monasticism*. Cambridge, 1896.

Eleazar, Edwin. ' "With Us Ther Was a Doctour of Phisik" '. *Chaucer's Pilgrims: An Historical Guide to the Pilgrims in the Canterbury Tales*. Eds Laura C. Lambdin and Robert T. Lambdin. Westport, CT, 1996, 220–42.

The Ellesmere Miniatures of the Canterbury Pilgrims. Ed. Theo Stemmler. Mannheim, 1977.

Emmerson, Richard K. 'Text and Image in the Ellesmere Portraits of the Tale-Tellers'. *The Ellesmere Chaucer: Essays in Interpretation*. Eds Martin Stevens and Daniel Woodward. San Marino, CA, 1995, 143–70.

Emmerson, Richard K., and Ronald B. Herzman. *The Apocalyptic Imagination in Medieval Literature*. Philadelphia, 1992.

Engelhardt, George J. 'The Ecclesiastical Pilgrims of the *Canterbury Tales*: A Study in Ethology'. *Mediaeval Studies* (Toronto) 37 (1975): 287–315.

English Historical Documents. Vol. 4. Ed. A. R. Myers. New York, 1969.

D'Etienne de Bourbon. *Anecdotes Historiques: Legendes et Apologues*. Paris, 1877.

Evans, Joan. *Dress in Mediaeval France*. Oxford, 1952.

———. *English Posies and Posy Rings*. London, 1931.

———, ed. *The Flowering of the Middle Ages*. New York, 1966.

———. *A History of Jewellery 1100–1870*. Boston, 1970.

———. *Magical Jewels of the Middle Ages and the Renaissance Particularly in England*. New York, 1976.

Evans, Joan, and M. S. Serjeantson, eds. *English Medieval Lapidaries*. EETS, OS 190. Oxford, 1933.

Everett, Walter Kennedy. 'A Critical Edition of the Confession Section of *The Clensyng of Mannes Soule*'. Diss., University of North Carolina at Chapel Hill, 1974.

Ewing, Elizabeth. *Fur in Dress*. London, 1981.

———. *Women in Uniform: Through the Centuries*. London, 1973.

Fairholt, F. W. *Costume in England: A History of Dress to the End of the Eighteenth Century*. 4th edn rev., H. A. Dillon. 2 vols. London, 1909.

A Fifteenth-Century Courtesy Book and Two Fifteenth-Century Franciscan Rules. Eds R. W. Chambers and Walter W. Seton. EETS, OS 148. London, 1914.

The Fifty Earliest English Wills in the Court of Probate, London: A.D. 1387–1439. Ed. F. J. Furnivall. EETS, OS 78. London, 1882.

Fleming, John V. 'Chaucer and the Visual Arts of His Time'. *New Perspectives in Chaucer Criticism*. Ed. Donald M. Ross. Norman, OK, 1981, 121–36.

———. 'Chaucer's Ascetical Images'. *C&L* 28.4 (1979): 19–26.

———. 'Daun Piers and Dom Pier: Waterless Fish and Unholy Hunters'. *ChauR* 15 (1981): 287–94.

———. 'Gospel Asceticism: Some Chaucerian Images of Perfection'. *Chaucer and Scriptual Tradition*. Ed. David Lyle Jeffrey. Ottawa, 1984, 183–95.

———. *An Introduction to the Franciscan Literature of the Middle Ages*. Chicago, 1977.

Fletcher, Alan J. 'A Critical Edition of Selected Sermons from an Unpublished Fifteenth-Century *de Tempore* Sermon Cycle'. B. Litt. Thesis, Oxford University, 1978.

———. 'The Topical Hypocrisy of Chaucer's Pardoner'. *ChauR* 25 (1990): 110–26.

Flury-Lemberg, Mechtild. *Textile Conservation and Research*. Bern, 1988.

Frank, Mary Hardy Long. 'Chaucer's Prioress and the Blessed Virgin'. *ChauR* 13 (1979): 346–62.

———. 'The Prioress and the Puys: A Study of the Cult of the Virgin and the Medieval Puys in Relation to Chaucer's Prioress and Her Tale'. Diss., University of Colorado, 1970.

———. 'Seeing the Prioress Whole'. *ChauR* 25 (1991): 229–37.

Frank, Robert Worth, Jr. 'Chaucer and the London Bell-Founders'. *MLN* 68 (1953): 524–8.

Fredell, Joel. 'Late Gothic Portraiture: The Prioress and Philippa'. *ChauR* 23 (1989): 181–91.

French, Gilbert J. *The Tippets of the Canons Ecclesiastical*. London, 1850.

De Frere Denise. The French Fabliau: B.N. MS. 837. Eds and trans. Raymond Eichmann and John DuVal. Vol. 2. Garland Library of Medieval Literature, Series A, 17. New York, 1985.

Frese, Dolores Warwick. 'The Names of Women in the *CT* [sic]: Chaucer's Hidden Art of Involucral Nomenclature'. *A Wyf Ther Was: Essays in Honour of Paule Mertens-Fonck*. Ed. Juliette Dor. Liège, 1992, 155–66.

Friedman, John B. 'The Friar Portrait in Bodleian Library MS. Douce 104: Contemporary Satire'. *YLS* 8 (1995): 177–85.

———. 'The Prioress's Beads "of smal coral" '. *MÆ* 39 (1970): 301–5.

Gallo, Ernest. *The 'Poetria Nova' and its Sources in Early Rhetorical Doctrine*. The Hague, 1971.

Ganter, Bernard J. *Clerical Attire: A Historical Synopsis and a Commentary*. Washington, D.C., 1955.

Gardner, Arthur. 'Hair and Head-Dress, 1050–1600'. *JBAA*, Series 3, 13 (1950): 4–13.

Gasquet, Francis A. *English Monastic Life*. 2nd edn rev. London, 1904.

Gautier de Coinci. *Le sermon en vers de la chasteé as nonains. Suomalaisen Tiedeakatemian Toimituksia: Annales Academiae Scientiarum Fennicae*. Sarja B. nid. 38. Suomalainen Tiedeakatemia, no. 10. Helsinki, 1938.

Gaylord, Alan T. 'The Unconquered Tale of the Prioress'. *Papers of the Michigan Academy of Science, Arts and Letters* 47 (1962): 613–36.

Gerard, John. *The Herbal, or General History of Plants: The Complete 1633 Edition as Revised and Enlarged by Thomas Johnson*. New York, 1975.

Gibbons, Alfred. *Early Lincoln Wills 1280–1547*. Lincoln, 1888.

Gibbs, Marion, and Jane Lang. *Bishops and Reform: 1215–1272, With Special Reference to the Lateran Council of 1215*. Oxford, 1934; rpt. 1962.

Gibson, Gail McMurry. *The Theater of Devotion: East Anglian Drama and Society in the Middle Ages*. Chicago, 1989.

Gibson, Strickland, ed. *Statuta Antiqua Universitatis Oxoniensis*. Oxford, 1931.

Gilchrist, Roberta. *Gender and Material Culture: The Archeology of Religious Women*. London, 1994.

Gioanventura Rosetti. *The Plictho: Instructions in the Art of the Dyers which Teaches the Dyeing of Woolen Cloths, Linens, Cottons, and Silk by the Great Art as Well as by the Common*. Trans. of the 1st edn of 1548, Sidney M. Edelstein and Hector C. Borghetty. Cambridge, MA, 1969.

Godefroy, Frédéric. *Dictionnaire de L'Ancienne Langue Française et de tous ses dialectes*. Vol. 3. 1884; rpt. New York, 1961.

Gordon, Stewart. 'Robes, Kings, and Semiotic Ambiguity'. *Robes and Honor: The Medieval World of Investiture*. Ed. Stewart Gordon. New York, 2001, 379–85.

———. 'A World of Investiture'. *Robes and Honor: The Medieval World of Investiture*. Ed. Stewart Gordon. New York, 2001, 1–19.

The Gospels Book of Days: According to St Matthew, St Mark, St Luke & St John. London, 1993.

Gottfried, Robert S. *Doctors and Medicine in Medieval England: 1340–1530*. Princeton, 1986.

Gower, John. *Mirour de l'Omme. Complete Works of John Gower*. Vol. 1. Ed. G. C. Macaulay. Oxford, 1899; 1968.

———. *Mirour de l'Omme*. Trans. William Burton Wilson. East Lansing, MI, 1992.

———. *Vox clamantis. Complete Works of John Gower*. Vol. 4. Ed. G. C. Macaulay. Oxford, 1902, 1968.

Gray, H. L. 'The Production and Export of English Woollens in the Fourteenth Century'. *EHR* 39 (1924): 13–35.

Green, A. Wigfall. 'Chaucer's Clerks and the Mediaeval Scholarly Tradition as Represented by Richard de Bury's *Philobiblon*'. *ELH* 18 (1951): 1–6.

Green, Richard Firth. 'John Ball's Letters: Literary History and Historical Literature'. *Chaucer's England: Literature in Historical Context*. Ed. Barbara Hanawalt. Medieval Studies at Minnesota 4. Minneapolis, 1992, 176–200.

———. 'The Pardoner's Pants (and Why They Matter)'. *SAC* 15 (1993): 131–45.

Grigsby, Bryon. 'The Social Position of the Surgeon in London, 1350–1450'. *Essays in Medieval Studies* 13 (1996). <http://www.luc.edu/publications/medieval/vol13/grigsby.html>.

Guibertus, Tornacensis. *Sermones ad oes status de novo correcti & emendati*. Ab. S. Guenyard, [1510?].

Guide to Saint Peter's Basilica. Rome, 1995.

Guillaume de Lorris and Jean de Meun. *The Romance of the Rose*. Trans. Charles Dahlberg. 1971; Hanover, NH, 1983.

———. *Le Roman de la rose*. Ed. Daniel Poirion. Paris, 1974.

Günther, Robert W. T. Preface. 'A Description of Brasses and other Funeral Monuments in the Chapel'. *A Register of the Members of St Mary Magdalen College, Oxford*. NS 8. Ed. William Dunn Macray. London, 1915.

Hahn, Thomas. 'The Performance of Gender in the Prioress'. *ChauY* 1 (1992): 11–34.

———, and Richard W. Kaeuper. 'Text and Context: Chaucer's *Friar's Tale*'. *SAC* 5 (1983): 67–101.

Hall, James. *Hall's Dictionary of Subjects and Symbols in Art*. London, 1984.

Hall, Thomas N. 'The *Euangelium Nichodemi* and *Vindicta saluatoris* in Anglo-Saxon England'. *Two Old English Apocrypha and their Manuscript Sources*. Eds J. E. Cross et al. Cambridge, 1996, 36–81.

Halligan, Theresa A. *The Booke of Gostlye Grace of Mechtild of Hackeborn*. Toronto, 1979.

Halverson, John. 'Chaucer's Pardoner and the Progress of Criticism'. *ChauR* 4 (1970): 184–202.

Hamilton, Marie Padgett. 'The Clerical Status of Chaucer's Alchemist'. *Speculum* 16 (1941): 103–8.

———. 'The Credentials of Chaucer's Pardoner'. *JEGP* 40 (1941): 48–72.

Hargreaves-Mawdsley, W. N. *A History of Academical Dress in Europe until the End of the Eighteenth Century*. Oxford, 1963; rpt. Westport, CT, 1978.

Harthan, John. *Books of Hours*. London, 1977; rpt. 1982.

Hartley, Dorothy R. *Mediaeval Costume and Life*. London, 1931.

Hartshorne, A. 'The gold chains, the pendants, the paternosters and the zones of the Middle Ages, the Renaissance and later times'. *Archaeol J* 66 (1909): 77–102.

Harvey, Barbara. *Monastic Dress in the Middle Ages: Precept and Practice*. Canterbury, 1988.

Harwood, Britton J. 'Chaucer's Pardoner: The Dialectics of Inside and Outside'. *PQ* 67 (1988): 409–22.

Haselmayer, Louis A. 'The Apparitor and Chaucer's Summoner'. *Speculum* 12 (1937): 43–57.

Hatton, Thomas J. 'Chaucer's Miller's Curious Characters'. *Proceedings of the Medieval Association of the Midwest* 2 (1993): 81–9.

Hauser, Arnold. *The Social History of Art* I. New York, 1952.

Havely, Nicolas. 'Chaucer, Boccaccio, and the Friars'. *Chaucer and the Italian Trecento*. Ed. Piero Boitani. Cambridge, 1983, 249–68.

———. 'Chaucer's Friar and Merchant'. *ChauR* 13 (1979): 337–45.

Heath, Peter. *The English Parish Clergy on the Eve of the Reformation*. London, 1969.

Heath, Sidney. *Pilgrim Life in the Middle Ages*. London, 1911.

'The "Heilig-Rock" Pilgrimage'. Eds Hans Casel, Christoph Rosenzweig, Hans Georg Schneider, and Alfons Waschbüsch. Trier, n.d.

Henryson, Robert. *The Testament of Crisseid. The Story of Troilus.* Ed. Robert Kay Gordon. Toronto, 1978.

Herrade de Landsberg Hortus Deliciarum. Eds A. Straub and G. Keller. 1899; rpt. Strasbourg–Paris, 1952.

Higgs, Elton D. 'The Old Order and the "Newe World" in the General Prologue to the *Canterbury Tales*'. *HLQ* 45 (1982): 155–73.

Hildegard of Bingen. *The Physica.* Trans. Priscilla Throop. Rochester, VT, 1998.

Hingeston-Randolph, Revd F. C. *The Register of Edmund Stafford (A.D. 1395–1419).* London, 1886.

The History of Reynard the Fox: Translated and Printed by William Caxton in 1481. Ed. Donald B. Sands. Cambridge, MA, 1960.

Hoccleve's Works, III: The Regement of Princes. Ed. F. J. Furnivall. EETS, ES 72. London, 1897.

Hodges, Laura F. *Chaucer and Costume: The Secular Pilgrims in the General Prologue.* Chaucer Studies XXVI. Cambridge, 2000.

———. 'Dyes and Pigments'. *Trade, Travel, and Exploration in the Middle Ages: An Encyclopedia.* Eds John B. Friedman and Kristin Mossler Figg. New York, 2000, 154–6.

———. 'Noe's Wife: Type of Eve and Wakefield Spinner'. *Equally in God's Image: Women in the Middle Ages.* Eds Julia Bolton Holloway, Constance S. Wright, and Joan Bechtold. New York, 1990, 30–9.

———. 'The Sartorial Signs in *Troilus and Criseyde*'. *ChauR* 35 (2001): 223–59.

Hodgson, Phyllis, ed. *Chaucer: General Prologue, The Canterbury Tales.* London, 1969.

Hoepfner, E. 'Pers en ancien Française'. *Romania* 49 (1923): 592–7.

Hoerner, Fred. 'Church Office, Routine, and Self-Exile in Chaucer's Pardoner'. *SAC* 16 (1994): 69–98.

Holloway, Julia Bolton. 'The Figure of the Pilgrim in Medieval Poetry'. Diss., University of California, Berkeley, 1974.

———. *The Pilgrim and the Book: A Study of Dante, Langland, and Chaucer.* New York, 1987.

———, trans. *Saint Bride and Her Book: Birgitta of Sweden's Revelations.* Newburyport, MA, 1992.

The Holy Bible. Douay Rheims Version. 1899; Rockford, IL, 1971.

Hope, W. H. St John. *Heraldry for Craftsmen and Designers.* New York, 1913.

Houghton, Helen Sherwood. ' "Degree" and "Array" in Chaucer's Portrait of the Reeve: A Study of Idiom and Meaning'. 2 vols. Diss., University of York, 1975.

Houston, Mary G. *Medieval Costume in England & France: The 13th, 14th and 15th Centuries.* London, 1965; New York, 1996.

'How a Louer Prayseth Hys Lady'. MS Bodl. Fairfax 16, Fol. 306a.

Howard, Donald. *Chaucer and the Medieval World.* London, 1987.

———. *Writers and Pilgrims: Medieval Pilgrimage Narratives and Their Posterity.* Berkeley, CA, 1980.

Hudson, Anne. *The Premature Reformation: Wycliffite Texts and Lollard History.* Oxford, 1988.

Hudson, Vivian Kay. 'Clothing and Adornment Imagery in "The Scale of Perfection": A Reflection of Contemplation'. *Studies in Spirituality* 4 (1994): 116–45.

Hunter, G. K. 'Flatcaps and Bluecoats: Visual Signals on the Elizabethan Stage'. *E&S*, n.s. 33. Ed. Inga-Stina Ewbank. Atlantic Highlands, NJ, 1980, 16–47.

'Illuminating the Mind's Eye: Memory & Medieval Book Arts'. [pamphlet] The J. Paul Getty Museum, 1996.

The Imperial City Museum [handout], Rothenburg ob der Taub, Germany, n.d.

Jacob, E. F. *Essays in the Conciliar Epoch*, 3rd edn rev. Manchester, 1963.

Jacob's Well, an Englisht Treatise on the Cleansing of Man's Conscience. Ed. A. Brandeis. EETS, OS 115. London, 1900.

Jacobs, Edward Craney. 'Further Biblical Allusions for Chaucer's Prioress'. *ChauR* 15 (1980): 151–4.

James, John. *History of the Worsted Manufacture in England*. London, 1968.

James, M. R. [Monk's Sketchbook.] *Walpole Society, Annual* 13 (1924–25). Oxford, 1925.

Jankofsky, Klaus P. 'Love and Death and the Prioress's Beads'. Paper presented at the 30th International Congress on Medieval Studies, May 1995, at Western Michigan University, Kalamazoo, MI.

Jeffrey, David Lyle. 'The Friar's Rent'. *JEGP* 70 (1971): 600–6.

Jenkins, J. Geraint, ed. *The Wool Textile Industry in Great Britain*. London, 1972.

John of Arderne, *Treatise in Fistula in Ano*. Ed. D'Arcy Power. EETS, OS 139. 1910; rpt. in 'A surgeon's code of behaviour and ethics, c. 1376', #696. *English Historical Documents*. Vol. 4. New York, 1969, 1185.

Jones, George F. 'Realism and Social Satire in Heinrich Wittenwiler's Ring'. Columbia Diss., Univ. Microfilms (Ann Arbor, 1950), no. 1864.

Jones, Ida B. 'Popular Medical Knowledge in Fourteenth-Century English Literature', Pts 1–2. *BIHM* 5 (May 1937): 405–51, 538–88.

Jones, Peter Murray. *Medieval Medical Miniatures*. Austin, TX, 1984.

Julian of Norwich. *A Book of Showings to the Anchoress Julian of Norwich*. 2 vols. Eds Edmund Colledge and James Walsh. *Studies and Texts* 35. Toronto, 1928.

———. *The Shewings of Julian of Norwich*. Ed. Georgia Ronan Crampton. TEAMS Middle English Text Series. Kalamazoo, MI, 1993.

———. *The Shewings of Julian of Norwich*. TEAMS online edn <http://www.lib.rochester.edu/camelot/teams/julianfr.htm>.

Jungman, Robert E. 'The Pardoner's Quarrel with the Host'. *PQ* 55 (1976): 279–81.

Jusserand, J. J. 'Chaucer's Pardoner and the Pope's Pardoners'. *Chaucer Society Essays*, Pt 5, Second Series 19. London, 1884, 424–36.

———. *English Wayfaring Life in the Middle Ages: XIVth Century*. 3rd edn. Trans. Lucy Toulmin Smith. London, 1925.

Katzenellenbogen, Adolf. *Allegories of the Virtues and Vices in Mediaeval Art: From Early Christian Times to the Thirteenth Century*. New York, 1964; rpt. Toronto, 1989.

Keller, James. ' "A Sumonour Was Ther With Us In That Place" '. *Chaucer's Pilgrims: An Historical Guide to the Pilgrims in The Canterbury Tales*. Eds Laura C. Lambdin and Robert T. Lambdin. Westport, CT, 1996, 300–13.

Kellogg, Alfred L. 'An Augustinian Interpretation of Chaucer's Pardoner'. *Speculum* 26 (1951): 465–81.

Kellogg, Alfred L., and Louis A. Haselmayer. 'Chaucer's Satire of the Pardoner'. *PMLA* 66 (1951): 251–77; rpt. in Kellogg, Alfred L. *Chaucer, Langland, Arthur: Essays in Middle English Literature*. New Brunswick, NJ, 1972, 212–44.

Kelly, Douglas. 'The Art of Description'. *The Legacy of Chrétien de Troyes*. Vol. 1. Eds Norris J. Lacy, Douglas Kelly, and Keith Busby. Amsterdam, 1987, 191–221.

Kelly, Francis M., and Randolph Schwabe. *A Short History of Costume and Armor in England, Volume I: 1066–1485*. London, 1931; [New York], 1968.

Kelly, Henry Ansgar. 'Bishop, Prioress, and Bawd in the Stews of Southwark', *Speculum* 75 (2000): 342–88.

———. 'A Neo-Revisionist Look at Chaucer's Nuns', *ChauR* 31 (1996–97): 115–32.

Kendall, Alan. *Medieval Pilgrims*. London, 1970.

Kennard, Joseph Spencer. *The Friar in Fiction, Sincerity in Art, and Other Essays*. New York, 1923.

Kessler, Herbert L., and Johanna Zacharias. *Rome, 1300: On the Path of the Pilgrim*. New Haven, CT, 2000.

Kiehl, James M. 'Dryden's Zimri and Chaucer's Pardoner: A Comparative Study in Verse Portraiture'. *Thoth* 6 (1965): 3–12.

Kiernan, Kevin S. 'The Art of the Descending Catalogue, and a Fresh Look at Alisoun'. *ChauR* 10 (1975): 1–16.

Klapisch-Zuber, Christiane. *Women, Family, and Ritual in Renaissance Italy*. Trans. Lydia Cochrane. Chicago, 1985.

Knight, S. T. ' "Almoost a spanne brood" '. *Neophil* 52 (1968): 178–80.

Knowles, Dom David. *The Religious Orders in England: The End of the Middle Ages*. Vol. 2. Cambridge, 1957.

Koslin, Désirée. 'The Robe of Simplicity: Initiation, Robing, and Veiling of Nuns in the Middle Ages'. *Robes and Honor: The Medieval World of Investiture*. Ed. Stewart Gordon. New York, 2001, 255–74.

———. 'Textiles, Decorative'. *Trade, Travel, and Exploration in the Middle Ages: An Encyclopedia*. Eds John B. Friedman and Kristin Mossler Figg. New York, 2000, 597–8.

Krapp, J. P. *The Legend of St Patrick's Purgatory; Its Later Literary History*. Baltimore, 1899.

Kunz, George Frederick. *The Curious Lore of Precious Stones*. Philadelphia, 1913.

Kuryluk, Ewa. *Veronica and her Cloth: History, Symbolism and Structure of 'True' Image*. Oxford, 1991.

Labarge, Margaret Wade. *A Baronial Household of the Thirteenth Century*. New York, 1965.

'The Land of Cokaygne'. *Early English Poems and Lives of Saints*. Ed. F. J. Furnivall. Transactions of the Philological Society. Berlin, 1858, 156–61.

Landrum, Graham. 'The Convent Crowd and the Feminist Nun'. *TPB* 13 (1976): 5–12.

Langland, William. *Piers Plowman: The B Version*. Eds George Kane and E. Talbot Donaldson. University of London, 1975.

———. *Piers the Plowman*. Trans. J. F. Goodridge. New York, 1980.

Lanham, Richard A. *A Handlist of Rhetorical Terms*. Berkeley, CA, 1969.

Latham, R. E. *Dictionary of Medieval Latin*. London, 1975.

———. *Revised Medieval Word-List from British and Irish Sources*. Oxford, 1965.

Laver, James. *Modesty in Dress*. Boston, 1967.

Leech, Patrick. 'Who Says Manchester Says Cotton: Textile Terminology in the Oxford English Dictionary (1000–1960)'. *TRA linea* 2 (1999). <http://www.intralinea.it/vol2/leech/default.htm>.

Lescher, Wilfrid. *The Rosary*. London, 1888.

Lewis, Charlton T. *Elementary Latin Dictionary*. Oxford, 1979.

The Liber Celestis of St Bridget of Sweden. Vol. 1. Ed. Roger Ellis. EETS, OS 291. Oxford, 1987.

Lightbown, Ronald W. *Mediaeval European Jewellery: with a catalogue of the collection in the Victoria and Albert Museum*. [London], 1992.

Lincoln Diocese Documents 1450–1544. Ed. Andrew Clark. EETS, OS 149. London, 1914.

Lloyd, A. H. *The Early History of Christ's College, Cambridge*. Cambridge, 1934.

The London Archaeologist. [cover picture]. 4.11 (Summer 1983).

Loomis, Roger Sherman. *A Mirror of Chaucer's World*. Princeton, 1965.

———. 'Was Chaucer a Laodicean?' *Essays and Studies in Honor of Carleton Brown*. New York, 1940, 129–48.

Lowes, John Livingston. *Convention and Revolt in Poetry*. London, 1930.

———. 'Illustrations of Chaucer. Drawn Chiefly from Deschamps'. *RR* 2 (1911): 113–28.

———. 'The Prioress's Oath'. *RR* 5 (1914): 368–85.

Lumiansky, Robert M. *Of Sondry Folk: The Dramatic Principle in The Canterbury Tales*. Austin, TX, 1955.

Lydgate, John. *Minor Poems*. Ed. H. N. MacCracken. EETS, OS 192. London, 1934; rpt. 1961.

———. *Pilgrimage of the Life of Man*, From the French of Guillaume De Deguileville, A.D. 1335. Ed. F. J. Furnivall. EETS, ES 77. London, 1899.

———. Prologue to the *Siege of Thebes*. Ed. John M. Bowers. *The Canterbury Tales: Fifteenth Century Continuations and Additions*. TEAMS Middle English Texts Series. Kalamazoo, MI, 1992, 13–18.

———. *The Temple of Glas*. Ed. J. Schick. EETS, ES 60. London, 1891.

MacIntyre, Jean, and Garrett P. J. Epp. ' "Cloathes worth all the rest": Costumes and Properties'. *A New History of Early English Drama*. Eds John D. Cox and David Scott Kastan. New York, 1997, 269–85.

MacKinney, Loren. *Medical Illustrations in Medieval Manuscripts*. Publications of the Wellcome Historical Medical Library, n.s. 5. London, 1965.

MacKinney, L. C., and Harry Bober. 'A thirteenth-century medical case history in miniatures'. *Speculum* 35 (1960): 251–9.

Macklin, H. W. *The Brasses of England*. London, 1907.

Madeleva, Sr M. 'Chaucer's Nuns'. *Chaucer's Nuns and Other Essays*. Port Washington, NY, 1965, 3–42.

Maleski, Mary A. 'The Culpability of Chaucer's Prioress'. *ChauY* 5 (1998): 41–60.

Malory, Thomas. 'The Knight with the Two Swords'. *Malory: Works*. 2nd edn. Ed. Eugène Vinaver. Oxford, 1977.

Mankind. The Macro Plays. Ed. Mark Eccles. EETS, OS 262. London, 1969.

Manley, Francis. 'Chaucer's Rosary and Donne's Bracelet: Ambiguous Coral'. *MLN* 74 (1959): 385–8.

Manly, John Matthews. Introduction, Notes, and Glossary. *Canterbury Tales by Geoffrey Chaucer*. New York, 1928; rpt. 1947.

Mann, Jill. *Chaucer and Medieval Estates Satire: The Literature of Social Classes and the General Prologue to the Canterbury Tales*. Cambridge, 1973.

Mann, Maurice. 'Le couleur perse en ancien française et chez Dante'. *Romania* 49 (1923): 186–203.

Markert, Emil. *Chaucers Canterbury-Pilger und ihre Tracht*. Würzburg, 1911.

de Marly, Diana. *Fashion For Men: An Illustrated History*. New York, 1985.

Martin, Janet. *Treasure of the Land of Darkness: The Fur Trade and its Significance for Medieval Russia*. Cambridge, 1986.

Mathew, Gervase. *The Court of Richard II*. New York, 1968.

Maxfield, David K. 'St Mary Rouncivale, Charing Cross: The Hospital of Chaucer's Pardoner'. *ChauR* 28 (1993): 148–63.

Mayo, Janet. *A History of Ecclesiastical Dress*. New York, 1984.

McBride, M. F. *Chaucer's Physician and Fourteenth-Century Medicine: A Compendium for Students*. University Monograph Series. Bristol, IN, 1985.

McCloud, Revd Henry J. *Clerical Dress and Insignia of the Roman Catholic Church*. Milwaukee, 1948.

McConnell, Sophie (text), and Alvin Grossman (design). *Metropolitan Jewelry*. The Metropolitan Museum of Art, New York. Boston, 1991.

McCracken, Grant. 'Clothing as Language: An Object Lesson in the Study of the Expressive Properties of Material Culture'. *Material Anthropology*. Eds Barrie Reynolds and Margaret A. Stott. Lanham, MD, 1987, 103–28.

McNamara, Jo Ann. *Sisters in Arms*. Cambridge, MA, 1996.

McVaugh, Michael R. 'Moments of Inflection: The Careers of Arnau de Vilanova'. *Religion and Medicine in the Middle Ages*. Eds Peter Biller and Joseph Ziegler. York Studies in Medieval Theology 3. Woodbridge, 2001, 47–67.

McVeigh, Terrence A. 'Chaucer's Portraits of the Pardoner and the Summoner and Wyclif's *Tractatus De Simonia*'. *Classical Folia* 29 (1975): 54–8.

Medieval Eloquence: Studies in the Theory and Practice of Medieval Rhetoric. Ed. James J. Murphy. Berkeley, CA, 1978.

Medicine: A Treasury of Art and Literature. Eds Ann G. Carmichael and Richard M. Ratzan. New York, 1991.

Meiss, Millard. *French Painting in the Time of Jean de Berry: The Boucicaut Master*. New York, 1968.

Mellinkoff, Ruth. *Outcasts: Signs of Otherness in Northern-European Art of the Late Middle Ages*. 2 vols. Berkeley, CA, 1993.

'Du Mercier'. *Satirical Songs and Poems on Costume From the 13th to the 19th Century*. Ed. Frederick W. Fairholt. London, 1849, 7–15.

Meyer, Claudius F. 'A Medieval English Leechbook and its 14th Century Poem on Bloodletting'. *Bulletin of the History of Medicine* 7 (1939): 380–91.

The Middle English Translations of Robert Grosseteste's Chateau d'Amour. Ed. Kari Sajavaara. Helsinki, 1967.

The Middle-English Versions of Partonope of Blois. Ed. A. Trampe Bödtker. EETS, ES 109. London, 1912.

The Middle-English Versions of The Rule of St Benet and Two Contemporary Rituals for the Ordination of Nuns. Ed. Ernst A. Kock. EETS, OS 120. London, 1902.

Milburn, R. L. P. *Saints and Their Emblems in English Churches*. Oxford, 1957.

Miller, Clarence H., and Roberta Bosse. 'Chaucer's Pardoner and the Mass'. *ChauR* 6 (1972): 171–84.

Miller, Edward. 'The Fortunes of the English Textile Industry during the Thirteenth Century'. *Econ. Hist Rev* 18, 2nd series (1965): 64–82.

Miller, Robert P. *Chaucer: Sources and Backgrounds*. New York, 1977.

————. 'Chaucer's Pardoner, the Scriptural Eunuch, and the Pardoner's Tale'. *Speculum* 30 (1955): 180–99.

[Mirk, John]. *Mirk's Festial: A Collection of Homilies by Johannes Mirkus*. Ed. Theodor Erbe. EETS, ES 96. London, 1905; rpt. 1987.

Mirus, John [John Mirk]. *Instructions for Parish Priests*. Ed. Edward Peacock. EETS, OS 31. London, 1868; rev. 1902; rpt. 1996.

Mohl, Ruth. *The Three Estates in Medieval and Renaissance Literature*. 1933; rpt. New York, 1962.

Monnas, Lisa. 'Silk Cloths Purchased for the Great Wardrobe of the Kings of England, 1325–1462'. *Ancient and Medieval Textiles: Studies in Honour of Donald King*. Eds Lisa Monnas and Hero Granger-Taylor. *Text Hist* 20.2 (1989): 283–307.

Monumenta Franciscana. Ed. J. S. Brewer. Vol. 1. London, 1858; Germany, 1965.

Monumenta Franciscana. Ed. Richard Howlett. Vol. 2. London, 1882; Germany, 1965.

Moore, Ellen Wedemeyer. *The Fairs of Medieval England: An Introductory Study*. Studies and Texts 72. Toronto, 1985.

Moorman, Charles. 'The Prioress as Pearly Queen'. *ChauR* 13 (1978): 25–33.

Moorman, John R. H. *A History of the Franciscan Order*. Oxford, 1968; rpt. 1988.

Morey, Charles Rufus. *Mediaeval Art*. New York, 1942.

Morgan, Gerald. 'The Design of the *General Prologue* to the *Canterbury Tales*'. *ES* 59 (1978): 481–98.

————. 'The Universality of the Portraits in the *General Prologue* to the *Canterbury Tales*'. *ES* 58 (1977): 481–93.

Moriarty, Catherine, ed. *The Voice of the Middle Age*. New York, 1989.

Morris, Revd Richard, ed. *Chaucer: the Prologue, the Knightes Tale, the Nonnes Prestes Tale, from the Canterbury Tales*. 3rd rev. edn. Oxford, 1874.

Morse, J. Mitchell. 'The Philosophy of the Clerk of Oxenford'. *MLQ* 19 (1958): 3–20.

Mullaney, Samantha. 'Fashion and Morality in BL MS Add. 37049'. *Texts and their Contexts: Papers From the Early Book Society (1997)*. Eds John Scattergood and Julia Boffey. Dublin, 1997, 71–86.

————. 'The Language of Costume in the Ellesmere Portraits'. *Sources, Exemplars and Copy-Texts: Influence and Transmission*, special edn, *Trivium* 31 (1999): 33–57.

Muscatine, Charles. *Chaucer and the French Tradition: A Study in Style and Meaning*. Berkeley, CA, 1957.

————. 'The Name of Chaucer's Friar'. *MLN* 70 (1955): 169–72.

Muthesius, Anna. 'Silk in the Medieval World'. *The Cambridge History of Western Textiles*. Vol. 1. Ed. David Jenkins. Cambridge, 2003, 325–54.

Nevinson, J. L. 'Buttons and Buttonholes in the Fourteenth Century'. *The Journal of the Costume Society* 11 (1977): 38–44.

New Catholic Encyclopedia. New York, 1967.

Newhauser, Richard. *The Early History of Greed: The Sin of Avarice in Early Medieval Thought and Literature*. Cambridge Studies in Medieval Literature 41. Cambridge, 2000.

Newton, Stella Mary. *Fashion in the Age of the Black Prince: A Study of the Years 1340–1365*. Woodbridge, 1980; rpt. 1999.

————, and Mary M. Giza. 'Frilled Edges'. *Text Hist* 14 (1983): 141–52.

Nicholls, Albert G. 'Medicine in Chaucer's Day'. *Dalhousie Review* 12 (1932): 218–30.

Nicholls, John, comp. *Illustrations of the Manners and Expences of Antient Times in England, In the Fifteenth, Sixteenth, and Seventeenth Centuries, Deduced From The Accompts of Churchwardens, and Other Authentic Documents, Collected From Various Parts of the Kingdom, with Explanatory Notes*. London, 1797; rpt. London, 1973.

Nichols, John. *History and Antiquities of the County of Leicester*. London, 1795–1815.

Nigel De Longchamps. *Speculum Stultorum*. Eds John H. Mozley and Robert R. Raymo. Berkeley and Los Angeles, 1960.

Nigel Longchamp. *A Mirror for Fools: The Book of Burnel the Ass*. Trans. J. H. Mozley. Notre Dame, IN, 1963.

Nohl, Johannes. *The Black Death*. Trans. C. H. Clarke. New York, n.d.

Norris, Herbert. *Costume & Fashion: Senlac to Bosworth 1066–1485*. Vol. 2. New York, 1950.

————. *Medieval Costume and Fashion*. Mineola, NY, 1999.

'Of Men Lif þat Woniþ in Lond'. *Early English Poems and Lives of Saints*. Ed. F. J. Furnivall. Transactions of the Philological Society. Berlin, 1858, 152–6.

Oliva, Marilyn. *The Convent and the Community in Late Medieval England: Female Monasteries in the Diocese of Norwich, 1350–1540*. Studies in the History of Medieval Religion 12. Woodbridge, 1998.

Olson, Roberta J. M. 'The Rosary and its Iconography, Part I: Background for Devotional Tondi'. *Arte Cristiani* 86 (1998): 263–76.

Olsson, Kurt. 'Grammar, Manhood, and Tears: The Curiosity of Chaucer's Monk'. *MP* 76 (1978): 1–17.

O'Mara, V[eronica] M. *A Study and Edition of Selected Middle English Sermons*. Leeds Texts and Monographs, n.s. 13, 1994.

'On the Deposition of Richard II'. *Political Poems and Songs Relating to English History, Composed During the Period From the Accession of Edw.III to that of Ric.III*. Vol. I. Ed. Thomas Wright. London, 1859, 368–416.

'On the times'. *Political Poems and Songs Relating to English History, Composed During the Period From the Accession of Edw.III to that of Ric.III*. Vol. I. Ed. Thomas Wright. London, 1859, 270–8.

'The Order of Fair-Ease' ['Ordre de Bel-Eyse']. *The Political Songs of England From the Reign of John to that of Edward II*. EETS, OS 6. Ed. and trans. Thomas Wright. London, 1839, 137–48.

'An Orison of the Five Joys'. No. 26. *Religious Lyrics of the XIVth Century*. Ed. Carleton Brown., 2nd edn rev., G. V. Smithers. 1924; Oxford, 1957, 29–31.

Orme, Nicholas. 'Chaucer and Education'. *ChauR* 16 (1981): 38–59.

————. 'Education and Learning at a Medieval English Cathedral: Exeter 1380–1548'. *Journal of Ecclesiastical History* 32 (1981): 265–83.

————. *English Schools in the Middle Ages*. London, 1973.

————. *From Childhood to Chivalry: The Education of the English Kings and Aristocracy 1066–1530*. London, 1984.

————. 'Langland and Education'. *History of Education* 11 (1982): 251–66.

————. 'Schoolmasters, 1307–1509'. *Profession, Vocation, and Culture in Later Medieval England*. Ed. Cecil H. Clough. Liverpool, 1982, 218–41.

Owen-Crocker, Gale R. *Dress in Anglo-Saxon England*. Manchester, 1986.

Pächt, Otto, and J. J. G. Alexander, *Illuminated Manuscripts in the Bodleian Library Oxford.3: British, Irish, and Icelandic Schools*. Oxford, 1973.

Pantin, William Abel, ed. *Documents Illustrating the Activities of the General and Provincial Chapters of the English Black Monks 1215–1540*. 3 vols. Camden Society, 3rd Series, 45, 47, 54. London, 1931–37.

Parisse, Michel. *Les nonnes au Moyen Âge*. Paris, 1983.

Pastors and the Care of Souls: in Medieval England. Eds John Shinners and William J. Dohar. Notre Dame, IN, 1998.

Pastoureau, Michel. 'Ceci est mon sang. Le christianisme medieval et la couleur rouge'. *Le Pressoir mystique: Actes du Colloque de Recloses*. Paris, 1990, 43–56.

Patterson, Lee. 'Chaucer's Pardoner on the Couch: Psyche and Clio in Medieval Literary Studies'. *Speculum* 76 (2001): 638–80.

Pearsall, Derek. *The Life of Geoffrey Chaucer: A Critical Biography*. Oxford, 1992; rpt. 1994.

Pendrill, Charles. *London Life in the 14th Century*. Port Washington, NY, 1971.

Pépin, Jean. 'Saint Augustin et le symbolisme néoplatonicien de la vêture'. *Augustinus Magister, Congrès international augustinien, Paris, 21–24 Septembre 1954*. 1 (1954–55): 293–306.

Pierce the Ploughmans Crede. Ed. and trans. Walter W. Skeat. EETS, OS 30. London, 1867.

Piponnier, Françoise, and Perrine Mane. *Dress in the Middle Ages*. Trans. Caroline Beamish. New Haven, CT, 1997.

Planché, James Robinson. *A Cyclopaedia of Costume or Dictionary of Dress*. 2 vols. London, 1876.

————. *An Illustrated Dictionary of Historic Costume: From the First Century B.C. to c.1760*. Mineola, NY, 2003.

'Plangit nonna fletibus'. *Medieval Latin and the Rise of the European Love Lyric*. Vol. 2. Ed. Peter Dronke. Oxford, 1966, 357.

The Plowman's Tale. Six Ecclesiastical Satires. Ed. James M. Dean. Kalamazoo, MI, 1991.

'Poem on the Evil Times of Edward II'. *The Political Songs of England From the Reign of John to that of Edward II*. Ed. and trans. Thomas Wright. EETS, OS 6. London: The Camden Society, 1839, 334–7.

'Poem on the Passion of Christ', Bodleian Library MS Bodley Rolls 16.

Political Poems and Songs Relating to English History, Composed During the Period From the Accession of Edw. III to that of Ric. III. Vols 1–2. Ed. Thomas Wright. London, 1859, 1861; rpt. Germany, 1965.

The Political Songs of England From the Reign of John to that of Edward II. London: The Camden Society, 1839.

Ponting, Kenneth G. *A Dictionary of Dyes and Dyeing*. London, 1980.

————. *The Woolen Industry of South-West England*. Bath, 1971.

Postlethwayt, Malachy. *The Universal Dictionary of Trade and Commerce: Translated from the French of the Celebrated Monsieur Savary*. Vol. 2. London, 1755.

Power, Eileen. *Medieval English Nunneries*. Cambridge Studies in Medieval Life and Thought. Ed. G. G. Coulton. London, 1922.

————. *Medieval People*. 2nd edn. Boston, 1925.

Preston, Raymond. *Chaucer*. London, 1952.

Price, John Edward. *A Descriptive Account of the Guildhall of the City of London: Its History and Associations*. London, 1886.

'Priere d'amour d'une nonnain a un jeune adolescent'. *Recueil de poesies françoises des xve^e et xvie siècles*. Vol. 8. Ed. Anatole de Montaiglon. Paris, 1858, 170–5.

Prior, Sandra Pierson. *The Fayre Formez of the Pearl Poet*. Medieval Texts and Studies 18. East Lansing, MI, 1996.

Puff, Helmut. 'Sodomite Clothes'. *The Material Culture of Sex, Procreation, and Marriage in Premodern Europe*. Eds Anne L. McClanan and Karen Rosoff. New York, 2001, 251–72.

Racinet, Auguste. *Racinet's Full-Color Pictorial History of Western Costume*. New York, 1987.

Ragen, Brian Abel. 'Chaucer, Jean de Meun, and Proverbs 30:20'. *N&Q* 35.3 (Sept. 1988): 295–6.

Rashdall, Hastings. *The Universities of Europe in the Middle Ages*. Rev. edn. Eds F. M. Powicke and A. B. Emden. 3 vols. Oxford, 1936.

Rawcliffe, Carole. *Medicine & Society in Later Medieval England*. Stroud, 1995.

Read, John. *Alchemist in Life, Literature and Art*. 1947; London, n.d.

Registrum Thome Bourgchier: Cantuariensis Archiepiscopi. Ed. F. R. H. Du Boulay. Oxford, 1957.

Reiss, Edmund. 'The Symbolic Surface of the *Canterbury Tales*: The Monk's Portrait, Part I'. *ChauR* 2 (1968a): 254–72.

————. 'The Symbolic Surface of the *Canterbury Tales*: The Monk's Portrait, Part II'. *ChauR* 3 (1968b): 12–28.

De Remediis utriusque fortunae. English & Latin. A Dialogue Between Reason and Adversity: A Late Middle English Version of Petrarch's De Remediis. Ed. F. N. M. Diekstra. Assen, 1968.

Renn, George A. 'Chaucer's Doctour of Phisik'. *Expl* 45.2 (1987): 4–5.

Renoir, Alain. 'Bayard and Troilus: Chaucerian Non-paradox in the Reader'. *Orbis Litterarum* 36.2 (1981): 116–40.

'The Reply of Friar Daw Topias, with Jack Upland's Rejoinder'. *Political Poems and Songs Relating to English History, Composed During the Period from the Accession of Edw. III to that of Ric. III*. Vol. 2. Ed. Thomas Wright. London, 1861; rpt. Germany, 1965, 39–113.

Revard, Carter. 'The Lecher, the Legal Eagle, and the Papelard Priest: Middle English Confessional Satires in MS Harley 2253 and Elsewhere'. *His Firm Estate: Essays in Honor of Franklin James Eikenberry by Former Students*. The University of Tulsa Department of English 2. Ed. Donald E. Hayden. Tulsa, OK, 1967, 54–71.

The Revelations of Saint Birgitta. Ed. William Patterson Cumming. EETS, OS 178. London, 1929.

Reynolds, William Donald. 'The Ovidius Moralizatus of Petrus Berchorius: An Introduction and Translation'. Diss., University of Illinois at Urbana-Champaign, 1971. Ann Arbor, MI, 1971

Rex, Richard. *'The Sins of Madame Eglentyne' and other Essays on Chaucer*. Newark, NJ, 1995.

Rhodes, James F. 'The Pardoner's *Vernycle* and his *Vera Icon*'. *MLS* 13.2 (1983): 34–40.

Richardson, Janette. 'Friar and Summoner, The Art of Balance'. *ChauR* 9 (1975): 227–36.

Rickert, Edith, comp. *Chaucer's World*. Eds Clair C. Olson and Martin M. Crow. New York, 1948.

Rickert, Margaret. *Painting in Britain: The Middle Ages*. 2nd edn. Baltimore, 1965.

Ridley, Florence H. *The Prioress and the Critics*. Berkeley and Los Angeles, 1965.

Rigby, S. H. *Chaucer in Context: Society, Allegory, and Gender*. Manchester, 1996.

———. *English Society in the Later Middle Ages: Class, Status and Gender*. New York, 1995.

———. 'The Wife of Bath, Christine de Pizan, and the Medieval Case for Women'. *ChauR* 35 (2000): 133–65.

Riley, Henry Thomas, ed. Introduction. *Munimenta Gildhallae Londoniensis: Liber Albus, Liber Custumarum et Liber Horn*. Vol. 1. London, 1859.

Robert of Cisyle. Amis and Amiloun, Robert of Cisyle, and Sir Amadace. Ed. Edward E. Foster. TEAMS, Medieval Institute Publications. Kalamazoo, MI, 1997, 96–110.

Robertson, D. W., Jr. *A Preface to Chaucer*. Princeton, 1973.

———, and Bernard F. Huppé. *Piers Plowman and Scriptural Tradition*. Princeton, 1951.

Rock, Daniel. *Hierugia; or, The Holy Sacrifice of the Mass*. Vol. 2. 3rd edn, rev. Ed. W. H. James Weale. London, 1892.

Rodes, Robert E., Jr. *Ecclesiastical Administration in Late Medieval England: The Anglo-Saxons to the Reformation*. Notre Dame, IN, 1977.

Rogers, James E. Thorold. *A History of Agriculture and Prices in England*. 4 vols. Oxford, 1892; rpt. Vaduz, 1963.

Rogers, P. Burwell. 'The Names of the Canterbury Pilgrims'. *Names* 16 (1968): 339–46.

Rolle (de Hampole), Richard. *Pricke of Conscience*. Ed. Richard Morris. Philological Society. Berlin, 1863.

Roney, Lois. 'Chaucer's Clerk: Arts Education, Insoluble Tale, Obedience Ethic'. Forthcoming.

Ronig, Franz. *Trier Cathedral*. Trans. M. C. Maxwell. 4th edn. Trier, 1986.

Rosetti, Gioanventura. *The Plictho: Instructions in the Art of the Dyers which Teaches the Dyeing of Woolen Cloths, Linens, Cottons, and Silk by the Great Art as Well as by the Common*. Trans. Sidney M. Edelstein and Hector C. Borghetty. Cambridge, MA, 1969.

Roulin, E. A. *Vestments and Vesture, A Manual of Liturgical Art*. Trans. Justin McCann. Westminster, MD, 1950.

Rousselot [l'abbé Pierre Jean]. 'La sainte Vierge dans la poésie française du moyen âge'. *Revue du clergé français* 42 (1905): 457–81.

Rowland, Beryl. 'The Physician's "Historial Thyng Notable" and the Man of Law'. *ELH* 40 (1973): 165–78.

Rubin, Stanley. *Medieval English Medicine*. New York, 1974.

Ruiz, Juan. *Libro de buen amor*. Ed. Giorgio Chiarini. Milan, 1964.

The Rule of St Benedict. 4th edn, rev. Ed. and trans. D. Oswald Hunter Blair. Fort Augustus, 1934.

Rule of St Benedict: A Commentary by the Right Rev. Dom Paul Delatte. Trans. Justin McCann. New York, 1921.

Rutebeuf. 'La Chanson des ordres'. *Fabliaux et contes des poètes François Des XI, XII, XIII, XIV et XVe siècles*. Vol. 2. Ed. E. Barbazan. Paris, 1808, 299–301.

———. 'Les Ordres de Paris'. *Fabliaux et contes des poètes François Des XI, XII, XIII, XIV et XVe siècles*. Vol. 2. Ed. E. Barbazan. Paris, 1808, 293–8.

Sadowski, Piotr. 'The Greeness of the Green Knight: A Study of Medieval Colour Symbolism'. *Ethnologia Polona* 15–16 (1991): 61–79.

Salter, Elizabeth. *Chaucer: The Knight's Tale and the Clerk's Tale*. Studies in English Literature 5. Gen. Ed. David Daiches. Woodbury, NY, 1962.

Salzman, L. F. *English Industries of the Middle Ages*. Oxford, 1923.

Sandler, Lucy Freeman. *Omne Bonum: A Fourteenth-Century Encyclopedia of Universal Knowledge [BL MSS Royal 6 E VI–6 E VII]*. 2 vols. London, 1996.

'Satyre on the Consistory Courts'. *The Political Songs of England: From the Reign of John to that of Edward II*. Ed. and trans. Thomas Wright. London: The Camden Society, 1839, 155–9.

Scase, Wendy. ' "Proud Gallants and Popeholy Priests": The Context and Function of a Fifteenth-Century Satirical Poem'. *MÆ* 63.2 (1994): 275–86.

Scattergood, John. 'Fashion and Morality in the Late Middle Ages'. *England in the Fifteenth Century: Proceedings of the 1986 Harlaxton Symposium*. Ed. Daniel Williams. Woodbridge, 1987, 255–72.

———. '*The Two Ways*: An Unpublished Religious Treatise by Sir John Clanvowe'. *English Philological Studies* 10 (1967): 33–56.

Schachner, Nathan. *The Medieval Universities*. New York, 1938.

Schramm, Wilbur Lang. 'The Cost of Books in Chaucer's Time'. *MLN* 48 (1933): 139–45.

Scott, Kathleen. Catalogue of Illustrations. *Piers Plowman: A Facsimile of Bodleian Library, Oxford, MS Douce 104*. Introduction, Derek Pearsall. Cambridge, 1992, xxvii–lxxxii.

Scott, Margaret. *Late Gothic Europe, 1400–1500*. The History of Dress. Ed. Aileen Ribeiro. Atlantic Highlands, NJ, 1980.

Sequeira, Isaac. 'Clerical Satire in the Portrait of the Monk and the Prologue to *The Monk's Tale*'. *Literary Studies: Homage to Dr A. Sivaramasubramonia Aiyer*. Eds K. P. K. Menon, M. Manuel, and K. Ayyappa Paniker. Trivandrum, 1973, 34–43.

Shakespeare, William. *Twelfth Night. The Complete Signet Classic Shakespeare*. New York, 1972.

The Siege of Jerusalem. Eds E. Kölbing and Mabel Day. EETS, OS 188. London, 1932.

Sirasi, Nancy G. *Medieval and Early Renaissance Medicine: An Introduction to Knowledge and Practice*. Chicago, 1990.

———. 'The Music of Pulse in the Writings of Italian Academic Physicians (Fourteenth and Fifteenth Centuries)'. *Speculum* 50 (1975): 689–710.

'The Sisters' Clothes'; 'From *The Rule of Our Saviour*'. *Women's Writing in Middle English*. Ed. Alexandra Barratt. New York, 1992, 91–3.

Sitwell, Sacheverell. *Monks, Nuns and Monasteries*. New York, 1965.

Skeat, Walter W., ed. *Chaucerian and Other Pieces: Being a Supplement to The Complete Works of Geoffrey Chaucer*. Oxford, 1897.

Sklute, Larry. 'Catalogue Form and Catalogue Style in the *General Prologue* of the *Canterbury Tales*'. *SN* 52 (1980): 35–46.

Smith, H. Clifford. *Jewellery*. London, 1908; rpt. 1973.

Smith, Sarah Stanbury. ' "Game in myn hood": The Tradition of a Comic Proverb'. *SIcon* 9 (1983): 1–12.

Snape, R. H. *English Monastic Finances in the Later Middle Ages*. Cambridge Studies in Medieval Life and Thought. Ed. G. G. Coulton. Cambridge, 1926.

Snyder, James. *Northern Renaissance Art: Painting, Sculpture, The Graphic Arts From 1350–1575*. New York, 1985.

Social England: A Record of the Progress of the People. Eds H. D. Traill and J. S. Mann. Vol. 2. New York, 1969.

'A Song Against the Friars'. *Political Poems and Songs Relating to English History, Composed During the Period From the Accession of Edw. III to that of Ric. III*. Vol. 1. Ed. Thomas Wright. London, 1859, 1861; rpt. Germany, 1965, 263–8.

'Song of the Corruptions of the Time'. *The Political Songs of England: From the Reign of John to that of Edward II*. Ed. and trans. Thomas Wright. London: Camden Society, 1839, 27–36.

Specht, Henrik. 'The Beautiful, the Handsome, and the Ugly: Some Aspects of the Art of Character Portrayal in Medieval Literature'. *SN* 56 (1984): 129–46.

Speed, Peter, ed. *Those Who Worked: An Anthology of Medieval Sources*. New York, 1997.

Spencer, Brian. 'London–St Alban's Return'. *The London Archaeologist*, n.vol. (Spring 1969): 34–5, 45.

———. *Pilgrim Souvenirs and Secular Badges*. Medieval Finds from Excavations in London 7. London, 1998.

———. *Pilgrim Souvenirs and Secular Badges*. Salisbury Museum Medieval Catalogue, Pt 2. Salisbury, 1990.

Spencer, William. 'Are Chaucer's Pilgrims Keyed to the Zodiac?' *ChauR* 4 (1970): 147–70.

Staley, Lynn. 'The Man in Foul Clothes and a Late Fourteenth-Century Conversation About Sin'. *SAC* 24 (2002): 1–47.

Staniland, Kay. 'Clothing and Textiles at the Court of Edward III 1342–1352'. *Collectanea Londiniensia: Studies in London Archaeology and History Presented to Ralph Merrifield*. Eds Joanna Bird, Hugh Chapman, and John Clark. London and Middlesex Archaeological Society, Special Papers 2. London, 1978, 223–34.

———. *Medieval Craftsmen: Embroiderers*. Toronto, 1991.

The Statutes of the Realm. Vol. 1. London, 1910; Netherlands, 1963.

Steadman, John M. 'The Prioress's Brooch and St. Leonard'. *ES* 44 (1963): 350–3.

Stemmler, Theo, ed. *The Ellesmere Miniatures of the Canterbury Pilgrims*. Poetria Mediaevalis 2. 3rd edn. Mannheim, 1979.

Stoian, Gabriel. *An Illustrated Herbal*. <http://www.magdalin.com/herbal/plants_pages/b/burdock.htm>.

Stokes, A. E. *Christ Church Cathedral, Dublin*. The Irish Heritage Series, no. 12. N.p., n.d.

Storm, Melvin. 'The Pardoner's Invitation: Quaestor's Bag or Becket's Shrine?' *PMLA* 97.5 (1982): 810–18.

The Story of Medicine in Art. Exhibition catalogue. The Milwaukee Art Institute, Sept. 11–Oct. 25, 1953. Milwaukee, 1953.

Strohm, Paul. *Social Chaucer*. Cambridge, MA, 1989.

Strutt, Joseph. *A Complete View of the Dress and Habits of the People of England, from the Establishment of the Saxons in Britain to the Present Time: Illustrated by*

Engravings Taken from the Most Authentic Remains of Antiquity. Critical and explanatory notes by J. R. Planché. 2 vols. London, 1842; London, 1970.

Studer, Paul, and Joan Evans. *Anglo-Norman Lapidaries*. Paris, 1924.

Summa virtutum de remediis anime. Ed. and trans. Siegfried Wenzel. The Chaucer Library. Athens, GA, 1984.

Sumption, Jonathan. *Pilgrimage: An Image of Medieval Religion*. Totowa, NJ, 1975.

Swanson, Robert N. 'Chaucer's Parson and Other Priests'. *SAC* 13 (1991): 41–80.

———. *Church and Society in Late Medieval England*. Oxford, 1989.

Swart, J. 'Chaucer's Pardoner'. *Neophil* 36 (1952): 45–50.

Szittya, P[enn]. R. *The Antifraternal Tradition*. Princeton, 1986.

———. 'The Antifraternal Tradition in Middle English Literature'. *Speculum* 52 (1977): 287–313.

Taitt, Peter S. *Incubus and Ideal: Ecclesiastical Figures in Chaucer and Langland*. Salzburg Studies in English Literature 44. Salzburg, 1975.

Talbot, C. H. *Medicine in Medieval England*. London, 1973.

———. and E. A. Hammond. *The Medical Practitioners In Medieval England: A Biographical Register*. London, 1965.

Tatlock, J[ohn] S. P. 'Chaucer's Monk'. *MLN* 55 (1940): 350–4.

———. 'The Date of the *Troilus* and Minor Chauceriana'. *MLN* 50 (1935): 277–96.

Testamenta Eboracensia, or Wills Registered at York Illustrative of the History, Manners, Language, Statistics, &c., of the Province of York, From the Year MCCC. Downwards. Vols 1 and 3. Ed. James Raine. London, 1836–1902.

Thomas, Marcel. *The Golden Age*. New York, 1979.

Thompson, Daniel V. *The Materials and Techniques of Medieval Painting*. Foreword by Bernard Berenson. New York, 1956.

Thorndike, Lynn. *University Records and Life in the Middle Ages*. New York, 1944; rpt. 1949.

Three Middle-English Versions of the Rule of St. Benet and Two Contemporary Rituals for the Ordination of Nuns. Ed. Ernst A. Kock. EETS, OS 120. London, 1902.

Thurston, Herbert. *The Holy Year of Jubilee*. Westminster, MD, 1949.

Tierney, Brian. *The Medieval Poor Law: A Sketch of Canonical Theory and Its Application in England*. Berkeley and Los Angeles, 1959.

Tiron, Abbé. *Histoire et costume des ordres religieux, civils et militaires*. 2nd edn. 2 vols. Bruxelles, 1845.

Tischendorf, Christine. *Evangelica Apocrypha*. Leipzig, 1853.

Todd, Revd Henry J. *Illustrations of the Lives and Writings of Chaucer and Gower: Collected from Authentic Documents*. London, 1810.

Tommaso da Celano, Fra. *The Life of St. Clare Virgin*. Trans. Catherine Bolton Magrini. Assisi, n.d.

Tonnochy, A. B. *Catalogue of British Seal-dies in the British Museum*. London, 1954.

Toynbee, Arnold. *A Study of History*. Rev. edn. Eds Arnold Toynbee and Jane Caplan. New York, 1972.

Traill, H. D., and J. S. Mann, eds. *Social England: A Record of the Progress of the People*. New York, 1969.

Two Old English Apocrypha and their Manuscript Sources. Eds J. E. Cross, et al. Cambridge, 1996.

Two Wycliffite Texts: The Sermon of William Taylor 1406; The Testimony of William Thorpe 1407. EETS, OS 301. Oxford, 1993.

Ussery, Huling E. *Chaucer's Physician: Medicine and Literature in Fourteenth-Century England*. TSE, 19. New Orleans, 1971.

———. 'Fourteenth Century English Logicians: Possible Models for Chaucer's Clerk'. *TSE* 18 (1970): 1–15.

———. 'How Old Was Chaucer's Clerk?' *TSE* 15 (1967): 1–18.

———. 'The Status of Chaucer's Monk: Clerical, Official, Social, and Moral'. *TSE* 17 (1969): 1–30.

van Uytven, Raymond. 'Cloth in Medieval Literature of Western Europe'. *Cloth and Clothing in Medieval Europe: Essays in the Memory of Professor E. M. Carus-Wilson*. Eds N. B. Harte and K. G. Ponting. *Pasold Studies in Textile History* 2. London, 1983, 151–83.

Vance, Eugene. 'Chaucer's Pardoner: Relics, Discourse, and Frames of Propriety'. *NLH* 20 (1989): 723–45.

Varty, Kenneth. *Reynard the Fox: A Study of the Fox in Medieval English Art*. [Leicester], 1967.

Veale, Elspeth M. *The English Fur Trade in the Later Middle Ages*. Oxford, 1960.

The Victoria History of the Counties of England: Yorkshire. Vol. 3. Ed. William Page. London, 1913.

Vigourel, Revd Adrian. *A Synthetical Manual of Liturgy*. Trans. Revd John A. Nainfa. New York, 1907.

Visitations of Religious Houses in the Diocese of Lincoln: Alnwick's Visitations (1436–49). Vol. 2, pt 1. Ed. Alexander Hamilton Thompson. Canterbury and York Society 24. London, 1919.

Visitations of Religious Houses in the Diocese of Lincoln: Alnwick's Visitations (1436–49). Vol. 3, pt 2. Ed. Alexander Hamilton Thompson. Canterbury and York Society 33. Oxford, 1929.

Visitations of Religious Houses in the Diocese of Lincoln: Injunctions and other Documents from the Registers of Richard Flemyng and William Gray, Bishops of Lincoln A.D. 1420–A.D. 1436. Vol. 1. Ed. Alexander Hamilton Thompson. Horncastle, 1914.

Visitations of Religious Houses in the Diocese of Lincoln: Records of Visitations Held by William Alnwick, Bishop of Lincoln A.D. 1436 to A.D. 1449. Vol. 2, pt 1. Ed. Alexander Hamilton Thompson. Horncastle, 1918.

Visitations of Religious Houses in the Diocese of Lincoln: Records of Visitations Held by William Alnwick, Bishop of Lincoln A.D. 1436 to A.D. 1449. Vol. 3. Ed. Alexander Hamilton Thompson. Lincoln, 1929.

Warthin, Aldred Scott. *The Physician of the Dance of Death*. New York, 1931.

Webb, Diana. *Pilgrims and Pilgrimage in the Medieval West*. London, 1999.

Weiner, Annette B., and Jane Schneider. *Cloth and Human Experience*. Washington, D.C., 1989.

Weisheipl, James A. 'Curriculum of the Faculty of Arts at Oxford in the Early Fourteenth Century'. *MS* 26 (1964): 143–85.

Weissman, Hope Phyllis. 'Antifeminism and Chaucer's Characterization of Women'. *Geoffrey Chaucer: A Collection of Original Articles*. Ed. George D. Economou. New York, 1975, 93–110.

————. 'The Pardoner's Vernicle, the Wife's Coverchiefs, and Saint Paul'. *ChauN* 1.2 (1979): 10–12.

Wenzel, Siegfried. 'Chaucer's Pardoner and His Relics'. *SAC* 11 (1989): 37–41.

Whitaker, Elaine E. 'John of Arderne and Chaucer's Physician'. *ANQ: A Quarterly Journal of Short Articles, Notes, and Reviews* 8.1 (Winter 1995): 3–8.

White, Robert B., Jr. 'Chaucer's Daun Piers and the Rule of St Benedict: The Failure of an Ideal'. *JEGP* 70 (1971): 13–30.

Whitmore, Sr Mary Ernestine. *Medieval English Domestic Life and Amusements in the Works of Chaucer.* New York, 1972.

'Why I Can't Be a Nun'. *Early English Poems and Lives of Saints.* Ed. F. J. Furnivall. Transactions of the Philological Society. Berlin, 1858, 138–48.

Wieck, Roger S. *Time Sanctified: The Book of Hours in Medieval Art and Life.* New York, 1988.

Wilkins, David. *Concilia Magnae Britanniae et Hiberniae.* Vol. 1. Londini, 1737.

————. *Concilia Magnae Britanniae et Hiberniae, Ab Anno MCCLXVIII Ad Annum MCCCXLIX.* Vol. 2. London, 1737; rpt. Brussels, 1964.

————. *Concilia Magnae Britanniae et Hiberniae, Ab Anno MCCCL Ad Annum MDXLV.* Vol. 3. London, 1737; rpt. Brussels, 1964.

Wilkins, Eithne. *The Rose-Garden Game: The Symbolic Background to the European Prayer-Beads.* London, 1969.

Williams, Arnold. 'Chaucer and the Friars'. *Chaucer Criticism*: Vol. 1, 'The Canterbury Tales'. Eds Richard J. Schoeck and Jerome Taylor. Notre Dame, IN, 1960, 63–83; rpt. from *Speculum* 28 (1953): 499–513.

————. 'Some Documents on English Pardoners, 1300–1400'. *Medieval Studies in Honor of Urban Tigner Holmes, Jr.* University of North Carolina Studies in the Romance Languages and Literatures 56. Chapel Hill, NC, 1965, 197–207.

————. 'Two Notes on Chaucer's Friars'. *MP* 54 (1956–57): 117–20.

Wilson, Kax. *A History of Textiles.* Boulder, CO, 1979.

Winston-Allen, Anne. *Stories of the Rose: The Making of the Rosary in the Middle Ages.* University Park, PA, 1997.

————. 'Tracing the Origins of the Rosary: German Vernacular Texts'. *Speculum* 68 (1993): 619–36.

Wolfram von Eschenbach. *Parzival.* Trans. A. T. Hatto. New York, 1980.

Wood, Chauncey. 'Chaucer's Clerk and Chalcidius'. *ELN* 4 (1966–67): 166–72.

————. 'Chaucer's Use of Signs in his Portrait of the Prioress'. *Signs and Symbols in Chaucer's Poetry.* Eds John P. Hermann and John J. Burke, Jr. University, AL, 1981, 81–101.

Wright, Stephen K. *The Vengeance of Our Lord: Medieval Dramatizations of the Destruction of Jerusalem.* Studies and Texts 89. Toronto, 1989.

Wurtele, Douglas. Review of Richard Rex, '*The Sins of Madame Eglantyne' and other Essays on Chaucer. SAC* 19 (1997): 292–4.

Wyclif, Iohannis. *Operis Evangelici Liber Tertius et Quartus sive De Antichristo Liber Primus et Secundus.* Notes, Iohann Loserth and F. D. Matthew. Vols. 3–4. London, 1896.

————. *Sermones.* Vol. 3. Ed. Iohann Loserth. Notes by F. D. Matthew. 1889; rpt. New York, 1966.

[Wyclif, John]. *The English Works of Wyclif Hitherto Unprinted.* Ed. F. D. Matthew. EETS, OS 74. London, 1880; 1896.

Zacher, Christian K. *Curiosity and Pilgrimage: The Literature of Discovery in Four-teenth-Century England*. Baltimore, 1976.

Ziegler, Joseph. Introduction. *Religion and Medicine in the Middle Ages*. Eds Peter Biller and Joseph Ziegler. York Studies in Medieval Theology 3. York, 2001, 3–14.

Zigrosser, Carl. *Medicine and the Artist*. 3rd enl. edn. New York, 1970.

Index

abuses, sartorial: 13, 17–24, 258; Adam,
14; by canons, 116, 243; by clerks, 3–4,
171, 174–5, 193; by friars, 20, 24, 94,
137, 139, 145, 148–9, 152–3, 155; by
laybrothers, 94, 116; by monks, 27–8,
115–18, 121–3, 125–8; by nuns,
prioresses, abbesses, 24–8, 30–4, 43,
65–73, 75–6, 79, 89–91, 95–6; by
priests, 246, 264–5, 269
academical dress: c.pl. VI, pl. 10, 135,
162–6, 172–5, 190, 201, 203–6,
208–10, 218–20, 222–4, 228; costs,
172–3; *cappa clausa*, overtunic, pl. 11,
174–5, 205, 207; *cappa manicata*, 205,
211; for physicians, 205–6; furs, 222;
for non-academic functions, 174;
hoods, 210; Master's academic robe of
sangwyn, c.pl. VI, 215; *pileus*, pl. 10,
205–6, 243, definition, 205; tunic,
upper, 174–5; *tunic talaris*, 217; silk
linings, 218
academics, medieval: Nicholas Lynne,
190; Richard Harward, Master,
Winchester, 173
Adam, garments: 14, 175–6; symbolism,
176
Alan of Lille: *Anticlaudianus*, 41, 189,
246; *Complaint of Nature*: Nature,
177–8
alchemists: 184–5, 187; Johannes Pygas,
monk, Bristol, 184–5; William de
Brumley, canon-chaplain,
Harmandsworth, 184–5
Alcock, John, Bishop, Ely: 13, 46, 80;
*Exhortacyon Made to Relygyous
Systers*, 80
Aldhelm, *De Virginitate*': 72, 80, 115–16
Alexander, J. J. G., 2
Alford, John A., 201
Alighieri, Dante: 236, 239; *Inferno*, Frate
Gaudenti, 156–7; *Paradiso*, 126, 153,
236, 249; *La Vita Nuova*, 236
allegory: 4; Wisdom's clothes, 23
almuce: 120–3; definition, 120;

lambskin-lined, 123; of black
cloth/muslin, black budget fur, 120; of
fur with tails, lappets, 173; of gray fur,
120, 122, 124
Alnwick, William, Bishop, Lincoln: 9,
30–2, 43, 58, 72, 90–1, 116–17, 171
Alphabet of Tales, 22
amulets, 235–6
Ancren[e] Riwle, 11, 40, 44, 66
Ancrene Wisse, 44
Andere, Mary, 141
Andrew, Malcolm, 29, 33, 160, 173,
199–200, 241–2, 248, 252–3
Anglo-Saxon Legends, 233–4
Aquinas, Thomas, *Summa Theologica*, 197
arms: 165; anelace, 7; armor, 58, 114;
buckler, 153; helm, 251; shield, 251;
sword, 153, 165; *see* knives
Armstrong, Nancy, 236
Arundel, Archbishop, 270–1
Ashwardly, John, Vicar, St Mary's, 153
Astell, Ann, 37, 163, 198
Atchley, E. G. Cuthbert F., 102, 214–15
Aungier, George James, 11–12, 14, 44

Backhouse, Janet, 208
*Baines's Account of the Woollen
Manufacture of England*, 145–6
Baldwin, Frances Elizabeth, 15–17, 93,
119–20, 128–9, 217
Baldwin, John W., 178
'Ballad Against Excess in Apparel', 264–5
Barratt, Alexandra, 14
Barron, Caroline M., 61–2
Barthes, Roland, 3, 262
Bartlett, Anne Clark, 39
Beard, Charles, 166–7, 228
Becchio, Silvana, 134
Beck, S. William, 218
bedclothes, 22, 70, 124
Beichner, Paul, 112–13, 126, 240
belt, *see* girdle
Bennett, H. S., 117
Bennett, J. A. W., 160, 173

Benson, C. David, 202–3
Berchorius, Petrus, *Ovidius Moralizatus*, 221, 224
Besserman, Lawrence, 148, 150
Bettmann, Otto L., 221
Binski, Paul, 58
Birgitta of Sweden's Revelations, 108
Bishop, W. J., 200, 220–21
Blaunkfront, Joan, 34
Blessed Virgin Mary: 35, 37–9, 41–2, 63–4, 73, 76, 99, 101–2, 106–8, 229, 238, 249–50, 253–4; veil, 249–50
Bloomfield, Morton W., 113, 184
Bober, Harry, 205
Boccaccio, Giovanni: 137, 221; *Decameron*, 46–7, 61, 148–9, 156; *de Casu illustrium virorum et feminarum*, 77–8; Fortune, 78; Glad Poverty, 77–8
Boethius: *The Consolation of Philosophy*, Philosophy, 177–8
'The Book of Physiognomy', 32–3
The Book of Vices and Virtues, 40, 81, 111
Book to a Mother, 28
boots, half-boots: 152; *see* Monk, monks
Bosse, Roberta, 241
Bourchier, Thomas, Archbishop, 120
Bowden, Muriel, 32–3, 160, 220, 252
Boyd, Beverly, 101
bracelet: 84, 95, 103; *see* Prioress, pejorative language
Braddy, Haldeen, 102
Bradley, Sr Ritamary, 136, 175–6
Bragg, Lois, 243
Brant, Sebastian, 192
Braun, Joseph, 217
Brearley, Denis, 232
Bressie, Ramona, 122, 127, 129
Breugel, Pieter, 236
Breward, Christopher, 4
Bridbury, A. R., 214
Brightman, F. E., 205, 208
britches (braies, breeches, drawers): 8, 66, 115, 124, 180, 240; Thomas Becket's hair breeches, 249
Brocchieri, Mariateresa Fumagalli Beonio, 191, 195
brooch: pl. 7, 82–5, 91, 93, 98, 104–5, 124, 131, 222, 267, 269; decorative, 17, 22, 48, 82–3, 89–93, 95, 108, 128; fastening, 68, 103, 108, 127–8, 131–2, 269; fraternal emblem, pl. 8, 269, *see* Monk, pyn; in visual arts, 222; love

gifts, 103; morse, 127; of Robert de Hereford, 127; ornamenting hood, 128; *see* Prioress, rosary
Brosnahan, Leger, 85
brothers, Austin: John Overtone, 116, Ralph Carnelle, 116; habits: cassocks, buttoned, 116; lambskin-lined cassocks, hoods, 121; woolen shirt, 116; forbidden lay dress: hood, 116; gowns of russet, 116; linen shirts, 116; riding cloak, 116; tunics, laced, 116
Broughton, Laurel, 181, 186
Bullough, Vern L., 203
Burnham, Dorothy K., 123
Burns, E. Jane, 180
buttons, 17, 72, 90, 103, 116, 127, 153, 167, 221
Buxtehude altarpiece, 2
Buxton, L. H. Dudley, 210

Caesarius of Heisterbach, *The Dialogue on Miracles*, 23
Calendar Inquisitions Misc., 152
Calendar of Wills...Court of Husting, London, 90
Cambridge History of Western Textiles, 68
Camille, Michael, 53, 108
Campbell, Marian, 105
Candon, Sr Mary Patrick, ed., *The Doctrine of the Hert*, 40
canon's habit: 68, 147, 185–6, 240; birettum, 240, 243; cap, 243; cloaks, 116, 186–7; hood, attached, 186, 240, 243; *pileus*, 240; surplice, 185; tippets, 120, 229, *see* Friar; forbidden: belts, purses, with silver bars, orphreys, 116
cape: 10, 44, 80, 120–2, 131, 134–5, 152, 229, 261; of St Clare, 183; *see* clerks, tippet, Friar
Carr, Annemarie Weyl, 249
Carter, John, 53, 61, 103, 114
Cartwright, Frederick F., 200–2, 204
Carus-Wilson, E. M., 215
Casagrande, Carla, 134
Caxton: 150; *Caxton Abstract of the Rule of St Benet*, 10
Chance, Jane, 221, 240
chains (neck), 17, 78, 93, 96, 101
chainse: 178; definition, 178; symbolism, 178–9
Chapters of the Augustinian Canons, 243

Chaucer: *General Prologue*, 3–4, 239, 244;
    Cook, 7; Franklin, 7, 172, 219;
    Guildsmen, 7, 199; Host, 7, 123,
    186–7, 247; Knight, 219, 227;
    Manciple, 7; Merchant, 7, 141, 172,
    219; Reeve, 215; Second Nun, 52;
    Sergeant of the Law, 7, 172 219;
    Shipman, 199; Squire, 219, 254; Wife
    of Bath, 7–8, 85, 95, 107, 113, 199,
    219, 246, 251, 262; Yeoman, 107, 131;
    see Clerk, Doctour of Phisik, Friar,
    Monk, Pardoner, Parson, Prioress,
    Summoner; *Book of the Duchess*, 38,
    Black Knight, 38, Blanche, 38; *Canon's
    Yeoman's Tale*, 184–5, Cannon, 184–7,
    Yeoman, 184–5, 187; *Clerk's Tale*, 180,
    Prologue, 196, Griselda, 179–80,
    196–7, Walter, 179–80, 197, the father,
    180; *Friar's Tale*, 185, 251, Summoner,
    139, 144, Yeoman, 144, 168; *House of
    Fame*, 58; *Knight's Tale*, 8, 21, 180,
    213, 227, 239, 245, Theseus, 8; *Legend
    of Good Women*, 244, Aeneas, 244,
    Dido, 244, Lucrece, 244; *Manciple's
    Tale*, 245, Phebus, 245; *Melibee, Tale
    of*, 245; *Merchant's Tale*, 245–6,
    January, 246; *Miller's Tale*, Absalon,
    170–71, Nicholas, 138, 174; *Nun's
    Priest's Tale*, 83, 239, Nun's Priest, 135,
    Pertelote, 83; *Pardoner's Tale*, 227,
    240, 249, Introduction, 247; *Parliament
    of the Fowls*, 244; *Parson's Tale*, 161,
    184, 193–4, 245–7, 262; *Prioress's
    Tale*, 64; *Reeve's Tale*, Aleyn, 174,
    John, 174; *Romaunt of the Rose*, 100,
    Avarice, 166, 169–70, 177, Poverty,
    183, Rychesse, 100; *Shipman's Tale*,
    130; *Squire's Tale*, 245; *Summoner's
    Tale*, 137, 230, friar, 144; *Troilus and
    Criseyde*, 180, 243, 245, Pandarus, 243,
    245, Troilus 245
Chaucer Life-Records, 229
chemise (*stamen*, shift, smock, shirt): 63,
    66, 178–9, 197; cloth of Rennes, 33,
    71, 76; fine linen, 80; haircloth, 66,
    113, 128; hedgehogskins, 66; white
    flannel, 13
Chism, Christine N., 186
Chrétien de Troyes: *Erec et Enide*, 178;
    Perceval, 178–9; *Yvain*, 178, 180
Christine de Pizan: 33, 113; *The Eipstle of
    Othea to Hector*, 33

Cigman, Gloria, 121, 158, 238
Clanvowe, Sir John, 254
Clark, John, 61
Clark, John Willis, ed., 122
Clark, Thomas Blake, 32
Clarke, E. C., 163, 190, 203, 205, 208,
    210, 218–20, 222–3
Clark-Maxwell, Revd W. G., 10
cleanness: 45, 47, 74–5, 176, 264; laundry,
    13; manners, 35, 40; spiritual
    cleanness, 40, 45, 74, 103, 109–10
Cleanness, 5–6, 246, 264–5
Clensyng of Mannes Soule, 28, 265
clerical dress: 3–4, 10, 144–5, 164–5, 173,
    204–5, 208, 220–1, 229, 239–40, 243,
    258, 260; definition, 164; garments:
    cassock, 164, 173, with fur-lined cuffs,
    173; fur-lined sub-tunica, 121, 123,
    173; furs, 14, 27, 47–8, 118, 120–21,
    131, 152–3, 217, 220, 227; mantle,
    165; in visual arts, 260–1; regulations,
    24–6, 28, 165; sumptuary laws 120,
    217; worn by physicians, 204, 220–1;
    see clerks, furs, pilch, 'long robes',
    Monk; monk's habit, monks
Clerk, the (Chaucer): 160–98, 201,
    268–70; clothing: courtepy, 160–1,
    166–70, 173–5, 177–8, 183–4, 187–9,
    193, 195–8, 214, 268–70, definition,
    166, synonyms: *cote-hardie*, 167,
    doublet (aketon), 168, *haincelin*, 167,
    245, *garnache* 167, *garde corps*, 167,
    gown, 166–7, houppelande, 166–7,
    super tunic, 167, surcoat, 166–7,
    tabard, 167; condition of courtepy:
    168–9, thredbare, 144, 148, 160–1,
    170, 173, 175–85, 187–9, 191, 193–8,
    268, 270, definition, 177, symbolism,
    177, 184, 187–8, 191, 193–5, 198, pied,
    167, 268; layman's dress, pl. 9, 160,
    162, 175; overeste, 160–1, 165–6, 168,
    173, 197; value, 168; education:
    189–91, 193–8; Aristotle, 189, 191,
    193–5; Petrarch, 191–2, 196, 221–2;
    philosophy, 177, 189, 193–5; sins:
    avarice, 189, 196; coveting, 189, 196;
    curiositas, 161, 185–7, 189–93, 196–8,
    definition 185; vanity, 196; spending:
    195; books, 161, 174, 189, 192–8;
    'robes riche', 161, 194, 268;
    see clerks, doublet, poor scholars

clerks: 24, 120; copyists, 194, medical practitioners, 200–2, 2004; in visual arts, 160–1, 163–5; poor scholars, 173–5, 181, 269–70; status, 171–2; sumptuary laws, 15–16, 120, 215, 217
clothing: boots, 164, cape, tippet, *caputium*, 164; *cappa clausa* (sub-tunica), pl. 11, 164–5, 173, 175, 205, 207; 'clerkly garments', 160, 162–3, 166, 172–3, 205–8, 220; clerk's gown, 163; gloves, 164; hood, furred (Bachelor), 190; silk-lined, 218; long robe (*vestis talaris*), c.pl. V, pls. 9–10, 3–4, 160, 162–5, 168, 206, 208, 217, 220–1; mittens, 174; *pileus*, cap, pl. 10, 164, 166, 173, 205–6, 208, 243; scarves, 165; shoes, 164, 174; surplice, 171, 173; vesture, 171; tabard, academical, 165–7, 190, 218; lay dress: pl. 9, 160, 162, 164, 171, 175, non-academic dress, 174; livery, 218; *see* tunic
forbidden: bearing arms, 164–6, 171–2; boots, visible, 165; girdles, embroidered in gold, silver, 172; garments too brief, tight, 165, 172; gowns too long, 184, symbolism, 184; hoods, fancy, 172; hose of red, green, 165, 171; indecent dress, 165; mantles worn improperly, 175; pointed shoes, 165, 170; puffed sleeves, 165; shoes, red, green, 172; sleeveless tunics, 175; tabards worn improperly, 175; trunk hose, 165; *see* scholars
clerks, medieval: Thomas Adams, 171; John Clerke, 172; John Bracebrigge, 194; John More, 171; John Thorp, 172; John Wetlee, 194
The Clerk's Book, 160, 171
Clode, C. M., 218
cloak, mantle: 6, 10, 28, 52, 69–71, 73, 75–8, 117, 121, 152, 169; *armilansa*, 27; black cloak, furred with gris, 69; blue cloak, 78; *clamides*, 69; for London, 28; fur-lined cloak, 59, 68, 120, 132, 209; furred mantle, 69, 116; furred with half-vair, 69; hip-mantle of Wife of Bath, 7; lining, white cloth, 70; mantle, 9–10, 14, 23, 25–6, 46, 182; 'mantel furres', 14, 65; mantle not

worn, 27; murrey cloth with budge, 69; of Avarice, 170; of *blod*, 168; of gray cloth, 13, 77; of Jack Upland, 136–7; of lead, 156–7; of murrey cloth of Ypres, 27; of Poverty, 182–3; of russet, 70, 77, 152; lambskin lining, 152; of St Clare, 80, 138; of scarlet, 182; of worsted, 71; nun's cloak, 63, 65; riding cloak of burnet, 121; rochet, 69, definition 10; *rotundello*, 156; *see* Friar; monks; Prioress
'clote-leef' (burdock), 186
coat (cote): 9, 14, 123–4, 153, 169; Jack Upland's, 136; Avarice's, burnet, 169–70; friar's, 15; Griselda's coat, 180; Haukyn's 'cote', 188–9; Poverty's coat, 182–3; short coat, Hugh, Austin friar, 153
Cobcote, Prioress Dame Eleanor, 26
Colby, Alice, 178
colors: 267–8, 70–2; black: 10–12, 25, 27–8, 38–9, 44, 46, 52, 67–70, 77–9, 109, 116, 117–18, 120–1, 124–6, 138–9, 154, 161, 165, 228, 247, 260, 267, symbolism, 154, 181, 185–7, 204–5, 208–10; blue: 67–8, 70, 77–80, 96, 102, 117, 140, 149, 161, 166, 171, 188, 208–11, 215–17, 219, 221–2, 225–6, 229, 267–8, *blodi, blodius*, 70, 168[?], 214, symbolism, 102; brown: 78, 117–18, 121, 139, 161, 163, 169, 209, 267; gray: 13–14, 44, 77–8, 80, 121, 136, 138–40, 209, 215, 222, 236, 267; green: 78, 83, 88, 94, 99, 101–2, 108, 117–18, 161, 168, 172, 181, 185, 209, 214, 218–19, 222, 261, 267, symbolism, 102–3; mauve: 78, 161, 209, 222; orange: 77–8, 117, 157, 161, 181; pink: 208; purple: 78, 221; red: 1, 12, 38–9, 42, 68, 71, 80, 97, 99, 110, 117–8, 134, 152, 161, 172, 204, 208–11, 213–17, 219, 221–2, 225, 227–9, 247, 253–4, 259–61, 267–8, confusion with *blodi*, 168[?], 214, rose, 42, 228, scarlet, 41, 163, 229, symbolism 1, 12, 99, 211, 213; tan, 140, 161; violet: 71, 209; white: 10–12, 21, 25, 38–9, 41, 43–4, 47, 49, 52, 72, 77–9, 96, 108–10, 114, 120, 124, 140, 143, 152, 154, 161, 171, 175, 185–6, 208–9, 211, 215, 228–9, 247, 253–4, 267, symbolism, 154, ivory, 38, 41;

yellow: 67–8, 78, 96; colors used in visual arts: 208
Concilia Magnae Britanniae et Hiberniae, 18, 24–6, 67–8, 70, 118, 126, 243
Condren, Edward I., 236–8, 240, 250
confession, costume sins, 28, 265
Conrad, Lawrence I., 200–2, 204
consecration ceremonies, 12–13, 43, 66
cope: 108, 118, 120, 123, 127, 131, 135, 153, 169, definition, 123, 151, 169, 185; choir cope, 120, 151; Syon Cope, 151; *see* Friar, semycope
Corboys, William, Archbishop, Canterbury, 13
coronet, 22, 47–8
Corley, Brigitte, 256
Corrigan, Peter, 7
costume rhetoric: 5–8, 28, 266–72, definition, 3, as communication, 4; models: *Actual Garment/Accessory*, 7, 183; *Emblematic Dress*, 7, 266–7; *False Vestments*, 5–7, 19, 47, 74–6, 144, 264; *Generalized Costume*, 8; *Omitted Clothing*, 7, 244–5, 260; *Social Mirror*, 8, 173; *Spiritual Mirror*, 6, 19, 47, 75, 159, 183–4, 261–2, 266–7; *see* metaphors
Coulton, G. G., 15, 28, 32, 34, 41–2, 48, 51, 114–17, 131, 139, 153, 158, 255
Courtenay, William J., 183, 195, 201–2
The Court of Love, 20, 35, 47
cowl: 7–8, 10–12, 26, 28, 80, 115, 121, 124, 139–40, 151, 156, 161; of St Francis, 80, 138, 183; *see* friar's habit, monk's habit, monks
Craik, T. W., 152
Crane, Susan, 166
Crawfurd, Raymond, 200
Cross, J. E., 232–3
crown, 11–12, 52, 58, 79
Cunningham, D. J., 204–5
Cunnington, C. Willett, 49, 51, 117–18, 124–6, 166–7, 227–8
Cunnington, Phillis, 49, 51, 117–18, 123–6, 165–7, 205, 227–8
Cura sanitatis Tiberii, 233–4
curious, *ouer* curyous: definition, 11; 11–14, 19, 25–6, 28, 45, 65, 82, 89, 97, 110–11, 130–2, 267
Curry, Walter Clyde, 225, 248
Cutts, Edward L., 3, 53, 139, 163, 262

Dagenais, John, 157
Daichman, Graciela S., 22
Dalby, Thomas, Archdeacon, Richmond, 27
Dane, Joseph A., 42
Dauby, Hélène, 211, 213
Davis, R. Evan, 96
Day, Mildred, 232–4
Decalogus evangelice paupertatis, 139
Decun, Dame Alice, 31
Deevy, Mary B., 108
Delatte, Dom Paul, 114, 121, 124–5, 129
Demus, Otto, 57
Dennys, Rodney, 237
Derbes, Anne, 1
La Destruction de Jerusalem, 235
Dillon, Bert, 192–3
dirtiness, 6, 184, 187–9
disguise, 5–7
'A Disputation between a Christian and a Jew', 21
Dives et Pauper, 131
doctors (physicians, surgeons): fees and robes, 201, 204, 219–20, 223–5; knowledge of astronomy, astrology, 202; in visual arts, c.pl. VI, pls. 12–13, 205, 208–12, 222–5, 267
  in fashionable dress: 209, 221–5; buttons of gold, 221; caps, brimless, conical, 222; chaperon, 209; cloak of 'Calabre', 221; furs, 222; gilded spurs, 221; gold accessories, 222; gowns of purple, 221; gowns of scarlet, 222; hood, furred, 221; red, 222; puffed sleeves, 209; rings, 221; *see* academical costume
  medical costume: 200, 209, 220–1, 223–5; academic garments, 204; biretta, 208; 'clerkly' dress, 220, *see* clerks; ecclesiastical garments, 204; furs, 215; gown with hood, 208; long robes, 204, 208; monastic styles, 204; plague costume, 200; scholar's dress, 220; surgeon's dress, pl. 12, 220; short tunics, 204, 212; tabard, sleeveless, 208; undertunic, 208
  medical men, medieval: Adelard of Bath, 202; Arnau de Vilanova, 201; Avicenna, 216; Daniel Morley, 202; Galen, 211, 216, 222; Guy de Chauliac, 203; Henri Mondeville,

203; John de Middleton, 220; John de Mirfeld, 203; John of Arderne, 219–20; John of Bosnia, 202; John of Cella, 202; John of Gaddesden, 203; Lanfrank, 203; Br Matthew, 202; Robert of Chester, 202; Simon Bredon, 202–3; Thomas Brown, 202; Br Warin, 202; William Appleton, 204; William Holme, king's physician, 220; William of Bedford, 202; William Scheves, 202
Doctour of Phisik, the (Chaucer): 199–225, 267–70; character: fees and robes, 219–20; gold, 200; education, 200–4, 216–7, 220, 223, 225, 269; plague, 200, 225; status, 199–200, 210, 267, in holy orders, 199, 201–4; surgeon, 203–4; vice, greed(?), 270; clothing: color choices, 201, 221, 267, 270; fabrics, 200–1, 208, 210–11, 213–17, 219, 221, 223, 225, 268–70; pers, 199, 211, 215–17, 219, 221, 268, prices, 215–16, 225; sangwyn, c.pl. VI, 199, 211, 213–17, 219, 221–2, 268, definition 211, 213, 225, prices, 213–14; sendal, 199, 218–19, 268, lining, 269; taffata, 199, 217–19, 221, 268, lining, 269; silk prices, 217–19
Dodwell, C. R., 58
Dohar, William J., 172, 262
Donaldson, E. Talbot, 169
Donavan, J. F., 250
doublet (aketon): 168, 244, 261, 265; pourpoint, 167, 229
Druitt, Herbert, 113, 122
Duncan, Edgar H., 184–5, 187
Duranti, 14
dyes, 28, 65, 67–8, 211, 213–17

'Earth to Earth', 18, 22, 75
Eckenstein, Lina, 25, 72
Eleazar, Edwin, 100–2, 203, 211
Ellesmere miniatures, 52, 55, 61–2, 119, 209–10, 225–30, 240, 246–7, 253–4, 260
embroidery (ornamention): 17, 45, 72, 89, 93–4, 151, 219; as metaphor, 46; gold and silver, 11–12, 27, 65, 67–8, 72, 76, 89–90, 168, 172, 178, on *dyapre*, 21, 27; jewels, 93; lovers' knots, 129; necklines, sleeves, 80; silk, 12, 68, 76, 89

Emmerson, Richard K., 248, 260
enamelling, 17, 93, 127–8
Engelhardt, George J., 141, 187, 189, 246, 255–6, 262
Episcopal Register of John de Grandisson, 239
Epp, Garrett P. J., 181, 246
D'Etienne de Bourbon, 14
Euangelium Nichodemi, 233, 237
Evans, Joan, 35–6, 77, 93, 96, 98–106, 108, 131–2, 138–9, 154, 236, 251
Everett, Walter Kennedy, 28, 265
Ewing, Elizabeth, 14, 109

fabric: 70, 146–7, 150, 183, 267–8, 270–2; measurements: 146–9, quarter, 146, ell, 33, 146–7; prices, 146–9; quality: 168–70; dirty, 184, 187–9; foul, 176; old, 175–82, 193, 198, symbolism, 179, 181; ragged, 136, 169, 176–9, 181–2; tears, 6, 19, 169–70, 175–83, 187–8, 198, 264, symbolism 179, 181, 183, 187; threadbare, 144, 148, definition, 177–8, symbolism, 177, 179–80, 184–9, 191, 268–9; *see* Clerk, threadbare; patches
types: Aylesham cloths, 148; black cloth, 27; blanket, 16, 147, 152, 168; broadcloth, 147; brocade, 217; burel, 26; burnet, 24, 46, 67, 121, 123–4, 169, glossed, 169; camels' hair, 217; canons' cloth, 76, 123, 146–7; canvas, 66, 124, 152; cendal, 218–19; checkered green cloth, 118; cloth of gold, 17, 91, 93, silver, 17; cloth of Rennes, 33; coarse ('vyle') cloth, 148; cotton, 217; *diapre*, 21–2, 27, 76; felt, 124–5; fine linen, 80, 116, violet, 71; of flax, 66; frieze, 124; fustian, 68, 76, 219; goats' hair, 217; gray, 13, 44, 77, 136, 138, 140, symbolism, humility, 15; haircloth, 66; Holland, 171; humble, 72; Kersey, 124; Lincoln says, 124; linen, 10, 12, 14, 39, 44, 49, 80, 124–5, 178, black, 44, white, 49; 'Linure' (lawn), 173; medley, 219; monks' cloth, 76, 146–7, 219, 268; motley, 145; murrey, 27, 69; muslin (cyndon), 124; of Rennes, 33; pers, 215–17, 219; russet, 16, 69–70, 77–9, 132, 140, 152, 154,

symbolism, 154; sanguine, 213–15, 219; satin, 219; scarlet, 147–8, 182, 188, 214; scarlet gytes, 8; serge, 28, 124; silk, 124, 132, 136, 217–19, 219, 269; sindon, 147; 'Stafford blew', 149; *stamineum* (linsey-woolsey), 124; taffeta, 217–19, 221; tartaryn/tantaryn, 147, 218; 'tweny medley', 213; velvet, 219, gold velvet, 217; wilkoc(?), 124; woolen, 68, 116, 145–7, 152, 159, 211, 268; worsted: 28, 68, 71, 76, 123–4, 145–8, 211, measurements, 146–9; double worsted, 73, 76, 128, 132, 144–9, 219, definition, 145, significance, 148–9; half double worsted, 145; single worsted, 146; worsted ray, 145, 152; worsted say, 145; dyed, 44–5, 65, 67–8, 72, in grain, 147; cloths: inexpensive, 43; suitable for friars, 15; suitable for nuns, 14–15; *see* Friar, silk

Fairholt, F. W., 43, 205

Fanning, William H. W., 202, 223–4

fashionable (luxurious) dress: 6, 33, 43, 45, 58–9, 69, 71–2, 75, 246; anglice 'gounes', 27; barred girdles, plaited belts, 68; delicate or colored furs, 67; dresses with trains, 68, 76; dresses with pleats, 68, 76, 89; fastenings of laces, brooches, 68, 89, 131; fur at wrist, 68; gowns, with wide bottoms, 68; *houppelandes*, 68; kirtles of fustian, worsted, 68, 76, 152, laced with silk, 71, 76; laced shoes, 68; large collars, 68; long [excessive] supertunics, 68; mantles, kirtles with seam openings, 68; narrow-cut tunics, 69; narrow-cut rochets, 69; pleated girdle, 76; red dresses, 68; rosaries (fifteen-century fashion), 91, 95; secular rings, 68, 89–90; silk garments, veils, 68, 71, 76; sleeves, turned-back, 68

Fayrfax, John, Rector of Presscot: bequest, 27, 69, 76

Fayrfax, Prioress Margaret, 27, 34, 69, 76

Fleming, John V., 126, 139, 170, 242, 251–2

Fletcher, Alan J., 91, 240

Flury-Lemberg, Mechtild, 114, 138, 183

fools, jesters, *jongleurs*, minstrels: 134, 220, 270; *see* metaphors: *joculators Dei*

fops, dandies, gallants, 24, 170, 173–4, 246

Frank, Mary Hardy Long, 29–30, 34, 37, 42, 64

Frank, Robert Worth, Jr., 157

Fredell, Joel, 35

French, Gilbert J., 120, 123, 134, 151, 204, 229, 260–1

De Frere Denise, 155

Frese, Dolores Warwick, 42, 129–30

Friar: 8, 133–59, 173–4, 267–70, 272; figure of Sire *Penetrans Domos*, 142–4, 158; vices: 'covetyse', doubleness, greed, hypocrisy, pride, lechery, 133, 143–4, 149–50, 155, 158–9; clothing: cope: 23, 144–5, 150–1, 153, definition, 151; headcovering: 144; hood, 144, 148, 151, 158; 'typet', 133–6, 140–1, 143–5, 153, 158–9, definition, 134–5, 153, 269, 272; 'semycope': 76, 123, 133–4, 144–5, 150–9, 173–4, 219, 269, symbolism, 156; bell-shape, 134, 136–7, 144, 150, 155–7, 159; rounded, 144–5, 150, 155–7, 269; not thredbare, 144, 148, double-worsted, 76, 132, 134, 144–9, 159, 173–4, 219, 268–9, definition, 145; tippet goods: knives, pins, 134–5, 139, 141–3, 158

friars: 5–6, 158, 241, 268; habits: 15, 19–20, 135–9, 143, 147, 154–6; Franciscan: 137–8, 151–2, dimensions, 151; belt, 152; coarse ('vyle') cloth, 148, 151, russet, 154, symbolism, 154; cote with hood, 138, 159; cowl of gray, 140; 'freresgerdle', 152; frock, 139, 153; girdle of cord, knotted, 138–9, 150, 156, symbolism, 154; hood, c.pl. IV, 137–41, 143, 152; patches of sack cloth, 138, 159; rope belt, knotted, 109, 137, 150, 154, 156, symbolism, 154; sandals, 137, 139; shoes, necessary, 138; (1) tunic, 137, 139; forbidden clothing: (2) coats, 137, 150; [garments] curiously made, 151; 'fine copes', 145; leather belt, 137; pleats, creases, 153; purses with money, 137, 139; [garments]'pynched aboute the neck', 151; scrip, 137; shoes (unnecessary), 137; staff, 137; wallets, 137, 139, 152; wide garments, broad hems, 155–6; *see* peddlers, 'Reply of Friar Daw Topias', rules

friars, medieval: Hugh, Austin friar, in
lay garments, 152–3; Richard
Ruston, friar minor, wardrobe, 152
Friedman, John B., 84, 89, 99, 142
furs: 10, 13–16, 22, 25, 27, 68, 72, 75,
117–23, 166, 173, 190, 220, 222,
267–9; prices 215, 222; bedclothes, 22;
delicate or colored, 68; lining for cloak,
59, 79; lining for *pellicea*, 71; legacies,
27; on cap of estate, 30; 'mantel
furres', 14, 65; showing at wrist, 68;
sumptuary laws, 15–17; types: badger,
222; beaver, 153; 'bifle', 14; budge, 27,
30, 33, 69, 71, 118, 141, definition, 17;
'byse', 141; calaber, 14, 221–2; cat, 14,
16–17; coney, 16–17, 269; ermine, 22,
27, 48, 79, 93, 120, 211, 215–16, 222,
erminette, 76; 'foyns', 153; fox, 16–17;
furs, red, 71; gris (*grys*), 14, 27, 68, 73,
76, 117, 119–23, 128, 136, 141, 215,
219, 222, 267–9; lamb, 14, 16–17, 118,
152, 169–70, 215, 222, 227, 229, 269,
sheep's fleece, 128; lettice ('Letuses'),
93, 120, 215; miniver, 118, 120–1, 205,
214–15, 222; rabbit, 70, 215; sable,
215; shankes, 70; vair, 33, 69, 71, 76,
128, 141, 215; squirrel, 118; strandling,
118; *see* Monk, purfled

Gallo, Ernest, 38
Ganter, Bernard J., c.pl. V, 164–6
Garbáty, Thomas, 253
Gardner, Arthur, 33
garment construction methods: 267–71;
fronciées (fruncyd), 25–6; dimensions,
proper, 13, 23–4, 28, 151, 172;
openings: front and side, 28, seams, 68;
pleats, pl. 4, 23, 25–8, 35, 39, 43–4,
46–7, 49, 51, 59, 62, 89; pynched (in a
mantle), 26, 151; tucks, 23, 49, 51, 59
'garnach', with vair, 69
Gasquet, Francis A., 9–10, 28, 40, 115, 125
Gautier de Coinci, *La Chasteé as nonains*,
38–40, 46–7, 75–6
Gaylord, Alan T, 29, 84
Geoffroi de Vinsauf, *The Poetria Nova*, 38,
51, 271
Gerard, John, 186
Gerbert de Montreuil, 178
Getz, Faye, 201
Gibbons, Alfred (abstr.), 194
Gibbs, Marion, 24, 163

Gibson, Gail McMurry, 2
Gibson, Strickland, 210
Gilchrist, Roberta, 11–12
Ginsberg, Warren S., 160
Gioanventura Rosetti, *The Plictho*, 67, 211
Giotto, 1, 182
girdle (belt): 7, 9, 12, 17, 44, 63, 71–2, 75,
110, 131, 141, 159, 178, 229; and
buckle, stone of vertu, 100; and gold
buckle[?], 228; barred, 67, 76;
embroidered, 67, 72, 76, 89–90, 172;
for sleeping, 66; of cord, 138, 150; of
gold, 222; of rope, 15, 109; of silk, 67;
of silver and overgilt, 12, 33, 65, 71–2,
89–90; plaited belt, 68; pleated girdle,
76; *see* friars' habit, monks' habit,
monks
Giza, Mary M., 36, 49
gloves, 89, 116, 141, 164, 174
Godefroy, Frédéric, 65–7
gold: 16–17, 91, 93, 97, 105, 228, 249; as
braid, 78–9; as color, 38; as cloth, 17,
91, 93; as gilding, 156–7; as 'harneis',
93, 116, 136; as medicine, 200; as
metal, 1, 11–12, 16, 18, 25, 27, 93–4,
252; as money, 137, 195, 200; as
thread, 21, 129; crosses, 101; goldleaf,
77; horse trappings, 94; overgilt, 22–3,
33, 71; ribbons, 93; spurs, 116, 221;
tiraz, pl. 5a-c, 86–9; symbolism, 1; *see*
brooches, chains, crown, embroidery,
Monk, pins, Prioress, rings, rosaries
Goodridge, J. F., 169, 188
Gordon, Stewart, 12–13
The Gospels Book of Days, 231
Gottfried, Robert S., 199, 215
Gower, John: *Mirour de l'Omme*, 127–8,
132, 140, 199, 223; *Vox clamantis*, 85,
140
gown: 152; Jack Upland's, 136; Lollard's
blue gown, 187–8; *see* Clerk's courtepy,
clerks, lay and fashionable dress
Gray, H. L., 146
Green, A. Wigfall, 192–3
Green, Richard Firth, 204, 240
Grigsby, Bryon, 210
Grillinger, Peter, canon, 122
Grosse, Max, 157
Grossman, Alvin, 101
Guibertus, Tornacensis, 38, 40–1
Guillaume de Lorris and Jean de Meun: *Le
Roman de la rose*, 5–6, 50, 61, 64, 67,

74–9, 85, 100, 109–10, 158, 169–70, 180, 182, 240, 254; Amis, 110; Avarice, 169–70; Chastity, 61; Constrained Abstinence, 6, 64, 76, 79, 109–10; Courtesy, 85; Fair Welcome, 85; False Seeming, 5, 64, 67, 74–6, 109, 158, 240; Idleness, 64, 85; Lady Poverty, 182–3; Lover, 110; Pope Holiness, 6, 76, 109; Tristece, 180

Günther, Robert W. T., 134, 205, 208

Guy de Chaulia, *Cyrugie*, 186

Hahn, Thomas, 37, 48, 251

Hall, James, 231

Hall, Thomas N., 233, 237

Halligan, Theresa A., 32

Halverson, John, 241, 244, 250

Hamilton, Marie Padgett, 240, 243, 247

Hammond, E. A., 172, 199, 202–4, 220

Hargreaves-Mawdsley, W. N., 135, 164, 201, 205, 208–10, 219, 222, 224, 228, 240

Harper, Gordon H., 32

Harthan, John, 153

Hartley, Dorothy R., 135, 163

Hartshorne, A., 101

Harvey, Barbara, 9–10, 14–15, 23, 26, 28, 72, 115, 121, 123–5, 164

Harwood, Britton J., 242

Haselmayer, Louis A., 241–2, 251

Hatton, Thomas J., 185

Hauser, Arnold, 266–7

Havely, Nicolas, 137, 141

headcoverings (masculine): 230, 244, 246, 250; bareheaded, 244–5; cap: 11–12, 25, 161, 205, 228, coif, 244–5, flatcaps, 226, of estate, 31, 33, 71, furred, 30, 33, 71; garland, 252–6; hats: 188, 205, 236, 244–5; berets, 175; biretta, 205, 208, 243; *bourrelet*, 228, defined 228; chaperon, 135, 209, 222, 228, definition, 228; fez style, 209; Jewish, 53; red, 134; turban, 231; wide- brimmed, 77–8, 119, 251; mitre, 128; hoods: c.pl. IV, 52, 119, 120–1, 134–41, 143, 161, 166, 172, 186; clerk's nonacademic hood, 174; Coueitise, 188, 190; 'feend', 185; Friar Daw Topias, 136–7; friar's, 15; fur-lined hoods, 25, 27, 121–2, 209–10, 264–5; furs for hoods, 118; harlot's, 6, 264; gray cloth, 13, 77; Pardoner's hood, 7, 228, with liripipe,

166, with a 'poke', 134; *see* Friar, monks, Pardoner, pilgrim's weeds

headdresses (feminine): 27, 43–53, 58, 83; beribboned, 71, 80; coverchiefs, 246; fifteenth-century, 33–4, 58; fillet, 12; goffered, 49–50, 59; nebula, 49; nuns' headdresses, pl. 2, 50, 76–7, definition, 35, in visual arts, 51–63, 76; laywomen's, worn by Vices, 58; of color, 24, 80; of Wife of Bath, 8; veil: 71, 73, definition, 35–6, 78, overveil, underveil definition, 35, symbolism, 45–6, 59, bridal, 22, colored, 68, goffered, 49, laywomen's, 17, gauze-like, 28, of silk, 17, 25–7, 43, 45–6, 68, 71, nun's, 7, 10–13, 34, 36, 43–5, 50, 76–7, in visual arts, pl. 2, 51–63, 76; position: forehead, 31–3, 45–6; *see* Prioress

Heath, Peter, 24, 163

Heath, Sidney, 95, 112, 232, 262

Heloise, 54–5, 79, 131

Henry de Knyghton, 145

Henryson, Robert: 140; *The Testament of Crisseid*, 221–2; Doctour in phisik, 222

Herrade de Landsberg, *Hortus Deliciarum*, 58

Hervey, Isabel, Abbess, Elstow, 43

Herzman, Ronald B., 248

Heywood, John, 250

Higgs, Elton D., 197, 245

Hilary, Christine Ryan, 239

Hildegard of Bingen, *The Physica*, 186

Hilton, Walter, 12

Hinckley, Henry Barrett, 240

Hingeston-Randolph, Revd F. C., 94, 98

Hoccleve, Thomas: 177; *Regement of Princes*, 23, 64, 96

Hodges, Laura F., 3, 5, 7–8, 23, 49, 107, 149, 168, 177, 180, 199, 214–16, 242–3, 246, 261–2, 264, 266

Hodgson, Phyllis, 64–5, 85

Hoepfner, E., 215

Hoerner, Fred, 238–9, 250

Holloway, Julia Bolton, 11, 15, 31, 64, 108, 227

Hope, W. H. St John, 129

Houghton, Helen Sherwood, 215

houppeland: 65, 68; *see* Clerk's courtepy, clerks

Houston, Mary G., 33, 36, 58, 121, 134, 151, 163–4, 167, 173

'How a Louer Prayseth Hys Lady', 49
Howard, Donald, 59, 105
Hudson, Anne, 188
Hudson, Vivian Kay, 12, 37
Hunter, G. K., 226, 244–5
Huppé, Bernard F., 176–7, 197

Jacob, E. F., 163, 183
Jacob's Well, 103
Jacobs, Edward Craney, 64–5, 85, 88
jacke: of defense, 152; short, 168, 246–7
James, John, 123, 145–6, 211
James le Palmer (Jacobus): 163; *Omne
   bonum*, 50, 53, 79, 97, 108, 113, 161–5,
   171, 173, 206, 224
James, M. R., 123
Jankofsky, Klaus P., pl. 5a-c, 86–8
Jean Renart, 178
Jeffrey, David Lyle, 158
Jenkins, J. Geraint, 145
jerkin, 168
jewelry: 94, 132, 236; definition, 105
jewels: 16–17, 27, 33, 46–7, 68, 82–3,
   90–1, 93–108, 128–9, 236, 252; morse,
   108, 127; on copes, 131; on hoods, 128;
   stones of vertu, 100–1; rings: 22,
   89–91, 93, 97, 99, 118, 128,
   consecration, 68, of gold, silver, 17, 33,
   82, 89–90, 97, secular, 68; *see*
   embroidery, metaphors
Joan of Swine, Prioress, 27, 69
John of Arderne, *Treatise in Fistula in
   Ano*, 220
John of Gaunt, 204
John of Wales, 192
Jones, George F., 223, 239
Jones, Ida B., 200
Jones, Peter Murray, 199, 205, 208
Jonson, Ben, *Alchemist*, 185
Julian of Norwich, *Showings*, 136, 175–6,
   256, 272
Jungman, Robert E., 238
jupis, 27
Jusserand, J. J., 118, 126, 141, 232, 238–9

Kaeupner, Richard W., 251
Katzenellenbogen, Adolf, 58–9, 110
Keller, James, 226, 251, 254
Kellogg, Alfred L., 238, 241–2
Kelly, Douglas, 178
Kelly, Francis M., 135
Kelly, Henry Ansgar, 30, 32, 83, 251

Kendall, Alan, 262
Kennard, Joseph Spencer, 158, 240–1
Kessler, Herbert L., 231–2, 235, 237
Kiehl, James M., 242
Kiernan, Kevin S., 32, 37–8
kirtle: 9, 26, 244; definition, 170–1;
   Absalon's, 170; Christ's, 175; laced, 33,
   72; of fustian, 68; of worsted, 68
Kittredge, George Lyman, 240
Klapisch-Zuber, Christiane, 179
Knight, S. T., 35
knights: 227, 251; Lord Robert of
   Robertstone, Annandale, 255;
   Hospitalers, 21; sumptuary laws,
   15–17, 93, 120, 128, 173, 215
knives, 7, 17, 118, 152, 172
Knowles, Dom David, 112–13
Koslin, Désirée, 10, 12–13, 45, 215
Krapp, J. P., *The Legend of St. Patrick's
   Purgatory*, 22, 90
Kunz, George Frederick, 100
Kuryluk, Ewa, 2, 231, 233–4, 237, 256

Labarge, Margaret Wade, 214–17
laborer's dress, 175–6
lace: 72; for neck (necklace), 22, 48, 90–1;
   of scarlet, 41; of silk, 34
'The Land of Cokaygne', 22
Landrum, Graham, 84
Lanercost Chronicle, 255
Lang, Jane, 24, 163
Langland, William: 85, 189, 227, 236,
   239–41, 251–2, 265; *Piers Plowman*,
   5–6, 8, 106, 113, 135–6, 140, 142–4,
   149, 152, 161, 166, 169–70, 176–7,
   184, 188–9, 221–2, 228. 236. 239, 265;
   Anima, 106, 189; Charity, 136;
   Conscience, 135; Coueitise, 188; Guile,
   149; Haukyn, 6, 187–9; Imaginatif,
   161; Lady Meed, 251–2; Palmer, 227,
   236; Patience, 188; Phisik, 221; Piers,
   169; Sire *Penetrans Domos*, 142–4; Sloth,
   265; Truth, 228; Will, 189; Wit, 197
Langton, Stephen, 164, 205, 208
Lanham. Richard A., 133
Latham, R. E., 70, 214
Laver, James, 204
Lay Folks' Catechism, 114
leather: suitability for nuns, 14; skins: 7,
   13; well-tawed, 11
Leech, Patrick, 217
Legenda Aurea, 234–5

leggings, 6
leper's dress, 248
Lescher, Wilfrid, 96
Lewis, Charlton T., 185
Liber Celestis of St Bridget, 31, 33
Lightbown, Ronald W., 89, 91, 95–7, 99,
  101–4, 129, 131, 235, 253
Lincoln Diocese Documents, 95
liripipe: 134–5, 228; symbolism, 134; *see*
  Friar
livery, 15, 28, 267, 269–70
Lloyd, A. H., 173
Lollards, 145–6, 187–8
Loomis, Roger Sherman, 160, 228
Lowes, John Livingston, 42, 84–5, 94,
  156
Lucas, Catherine, 123, 165, 205
Lumiansky, Robert M., 223
Lydgate, John: *Amor Vincit Omnia*
  Mentiris Quod Pecunia, 106; *The*
  Pilgrimage of the Life of Man, 114;
  Prologue to the *Siege of Thebes*, 118,
  185–6; *The Temple of Glas*, 20

MacIntyre, Jean, 181, 246
MacKinney, L. C., 205
MacKinney, Loren, 211
Macklin, H. W., 113, 139, 165
Madeleva, Sr M., 30, 49, 88–9, 103, 108
Maidstone, Richard, priest, 153
male (pouch, wallet): 7, 118, 185–6,
  228–9, 237, 240–3, 246, 249–50; *see*
  Pardoner
Maleski, Mary A., 34
Malory, Thomas, *The Knight with the Two*
  Swords, 3, 271
Mane, Perrine, 49, 167
Mankind: Mankynde, 152, 168, 246; New
  Guise, 152, 246
Manley, Francis, 84
Manly, John Matthews, 184, 239
Mann, Jill, 22, 29, 39, 44, 47–8, 112,
  125–7, 133, 149, 154, 160, 195, 222–3,
  240, 246, 252, 254
Mann, Maurice, 215
Marchand, Jim, 157
Marchant, Guyot, 209
Markert, Emil, 229
de Marly, Diana, 167
Martin, Janet, 120
Mathew, Gervase, 167
Maxfield, David K., 239, 241

Mayo, Janet, 10, 14–15, 24, 34, 115, 123,
  129, 139, 151, 163
McBride, M. F., 216
McCloud, Revd Henry J., 18, 205, 220
McConnell, Sophie, 101
McCracken, Grant, 4
McNamara, Jo Ann, 12, 68
McVaugh, Michael R., 201
McVeigh, Terrence A., 248
medal, St Christopher, 107, 131
Medforde, Clemence, Prioress,
  Ankerwyke, 30, 33–4, 71, 90
Meier, Gabriel, 223
Meiss, Millard, 182
Mellinkoff, Ruth, 134–5, 139, 181, 244,
  246, 248
merchants, 120
'Du Mercier', 126–7
Melton, Archbishop, 69–70, 77–8
metaphors: 17–24, 28, 81; Augustinian
  garment metaphors, 262, 264; beloved,
  in Song of Songs, 37; Blessed Virgin as
  courtly lady, 37; bridal veil, 47–8;
  brideclothes/array, 40–1, 136; bride of
  Christ, 37–8, 40–1, 75; brooch, as
  Passion of Christ, 108; buckler made of
  cake, 251; cakes and ale church, 252;
  caritas as brideclothes, 264; Christ as
  courtly lover, 39–40, 75; Christ in
  servant's clothes, 175–7; cleanness as
  spiritual health, 264; cloak of pope-
  holiness, 75; clothed in virtues, 7; 'cote
  of cristendom', 188–9, 193, 196–7;
  crown of glory, 259; dance of death,
  201, 209; dressed in Christ's love, 272;
  earthly treasure as spiritual poverty,
  189; enlarged hems of copes, 134;
  embroidered with virtues, 46; foxes as
  doctors, apothecaries, 223; friar's habit
  as sign of poverty, chastity, 144; foxes
  as tricky friars, 140; friars as '*jongleurs*
  de Dieu', 134; holy habits, sign of
  vows, 247, 266–7, 272; 'get a cowl', as
  become a friar, monk, nun, 151; good
  shepherd, 259, 261–2, 265; good works
  clothing the soul, 258–9, 262, 264,
  267–8; jewels as virtues, 46, 80, 272;
  joculators Dei, 158; large robes (length,
  width), 18–21, 73, 75–6, 135–6;
  leprosy as simony, 248; life as
  pilgrimage, 265; mantle of authority,
  154; Mantle of Church Authority, 150;

naked in his/her smock, 179–80; new guise as current fashion, 152; nun as Christ's courtly lady, 40; nun's cloak (mantle) of faith, 63, seams, 63–4, 66; old man, new man, as spiritual images, 259; 'Purs is the ercedekenes helle', 242, 252; robe of religion, 74; robe of virginity, 40; shoes, not well-tawed, 22; short cloak as disobedience, 157; shortness of garment as lack of moral character, 152–3; Sire *Penetrans Domos*, 142–3; skins, well-tawed, 66; spots as sins, 40, 188; tavern sign signifying contents, 258; torn clothes, 6, 19, 169, 175–83, 187–8, 198, 264; veil as psalter, 46–7; veil, taking the, 20, 36, 43, 47; *vestis talaris* (*talaris tunica*, *pellicea*) signifying life of religion, 18, 23; Virtues as nuns, 37, 51, 59; virtues as vesture of soul, 39, 75, whited sepulchre, 153; wide and long garments, 17–21, 23, 68, 73, 148, 150; 'wide copis', 19–20; wolf in sheep's clothing, 133, 140, 149, 159; *see* jewels/virtues; Lydgate, Wyclif, Virtues, Vices
Meyer, Claudius F., 211
Milburn, R. L. P., 54
Miller, Clarence H., 241
Miller, Edward, 147
Miller, Robert P., 138–9, 192, 241, 246
Mirus, John [John Mirk]: *Instructions for Parish Priests*, 8, 239, 246, 261; *Mirk's Festial*: 253
Mohl, Ruth, 223
Monk, the (Chaucer): 112–32, 185, 193–4, 219, 267–9; in visual arts, c.pl. III, 119; character: status, 128; vices: gluttony, 112; lechery, vanity(?), 129; pride[?], 269; clothing: boots, 7, 112, 124–7, 131–2; cope, wide, c.pl. III, 123, 267, definition, 123; pyn, of gold: pl. 8, 11, 112, 119, 127–32, 267, 269; curious, 65, 119, 127–8, 130–2, 267; love-knotte, 119, 124, 127, 129–30, symbolism, 129; sleeves, purfiled: 119–21, 131–2, 267–9; *gris* (*grys*), 76, 112, 117, 119–23, 267–9
monks: 67, 204; habit: 8–9, 67–8, 113–14, 116, 118–19, 147–8, 150; in visual arts, c.pl. III, 118–19, 123–4; alb, 114,

definition, 114; boots, sandals, *caligae* (defined 126), *caligae clavatae*, 124–6; breeches, 115, 124; cap (nightcap), 124; cincture (belt), 114, 272, definition, 114, symbolism, 114; cloak, 148, 150–1, 153, symbolism, 153; cowl, 114–15, 118, 124; frock, 124; furs, 15, of black, 117; garments of black, 117; girdle for night, 124; girdle with pouch, 124; *indumenta pedum*, 125; mantle, 148; *pelisse*, 15; pilch, 124, 272; scapular, 114–15, definition, 115; shoes and stockings (*pedules*?), 14, 114, 124–6; shoes, round toes, 116; shirts, 124; sub-tunic, fur-lined, 123; *staminorum* (wool shirts), 124; tunic, 114, 124, 148; investiture, 114; lay dress forbidden: 123; belts of silk, 117, with silver ornaments, 117; boots: pointed toes, 116–17, 126, too tight, 117, 126, half-boots of red, 118, 126; cloaks, colored, 116, non-standard cloaks, riding capes, 117–18; cap, 116, *pilio*, 117; doublets, short, 116; fur (other than black) on hoods, collars, 117; garments too long, wide, 117, 123, 148, 150, green, blue, red, brown 117, checkered green, 118; girdles of magnitude, 118; gloves with fingers, 116; hose, tight, 116; knives worn at side, 118; mantle, furred, 116; purses, enameled, gilt, 118; rings, 118, 128; shoes: pointed toes, 116, 118, with cut-out design, 118, 126, with thong ties, 116; sleeves too long, wide, 117; surcoats, sleeved/unsleeved, 117; tunic, 116, split, buttoned, pleated, too short, 117, 127
monks, medieval: John Gedeney, 116; William Hornyng, 126; Richard Norwich, cellera, 126
Monnas, Lisa, 218
Montaigne, Michel de, 236
Monumenta Franciscana, 15, 19, 138, 148, 151–2
Moore, Ellen Wedemeyer, 118, 124, 147
Moorman, Charles, 65, 83
Moorman, John R. H., 137, 139
Morey, Charles Rufus, 113
Morgan, Gerald, 34, 64, 112–13, 172, 199, 223

Moriarty, Catherine, 221
Morris, Revd Richard, 239, 250
Morse, J. Mitchell, 160
Mors Pilati, 249
mottoes, 83–7, 103–7, 236
mourning weeds, 244
Mullaney, Samantha, 6, 52, 62, 84, 119, 124, 126, 260
Muscatine, Charles, 38, 140
Muthesius, Anna, 218

nakedness, 7, 19
Neve, Michael, 200–2, 204
Nevinson, J. L., 127
Newhauser, Richard, 189
Newton, Stella Mary, 25, 36, 49, 78, 164–5, 168, 214–15, 218, 229
Nicholas of Lynn, *Kalendarium*, 202
Nicholls, Albert G., 216, 223
Nicholls, John, 171
Nichols, John, pl. 8, 125, 129–30
Nigel De Longchamps, *Speculum Stultorum*, 19, 121
Nohl, Johannes, 200
Norris, Herbert, 129, 134, 167–8
nuns' habits: 17, 67–75, 77–9, 83; Franciscan, mauve cloaks, 78; measurements, 72–3; of Fontevrault, 78; *see* rules
Nutton, Vivian, 200–2, 204

'Of Men Lif þat Woniþ in Lond', 22
Oliva, Marilyn, 10, 27, 48, 64
Olson, Roberta J. M., 110
Olsson, Kurt, 185
O'Mara, V[eronica] M., 45, 64
'On the Deposition of Richard II', 23
'On the times', 23
Orchard, Andy, 232
'The Order of Fair-Ease', 19, 21, 126
'An Orison of the Five Joys', 38–9, 42
Orme, Nicholas, 40, 173–4, 184, 189–90, 194
Owen-Crocker, Gale R., 9, 25

Pace, E. A., 201
Pächt, Otto, 2
pallium: 208; definition, 208
paltok, 152, 167, 229, 246–7
Pantin, William Abel, ed., 117–18, 123, 126–7, 192
Pardoner, the (Chaucer): c.pl. VII, 7–8,

107, 132, 139, 144, 226–32, 236–49, 252, 256–7, 267, 269–70, 272; in visual arts, 226–31, 241; character: crucifix, 227–8, 249; *illusor*, 246; pardons, 237, 240, 242, 246–7; *quaestor*, 247; relics, 226, 231–7, 239–42, 249; vices: avarice, 238, 242–3; *cupiditas*, 238; gluttony, 238; greed, 242–3; *gula*, 238; hypocrisy, 238; insolence, 246; irreverence, 246; lechery, 238; *luxuria*, 238; pride, 246; simony, 238; sodomy, 238; shamelessness, 246; *superbia*, 238; vanity, 238; bags: male, 7, 228, 237, 240–2, 247, 249–50; purse, 139, 242, 252; walet, 139, 228, 240–3, 246–7; habit, 239–40; headcovering: 246; cap, 226, 228, 230, 237, 239–45, 247, definition, 243; hood, 7, 240–1, 243, 245–7, 250, 269; fashion: 'dischevelee', 241, 243–4, 247, 269–70, definition 244; 'jolitee', 244–5, 250, definition, 245–6; 'newe jet', 241, 244, 246–7; livery, 239–40; vernicle: 7, 107, 226–8, 230–7, 239–41, 246–50, 256, 272; Christ's crown of thorns, pl. 15, 231, 237, 255–6; powers, 235–7
pardoners: 227–8, 239, 268; false, 238–40; pardons, 240, false, 238–40; *quaestore*, 241
Paris, Matthew, 114
Parisse, Michel, 9
Parson, the (Chaucer): 7, 229, 258–65, 267–9, 272; in Ellesmere portrait, 260; pilgrim staff, pl. 16, 261–3, 265, in visual arts, 262; status, 260; virtues: charity, 258–9, 261–2, 264, 268; humility, 258–61, 264, 268, wisdom, 268
Partonope of Blois, Partenope, 179
Pastoureau, Michel, 213
patches: 6, 15, 77–8, 80, 138, 170, 176, 181–3, 198; symbolism, 183
Patterson, Lee, 238–40, 249
Pearl Poet: *Pearl*, 6, 74, 102, Pearl maiden, 6; *Cleanness*, 74, 129, 264–5
peasant dress, 139
peddlers (tinkers): 140–1, 143, 150, 158–9, 269; *see* vagabonds
Pelbart, Oswald, 42
Pemberton, Maureen, 101, 208, 223
Pendrill, Charles, 220
Pépin, Jean, 262, 264

Petrarch, F., 191–2, 196, 221–2, 236
Pierce the Ploughmans Crede, 135, 140, 149, 153
pilch: 10, 14, 70–1, 152, 272; definition, 14; measurements, 14; *see* fur
pilgrim: 64, 76–8, 82, 95, 108–9, 112, 223, 230–2, 235–6, 247, 249–51, 258, 260–2, 265, 266–72; fox as pilgrim, 140
pilgrim badge: pl. 16, 95, 104, 107, 231, 235–6; powers, 235–6, 247, 256, 262–3, 272
pilgrim weeds: 82; hat, 227, 236, 251; headdress, 230; scrip, wallet, 77–8, 109, 152, 265; staff, pl. 16, 77–8, 95, 109–10, 140, 261–3, 265, in visual arts, 262; tabard, sclavin, 236
pins, tiring: 11–12, 31, 44–7, 49, 71–2; of gold and/or silver, 11–12, 25–6, 31, 33, 45–6, 71–2, 89–90
Piponnier, Françoise, 49, 167
Planché, James Robinson, 14, 35, 134
'Plangit nonna fletibus', 22, 47–8
Plowman's Tale: 128, 135, 239
'Poem on the Evil Times of Edward II', 222
'Poem on the Passion of Christ', 2
Ponting, Kenneth G., 67–8, 145
Porter, Roy, 201–2, 204
Postlethwayt, Malachy, 216–17
Power, Eileen, 11–12, 26–8, 30, 32–3, 43–4, 48, 65, 68–9, 74, 77, 90
Preston, Raymond, 32, 240
Price, John Edward, 61
'Priere d'amour d'une nonnain a un jeune adolescent', 46–7, 74
priests: 144–5, 152, 204, 228–9, 239, 255, 259, 262; in visual arts, 260–1; clothing: dressed in red, 260; in larger hats, 265; in padded doublets, 265; in plaid gowns, 265; in short tunics, 265; instructions for, 262; in 'wyde fueryd hodes', 264; lay styles, 261; parson's wardrobe, 261; vestments, 261, 265; *see* red, Richard de Bury, Richard Maidstone
Prior, Sandra Pierson, 40
Prioress, the (Chaucer): 29–111, 251, 267–9; character: broadness, stature, 32–3, 35–6, 41–3, 81; cleanness and the Blessed Virgin, 35, 40; courtesy and the Blessed Virgin, 35, 37, 40–1,

manners, 35, 40, 80–1; dress as Marian: 35, 63–4, 81; cloak (mantle), 6, 33, 63–81, 109, 267–8, *fetys* (well-made), 6, 33, 42, 44, 63–8, 72–3, 76, 81, defininition, 65–7, 109, 268; veil, 11, 30–6, 38, 43, 45, 62–3, 81, 83, 109, 267, forehead, fair, 'revealed', 30–8, 41–3, 51, 53, 58–9, 62, 81; wimple, 7, 30, 32, 34–5, 43, 45, 47–9, 51, 81, 83, 109, 267, 'pynched', pleated, 30, 32, 44, 47–9, 62–3, 81; rosary, 11, 82–111, 267, definition, 82, symbolism, 82; brooch pendant, 11, 82–5, 88–9, 91, 103–8, 130, crowned 'A', 106–8, gold, 82, 267, motto, pl. 5a-c, 83–8, 103–7; coral, small, 82–5, 88–9, 91, 94, 99–101, 267; gauds, green, 83, 88, 91, 94, 99–103, 267; Eglentyne, 32–4, 35, 38, 40–3, 62–3, 73–5, 77, 79, 81, 83, 94, 110; in Ellesmere miniatures, 61–2; pejorative diction: 29–30, 33–4, 48–9, 51, 63–6, 81, 83–5, 88, 95–6, 103, 105, 107; 'elegance', 34–5, 62–5; fashionable, 34–5; 'fluted', 34–6, 48–9; reputed vices (pride, vanity, love of luxury), 63–4, 103, 107; status, 48, 85, 91, 102; *see* Blessed Virgin Mary; headdress, metaphors; rosaries; veil; virtues; wimple
Processus Noe cum Filiis: Noe, 149; Uxor, 149
'Proud Gallants and Popeholy Priests', 144
Puff, Helmut, 246
purse: 7, 118, 139, 152, 219, 242, 252; *see* monks, Pardoner
De Pyloto, 234–5

Racinet, Auguste, 33
Ragen, Brian Abel, 40
Rashdall, Hastings, 162–3, 165, 173, 175
Rawcliffe, Carole, 211
Read, John, 185
Reed, Karen, 157
Regimen Sanitatus Salernitanum, 225
Register of Thomas de Brantingham, 238
Registrum Thome Bourgchier, 24, 145
Reidy, John, 186
Reinecke, George, F., 240–1
Reiss, Edmund, 112, 125
relics: 226, 231–7, 239–42; *see* saints, St Thomas Becket

De Remediis utriusque fortunae in ME, 36–7
Renn, George A., 200
Renoir, Alain, 140
'The Reply of Friar Daw Topias, with Jack Upland's Rejoinder', 136
Revard, Carter, 255
The Revelations of Saint Birgitta, 15, 40–1
Reynard the Fox, 233
Reynolds, William Donald, 221
Rex, Richard, 29, 32, 91, 99
Rhodes, James F., 227, 233–4, 247, 249
ribbon: 22, 25, 47–8; beribboned headdress, 71, 80; of gold, 93
Richard de Bury, Bishop: 191–3, 196; *Philobiblon*, 192
Richard le Scrope, Archbishop, York, 238
Richardson, Janette, 144, 158, 248
Rickert, Edith, 97, 156, 168–9, 172, 184, 209, 213, 220
Rickert, Margaret, 151
Ridley, Florence H., 29, 32–3, 65, 81
Rigby, S. H., 4–5, 113, 145, 160, 171–4, 190, 195, 248, 260
Riley, Henry Thomas, 242
Robert de Hereford, deacon, 127
Robert of Cisyle: 215–16; King Robert, 216
Robert Grosseteste, *Chateau d'Amour*, 102
Robertson, D. W., Jr., 32, 129, 176–7, 197, 250
Robinson, F. N., ed., 34, 48, 83, 103
rochet: 69; definition, 10
Rock, Daniel, 14, 102, 121, 151
Rodes, Robert E., Jr., 3, 260
Rogers, James E. Thorold, 120, 125, 147, 172, 213–4, 216–18
Rogers, P. Burwell, 140
Rolle (de Hampole), Richard, *Pricke of Conscience*, 23
Roney, Lois, 190–1, 194–5
Ronig, Franz, 1
rosaries: 76–7, 82–3, 88–9, 91, 93–8, 101, 108–11, 253–4; Catherine of Cleves, large coral, c.pl. II, 91; Chaucer, 96; d'Evreaux, Queen Jean, 98–9; fifteenth-century fashion, 91; gold, silver beads, 91, 95, 97–9, 109; Henry VI's rosary, 91; Langdale Rosary, 98; materials, 96–9, 101–2; pendants (spiritual), c.pl. II, 88, 91, 96–7, 99, 101, 105, in visual arts, 108–10; St Hedwig, brooch pendant, pl. 6, 91–2,

108; worn by Christ, 101; *see* Prioress, rosary
Rosetti, Gioanventura, 211
Roulin, E. A., 208, 210
Rousselot, [l'abbé Pierre Jean], 41
Rowland, Beryl, 221
royal robes, 8, 79
Rubin, Stanley, 202
Ruiz, Juan, *Libro de buen amor*, 157
rules, religious dress: 1, 3–4, 6, 8–16, 30, 78, 113, 139, 266, 269; Augustinian, 10, 44, 243; Austin, 10; Benedictine, 8–13, 17, 27–8, 43–4, 52, 65–7, 69–70, 79, 113–15, 118–19, 121, 124–5, 267–9; Brigittine, 11–15, 18–19, 23, 31, 44–5, 64, 66, 77, 89–90; Cistercian, 69; Dominican, 79, 240; Franciscan, 15, 31, 138, 150–2, 159, 240, 272; *peculium*, 26–8; private gifts, 13–14, 26–8, 30, 68–70, 72, 82, 90, 94–5, 97; private ownership (*proprietas*), 13, 24, 26–7, 30, 71, 83, 94–5, 97, 115, 117, 128, 137, definition, 115; Poor Clares, 10, 15
Rutebeuf: 'La Chanson des ordres', 20; 'Les Ordres de Paris', 20

saints: St Agnes, 80, 107, 272; St Alban, 107, 113, 121, 123, 127, 132, 163; in visual arts, 79; St Aldhelm, 24–5, 71–2; St Andrew, 233; St Anthony, 114; St Augustine, 171, 177, 186; St Bartholomew, 116; St Benedict, 124, 126, 129; St Bernard, 37, 185, 249; St Bridget (Birgitta, Bride), 40–1, 79, 108; St Christopher, 99, 107, 129, 131, 250; St Clare, 76, 80, 96, 138, 183; St Cosmas, c.pl. VI, 223; St Cuthbert, 53; St Damian, c.pl. VI, 223; St Dominic, 154; St Eligius, 89; St Eloy, 94; St Ethelburger, 79; St Etheldreda, 79; St Francis, 80, 136–8, 153–4, 159, 182–3, 192–3; St Gertrude, c.pl. I, 53–4, 79; St Hedwig, pl. 6, 91–2, 95, 108; St Jerome, 170; St John the Evangelist, 100; St Joss[e], pl. 16, 95, 262–3; St Lawrence, 250; St Leonard, 103; St Margaret, 171; St Martin, 182; St Mary Magdalen, 49, 68, 134, 205; St Odile, 78; St Paul, 118, 142, 231, 256, 259, 265; St Peter, 100, 231–2, 235, 256, 259, 265; St Sebaldus, 235–6; St Severin, 101; St Thomas

Aquinas, 192, 197; St Thomas Becket, 58, 96, 249; St Veronica, 231–5, 237, 247, 249, in visual arts, 231–2, 255–6

Sadowski, Piotr, 102

Salter, Elizabeth, 180

Salzman, L. F., 148

Samborne, Joan, 10, 70

Sandler, Lucy Freeman, 53, 163–5

Sandona, Mark, 1

satire, 4, 18–24, 73, 76, 112–13, 121, 123, 125–6, 128, 132–3, 135, 137, 139, 142, 144, 148, 150, 154, 200, 223, 239–41, 252, 255, 258, 264–5

'Satyre on the Consistory Courts', 252

scapular: 63; definition, 10; *see* monk's habit

Scase, Wendy, 24, 123, 144–5

Scattergood, John, 23, 254

Schachner, Nathan, 225

Schaffner, Paul F., 186

Schneider, Jane, 1, 7

scholars: pls. 10–11, 183, 196–8, 202, 206–7, 220, 269–70; Ralph Strode, 198; Sir Richard of Chicester, 175; poor, 144, 173–4, 181; *see* Clerk, clerks, Richard de Bury

Schramm, Wilbur Lang, 161

Schwabe, Randolph, 135

Scott, Kathleen, 135, 138, 142, 144, 161, 181, 228

Scott, Margaret, 102

Sequeira, Isaac, 112

Serjeantson, M. S., 100–1

Sewardby, Elizabeth, 70, 77–8

Shakespeare, William: *Hamlet*, 244–5; *King Lear*, 241, 245; *Twelfth Night*, 252

Sheridan, James J., 177

Shinners, John, 172, 262

shoes: 9–10, 14–15, 22, 71, 75–6, 210; ankle shoes, 124; boots, 71, 124; laced, 68, 116; low-cut, 26; old, 6; overshoes, 125; pointed toed footwear, 119; 'pyked', 152; red, green, 172; sandals, 124–5; trimmed, red leather, 80; with cut-out patterns, 126, 170–1; with silver buckles, 23, 90; 'woolen' shoes, 125; *see* clerks, monk's habit, monks, stockings

The Siege of Jerusalem, 232–4

silk: 12, 16–17, 21–2, 25, 68, 72, 76; belts, 117; kerchiefs, 17; veil, bridal, 47–8; veils, 30–1, 33, 43–6, 68, 72; veils and robes, 26–7; not suitable for nuns, 14–15; *see* fabric, *dyapre*, Doctour of Phisik

silver: 11–12, 16, 25, 27; and overgilt buckles, 22–3; cloth of silver, 17; enamelled silver jewelry, 128; ornaments, 117; *see* embroidery

Sirasi, Nancy G., 200, 203–4, 213

Sitwell, Sacheverell, 34

Skeat, Walter W., 222, 239, 251

Skirlaw, Walter, Bishop, Durham: bequests, 27, 69

Sklute, Larry, 83, 89, 160

sleeves: dimensions: length, 13, 26, 68, 117, 267–9; width, 117; types: bag sleeves, 228–9; emboidered, 80, 168; fur-trimmed, 71, 267; lining, 78–9; striped with silk, 71; with cuffs, 168; with pendants, 134–5; *see* Friar, Monk

'sloppes', 246–7

Smith, H. Clifford, 91

Smith, Sarah Stanbury, 243

Snape, R. H., 124

Snyder, James, 256

Social England, 238, 262

'A Song Against the Friars', 140–1

Song of Songs, 37–8, 42

'Song of the Corruptions of the Time', 252

Specht, Henrik, 248

Speed, Peter, 200–1, 204

Spencer, Brian, 104, 235–6, 256

Spencer, William, 33, 213

squires, 21, 230

Staley, Lynn, 176

Staniland, Kay, 151, 218

Statuta Antiqua Universitatis Oxoniensis, 205

Statutes of the Hotel-Dieu of Troyes, 100

Statutes of the Realm, 15–17, 93, 128, 148, 173, 217

Steadman, John M., 103

Stemmler, Theo, 225

stockings (hose): 9, 14, 17, 66, 93, 209, 229; Absalon's, red, 171; Hamlet's, 244–5; leggings, leather, 125; linen, 125; socks, 71; soled hose, 124–5; tight, 116; without vamps, 66; *see* monk's habit

Stock, Lorraine, 144

Stoian, Gabriel, 186

Stokes, A. E., 140

Storm, Melvin, 247, 249

Stratford, John, Archbishop, Canterbury, 3–4
stripes: 28, 152; lining, 28
Strohm, Paul, 226
Strutt, Joseph, 23, 61, 77–9, 102, 110, 114, 120, 171, 237, 247
Studer, Paul, 100
Summa virtutum de remediis anime, 102
Summoner, the (Chaucer): 158, 226–7, 229–30, 247–57, 267, 269–70; in visual arts, 246–7, 254; character: leprosy, c.pl. VIII, 248, 250, skin disease, 247–8, 270; status, 226–7; vices: harlotry, 248; greed, 251, 254; lechery, 248; simony, 248; sodomy, 248; clothing: buckler, 226, 250–1, definition 250–1; garland, pl. 14, 226, 229–30, 250–7, 269–70, symbolism, 256–7; *see* Pardoner's vernicle
summoners: 139, 251–2, 255, 268; false summoners, 239; in visual arts, 226–7, 229–30; in lay dress, 229–30; livery, 229; standard dress, 229; status, 226–7
Sumption, Jonathan, 235
sumptuary laws: 4, 8, 15–17, 45, 63, 72–3, 93–4, 119–20, 199, 215, 217; grooms, 16–17, 93; esquires (gentlemen): 16–17, 93, 173, 215, 217; handicraftsmen, 16–17, 93, 217; servants of lords: 17, 93; wives and children, 17; yeomen, 16–17, 93; *see* clerical dress, clerks, furs, knights, esquires
surcoat: wide-sleeved, 10; *see* clerks, Clerk's courtepy
Swanson, Robert N., 239, 260
Swart, J., 238
symbolism: animal skins for pilch, 14; barbe, 46, 73; clothing, 184, 266–72; hood/'typet' with knives,pins, 143; linen covering for pilch, 14; mantle, 46; Mars, 213; nun's garments, 10, 46, 63, 74; of Poverty, 179–83; poor dress as poverty, 197; religious, 28, 46, 175–6, 182, 266–72; silk as vanity, 45; smock, old, as poverty, 197; veil, 45–6; wimple, pl. 4, 45–6; *see* fabric, quality
Synagoga, 181
Szittya, P[enn]. R., 137–40, 142–3, 154–6

tabard (sclavin): 236; Bachelor's, 290; physicians', 208, definition, 208; torn, 6, 188, 190; threadbare, 188–9; *see* fabric, quality
Tabard Inn, 110
Taitt, Peter S., 83–4, 103, 112, 126, 129, 158, 161, 187
Talbot, C. H., 172, 199, 202–5, 220
Tatlock, J[ohn] S. P., 127, 137
Tertullian, 189
Testamenta Eboracensia, 27, 69–70
Testimony of William Thorpe, 187–8, 270–1
Thomas, de la Mare, Abbot, 113–14, 117, 127
Thomas of Cantimpre, 99
Thomas, Marcel, 122
Thompson, Daniel V., 214
Thorndike, Lynn, 165, 173
Thurston, Herbert, 164, 205, 230–2, 236
Tierney, Brian, 173
tippet: 120, 229, 261; Friar Daw Topias, 136–7, 167; *see* clerks, Friar
tiraz, pl. 5a-c, 86–8
Tiron, Abbé, 77
Tischendorf, Christine, 233
Todd, Revd Henry J., 229
Tommaso da Celano, Fra., 80, 96
Tonnochy, A. B., 165
Toynbee, Arnold, 182
trains, 25
trousseau, 179
tunic: 23, 78, 103, 116–17; definition, 18; friar's, 15; monk's, 8, 27–8; nun's (gown, *cotte*), 10, 13, 25, 63, 77, 79; cassock, 173, defininition, 18; *pellicea, talaris tunica*, 18, 208, 217, 220–1; *pelisse*, fur-lined, 15; *superpellicium* (surplice), 14, 27, 76, 120–1, 171, 173, 185, symbolism, 121; supertunic, 65, 68; Christ's seamless: pl. 1, 1–2, 19, 153, 237, pilgrimage, 1; Synagoga's tunic, 181; tunic, blue, 70, 77, 80, green, 78; tunic, gathered (*fronciées*), 25–6; tunic of brightly dyed fabric, 27–8; narrow-cut, 69; pleated (*laqueatis*), 27, 89; scarlet, 71, 80; short, 18; striped lining, 28; woolen (*staminea*), 114; *see* monk's habit, friars, Richard Ruston
Tyrwhitt, Thomas, 240

Ussery, Huling E, 112, 126, 163, 173, 183, 190, 194, 198, 220

Uttranadhie, Alberto, 157

van Uytven, Raymond, 146
vagabonds (*vagabundus*): 139, 187; *see* peddlers
Vance, Eugene, 242, 248
van der Weyden, Roger, 49, 231
Varty, Kenneth, 223
Veale, Elspeth M., 120–1, 215, 222
vests, 71
vices and personifications: 3, 18, 58–9; apostasy, 27, 113, 153–4, 187; avarice, 58, 177, 191, 196, 221, 238, 242–3; 'colomy', 188; 'coueitise', 188, 191, 196, 245; *cupiditas*, 238; *curiositas*, 185–7, 189–93, 196–8; disobedience, 112; envy, 245; fraud, 221, 223; gluttony, 22, 238; greed, 133, 140, 143, 150, 188–9, 223, 242–3, 252, 254, 270; guile, 153; *gula*, 238; harlotry, 248; hypocrisy, 5, 19, 110, 238; idleness, 64; ignorance, 223; insolence, 80; ire, 245; jolitee, 245; lechery, 28, 143, 192, 238, 248; *luxuria*, 18, 58, 63, 134, 238; murder, 245; pope-holiness, 5, 24, 75, 123, 255, 264; presumption, 221; pride, 6, 18, 24, 28, 46, 63–4, 134–5, 165, 184, 221, 245, 258–60, 264–5, 268–9; promiscuity, 19; recklessness, 181; simony, 238, 248; sodomy, 238, 248; *superbia*, 238; vainglory, 18; vanity, 12, 18–19, 30, 45–6, 49, 63, 80, 103, 129, 134, 191, 196, 238; violence, 58; worldliness, 6
Vigourel, Revd Adrian, 9, 18, 114, 151
Vindicta saluatoris (Latin), 232–4
Vindicta saluatoris (Old English), 232–4, 237
virtues and personifications: 3, 7, 17, 37, 39, 76; Cardinal Virtues, pl. 3, 60; of Christian *viator*, 262; of Good Shepherd, 262; in visual arts, pl. 3, 51–63, 81; abstinence, 46; benignity, 259; charity, 46, 64, 106, 258–9, 261–2, 264, 268; chastity, 18, 58, 61, 272; compassion, 259; continence, 61; discipline, pl. 4, 61–2; faith, 46, 61; fortitude, 59–60; glad poverty, 61, 77–8, 144–6, 148; hope, 46; humility, 15, 46, 175–6, 258–61, 264, 268; justice, 60; mercy, 259; modesty, 259; obedience, 46, 259;

patience, 188, 259; prudence, 18, 37, 41–2, 46, 51, 58–62; respectfulness, 259; reverence, 259; sobriety, 59; *studiositas*, 197, definition 197; submissiveness, 259; temperance, 61, 192, 197; wisdom, 18, 268; *see* metaphors

Waltham, Robert, precentor, Salisbury, pl. 7, 121–2, 131
Warthin, Aldred Scott, 201, 209
Wear, Andrew, 201–2, 204
Webb, Diana, 95, 232, 237, 265
Weiner, Annette B., 1, 7
Weisheipl, James A., 172, 190–1, 195
Weissman, Hope Phyllis, 34, 246, 250
Wenzel, Siegfried, 240
Whethamstede, John, Abbot, 123
Whitaker, Elaine E., 220
White, Robert B., Jr., 112, 126
Whitmore, Sr Mary Ernestine, 88, 115–16, 118, 123, 138, 161, 170–1, 175, 187, 218
'Why I Can't Be a Nun', 46, 73–4
Wieck, Roger S., 231, 237
Wilkins, Eithne, 91, 94–6, 98, 101–2, 110, 253–4
Williams, Arnold, 153, 158, 238
Wilson, Kax, 217
wimple: pls. 2–4, 7, 10–12, 23, 36, 43–6, 49, 50–63, 73, 78; definition, 35–6; in visual arts, pls. 2–4, 51–63; symbolism of, 45–6; barbe, 46, 73, definition, 35, pleated, 35, 43, 61–2; fillets, 36, 44; goffered, 49; of silk, 25, 46
Winston-Allen, Anne, 89, 95–6, 253
Wolfram von Eschenbach, *Parzival*: 179; Gahmuret, 179; Jeschute, 179
Wood, Chauncey, 34, 84–5, 189
Wright, Stephen K., 233–4
Wurtele, Douglas, 32
Wyclif, John (Iohannis), 19–20, 119, 123, 129, 135–6, 140, 153–6, 188, 248, 262, 264, 270–1
Wykeham, William, 68, 107–8, 123, 165

Zacharias, Johanna, 231–2, 235, 237
Zacher, Christian K., 185, 190–3, 196–7
Ziegler, Joseph, 201
Zigrosser, Carl, 209

CHAUCER STUDIES

I   MUSIC IN THE AGE OF CHAUCER, *Nigel Wilkins*

II   CHAUCER'S LANGUAGE AND THE PHILOSOPHERS' TRADITION, *J. D. Burnley*

III   ESSAYS ON TROILUS AND CRISEYDE, *edited by Mary Salu*

IV   CHAUCER SONGS, *Nigel Wilkins*

V   CHAUCER'S BOCCACCIO: Sources of Troilus and the Knight's and Franklin's Tales, *edited and translated by N. R. Havely*

VI   SYNTAX AND STYLE IN CHAUCER'S POETRY, *G. H. Roscow*

VII   CHAUCER'S DREAM POETRY: Sources and Analogues, *B. A. Windeatt*

VIII   CHAUCER AND PAGAN ANTIQUITY, *Alastair Minnis*

IX   CHAUCER AND THE POEMS OF 'CH' in University of Pennsylvania MS French 15, *James I. Wimsatt*

X   CHAUCER AND THE IMAGINARY WORLD OF FAME, *Piero Boitani*

XI   INTRODUCTION TO CHAUCERIAN ENGLISH, *Arthur O. Sandved*

XII   CHAUCER AND THE EARLY WRITINGS OF BOCCACCIO, *David Wallace*

XIII   CHAUCER'S NARRATORS, *David Lawton*

XIV   CHAUCER: COMPLAINT AND NARRATIVE, *W. A. Davenport*

XV   CHAUCER'S RELIGIOUS TALES, *edited by C. David Benson and Elizabeth Robertson*

XVI   EIGHTEENTH-CENTURY MODERNIZATIONS FROM THE *CANTERBURY TALES*, *edited by Betsy Bowden*

XVII   THE MANUSCRIPTS OF THE *CANTERBURY TALES*, *Charles A. Owen Jr*

XVIII   CHAUCER'S *BOECE* AND THE MEDIEVAL TRADITION OF BOETHIUS, *edited by A. J. Minnis*

XIX   THE AUTHORSHIP OF *THE EQUATORIE OF THE PLANETIS*, *Kari Anne Rand Schmidt*

XX   CHAUCERIAN REALISM, *Robert Myles*

XXI   CHAUCER ON LOVE, KNOWLEDGE AND SIGHT, *Norman Klassen*

XXII   CONQUERING THE REIGN OF FEMENY: GENDER AND GENRE IN CHAUCER'S ROMANCE, *Angela Jane Weisl*

XXIII   CHAUCER'S APPROACH TO GENDER IN THE *CANTERBURY TALES*, *Anne Laskaya*

XXIV   CHAUCERIAN TRAGEDY, *Henry Ansgar Kelly*

XXV   MASCULINITIES IN CHAUCER: Approaches to Maleness in the *Canterbury Tales* and *Troilus and Criseyde*, *edited by Peter G. Beidler*

XXVI   CHAUCER AND COSTUME: The Secular Pilgrims in the General Prologue, *Laura F. Hodges*

XXVII   CHAUCER'S PHILOSOPHICAL VISIONS, *Kathryn L. Lynch*

XXVIII   SOURCES AND ANALOGUES OF THE CANTERBURY TALES [I], *edited by Robert M. Correale with Mary Hamel*

XXX   FEMINIZING CHAUCER, *Jill Mann*

XXXI   NEW READINGS OF CHAUCER'S POETRY, *edited by Robert G. Benson and Susan J. Ridyard*

XXXII   THE LANGUAGE OF THE CHAUCER TRADITION, *Simon Horobin*

XXXIII ETHICS AND EXEMPLARY NARRATIVE IN CHAUCER AND GOWER, *J. Allan Mitchell*